Introduction to Kalophony, the Byzantine *Ars Nova*

Studies in Eastern Orthodoxy

Series Editors
RENÉ GOTHÓNI
and
GRAHAM SPEAKE

PETER LANG
Oxford · Bern · Berlin · Bruxelles · Frankfurt am Main · New York · Wien

Introduction to Kalophony, the Byzantine *Ars Nova*

The *Anagrammatismoi* and *Mathēmata* of Byzantine Chant

GREGORIOS STATHIS

TRANSLATED AND REVISED BY
KONSTANTINOS TERZOPOULOS

PETER LANG
Oxford · Bern · Berlin · Bruxelles · Frankfurt am Main · New York · Wien

Bibliographic information published by Die Deutsche Nationalbibliothek.
Die Deutsche Nationalbibliothek lists this publication in the Deutsche National-
bibliografie; detailed bibliographic data is available on the Internet at http://dnb.d-nb.de.

A catalogue record for this book is available from the British Library.

Library of Congress Control Number: 2014946250

This publication has been translated, revised and updated by Konstantinos Terzopoulos from the original edition: *Οἱ ἀναγραμματισμοὶ καὶ τὰ μαθήματα τῆς βυζαντινῆς μελοποιίας καὶ πανομοιότυπος ἔκδοσις τοῦ καλοφωνικοῦ στιχηροῦ τῆς Μεταμορφώσεως «Προτυπῶν τὴν ἀνάστασιν», μεθ'ὅλων τῶν ποδῶν καὶ ἀναγραμματισμῶν αὐτοῦ, ἐκ τοῦ Μαθηματαρίου τοῦ Χουρμουζίου Χαρτοφύλακος*. Athens: Institute of Byzantine Musicology: Meletai 3, 1979.

ISSN 2235-1930
ISBN 978-3-0343-0912-7 (print)
ISBN 978-3-0353-0357-5 (eBook)

© Peter Lang AG, International Academic Publishers, Bern 2014
Hochfeldstrasse 32, CH-3012 Bern, Switzerland
info@peterlang.com, www.peterlang.com, www.peterlang.net

All rights reserved.
All parts of this publication are protected by copyright.
Any utilisation outside the strict limits of the copyright law, without the permission of the publisher, is forbidden and liable to prosecution.
This applies in particular to reproductions, translations, microfilming, and storage and processing in electronic retrieval systems.

This publication has been peer reviewed.

Printed in Germany

*To my beloved wife Penelope (†26 March 2008),
and our children, Petros, Eleni, Maria and Katerina*

Contents

Author's preface to the English edition   xiii

Translator's note   xix

PART ONE   1

CHAPTER 1

A synoptic review of Byzantine ecclesiastical melopœïa   3
- Introductory: terminology   3
- The genera and forms of Byzantine melopœïa   19
  - First genus: stichērarikon, with the following necessary distinctions   30
  - Second genus: heirmologikon, with the following necessary distinctions   30
  - Third genus: papadikon, with the following necessary distinctions   31
- Periods of Byzantine melopœïa and parallel development of Byzantine notation   32

CHAPTER 2

The form of the Mathēmatarion   49
- The genesis   49
  - *The fully developed appearance of the Mathēmatarion eidos and its codification: AD 1336 as milieu*   49
  - *Kalophony [kalophōnia or kalliphōnia] as 'ars nova' in the fourteenth century and its defining elements*   56
  - *The first appearances of the kalophonic melos and the favourable historic circumstances surrounding its development*   62
  - *The terms: anagrammatismos, anapodismos, mathēma and others related to them, epiphōnēma, anaphōnēma, allagma, epibolē, parekbolē, prologos, katabasia, homonoia*   70

CHAPTER 3

The tradition of the kalophonic melos   95

The formation and tradition of the related codices beginning from the fourteenth century   95
The Papadikē   96
The Kratēmatarion   110
The Kalophōnon Stichērarion or Mathēmatarion   115
Kontakarion or Oikēmatarion and the Akathistos   120

The principal composers of the kalophonic melos of the mathēmatarion   125
The brilliant ensemble of composers: Nikēphoros Ēthikos, Iohannes Glykys, Iohannes Koukouzelēs, and Xenos Korōnēs (first half of the fourteenth century)   125
Melourgoi contemporary to Iohannes Kladas the lampadarios (c. 1400)   128
Melourgoi contemporary to Manuel Chrysaphēs the lampadarios (c. 1453)   129
The sixteenth- and seventeenth-century transmitters and renewers of the tradition   131
Last appearance of the form of the mathēmata in the eighteenth and nineteenth centuries   133

CHAPTER 4

The analysis of the mathēmata   135

The text of the mathēmata   135
First Category: psalmic verses   135
Second Category: the mathēmata, proper   143

The forms based on content   150
Triadika (triadic – trinitarian)   150
Anastasima (resurrectional)   151
Dogmatika (dogmatic)   151
Doxastika   152
Theotokia   152

The morphological types of composition of the mathēmata proper   156

PART TWO 171

CHAPTER 5
Incipits of the anagrams and mathēmata in the Mathēmatarion
transcribed by Chourmouzios 173
   Introductory note 173
   ΜΠΤ 727: Mathēmatarion (volume I) 176
   ΜΠΤ 728: Mathēmatarion (volume II) 180
   ΜΠΤ 729: Mathēmatarion (volume III) 186
   ΜΠΤ 730: Mathēmatarion (volume IV) 192
   ΜΠΤ 731: Mathēmatarion (volume V) 200
   ΜΠΤ 732: Mathēmatarion (volume VI) 207
   ΜΠΤ 733: Mathēmatarion (volume VII — triōdion) 215
   ΜΠΤ 734: Mathēmatarion (volume VIII — pentēcostarion) 222
   ΜΠΤ 706: Papadikē (theotokiōn) 226
   ΜΠΤ 706: Papadikē (volume V) 230
   ΜΠΤ 712: Hapanta of Petros Bereketēs 234

CHAPTER 6
Reproduction of the kalophonic stichēron Προτυπων την
αναστασιν from the feast of the transfiguration 239
   Preliminary remarks 239
   Transcriptions of the kalophonic stichēron προτυπων την αναστασιν 241
      Text of the Doxastikon of the vespers for the feast of the Transfiguration 249
   The text of the kalophonic stichēron from the chourmouzios
      mathēmatarion (ΜΠΤ 732) 250
   Images of ΜΠΤ 732 255

Epilogue 293

Bibliography 297
   Manuscripts used 297
      Athos 297
         Chilandariou 297

  Dionysiou   297
  Docheiariou   297
  Gregoriou   297
  Hagiou Pavlou   297
  Iberon   297
  Koutloumousiou   298
  Konstamonitou   298
  M. Lavra   298
  Panteleimon   298
  Philotheou   298
  Vatopedi   299
  Xenophontos   299
 Athens   299
  Hidryma Byzantines Mousikologias (ΙΒΜ)   299
  Historikes kai Ethnologikes Hetaireias (ΙΕΕ)   299
  National Library of Greece (ΕΒΕ)   299
 Constantinople   299
  Metochion Panagiou Taphou (ΜΠΤ)   299
 Meteora   300
  Holy Transfiguration Monastery   300
 Messina   300
  Bibl. Regionale Universitaria   300
 Paris   300
  Bibliotèque nationale de France   300
 Patmos   300
  Monastery of Saint John the Theologian   300
 Rome   300
  Grottaferrata Badia Graeca   300
 Sinai   300
  Saint Catherine's Monastery   300
 St. Petersburg–Leningrad   300
  National Library of Russia   300

Vienna	300
Österreichische Nationalbibliothek	300
Works cited	301
Index of manuscripts	313
Index of topics and names	319

Author's preface to the English edition

The anagrams [*anagrammatismoi*], or more generally, the *mathēmata* and morphologically related kalophonic forms [*eidē*] of Byzantine melopœïa — *anapodismoi, podes, anaphonēmata, allagma, epibolē, parekbolē, prologos, kratēma,* etc. — constitute the artistic creations by which Psaltic Art [*psaltikē technē*] is known in all its splendour and becomes an object of admiration. Kalophony as *ars nova* was born following the recovery of the city of Constantinople after the Latin occupation of Byzantium (AD 1204–1261) during the long reign of Andronicus II (1282–1328) and reached its final form in the first half of the fourteenth century. During the years 1300–1350, four composers and teachers of the Psaltic Art, Nikēphoros Ēthikos the domestikos, Iohannēs prōtopsaltēs Glykys, Iohannēs maïstor Koukouzelēs and Xenos Korōnēs, imposed a new attitude of melic composition on the pre-existing forms and designated new compositional techniques dominated by the beautifying kallopistic element, which resulted in the lengthening of those works. Together with their contemporary composers, they created new compositions in the new spirit of *kallōpismos* and musical verbosity. This new musical creation was christened with the term *kalophōnia*, kalophony, and this period is the golden age of Byzantine Music, that is, of the Hellenic Psaltic Art of Orthodox Christian worship.

Kalophony has three basic elements: (i) the elaborate and long melos; (ii) the reworking of the poetic text, the anagrams, through the repetition of words and phrases or insertion of new text; and (iii) the insertion of the *kratēma* — a specific melody using the syllables *nena, titi, toto, tororo* and especially the *terirem* — one, two, three or more times at particular points within the kalophonic work. That third element defines the morphological type of composition as single-part, two-part, three-part, many-part or *oktaēchon* [eight-modal]. In this way, the composers 'sign' their creations and the musical art form becomes eponymous and autonomous. Thanks to the wise system of Hellenic music notation born of the Greek alphabet in the mid-tenth century, middle Byzantium, a plethora of composers with their oceanic corpus of works created one of the largest musical cultures of the world (take, for instance, the Polyeleos composition in Constantinople and all the world, works by various ancient and newer composers, Athens, Nat. Libr. Ms. 2458 from the year 1336, fol. 75r). The fourteenth-century chant compositions of kalophony are masterpieces that filled the magnificent Byzantine Church structures such as the Hagia Sophia, with their evocative mosaics, frescoes and ever-increasing iconographic programmes. As artists, these magnificent composers of chant music are equal in cultural value to the great painters, poets and philosophers of the same noble and aristocratic spirit that would be the last shining moments of the Byzantine Empire, the highest form of artistic and cultural originality and expression that can be observed throughout the long history of Byzantine civilization.

The book in hand, originally published under the title *Οἱ ἀναγραμματισμοὶ καὶ τὰ μαθήματα τῆς βυζαντινῆς μελοποιίας* (Stathēs 1979a), thoroughly investigates and reveals for the first time the entire magnitude of Byzantine kalophony with its individual forms [*eidē*] of melic composition, basically serving as a systematic introduction to the Greek Byzantine music culture, that of the Byzantine Psaltic Art at the height of its expression.

To sketch the historical and morphological frame within which these truly wondrous monuments of monophonic Byzantine and post-Byzantine melic composition hold the primary position of honour, Part One embarks on a necessary introduction to the related terminology, the genera [*genē*] and forms [*eidē*] of melopœïa, as well as the developmental periods. All that is examined and said thereafter, on the genesis of the form of the *mathēma*, the appearance of kalophony and its components, its specialized structures of composition and legacy, even regarding the composers — creators of these compositions and their morphology from the aspects of text and melody — serves to make more understandable and clarify every facet of the principal topic of the kalophony of the Psaltic Art.

Part Two proffers the incipits of the *mathēmata* with their epigraphic description from the eight-volume manuscript *Mathēmatarion* and three more volumes of the *Papadikē*, according to the *exēgēsis* transcription into the New Method of analytical chant notation by Chourmouzios Chartophylax (c. 1825). The internal order of the contents of these codices

Author's preface to the English edition

follows the liturgical calendar as it unfolds in the *Menologion, Triodion* and *Pentekostarion* ecclesiastical hymnbooks. The usefulness of these descriptions and their publication is obvious, for it makes almost the entire corpus of the fourteenth- to fifteenth-century and seventeenth- to eighteenth-century *mathēmata* available to modern chanters and contemporary chant musicologists, transcribed into the present form of chant notation from 1814–1815. Reviewing the folios of those manuscripts, we can chant and enjoy the kalophony of the Psaltic Art. An opportunity to sample this cultural treasure is provided with the stichēron idiomelon *Προτυπῶν τὴν ἀνάστασιν* from the feast of the Transfiguration as preserved on the pages of *Metochion Panagiou Taphou* (MΠT) Ms. 732, fols. 234r–251v (used with permission), and the accompanying comparative transcription into western staff notation and the fifteenth-century Athens, Nat. Libr. Ms. 886, fol. 379v.

The manifestation of Byzantine kalophony in all its scope and splendour enchanted an entire generation of modern musicologists, made up of the chorus of my many students and doctoral candidates, fifty all together. Twelve of them dealt with aspects of kalophony in their dissertations and it is both worthy and right to list their names here along with the titles of their papers as it is impossible for me to now go back and reference their works in detail. These papers, as well as others dealing with different aspects of Byzantine chant, are published in the series *Meletae* of the Institute of Byzantine Musicology of the Holy Synod of the Church of Greece.

Anastasiou, Gregorios (2005), *Τὰ κρατήματα στὴν Ψαλτικὴ Τέχνη*, ed. Grēgorios Th. Stathēs (Meletai, 12; Athens: Institute of Byzantine Musicology).
Apostolopoulos, Thomas (2002), *Ὁ Ἀπόστολος Κώνστας ὁ Χῖος καὶ ἡ συμβολή του στὴ θεωρία τῆς Μουσικῆς Τέχνης*, ed. Institute of Byzantine Musicology of the Holy Synod of the Church of Greece (Meletai, 4; Athens).
Balageōrgos, Dēmētrios (2003), *Ἡ ψαλτικὴ παράδοση τῶν Ἀκολουθιῶν τοῦ Βυζαντινοῦ Κοσμικοῦ Τυπικοῦ*, ed. Grēgorios Th. Stathēs (Meletai, 6; Athens: Institute of Byzantine Musicology).
Chaldaiakēs, Achileas (2003), *Ὁ Πολυέλεος στὴ βυζαντινὴ καὶ μεταβυζαντινὴ μελοποιία*, ed. Grēgorios Th. Stathēs (Meletai, 5; Athens: Institute of Byzantine Musicology).
Giannopoulos, Emmanouel St. (2004), *Ἡ ἄνθηση τῆς Ψαλτικῆς Τέχνης στὴν Κρήτη (1566–1669)*, ed. Grēgorios Th. Stathēs (Meletai, 11; Athens: Institute of Byzantine Musicology).

Karagounēs, Kōnstantinos (2003), *Ἡ παράδοση καὶ ἐξήγηση τοῦ μέλους τῶν Χερουβικῶν τῆς βυζαντινῆς καὶ μεταβυζαντινῆς μελοποιίας*, ed. Grēgorios Th. Stathēs (Meletai, 7; Athens: Institute of Byzantine Musicology).

Karanos, Grammenos (forthcoming), *Τὸ Καλοφωνικὸ Εἱρμολόγιο*, ed. Grēgorios Th. Stathēs (Meletai; Athens: Institute of Byzantine Musicology).

Krētikou, Flōra (2004), *Ὁ Ἀκάθιστος Ὕμνος στὴ βυζαντινὴ καὶ μεταβυζαντινὴ μελοποιία*, ed. Grēgorios Th. Stathēs (Meletai, 10; Athens: Institute of Byzantine Musicology).

Liakos, Iōannēs (2007), *Ἡ βυζαντινὴ ψαλτικὴ παράδοση τῆς Θεσσαλονίκης κατὰ τὸν ιδ΄ αἰῶνα*, ed. Grēgorios Th. Stathēs (Meletai, 15; Athens: Institute of Byzantine Musicology).

Mazera-Mamalē, Sebē (2007), *Τὰ Μεγαλυνάρια Θεοτοκία τῆς Ψαλτικῆς Τέχνης*, ed. Grēgorios Th. Stathēs (Meletai, 15; Athens: Institute of Byzantine Musicology).

Spyrakou, Euangelia (2008), *Οἱ Χοροὶ Ψαλτῶν κατὰ τὴν βυζαντινὴ παράδοση*, ed. Gr. Th. Stathes (Meletai, 14; Athens: Institute of Byzantine Musicology).

Terzopoulos, Kōnstantinos (2004), *Ὁ πρωτοψάλτης τῆς Μεγάλης τοῦ Χριστοῦ Ἐκκλησίας Κωνσταντῖνος Βυζάντιος († 30 Ἰουνίου 1862)· ἡ συμβολή του στὴν Ψαλτικὴ Τέχνη*, ed. Gr. Th. Stathis (Meletai, 9; Athens: Institute of Byzantine Musicology).

Having reached the end of the present work for a second time, I extend once again my heartfelt gratitude to all those who contributed to the writing and publication of this book in its first edition. As an academic textbook used during my twenty-five years as professor at the National and Kapodistrian University of Athens, it is already in its seventh printing since first being published by the Institute of Byzantine Musicology in 1979. It is now made available in English translation for the first time owing to the efforts of my doctoral student, the Revd Dr Konstantinos Terzopoulos. Through his dedication in promoting the advancement of Byzantine and post-Byzantine Hellenic Psaltic Art, with the hope of substantially contributing to the historical and theoretical documentation for a growing international following, including the area of Orthodox worship all around the world, and interest in the study of the notation of this wondrous Psaltic Art, Dr Terzopoulos has taken care to offer the contents of this book in a coherent and vibrant fashion; I thank him wholeheartedly.

Although I cannot worthily express my gratitude, special appreciation must be directed to THE J. F. COSTOPOULOS FOUNDATION for its kind support toward covering the majority of the costs for publication.

Author's preface to the English edition

Also, a grant from PSALTIKI, INC., an American non-profit organisation dedicated to the Byzantine chant heritage, faithfully covered the remaining publication expenses. We wish them continued success in their mission.

Finally, this author is also grateful to Peter Lang International Academic Publishers for the unique honour of inaugurating their new series, *Studies in Eastern Orthodoxy*. I congratulate them on their new series and sincerely thank them.

6 August 2013
Gregorios Stathēs, professor emeritus of the University of Athens

Translator's note

Although Byzantium has been the subject of much study in recent decades for inspiring religious splendour through its artistic, especially iconographic and architectural artefacts of the Middle Byzantine period (AD 843–1204) and the so-called Palaeologan Renaissance (1261–1325), including the areas of literature, learning, theological controversy and liturgy, the opposite is mostly true of Byzantine musical culture. Clearly, the main reason for this is that the analysis of the preserved artefacts of Byzantium's musical life, namely, the Medieval manuscripts containing Byzantine chant notation, have been the specialized domain of musicologists, whose observations have been largely unavailable to an English-reading audience.

Even in optimal circumstances, no single scholar could ever be expected to sift through the thousands of extant Byzantine music manuscripts, presupposing the necessary permissions, time and resources to travel to remote locations for the painstaking and tedious task of manual inspection. This is exactly why this important, seminal study by Grēgorios Stathēs, an internationally renowned Byzantine musicologist, professor emeritus of the National and Kapodistrian University of Athens and my doctoral professor, is such a significant contribution to the discussion of Byzantium's musical legacy. He possesses an intimate knowledge of the vast caches of Medieval manuscripts containing Byzantine chant notation in the numerous libraries on the Monastic Republic of Mount Athos in northern Greece and beyond — and his monumental cataloguing is now in its fifth volume.

Within the great multiplicity of styles and forms utilized in the Byzantine chant repertoire, there exists the compositional technique referred to as kalophony [*kalophōnia*], meaning *beautiful voice* or *beautiful singing*. This highly artistic and virtuosic musical expression, that reached its height in the fourteenth-century *homo byzantinus*, is the *ars nova* of the latter Byzantine spirit. The publication of this *Introduction to Kalophony*, translated into English for the first time, brings this lesser-known and often misunderstood chapter in the cultural and musical history of Byzantium to an English-speaking readership, thus making it more available to musicians, scholars and students of music history and Byzantium.

While much has transpired since the writing of this original work in 1979,[1] it still remains an essential resource for anyone interested in attaining an informed knowledge regarding Byzantine chant because the work succinctly, and yet in a detailed and thorough manner, covers all the basic genera [*genē*] and forms [*eidē*] of melopœïa, thus simultaneously offering the reader a foundation upon which to stand when approaching any other aspect of the rich Byzantine chant heritage.

For this reason, special care has been taken in the translation to assure technical accuracy in the terminology used here. In this way, even the novice and non-musical reader is initiated into the Byzantine Music lexicon foundational for further study. Toula Polygalaktos, Dr Peter Jeffreys and Oonagh Walker provided many helpful suggestions in their proofs of my translation for which I express genuine appreciation.

This work is broader than most of its kind. Those who can take in its contents will receive an advanced education. It is my distinct honour and pleasure to contribute in this way to the advancement of the world treasure that is our Byzantine chant heritage.

KT
Aegina Island, 2014

---

[1] In addition to the works listed in the author's preface above, the following may serve as starting points for a survey of more recent scholarship concerning kalophony: Alexandru 2011–2012; Conomos 2001; Ioannidou 2009; Jung 1998; Krētikou 2008; Lingas 2004; Schartau 2008; Troelgård 2004, 2008. In the area of Slavonic chant notations, increasingly important to the study of early Byzantine chant notations, welcome additions to the English bibliography include the following important works by Constantin Floros: Floros and Moran 2005; Floros 2009.

PART ONE

CHAPTER 1

A synoptic review of Byzantine ecclesiastical melopœïa

INTRODUCTORY: TERMINOLOGY

Melopœïa[1] [melic composition] and *melourgia* are terms that designate the art of the composition of melodies based on particular rules for the correct use of poetic and musical elements primarily destined for ecclesiastical use. This is indicated by the use of the word *melos* in both terms.

Melos[2] is every musically enunciated utterance, that is, anything sung by the human voice. This utterance, the words of the verses in a sung text, can have meaning, but they can also be without meaning, as is the case

1   For the terms *melopœïa* (from the verb μελοποιέω -ῶ) and *melourgia* (from the verb μελουργέω -ῶ); cfr Liddell *et al.* 1996; see Murray 1933: s.v. melopœïa for the English word. It is characteristic that the terms are used for lyric poetry and music interchangeably. Chrysanthos of Madytus, Byzantine music theoretician according to its analytical notation, states, 'melopœïa is the ability to create melos. Melos is created not simply by repeating known psalmodies, but by inventing and writing one's own melē pleasing to the listeners' (Chrysanthos ek Madyton 1832: 174, § 389). A similar statement is given by Theodōros Phōkaeus in his work: 'μελοποιία είναι δύναμις κατασκευαστική μέλους. Διαφέρει (ἀπὸ τὴν μελῳδίαν) ἐπειδὴ ἡ μελῳδία είναι ἀπαγγελία μέλους, ἡ δὲ μελοποιία είναι ἕξις ποιητική'. [Melopœïa is the power to construct melos. It is different (from melody) because melody is the reciting of melos, while melopœïa is a poetic state.] (Theodōros Phōkaeus 1842: 69).
2   According to Liddell-Scott, *melos* is related to lyric poetry, a lyrical musical phrase and song (Liddell *et al.* 1996: s.v. μέλος). In the *Republic* (398d) Plato states that 'the song is composed of three things, the words, the tune and the rhythm' [τὸ μέλος ἐκ τριῶν ἐστιν συγκείμενον, λόγου τε καὶ ἁρμονίας καὶ ῥυθμοῦ]. Musically 'melos is a series of disparate voices [*phthongoi*] according to highness [*oxytēta*] and lowness

with the *ēchēmata* or *kratēmata*[3] — *te-ri-rem, te-ne-na, ti-ti-ti, to-ro-ron* and so on. In any case, the presupposition for melos is that the syllables be pronounced by the human voice. Melos, then, literally and properly speaking belongs to the musical category termed 'vocal' and only by exception is it applied to instrumental music.[4] This is the organic, essential reason that the term melos is preferred over the other terms generally used in art music. These other terms would include the following: *melōdia, psalmōdia, psalmos, psalma*, and music composition. From these terms, the first four, even by their etymology, signify a sung poetic text vocally uttered and clad in a musical garb. These terms, however, simultaneously signify a particular poetic text that submits to the musical expression, regardless of the fact that they later attained a generalized meaning and came to refer to anything sung. The meanings of the terms *hymnos, epos,*[5] *poiēma, odē, ainos, asma, deēsis* and *proseuchē* should also be understood in this light; that is, the original meanings of these words signified specific, unique types[6] of poetic texts. They later lost their original technical meaning and came to denote anything sung in worship unto the doxology and thanksgiving of God or the praise of the Saints and the Mother of God and Theotokos.

From a musical standpoint, the Greek term *synthesis* [composition or arrangement] belongs chiefly to instrumental music; it signifies the combining of various elements, poetic and musical, the compounding of different voices based on the rules of harmony and the combining of both instruments and voices or just musical instruments. It does not assume the

---

[*barytēta*], i.e., according to ascent and descent in succession, as each voice comes after the other offering pleasure to the hearing'; cfr Theodōros Phōkaeus 1842: 3.

3   Regarding *kratēmata* see especially, below, p. 110.

4   The term *melodioso* can be found in instrumental music to describe the expression with which a part of a composition is to attain parallel with the lyrical expression of the human voice, which cannot be compared to any musical instrument.

5   According to A. Mai, Eustathius of Thessalonike characterized Iohannes Damascenus' canons as 'epos' (epic poetry); cfr Mai 1839: 164.

6   Specific as to the distinct conceptual meanings, because during the early Christian period there was general confusion as to the characterisation of poetic creation; cfr Metsakes 1971: 190. The terms currently being discussed were also used as acrostics in kontakia and canons; cfr Tomadakes 1965a: 56.

existence of a poetic text. It is only recently and by exception that we consider the musical embellishment of a poetic text as a *synthesis* or composition for a text intended for ecclesiastical use. Nevertheless, it is useful as a technical term with the meaning of *composition* in referring generally to the creations of Byzantine Chant; this is convenient for the categorisation of these works into types in order to better understand and study them.

The terms *troparion*,[7] *kontakion, kanōn*,[8] *stichēron idiomelon, automelon prosomoion* and *prologos*, which signify a particular poetic form [*eidos*], albeit developed in a specific musical context, require special consideration.

These terms are the basic objects of study for the field of Byzantine Hymnography.[9] They regard poetry and signify the different forms [*eidē*] of poetry used in Christian worship. Music, however, lent a defining tone to a number of them. Thus, in contrast to the first set of terms considered above, regarding generally anything sung, these hymnographic terms cannot be generalized, each one signifying a particular poetic form, *eidos* in Greek, of melopœïa; however, two or more can be grouped together and categorized into a single form.

From everything presented thus far, it becomes clear that the only fitting term regarding Byzantine melopœïa in general, that clearly expresses the musical enrichment and affect on the poetic text with ecclesiastical character, is *melos*. This particular meaning of the term — referring specifically to the Church's teleturgic — is strengthened by the descriptions of other melodies, such as 'Ambrosian melos', 'Gregorian melos' and 'Mozambican melos', which are employed to point to the particular ecclesiastical chant

---

7   In Byzantine Hymnography and Music, generally, the term 'troparion' characterizes almost anything sung, regardless of the specific forms and their particular names. This points to the fact that it was used as the nucleus for the evolution of Byzantine hymnography, whether used as a refrain to psalmic verses or as a fully developed autonomous strophe. J.-B. Pitra writes the following concerning the troparion: 'A tropariis sic omnia pendent, ut canones et cetera nihil esse videatur, quam tropariorum systemata, quae continua serie et diverso agmine instruntur' (Pitra 1876: p. v).
8   Regarding early canons cfr Metsakes 1971: 72–77.
9   Cfr Tomadakes 1965a: 45–48, 51–52; Trembelas 1949: η΄-ιβ΄, λα΄-λζ΄.

forms of a specific ecclesiastical character suitable to the purpose of the faithful's dialogue with God the Father.[10]

This specialized meaning of the term in the ecclesiastical climate forces us to make a distinction between the ecclesiastical melos and secular melos, referred to as 'exoteric' [*exōterikon*] in Byzantium. The exoteric melos is usually characterized as *ethnikon melos*; in Byzantine Music the *ethnikon melos* refers specifically to the melos of the eastern peoples of other faiths. This is further defined through terms such as *persikon*, or *ismaēlitikon*, *organikon* and so on.[11] The terms *melos dytikon* or *melos frangikon* are encountered less frequently and always after the Latin occupation of Constantinople (AD 1204).

During the first period of Byzantine Hymnography (up to Iconoclasm and the fourteenth century), the characterisation *exōterikon melos* refers to the melos of heretical hymnography, through which the heretical doctrines were disseminated. The heretical hymnographers knew the power of music to penetrate and corrupt opinion, and wrote their heretical hymns

---

10 Sozomenus, the historian of the early Christian Church, offers an explanation in Book III, Chapter 16 of his *Historia Ecclesiastica* (Socrates Scholasticus 1865: 1089B): 'When Ephraim perceived that the Syrians were charmed with the elegance of the diction and the rhythm of the melody, he became apprehensive, lest they should imbibe the same opinions; and therefore, although he was ignorant of Grecian learning, he applied himself to the understanding of the metres of Harmonius, and composed similar poems in accordance with the doctrines of the Church, and wrought also in sacred hymns and in the praises of passionless men' (Socrates Scholasticus 1886, 2004–2007).

11 For an indication, see Athos Xeropotamou 383 (second half of the fifteenth century), fols. 149v–150r: 'ἕτερον μαγαλυνάριον εἰς τὴν αὐτὴν ἑορτήν, κυροῦ Ἰωάννου τοῦ λαμπαδαρίου [Κλαδᾶ], τὸ μέλος ἐκ Περσῶν· τετράφωνος αʹ Ἀκατάληπτόν ἐστιν'; Athos, Koutloumousiou 446 (AD 1757), fols. 505r–v: 'ἕτερα κρατήματα λεγόμενα νάϊα, πάνυ ἔντεχνα καὶ χαρμόσυνα, συντεθέντα ἐκ τῶν ἔξω'; Fol. 517v: 'τοῦ Καρύκη, ὅλον ἐθνικόν'; fol. 521r: 'ἕτερον νάϊον ἀτζέμικον [= Persian], πλ. δ''; cfr Stathēs 1975–: Vol. I, 291 and p. 110 below.

Two Bulgarian researchers concentrated on melē with the characterisation *boulgarikon* in their study, Stancev and Tonceva 1978.

A synoptic review of Byzantine ecclesiastical melopœïa

to already existing melodies.[12] In order to protect the Orthodox faithful from this onslaught, the Church Fathers responded with new Orthodox hymnography, whose melodies, even though similar to the heretical melodies, eventually defined the boundaries of another genuinely ecclesiastical melos. From then on, the difference between ecclesiastical and *exōterikon melos* became even more distinct,[13] and is eventually finalized in the eighth century when, according to tradition, Iohannes Damascenus institutes the *oktōēchos*[14] system into Byzantine ecclesiastical melopœïa.

---

12   This activity by the heretics is recorded in many places; cfr the fourth-century Church historian Socrates: 'Ὠδὰς ἀντιφώνους πρὸς τὴν Ἀρειανὴν δόξαν συντιθέντες ᾖδον' (Socrates Scholasticus 2004–2007: VI, 8,6); and Philostorgius: 'διὰ τῆς ἐν ταῖς μελῳδίαις ἡδονῆς ἐκκλέπτων πρὸς τὴν οἰκείαν ἀσέβειαν τοὺς ἀμαθεστέρους τῶν ἀνθρώπων' (Philostorgius Cappadox 1981: Fragment 2,4).

13   Gregory the theologian urges, 'Let us take up hymns instead of timbrils, psalmody instead of profane talking and songs' (Gregorius Nazianzenus 1857–1866: 35; King 1888: 115). Chrysostom also expresses concern, 'John fearing lest any of the more simple should be drawn away from the church by such kind of hymns, opposed to them some of his own people, that they also employing themselves in chanting nocturnal hymns, might obscure the effort of the Arians, and confirm his own party in the profession of their faith' (Socrates Scholasticus 1886; 2004–2007: VI, 8).

14   Through the establishment of the oktōēchos in Orthodox worship many types of melē were excluded, particularly the 'exoteric', since it was forbidden for them to be used in the Church. The name of Iohannes Damascenus is especially connected with the psaltic *oktōēchia*, being considered the author of the idiomela troparia of the *Anastasimatarion* and many poetic canons in the eight modes (Orthodox Eastern Church and Apostolikē Diakonia 1976: p. 3). Nevertheless, the existence of an eight-mode musical system is witnessed to before Iohannes Damascenus. Until recently the earliest eight-mode hymnal was attributed to Severus (ca. 465–ca. 538) patriarch of Antioch; however, recent research has suggested an earlier origin to the eight-mode system centered in Jerusalem. For a discussion see Frøyshov 2007 and cfr Baumstark 1910: 45–48; Baumstark *et al.* 1958: 106; Cody 1982; Jeffery 2001. From other comments Jörgen Raasted, in his Raasted 1966: 158, is led to the following conclusion: 'the Noeane system showed with certainty that Byzantine intonations of some kind existed about AD 800. In their "classical" use these intonations are intimately linked to the eight modes that the intonation system [...] cannot be earlier than the *Oktōēchos* Systematisation. This important date cannot be fixed even approximately, but is in all likelihood earlier than the time of St. John of Damascus (ca. 750) the alleged inventor

It still remains, however, for the present introductory examination of the terminology of Byzantine Music and Hymnography, to consider the following terms: *melopœïa* — *melourgia* — *hymnographia*, together with the terms *melopoios* — *melourgos*, *melographos* — *melōdos* and *hymnographos*.

Melopœïa and *melourgia*, along with the corresponding terms *melopoios* — *melourgos* — *melōdos*, as well as *melographos*, are terms that correspond to the creation of a composed poetic text *and* melody by the same poet. In Byzantine Music it is noteworthy that the word *poiētēs* [poet] refers mainly to the musical composer and replaces the terms *melopoios*, *melōdos* and *melourgos*. Encountered mostly during the first period of Byzantine Hymnography up to the Iconoclastic controversy and derived from the above terms, *melōdoi*, *melopoioi* and *hymnōdoi*[15] are also included. From about the sixth century, the prosomoiac [*pros* + *homoion* = toward + the same] poetry of the troparia, however, belonging to various poetic forms themselves, contributed to the creation of the terms *hymnographia* [hymnography] and *hymnographos* [hymnographer]. These terms refer mainly to the creation of a poetic text for use with already established prototype melodies. This is how we have prosomoiac kontakia and prosomoiac canons. Surely, the hymnographer-poets of these works also knew music and many of them even created completely new compositions, whether they be kontakia, canons or idiomela troparia, but mostly stichēra, since they were not only hymnographers [composers of hymnic poems] but also *melōdoi* [composers of melos].

During the late Byzantine and post-Byzantine periods there is confusion regarding these terms. Having lost their original meaning, the majority have now been abandoned. Today, the terms *melopoios*, *melographos* and *melourgos* come to refer only to the composers of melody. The music aspires to another level and becomes the high art of melopœïa, which morphologically comes to recognize or, rather, define forms of composition. Some

---

of the *Oktōēchos*'; cfr Baumstark and Botte 1953: 106; Baumstark *et al.* 1958; Strunk 1977c; Trembelas 1949: 163; Wellesz 1980: 44, 140, 163; Werner 1948: 24; Wulstan 1971.

15 *Hymnōdos* connotes the creator of both the poetic text and melos.

melographoi even created new forms regarding the text, like the dekapentasyllabic mathēma,[16] and, until just recently, were completely unknown. The classification *melōdos* applied to the lampadarios Iohannes Kladas and Petros Bereketēs[17] refers to the melodic talent perceived in their compositions. This intention is also attested to by the description *glykys* [sweet] — *Iohannes protopsaltes ho Glykys* or *Petros Beretekēs ho neos Glykys*; the dexterity with which they composed and the quality of those melē are also expressed through these terms. Byzantine Music's development into an *ars perfecta* from the twelfth century is borne witness to by distinctly musical terms such as *maïstōr* [maestro] and *didaskalos tēs mousikēs* [teacher of music].

To complete this section on the related terminology, the terms *protopsaltes, lampadarios, domestikos, kanonarchos, monophōnarēs, bastaktai, choros* and *kalophōnarēs*[18] must also be addressed.

The terms *maïstōr*[19] and *didaskalos* [teacher] of music are equivalent and denote the paramount teacher of music, the ideal technician of the art [*technē*] of the modes [ēchoi], those who possess complete knowledge regarding the theory of music and are the source of the terms, rules and *methodoi* [methods] of Music. The *maïstores* and teachers are usually endowed with sweet and melodic voices connoting virtuosity. They are also distinguished in their service at the *analogion* and *bēma* [the chanter's podium] in the sacred churches, in both the composition of melodies and the teaching of music. From these two terms, the second, *didaskalos tēs mousikēs*, can refer to all the known melodists of Byzantine Chant and, naturally, primarily to the most famous personalities. The term *maïstōr* is bestowed on only a few musicians and chiefly to Iohannes Koukouzelēs

---

16 The author's doctoral dissertation was dedicated to this branch of hymnography (Stathēs 1977).

17 Regarding the title *melōdos* for Petros Bereketēs cfr Stathēs 1971: 230; also, regarding references to the same *melōdos* in the Athonite music manuscripts cfr Stathēs 1975–: Vol. 1, 715–716; Vol 2, 902–903.

18 Other terms, mostly the ecclesiastical 'offices' [*ophphikia*] of *nomophylax, oikonomos, primikērios, megas rētōr, prōtopapas*, shall be examined as necessary; cfr Spyrakou 2008.

19 From the Latin *magister*.

Papadopoulos.[20] Because of Koukouzelēs' importance to Byzantine Music the term *maïstōr* holds special meaning and is considered the crown of musical titles. Other melodists with the title *maïstōr* are witnessed to in the manuscripts during the late Byzantine period (1200–1453) and include Iohannes Kallistos the maïstōr, Manuel Argyropoulos the maïstōr, Manuel Chrysaphēs the maïstōr and others.

The terms *protopsaltes, domestikos, laosynaktēs* and *primikērios*, together with the *archon of the kontakion*, are found in the seventh pentad of ecclesiastical offices [*ophphikia*] according to the enumeration of Ps.-Codinus.[21] The two domestikoi — of the first and second choir respectively — were the leaders and overseers of the melodies and singers during the divine services. It was understood that they were the teachers of the members of the choir [*choros*], responsible for the knowledge of every melody. In the Office of the Pannychis, the domestikoi made the *initus* [*enarxis*], proclaiming to the bishop or priest the *eulogēson, despota* [bless, master].[22] Regarding this particular rubric, we read in codex Athos, Konstamonitou 86 (first half of the fifteenth century): (fol. 39v) 'Πληρουμένων δὲ τούτων εὐθὺς ποιεῖ ὁ ἱερεὺς τὴν μεγάλην συναπτὴν καὶ μετὰ τὴν ἐκφώνησιν βάλλει ὁ κανονάρχος μετάνοιαν τὸν ἕτερον δομέστικον τοῦ β' χοροῦ καὶ ἄρχεται τὸ Μακάριος ἀνήρ, γεγονωτέρᾳ τῇ φωνῇ ἀπ' ἔξω εἰς διπλασμὸν' [when this is completed the priest straighaway does the great synaptē]; (fol. 51r) '[...] καὶ εὐθὺς ἄρχεται ὁ α' χορὸς καὶ ἀλλάσσει ὁ δομέστικος· ἀπὸ χοροῦ, ἀρχαῖον, ἦχος πλ. δ', πολίτικον, Ἀνοίξαντός σου τὴν χεῖρα' [the first choir immediate begins and the domestikos changes; from the choir, ancient, mode IV plagal]; (fol. 56v) 'Εἶτα γίνεται μεγάλη συναπτὴ καὶ εὐθὺς ὁ δομέστικος ἀπ' ἔξω, ἦχος πλ. δ' *Μακάριος ἀνήρ* [then the great synaptē and straightaway the domestikos from outside, mode IV plagal *Makarios anēr*]; (fol. 106r) '[...] ὁ δομέστικος τοῦ ἄρχοντος χοροῦ· ἦχος α' *Κύριε ἐκέκραξα*' [the domestikos of the chief choir; mode I

---

20 Cfr Eustratiades 1938: 1–27; Petrov and Kodov 1973: 40–48; R. Palikarova 1953: 193–210; Stathēs 1977: 101–102; Williams 1972: 211–229 and the booklet accompanying Stathēs and Maïstores tēs psaltikēs tecknēs 1988.
21 According to Goar 1960; cfr Demetriou 1927: 25.
22 Cfr Rallēs and Potlēs 1852–1859: Vol. 5, 413.

Kyrie ekekraxa]; and, (fol. 125v) Ὁ δομέστικος εὐθὺς τὸ *Πᾶσα πνοὴ* πλ. δ'' [immediately, the domestikos performs the *Pasa pnoē*].[23]

The term *protopsaltes* refers to the main chanter of the first choir. During the Byzantine period the term referred specifically to the chanter presiding over the singers of the imperial palace.[24] The presiding chanter of the second choir came to be referred to as the *lampadarios*,[25] since he would hold the emperor's taper during the royal ceremonies[26] or other services he attended.

The *kanonarchos*, as *prōtokanonarchos* in Ps.-Codinus,[27] is found in some manuscript typikon diataxeis, especially at the beginning of the Great Vespers: 'βάζει ὁ κανονάρχος μετάνοιαν τοῦ δομεστίκου τοῦ δεξιοῦ [ἢ ἀριστεροῦ] χοροῦ ...' ,[28] whereas some other manuscripts mention the *anagnōstēs*[29] instead of the kanonarchos, even though quite seldom and possibly through some confusion of the term. The *bastaktai* are the *isokratai*;

23 Many other Papadikai bear witness to the same; cfr Stathēs 1975–: Vol. 1, 658.
24 The imperial clergy included four offices for the chanters, the protopsaltes, domestikos, lampadarios and maïstōr, as witnessed to by Ps.-Codinus specifically regarding the Great Church: 'ὡσαύτως, οὐδὲ πρωτοψάλτην ἔχει ἡ Ἐκκλησία, ἀλλὰ δομέστικον, ὁ δὲ βασιλικὸς κλῆρος καὶ ἀμφοτέρους. Καὶ ὁ μὲν πρωτοψάλτης τοῦ βασιλικοῦ ἔξαρχος κλήρου, ὁ δέ γε δομέστικος τοῦ δεποινικοῦ· καὶ ποτὲ μὲν ἔχει καὶ ἡ ἐκκλησία ἕτερον δομέστικον παρὰ τὸν δεσποινικόν, ποτὲ δὲ ὁ αὐτὸς καὶ ἀμφοτέροις τοῖς κλήροις ὑπηρετεῖ, ὥσπερ καὶ ὁ πρωτοπαπᾶς' (Verpeaux and Codinus 1976: 214, 265–266).
25 Cfr Rallēs and Potlēs 1934: 259–261; 1936: 66–69.
26 'Προανέρχεται γοῦν ὁ λαμπαδάριος εἰς τὸν περίπατον λαμπαδηφορῶν, ψάλλων ὅλον τὸ ἰδιόμελον, τό, Ἐξέλθετε ἔθνη, ἐξέλθετε καὶ λαοὶ καὶ θεάσασθε σήμερον τὸν βασιλέα τῶν οὐρανῶν' (Verpeaux and Codinus 1976: 225).
27 Cfr Verpeaux and Codinus 1976: 356. Also, Symeon of Thessalonike, in his treatise on the asmatic akolouthia in Athens, Nat. Libr. 2047 (fol. 8v), relates: 'Οἱ ψάλται δὲ εἰς δύο γίνονται χοροὺς ἑκατέρωθεν, τοῦ πρωτοκανονάρχου μέσον πορευομένου'; cfr Phountoules 1976: 134.
28 Cfr Athos, Konstamonitou 86, fol. 39v (Stathēs 1975–: Vol. 1, 658).
29 The *anagnōstēs* was used mainly for readings, specifically the Epistle and Prophecy readings. Cfr Athos, Iviron 1120, fol. 494v: 'εἶτα λέγει ὁ ἀναγνώστης ἀπ' ἔξω· τῆς Θεοτόκου, Ψαλμὸς τῷ Δαβίδ ... Μετὰ τὸν Ἀπόστολον πάλιν λέγει ὁ ἀναγνώστης, Ἀλληλούια'. For the same instance, also see Athos, Koutloumousiou 457 (second half of fourteenth century), fols. 104v and 106r.

this is clearly referred to in the manuscripts as 'the holders of the ison' and with indications like 'this is chanted with the bastaktai'[30] or 'the domestikos chants with the bastaktai'.[31] The chanting of the actual melos is done with the bastaktai holding the ison or chanting in unison, while the melos is performed by the choir — *apo chorou* or *holoi homou*, either by the monophōnarēs and kalophōnarēs (terms used in the manuscripts)[32] with one or two bastaktai, by the protopsaltes, lampadarios or domestikos.[33] *Kalophōnarēs* and *monophōnarēs* seem to be synonymous;[34] nevertheless, the performance of a kalophonic melody by either of them was embellished, virtuosic and designated beforehand. These indications are witnessed to in the kalophonic verses, prokeimena,[35] cheroubika, and less commonly, in the koinonika, anthems to the emperors and other hymns.

30   Cfr Athos Koutloumousiou 588 (eighteenth century), fol. 115r: 'Χριστοφόρου Μυστάκωνος, μετὰ βαστακτῶν, ἦχος α' Οἶκος Ἰσραήλ'; fol. 122v: an indication that a kratēma 'ψάλλεται μετὰ βαστακτῶν'; and fol. 123r: another kratēma, 'ὁ α' μετὰ τῶν βαστακτῶν'.

31   Cfr Athos Iviron 1120, fol. 489r: 'Εἶτα πάλιν ὁ δομέστικος μετὰ τῶν σὺν αὐτῷ, τὸ Νεάγιε, πλ. δ' Νεαγιε Δόξα Πατρί'. See below, p.18n.54.

32   Cfr Athos Iviron 1120, fol. 566χr: 'Ἀρχὴ τῆς θείας Λειτουργίας τῶν Προηγιασμένων. Μετὰ τὴν συμπλήρωσιν τῶν ἀναγνωσμάτων ἄρχεται ὁ δομέστικος, ἀπὸ χοροῦ· πλ. β' Κετευθυνθήτω. Εἶτα εὐθὺς ἄρχεται ὁ μονοφωνάρης, γεγονωτέρᾳ τῇ φωνῇ, ταῦτα· ἦχος β' Κύριε ἐκέκραξα ... '; fol. 567χv: 'Ὁ δομέστικος ἀπ' ἔξω, τὸ τέλος· ἔπαρσις τῶν χειρῶν μου'.

33   In his important manuscript *Papadikē*, Athos, Iviron 1120 (which we will often refer to in this work), Manuel Doukas Chrysaphēs the lampadarios offers the following concerning the function of the protopsaltes and domestikos (fol. 203v): 'Εἶτα γίνεται μικρὰ συναπτή· καὶ μετὰ τὴν ἐκφώνησιν ἄρχεται ὁ πρωτοψάλτης ἢ ὁ δομέστικος τὸ Κύριε, ἐκέκραξα, εἰς ἦχον τῆς ἑορτῆς, κατ' ἦχον'.

34   A clarifying note can be found in Athos, Konstamonitou 86, fol. 252v: 'Τοῦτο μὲν ἀπὸ χοροῦ καὶ δίχορον ὡς ὁρᾷς [referring to the mathēma Ἄνωθεν οἱ προφῆται], τοῦτο δὲ καλλιφωνικὸν μονοφωνάρικον καὶ ἴδιον τοῦ λαμπαδαρίου [Ιωhannes Kladas] ποίημα' (Stathēs 1975–: Vol. 1, 666).

35   In Athos, Konstamonitou 86, fol. 123v: 'Ὁ μονοφωνάρης, ἦχος β' Ἐν πάσῃ γενεᾷ καὶ γενεᾷ'; fol. 124r: 'Ὁ μονοφωνάρης, ἦχος β' Καὶ ἐλπιεῖ ἐπ' αὐτὸν ὁ δίκαιος' (Stathēs 1975–: Vol. 1, 661). Also, Athos, Koutloumousiou 457, fols. 68r–69v, and especially 70r: 'Εἶθ' οὕτως ἄρχεται ὁ μονοφωνάρης ἐπὶ ἄμβωνος τοῦτο· ποίημα τοῦ μαΐστορος Ἰωάννου τοῦ

A synoptic review of Byzantine ecclesiastical melopœia

The following citation from Gabriel hieromonachos' theory helps clarify the meanings of these terms:

11. Μέθοδος πῶς δεῖ ἀνέρχεσθαι τῆς καλοφωνίας. Μετὰ ταῦτα ἔδοξέ μοι καὶ ἔφοδον ἐκθεῖναι, ᾗ τινί τις ἑπόμενος, καλῶς ἂν τὰς κατ' ἀρχὰς τῆς καλοφωνίας ποιοῖτο καὶ οὐδέποτ' ἂν ἐξέλθοι ἐπὸ τὸ πλέον τοῦ δέοντος ἢ ἐπὶ τῷ ἄνω ἢ ἐπὶ τῷ κάτω. [...] Ταῦτα γοῦν πάντα ἔχων καθ' ἑαυτὸν ὁ μέλλων καλοφωνῆσαι, σκόπει μέχρι πόσων φωνῶν προέρχεται τὸ προκείμενον καλοφωνικόν. Καὶ εἰ μὲν μέχρι τετραφωνίας ἢ πενταφωνίας, γύμνασον τὴν φωνήν σου πρὸ τοῦ ἐλθεῖν τὸν καιρὸν τῆς καλοφωνίας καὶ ἀναβίβασον ταύτην ἐπὶ τὸ ὑψηλότερον· εἶτα ἐπιστρέψας κάτελθε μέχρι τῆς φωνῆς ἧς μέλλεις ποιῆσαι τὴν ἀρχήν, εἶτα κατάβαινε καὶ ἑτέραν μίαν καὶ οὕτως ἄρχου, διότι ἡ φωνὴ ἀεὶ προέρχεται λεληθότως· ἀλλὰ κρεῖττόν ἐστιν ἔχειν τὴν φωνήν σου ἐλευθέραν ἢ ἀναγκάζεσθαι. [...] Δεῖ δὲ ἔχειν μετὰ σοῦ καὶ ἕτερον βοηθὸν ἢ καὶ δύο, πλείονας δὲ οὐδαμῶς· τότε γὰρ οὐ καλοφωνία ἀλλὰ τὸ λεγόμενον ἀπὸ χοροῦ γενήσεται. Ἀλλὰ τοῦτο ὀφείλει γίνεσθαι ἐὰν αἱ φωναὶ ὦσιν ἐπιτήδιαι καὶ καλαί· εἰ δὲ μὴ οὕτως ἔχει ἡ τοῦ καλοφωνοῦντος φωνή, πάντας λαμβανέτω βοηθούς. Ὀφείλουσι δὲ οἱ ψάλλοντες εἶναι καὶ συνήθεις καὶ σχεδὸν προμελετηκότες ἕκαστος τὸ ἑκάστου κοινῶς, ἵνα συμφωνῶσι καὶ ἡδίων οὕτω φανείη ἡ ψαλτική. (Gabriel hieromonachos *et al.* 1985: 94,609–96,658)

11. Method regarding the commencement of kalophony. After all these remarks, it seemed to me advisable also to provide access to the commencement of kalophony. Anyone who is to commence kalophony will be able to follow this and never fall out of the necessary range, either too high or too low. [...] Anyone desiring to begin kalophony must be in control of all these. He must examine to which interval the kalophonic piece ascends. If it ascends to the tetraphony or pentaphony, then train your voice before kalophony occurs and raise your voice to the necessary range. Then sing downward to the tone where you want to begin. Go yet another tone down and begin there. The voice always rises unexpectedly. Yet, it is always better to keep your voice free rather than it being restricted. [...] It is certainly also necessary that you have the support of one or two singers, but not more. Otherwise, it is no longer kalophony, but choral singing. However, this is acceptable if the voices are trained and good; if, however, the voice of the one singing kalophony is not good, all voices should be a support. The singers must be accustomed to being together, and everyone must know his part beforehand in order to be in symphony and the psaltike will ring out more pleasantly. (Gabriel hieromonachos *et al.* 1985: XI)

Κουκουζέλη, πλ. δ' *Πᾶσα πνοή* regarding the lengthy kalophonic mathēma, pasapnoarion of the morning Gospel.

It is important that certain other technical musical terms also be clarified, the main ones being *parallagē, metrophōnia, melos*,[36] *thesis, diplophōnia, antiphōnia, ēchoi* (*diphōnos, triphōnos, tetraphōnos, pentaphōnos, heptaphōnos* and *kyrios, plagios, mesos, paramesos, paraplagios*) and *ison*.

The corresponding paragraph from Chrysanthos' *Theōrētikon Mega tēs moysikēs* (Chrysanthos ek Madyton 1832) clarifies the first three:

Ἢν δὲ παραλλαγὴ μὲν τὸ νὰ ἐφαρμόζωσι τοὺς πολυσυλλάβους φθόγγους ἐπάνω εἰς τοὺς ἐγκεχαραγμένους χαρακτῆρας τοῦ ποσοῦ τῆς μελῳδίας, ψάλλοντες αὐτοὺς συνεχῶς ἐπὶ τὸ ὀξὺ καὶ ἐπὶ τὸ βαρὺ καὶ οὐδέποτε ἐπὶ τὸ ἴσον ἢ ὑπερβατῶς. Μετροφωνία δὲ ἦν, τὸ νὰ ψάλλωσι τὸ μεμελισμένον τροπάριον καθὼς ζητοῦσιν μόνον οἱ χαρακτῆρες, οἵτινες γράφουσι τὸ ποσὸν τῆς μελῳδίας, χωρὶς νὰ παρατηρῆται τὸ ζητούμενον ἀπὸ τὰς ὑποστάσεις καὶ θέσεις. Μέλος δὲ ἦν, τὸ νὰ ψάλλωσι τὸ μεμελισμένον τροπάριον καθὼς ζητοῦσιν αἱ θέσεις τῶν χαρακτήρων μετὰ τῶν ὑποστάσεων, δι' ὧν γράφεται ὄχι μόνον τὸ ποσὸν τῆς μελῳδίας ἀλλὰ καὶ τὸ ποιόν, χωρὶς νὰ παρατρέχηται καὶ τὸ κείμενον τῶν λέξεων. (Chrysanthos ek Madyton 1832: 36–37n4)

Parallagē is the application of the polysyllabic notes[37] of the signs of melodic quantity, continuously chanting them as they ascend and descend, but never the ison or jumps. Metrophonia is to chant the composed troparion by the quantitative signs, not regarding the *hypostaseis* and *theseis*. Melos is the chanting of the troparion as required by the theseis of the signs with their hypostaseis, which express not only the quantity of the melody, but also the quality, without rushing the text.

The theories of *Psaltikē* preceding Chrysanthos's which he follows, also speak of *parallagē* and *metrophōnia*, even though he is in essence referring

---

36 The word *melos* is used as a technical term here, to indicate the perfect performance of the musical phrase [*thesis*] or general composition. This is made clear by Chrysanthos' *Theory* quoted below.

37 The polysyllabic notes [*phthongoi*] according to the *parallagē* pre-1814 notation were, according to the diatonic genus and the system of the *trochos*, as follows; in ascent: *Ananes, Neanes, Nana, Agia, Ananes*; and in descent: *Ananes, Neagie, Aanes, Necheanes, Aneanes*; according to the chromatic genus, in ascent: *Necheanes, Nenanō, Neanes, Nenanō*; in descent: *Necheanes, Nenanō, Necheanes, Nenanō, Necheanes*. Cfr Chrysanthos ek Madyton 1832: § 69, 28–31; §88, 40; § 246, 110; § 257–264, 110; §263, 116.

to something else.[38] These *theoriai* include those written by Manuel Dukas Chrysaphēs,[39] Iohannes Plousiadēnos hiereus,[40] the monachos Pachomios Rousanos,[41] the Gabriel hieromonachos,[42] Cyril Marmarēnos,[43] former bishop of the island of Tenos, Apostolos Kōnstas Chiou[44] and others.[45]

As a musical term, *thesis* (pl. *theseis*) is of primary importance in Byzantine Chant especially when it refers to the older notations. Manuel Chrysaphēs gave the following concise definition:

[38] Chrysanthos' *metrophōnia* does not agree with the content of the term, which the ancient theoricians define better, especially Gabriel hieromonachus and Pachōmius Rousanos; cfr Bamboudakes 1938: 60–76.

[39] For his treatise *On the theory of the art of chanting and on certain erroneous views that some hold about it* cfr Bamboudakes 1938: 35–45; Manuel Chrysaphēs and Conomos 1985; Tardo 1938: 230–243.

[40] See the autograph Athos, Dionysiou 570, fols. 110r–123v; cfr Stathēs 1975–: Vol. 2, 705 and Manussaca 1959: 28–51.

[41] In his treatise one reads: 'Ἡ μὲν γὰρ παραλλαγὴ ἀπαρίθμησίς ἐστι τῶν φωνῶν, τὸ δὲ ἤχημα ἡ τῶν φωνῶν ποιότης· μᾶλλον δὲ παραλλαγή ἐστι μετροφωνία μετὰ ἠχήματος, διὸ καὶ ἀσύστατον ἕκαστον ἄνευ θατέρου' (Bamboudakes 1938: 47; Rousanus 1903: 3).

[42] Regarding *parallagē* cfr Gabriel hieromonachos *et al.* 1985: 88 sq.; Gabriel hieromonachos and Schartau 1990.

[43] In his unpublished treatise, *Eisagōgē mousikēs kat' erōtapokrisin eis raoteran katalēpsin tōn mathēmatōn*, his own description reads: 'ἧς ὁ λόγος περί τε τῶν ἀνιουσῶν καὶ κατιουσῶν φωνῶν, σωμάτων τε καὶ πνευμάτων, ἢ καθ' ἑαυτὰ καὶ ᾗ πρὸς ἄλληλα ἔχουσιν, ἔν τε συνθέσει καὶ συντάξει καὶ περὶ τῶν ἐνεργειῶν τε καὶ σχημάτων, τῶν κοινῶς λεγομένων μεγάλων σημαδίων, παρά τε τοῖς πάλαι καὶ νῦν ἐπὶ παντὸς ἤχου, φθορῶν τε αὐτῶν καὶ φωνουργιῶν καὶ λήξεων καὶ τινων ἄλλων παρεπομένων αὐτοῖς, ποιηθεῖσα παρ' ἐμοῦ Κυρίλλου ἀρχιερέως Τήνου τοῦ Μαρμαρηνοῦ' (Athens, Historikēs kai Ethnologikēs Hetaireias 305, fol. 17r). In his autograph Athos, Xeropotamou 330 (fols. 2–7) Demetrius Lotos anthologizes the first part of Cyril's theory; cfr Lampros 1926: 276; Stathēs 1975–: Vol. 1, 190.

[44] Apostolos Kōnstas Chios is an important musician and prolific codex writer (about 140) of Byzantine chant and author of a theory of chant, which he personally copied at least seven times; cfr Apostolopoulos 2002; Stathēs 1978: 25–38.

[45] Basileios Stephanides should be noted as a contemporary of Chrysanthos; cfr Stephanides 1900–1902.

Θέσις γὰρ λέγεται ἡ τῶν σημαδίων ἕνωσις, ἥτις ἀποτελεῖ τὸ μέλος· καθὼς γὰρ ἐν τῇ γραμματικῇ τῶν εἰκοσιτεσσάρων στοιχείων ἡ ἕνωσις συλλαβηθεῖσα ἀποτελεῖ τὸν λόγον, τὸν αὐτὸν τρόπον καὶ τὰ σημεῖα τῶν φωνῶν ἑνοῦνται ἐπιστημόνως ἀποτελοῦσι τὸ μέλος, καὶ λέγεται τὸ τοιοῦτον τότε θέσις. (Manuel Chrysaphēs and Conomos 1985: 40, 91–96)

Thesis means the union of signs that form the melody. As in grammar, the union of the twenty-four letter forms words in syllables, in the same way, the signs of the sounds are united scientifically and form the melody. This, then, is called *thesis*. (Manuel Chrysaphēs and Conomos 1985: 41)

The united signs used to create any particular *thesis* are the voiced signs [*phōnētika sēmadia*] and voiceless signs [*aphōna sēmadia*], or the so-called great hypostases of cheironomy [*megalai hypostaseis cheironomias*].[46] In referring to the way that the older composers made melody, Chrysanthos writes: 'They composed *theseis* of musical signs to write the chanted melody in a synoptic manner, and thus, pass on their compositions to their students in a methodological way' (Chrysanthos ek Madyton 1832: § 400, 178). The *theseis*, then, are a basic component[47] for the art of *melopœïa*. The *sticherarikon* and *papadikon* genera [*genē*], to which the *Mathēmatarion* belongs (the discussion will return to both below), are distinguished by their differing melodies of these *theseis*. The combination of the genera and forms is nothing other than the succession and combining of *theseis* for each specific genus [*genos*].[48] Knowledge of the *theseis* is therefore fundamental to the analysis of any composition.

46 They are characterized and enumerated in all the *Papadikai* and above-mentioned theories, divided into groups of (a) expression, (b) time and (c) augmentation of the melos; cfr Stathēs 1975: 196–197, 206.
47 'The creative art of a composer of this period should not be misunderstood [...]; his main task was to adapt an already existing melody to the words of a new poem, or to compose a melody based on already existing formulae [*theseis*], and to combine these formulae with connecting passages' (Wellesz 1947: 81).
48 'The ecclesiastical musicians chanted and wrote according to the different forms [*eidē*] of psalmody with rhythms they indicated using cheironomy, inventing melē suiting [*harmozonta*] their needs' Chrysanthos ek Madyton 1832, §400 p. 178). 'But, O my friend, do not think that the manner of the whole musical art and its practice is so simple and uniform that the composer of a kalophonic sticheron with appropriate

As is taught in the *Protheōria of the Papadikē*[49] chant books, the terms *diplophōnia, heptaphōnia* and *antiphōnia* denote the chanting of the same melos by two chanters at different *baseis*, an octave apart, or by a single chanter an octave above the normal *basis* (starting tone) of the mode; this is called *diplasmos* (doubling).

Beyond its more general musical meaning, the term ēchos is also of seminal importance for Byzantine Music. It denotes, according to the ancient Greeks, a *tropos* [*modus*, way],[50] a scale or a succession of intervals that differs from some other scale. Byzantine Music used eight ēchoi based on a pentachord system called the *trochos* or 'wheel'. The modes are divided into authentic and plagal modes. Beyond this division though, the relationship between them leads to their also being termed as *mesos, paramesos* and *paraplagios*. In accordance once again with the *protheōria* in the *Papadikai*, but also according to practice, the modes are furthermore recognized as being *diphōnos* (when the beginning of the mode is initiated two steps above its normal *basis*), as *triphōnos* (when initiated three steps above the basis), *tetraphōnos* (when initiated four steps above), *pentaphōnos* (initiated five steps above) and *heptaphōnos* (initiated seven steps above

---

[*harmodiōn*] *theseis* who does not adhere to the manner of the old sticheron can think that he has done well and that he has written quite well and free from every condemnation — since, if what he has composed does not include the method of the old sticheron, it is not correct' (Manuel Chrysaphēs and Conomos 1985: 41–43). In the numbering of the six chapters of his treatise, this same Chrysaphēs, sine qua non, refers first of all to the knowledge of the appropriate *theseis*: 'First, therefore, there is the ability to compose appropriate [*prosēkousas*] and fitting [*harmodias*] *theseis* following the rules of the art' (Manuel Chrysaphēs and Conomos 1985: 47).

49 The *Propaideia* or *Protheōria tēs Psaltikēs Technēs* is found in the beginning of the *Papadikai* music manuscripts or other codices, as *Stichērarion, Anastasimatarion* and especially *Anthologiai*. A general text of the *Protheōria* can be found in Tardo 1938: 151–230. The theoricians Manuel Chrysaphes, Gabriel hieromonachus and Pachōmius Rousanus also discuss these terms in their works.

50 The *tropoi* of ancient Greek music were based on a tetrachord system where the placement of the hemitonic interval determined the type of tetrachord as Dorian, Phrygian and Lydian; cfr Asioli and Coli 1832: 49–50.

or the lower antiphony of the *basis* of the mode). The knowledge[51] of this eight-mode system, referred to as *oktōēchia*, is necessary for the precise establishment of the *basis* [initial tone, note] in any composition and for the correct operation of any accidentals and modulations in the melos, but also for the correct utilisation of the *isokratēma*.

What still remains is the clarification of *ison*, not as a sign — because as a sign it is the 'ἀρχή, μέση, τέλος καὶ σύστημα πάντων τῶν σημαδίων τῆς Μουσικῆς Τέχνης ...' [beginning, middle and end and the system of all the signs of the Musical Art ...][52] — but as a continuous, accompanying unison on the *basis* of the tetrachord or pentachord of any melos chanted by the *choros*, *monophōnarēs-kalophōnarēs*, or *domestikos*.

As monophonic, vocal or even *tropic*, Byzantine Music is based on the tetrachord and pentachord *systēma* and knows no other harmony, in the Western sense of the word, except for that of the ancient *symphōnoi phthongoi* [symphonic notes].[53] The ison-isokratēma, or continuous unison, is created on the *basis* tone of each tetrachord or pentachord used by the melos. The existence of the isokratēma is witnessed to in the Byzantine music manuscripts when they mention 'the holders of the ison', 'this is chanted with ison' or 'the *domestikos* with the *bastaktai*' and the like.[54] The

---

51   The *Protheōriai of the Papadikai* also contain *methodoi tēs sophōtatēs parallagēs* or *Trochos* of Iohannes Koukouzelēs, as well as the *methodos tetrachordōn* of Iohannes Plousiadenus, through which the relationships between the modes were expressed.
52   This is the normal beginning for the *Protheōriai of the Papadikai*; cfr Athos, Iviron 1120, fol. 2r.
53   'According to Euclides, symphony is the attack and blending of two notes [*phthongoi*] differing in sharpness [*oxytis*] and heaviness [*barytis*]. That is, symphony [*symphōnia*] is the falling of two notes together, even though one is higher than the other, so that they unite. Hence, when they reach the ears of the listener they are indistinguishable the one from the other, while they produce a well-accepted feeling, pleasant, that is the consonance' (Chrysanthos ek Madyton 1832: § 55, 22). Aristoxenus contended that there are four *symphōniai*; by fourths, fifth and octaves, and every symphonous interval across the diapason. The third is not included among the symphonous according to the ancient harmonists; cfr Meibomius 1652.
54   Similar indications include the following examples. Athos, Koutloumousiou 588 (eighteenth century), fol. 115r: 'Χριστοφόρου Μυστάκωνος, μετὰ βαστακτῶν, ἦχος

A synoptic review of Byzantine ecclesiastical melopœia

ison, then, is a necessary element for the performance of the Byzantine melodies. Through it, the necessary and permissible *symphōnia* is accomplished in Byzantine Chant. The establishment of this continuous unison is not an easy subject; it presupposes a deep knowledge of the Psaltic Art and of the contour and progress of each melody.

THE GENERA AND FORMS OF BYZANTINE MELOPŒÏA

Anyone concerning themselves with Hymnography and Musicology will clearly distinguish different genera and forms of melopœïa in manuscripts containing Byzantine chant notation.[55] The names of these genera and

---

α΄ Οἶκος Ἰσραήλ; fol. 122r: Ψάλλεται μετὰ βαστακτῶν [kratēma]'; fol. 123r: "Ο α΄ μετὰ τῶν βαστακτῶν [kratēma]'. Other witnesses from among the many, Athos, Koutloumousiou 455 (fifteenth–sixteenth century), fol. 12v: 'Πρόλογος μετὰ ἴσου, τοῦ, Χρυσάφη [Manuel], ἦχος δ΄ Ερερρερε'; Koutloumousiou 457 (fourteenth century), fol. 61r: ' Ἐνταῦθα ἄρχεται ὁ δεξιὸς χορός, ἴσα καὶ ἀργά, οἱ ὅλοι ὁμοῦ· πλ. δ΄ Πάντα ἐν σοφίᾳ; fol. 104v: Εἶτα ἠχίζει ὁ δομέστικος καὶ ψάλλουσι ἔξω ὅλοι τοῦτο, οὕτως ἀργὰ καὶ ἴσα, β΄ Δόξα ἐν ὑψίστοις Θεῷ καὶ ἐπὶ γῆς εἰρήνη [kalophōnikon]'; Docheiariou 379 (seventeenth century), fol. 105r: 'Εἱρμοὶ καλοφωνικοὶ ... ψάλλονται ἀργὰ καὶ ἴσα' [cfr Stathēs 1975–: Vol. 1, 529]. From these instances we can confer how the need for ison is emphasized for the kalophonic melē, which must also be chanted slowly [*arga*], or rather, *argòs kai meta melous*. It is evident that the ison is an instrumental [*organikon*] element of the melos. We reference the following: Athos, Panteleimon 927 (eighteenth century), fol. 49v: 'εἰς τὸν ἀκάθιστον ὕμνον, ἀργῶς καὶ μετὰ μέλους· ἦχος πλ. δ΄ Θεὸς Κύριος' [cfr Stathēs 1975–: Vol. 2, 223]; And Panteleimon 1008 (autograph of Balasius hiereus), fol. 121r: 'Τρισάγιον νεκρώσιμον, ἀθηναῖον, ψάλλεται δὲ ὅλον ἀργὸν μετὰ παραδόσεως, πλ. β΄ Ἅγιος ὁ Θεός' [cfr Stathēs 1975–: Vol. 2, 421].
Regarding the *bastaktai*, the witness of Athos, Iviron 973 (fifteenth century), fol. 16r is considerably sufficient: 'Ὁ δομέστικος ἀπὸ χοροῦ, μετὰ τῶν βαστακτῶν αὐτοῦ, οἷον ἀναγνωστῶν καὶ λοιποῦ λαοῦ αὐτοῦ, ἦχος πλ. α΄ Ἰδοὺ δὴ εὐλογεῖτε'. It is clear from this that the *bastaktai* had as their task the 'holding' of the ison.

55 This paragraph was adapted for use in my general Introduction in Stathēs 1975–: κδ΄ – λ΄; noted on ξη΄.

forms are related mainly to the content of the poetic text, most of which are also the object of study for the field of Byzantine Hymnology. From the musical standpoint, however, both the genera and forms are of great importance, because each requires a distinct musical application and simultaneously points to the variety of forms in Byzantine chant, as well as to the wondrous achievement of this Byzantine art form. This is easily revealed when we analyse the various Byzantine compositions.

Beyond the manuscript codices, the theoretic works regarding Byzantine Music composed at different times contain specific information on the forms of melic composition, some only in passing and others in great detail. In his *Introduction Concerning the Theory of the Psaltic Art and on Certain Erroneous Views that Some Hold About It* (Manuel Chrysaphēs and Conomos 1985), a truly significant treatise in many ways, Manuel Chrysaphēs, the lampadarios, writes so as to defend the variety of forms in Byzantine Chant.

> Ἀλλὰ μηδὲ τὸν δρόμον, ὦ οὗτος, τῆς μουσικῆς ἁπάσης τέχνης καὶ τὴν μεταχείρισιν ἁπλῆν τινα νομίσῃς εἶναι καὶ μονοειδῆ· ὥστε τὸν ποιήσαντα στιχηρὸν καλλιφωνικὸν μετὰ θέσεων ἁρμοδίων, μὴ μέντοιγε καὶ ὁδὸν τηρήσαντα στιχηροῦ καλῶς ἡγεῖσθαι τοῦτον πεποιηκέναι, καὶ τὸ ποιηθὲν ὑπ' αὐτοῦ καλὸν ἁπλῶς εἶναι καὶ μώμου παντὸς ἀνεπίδεκτον· ἐπεὶ εἰ καὶ μεταχείρισιν στιχηροῦ τὸ ὑπ' αὐτοῦ γινόμενον οὐκ ἔχει, τῷ ὄντι οὐκ ἔστιν ἀνεπίληπτον. Μὴ τοίνυν νόμιζε ἁπλῆν εἶναι τὴν τῆς Ψαλτικῆς μεταχείρισιν, ἀλλὰ ποικίλην τε καὶ πολυσχιδῆ· καὶ πολύ τι διαφέρειν ἀλλήλων γίνωσκε τὰ στιχηρὰ καὶ τὰ κρατήματα καὶ τὰ κατανυκτικὰ καὶ τὰ μεγαλυνάρια καὶ οἱ οἶκοι κατὰ τὰς μεταχειρίσεις αὐτῶν καὶ τὰ λοιπά, περὶ ἃ ἡ τέχνη καταγίνεται· ἄλλη γὰ ὁδὸς καὶ μεταχείρισις στιχηροῦ καὶ ἄλλη κατανυκτικοῦ καὶ ἑτέρα κρατήματος· ἄλλη μεγαλυναρίου καὶ τῶν οἴκων ἑτέρα καὶ ἄλλη χερουβικοῦ καὶ ἀλληλουιαρίου ἑτέρα [...] καὶ τὸν ἐκεῖσε πάντες δρόμον παρ' ὅλον τὸ ποίημα τρέχουσιν ἀμετατρέπτει καὶ τῷ προτέρῳ τῶν ποιητῶν ἀεὶ ὁ δεύτερος ἕπεται καὶ τούτῳ ὁ μετ' αὐτὸν καὶ πάντες ἁπλῶς ἔχονται τῆς τέχνης ὁδοῦ [...]. Κἂν τοῖς κατανυκτικοῖς δὲ τὸν πρὸ αὐτοῦ τῇ τέχνῃ ἐνευδοκιμήσαντα μιμεῖται ὁ μετ' αὐτόν, καὶ ἐν τοῖς κρατήμασι καὶ τοῖς μεγαλυναρίοις ὁμοίως. Ἀλλὰ καὶ ἐν τοῖς χερουβικοῖς ὕμνοις, κομματιαστῶν τῶν ἐν αὐτοῖς μελῶν ὄντων, εὕροι τις ἂν τοὺς πάντας ποιητὰς σκοπούμενος ἀκριβῶς ἐπίσης τε χρωμένοις αὐτοῖς καὶ συμφωνοῦντας ἀλλήλοις. Οὐ μὲν δὲ ἀλλὰ κἂν τῷ πολυελέῳ δὲ καὶ τοῖς ἀντιφώνοις λεγομένοις καὶ τοῖς οἴκοις ὁμοίως. (Manuel Chrysaphēs and Conomos 1985: 40,96–44,142)

But, O my friend, do not think that the manner of the whole musical art and its practice is so simple and uniform that the composer of a kalophonic sticherōn with appropriate *theseis* who does not adhere to the manner of the old stichērōn can think that he has done well and that which he has written quite good and free from every condemnation — since, if what he has composed does not include the method of the old stichēron, it is not correct. Do not think, therefore, that the performance of chant is simple, but rather that it is complex and of many forms [*eidē*]. Know that the *stichēra* and the *kratēmata* and the *katanyktika* and the *megalynaria* and the *oikoi* differ greatly from each other according to their use and in other matters about which the art is concerned. For one kind of manner and practice pertains to the *stichēron*, another to the *alleluarion*, another to the *kratēma*, another to the *megalynarion*, another to the *oikoi*, another to the *cherubikon*, and another to the *alleluarion* [...] Therefore, they take over some melodies unchanged from tradition and from the music thus preserved (as it is recorded in the *Stichērarion*), and they all follow the path unaltered throughout the entire composition. The second composer always follows his predecessor and his successor follows him and, to put it simply, everyone retains the technique of the art ... In the *katanyktika* the composer imitates his predecessor who was successful in this art; and the same applies to the *kratēmata* and to the *megalynaria*. And even in the Cherubic hymns, although their melodies are segmented, one would find on examining all the composers in detail that they were still using the same melodies and were in agreement with each other. Equally in Great Vespers they use the same rule and the same procedure; as well as in the *polyeleos* and in the so-called antiphons, and also in the *oikoi*. (Manuel Chrysaphēs and Conomos 1985: 41–45)

The existence of the variety of forms in the Psaltic Art is apparent from this lengthy citation. Other theoreticians also write concerning these forms. It is of no small consequence that all teachers emphasize the role of mimesis[56] as a great virtue in the pursuit of melopœïa: the younger students imitated

---

56 Cfr 'In the *katanyktika* the composer imitates his predecessor who was successful in his art; and the same applies to the *kratemata* and to the *megalynaria*. And even in the Cherubic hymns, although their melodies are segmented, one would find on examining all the composers in detail that they were still using the same melodies and were in agreement with each other. Equally in Great Vespers they use the same rule and the same procedure; as well as in the *polyeleos*, in the so-called antiphons, and also in the *oikoi*' (Manuel Chrysaphēs and Conomos 1985: 44,134–143; 45). With regards to this Stephanides 1900–1902: 274 writes how it is assumed that the ecclesiastical musician learns, as much as is possible, from tradition the melē and the power of the notational signs; 'οὐδὲ ἐκκλησιαστικὸς μουσικὸς λέγεται πρεπόντως ὁ μὴ μαθὼν ὅσον τὸ δυνατὸν ἐκ παραδόσεως τὰ μέλη καὶ τοὺς σχηματισμοὺς αὐτῶν τῶν σημαδίων'.

their teachers. This is especially so, according to Chrysanthos, because 'this has contributed to the preservation of the differences of melodies and forms of psalmody up to our time' (Chrysanthos ek Madyton 1832: § 400, 178).

This same Chrysanthos of Madytus, to some extent, codifier of the theory of the New Method of Byzantine Chant through his work *Theōrētikon Mega tēs Mousikēs*, enumerates the following forms of psalmody: '*Anoixantaria, kekragaria, doxastika, stichēra, dochai,*[57] *troparia, apolytikia, anastasima, kathismata, hypakoai, antiphōna,*[58] *polyeleoi, pasapnoaria,* canons, *odai, heirmoi, katabasiai, kontakia, oikoi, megalynaria, exaposteilaria, ainoi, prosomoia, idiomela, heōthina, doxologiai, asmatika, mathēmata,*[59] *typika, makarismoi, eisodika, trisagia, alleluiaria, cherubika, koinonika, kratēmata,* kalophonic *heirmoi,* and the rest' (Chrysanthos ek Madyton 1832: §401, pp. 178–179). Although the term *anagrammatismos,* with which the present work concerns itself, is not specifically mentioned by Chrysanthos, it is most definitely alluded to in the term *mathēmata.*

These forms of psalmody are ordered according to four genera of melodies. Chrysanthos again instructs, 'These forms of psalmody refer to four genera of melos: the old stichēraric, the new stichēraric, the papadic and the heirmologic' (Chrysanthos ek Madyton 1832: § 402, 179).

---

57 Dochai are the prokeimena of the vespers and orthros. There exist small [*mikra*], great [*megalai*] and artistic [*entechna*] dochai. Cfr Athos, Iviron 1120, fol. 223r: Ἀρχὴ τῶν μικρῶν καὶ μεγάλων δοχῶν τῆς ὅλης ἑβδομάδος'; and Athens, Nat. Libr. 2458, fol. 37r: Τὰ λυχνικὰ μετὰ τῶν δοχῶν', and fols. 66v sq. The dochai are also a part of the classical repertiore of the *Psaltikon*, a hymnbook discussed below; cfr Thodberg and Hamann 1966: § 6, 14.

58 These antiphons refer to those chanted after the Polyeleos in the orthros or verses special to particular feasts chanted antiphonally. Cfr Athens, Nat. Libr. 2458, fol. 113v: ἀντίφωνα ψαλλόμενα εἰς τὴν ὑπεραγίαν Θεοτόκος· Ἐπακούσαι σου Κύριος'; fol. 116r: ἕτερα ἀντίφωνα ψαλλόμενα εἰς τὰς ἑορτάς· ἦχος δ΄ Τὸν Κύριον, ἀλληλούια'; and fol. 123r: ἕτερα ἀντίφωνα εἰς τοὺς ἀρχιστρατήγους· ἦχος πλ. β΄ Δόξα ἐν ὑψίστοις Θεῷ'; add to this Athos, Iviron 1120, fols. 353r, 366r, 377r and 399r.

59 With this term Chrysanthos is mainly referring to the kalophonic stichera and heirmoi, which are the basic content of the *Mathēmatarion* in the post-Byzantine period, as was known to him. This term also refers to the *anapodismoi* and feet [*podes*]. The next chapter below deals exclusively with this form.

A synoptic review of Byzantine ecclesiastical melopœïa

In examining our subject, these four paragraphs from Chrysanthos' *Theōrētikon* (Chrysanthos ek Madyton 1832: §402–405, pp. 179–180) to be quoted here in full are worthy of our attention and quite useful. This shall facilitate the discussion to follow.

§ 402. Καὶ τὸ μὲν παλαιὸν στιχηραρικὸν μέλος εἶναι τοιοῦτον, οἷον εὑρίσκεται εἰς τὸ παλαιὸν Ἀναστασιματάριον, εἰς τὰ παλαιὰ Στιχηράρια καὶ εἰς τὸ Δοξαστάριον Ἰακώβου. Μελίζονται λοιπὸν μὲ στιχηραρικὸν μέλος δοξαστικά, στιχηρά, ἀναστάσιμα, αἶνοι, προσόμοια, ἰδιόμελα, ἑωθινά. (Chrysanthos ek Madyton 1832: 179)

And the old sticheraric melos is that which is found in the old *Anastasimatarion*, in the old *Sticherāria* and in Iakovos' *Doxastarion*. The *doxastika, stichēra, anastasima, ainoi, prosomoia, idiomela* and *heōthina* are composed using the old sticheraric melos.

§ 403. Τὸ δὲ νέον στιχηραρικὸν μέλος εἶναι τοιοῦτον, οἷον εὑρίσκεται εἰς τὸ Ἀναστασιματάριον Πέτρου τοῦ Πελοποννησίου. Μελίζονται λοιπὸν μὲ τοιοῦτον μέλος δοξαστικά, στιχηρά, ἀναστάσιμα, ἐξαποστειλάρια, αἶνοι, προσόμοια, ἰδιόμελα, ἑωθινά, καθίσματα, ἀντίφωνα, εἰσοδικά. (Chrysanthos ek Madyton 1832: 179)

The new sticheraric melos is that which is found in Petros Peloponnēsios's *Anastasimatarion*. The *doxastika, stichēra, anastasima, exaposteilaria, ainoi, prosomoia, idiomela, heōthina, kathismata, antiphōna* and *eisodika* are composed with this melos.

§ 404. Τὸ δὲ παπαδικὸν μέλος εἶναι τοιοῦτον, οἷον εὑρίσκεται εἰς τὰ κοινωνικὰ καὶ χερουβικά. Μελίζονται λοιπὸν μὲ τοιοῦτον μέλος ἀνοιξαντάρια, κεκραγάρια, δοχαί, πολυέλεοι, πασαπνοάρια, οἶκοι, μεγαλυνάρια, ἀσματικά, μαθήματα, εἰσοδικά, τρισάγια, ἀλληλουϊάρια, χερουβικά, κρατήματα. Αἱ δὲ δοξολογίαι, οἱ στίχοι τῶν πολυελέων, τὸ Μακάριος ἀνήρ, καὶ τὰ τοιαῦτα, μετέχουσι τοῦ νέου στιχηραρικοῦ καὶ τοῦ παπαδικοῦ μέλους. (Chrysanthos ek Madyton 1832: 179)

The papadikon melos is that which is used in the cherubic and communion hymns. *Anoixantaria, kekragaria, dochai, polyeleoi, pasapnoaria, oikoi, megalynaria, asmatika, mathēmata, eisodika, trisagia, allelouiaria,* cherubic hymns and *kratēmata* are composed in this melos. The doxologies, verses of the *polyeleoi,* the *Blessed is the man* and such partake of both the sticheraric and papadic melos.

§ 405. Τὸ δὲ εἱρμολογικὸν μέλος εἶναι τοιοῦτον, οἷον εὑρίσκεται εἰς τὸ Εἱρμολόγιον τοῦ Βυζαντίου Πέτρου. Μελίζονται λοιπὸν μὲ τοιοῦτον μέλος τροπάρια, ἀπολυτίκια, ἀναστάσιμα καὶ μάλιστα τὰ τῶν ἀπὸ στίχου, καθίσματα, ὑπακοαί, ἀντίφωνα, κανόνες, ᾠδαί, εἱρμοί, κοντάκια, μεγαλυνάρια, ἐξαποστειλάρια, αἶνοι, μακαρισμοί, στίχοι τῶν

Θοῦ Κύριε, καὶ λοιποί, δοξολογίαι, τυπικά, εἰσοδικά, καὶ ἔτι αἱ καταβαρίαι αἱ ἀργότερον ψαλλόμεναι. Τὸ δὲ Καλοφωνικὸν Εἱρμολόγιον μετέχει καὶ τοῦ εἱρμολογικοῦ καὶ τοῦ παπαδικοῦ μέλους. (Chrysanthos ek Madyton 1832: 179–180)

The heirmologic melos is that which is found in the *Heirmologion* of Petros Byzantios. *Troparia, apolytikia, anastasima* and the *aposticha, kathismata, hypakoai,* antiphons, canons, odes, *heirmoi, kontakia, megalynaria, exaposteilaria, ainoi, makarismoi,* verses of the *Lord, set a guard* and the remaining doxologies, *typika, eisodika,* in addition to the slow (*argai*) *katabasiai*. The *Kalophonic Heirmologion* partakes of both the heirmologic and papadic melos.

In this ordering of the four genera of melos of the forms of psalmody by Chrysanthos, we note that the forms belong to two, three or four genera of melodies. Basically, the troparia of the *Sticherarion*, that is, the forms of psalmody belonging to the old and new sticheraric genus or melos, are one and the same. From them, the resurrectional [*anastasima*], the verse troparia and *ainoi* are also found in the fourth form, the heirmologic. If we take into account the fact that the term *mathēma* in the third genus, namely, the papadic, refers to stichera idiomela, prosomoia, kontakia, apolytikia, etc., it is evident that the troparia of the *Sticherarion* exist in all four genera of melos.

If a more precise ordering of the forms and genera of psalmody is to be undertaken, it is necessary that two further points be clarified in Chrysanthos' ordering.

First, the new sticheraric melos 'found in Petros Peloponnēsios's *Anastasimatarion*' must be doubly considered as *argon* and *syntomon*. The same troparion, then, is treated differently from the viewpoint of melic composition, either as *argon* or *syntomon*. The basic difference lies in the tempo [*agogē*] utilized in the notes-per-syllable ratio, the *argon* at least doubling the time of the *syntomon*. Beyond this difference, the *argon* character of any sticheraric troparion also lies in the *theseis* the composer is called to use in the one or another genus. As observed above, these appropriate sticheraric *theseis* of the new sticheraric melos are composed with different *theseis* from the old sticheraric melos and the *argon* heirmologic melos. This different application of the same troparion according to melopœïa is more precisely termed by the theories of Byzantine Music, and even by

Chrysanthos himself, as *dromos*[60] — which means 'road' or 'path' (even, 'technique'); hence, we speak of the *argon dromos* and the *syntomon dromos*.

Second, in regard to the heirmological melos — the fourth genus of the forms of psalmody — Chrysanthos recognizes the 'quick road' [*tachys dromos*][61] as referring basically to the troparia of the *Heirmologion* and only by extension to the other troparia, especially the *prologoi* and *stichoi* [verses] of the *Anastasimatarion*. We know, however, that the troparia of the *Heirmologion* are put to melody and chanted according to the two *dromoi* — the *argon* and the *syntomon*. In its worship the Church today accepts and uses the *Heirmologion* of Petros Peloponnēsios[62] with the additions by Petros Byzantios[63] and Gregorios Protopsaltes,[64] added since the time of Petros Peloponnēsios (d. 1777). Before Petros Peloponnēsios, however, the *Heirmologion* of Balasios hiereus and Nomophylax[65] was well-known and

---

60 'The rest, those chanted with a faster tempo (because the heirmological melē can be performed with either a fast or slow tempo, while the stichēraric require a slow tempo) were put to melody by the teachers Petros Peloponnēsios and Petros Byzantios' (Chrysanthos ek Madyton 1832: § 425, 189; Manuel Chrysaphēs and Conomos 1985: 44,134–143; 45). Also, Apostolos Kōnstas Chios, in his *Mousikē technē*, Athos, Docheiariou 389, fol. 54r, regards the scale [*klimax*] as *dromos*; interestingly, he writes the following: Ἱερὶ χειρονομίασ καὶ δρόμου τῶν ἤχων. Τὸ δὲ μάθημα τοῦ πρώτου δρόμου (κλίμαξ α΄ καὶ πλ. α΄ ἤχων) ἔστι εἰς τέσσαρας τρόπους. Καὶ ὁ μὲν πρῶτος τρόπος ἐστὶ κατὰ παπαδικήν· ἤγουν ἀργὸν μέλος. Ὁ δεύτερος κατὰ στιχηράριον· ὁ τρίτος εἰρμολογικός· καὶ ὁ τέταρτος ταχύς, ὡς προέγραψα. Ὁμοίως καὶ πᾶσα ἡ τέχνη εἰς τέσσαρας τρόπους ψάλλεται.
61 Cfr autograph Paris, BnF Suppl. Gr. 1047, fol. 2r.
62 Third quarter of eighteenth century; cfr Patrinelis 1969: 85, 89; 1973; Stathēs 1971: 228–229.
63 Petros protopsaltes ho Byzantios was a student of Petros Peloponnēsios and filled his teacher's compositional lacunae, i.e., the katabasiai of the first three Sundays of the *Triōdion* (Publican and Pharisee, Prodigal and Meat-fare) and the first Sunday of the Fast, as well as Mid-Pentecost; cfr Patrinelis 1969, 1973; Stathēs 1971.
64 Gregorios was the student of Petros Byzantios and composed heirmoi filling his teacher's compositional lacunae, as well as the argon kathismata of the orthros of Holy Week. Regarding his life and work, refer to the liner notes in Stathēs *et al.* 1977.
65 A large number of manuscripts preserve Balasios' (second half of seventeenth century) *Heirmologion*, the oldest of which seems to be Athos, Iviron 1048, from the year

widely disseminated in the manuscript tradition. Subsequently, it was his *Heirmologion* that Petros Peloponnēsios abridged in his own *Heirmologion*. Balasios' teacher was Germanos, bishop of New Patras,[66] and his teacher was the New Chrysaphēs and Protopsaltes of the Great Church;[67] before Balasios, both these teachers — Germanos and the New Chrysaphēs — produced the melodies of the *katabasiai* and many canons for the great feasts. It was with another of Germanos's students, hieromonachos Cosmas Ivēritis and Macedonian,[68] that Balasios composed a complete *Heirmologion*. These seventeenth-century *Heirmologia* contain *kallopismoi* [literally, to make beautiful or embellishments, but not to be confused with improvisations] of the *Heirmologia* of Theophanēs Karykēs[69] and Iohasaph the New Koukouzelēs.[70] These last two Masters, in turn, reflect the tradition of the sixteenth and fifteenth centuries and are also the measure by which we can judge the evolution that the melos of the old *Heirmologion* underwent. The argon *Heirmologion* of Petros Peloponnēsios, then, is the argon tradition of the heirmologic melos and the syntomon *Heirmologion*[71] attributed

---

1686, copied by Kosmas the Macedonian: Ἀρχὴ σὺν Θεῷ ἁγίῳ τοῦ Εἱρμολογίου τοῦ καλλωπισθέντος παρὰ τοῦ τιμιωτάτου νομοφύλακος τῆς μεγάλης Ἐκκλησίας ἐν ἱερεῦσι κυροῦ Μπαλασίου'. His original autograph has not been identified. An *exēgēsis* of his *Heirmologion* was prepared by Simon Karas, but never published; cfr Stathēs 1977: 119–120; 1992.

66 Germanos is the main musical personality during the second half of seventeenth century; cfr Lainas 1960: 145; 1973; Stathēs 1977: 117–118; 1979b, 1998.
67 Cfr Patrinelis 1969: 73–74; 1973; Stathēs 1977: 115–116.
68 Athos, Iviron 1074, fol. 51r: 'Εἱρμολόγιον σὺν Θεῷ ἁγίῳ καλλωπισθὲν ὑπ' ἐμοῦ εὐτελοῦς Κοσμᾶ τοῦ Μακεδόνος' (Lampros 1966: Vol. 2, 249).
69 Athos, Iviron 1154 and Iviron 1155, and Xenophontos 159 from the year 1610. The last is entitled (p. 6): Εἱρμολόγιον σὺν Θεῷ ἁγίῳ περιέχον πάντας τοὺς εἱρμοὺς τῆς Ὀχτωήχου καὶ τῶν δεσποτικῶν ἑορτῶν καὶ τῆς Θεοτόκου. Καλλωπισμὸς τοῦ Καρύκη'; cfr image of the same Ms. in Stathēs 1975–: Vol. 2, 124.
70 Athos, Iviron 1192, M. Lavra K 158, Vaticanus Bibl. Apost. Gr. 301. In Iviron 1192 (seventeenth century) we read: 'Ἀρχὴ σὺν Θεῷ ἁγίῳ τοῦ Εἱρμολογίου τοῦ ὅλου ἐνιαυτοῦ, καθὼς ψάλλεται εἰς τὸ Ἅγιον Ὄρος. Ἐκαλλωπίσθη δὲ μικρὸν παρὰ τοῦ ἐν μοναχοῖς Ἰωάσαφ τοῦ νέου Κουκουζέλους'.
71 The syntomon *Heirmologion* of Petros Byzantios was first published together with the *Heirmologion* of Petros Peloponnēsios, according to the exegesis of Gregorios

to Petros Byzantios is the syntomon tradition, the 'quick road' [*syntomos dromos*] of the heirmologic melos. In more recent times this syntomon melos was broadened and adapted for forms of psalmody that were not heirmological, whenever shorter chants were desired.

Beyond the heirmoi of the canons, both as a book and form of psalmody, the *Heirmologion* also contains the prologoi and other prosomoiac troparia, specifically, the prologoi of the prosomoiac stichera for each mode, sometimes characterized as '*katabasiai*', the kathismata for each mode, the antiphons for each mode, the exaposteilaria and occasionally a few kontakia. All of these troparia mentioned can be chanted using either the argon or syntomon technique or *dromos*.

The *Kalophonic Heirmologion* which, Chrysanthos says, 'partakes of the heirmologic and papadic melē', should be regarded as a newer melos. The melos of the kalophonic heirmologic form consists of a skilful broadening [*platismos*] of the heirmologic *theseis* with a panegyric character, the very goal of kalophony as an artistic virtuosic technique. The desired end then is the artistic delight of the listener. The truth that 'it partakes of the papadic melos' (Chrysanthos ek Madyton 1832: §404, 179) relates to the fact that a kratēma is added at the end of each kalophonic heirmos; beyond this, some heirmoi contain papadic *theseis*, either in their entirety or in some abridged [*syntetmēmenon*] form. The origin of the *Kalophonic Heirmologion* must be attributed to Theophanēs Karykēs.[72] For its perfection as a form,

---

Protopsaltes, which was replaced with the *Syntomon Heirmologion* of Iohannes Lampadarios in later editions. The latter is no more than a reworking or interpretation of Petros Byzantios' work. The *Syntomon Heirmologion* of Petros Byzantios is characterized in the Athos, Panteleimon 917 (nineteenth century) as being 'κατὰ τὸ ὕφος τῆς τοῦ Χριστοῦ Μεγάλης Ἐκκλησίας· ὕφος σύντομον'. Cfr Stathēs 1975–: Vol. 2, 208.

72 This opinion is strengthened by the instances encountered in the music manuscripts, when a kratema is added to an heirmos in the Karykes *Heirmologion*. In these cases the heirmos replaces the prologos, as shall be obvious below. Cfr Athos, Xeropotamou 279, fols. 90r–v, 96r, 100r in Stathēs 1975–: Vol. 1, 42; Athos, Panteleimon 959, fols. 184v–191r in Stathēs 1975–: Vol. 2, 293.

however, much is owed to Germanos Bishop Neōn Patrōn, Balasios hiereus the Nomophylax, but especially Petros Bereketēs the Melōdos.[73]

Following these definitions, some additional points still require clarification regarding the *papadikon melos*. The papadic melos consists mainly of extended or broad musical *theseis* applied to a single syllable of poetic text, usually in a drawn out manner resulting in a long, melismatic chant. As a book, the *Papadikē* contains these long melodies chanted in the *akolouthiai* [services or offices] — hence the original name by which the *Papadikē* hymnbook was known, *Akolouthia*.[74] Examining the content of the *Papadikē* in its oldest chronological form via the Athens codex, Nat. Libr. 2458 from the year 1336, we see that it consists of compositions collected from two different music books, the *Psaltikon* and the *Asmatikon*, along with a few other melodies from the daily office.

Researchers[75] characterize the *Psaltikon* as the book of the protopsaltes or soloist, while the *Asmatikon* is considered the book of the choir. The

---

73 Following the two preceding composers, Germanos and Balasios, Petros Bereketes surpassed them in both the art and number of kalophonic heirmoi produced, approximately 45; cfr Stathēs 1971: 238–240. Regarding Bereketes Chrysanthos writes, 'He surpassed all musicians in the sweetness of his heirmoi compositions, those termed kalophonic. A contemporary of Panagiōtēs [Chalatzoglou], he was protopsaltes at Emathia. He was called Pereketes because when he was teaching the heirmoi and his students would ask him if there were more heirmoi, he would respond "pereketi" [meaning *abundance* in the Turkish language]. It seems that he wrote more than all the other melodes that we have catalogued here, except for Petros of Lacedaemon' (Chrysanthos ek Madyton 1832: XLn.α ́); cfr Stathēs 1977: 121–122.

74 The oldest dated manuscript *Akolouthia, Papadikē* or *Anthologia* is the Athens, Nat. Libr. 2458 from the year 1336. A summary of its contents is provided below. The first synthesis of its repertoire is attributed to Iohannes Maïstōr Koukouzelēs, who knew well the earlier tradition of the *Psaltikē* and *Asmatikon*. Cfr Athens Nat. Libr. 2458, fol. 151r: 'Ἀλληλουιάρια τῶν μεγάλων ἑορτῶν συντεθέντα καὶ καλοποιηθέντα παρὰ τοῦ Μαΐστορος κὺρ Ἰωάννου τοῦ Κουκουζέλους· ἀρχόμεθα ἀπὸ τὴν Χριστοῦ γέννησιν καθὼς ἄρχονται καὶ ἐν τῷ Ψαλτικῷ βιβλίῳ'.

75 Cfr Strunk 1977d: 46; Wellesz 1980: 143–144, as well as Thodberg and Hamann 1966: 12–19 where Thodberg gives the terms, 'Psaltikon ist die Bezeichung des Buches, in dem der Psaltes, der Solist des byzantinischen Gottesdienstes, die Gesänge fand, die er in der Heiligen Liturgie und in dem Studengottestienst vorzutragen hatte' (p. 12).

Monumenta Musicæ Byzantinæ (MMB) of Copenhagen published facsimiles of two codices deemed representative of these two types of chant in vols. IV and VI of its *Série Principale*, the Firenze, Biblioteca Medicea Laurenziana Ashburnhamense codex 64 *Psaltikon* and Moscow, Uspensky Sobor codex no. 9 *Asmatikon Kontakaria* (Bugge 1960; Høeg and Florence. Biblioteca mediceo-laurenziana. 1956).

The classic shape of the *Psaltikon* form is preserved in manuscripts dating from the end of the twelfth century, as in the codex at the Monastery of St John the Theologian, Patmos 221: fol. 1r, 'Ἀρχὴ σὺν Θεῷ Ψαλτικοῦ περιέχοντος τὴν πᾶσαν ἀκολουθίαν' [Beginning with God of the *Psaltikon* containing the entire *akolouthia*]. The classic repertory belonging to the *Psaltikon* consists of the prokeimena, the stichologia of the vespers for the Nativity and Theophany, the cycle of alleluiaria and the hypakoai, but the largest part is dedicated to the *Kontakarion*. The *Asmatikon*, for example, Messina, San Salvatore 129 (now at the Biblioteca Regionale Universitaria Giacomo Longo di Messina), together with the finales *apo chorou* [by the choir] and the *Kontakarion* also contains the cycle of koinonika [communion hymns]. The *Akolouthia* or *Papadikē* books, then, clearly represent a blending of the contents of the *Psaltikon* and *Asmatikon* hymn books.

The great number of similar compositions of diverse forms within the papadic melos contributed to the creation of specialized books, the main ones being the *Mathēmatarion* or *Kalophōnon Sticharion*, but also the *Kontakarion* or *Oikēmatarion* and the *Kratēmatarion*, which will be discussed in another chapter below.[76]

Having addressed Chrysanthos' four genera of melos, we are now prepared to better define the forms of Byzantine melopœïa as being fundamentally three: the *stichērarikon*, the *heirmologikon* and the *papadikon*. Thus, preserving the examined differences, we may enumerate:

'Neben dem Psaltikonstil wird noch eine andere Stilart, der Asmatikonstil benuzzt' (p. 13). 'Der Asmatikon ist mit anderen Worten der Stil, in dem der Elitechor, der Chor der Psaltai, singt' (p. 14).

76   Cfr p. 95 sq.

First genus: stichērarikon, with the following necessary distinctions

a) The old stichēraric of the *Palaia Stichēraria* (twelfth-seventeenth century), based on the *Stichēraria* 'with some new *kallōpismos*[77] by Georgios from Athens, Panagiotēs Chrysaphēs the new, Germanos Neōn Patrōn, Cosmas the Macedonian, some stichēra belonging to Petros Peloponnēsios, the *Doxastarion* of Iakovos Protopsaltes (Iakōbos Prōtopsaltēs and Chourmouzios Chartophylax 1836) and Chourmouzios Chartophylax's *Doxastarion of the Aposticha* (Chourmouzios Chartophylax and Theodōros Phōkaeus 1859; Chourmouzios Chartophylax 1901).

b) The new argon stichēraric based on the *Anastasimatarion* and *Doxastarion* of Petros Lampadarios Peloponnēsios.

c) The new syntomon stichēraric based on Petros Peloponnēsios's *Syntomon Anastasimatarion*. The melos of the syntomon heirmologic style of Petros Byzantios and some other melodies similar to it.

Second genus: heirmologikon, with the following necessary distinctions

a) *Heirmologikon argon*: its pillar is the *Argon Heirmologion* of Petros Peloponnēsios and, in reverse development, the *Heirmologia* of Balasios the priest, Cosmas the Macedonian and Germanos Neōn Patrōn.

---

77 The *kainon* or *kainophanēs kallopismos* in the melos of the *Palaion Stichērarion* is encountered in the middle of the seventeenth century mostly in the *Stichērarion* of Chrysaphēs the new and Germanos Neōn Patrōn. There also exists the tradition of the *kekallopismenon Stichērarion* of Geōrgios oikonomos tou ex Athenōn, regarding whom cfr Athos Iviron 1108, f. 1r: 'Ἀνθολόγιον σὺν Θεῷ ἁγίῳ περιέχον τὴν ἅπασαν αὐτῷ ἀκολουθίαν τῶν δεσποτικῶν ἑορτῶν καὶ δοξαζομένων ἁγίων· συντεθὲν δὲ καὶ ὡραίως καλλωπισθὲν παρὰ τοῦ μουσικωτάτου κὺρ Γεωργίου τοῦ οἰκονόμου καὶ πρωτοψάλτου Ἀθηνῶν'.

b) *Heirmologikon syntomon*: the *Syntomon Heirmologion* of Petros Byzantios and the *Old Heirmologion* of Iohannes the lampadarios and protopsaltes are its foundational representatives.
c) *Kalophonikon Heirmologikon*: this new style is found in Gregorios Protopsaltes's[78] collection of kalophonic heirmoi.

Third genus: papadikon, with the following necessary distinctions

a) *The authentic papadic* melos of the asmatika, alleluiaria, cherubika and koinonika; but also, the anoixantaria, kekragaria, the *Makarios anēr*, the dochai, Polyeleoi, antiphons and Amōmos.
b) *The melos of the Kontakarion or Oikematarion*.
c) *The melos of the Mathēmatarion*, with the mathēmata, that is, the anagrams and anapodismoi of the stichēra, theotokia, and katanyktika. The kalophonic verses of the *Makarios anēr*, the Polyeleoi and the Amōmos, the asmatic heirmoi, and others belonging to this eidos.
d) *The melos of the Kratēmatarion*. The anoixantaria, *Makarios anēr* (except for the kalophonic verses), the dochai, the verses of the Polyeleoi, the antiphons and the Amōmos (except for the kalophonic verses), the megalynaria, the asmatika (mostly trisagia) are purely papadic melodies of the first branch or eidos of authentic papadic melē; the initial part of the compositions in the *Methematarion* belong to this eidos. For this reason they are examined together with the kalophonic verses in the large group of Psalmic mathēmata.[79]

From this point on, the present study will concern itself with the papadic genus, and within it, especially the third form, the melos of the

---

78 Gregorios protopsaltes selected the kalophonic heirmoi *kat' echon* and transcribed them by way of *exēgēsis* into the New Method of analytical notation, appending appropriate *kat' ēchon* kratemata, which he also transcribed. This codex was published by Theodoros Phōkaeus in the year 1835, in Constantinople as the *Kalophōnikon Heirmologion* (Theodōros Phōkaeus and Gregorios Prōtopsaltēs 1835).
79 Cfr pp. 49 and 135.

Mathēmatarion. As we shall see, the skilled papadic melos of the first authentic papadic and second kontakarian forms, together with the kratēmata, or fourth form, will all be considered. Hence, references to all forms of the papadic genus will follow.

PERIODS OF BYZANTINE MELOPŒÏA AND PARALLEL DEVELOPMENT OF BYZANTINE NOTATION

The development of Byzantine melopœïa or the melic composition of hymns according to the various genera and forms of the melourgic art parallels with the evolution of Byzantine notation.[80] They are two things that bear a close dependency one on the other, and the aim of the one beneficially influences the other. Specifically, the search for a more explicit, analytical expression of the melos aids in the development of a more perfected combination and function of notational elements. Conversely, when the notation reaches the point of being a more refined system, with inexhaustible possibilities of expression, the creation of works moves to a new plateau and is opened up to the wonderful artistry of sententious elements belonging to a high art, in this case, the Psaltic Art [*Psaltikē*].

The following must be discussed vis-à-vis the notation used in Byzantine chant, albeit in a cursory manner. There exist four categories of

80   The terminology *semeiographia* and the more widely used 'notation' [*parasēmantikē*] refer to the *parasemantics* via *sēmeia* or *sēmadia* of the melē of Byzantine chant. The term *parasēmantikē* comes to us from ancient Greek music theory, first encountered in Aristoxenus Tarentinus (IV bc): 'οὐ γὰρ ὅτι πέρας τῆς ἁρμονικῆς ἐπιστήμης ἐστὶν ἡ παρασημαντική, ἀλλ' οὐδὲ μέρος οὐδέν, εἰ μὴ καὶ τῆς μετρικῆς τὸ γράψασθαι τῶν μέτρων ἕκαστον' (Aristoxenus Tarentinus 1954: 49,7–9) ['so far from being the limit of harmonic science, notation [*parasēmantikē*] is not even a part of it, unless writing down metres is also a part of the science of metre'] (Barker 1984: 155,11–156,2). Our discussion will soon address the earliest appearance and evolution of Byzantine notation later in this chapter.

signs [*sēmadia*] that achieve the written articulation or recording of the melē through their correct combination and arrangement. Specifically, the first basic category of signs contains fifteen voiced signs called *emphōna* or *phōnētika sēmadia* written with black ink in the manuscripts. The second large category contains over forty so-called voiceless signs written in red ink and known as voiceless signs [*aphōna sēmadia*]. With few exceptions, the voiceless signs are also known by the long name *megalai hypostaseis cheironomias* [great hypostases of cheironomy] and indicate the *melodēmata*, or shape of the melody.

Of primary importance are also the other two categories of signs. The third category of signs is ēchetic and known as *martyriai* [literally, *witnesses*, meaning modal signs in this instance] of the modes. The fourth category is composed of the various phthoric signs called *phthorai*, and which act as signs of modulation delineating changes in the melos according to the rules of the art; these signs are also written in red ink. These four categories of signs have existed since the notation made its first appearance.

Byzantine chant notation has now been in existence for over a millennium and its evolution can be divided into historical periods of development. In order correctly to ascertain these periods of notational development — and correspondingly, those of Byzantine melopœïa — primary importance is given to the signs [*sēmadia*] and the hypostases [*hypostaseis*] through which the melos is expressed. More specifically, since the evolution and the definition of the developmental periods of notation is not dictated by particular historical events that may have occurred around the time of the changes and that might have influenced them, but precisely to the internal operations and criteria of notation, special attention must be given to:

a) the number and the chronological genesis or appearance of the signs;
b) their dynamic *energeia* [function];
c) the falling into disuse or complete disappearance of certain signs;

d)   the transcription or conversion[81] of older signs and melē into newer ones.

When one, two, three or all of these above criteria are met in a particular historical period and become permanent, it is possible to distinguish the following chronological periods of development of Byzantine chant notation:

a)   First Period: *Early Byzantine Notation (AD 950–1177)*
b)   Second Period: *Middle, Fully Developed Byzantine Notation* or the so-called *Round Notation (AD 1177–c. 1670)*
c)   Third Period: *Transitional, 'exegetic' Byzantine Notation (c. AD 1670–1814)*
d)   Fourth Period: *New Analytical Byzantine Notation* or simply, *New Method (1814–present)*

The year 1177, which is a milestone between the first and second periods, is, by a fortunate linking of circumstances, the year in which two musical codices now housed in St Catherine Monastery on Sinai were written. They are the Triodion Codex Sinaiticus 754 — half of which was written using the partial Hagiorite notation and the other in the full Byzantine notation — and the Codex Sinaiticus 1218 — a *Stichērarion* also in the full Byzantine notation.[82] The other benchmark, from circa 1670, is established with the Athonite Codex Iviron 1250, a *Papadikē* written by the composer Balasēs hiereus and nomophylax, which contains a clear *exēgēsis* of the Trisagion hymn. The year 1814 is also the year when the notational reform occurred in Constantinople and from which arose the 'New System' or 'New Method' of analytical chant notation, as it has come to be known.

---

81   The transcription from one notation or, rather, one notation type into another has always been significant, for the very reason that it points without a doubt to the change in Byzantine melos. Through the instances of transcription or conversion one can compare the function of the signs in one notation to another. A classic example of conversion during the Byzantine era from the early Coislin Notation into the Round Notation can be observed in Raasted 1968: 33.
82   Strunk 1966a: 7–8.

A synoptic review of Byzantine ecclesiastical melopœïa

The corresponding criteria for the determination of these four periods of notational development include the following:

FIRST PERIOD: the genesis of new signs; unstable *energeia* or dynamic function.
SECOND PERIOD: the genesis and combination of all symbols and hypostases; stable diastematic or other function; falling into disuse; conversion of the shapes of some older signs; conversion of melodies from older forms of notations into another system.
THIRD PERIOD: the fluctuating combination[83] of symbols and erratic frequency of use and shape; falling into disuse and eventual disappearance of certain great hypostases due to the attempted analysis or *exēgēsis* of the melodic content of the hymns and their analytical melic expression.
FOURTH PERIOD: the falling into disuse and complete disappearance of all *hypostaseis* (with the exception of six) and some other (five) phonetic signs in the New Method; the genesis of new symbols and signs; defined, stable function of elements of this analytical notation; and, most important, the transcription of the melodies of the second and third periods of notation into the notation of the New Method of the so-called Three Teachers (Chrysanthos, Gregorios, Chourmouzios) in 1814.

With regards to the first and fourth periods, my organisation of the historical periods of Byzantine chant notation concur with those of the newer theoreticians of Byzantine music palæography, namely, Egon Wellesz,[84] H. J. W. Tillyard[85] and Oliver Strunk,[86] each of which were considering, in turn, classifications of earlier researchers such as J. Thibaut,[87] A. Gastoué,[88] O. Fleischer,[89] H. Riemann,[90] L. Tardo,[91] J. Petresco[92] and O. Tiby.[93]

---

83 Cfr Stathēs 1975–: 44–45.
84 Cfr Wellesz 1916: 91–125; 1980: 262.
85 Cfr Tillyard 1935: 13–18.
86 Cfr Strunk 1966a.
87 Cfr Thibaut 1907: 33, 101.
88 Cfr Gastoué 1907: 12–23.
89 Cfr Fleischer 1904.
90 Cfr Riemann 1909: 57, 73.
91 Cfr Tardo 1931: 6; 1938: 45–47.
92 Cfr Petresco 1932: 41.
93 Cfr Tiby 1938.

Regarding the second and third historical periods, however, these three important researchers disagree chronologically, the middle of the fifteenth century serving as a distinguishing period among them. Thus, Egon Wellesz suggests the following:[94]

- Middle Byzantine Notation (Hagiopolite — Round): twelfth through fourteenth century
- Late Byzantine Notation (Koukouzelian, Hagiopolite — Psaltique): fourteenth through nineteenth century

And Tillyard as follows:[95]

- Middle Byzantine Notation or Round Notation: c. 1100–1450
- Late Byzantine Notation: 1400–1821

Oliver Strunk[96] offers the year 1177 as the beginning of the Middle Byzantine Notation. The rest of his categories follow Tillyard's, although he did not deal with the notation of post-Byzantine times.

This fifteenth-century dividing line, nonetheless, seems to follow the historical division between Byzantine and post-Byzantine periods and not some distinct change in the chant notation. Hence, from this point of departure all three scholars believed in an oppressive influence of the Ottoman music on Byzantine melos during the Late Byzantine Notation Period (1400–1821): 'And the new works [...] showed, in their florid and chromatic ornamentation, the growing influence of the East [...]. The Fall of Constantinople brought to a rude cessation the activities of Greek musicians [...]. The influence of the East was overwhelming: Greek musicians composed Turkish songs, while they naturally borrowed from Oriental sources much of the new melodic material used in the setting of Byzantine hymns' (Tillyard 1935: 15).

---

94   Cfr Wellesz 1980: 262.
95   Cfr Tillyard 1935: 14–15.
96   Cfr Strunk 1966a: 1, 7, 15.

They were not able, however, to substantiate this division to their satisfaction. Wellesz confesses, 'It would be even more correct to say that studies in Byzantine Music must begin with a thorough study of the theoretical treatises in which the significance of the numerous signs is explained. Though these treatises were written in the fifteenth and sixteenth centuries and referred therefore to Late Byzantine notation, they are reliable for explaining the Middle Byzantine notation, since the latter stage represents only an amplification of the former' (Wellesz 1980: 284).

Regarding the Late Byzantine notation, Tillyard notes how 'the interval-signs remain unchanged; but, to cope with a more elaborate rhythm, the composers employ a great number of symbols intended to give a summary view of various conventional figures, or to indicate the primary and secondary accents with greater precision, or to divide the unit of time. Most[97] of these symbols had already been invented and were illustrated in a study by the precentor Cucuzeles (AD 1300)' (Tillyard 1935: 15).

Oliver Strunk is quite clear when he states, 'from about 1175 until the time of Chrysanthos, whose first publication appeared in 1821, the notation used in the transmission of Byzantine Chant underwent no radical change' (Strunk 1966a: 1).

All this clearly shows how the division into Middle and Late Byzantine notational periods in the middle of the fifteenth century does not flow from the criteria for the classification of notational periods expounded above. Such a division should, however, be sought and actually exists later on, in the middle of the seventeenth century. Tillyard explains the 'how' only vaguely, conjecturing about a change in notation during this period, though he does not seek proof because this would disrupt his theories: 'but from 1660 onwards there was a vast output of Church music. Some scribes copied the older hymns, with little change, from the manuscripts of the fifteenth century. Many composers made ornamental or embellished versions, often with almost incredible elaboration: while others, again, simplified the more difficult tunes to suit beginners or village singers' (Tillyard 1935: 15).

---

97 My own contention is not 'most', but all the symbols had been already invented. From the time of Koukouzelēs on, no other signs exist or are used in Byzantine notation.

These elements, appearing in the middle of the seventeenth century, are carefully analysed in the third part of this writer's introductory tetralogy on the millennium of Byzantine Musical notation (Stathēs 1972b). In that work, the third period of Late Byzantine notation, as defined by many western musicologists, is divided into two notational developmental periods never before defined by the other scholars of Byzantine musicology.[98] 'If we link this event of the analysis or explanation of the notation system with the existence of *kalophōnia* in the *Stichērarion* and *Heirmologion*, where the notation takes on a new form, we can then speak of a new stage of notational development for Byzantine chant. The middle of the seventeenth century is then the end of the Round Notation, as well as the beginning of a period stretching from the mid-seventeenth century to the year 1814 of notational analysis' (Stathēs 1972b: 420).

The three elements dictating the division of the period of notational development from the middle of the seventeenth century into two are: first, the *kainos* (new) or *kainophanēs kallōpismos* [newly-appeared beautification][99] applied to the *Stichērarion* and *Heirmologion* by the musicians Panagiōtēs the New Chrysaphēs and protopsaltes of the Great Church, Germanos Neōn Patrōn,[100] Geōrgios oikonomos from Athens,

---

98 In his Karas 1933: 5, 8–10 S. Karas verifies the change in notation, placing it, however, at 'the beginning or probably middle of the eighteenth century'; nevertheless, he hesitates to place the change earlier even though he mentions the names of Balasios hiereus and Akakios Chalkeopoulos.

99 In the colophon of Athos, Xenophontos 128, fol. 250r, and in the year 1671, Chrysaphes the new writes, 'ἐγράφη δὲ καὶ παρ' ἐμοῦ τοῦ εὐτελοῦς, ἐλαχίστου τε καὶ ἀμαθοῦς, ἁμαρτωλοῦ τε ὑπὲρ πάντας Χρυσάφου δῆθεν καὶ πρωτοψάλτου τῆς Μεγάλης τοῦ Χριστοῦ Ἐκκλησίας, οὐ μέντοι κατὰ τὸ κείμενον τῶν παλαιῶν ἐκτονισθεῖσα, ἀλλ' ἐν καινῷ τινι καλλωπισμῷ καὶ μελιρρυτοφθόγγοις νεοφανέσι θέσεσι, καθάπερ τὰ νῦν ᾀσματολογεῖται τοῖς μελῳδοῦσιν ἐν Κωνσταντινουπόλει. Τοῦτο τοίνυν, ὅσον τὸ κατ' ἐμὲ ἐφικτὸν παρ' ἐμαυτοῦ γέγονε, κατὰ τὴν ἣν παρέλαβον εἰσήγησιν παρὰ τοῦ ἐμοῦ διδασκάλου κὺρ Γεωργίου τοῦ Ῥαιδεστηνοῦ, καὶ πρωτοψάλτου τῆς τοῦ Χριστοῦ Μεγάλης Ἐκκλησίας ἐκτεθεικὼς καὶ τονίσας [...]'; cfr Papadopoulos-Kerameus 1891–1915: Vol. 5, 325–326; Stathēs 1975–: Vol. 2, 65–68.

100 In his autograph codex, Monastery of St. John the Theologian, Patmos 930, fols. 425v–426r, Germanos testifies to *kallopistmos*, 'τούτου χάριν κἀγὼ ὁ ἐν ἀρχιερεῦσι

Kosmas Ibēritēs the Macedonian, Balasios hiereus the nomophylax, and, a little earlier, Geōrgios Raidestēnos, Theophanēs Karykēs, and Iohasaph Neos Koukouzelēs. From this point on, the *kallopismoi* were also applied to the papadic melos.

Secondly, the earliest attempt of *exēgēsis*[101] of the Middle Byzantine notation was made by Balasios hiereus and is found in his autograph codex *Papadikē*, Athos, Iviron 1250, written around the year 1670. On fol. 211v of this manuscript we read the following: Τρισάγιον νεκρώσιμον, καλούμενον ἀθηναϊκον, ψαλλόμενον ἀργόν· ἦχος πλ. β' Ἅγιος ὁ Θεός' [*Nekrōsimon trisagion*, called Athenean, chanted *argon*; mode II plagal, *Holy God*]; and on fol. 212r, just after the above composition, Τὸ αὐτό, ἐξηγήθη παρ' ἐμοῦ· ἦχος πλ. β' Ἅγιος ὁ Θεός' [the same, my own [Balasios'] *exēgēsis*; mode II plagal, *Holy God*].[102] Examining the notation of the *exēgēsis* of this *nekrōsimon trisagion*, we observe almost double the number of notational signs and how the great *hypostaseis* have disappeared, since the melodic line they expressed was written in a more analytical fashion, i.e., utilising a greater number of notational *sēmadia*. This same *exēgēsis* by Balasios was anthologized by his fellow student, Kosmas the Macedonian.[103] Later, Athanasios the Patriarch from Andrianoupolis also attempts an *exēgēsis* of the same *nekrōsimon* trisagion.[104] During the eighteenth century, about fifty *exēgētai*[105] will follow, making *exēgēseis* for a large part of the melodies of the Middle Byzantine

---

ταπεινὸς Νέων Πατρῶν Γερμανός […] συνέγραψα ἐκ πολλῶν πρωτοτύπων, παλαιῶν τε καὶ νέων ἀναλεξάμενος· ἔνια καὶ παρ' ἐμαυτοῦ ἐστιν, ἃ προσθεὶς καλλονῆς ἔνεκα, οἷα που πρὸς τῶν ἐμοῦ καθηγητῶν, προκρίτως δὲ πρὸς τοῦ λογιωτάτου καὶ μουσικωτάτου κυρίου Χρυσάφου πρωτοψάλτου τῆς Μεγάλης Ἐκκλησίας ἐδιδάχθην […] χρόνος ,αχξε' μηνὶ Αὐγούστῳ'; cfr Komines 1968: 49–50.

101 *Exēgēsis* and analysis of the Middle Byzantine notation is the act of recording the melos of the *theseis* and the great hypostatic signs of cheironomy using only the signs of quantity [*posotis*]; cfr Stathēs 1973: 778–781; 1975: 214–216; 1978: 85–95.
102 Cfr Stathēs 1975: p. 214 and Pinakes 17, 18 and 19; 1992.
103 Cfr Athos, Iviron 970, fol. 119r from the year 1686 '*exēgēton*' trisagion.
104 Codex Athos, Chilandar 970, p. 651: 'τὸ ἀθηναϊκον [trisagion], ἐξηγήθη ὑπὸ κὺρ Ἀθανασίου πατριάρχου· ἡ ἐρυθρὰ ἐξήγησις τοῦ Μπαλασίου'; cfr Paris, BnF Suppl. Gr. 1135, fols. 152–163 (Astruc *et al.* 1989: 250).
105 The names can be found in Stathēs 1971: 244n.90; 1975: 214–215.

notational period, essentially rendering the signs of the *megalai hypostaseis cheironomiai* unnecessary. The atrophy and eventual disappearance of many voiceless signs was not correctly understood by Tillyard because the melos they indicated was being analytically expressed, utilising the voiced signs. This was the reason for his accusation that, 'with the growing influence of the East [...] many composers [of that period] made ornamental or embellished versions, often with almost incredible elaboration.'[106]

Akakios Chalkeopoulos's[107] case of *exēgēsis* in Crete during the first half or middle of the sixteenth century is of special interest. However, while his case precedes the *exēgēseis* of Balasios and Athanasios the patriarch, it had no imitators and was not accompanied by any of the other distinguishing criteria that would allow us to define his epoch as initiating the change in notation; nevertheless, Akakios Chalkeopoulos most definitely remains the distant forerunner of *exēgēsis* in Byzantine Musical notation.

Thirdly, the *syntmēsis* [abridgement][108] of the old melodies is a secondary element as far as the development of Byzantine chant notation is concerned. Without a doubt, though, it is indicative of the demands of the times for a change moving toward shorter melē, while at the same time

106 Tillyard 1935: 13–18.
107 As things should have it, luckily, we have an autograph from Akakios Chalkeopoulos in the codex Athens, Nat. Libr. 917, from which we can draw important data regarding a number of musical issues, but mainly about the need for the analysis of the notation for the correct preservation and dissemination of the art. His comment at the outset of his *exēgēsis* of the kekragarion for mode I by Iohannes Damascenus on fol. 15r: Ἐπειδὴ τινες διδάσκαλοι τὸν τῆς μουσικῆς Ἐπιστήμης διηγήσαντο περὶ τῶν σχημάτων μου, ὅτι ἀπόντος κἀμοῦ Ἀκακίου Χαλκεοπούλου καὶ θανόντος διαμένουσι τὰ σχήματα εἰς τοὺς μαθητάς μου· διότι τὰ γινώσκουσι καὶ ψάλλονται. Ἀποθανόντων δὲ καὶ τῶν μαθητῶν μου, διαμένουσι τὰ σχήματα ἀκίνητα καὶ ἀνενέργητα. Διότι οὐδεὶς τῶν διδασκάλων γινώσκει νὰ τὰ ψάλη. Νῦν δὲ ἐμεταμελήθηκα ἐν τοῖς ὑστέροις μου καὶ ἔτρεψα τὰ σχήματα εἰς τὸ κείμενον· καὶ τὸ κείμενον ζητεῖ τὸ σχῆμα. Καὶ ὅστις διδάσκαλος ἀναπτύσσει καὶ βούλεται ψάλλειν τὸ κείμενον, λέγει τὰ πάντα ἀσφαλῶς, ὥσπερ ψάλλεται καὶ τὸ ἐμὸν στιχηράριον· καὶ οὕτως διαλαμβάνεται.
108 When the abridgers recorded part of a melos, they used a more analytical notation and, hence, more signs of quantity; thus, the written presentation of a *thesis* is always optically larger, sometimes with twice as many signs than the prototype; cfr Stathēs 1983.

preserving the primary elements of Byzantine musical composition. This tendency for abridgement contributed to the creation of the new sticheraric and syntomon heirmologic melos. *Syntmēsis*, as a practice, means two things: Firstly, the abridgement of the melos of a composition resulting in the reduction of the time it takes to perform; secondly, it indicates the reduction of signs with which the composition is notated. By shortening some of the extended passages of the original composition and reducing some of its voiceless sounds, it can again be seen that some of the voiceless sounds are first abandoned and then completely disappear. Towards the end of this period, when a new practice of composition had been established using the analytical notation, the phenomenon of *syntmēsis* presents the following rather odd picture. The voiced signs used to indicate part of a *thesis* remaining after the abridgement are always many more than the voiced signs of the entire, unabridged *thesis* as notated in the original script. Hence, this is additional evidence for the fact that the melos was once longer.[109]

I believe that these phenomena support the acceptance of the genesis of a new period — and, by definition, the end of the previous one — in the development of the Byzantine chant notation as defined above.

After this appointment of the chronological periods of the development of Byzantine chant notation, some specific points can be summarized for each period.

First Period. This period was examined in all its breadth and depth by Oliver Strunk's truly expert research. He also collected the 'Atlas' for this notational period in his *Specimina notationum antiquiorum* (Strunk 1966a: 49n4). In the introductory 'Pars Suppletoria' of that work, Strunk distinguishes two types of notation: the so-called Chartes and Coislin notations, further subdividing them into 'archaic' and 'fully developed' forms. He attributes both to a common prototype, contrasting them with the names used by other musicologists.[110] During this period, 'almost equally critical were the years just before and after the middle of the eleventh [century]' (Strunk 1966a: 16). Archaic Chartres and archaic Coislin notations

---

109 Cfr Balageōrgos 2003; Stathēs 1983, 2001.
110 Cfr Strunk 1966a: 4–5, Table 1.

utilize — and not over each syllable of the text, as well as without a stable diastematic value — the following signs that exist in Athos, Lavra Γ 67, fol. 159.[111]

> Σὺν Θεῷ, ἀρχαὶ τῶν μελωδημάτων ... ὀλίγον, γοργόν, ψιλόν, χαμηλόν, βαθύ, ἴσον σαξίματα, πάρηχον, σταυρός, ἀπόδειξις, ὀξεῖαι, βαρεῖαι, ἀπόστροφος, ἀπόδερμα, ἀπόθεμα, κλάσμα, ρεῦμα, πίασμα, τίναγμα, ἀνατρίχισμα, σεῖσμα, σύναγμα, μετὰ σταυροῦ [σύναγμα], οὐράνισμα, θέμα, λεμοί, τρία, τέσσαρα, κρατήματα, ἀπ' ἔσω ἔξω, δύο, φθορά, ἡμίφθορα, καταβατρομικόν, πελαστόν, ψηφιστόν, κόνδευμα, χόρευμα, ῥάπισμα, παρακάλεσμα, παρακλητική, ἠχάδιν, νανά, πέτασμα, κόνδευμα [ἄλλο], τρομικόν, στραγγίσματα, γρονθίσματα.

> [With God, beginning of the melōdēmata ... oligon, gorgon, psilon, chamēlon, bathy, ison saximata, parēchon, stauros, apodeixis, oxeiai, bareiai, apostrophos, apoderma, apothema, klasma, reuma, piasma, tinagma, anatrichisma, seisma, synagma, [synagma] meta staurou, ouranisma, thema, lemoi, tria, tessara, kratēma, ap' esō exō, duo, fthora, hēmiphthora, katabatromikon, pelaston, psēphiston, kondeuma, choreuma, rapisma, parakalesma, paraklētikē, ēchadin, nana, petasma, [another] kondeuma, tromikon, strangismata, gronthismata.]

In the above list of *melōdemata*, the names of entire *theseis* are included. The chronological ordering of these notations is as follows: archaic Chartres, fully developed Chartres, archaic Coislin and fully developed Coislin, which around the middle of the twelfth century coexists with the Middle Byzantine notation.

These two types of notation are known by the French names, respectively, of Coislin and Chartres: *Coislin* after Codex 220 of the Coislin collection at the Biliothèque Nationale in Paris, an eleventh-century *Heirmologion* originally from Jerusalem; and *Chartres* after the so-called 'Chartres fragments' consisting of six leaves (nos. 61–66) from the Athonite codex Γ 76 of the Great Lavra, which the director of the National Library in Chartres, Paul Durand, extracted and carried back to the city in the year 1840. Despite the fact that research has proved that these six folios did, indeed, belong to the Athos Codex M. Lavra Γ 76, still in that library on Mount Athos, and moreover, that the six folios no longer exist, having been destroyed in the

---

111   Cfr Strunk 1966a: Table 12; Wellesz 1980: 273.

allied bombardment of 26 May 1944,[112] this type of notation continues to be known as 'Chartres notation', perhaps as a reminder of the shameless theft by which it was originally acquired.

It is, however, clear that musicologists talking about Byzantine Music refer to it by two 'foreign' names, *Coislin* and *Chartres*, both of which are French. Following consistent admonition in my personal writings, Greek music scholarship has initiated the correct nomenclature for these two notational types of the first period: *Aghioreitiki (Hagion Oros Athos)* for the tenth-century Athonite Codex M. Lavra Γ 67 previously referred to as Chartres notation; and *Aghiopolitiki notation (Holy City)* for the eleventh-century Paris Bibliotèque Nationale Coislin codex 220 *Heirmologion* written in the Holy City *(hagia polis)* of Jerusalem, which echoes the chant tradition of the Lavra of Saint Sabbas, up to now referred to as *Coislin notation*.

Second Period. Again, Oliver Strunk fixes the beginning of this period chronologically. 'At the opposite extreme is the Triodion Sinai 754, completed in the year 1177, the latest dated ms in which the Coislin Notation is appropriately used. And by a curious coincidence, this same year also saw the completion of our earliest dated example of the Middle Byzantine notation, the *Sticherarion* Sinai 1218 [...]. As we have already seen, the third quarter of the twelfth century was a crucial time for the development of Byzantine notation' (Strunk 1966a: 7–8, 16).

Now, all the *sēmadophōna* or notational signs in this period come with a clearly defined diastematic value, as well as the full number of *megalai hypostaseis*, while some notational signs belonging to the previous period have ceased to be used. These signs have been classified by Iohannes Maïstōr Koukouzelēs,[113] whose name was used as the primary classification of the

---

112   Cfr Strunk 1966b.
113   The infamous *Mega Ison* of Iohannes Koukouzelēs (called this because of the beginning words, *Ison, oligon, oxeia*) preserves for us the names of the great hypostatic signs of cheironomy and the melodic shapes of the *theseis*. It is anthologized in most *Papadikai* and *Anthologiai*. It was transcribed by means of *exēgēsis* by Petros Peloponnēsios and came to be in the New Method of analytical notation by Chourmouzios Chartophylax and Matthaios hieromonachos Batopēdenos (cfr Athos, Xenophontos 120, fols. 1–10, and the entirety of Xenophontos 183); cfr Stathēs 1975–: Vol. 2, 39–42, 145–146;

notation for this period by the older musicologists due to his musical genius. This notation remains unchanged[114] until the middle of the seventeenth century, as we have discussed above.

Third Period. Regarding composition, the '*neos kallōpismos*' of the *Sticherarion, Heirmologion* and, by extension, the papadic melos typifies this period in its early stages, as well as the more precise or analytical codification of the melos of the *theseis* and *hypostaseis* through the use of more notational signs. As we have seen, we call this phenomenon *exēgēsis*. During the process of *exēgēsis*, the great hypostases of cheironomy or, otherwise, the *aphōna sēmadia* are analysed, explained and abolished as notational signs. From the middle of the eighteenth century, we also have an essential differentiation[115] in the music itself, mainly with regard to the sticheraric melos. We have the genesis of the new sticheraric melos of Petros Peloponnēsios, following in the tradition of Daniel the Protopsaltes. Correspondingly, regarding the dissemination of the tradition, Iakovos Protopsaltes abridges[116] the old sticheraric melos, possibly dictated by the necessity to use less liturgical time. The occurrence of *exēgēsis* during the mid-eighteenth century, however, serves as a true fermentation of the chant notation.

1997. It was published in Kyriazides 1896: 127–144 and the text, without notation, is in Chrysanthos ek Madyton 1832: xliv.

114 An exception must be noted, possibly the only one which did not have a noble effect on things. Around the years 1549–1559 a student of Iohseph Tsarlinos' in Venice, Hierōnymos Tragōdistēs of Cyprus attempted reforming the system of signs and the stabilisation (of some) at particular pitches. His *Theōrētikon* is preserved in Sinai Gr. 1764; cfr Beneshevich 1937: 186; Hierōnymos Tragōdistēs and Schartau 1990; Stathēs 1972a: 271–308; Strunk 1962: 101–113.

115 The differentiation referred to here concerns mainly the prevalence of the shorter melē in comparison to the older ones and a slight avoidance of compositions by the old teachers. The Byzantine chant used today in the worship of the Greek Church is basically that of the tradition of the second half of the eighteenth century.

116 In Iakovos Prōtopsaltēs and Chourmouzios Chartophylax 1836 his work is referred to as being quicker in its unfolding of the sticheraric and heirmological *theseis*, but also his series of kekragaria and of the eleven heothina doxastiaka, which carry the following note: 'συντετμημένα ἐκ τῶν παλαιῶν μετὰ καλλωπισμοῦ'; cfr Athos, Xeropotamou 289 (year 1807) and Xeropotamou 295, Docheiariou 361 and many others, as in Stathēs 1975–: Vol. 1, 61–63, 69–70, 480–481.

Fourth Period. The fourth period begins between the years 1814–1815 with the reform of the notation by the Three Teachers.[117] During this period we witness the abolition of five *sēmadophōna*[118] and all the great signs of cheironomy except for six.[119] New signs were introduced, *martyriai* and *phthorai*, and time is divided and indicated. Monosyllabic *parallagē* [solmization][120] is introduced, abolishing the polysyllabic[121] that preceded it. Scale intervals were defined, as was the exact actualisation, dynamic *energeia* of the *phthorai*. But the most important component is that the content of the *theseis* and *megalai hypostaseis* were fully transcribed into the analytical New Method notational through the work of the Three Teachers and their first students,[122] a work of enormous dimension and importance, creating a corpus of over sixty-two[123] manuscript volumes of transcriptions, all unpublished.

117 The so-called Three Teachers of Music and reformers of Byzantine chant notation during the years 1814–1815 are Chrysanthos of Madytus, then archimandrite and later Metropolitan of Dyrrachius, Smyrna and Proussa, respectively; Gregorius Byzantius, then lampadarios and later protopsaltes of the Great Church of Christ; and the *mousikodidaskalos* Chourmouzios Georgiou the Giamalēs, later Chartophylax of the Great Church; cfr Aristoklis 1866: 61–63; Chrysanthos ek Madyton 1832: xxxv–xlii; Papadopoulos 1890: 329–335; Psachos 1917: 46–48.
118 The *oxeia, pelaston, kouphisma, dyo apostrophoi and kratēmoÿporröon.*
119 The *bareia, psēphiston, antikenoma, homalon, heteron* or *syndesmos* and *stauros.*
120 The syllables instituted were based on the first letters of the Greek alphabet, from alpha to ēta, with the addition of consonants or vowels for pronunciation: πA, Boυ, Ἰα, Δι, κE, Ζω, νH.
121 Specifically, *Ananes, Neanes, Nana, Agia*; cfr note 37 on p. 14.
122 After the Three Teachers, the primary exegetes were their students, Petros Ephesios and Petros Hagiotaphitēs, both to a limited degree, and on a larger scale, Iohasaph hieromonachos Dionysiates, Matthaios hieromonachos Batopedēnos, Nikolaos hieromonachos Docheiaritēs, Nikēphoros hieromonachos Docheiaritēs and Theophanēs hieromonachos Pantokratorinos. Cfr especially *Eisagoge B* in Stathēs 1975–: Vol. 2, ια΄–ιε΄ on the unpublished and published *exēgēseis* — transcriptions into the New Method of analytical notation of the pre-1814 Byzantine melē.
123 The final number of these codices can only be attained subsequent to the cataloguing of all manuscripts containing Byzantine chant notation. At any rate, the autograph manuscripts of Chourmouzios and some belonging to Gregorius are enumerated in

Returning now to the eidē of Byzantine melopœïa, we note the following: the *Heirmologia, Sticheraria* and *Kontakaria* hymnbooks are written during the first notational period. During the second notational period, the above eidē are expanded, sometimes transcribed into the Middle Byzantine notation where the *Papadikē* appears under the name *Psaltikon* and, later, *Akolouthiai*, 'composed by the maïstōr Iohannes Koukouzelēs', in whose *Papadikē* are collected all the forms of the papadic genus. The greatest number of particular forms, however, their proper and particular compositions, and, from the fourteenth century, their melismatic ornamentations were brought together with the creation of particular books like the *Oikēmatarion* or *Kontakarion*, the *Kalophonic Sticherarion* for the entire liturgical year, later called the *Mathēmatarion* and the *Kratēmatarion*.

During the third notational period, the very same eidē continue to be collected while the new sticherāric melos and the *Kalophōnikon Heirmologion* make their first appearance.

During the fourth notational period all the eidē are preserved by transcription, the exception being that the old sticherāric melos is neglected;[124] the *Kontakarion* ceases to be used and the *Mathēmatarion* and *Kratēmatarion* slowly disappear.

Papadopoulos-Kerameus 1891–1915: Vol. 5, in the section describing the manuscripts in the Metochion of the All-holy Tomb (Jerusalem) in Constantinople (ΜΠΤ). Autograph codices of Grēgorios are in the K. Psachos Library, now housed in the Department of Musicology in the National and Capodistrian University of Athens; cfr Psachos 1917: 48n.55. Information call also be gathered from Chatzegiakoumes 1975: 282–286 for Gregorius and 389–391 for Chourmouzios and Stathēs 1975–: I, xii–xiv. The author has prepared a forthcoming analytical catalogue of the 62 principal manuscripts of the Three Teachers of the New Method, which was announced with an analytical table of their manuscripts in Stathēs 2007.

124 From the post 1814 teachers of music, some borrow *theseis* from the old *Sticherarion* in some of their own doxastika, as do Geōrgios Raidestēnos II and Geōrgios Biolakēs the prōtopsaltai. Systematic composition according to the old sticheraric melos can be found in Chourmouzios Chartophylax and Theodōros Phōkaeus 1859; Chourmouzios Chartophylax 1901, imitating Iakovos' *Doxastarion* (Iakōbos Prōtopsaltēs and Chourmouzios Chartophylax 1836); cfr the 1901, 2nd edition *parartēma* by

From this point on in the present study, the second and third periods and the papadic genus will be the focus of our general attention and, specifically, the *Mathēmatarion*.

N. K. Soubatzoglou adding melē according to the old sticheraric type by Matthaios and Spyridōn of Batopedē.

CHAPTER 2

The form of the Mathēmatarion

THE GENESIS

As we have already observed (p. 31), the form of the *Mathēmatarion* belongs to the papadic genus of Byzantine melopœïa. Before delving more deeply and examining our subject more closely, however, it is necessary to review the papadic genus, albeit in summary form. Considering the present overview, based on the manuscript tradition, it should be said in advance that during the middle of the fourteenth century the papadic genus and its branches, the *eidē* of melos, have already inherently developed into a high art form and reveal an amazing level of accomplishment from a morphological point of view. This means that a pre-existent change in composition has already long taken place, insofar as we are presented with an autonomous art form in its own right, represented by many famous masters, known in Greek as *didaskaloi*. It is through the works of these composers that we arrive at the preceding years and are able to perceive how this change in the asmatic tradition of Byzantine worship gradually occurred during the first century of the Palaeologian era (AD 1261–1360).[1]

The fully developed appearance of the Mathēmatarion eidos and its codification: AD 1336 as milieu

As discussed earlier, the papadic genus of Byzantine melopœïa with all its subdivisions is the most embellished and melodic in relation to the

---

[1] Cfr Levy 1976: 283.

sticheraric and heirmologic genera. The origins of this melodic form must be sought in the first Byzantine years and, hypothetically, must be found even before the first appearance of Byzantine notation, more specifically, in the eighth and ninth centuries. This backward tracing is supported by (a) the existence of the *Psaltikon* and *Asmatikon* books containing the chant repertoire because, from very early on, they contain mostly kontakia and, on the other hand, from (b) the fact that the *spinae medulla* of the papadic genus is dominated by the use of verses from the *Psalter*. Certainly, the psalmic verses [*stichoi*] and kontakia existed before the appearance of Byzantine notation[2] and their melismatic codification from the tenth century clearly reflects this embellishment during the previous years, easily determined from the manuscript tradition. Notably, the simple-syllabic and melismatic, asmatic or kalophonic forms of composition exist for the same troparia or various forms of hymnography; it would thus seem that this must also be true for the years before the ninth century.[3]

The makeup or repertoire of the *Papadike* as a hymnbook for both chanters and choirs is standardized during the fourteenth century, subsequent to a mixing of the *Psaltikon* and *Asmatikon* with other troparia.[4] The manuscript tradition attributes the honour of compilation as well as the standardisation of the contents of the *Papadike* into the form with which it has been passed down to our own day to Iohannes Papadopoulos, the *maïstōr* and Koukouzelēs. Undoubtedly, the *Papadike* was subsequently enriched with new compositions; these compositions, though, belonged to the same eidos and only the collection of kalophonic heirmoi from the end of the seventeenth century can properly be regarded as a new addition.

---

2   According to chronological conspectus in Strunk 1966a: 7–16, the first manuscript containing Byzantine Music was written no earlier than AD 950.
3   It should be noted here that the oral asmatic tradition from the years before the appearance of the notation preserves this difference between the syntomon and argon melos. The argon papadikon melos of the hymns repeated often in the daily offices were more common than the syntomon melē of the troparia chanted once a year. Since it was more difficult to recall the less-used, syllabic melē from memory they were codified first.
4   Cfr Strunk 1977d: 45–54.

The form of the Mathēmatarion

Two manuscripts from the fourteenth and fifteenth centuries attributing their authorship to Iohannes Koukouzelēs will occupy us in this endeavour. The first and oldest dated manuscript of its genus is the Athens, Nat. Libr. 2458, written in the year 1336, probably under Iohannes Koukouzelēs' supervision. The second manuscript is an important and rich *Papadikē* written by Manuel Doukas Chrysaphēs in the year 1458, the Athos, Iviron 1120.[5]

So as to recognize the forms of melos that constitute the papadic genus more easily, a preliminary inventory is presented here of Athens, Nat. Libr. 2458 according to its larger unities and comprising the mathēmata *eidos*.

Fol. 11r. *Akolouthiai* compiled by the maïstōr kyr Iohannes Koukouzelēs, from the beginning of the great vespers through to the completion of the Divine Liturgy.

Anoixantaria; *Makarios anēr*; kalophonic verses from Psalm 2 Ἵνα τί ἐφρύαξαν; kekragaria, *ta Lychnika* with their *dochai*; *dochai* with epiphōnēmata.

Fol. 46r. Here ends the vespers. Bright [*lampran*] orthros begins.

Ὁδηγήσει με ἐν γῇ εὐθείᾳ (end of *hexapsalmos*) —Θεὸς Κύριος —Ἀλληλούια, by mode [*kat' ēchon*] —prokeimena, the monophōnarēs (anagrams) —Πᾶσα πνοή —the monophōnarēs —Ἐλέησόν με ὁ Θεὸς —Megalynaria (kalophonic, Ninth Biblical Ode) —fol. 62r 'by the lampadarios sir Xenos Korōnēs' [Τὴν ὄντως Θεοτόκον] (anagram) —Ἅγιος Κύριος, by mode —Πᾶσα πνοή, of the *ainoi* —Δόξα Πατρί, verse and beginning of the heōthina —those for after the doxology and prekeimena.

Fol. 71v. The orthros has passed and finishes here; the prokeimena of new week begin.

Prekeimena of the Week of New Creation —resurrectional prokeimena —(fol.75r) Polyeleos chanted in Constantinople and all the world; by various composers, old and new. —(fol. 95r) mode I [Ἄσωμεν πάντες ἄσωμεν τὴν μόνην Θεοτόκον] (dekapentasyllabic composition at end of Polyeleos) —kalophonic verses of the Polyeleos [Στόμα ἔχουσι ...] —(fol. 113v). Antiphons chanted to the all-holy Theotokos [Ἐπακούσαι σου Κύριος] —*Hetera* antiphons for the commemorations of saints (the so-called *eklogai*) —(fol. 123v). In the holy city of Thessalonikē [Ἐx

---

5 This codex is described in the unpublished Vol. 4 of Stathēs 1975–, but a summary of the description is provided below on p. 96; also a detailed description can be found in Stathēs 1989.

τῶν οὐρανῶν, ἀλληλούια] (antiphons, anagram) —Amōmos —Kontakion for those who have fallen asleep, by the protopsaltes sir Andras [*Αὐτὸς μόνος ὑπάρχεις ἀθάνατος*] (anagram) —Amōmos to the Theotokos and saints (with kalophonic) —Theotokia (= *'ta archontika'* [*Ἄρχοντες κατεδίωξάν με δωρεάν*]) —verses without music.

Fol. 142v. Ἀρχὴ τῆς Θείας καὶ Ἱερᾶς Λειτουργίας· ἄρχονται δὲ τὰ Τυπικά.

[*Εὐλόγει ἡ ψυχή μου*] —Makarismoi —Entrance hymn [*eisodikon*] —[*Πολλὰ τὰ ἔτη τῶν βασιλέων*] (phēmai) —Trisagion of the Epistle —Prokeimena without commemoration, *kat' ēchon* —Alleluiaria without commemorations, *kat' ēchon* —Prokeimena of the week.

Fol. 151r. Alleluiaria of the great feasts, compiled and embellished [*kallōpisthenta*] by the maïstōr sir Iohannes Koukouzelēs.

Then, cherubic hymns, —Liturgy of Basil the Great [*Ἅγιος* (Sanctus) —*Ἀμὴν* —*Σὲ ὑμνοῦμεν* —*Ἐπὶ σοὶ χαίρει*] —Communion Hymns —[*Πληρωθήτω τὸ στόμα μου*] —(fol. 172v) Beginning of the Service of the Pre-sanctified [*Νῦν αἱ δυνάμεις*—*Γεύσασθε*].

Fol. 176r. Year 6844 [= 1336], fourth Indiction, month of March

Fol. 179r. (By the same hand). Katanyktika *kat' ēchon*; by the maïstōr, sir Iohannes Koukouzelēs:

Dekapentasyllabic compositions. Kratēmata —prologoi followed with kratēmata.

Fol. 191r. Akathistos by the protopsaltes sir Iohannes (Glykys) *Ἄγγελος πρωτοστάτης*.

Fol. 203r. Kratēmata *kat' ēchon*.

Fol. 211r. *Τὴν χεῖρά σου·* (asmatic· doxastikon for the Ninth Hour of Theophany).

Fol. 218r. Anagram by sir Iohannes Koukouzelēs; *Ἴδωμεν πάντες* from the stichēron of Theophany, Σήμερον ἡ κτίσις φωτίζεται.

From this summary of the contents of this important codex emerges the fact that it contains a collection of old melē, syntomon with regard to their form, but extendedly melismatic regarding their artistic kalophonic melodies, representing the new tendency and new artistic style of melodic ornamentation. Specifically, they present us with the following elements of seminal importance for the study of the eidos of the mathēmata:

i) The terms *kalophōnia* — *stichoi 'kalophōnikoi'* — *entechnos dochē* — the *monophōnarēs*, who, it is understood, is the performer of the kalophonic hymns, hence, the term *kalophōnarēs*. All these terms bear witness to a new practice in composition.

ii) *Anagrammatismoi* [anagrams][6] are observed, which are applied to the kalophonic verses [*stichoi*], and the actual term *anagrammatismos* is indicated (fol. 218r), which appears with a stichēron idiomelon, also with the term *anapodismos* (fol. 103r) referring to the kalophonic verse Ὀφθαλμὸν ἔχουσι τὰ εἴδωλα.

iii) Kontakia are found with both anagrams and kratēmata [(fols. 136v–138r) Αὐτὸς μόνος ὑπάρχεις ἀθάνατος] and (fol. 191r) the Akathistos of Iohannes Glykys.

iv) Dekapentasyllabic compositions are presented: the first (fol. 95r) is at the end of the Polyeleos and the second (fol. 179r) in the same section with the term *katanyktika* [compunctual].[7]

v) In the same section (fol. 203r) the kratēmata are found as both self-contained, independent compositions or with a prologos; they are mainly found with all the kalophonic compositions as a necessary element.

vi) Through the existence of the asmatic doxastikon of the Ninth Hour for Theophany (fol. 211r) [Τὴν χεῖρά σου] we are able to conclude that the asmatic practice used at times in various services is very old and that this most certainly influenced the evolution of the mathēmata of the kalophonic melos.

Apart from these observations and considering the content of the codex from a different angle, as it is possible to make other comments as well,

---

6 On the term *anagrammatismos*, see p. 70 below.
7 Cfr below, at p. 155, as well as Stathēs 1977: 79.

among which the main point is that the new compositions are eponymous and the old are distinguished by the characteristically anonymous indication '*palaion*' [old]. Named authorship asserts autonomy of art and composition, expressing the identity of a personal style belonging to particular composers. This autonomy is presented as being of value in and of itself and as a witness of creative freedom. The creative freedom, exercised by the Byzantine composers of the fourteenth century, possesses all the elements of a reformed asmatic chant tradition characterized mainly by the prevalence of the cathedral rite, overriding the simpler monastic liturgical *asma*.[8] The Byzantine chanters now acquired a degree of artistic freedom. They are designated *didaskalos* or *maïstōr* of music and prove themselves as gifted composers and unsurpassed interpreters of the Byzantine Psaltic Art. The codification of the kalophonic heirmoi, kratēmata, and katanyktika into specific groups reveals the full height of melodic ornamentation that Byzantine chant composition had reached by the year 1336.

Another vital comment that should be made is that the majority of the compositions in the *Papadikē* are of psalmic verses, and that kalophony [*kalophōnia*] is presented as a new element in relation to the pre-existing melos for the same verses. Of course, this phenomenon is natural since the psalmic verses, whether they be in a simple or a kalophonic melos, make up the natural corpus of the *Papadikē* book in which they were collected and from which, with the exception of a few isolated cases, they

---

8   Resonances of this are to be found in many manuscripts like the *Papadikē* from the year 1336, where a melos characterized as being that of the monks [*tōn kalogerōn*] is simple, frugal, *ekklesiastikon*, when compared to the *politikon* (Constantinopolitan), *thessalonikaion* or any kalophonic composition. In the service of the Amōmos, for example, Athens, Nat. Libr. 2458 preserves verses on the folios 134r–v by Phardiboukēs, Ἄρχοντες κατεδίωξάν με — Ἡ καρδία μου, ἄρχοντες — Ἠγάπησα, ἀδικίαν ἐμίσησα, as kalophonia. Immediately after then, on fol. 135v, we read, 'οὕτως ψάλλονται ἐν Κωνσταντινουπόλει εἰς τοὺς μοναχούς· πλ. α' Ἄρχοντες κατεδίωξάν με', and then observe the same verses with a *syntomon* melos. Further along, on fol. 136v, 'ἕτερος Ἄμωμος καλογερικός', where only the beginning of the three sections [*staseis*] of the Psalm are written, again *syntomon*. Recent scholarship is now thoroughly engaged with the asmatic office; early attempts at dealing with the musical aspects include Antoniades 1950; Strunk 1977b; Williams 1968.

were never separated. On the contrary, the above mentioned ii., iii., iv.–vi. kalophonic melē, whose texts are not psalmic, were eventually separated from the *Papadikē* and, as we shall soon see, came to make up their own hymn book, the *Mathēmatarion*.

Accordingly, the separation and organisation of the kalophonic mathēmata is ordered into two large categories: (a) the category of *psalmic mathēmata* belonging to the *Papadikē*; and (b) the category of *mathēmata proper*, belonging to the *Mathēmatarion*.

By general shape, and as revealed by the content of the above codex and others like it,⁹ the kalophony of the *Papadikē* relates to the following forms according to the order of the daily offices [*akolouthiai*].¹⁰

a) Kalophonic verses of the vespers:

i.) from Psalm 2, Ἵνα τί ἐφρύαξαν ἔθνη
ii.) the skilled, virtuosic [*entechnoi*] dochai, prokeimena
iii.) the prokeimena with *epiphōnēmata* or *anaphōnēmata*

b) Kalophonic verses of the orthros:

i.) the prokeimena before the orthros [*heōthinon*] Gospel
ii.) the pasapnoaria before the orthros [*heōthinon*] Gospel
iii.) the megalynaria of the Ninth Biblical Ode [Καθεῖλε δυνάστας] and their anagrams
iv.) the kalophonic verses of the Polyeleoi and all antiphons (*eklogai* [= selection]) and their *Doxa – Kai nyn*, with or without triadic or theotokion verses, respectively
v.) the Amōmos and specifically the kalophonic verses, so-called, '*archontika*' and the *Epitaphios*

---

9   Similar codices include fourteenth through fifteenth century Athens, Nat. Libr. 2444, Nat. Libr. 899, Nat. Libr. 2599, Nat. Libr. 2456, Nat. Libr. 2401, Nat. Libr. 2406 (from the year 1453) and Nat. Libr. 2837 (from the year 1457).
10 This order shall be addressed below, p. 135.

c) Kalophonic verses or kalophony of the Divine Liturgy:

i.) the Trisagion hymn — *Dynamis* 'asmatika' and the hymns used in place of the Trisagion for great feasts of the Lord
ii.) the Allelouiaria of the Epistle
iii.) the cherubic hymns, the so-called *asmatika*
iv.) the koinonika [communion hymns]
v.) the verses at the dismissal [Εἴη τὸ ὄνομα — Εὐλογήσω τὸν Κύριον]

The variety and abundant use of the kalophonic verses in the akolouthiai that engaged all the great composers down through the years with the creation of these compositions requires specialized research and study; such study has been attempted for some forms, even if only for those of the fourteenth and fifteenth centuries.[11] These forms are compared in the present study because their examination assists in the clarification of a terminology of kalophony, as well as illustrating the defining marks of kalophonic elements and, hence, of the melodic shape throughout.

The actual mathēmata of the other category are based on the texts of the diverse forms of Byzantine hymnography, especially the stichēra idiomela, kontakia, heirmoi and canon troparia. They will be treated in their own chapter below (p. 149).

Kalophony [kalophōnia or kalliphōnia] as 'ars nova' in the fourteenth century and its defining elements

As we have seen in the Athens, Nat. Libr. 2458 above, the terms *kalophōnia* and *kalliphōnia* or the designation *kalophōnikon* are found in the manuscripts of the fourteenth century and, sporadically, toward the end of the thirteenth century.[12] However, as a form of Byzantine melopœïa it existed

---

11   Cfr Conomos 1972; Morgan 1972; Touliatos-Banker 1976, 1984; Williams 1971.
12   The term is found in two manuscripts from the thirteenth century, Messina, Bibl. Regionale Universitaria 161, fol. 20 and Grottaferrata Badia greca, Cod. Crypt. Γ.γ.4, fol. 97.

The form of the Mathēmatarion 57

earlier, in the first part of the thirteenth century, and especially in the *Kontakaria*.[13]

The elements that constitute kalophony and lend a specific shape and character, that of the *kalophōnikon* or *melismatikon*, are easily extracted from the analysis of a single vesporal kalophonic verse. For instance, the text to the common [*koinon*] melos for the same verse can be compared to the kalophonic one.

We take the following kalophonic verse by Iohannes Koukouzelēs the maïstōr, Ἵνα τί ἐφρύαξαν ἔθνη, for examination.

a) The psalmic verse as found in the Greek Septuagint is as follows:

i.) Ἵνα τί ἐφρύαξαν ἔθνη καὶ λαοί [*Why do the nations conspire*][14] <ἔθνη καὶ λαοί> ἐμελέτησαν κενά; ἀλληλούια. [*and the peoples plot in vain? Alleluia.*]

ii.) Παρέστησαν οἱ βασιλεῖς τῆς γῆς· ἀλληλούια. [*The kings of the earth set themselves,*]

iii.) Καὶ οἱ ἄρχοντες συνήχθησαν ἐπὶ τὸ αὐτό· ἀλληλούια. [*And the rulers take counsel together, alleluia.*]

iv.) Κατὰ τοῦ Κυρίου καὶ κατὰ τοῦ Χριστοῦ αὐτοῦ. Ἀλληλούια. [*Against the Lord and his anointed, alleluia.*]

The melos of the verses, divided into four strophes, is extensive: the common [*koinon*] papadic melos.

b) According to kalophony,[15] the above psalmic text becomes as follows:

Ἵνα τί ... χικινι ... ιιι ...
Ἵνα τί ἐφρύαξαν ἔ ... τὰ ἔθνη

---

13 'Dem Psaltikonstil begegnen wir in den Hss. aus dem Ende des 12. und dem Anfang des 13. Jahrhurderts bis zum 14.–15. Jh.' (Thodberg and Hamann 1966: 13). The majority of the kontakia are to be found in the *Psaltikon*.
14 The English translation is from the Revised Standard Version.
15 The text was lifted from Chourmouzios' autograph *Papadikē*, Athens, Nat. Libr. ΜΠΤ 703, fol. 227v.

καὶ λαοὶ ἐμελέτησαν κενά;
Ἵνα τί ἐφρύαξαν ἔθνη καὶ λαοί;
ἔθνη καὶ λαοί
λαοὶ ἐμελέτη ... ἐμελέτησαν, ἐμελέτησαν κενά;
ἵνα τί ἐμελέτησαν κενά;
ἵνα τί ἐφρύαξαν ἔ ... τὰ ἔθνη
καὶ λαοὶ ἐμελέτησαν κενά;
Ἵνα τί οἱ βασιλεῖς καὶ οἱ ἄρχοντες
συνήχθησαν ἐπὶ τὸ αὐτό. —πάλιν
Ἵνα τί συνήχθησαν κατὰ τοῦ Κυρίου· —πάλιν
Ἵνα τί παρέ ... ἵνα τί παρέστησαν κατὰ τοῦ Κυρίου
Ἵνα τί παρέστησαν
ἵνα τί συνήχθησαν
λαοὶ συνήχθησαν κατὰ τοῦ Κυρίου
καὶ κατὰ τοῦ Χριστοῦ αὐτοῦ.
Ἵνα τί ... Τιριριν [κράτημα].
Ἵνα τί ἐφρύαξαν ἔθνη
τί ... τι τι τι ... τιριριν [κράτημα]
Ἔθνη καὶ λαοὶ ἐμελέτησαν κενά.
Ἀλληλούια.

As expected, the melos of the kalophonic verse is elaborate and embellished [*kekallōpismenon*] with elements that lend to its festive character, emphasising the text's dramatic and conjectural nature, and sealing the entire composition as the product of a high and wondrous art form. Regarding the other elements — the instrumental nature of the melody, the *theseis* and great signs of cheironomy, the *phthorai* and modulations [*allagas*] according to the progression of the melos — they are all relative to kalophony and without them kalophony does not exist. The following three elements, however, are distinctive and can be isolated.

First, the kalophonic melos proper. In relation to the common [*koinon*] papadic melos, the kalophonic melos is more elaborate and eloquent. From a purely melodic standpoint, this is accomplished through the power of the suitable kalophonic *theseis* represented by the 'great signs of cheironomy' and through the *allagē* [change, modulation] of the melody from

The form of the Mathēmatarion

genus to genus, from mode to mode and from ethos to ethos.[16] This change is declared and achieved through the special signs known as *phthorai*. According to Manuel Chrysaphēs, 'Φθορά ἐστι τὸ παρ' ἐλπίδα φθείρειν τὸ μέλος τοῦ ψαλλομένου ἤχου' [a *phthora* is the unexpected destruction of the melos of the mode being chanted] (Manuel Chrysaphēs and Conomos 1985: 48,218–219).[17] The melodic affectations and *platysmoi* [broadening] make the textual repetitions almost necessary, specifically, of one or many syllables, of one or more words or even of an entire phrase, especially so that the continuity and meaning of the text is not lost.[18] Also belonging to this melodic embellishment and lengthening of the melos and text is the perceived expansion of the text through the addition of another text from another troparion, or in some circumstances, like this one, of a text authored by the same composer, mostly in verse of metrical improvisation.[19]

The second element is that of the *anagrammatismoi* or *anapodismoi* of the poetic text, its rearrangement. In the above vesporal kalophonic verse, we have: Ἵνα τί ἐμελέτησαν κενὰ — ἵνα τί ἐφρύαξαν ἔ... τὰ ἔθνη — καὶ λαοὶ ἐμελέτησαν κενὰ instead of 'Ἵνα τί ἐφρύαξαν ἔθνη — καὶ λαοὶ ἐμελέτησαν κενά. Numerous anagrams of entire phrases with repetitions of single letters,

---

16   Cfr Chrysanthos ek Madyton 1832: 169; Panagiotopoulos 1947: 130–131.
17   It is characteristic that despite all the examples of phthorai by mode in his treatise, Manuel Chrysaphēs has in mind only the kalophonic compositions. The practice is more clearly described by Gabriel hieromonachos: 'Sometimes, however, whether by the diligent efforts of the composer, or aesthetic reasons, or out of some necessity one mode falls into another and its characteristic melos is made evident. This modulation occurs either by melos or by parallagē; if by parallagē, the modulated mode is indication; if, however, it is by melos, the mode is not indicated, but the phthora' (Gabriel hieromonachos *et al.* 1985: 565–570).
18   In Williams 1971: 179–180 the main elements of the kalophonic verse are enumerated. Williams observes (1) the repetition of syllables, (2) the repetition of words or phrases, (3) the rearrangement of words, (4) the rearrangement of continuous verses and (5) the interpolation of sections from various verses. Elementa (1) and (2), and often also (3) are so alike as to make up the organic element of the extended and elaborated melos and, therefore, should not be understood as separate.
19   This occurs in the verses of the great *anoixantaria*, the last verses of the Polyeleos and especially in the magalynaria and some encomia theotokia troparia.

syllables and words are observed in the text of the above kalophonic verse
Ἵνα τί ἐφρύαξαν ἔθνη. It is characteristic in this codex that, throughout the kalophonic verse from the Polyeleos, the somewhat similar term of *anapodismos*[20] is used when the phrases are rearranged and the meanings of two or three verses are alluded to, utilising various emphases or different compositions or expressions of the textual meaning by the composer.

Thirdly, the ēchēmata or, more commonly, *kratēmata* that are introduced in the beginning and are mainly inserted a little before the end of the composition. In the above kalophonic verse, Ἵνα τί ἐφρύαξαν ἔθνη, we observe a small extension of the melody in the beginning with the ēchēmata[21] χι χι

20 Cfr Athens, Nat. Libr. 2458, fols. 102v–103v: "Ἄλλον τοῦ μαΐστορος [Ioh. Koukouzelēs], ἦχος α´". Due to its importance, I add the verses of this kalophonic verses here:
Οὐδὲ γάρ ἐστι πνεῦμα ἐν τῷ στόματι αὐτῶν
καὶ οὐ λαλήσουσι, τὰ εἴδωλα τῶν ἐθνῶν.
Στόμα ἔχουσι, τὰ εἴδωλα, καὶ οὐ λαλήσουσι,
οὐ λαλήσουσι τὰ εἴδωλα.
Τὰ εἴδωλα τῶν ἐθνῶν ἀργύριον,
ἀργύριον καὶ χρυσίον.
Ἔργα χειρῶν ἀνθρώπων,
οὐ λαλήσουσι τὰ εἴδωλα.
Τὰ εἴδω – χωχω λα – χαχα τῶν ἐθνῶν
στόμα ἔχουσι καὶ οὐ λαλήσουσι.

Anapodismos 1:
Ὀφθαλμοὺς ἔχουσι τὰ εἴδωλα
καὶ οὐκ ὄψονται τὰ εἴδωλα
καὶ οὐ λαλήσουσι.
πλ. β´
Οὐδὲ γάρ ἐστι πνεῦμα ἐν τῷ στόματι αὐτῶν·
οὐ λαλήσουσι τὰ εἴδωλα τῶν ἐθνῶν.
Καὶ πάντες οἱ πεποιθότες ἐπ' αὐτοῖς
στόμα ἔχουσι καὶ οὐ λαλήσουσι.
Ἀλληλούια, ἀλληλούια, ἄλλη – Τιτιτι ... Ἀλληλούια.

21 *Ēchēmata*, less often referred to as *ēchismata*, is the melos of the meaningless syllables, especially *nena, chichi, kiki, niiii*, or the vowels of the first syllable of the first word of the troparion, which are used to lengthen the composition at the beginning and throughout. In the beginning the ēchēma also has the idea of announcement or establishment of the mode, a kind of introduction or prelude. This very introductory

The form of the Mathēmatarion

νι ιι ιι ... and two stanzas, first a short one and then a second more intricate one in the kratēma *τι ρι ριν* ... at the end of the composition. It is noteworthy that in the other kalophonic verse of the Polyeleos, Οὐδὲ γάρ ἐστι πνεῦμα, the circumstance in which the appropriate ēchēmata χω χω and χα χα are used at the word εἴδωλα [idols], as exclamations of weeping — εἴδω-χωχω-λα-χαχα. Many such circumstances are to be found in the kalophonic compositions when the appropriate syllables are drawn out from words expressing pain or embitterment,[22] fear or joy.

These three elements are the basic distinctive marks of kalophony or, more generally, of the form of the mathēmata of Byzantine melopœïa, whether they be kalophonic verses, kalophonic stichēra and their anagrams or anapodismoi, or whether they are oikoi of kontakia, heirmoi and troparia from canons, theotokia and katanyktika, etc., or compositions on dekapentasyllabic verse. It follows that the term *kalophōnikos -on* for the verses of the Psalms and the mathēmata refers specifically to the eidos of the *Mathēmatarion*. The term is found from the fifteenth century on as a specific designation — *Stichērarion to Kalophōnon*, or '*Archē ... ton kalophōnikon stichērōn tou holou eniautou*'.[23] The terms *kalophōnia* and *kalophōnikon* (the latter used less often) refer to the same entity and are simply variations on the same term.

---

purpose for the melos leads us to the ēchēmata of the modes as presented in the *Protheōriai of the Papadikai*. This practice began mainly with the embellished melē of the doxastika for the great feasts, with a special place for the doxastika of the offices of the Ninth Hour for the feasts of the Nativity of Christ, Theophany and Good Friday. Thus, in the manuscripts, with regards to these doxastika, we read, 'καὶ εὐθὺς ἠχίζει ὁ δομέστικος' in Athos, Xeropotamou 383 (end of fifteenth century), fol. 109v or 'ἠχίζει ὁ δομέστικος' on fol. 105r; cfr Stathēs 1975–: 290.

22 Cfr MΠΤ 733, fol. 213r (*exēgēsis* by Chourmouzios), the characteristic ēchēma *chochocho* on the word *pikron* of the *Τὴν ψυχωφελῆ πληρώσαντες*.

23 Indicitavely, cfr Athos, Vatopedi 1498 from the fifteenth century, *Stichērarion kalophōnikon tou holou eniautou*; Athos, Iviron 96 (fifteenth–seventeenth century), 'Ἀρχὴ σὺν Θεῷ ἁγίῳ τῶν καλοφωνικῶν ἀναγραμματισμῶν τοῦ ἐνιαυτοῦ, ψαλλομένων ἐν ταῖς ἐπισήμοις ἑορταῖς'; Athos, Iviron 964 (AD 1562), fol. 1r, 'Ἀρχὴ σὺν Θεῷ ἁγίῳ τῶν καλοφωνικῶν καὶ ἀναγραμματισμῶν τοῦ ὅλου ἐνιαυτοῦ'; Athos, Iviron 991 (AD 1670), fol. 1r, 'Μαθηματάριον, σὺν Θεῷ ἁγίῳ περιέχον πασῶν (sic) τῶν ἑορταζομένων ἁγίων τοῦ ὅλου ἐνιαυτοῦ στιχηρὰ καλοφωνικά, παλαιά τε καὶ νέα'.

In any event, from the end of the seventeenth century to our own day the term *kalophōnikos* characterizes only the new *kekallōpismenon* heirmologic form; hence, we come across the terms '*heimous kalophōnikous kai panegyrikous, pany charmosynous*,'[24] and *Kalophōnikon Heirmologion*, which we have already discussed above (p. 31).

The three lengthening and distinguishing elements of kalophony converge into one composition and are at the same time the surest indicators of the new style after it has already passed a long period of development, emerging out of the first half of the fourteenth century into the ocean of the new, more expansive musical ephos. Kalophony, then, in this sense can be considered the *ars nova* of Byzantine melopœïa.

The first appearances of the kalophonic melos and the favourable historic circumstances surrounding its development

Identifying the above elements belonging to kalophony as it appears in full development by the fourteenth century and, having before us the general schema of the two basic categories of the forms of *asmatologia* to which kalophony belongs, let us now attempt to deconstruct the evidence in order to determine the first appearances of this kalophonic melos. All researchers easily ascertain the existence of kalophony by the fourteenth century and, apart from a few exceptions, pair the phenomenon with the name and the entire musical activity of Iohannes Koukouzelēs the maïstōr.[25] The easy explanation is that up to the years of Koukouzelēs, the existence of the melismatic style [*hyphos*] of music was anonymous and probably to a large extent orally transmitted. This is easily deduced from the fact that a single special book containing such compositions did not exist in which these melodies could be found and disseminated. It is not by chance that the full appearance of

---

24 Cfr Athos, Xeropotamou 323 from AD 1708, where the terms *kalophōnikoi, panēgyrikoi, pany charmosynoi, hēdeis, hōraioi* and *entechnoi* are encountered in the collection of kalophonic heirmoi at the end of the *Anthologia* (Stathēs 1975–: Vol. 1, 168–170).
25 The height of his activity is detected during the early part of the fourteenth century.

precisely this kalophonic melos is due to the composition and publication of a single book, specifically, that of the *Papadikē*, which, again, appears to owe its existence to Iohannes Koukouzelēs. In this event we should, moreover, recognize an ingenious attempt at codification of the asmatic tradition and the embellishment of the music of the first Palaeologian period under Andronicus II (1282–1328) and not a sudden reformation and renewal in the asmatic tradition in the person of Koukouzelēs.

R. Palikarova Verdeil stated that the performance of the melismatic style in Koukouzelēs and his 'school', and its introduction through him of a new, foreign element into Byzantine Music, 'is not absolutely accurate because that kind of melismatic style has always existed in Byzantine Music' [n'est pas absolument exacte, car le genre mélismatique a toujours existé dans la musique byzantine] (R. Palikarova 1953: 207). A simple count of folios of the Slavic *Kontakaria* is sufficient, whose origins are to be found in the ninth century, Verdeil continues, for one to be convinced that the melodies are embellished to the same degree as those of Koukouzelēs' time.[26]

In a similar investigation back to the ninth century, when we encounter the first appearances of the melismatic style, Oliver Strunk presents without a doubt the strongest overview on the manuscript tradition of Byzantine Music in the first period of its development: 'Beginning about 850, radical changes were taking place. Particularly for doxastika and other liturgically prominent pieces, a new and more elaborate style was being developed' (Strunk 1977a: 194). This tendency spread into other forms of chant and especially to the heōthina, the doxastikon of Pentecost and the service of the Veneration of the Sacred Cross [*stauroproskynēsis*] on the third Sunday of the Great Fast.

From the other researchers, Kenneth Levy (Levy 1963: 156n48) identifies examples of the kalophonic melos in the beginning of the twelfth century, as does J. Raasted (Raasted 1966: 118), while in studying the *Psaltikon*

---

26 At another point in her publication, referring to the kontakarian notation of the ninth century in the Slavic manuscripts, she notes: 'C'est une écriture musicale très developpée, capable d'exprimer les chants mélismatuques pour lesquels elle fut créée: une voyelle est répétée parfois plus de dix fois, toujours munie de nouveaux signes musicaux' (R. Palikarova 1953: 274).

Christian Thodberg (Thodberg and Hamann 1966) sets its genesis to the end of the twelfth and beginning of the thirteenth century, as we saw above.

A definitive piece of evidence for the existence of the melismatic style in the chant of the tenth century is surely the existence of the Athos, M. Lavra catalogue 'of *melodēmata*'.[27] This is nothing other than a list of *theseis* of complete melē (Stathēs 1978: 37), because they are also found either as *theseis* or signs of cheironomy in Koukouzelēs's *Mega Ison*, but also in the notation of the Slavic *Kontakaria*. These melōdēmata were the best evidence for a semantic memory notation of the melē, especially of the embellished and long ones until a fuller development of the notation into the so-called Round stage.

In agreement with all the above, it is easily deduced that the melismatic, long and skilled manner of performance *[tropos]* always existed in Byzantine hymnology. Meanwhile, its progressive development and its circulation did not occur apart from the general evolution through the stabilisation of the hymnology of the daily services and the capabilities of the notation for its full and clear expression. This last point is worth special note. The mutual dependence of notation and melos is evident throughout the history of Byzantine Music.

We are lead in this way to the decisive point in the history of Byzantine notation, the year AD 1177. The origins of the kalophonic melos should be investigated in the manuscripts from 1177 on, not in its developed form, as described earlier, but as a blossoming and specially prepared melos in comparison to the *koinon*, simple melody. We discover traces of this melismatic style that grew out of the tendency of composers and chanters toward the embellished and skilled style in the repertory of the *Psaltikon* and primarily the kontakia. This tendency eventually led to kalophony.[28] The development, however, was slow and with great restraint in the evolution of the kalophonic

---

27 This most important table in found on folio 159r of the tenth century Athos, M. Lavra Γ 67; cfr R. Palikarova 1953: Table V; Strunk 1966a: No. 12.
28 Cfr Strunk 1977a and Levy 1976: 288, where the following is noted: 'We find the inevitable urge toward progress, toward the opening up of new styles and outlets for musical expression. The turn toward personalisation of style and the independent art-object must be accelerating'.

melos as it concerns Constantinopolitan practice; this restraint was a result of the period of Latin occupation (1204–1261).[29] During this time, the interest in the cultivation of chant was displaced and preserved, along with general Orthodox liturgical practice, on the Holy Mountain of Athos and in Thessalonike, other parts of Greece and the Magna Græca of Southern Italy.

The regaining of Constantinople in 1261 inspired the Orthodox to continue their cultural creativity through the cultivation of letters and the arts and to contend for the pure Orthodox faith, building a foundation for their theoretical power and the opulence of expression in all the forms of ecclesiastical art.[30] 'Letters [and generally during the Palaeologian era], classical learning and the arts were cultivated to a large extent; the initiation into Theology was for all who desired to belong to the aristocratic spirit. During the reign of Andronicus II (1282–13128), an imperial University was established in which prominent professors such as the Great Logothetis and humanist Theodōros Metochitēs taught, providing rare and highly specialized learning, while, during the reestablishment by Germanos III (1265–1267) in 1266 of the Patriarchal School, interior wisdom was wondrously cultivated to a high degree' (Dentakes 1969: 8–9).[31]

---

29 In Zakythenos 1972: 119 notice the following description of the situation in Constantinople at the time: 'Κατὰ τοὺς χρόνους τῆς Λατινικῆς κυριαρχίας ἡ πόλις εἶχεν ὑποστῆ μεγάλας καταστροφάς, ὁ πληθυσμὸς εἶχε διαρρεύσει. Ἐκ τῶν πρώτων μελημάτων τοῦ Παλαιολόγου ὑπῆρξεν ἡ ἀνακαίνισις αὐτῆς, ἡ ἀνίδρυσις τῶν ναῶν, ἡ ἀποκατάστασις τῶν ἀνακτόρων καὶ τῶν ἠρειπωμένων τειχῶν. Ἡ ἐρημωθεῖσα πρωτεύουσα ἐδέχετο τοὺς ἐπανακάμπτοντας κατοίκους ....'

30 The last two centuries of the Empire were undoubtedly centuries of struggle for the preservation of the Hellenic identity and culture. In writing about the hesychastic controversy, Tomadakes 1965b: Tom. A, 24–25 comments, 'ἡ Δύσις ἐκάλπαζε πρὸς τὴν δημιουργίαν τῆς ἐπιστήμης, ἡ ὁποία θ' ἀντικαθίστα τὴν πίστιν. Τοῦτο ἦτο ἀπαράδεκτον διὰ τοὺς θεωρητικοὺς τῆς Ἀνατολῆς, οἱ ὁποῖοι εἶχον πολὺν δυναμισμὸν ἀκόμη. Δι' αὐτὸ τὸ ἡσυχαστικὸν κίνημα [...] εἶναι βαθεῖα πνευματικὴ τομὴ μεταξὺ Ἀνατολῆς καὶ Δύσεως [...]. Εἰς τὴν δυνατότητα, τὴν ὁποίαν ἔσχε τὸ Βυζάντιον τὸν ΙΔ΄ αἰ. νὰ ἀποκοπῇ ἀπὸ τὴν Δύσιν ὀφείλεται ἡ διάσωσις τοῦ ἔθνους μετὰ τὴν ἅλωσιν'; cfr also (Konidares 1970: 142).

31 Cfr also, 'Mais comme souvent dans les époques de crise de la vie politique, la vie spirituelle florissait et mêne se manifestait d'une façon des plus brillantes. [...] Malgré tous les échecs politiques et économiques qu'avait subis le vieil Empire alors en agonie,

The first composers and poets of the kalophonic melos belong to this intellectual influence in Constantinople, which was transformed into an incredibly creative organism affecting all branches of the spirit after the regaining of the Empire.[32] Surely, their names are not revealed by the codices of their time, but are clearly deduced from later witnesses. In the *Papadikai* and *Mathēmataria* of the fourteenth through fifteenth centuries up to the present, a large number of composers whose kalophonic composition, anagrams and mathēmata are accompanied by the classification '*kath' heauto mathēmatōn*' and are embellished by the composers of the first half of the fourteenth century, Iohannes Glykys, Iohannes Koukouzelēs and Xenos Korōnēs. Chourmouzios Chartophylax's eight-volume *Mathēmatarion* (the description of which is found in Part Two of the present work) gives us the following table of composers who theoretically — for reasons already given — must have flourished after the year AD 1261.

Table 1. Composers flourishing after the year AD 1261.

Phōkas Philadelpheias:	*kalōpismoi* by Koukouzelēs	ΜΠΤ 728, 164v
Germanos monachos:	*kalōpismoi* by Koukouzelēs	ΜΠΤ 727, 115v
Abasiōtēs:	*kalōpismoi* by Koukouzelēs	ΜΠΤ 727, 94
Klōbas:	*kalōpismoi* by Koukouzelēs	ΜΠΤ 729, 116v ΜΠΤ 732 105v
Michael Patzados:	*kalōpismoi* by Koukouzelēs	ΜΠΤ 731, 147v, 247v ΜΠΤ 732, 353r ΜΠΤ 733, 120v

---

les lettres jetaient une dernière flamne claire et brillante, comme dans une chapelle sainte le cierge avant de s'éteindre' (Knös 1962: 90).

32   It was during this most interesting period between AD 1261–1360 that the development and stabilisation of the kalophonic melos occurred, the other arts and sciences cultivate important personalities, such as the historian Georgios Pachymeres (1242–c. 1310), the polymath and wise Nicēphorus Grēgoras (d. c. 1360), the poet Manuel Philēs (c. 1275–1340), the philologist Maximus Planoudēs (1260–1310), the theologian Gregory Palamas (c. 1296–1359), Nicolaus Cabasilas, Matthaios Blastarēs (d. c. 1350) and Theodorus Metochitēs.

The form of the Mathēmatarion

Nikolaos Kallistos:	*kalōpismoi* by Koukouzelēs and Korōnēs	ΜΠΤ 731, 322v ΜΠΤ 733, 314r
Nikolaos Kampanēs:	*kalōpismoi* by Koukouzelēs *kalōpismoi* by I. Glykys	ΜΠΤ 731, 373v ΜΠΤ 732, 17v, 154r ΜΠΤ 733, 271r
Symeōn Psēritzēs:	*kalōpismoi* by Koukouzelēs	ΜΠΤ 732, 303v
Karbounariōtēs:	*kalōpismoi* by Koukouzelēs and Magoulas	ΜΠΤ 732, 362v
	kalōpismoi by Koukouzelēs	ΜΠΤ 733, 58r, 290r
Theodōros Manourgas:	*kalōpismoi* by X. Korōnēs *kalōpismoi* by G. Kontopetrēs	ΜΠΤ 733, 255r ΜΠΤ 734, 103r
Leōn Almyriōtēs:	*kalōpismoi* by Glykys and Korōnēs	ΜΠΤ 733, 302r
Nikephoros Ēthikos:	*kalōpismoi* by Koukouzelēs	ΜΠΤ 733, 125r
Grēgorios domestikos:	*kalōpismoi* by Koukouzelēs	Xeropotamou 383, 113v

It is worth noting that in the above table Konstantinos Magoulas, Nikephoros Ēthikos and Grēgorios domestikos Glykys all precede Koukouzelēs. Also anterior to Koukouzelēs, and probably even his teacher, is Iohannes the protopsaltes *ho Glykys* [the sweet].[33]

The name Iohannes Koukouzelēs first appears in the AD 1302 codex *Heirmologion*, National Library of Russia, St. Petersburg–Leningrad 121 and again a second time in the *Heirmologion*, Sinai Gr. 1256 from AD 1309. Therefore, the period in which the previously mentioned composers developed the kalophonic style can now be further narrowed down to between the years 1261 and 1309. During this fifty-year period, the repertory of the *Psaltikon* took on its final shape as it appears in the Contacarium Ashburnamense 64 codex, dated AD 1289 (Høeg and Florence. Biblioteca

---

33   Cfr the well-known witness in Manuel Chrysaphēs and Conomos 1985: 40,71; also, the Athos, Panteleimon 938 *Mathēmatarion* provides the names of other melodes whose melē Koukouzelēs embellishes, namely, those of Basilikos, Eunouchos protopsaltes Philanthropinon, Komnēnos, Anapardas and Andrianoupolitēs, according to the kallopismos of Xenos Korōnēs; cfr Stathēs 1975–: Vol. 2, 244–245.

mediceo-laurenziana. 1956). Similarly, and possibly even influenced by or in imitation of the melismatic style of the allelouiaria, prokeimena and kontakia[34] of the *Psaltikon*, kalophony progresses on to the eidos of the stichēra idiomela and the ēchēmata begin to evolve into kratēmata in the eidos of the kalophonic verses.

As has already been mentioned, during this period the names of the first composers of the kalophonic melos are not directly mentioned in the sources, but the manuscript tradition supplies us with the term *kalophōnikon*. Two instances are drawn from the end of the thirteenth century (possibly the beginning of the fourteenth century): the manuscript Rome, Grottaferrata Badia greca, Cod. Crypt. Γ.γ.4, '*kalophōnikon eis ta hagia pathē*' (p. 97), and the important manuscript Gr. 161 of Bibl. Regionale Univ. di Messina, regarding which Lorenzo Tardo wrote (Tardo 1935: 170–176).

This important manuscript presents the following important points: fol. 20, '*Syn Theo kalophōnikon, archomenon apo tēs prōtēs melōdias*'. The kalophonic stichēra proper are found on the following fols.: 86r, 'ἦχος πλ. β´ τῇ Κυριακῇ τῶν Βαϊφόρων· *Κύριε ποῦ θέλεις*' — 87v, 'ἦχος πλ. β´ *Προτυπῶν τὸν Ἀνάστασιν*'[35] [for the feast of the Transfiguration] — 89 'ἦχος πλ. β´ *Ὅτε*

---

34   Grēgorius Bounēs' witness regarding the AD 1437 Sinai Gr. 1262 *Kontakarion*, fol. 1r, is extremely helpful: 'Ἀρχὴ σὺν Θεῷ ἁγίῳ τῶν κοντακίων τοῦ ὅλου ἐνιαυτοῦ ἀπ' ἀρχῆς τῆς ἰνδίκτου μέχρι συμπληρώσεως τοῦ Αὐγούστου μηνός. Ἐποιήθησαν μὲν παρὰ τοῦ δομεστίκου ἐκείνου κὺρ Μιχαὴλ Ἀνεώτου· ἐκαλλωπίσθησαν δὲ παρὰ τοῦ πρωτοψάλτου κὺρ Ἰωάννου Γλυκέος. Ὕστερον δὲ ἐγράφησαν καὶ παρὰ τοῦ μαΐστορος κὺρ Ἰωάννου Κουκουζέλη συντετμημένα καὶ σαφέστατα, καὶ οὐ γὰρ πολλὰς εἶχον μακρολογίας'. The indication that Koukouzelēs abridged [*synetame*] the embellished [*kekallopismenon*] melos of the kontakia shows that kalophony reached not only the pinnacle of perfection, but even the extremes of wordiness [*makrologias*].

35   The surprise in encountering these kalophonic melē in a manuscript of the XIIIth century led Tardo to the following remarks in Tardo 1938: 175–176: 'E chiaro che non è più l' ἰδιόμελον vero e proprio di S. Giovanni, ma è un' altra composizione melurgica completamente differente; differente anche dal genere dell' ἰδιόμελον, che per sè è più sobrio nell' ornamentazione melodica e più sostenuto, mentre il nuovo ἰδιόμελον καλοφωνικόν è pieno di gruppetti melodici, di abellimenti, di fioriture, in una parola è un canto καλοφωνικόν'. And regarding the kalophonic stichēron for

The form of the Mathēmatarion

ἡ μετάστασις᾽ [for the feast of the Dormition of the Theotokos]. On fol. 81v there is the kontakion 'Αὐτὸς μόνος ὑπάρχεις ἀθάνατος', mode IV plagal. Of special interest is also the instance in the section of theotokia, from fol. 76v, 'Ἀρχὴ τῶν θεοτοκαρίων', where we encounter verses of metrical improvisation foreign to the original text. Also, the type of katanyktikon on fol. 66v, mode II plagal, is extremely interesting:

Τί ἐπιμένεις, ὦ ψυχή μου, καὶ οὐκ ἐργάζου ἀγαθόν;
Ἐννόησον τὴν κρίσιν καὶ τὴν φλόγα τοῦ πυρός.
Λάβε κατὰ νοῦν τὴν κρίσιν τὴν μέλλουσαν κρίσιν·
Ἐννόησον τὴν κρίσιν καὶ τὴν φλόγα τοῦ πυρός.
Ἐννόησον καὶ στέναξον, ἐννόησον καὶ βόησον·
Ἱλάσθητι, συγχώρησον· καὶ στέναξον καὶ δάκρυσον
καὶ βόησον· Ἱλάσθητι καὶ βόησον τῷ κριτῇ·
ἥμαρτόν σοι, Κύριε, ἐλέησόν με. (Tardo 1938: 175)

In this example the basic elements of kalophony are clearly revealed: the melismatic, embellished melody, along with the repetition of words and insertion of imported texts and anagrams. The boldness of inserting verses of metrical improvisation into a pre-appointed ecclesiastical text opens a path to a freer technique in the shape of the melos and a tendency toward musical expansion [*platysmos*].

For the anagrams and mathēmata, the designation of the kalophonic melos will occur in the immediately following fifty-year period, between the years 1309 and 1360, through the work of great composers under the musical supervision and activity of Iohannes Koukouzelēs. The historical environment after the end of the Latin occupation of the Byzantine Empire was favourable for this development, as outlined above, while the

---

the Sunday of Palms, Κύριε, ποῦ θέλεις, he notes, 'da notare che in origine questo era un canto idiomelo. Qui invece il tesro servi a qualche Μαΐστωρ per essere lavorato con melismi e divenire un canto calofonicòn'; in this anonymous maïstōr we should recognize Theodoros Manougras.

hesychastic disputes surely contributed to the flowering of practical theology[36] and, with it, the liturgical arts.

The terms: anagrammatismos, anapodismos, mathēma and others related to them, epiphōnēma, anaphōnēma, allagma, epibolē, parekbolē, prologos, katabasia, homonoia

Anagrammatismos, anagram in English, and the less used *anapodismos* are terms first found in the fourteenth- and fifteenth-century *Papadikē* and later on in the Kalophonic *Sticheraria* or *Mathēmataria*. They primarily refer to the stichēra idiomela and, in only a few instances, to the megalynaria, Psalmic verses, kontakia, heirmoi and dekapentasyllabic compositions. The terms *anagramatismos* and *anapodismos* are not, however, absolutely synonymous. The term *anagramatismos* usually refers to the entire text of a stichēron that does not use the first textual phrase as its own beginning, but some other characteristic phrase and then rearranges the text according to its order of phrases and meanings. This rearrangement and recreation of the poetic text is called *anagramatismos*.[37]

We provided the example of anagrammatisation in the kalophonic verse Ἵνα τί ἐφρύαξαν ἔθνη above (p. 56).

As we observed above, on folio 218r of the Athens, Nat. Libr. 2458 we read: 'ἀναγραμματισμὸς κὺρ Ἰωάννου μαΐστορος τοῦ Κουκουζέλη· Ἴδωμεν πάντες, ἴδωμεν'. This phrase, with the repetition of the word *idōmen*, was taken from the stichēron idiomelon of the Office of Litē for Theophany, in mode IV plagal, Σήμερον ἡ κτίσις φωτίζεται. Here is the full text:

---

36 The general intellectual environment during the first half of the fourteenth century can be gleaned from Paschos 1978: 37–50, where, among other things, we read, 'αἱ λεγόμενοι Ἡσυχαστικαὶ ἔριδες, ὡς πιστεύομεν, κατέληξαν ὄχι ἁπλῶς νὰ ὠφελήσουν τὴν Ὀρθόδοξον Ἐκκλησίαν, ἀλλὰ καὶ νὰ δημιουργήσουν εὐκαιρίας καὶ προϋποθέσεις μιᾶς πραγματικῆς ἀνθήσεως τῆς ὀρθοδόξου θεολογίας, ἐνθυμιζούσης ἐν πολλοῖς τὸν χρυσοῦν αἰῶνα τῶν Πατερικῶν Γραμμάτων' (pp. 43–44).

37 It is obvious that the narrow definition is not assumed here to be that of the letters of a single word; rather, the context is larger, meaning the poetic text of a musical composition.

The form of the Mathēmatarion 71

Σήμερον ἡ κτίσις φωτίζεται·
σήμερον τὰ πάντα εὐφραίνονται,
τὰ οὐράνια ἅμα καὶ τὰ ἐπίγεια.
Ἄγγελοι καὶ ἄνθρωποι συμμίγνυνται·
ὅπου γὰρ βασιλέως παρουσία
καὶ ἡ τάξις παραγίνεται.
Δράμωμεν, τοίνυν ἐπὶ τὸν Ἰορδάνην.
Ἴδωμεν πάντες τὸν Ἰωάννην
πῶς βαπτίζει κορυφὴν
ἀχειροποίητον καὶ ἀναμάρτητον.
Διὸ ἀποστολικὴν φωνὴν προσᾴδοντες
συμφώνως βοήσωμεν·
Ἐπεφάνη ἡ χάρις τοῦ Θεοῦ
ἡ σωτήριος πᾶσιν ἀνθρώποις
καταυγάζουσα καὶ παρέχουσα πιστοῖς
τὸ μέγα ἔλεος.[38]

Iohannes Koukouzelēs's choice to begin his kalophonic composition with the verse Ἴδωμεν πάντες [ἴδωμεν] τὸν Ἰωάννην from this stichēron is most significant for a number of reasons.[39] It seems that Koukouzelēs wanted to give particular attention in his composition to the person of the venerable Forerunner and Baptist, John as if he were the representative of the human race in the feast of the Theophany. Having made the feast and the venerable personality obvious through the use of this verse for the composition's beginning, progressing forward he makes an anagram of the first half (two or three *metra* or feet) of the stichēron to emphasise the order

---

38 Orthodox Eastern Church and Apostolikē Diakonia 1967–1973: Ἰανουάριος, p. 80 in the Great Hagiasmos.
39 The significance of this idiomelon stichēron, as with the majority of stichēra, can be summarized in the following points: (a) Clearly, three feet can be ascertained, (i) Σήμερον ἡ κτίσις, (ii) Δράμωμεν τοίνυν, and (iii) Ἐπεφάνη ἡ χάρις. (b) There exist antithetical meanings that can almost be cross-chached via the similar endings of the words, specifically, συμμίγνυνται – παραγίνεται, Ἰορδάνην – Ἰωάννην. (c) It is offered by anagrammatisation, i.e., Ὅπου γὰρ βασιλέως παρουσία or Ἴδωμεν πάντες τὸν Ἰωάννην. (d) Two identical verses from the New Testament are included; specifically, we have the survival of the New Testamental hymns: Ἐπεφάνη ἡ χάρις τοῦ Θεοῦ / ἡ σωτήριος πᾶσιν ἀνθρώποις (Titus 2:11) with almost homotonic feet.

of meaning according to his liking. Here is how the kalophonic composition appears in his anagram for the stichēron as preserved in Athens, Nat. Libr. 2458 (fol. 218r):

Ἦχος πλ. δ΄ νανα

   Ἴδωμεν πάντες, ἴδωμεν, τὸν Ἰωάννην πῶς βαπτίζει
   κορυφὴν ἀχειροποίητον καὶ ἀναμάρτητον,
   πάντες ἴδωμεν.
πλ. δ΄ Σήμερον ἡ κτίσις φωτίζεται,
   σήμερον τὰ πάντα εὐφραίνονται,
δ΄ τὰ οὐράνια ἅμα καὶ τὰ ἐπίγεια.
α΄ Ἄγγελοι καὶ ἄνθρωποι — καὶ ἄνθρωποι συμμίγνυνται.
δ΄ Ὅπου γὰρ βασιλέως παρουσία
   παρουσία βασιλέως
   καὶ ἡ τάξις παραγίνεται, παραγίνεται.
β΄ Δράμωμεν τοίνυν ἐπὶ τὸν Ἰορδάνην.
α΄ Δράμωμεν πάντες
   καὶ ἴδωμεν τὸν Ἰωάννην
   πῶς βαπτίζει σήμερον
α΄ καρυφή ... τιριριτεριρε [long kratēma]
   καρυφὴν ἀχειροποίητον
   καὶ ἀναμάρτητον ... τοτοτο [short kratēma]
   καὶ ἀναμάρτητον.

It should be noted that through the repetition of the word *idōmen* a full first half-verse (oktasyllabic) iambic of a dekapentasyllabic verse was instituted. This is quite intentionally executed by Koukouzelēs. The sound of the iambic dekapentasyllabic verse was preferred to the sound of the verse 'ἴδωμεν πάντες τὸν Ἰωάννην'. This is so because the creation of full or half-dekapentasyllabic verses via small anagrams is often observed in the anagrams of verses. Compare, for example, the beginning of the anagram (second foot) of the stichēron for 1 September, *Τὸ μνημόσυνόν σου — Εἰ [γὰρ] καὶ μετέστης ἐξ ἡμῶν*, where a full half-verse of the dekapentasyllable is created by the omission of the word 'γάρ'.[40]

---

40 Cfr Athos, Hagiou Pavlou 128, p. 64, but also the *Methēmatarion* of Chourmouzios, Nat. Libr. ΜΠΤ 727, fol. 26v.

The contents of the oikos in the above codex, Athens, Nat. Libr. 2458, fols. 136v–138r, is also in the type of an anagram: Ἀυτὸς μόνος ὑπάρχεις ἀθάνατος, whose kontakion begins Μετὰ τῶν ἁγίων.

To further illustrate, we can examine a dekapentasyllabic anagram mathēma. The well-known troparion *Τῆς μετανοίας ἄνοιξόν μοι πύλας, Ζωοδότα*[41] is a dekapentasyllabic poem with four verses. In the manuscripts, it is normally referred to with the characteristic *pentēkostarin -ion*[42] because, as seems evident, in older practice it had the place of the troparion *Τὰ πλήθη τῶν πεπραγμένων μοι δεινῶν* and was chanted with the verses *Ἐλεῆμον, ἐλέησόν με, ὁ Θεός*, which is from Psalm 50 [*pentēkostos psalmos*]. The title *pentēkostarion* can still be upheld even though it is no longer chanted with the first verse of the fiftieth Psalm, since, in any event, it always follows the reading or chanting of the same Psalm in its entirety. The text of the troparion is as follows:

Τῆς μετανοίας ἄνοιξόν μοι πύλας, ζωοδότα·
ὀρθρίζει γὰρ τὸ πνεῦμά μου πρὸς
ναὸν <τὸν> ἅγιόν σου, ναὸν φέρων τοῦ σώματος ὅλον ἐσπιλωμένον.
Ἀλλ' ὡς οἰκτίρμων κάθαρον εὐσπλάγχνῳ σου ἐλέει.

Once again, Iohannes Koukouzelēs, the maïstōr and great teacher of the anagrams, takes the final verse for his beginning, *Ἀλλ' ὡς οἰκτίρμων, κάθαρον* and anagrammatizes[43] the poem as shown here:

Ἀλλ' ὡς οἰκτίρμων κάθαρον [κάθαρον] εὐσπλάγχνῳ σου ἐλέει.
Ὡς οἰκτίρμων κάθαρον εὐσπλάγχνῳ σου ἐλέει
κάθαρον ὡς οἰκτίρμων·
Ὀρθρίζει γὰρ τὸ πνεῦμά μου πρὸς ναὸν τὸν ἅγιόν σου
ναὸν φέρων τοῦ σώματος ὅλον ἐσπιλωμένον,

---

41 *Triōdion*, Sunday of the Publican and the Pharisee (Orthodox Eastern Church and Apostolikē Diakonia 1960: 6).
42 The term is addressed below, p. 155; cfr Stathēs 1977: 79–80.
43 It is characteristic that the Athos, Koutloumousiou 456 from the year AD 1443 contains a special unit in folios 120r–199v where all and only the anagrams of Iohannes Koukouzelēs for the feasts are indicated together with the beginning of the stichēron which has been anagrammatized; cfr Stathēs 1975–: Vol. 3, 347–351.

ὅλον ἐσπιλωμένον, κάθαρον, ζωοδότα, ναὸν ἐσπιλωμένον. Ἄνοιξον, Χριστέ μου, πύλας τῆς μετανοίας.
Ἄνοιξόν μοι πύλας, ζωοδότα, ἄνοιξόν μοι. — πάλιν
Ὀρθρίζει γὰρ τὸ πνεῦμά μου πρὸς ναὸν τὸν ἅγιόν σου, Ζωοδότα,
ναὸν φέρων τοῦ σώματος, ὅλον ἐσπιλωμένον·
κάθαρον, εὐσπλάγχνῳ σου ἐλέει, κάθαρον ... Τοτοτο ...
Ὡς οἰκτίρμων κάθαρον εὐπλάγχνῳ σου ἐλέει.[44]

This, then, is the technique of the anagrams as it relates to the rearranging of the text. Parallel to this technique exist another two elements of kalophony: the kratēma and the refined melos with its modulations [*enallagas*].

As we have already seen, the anagrams existed before Iohannes Koukouzelēs as performance practice in Byzantine melopœïa — at least by the middle of the thirteenth century. It seems, however, that by enriching this category with a myriad of compositions, Iohannes Koukouzelēs imparted to the genus the greatest possible grandeur and in a way set the inviolable defining bounds from a morphological perspective.[45] Regarding this issue, a certain interesting affirmation exists, made by Kosmas Macedōn in one of his autograph codices, a *Mathēmatarion* from the year 1670, the Athos, Iviron 991. In the lower margin of fol. 389r, there is a note that refers to the *parekbolas* [extrapolations] by G. Kontopetrēs in a composition by Thalassēnos, Γλῶσσαί ποτε συνεχέθησαν, in mode IV plagal; a stichēron idiomelon for Pentecost. Cosmas Macedōn writes:

Ὡς ἔοικεν, ὕστερον ἐκαλλωπίσθη τὸ στιχηρὸν ὑπὸ τοῦ Κοντοπετρῆ, ἑπόμενος τῇ ὁδῷ τοῦ ἀναγραμματισμοῦ, ἤτοι τοῦ μαΐστορος.

As is evident, the stichēron was later embellished by Kontopetrēs, following the road [*odos*] of the anagram, that is, of the maïstōr.

---

44 Athos, M. Lavra Λ 116, fol. 2r and ΜΠΤ 733, fol. 102r.
45 At the end of the kalophonic theotokion stichēron Ἀσπόρως ἐκ θείου πνεύματος (mode III), fol. 216r of Athos, Dionysiou 570 (autograph of Iohannes Plousiadēnos) there is a commemoration of Koukouzelēs: 'Αἰωνία σου ἡ μνήμη, Ἰωάννη Κουκουζέλη, μὲ τὸν δρόμον ὁποὺ ἐφανέρωσας τῆς αὐτῆς ἐπιστήμης'. By the term 'science' [*epistēmē*] is understand, generally, the Psaltic Art, and especially the art of the anagrams; cfr Stathēs 1975–: Vol. 2, 711.

It logically follows that the anagrams have their origin in the kalophony of Byzantine melopœïa.[46]

Anapodismos — pous — podes. *Anapodismos* means the rearrangement of the metrical feet of a stichēron. For this to be better understood, a few stichēra idiomela from the *Kalophonic Stichērarion* or *Mathēmatarion* have been laid out as examples below.

1. Stichēron idiomelon, first doxastikon of the vespers for the feast of the Divine Transfiguration. Mode II plagal.

Προτυπῶν τὴν ἀνάστασιν τὴν σήν,
Χριστὲ ὁ Θεός,
τότε παραλαμβάνεις τοὺς τρεῖς σου μαθητὰς
Πέτρον καὶ Ἰάκωβον καὶ Ἰωάννην, ἐν τῷ Θαβὼρ ἀνελθών.
Σοῦ δὲ Σωτὴρ μεταμορφουμένου
τὸ Θαβώριον ὄρος φωτὶ ἐσκέπετο.

The second foot:

Οἱ μαθηταί σου Λόγε,
ἔρριψαν ἑαυτοὺς ἐν τῷ ἐδάφει τῆς γῆς
μὴ φέροντες ὁρᾶν τὴν ἀθέατον μορφήν.
Ἄγγελοι διηκόνουν φόβῳ καὶ τρόμῳ.
Οὐρανοὶ ἔφριξαν,

46 The use of anagrams at the beginning of the psalms of the antiphons existed in all the akolouthiae of the Asmatic Typikon (Cathedral Rite) according to the witness of Symeon of Thessalonike: 'it is customary at the other services also to prefix a part of the verse of the following psalm always, preluding it either by "Alleluia" or "Glory to you" or some refrain (*hypopsalma*). This is called *hypopsalma* because it is sung together with the psalm by verses' (Symeon of Thessalonike and Simmons 1984: 72–73; Symeon Thessalonicensis 1865: 625D). The phenomenon of the anagrams has survived even into the contemporary daily worship. Today one can distinguish at least the following anagrams in Orthodox worship: 1) at the prokeimena of the vespers and orthros, 2) at the beginning of the Polyeleoi and antiphons or *Eklogai*, 3) at the second heōthinon prokeimenon Πᾶσα πνοὴ — Αἰνεσάτω πνοὴ πᾶσα, 4) at the bishop's supplication during the Divine Liturgy, Κύριε, Κύριε, ἐπίβλεψον — Ἐπίβλεψον Κύριε ... and 5) at the Εἴη τὸ ὄνομα Κυρίου — Τὸ ὄνομα Κυρίου εἴη ....

γῆ ἐτρόμαξεν
ὁρῶντες ἐπὶ γῆς
τῆς δόξης τὸν Κύριον.⁴⁷

2. Stichēron idiomelon, doxastikon from the Litē for the Sunday of Anti-Pascha (of Thomas).

Φιλάνθρωπε,
μέγα καὶ ἀνείκαστον
τὸ πλῆθος τῶν οἰκτιρμῶν σου·
ὅτι ἐμακροθύμησας
ὑπὸ Ἰουδαίων ῥαπιζόμενος,
ὑπὸ Ἀποστόλου ψηλαφώμενος
καὶ ὑπὸ τῶν ἀθετούντων σε πολυπραγμονούμενος.
Πῶς ἐσαρκώθης;
πῶς ἐσταυρώθης, ὁ ἀναμάρτητος;

The second foot:

Ἀλλὰ συνέτισον ἡμᾶς ὡς τὸν Θωμᾶν βοᾶν σοι·
ὁ Κύριός μου
καὶ ὁ Θεός μου, δόξα σοι.⁴⁸

According to the kalophonic usage many stichēra idiomela are clearly divided into two metric feet, as are the above two examples. In the

47 From Orthodox Eastern Church and Apostolikē Diakonia 1967–1973: Αὔγουστος, p. 46. For this stichēron exist the following anagrams and *anapodismoi*: 1) Theodoros Manougras and the *kallopismos* of Xenos Korōnēs, mode II plagal Προτυπῶν τὴν ἀνάστασιν; 2) foot by Iohannes Koukouzelēs, mode II Τὸ Θαβώριον ὄρος; 3) *palaion*, and another by Markos, metropolitan of Corinth, *heteros pous*, mode II plagal Οἱ μαθηταί σου, Λόγε; 4) anagram by Iohannes Koukouzelēs, mode I Οὐρανοὶ ἔφριξαν; 5) anagram by Manuel Chrysaphēs, mode II plagal Ἄγγελοι διηκόνουν φόβῳ καὶ τρόμῳ. In Chourmouzios' *Mathēmatarion* (ΜΠΤ 732, fol. 236r, a *parembole* by Korōnēs is also included, *nenano* Τοοτοτο Τὸ Θαβώριον ὄρος. Cfr Athos Xeropotamou 282 (fifteenth century), fols. 204v–209v; cfr Stathēs 1975–: Vol. 1, 293. Due to the importance of these consecutive kalophonic compositions within the span of two centuries I have included images below from Chourmouzios' *exegesis* in the present publication.

48 Orthodox Eastern Church *et al.* 1837: 25.

Kalophonic Sticheraria, there exist a few idiomela that are divided into three feet. The most commonly encountered are the following:

3. The idiomelon for the feast of the Annunciation, Εὐαγγελίζεται ὁ Γαβριὴλ:

First foot:

Εὐαγγελίζεται ὁ Γαβριὴλ
τῇ κεχαριτωμένῃ σήμερον

Second foot:

Χαῖρε ἀνύμφευτε ... Ἀρχάγγελός εἰμι

Third foot:

Ὄφις ἐξηπάτησεν ... ἕως τέλος.[49]

4. The idiomelon doxastikon of the aposticha for the feast of the Maccabees (1 August):

First foot:

Ψυχαὶ δικαίων ... ἕως, ἠγωνίσαντο δι' εὐσέβειαν.

Second foot:

Εὐσεβῶς γὰρ συντραφέντες ... πάντα Θεῷ ἀνέθετο.

Third foot:

Ψυχὴν γενναίαν ... ἕως, τέλος.[50]

---

49 The full text in Orthodox Eastern Church and Apostolikē Diakonia 1967–1973: Μάρτιος, p. 96.
50 The full text in Orthodox Eastern Church and Apostolikē Diakonia 1967–1973: Αὔγουστος, p. 6.

5. The idiomelon for the feast of Saint Eudokimos, the righteous wonderworker (31 July):

First foot:

Πῶς μὴ θαυμάσωμεν τὴν πολιτείαν σου

Second foot:

Τὸ πρᾶον καὶ ταπεινὸν καὶ ἡσύχιον

Third foot:

Ὅθεν ἀπόκειταί σοι.[51]

6. The stichēron idiomelon for the feast of Saint Demetrios (26 October):

First foot:

Τῇ τῶν ᾀσμάτων τερπνότητι

Second foot:

Πρόκειται γὰρ ἡμῖν

Third foot:

Καὶ γὰρ τὰς τῶν ἀνόμων.[52]

7. The doxastikon for this same feast of Saint Demetrios:

First foot:

Ἔχει μὲν ἡ θειοτάτη σου ψυχή

---

[51] Unpublished; the text is in the *Stichēraria* and *Mathēmataria*. Cfr ΜΠΤ 732, fols. 173r–181r.
[52] Orthodox Eastern Church and Apostolikē Diakonia 1967–1973: Ὀκτώβριος, p. 143.

Second foot:

Ἔχει δὲ καὶ τὸ πανέντιμον

Third foot:

Ἔνθα προστρέχοντες.[53]

Beyond these cases, however, wherein the feet of the stichēra are clearly marked in the manuscripts, the structure of the stichēra are such that most of them are easily separated into two or three feet and rarely into four[54] and five[55] feet. The division of the stichēra into feet is uncomplicated in the stichēra with dialogue content, the stichēra with quotations of Old Testament or New Testament sayings and in the usually long hymn-like stichēra containing salutations or invocations. Therefore, the basic guide for the division of stichēra into feet is (a) the meaning of one or more textual periods, an expansion of a preceding idea or its explanation, or (b) a snippet of quoted words attributed to a personage or from some biblical passage. In the first stichēron idiomelon above, Προτυπῶν τὴν ἀνάστασιν,

---

53 Orthodox Eastern Church and Apostolikē Diakonia 1967–1973: Ὀκτώβριος, p. 144. Other stichera divided into three feet according to their kalophonic usage include those for the feast of the Entrance (21 November) Μετὰ τὸ τεχθῆναί σε, the dekapentasyllabic stichēron for the feast of the Archangels (8 November) Ἄρχον δυνάμεως Θεοῦ, the translation of the relics of Iohannes Chrysostomus (27 January) Οὐκ ἔδει σε, Χρυσόστομε, the feast of Saint George (23 April) Ἀνέτειλε τὸ ἔαρ, the feast of the equal to the apostles Constantine and Helen (21 May) Σέλας φαεινόν, and some others. All the above mentioned stichera can be found in Chroumouzios' Mathēmatarion.

54 A stichēron divided into four feet is the Πνευματικῶς ἡμᾶς, πιστοί for the feast of Daniel the prophet (17 December). The feet are: 1) Πνευματικῶς ἡμᾶς, 2) Οὗτος γὰρ ὁ προφήτης, 3) Οὐ γὰρ ἐχώνευσεν αὐτούς, 4) Ὁ διαγαγὼν ἡμᾶς; cfr MΠT 729, fols. 214r–221v.

55 The only stichēron divided into five feet is for the feast of the Annunciation (25 March) Ἀπεστάλη ἄγγελος. The five feet and their kalophonic compositions are as follows: 1) Ἀπεστάλη ἄγγελος, 2) Εὐαγγελίσασθαι αὐτῇ, 3) Ἀπεστάλη δοῦλος ἀσώματος, 4) Χαῖρε θρόνε πυρίμορφε, 5) Χαῖρε ὄρος ἀλατόμητον; cfr MΠT 731, fols. 102r–118v.

the second foot, Οἱ μαθηταί σου, Λόγε, contains an entire meaning and simultaneously gives the impression of an expansion with regards to the previous meaning; that is, the Saviour is transfigured, Mount Tabor is overshadowed by light while the disciples throw themselves upon the surface of the earth. The next period that follows, Ἄγγελοι διηκόνουν φόβῳ καί τρόμῳ, can easily be taken as another foot, third in sequence. Furthermore, the fact that this verse served as the beginning of an anagram[56] is an excellent substantiation coming out of these manuscripts.

It should be stated here that the *Kalophonic Sticheraria* emerge from the common — not kalophonic — *Sticheraria* and from the fact that there exists a relationship between the kalophonic and non-kalophonic stichēron from a musical standpoint. This connection relates primarily to the mode with which each are chanted; the kalophonic follows the mode of the regular stichēron when it has the same beginning. A change of mode, however, can at times also be detected in the anagrams. The same can occur in the feet of the stichēra. Beyond this relationship and upon close study, we also find an internal connection between them: the feet, either the first or second, begin at the point where the non-kalophonic stichēra have martyriai or sometimes even entire modal enēchēmata indicating a change of melos. Jörgen Raasted first made this comment in his doctoral dissertation, where he deals specifically with the enēchēmata and martyriai in the Byzantine music manuscripts. Raasted states:

> The kalophonic stichera are frequently split up into sections called πόδες; the last πούς invariably ends with a short conclusion, sung ἀπὸ χοροῦ, of which only the incipit may be given. I have not been able to find descriptions and explanations of this πούς-system; but the way in which each πούς is normally signalized by an initial letter — and, sometimes, a clarifying rubric — shows that the division into πόδες corresponds to some actual feature of the performance (Raasted 1966: 141).

Consequently, the metric feet of the kalophonic stichēra quite often begin exactly where the non-kalophonic *Sticheraria* put their medial signatures. Additionally, at another point in the same study Raasted supports the

---

56   Cfr MΠT 732, fol. 243v.

The form of the Mathēmatarion

correct interpretation: 'It is natural to suppose that the change of the modality is the basic musical expression of this structuralisation of the text ...' (Raasted 1966: 92).

Moreover, the relationship between the kalophonic and non-kalophonic stichēra reveals the fact that the kalophonic stichēra sometimes borrow or quote the *koinon* melos for a particular phrase. This is distinguished in the manuscripts by the word *keimenon*, or, transversely, they begin with the common melos and *archontai tas kalophōnias*[57] from some other period or foot, or, finally, and this is more common, they end faithfully[58] with the *koinon* melos, with the indication *apo chorou* or *holoi homou*, and other related signals.

Following this analysis of the feet in the stichēra, the term *anapodismos* is now more easily understood. It is not identical to the term

---

[57] At the beginning of the kalophonic stichēron Προτυπῶν τὴν ἀνάστασιν by Manougras according to the *kallopismos* of Xenos Korōnēs the following is noted: 'ὁ δομέστικος, ἀπὸ χοροῦ, ἦχος πλ. β''. This command, *apo chorou* refers to the text Προτυπῶν τὴν ἀνάστασιν τὴν σήν, Χριστὲ ὁ Θεός; and immediately, 'εἶτα γίνεται καλλιφωνία, ὁ δομέστικος ἀπ' ἔξω· Τότε παραλαμβάνεις' from ΜΠΤ 732, fols. 234r–v. An identical instance is the stichēron for the Sunday of Palms Πρὸ ἓξ ἡμερῶν τοῦ Πάσχα; related to it we find the indication, 'εἶτα ἄρχεται ἡ καλλιφωνία· Κύριε, ποῦ θέλεις' from ΜΠΤ 733, fol. 225r–v; cfr the two instances in Athos, Gregoriou 3, fols. 261v and 217v; cfr Stathēs 1975–: Vol. 2, 589. Instead of the phrase *archetai hē kalliphōnia* in the stichēron Τάδε λέγει Ἰωσήφ (*apo chorou*) the is the indication 'εἶτα ἄρχεται ὁ μονοφωνάρης' in ΜΠΤ 729, fols. 264r–v.

[58] The loud-voiced comment by Chrysaphes is applicable: 'ἔνθεν τοι κἂν τοῖς καλοφωνικοῖς στιχηροῖς οἱ τούτων ποιηταὶ τῶν κατὰ τὰ ἰδιόμελα μελῶν οὐκ ἀπολείπονται, ἀλλὰ κατ' ἴχνος ἀκριβῶς ἀκολουθοῦσιν αὐτοῖς καὶ αὐτοῖς μέμνηνται. Ὡς γοῦν ἐν μέλεσι διὰ μαρτυρίας καὶ τῶν ἐκεῖσε κειμένων μελῶν ἔνια παραλαμβάνουσιν ἀπαραλλάκτως, καθάπερ δὲ καὶ ἐν τῷ σιχηραρίῳ ἔκκειντο, καὶ τὸν ἐκεῖσε πάντες δρόμον παρ' ὅλον τὸ ποίημα τρέχουσιν ἀμετατρεπτεὶ καὶ προτέρῳ τε τῶν ποιητῶν ἀεὶ ὁ δεύτερος ἕπεται καὶ τούτῳ ὁ μετ' αὐτόν, καὶ πάντες ἁπλῶς ἔχονται τῆς τέχνης ὁδοῦ' [Therefore, they take over some melodies unchanged from tradition and from the music this preserved (as it is recorded in the old *Sticherarion*), and they all follow the path unaltered throughout the entire composition. The second composer always follows his predecessor and his successor follows him and, to put it simply, everyone retains the technique of the art] (Manuel Chrysaphēs and Conomos 1985: 42,112–121 and 43).

anagrammatismos, even though the terms are sometimes confused as classifications of these types of compositions or are used interchangeably in the manuscripts. This is because anapodismos begins from the beginning of a particular foot and *anapodizei* [reverses, literally, *turns upside down*] or rearranges the feet of the sticheron, whereas the anagram does not always begin from the beginning of a particular foot. The anagram and anapodismos extend themselves over the entire content of the sticheron; the simple feet, however, less frequently anagrammatize only the foot of the text and do not spread to the other feet in the same sticheron. This comment allows us to distinguish and enumerate the feet as independent compositions.

Referring here to the clarification of terms, it should be noted that the forms of both the anagram and anapodismos are forms of kalophony in Byzantine melopœïa that grew out of the practice of the small anagrams and repetitions of words as an aphoristic element of kalophony. Only later did they evolve into a self-existing and autonomous unity, specifically, that of the anagrammatisation and anapodismos of the stichera for the entire year. It is this understanding of the kalophonic stichera that we find in the *Papadikai* from the fourteenth century on and from them the anagrams or anapodismoi. Considering only the melos, no difference exists between the kalophonic stichera and anagrams; this is proven from the same structure of the melos, as well as the existence of the distinctive kalophonic elements. The authoritative theoretical witness of these points belongs to Manuel Chrysaphēs, who, while speaking regarding the relationship of the kalophonic stichera with the normal stichera as found in the *Sticherarion*, adds: 'ὅτι δὲ ταῦθ' οὕτως ἔχει, καθάπερ ἐγώ φημι νῦν δῆλον ἐντεῦθεν. Ὁ γὰρ χαριτώνυμος μαΐστωρ, ὁ Κουκουζέλης, ἐν τοῖς ἀναγραμματισμοῖς αὐτοῦ τῶν παλαιῶν οὐκ ἐξίσταται στιχηρῶν, ἀλλὰ κατ' ἴχνος τούτοις ἀκολουθεῖ' [That things are as I now say can be seen from what follows. Iohannes Koukouzelēs, the maïstōr, does not alter the old stichera in his *anagrammatismoi*, but follows them step by step] (Manuel Chrysaphēs and Conomos 1985: 42,121–126).

Hence, Manuel Chrysaphēs speaks indiscriminately and without distinction regarding the kalophonic stichera and anagrams, seeing no difference of usage between one and the other in relation to the old stichera. It is significant that Manuel Chrysaphēs first makes the final equivalence:

anagrams equals kalophonic stichēra, or more generally, kalophony equals mathēmata, as is immediately understood.

Mathēma. The term *mathēma* as characteristic of the kalophonic compositions is first encountered, at least as far as research has progressed to date, in the theoretical treatise by Manuel Chrysaphēs, *On the Theory of the Psaltic Art* (Manuel Chrysaphēs and Conomos 1985) and coincides chronologically with the close of the Byzantine inheritance. Especially for this reason, it is a term with import; the Byzantine kalophonic compositions are mathēmata [lessons] for the coming generations of this high and remarkable art and should be the subject of special study toward the tradition's preservation.

Manuel Chrysaphēs uses the term mathēma to characterize kalophonic composition in two places. The first time: 'Εἰ μὲν οὖν θήσει τις εἰς μάθημα ψαλλόμενον τοῦ οἱουδήτινος ἤχου τοῦ πρώτου ἤχου φθοράν'. [Thus, if one places the phthora of the first mode in a mathēma chanted in any mode whatsoever] (Manuel Chrysaphēs and Conomos 1985: 50,248–249). It should be mentioned here that in Manuel Chrysaphēs' chapter on the phthorai he takes examples only from kalophonic compositions and the general correlation of the term mathēma with the kalophonic compositions is entirely clear:

> Εἰ δὲ θέλεις μαθεῖν καὶ εἰς ἄλλα καλοφωνικὰ καὶ κρατήματα πῶς τίθεται καὶ δεσμεῖ καὶ λύεται ὡς ἐν συντόμῳ, ἴδε εἰς ταῦτα τὰ προρρηθέντα ποιήματα[59] καὶ ἀλλαχοῦ εἰς ἄλλα μαθήματα, καὶ εἰς τὴν ἀρχὴν τοῦ *Ἄν βάρος με τῶν λυπηρῶν*, καὶ εἰς τὸ κράτημα τοῦ Κορώνη τοῦ πλαγίου δευτέρου, τὸ μέγα, περὶ τὴν ἀρχὴν καὶ εἰς τὸ ἔμπροσθεν [...] ἀλλὰ καὶ εἰς τὸ ἴδιόν μου κατανυκτικόν, ὃ ἐποίησα εἰς τὸν βαρὺν ἦχον, *Τὴν τετραυματισμένην μου ψυχήν*, περὶ τὴν ἀρχήν'.

> If you wish to know how it is used, bound and resolved in brief in other kalophonic chants and kratēmata, see the aforementioned compositions, and elsewhere in other lessons, and at the beginning of *Ἄν βάρος με τῶν λυπηρῶν*, and in the Great Kratēma of Korōnēs in the second plagal mode towards the beginning and at the outset [...]. Also towards the beginning of my own katanyktikon, which I composed in Barys

---

59   The other lessons are an Allelouiarion, the *phrangikon* and *Δουλεύσατε* regarding the end of the kratēma. They concern kalophonic compositions of the *Papadikē*.

mode, Τὴν τετραυματισμένην μου ψυχήν. (Manuel Chrysaphēs and Conomos 1985: pp. 62–64, lines 478–484, 486–489)

It is clear from this quotation that by the middle of the fifteenth century — when the codex type had already taken shape in the form of the *Kalophonic Stichērarion* — the term *mathēma* was associated with the kalophonic compositions in general.

In light of this general meaning of the term, evidently referring to all the kalophonic stichēra, it is also encountered in the theoretical treatise by Gabriel hieromonachos of Xanthopolis' (c. mid-fifteenth century) *Very Beneficial Explanation Regarding Chant* (Gabriel hieromonachos and Schartau 1990). The interesting pericope containing the term follows:

> Γίνεται δὲ ἀλλοία ἡ τοῦ πρώτου ἰδέα, ἄλλη ἡ τοῦ δευτέρου, ἄλλη ἡ τοῦ τρίτου καὶ ἄλλη ἡ τοῦ τετάρτου. Οὗτοι δὲ πάντες καὶ κοινὰ καὶ ἴδια κέκτηνται, καὶ ἴδιον μὲν ἑκάστῳ τὸ ποιεῖν τὸ γνωστικὸν αὐτοῦ μέλος, κοινὸν δὲ τὸ καταλέγειν καὶ τοὺς τέσσαρας ἔξω φωνὰς τρεῖς, παραδείγματα δὲ τούτων ταῦτα. Τοῦ μὲν πρώτου τό· *Εὐφραίνου ἐν κυρίῳ*, τοῦ δὲ δευτέρου τό· *Ἐν ταῖς αὐλαῖς σου ὑμνήσω σε*, τοῦ τρίτου ὁ τοῦ Ἠθικοῦ τρίτος, τοῦ τετάρτου σχεδὸν πάντα τὰ καλοφωνικὰ αὐτοῦ.

> The *idea* of mode I is different from that of mode II, different from that of the IVth. All the modes possess both that which is common and also their own, and each creates its characteristic melos, to whit the following three examples of the four *exo* voices: for the first, Εὐφραίνου ἐν κυρίῳ, of the second, Ἐν ταῖς αὐλαῖς σου ὑμνήσω σε, of the third is that of Ethekos, and for the fourth just about all his kalophonic compositions. (Gabriel hieromonachos and Schartau 1990: 76,443–78,452)[60]

In another anonymous theoretical treatise from around the end of the fifteenth century,[61] we find the combined use of both terms, *kalophōnia*

---

60 The word *mathēma* is replaced with the word *kalophōnika*. This occurs due to the scribe's preference for one or the other term from manuscript to manuscript. In a section on mode IV, Gabriel again refers to the word *mathēma* and the manuscripts retain a unified tradition in that case: 'εἰς αὐτὸν γὰρ ἔχει πλείονα χώραν τοῦτο τὸ μέλος ἢ εἰς τοὺς ἄλλους· καὶ τοσοῦτον, ὡς εὑρίσκεσθαί τινα μαθήματα ἐν αὐτῷ τῆς τοῦ μέσου ἰδέας ὄντα ἀπ' ἀρχῆς ἄχρι τέλους' (Gabriel hieromonachos and Schartau 1990: 503).

61 The said treatise is found on folios 2–15 of Athens, Nat. Libr. 899. This unit is written a little later than the main part of the codex. On fol. 6v is found an interesting

and *mathēma*: "Ὁ δὲ πλάγιος τοῦ β΄ οὐχ οὕτως τριφωνεῖ, ἀλλὰ μίαν καὶ μίαν τὰς φωνὰς ἀνέρχεται, διὰ τὸ τῆς φθορᾶς δέματος· λέγεται δὲ καὶ ἡ τούτου τριφωνία χωρὶς δέματος ἐν τῇ ἁπλῇ καταλογῇ· σπανίως δὲ καὶ ἐν καλλιφωνικοῖς μαθήμασι,[62] ὥσπερ τὸ Ὦ Παρθένε, καὶ τὸ Ὡς ὑπηρέτης τοῦ Λόγου". [Plagal of the second does not create triphōnia in this way, but one by one traverses the voices through the tying of the phthora; this is called triphōnia without the *tying* in the simple change; rare in the kalophonic mathēmata, like Ὦ Παρθένε and Ὡς ὑπηρέτης τοῦ Λόγου].

After these accounts and the passing of another half century, around the middle of the sixteenth century, the term *Mathēmatarion*[63] is established as the name of the codex containing 'stichēra and anagrams for the entire year'.

Accordingly, the term mathēma is conventional, referring primarily to the kalophonic application of a stichēron. Retaining as a given the commonality of all the kalophonic compositions one to the other, the term mathēma became the general identifying term for the eidos of the kalophonic compositions. Under the term mathēma, the kalophonic verses and the kalophonic stichēra are implied — especially the kalophonic kontakia, kalophonic heirmoi and the rest of the kalophonic compositions, that is, the prosomoia, apolytikia, dekapendasyllabic poems, katanyktika, phēmai, polychronismoi, etc.

There is no explanation in the manuscript tradition as to why the term mathēma came to imply the eidos of kalophonic Byzantine melopœïa. The

---

comment about the intervals: 'ὅπου γὰρ οὐ ψάλλεται φωνῆς τὸ ἥμισυ ἢ τὸ τρίτον ἢ τὸ τέταρτον οὐκ ἔνι φθορά'. The quoted text above is from fol. 11v. The same terminology is used by Iohannes Plousiadēnos in his Athos, Dionysiou 570, fol. 110r.

62 This unusual combination of terms, *kalliphōnikos* used as an adjective for *mathēma*, is found in the second half of the seventeenth century, but not at all common. We find it again in Athos, Iviron 961 from the end of the seventeenth century, where we read on fol. 167r: "Ἔκθεσίς τινων μαθημάτων καλοφωνικῶν, ψαλλομένων τὰς ἑορτὰς τῆς Θεοτόκου".

63 The beginning of Athos, Iviron 1204, most likely an autograph by Leontios Koukouzelēs the Dragousiarēs is as follows: 'Μαθηματάριον Ἀνθολόγιον, σὺν Θεῷ ἁγίῳ, στιχηρῶν τε καὶ ἀναγραμματισμῶν τοῦ ὅλου ἐνιαυτοῦ, ποιηθέντα (sic) παρὰ διαφόρων ποιητῶν'. This codex will be discussed more below.

most plausible explanation seems to be the very nature of these compositions themselves, which includes the many intricacies encountered that must be learned for performance. It assumes a long and difficult discipleship under a maïstōr or accomplished music teacher. It is from this reality that the kalophonic melē were characterized as mathēmata, that is, lessons.

The technical difficulty of these compositions, the mathēmata and kratēmata, is betrayed by the manuscripts when, for instance, their scribes noted 'another, very difficult, and requiring attention' [ἕτερον, πάνυ δύσκολον, καὶ πρόσχες], or 'phthoric and difficult' [φθορικὸν καὶ δύσκολον], or 'another, by Iohannes Koukouzelēs, the difficult one' [ἕτερον, κὺρ Ἰωάννου τοῦ Κουκουζέλη, τὸ δύσκολον], and others.[64]

The instance of the study of the 'difficult mathēmata', on the one hand, and the circumstances of the classification of the kalophonic compositions of the post-Byzantine (fourteenth–fifteenth centuries) as mathēma, on the other, are points worthy of consideration. Both bear witness to a fixed tradition as well as to its continuation in the years following the fall of Constantinople. Moreover, in and of themselves, these two points clarify the eidos as virtuosic Byzantine melopœïa.

Having outlined these terms via the analysis of the compositions to which they allude, it would also be useful to quickly clarify the following terms found in some compositions: *epiphōnēmata, anaphōnēmata, allagmata, epibolē, parekbolē, prologos*, and *katabasia*.

Epiphōnēmata. This term is primarily encountered in kalophony of the prokeimena, with anagrams in the vespers and orthros. The epiphōnēma, usually anagrammatized from the verses of the prokeimenon, is stereotypically repeated three times, usually four times or even five times during the duration of the melos. This repetition consists of the overflowing of enthusiasm of the faithful toward the glory of God; it inspires certainty through the power or mercy of God and lends interest to the entire composition, emphasizing the meaning of the verses. The characterisation *epiphōnēma* is substantiated in the stereotypical repetition of the phrase with the same

---

64 These indications are found in the *Mathēmataria* and *Papadikai*, especially in the prologoi and kratēmata of the kalophonic verses of the *Makarios anēr*; cfr Athos, Iviron 1120, fols. 70r–202v.

The form of the Mathēmatarion

or similar melos. The texts of the epiphōnēmata are written in red ink in the manuscripts, fundamentally, to easily stand out visually, possibly also because they may be chanted by a single *kalophōnos* chanter [soloist][65] for a better rendering of the desired expression and impression. This distinction is made even more clearly in some manuscripts with the inscription written in the margin, *to epiphōnēma*.

I transfer here three particular cases from the Athens, Nat. Libr. 2406:

a) fol. 63v. Ἀπὸ δὲ γίνεται καλοφωνία μετ' ἐπιφωνημάτων· ποίημα κὺρ Ἰωάννου μαΐστορος τοῦ Κουκουζέλη· ἦχος πλ. δ' Ἐνεδύσατο Κύριος'; the epiphōnēma, which is repeated four times, is 'δύναμιν ἐνεδύσατο καὶ περιεζώσατο'.

b) fol. 71v. Ἕτερον Ἐνεδύσατο· ποίημα κυροῦ Γρηγορίου ἱερομονάχου τοῦ Ἀλυάτου, παρόμοιον τοῦ μαΐστορος· ἦχος πλ. β' Ἐνεδύσατο Κύριος'; this epiphōnēma, also repeated twice, is 'δύναμιν ἐνεδύσατο ὁ Κύριος καὶ περιεζώσατο'.

c) fol. 159v. Τοῦ μαΐστορος [Iohannes Koukouzelēs], μετ' ἐπιφωνημάτων· ἦχος πλ. β' Ἐξομολογήσομαί σοι, Κύριε. The epiphōnēma, repeated here five times, is "Ὑψωθήτω ἡ χείρ σου, Κύριε, μὴ ἐπιλάθῃ τῶν πενήτων σου εἰς τέλος'.

Anaphōnēma. The anaphōnēmata are primarily encountered in the festive Polyeleoi and the Amōmos. The anaphōnēma is essentially an interpolation of another of the Psalms or of the choirs through a kratēma or ēchēma, or by employing a mirrored melos of the verses. The panygeric tone is strived for through the anaphōnēma and the sentiments of joy are expressed accordingly. So that the practice of the anaphōnēmata be better understood, let us use the example of the second stasis of the Polyeleos by Koukoumas, Ἐξομολογεῖσθε τῷ Κυρίῳ.

From the same Athens, Nat. Libr. 2406 above:

---

65   Cfr 'The ἐπιφωνήματα are usually written with red ink, an indication that they were not sung by those who chanted the rest of the text'; and, 'the leading principle would seem to be that red ink in these cases is a symbol meaning "sung by somebody else"' (Raasted 1966: 121n84 and 82).

Fol. 143r. Beginning, with holy God, of the second *stasis* of the Polyeleos, known as *Koukoumas*, work by the same maïstōr Koukoumas; the first choir, mode I *Ἐξομολογεῖσθε ...*.

Table 2. Second stasis from Koukoumas' Polyeleos.

Fol. 143v. Melos *heteron·* the left choir	Mode I	Ἐξομολογεῖσθε...
— allagma, right choir	Mode I	Ἐξομολογεῖσθε...
Fol. 144v. Verse, left choir; the same melos	Mode I	Τῷ ποιήσαντι...
Anaphōnēma, right choir	Mode I	Λέγε... Ἀλληλούια
Anaphōnēma, left choir	Mode I	Λέγε... Εἰς τὸν αἰῶνα
Allagma, right choir	Mode II	Τῷ ποιήσαντι τοὺς οὐρανούς...

In this way the Polyeleos progressively completes an oktaēchos, passing through each mode with anaphōnēmata and allagmata.

Allagma. As illustrated above, *allagma* is the term used to declare a change of melos, either within the same mode or through a modulation to another mode. This practice is clearly declared as noted above, *melos heteron.* The allagmata are found in the verses of the anoixantaria, the *Makarios anēr*, the Polyeleoi, the antiphons and the Amōmos,[66] only they are not always specifically indicated in the manuscripts.

Epibolē. The term is used in the mathēmata to indicate the insertion or, as the term suggests, imposition of some addition or *kallōpisma* [ornamentation] arranged by another composer to the text of yet someone else's composition. Without it being a hard and fast rule, the epibolē is usually short. The epibolē does not occur at the end of the piece, but in the middle;

---

66 In the *Papadikē* Athens, Nat. Libr. 2458 from the year AD 1336 one often finds the term *allagma*, sometimes with the complementary *palaion*. Quite interesting are the instances when Amōmon *allagma* is accompanied by a geographic designation for the melic tradition, such as, thettalikon, allagma (fols. 125r, 127v), or *thessalonikaion allagma* (fols. 126r, 129r), or *politikon allagma* (fols. 127r, 128v). These indications also designate sure changes in the melos, but also a comparable antiquity to the melic tradition; cfr Williams 1971: 174n3.

The form of the Mathēmatarion 89

the return to the melos of the first composition is indicated by the word 'text' [*keimenon*][67] in the margin and where the return actually takes place. The praxis of epibolē does not leave out the possibility of the withdrawal of a section of the first, older composition and its replacement with a new melos, which consists of the length of the epibolē.

A clear case is found on fol. 77v of the important Athens, Nat. Libr. 2406: 'Παλαιόν, ἐκαλλωπίσθη δὲ παρὰ τοῦ Κορώνη κὺρ Ξένου καὶ πρωτοψάλτου· ἦχος α´ Πᾶσα πνοή'; this is a mathēma, an anagram for before the heōthinon Gospel lectionary of the orthros. On fol. 78v, it is indicated without interrupting the flow of the composition: 'Ἐπιβολὴ τοῦ Κορώνη, πλ. δ´, *Oppov τον*'; this particular epibolē is composed of one kratēma — the most common type. On the same page, the word *keimenon* is indicated in the margin as an indicator to return to the first composition. In this specific case, the epibolē also introduces a new mode, initiating a modulation. This event is a kallopistic component because the melos is varied and a pleasant impression is presented to the listeners.[68]

As a phenomenon, the epibolē is surely encountered in the mathēmata on a very limited scale; in the kalophonic stichēra[69] it is found as independent compositions, since it is almost always concluded with a kratēma.

Parekbolē. The parekbolē is different from the epibolē in the following way; instead of simply inserting, it first extrapolates [*parekballō*] from somewhere else. It is a musical section added to an already existing composition that was not anticipated in the original composition. However, cases do exist where the parekbolē can easily refer to an epibolē and, hence, can be interchangeable in the manuscripts. In the manuscript used here, Athens, Nat. Libr. 2406, there exist examples of parekbolē. Consider: (fol. 243r)

---

67 These instances are met often in the *Mathēmataria* and mainly concern the finale of a composition; often at this point designations are found in the words *to telos* or *ho choros* or, more often, *apo chorou*.
68 Cfr Athos, Iviron 1120, fol. 593v.
69 For example, Athos, Iviron 991 from the year 1670 (autograph of Kosmas Makedōn): fol. 210v [20 June, anonymous] ἦχος πλ. δ´ *Τῶν τοῦ Θεοῦ δωρεῶν*; fol. 213r: 'ἐκ τοῦ αὐτοῦ στιχηροῦ ἐπιβολὴ τοῦ μαΐστορος Ἰωάννου Κουκουζέλη, ἦχος δ´ *Μακαρίσωμεν πάντες Θεόδωρον*'. Cfr Chourmouzios' *Mathēmatarion*, ΜΠΤ 731, fol. 330v.

Ἕτερον χερουβικόν· ποίημα κὺρ Μανουὴλ τοῦ Ἀγαλλιανοῦ· ἦχος β''; the entire cherubic hymn up to Ὡς τὸν βασιλέα τῶν ὅλων; followed by (fol. 243r–v) 'Παρεκβολὴ κὺρ Θεοδώρου τοῦ Κατακαλῶν, Ὡς τὸν βασιλέα ... τεριρεμ ... τῶν ὅλων ὑποδεξόμενοι' — (fol. 246r) 'Παρεκβολὴ κὺρ Μάρκου ἱερομονάχου ἐκ τῆς μονῆς τοῦ Ξανθοπούλων· Τὸν βασιλέα ... τεριρεμ ...'; the parekbolē refers to the cherubic hymn, the *dytikon*, by Agathon, in mode II plagal. In the *Papadikē*, the parekbolai are normally encountered in the cherubic hymns. In the *Mathēmatarion*, the parekbolē and epibolē are usually exceptions.

Many instances of the parekbolē exist in Iviron 991 (year 1670) by Kosmas Macedōn. Here are some examples:

302v (Aug. 29) [Μιχαὴλ] τοῦ Πατζάδος· πλ. β ', Γενεθλίων τελουμένων.
303r. Παρεκβολὴ τοῦ μαΐστορος [Ἰω. Κουκουζέλη]. πλ. β ', Καὶ ἐπληροῦτο ἡ διάθεσις.
304v. Παρεκβολὴ τοῦ Μαΐστορος [Ἰω. Κουκουζέλη]· βαρύς, Ἐφέρετο ὡς ὀψώνιον.

These two *ekbolai* refer to the same composition by Michael Patzados; an anagram by Iohannes Koukouzelēs follows: (fol. 305r) νενανω *Ἀλλ' ἡμεῖς τὸν βαπτιστήν*.

Another example from the same codex:

342r. Μ. Παρασκευῇ· Ἁλμυριώτου· ἦχος β ', Ὅτε τῷ σταυρῷ.
344r.Ἕτερον, τοῦ Μαΐστορος [Ἰω. Κουκουζέλη]· πλ. β ', Τίς ὑμᾶς ἐρρύσατο.
344v.Ἕτερον τέλος· Γεωργίου δομεστίκου Κοντοπετρῆ.
345r. Μαΐστορος [Ἰω. Κουκουζέλη]· πλ. β ', Τίς ὑμᾶς ἐρρύσατο.
346v. Παρεκβολή, Ἰωάννου Γλυκέος· ἦχος α ', Λοιπόν, καλῶ τὰ ἔθνη.
347v. Ἀναγραμματισμὸς Δημητρίου Δοκειανοῦ· πλ. δ ', Λοιπόν, καλῶ τὰ ἔθνη.
348r. Ἀναγραμματισμὸς Ἰω. Κουκουζέλη· πλ. δ ', Οὐκέτι στέργω λοιπόν.

Parekbolai are usually also anagrams. When they are sufficiently long they can even be regarded as autonomous compositions if they contain a kratēma. In the cases where the ekbolē is itself the addition of a kratēma, the text usually limits itself to a single distinctive phrase.[70]

70 In Chourmouzios' *Mathēmatarion*, ΜΠΤ 729, fol. 31v, we find the *parekbolē* of Korōnēs Παρεγένου ἐν ναῷ Κυρίου, Τοτοτο.

From both the examples shown here and the above instances of epibolē, it can be concluded that the epibolē and ekbolē are additions[71] to an already existing composition. These additions are made either by the actual composer, when they study and perform a mathēma, or by other teachers when they are attracted to a particularly beloved section of a composition by an older teacher, thus creating an epibolē [*epiballoun*] via addition or a parekbolē [*parekballoun*] via extrapolation and insertion/imposition. Instead of the terms *epibolē* and *parekbolē*, the term *parembolē* is rarely encountered indicating the same practice as the other two.

Prologos. A prologos is a short melos from a particular verse, usually in the collection of the kalophonic *Makarios anēr, Ἵνα τί ἐφρύαξαν*, which is followed by a long kratēma occasionally bearing its own name, like '*ethnikon*', '*ho anakaras*', '*ho choros*', etc. Consequently, the prologos is truly a prologue or introduction in the sense of a prelude to a kratēma that follows.

We come across many prologoi of this nature in Athos, Iviron 1120 by Manuel Chrysaphēs, referring to the kratēmata of the kalophonic verses Ἵνα τί ἐφρύαξαν and of the Polyeleos. The heirmoi, kalophonic or not, followed by a kratēma, occupy the place of a prologos, as observed in the section above on the origin of the *Kalophonic Heirmologion*. If the section is not lifted from the original related composition, the final verses of the kalophonic dogmatika of a kratēma of the same mode are also prologoi of the kratēmata and ēchēmata[72] chanted as preludes to the entrance during the service of vespers.

---

71 In Athos, Xeromotamou 383 (fifteenth century) the exact word *prosthēkē* is used to describe an *epibolē* or *parekbolē* on fol. 46v; cfr Stathēs 1975–: Vol. 1, 288. Also, on fol. 246r of Athos, Konstamonitou 86 we read: 'παρεκβολαὶ καὶ προσθέσεις καὶ καλλωπισμοί …'.

72 In the *Papadikai* and *Kratēmataria* the last verses of the dogmatic theotokia are anthologized with the kratēmata that follow and are described as prologoi. The following kratēma or more often ēchēma is short. Since the entrance of the vespers takes place during these dogmatika, the manuscripts often indicate *eis tēn megalēn eisodon tou hesperinou*; cfr Athos, Iviron 1120, fol. 207v: 'ἠχήματα κατ' ἦχον ψαλλόμενα εἰς ἑορτὰς ἐν τῇ εἰσόδῳ τοῦ ἑσπερινοῦ'.

Independent kratēmata, however, are clearly characterized as prologoi which, as understood, precede another composition. In the codex Athos, Iviron 1120, fol. 197v we read: 'Πρόλογος μουσικός, όργανικός, ψαλλόμενος διά τριών μελών έντέχνως. Μανουήλ λαμπαδαρίου τοῦ Χρυσάφη· ἦχος δ΄, Ετεν τεν τεν'. In the manuscript Athos, Koutloumousiou 455 (fifteenth–sixteenth century): fol. 12v 'Πρόλογος μετά ἴσου, τοῦ Χρυσάφη· ἦχος δ΄, Eppε ppε ppε — fol. 14r Πρόλογος τοῦ μαΐστορος, ὁ τροχός· πλ. δ΄, Ετερρετέ'. The comment on fol. 383r in Athens, Nat. Libr., 866 (end of fifteenth century) is very interesting: "Ο β΄ πούς· πρόλογος, ἐὰν βούλει·[73] ἦχος δ΄, Σύν..., τιτιτιτιρριτι'. The term refers to a preceding short kratēma[74] at the beginning of the second foot which follows, indicated again by the register 'ὁ β΄ πούς, ἦχος δ΄, Συ τιτιτι συλλαλοῦντες αὐτῷ'. Also, in Chourmouzios' *Mathēmatarion*, we encounter the term referring to a kratēma and functioning exactly as an introduction or prelude, according to international music terminology in manuscript Athens, Nat. Libr. ΜΠΤ 728, fol. 164v, "Ετερος πρόλογος', a kratēma; or, Athens, Nat. Libr. ΜΠΤ 729, fol. 35r "Ετερον, πρόλογος, Τατατα'. The above witnesses are illuminating and help in the clarification of the morphological types of the mathēmata, as will be evident below.

Katabasia. The term katabasia here, in the context of the discussion of the kalophonic compositions, has a different meaning from that of the normal characterisation of the heirmoi of the canons as katabasiai. In this case, it means the addition of a section of a kratēma at the end of another kratēma, as a conclusion or finale. This is the case in Athens, Nat. Libr. 2406, fol. 340v. 'Καταβασία Γρηγορίου Ἀλυάτου, [ἦχος] δ΄, Ερρετερε'. When the katabasia is notably long and tends toward maintaining an independent entity, except for the fact that it is placed at the end of another kratēma, it is then usually characterized as a *katabasia megalē*[75] [great katabasia].

---

73 The hypothetical *ei boulei*, which can be found in other instances also, offers the ability to forego the introductory kratēma to save time.

74 As a prelude, a kratēma carries the designation *apolytarisma* in Athos, Gregoriou 3 (end of seventeenth century), fol. 91r: 'τῇ Κυριακῇ πρὸ τῆς Χριστοῦ γεννήσεως, ἀκολοθία τῆς Καμίνου· λέγε πρῶτον τὸ παρὸν ἀπολυτάρισμα, κυρίου Ἰωάννου τοῦ Κλαδᾶ, ἦχος πλ. δ΄'.

75 The witness of Athens, Nat. Libr. 2604 (year 1463), fol. 234r clarifies: 'ἡ μεγάλη καταβασία ἔστιν αὔτη· γράφεται δὲ ἀπὸ τὸ Ἡμεῖς δὲ ταῦτα βλέποντες· ἐγὼ δὲ ἔγραψα

The form of the Mathēmatarion

Homonoia. The term *homonoia* is also found in the music manuscripts and always refers to a kratēma, indicating the meaning as katabasia, as we conclude from the Athens, Nat. Libr. 2406, fol. 18v, "Ὁμόνοια συνοπτική, ἥτις λέγεται καταβασία".[76] This practice is clarified by the witness in Athos, Koutloumousiou 456 (year 1443), fol. 466r, Ἕτερον ψαλλόμενον εἰς τὸ τέλος πάσης ἀκολουθίας, τὸ λεγόμενον ὁμόνοια, τοῦ Γλυκέος· ἦχος πλ. δ΄, *Εεερετερε*'. As with all the *homonoiai*, this kratēma is also short. Another occurrence specifies the asmatic practice; in Athos, Koutloumousiou 457 (second half of the fourteenth C), fol. 345r, we read: 'Μετὰ δὲ τὰς περισσάς, ὕστερον ἡ ὁμόνοια αὕτη· τοῦ πρωτοψάλτου κυροῦ Ἰωάννου τοῦ Γλυκύ· ἦχος δ΄, *Ετερρετε*'.[77] As found in the manuscript Athens 2601[78] (c. the year 1430), the *perissai* indicate the repetition of verses with ēchēmata or 'unto the more melodic' [*melismatikōteron*], or with the parembolē of other verses, according to the asmatic vespers and orthros[79] services. Hence, whether katabasia or homonoia, as 'τέλος πάσης ἀκολουθίας' [the finale of each service], they were used as closings or conclusions of a kalophonic unity.

ἐνταῦθα, διότι ἔχει ἐκεῖσε ὁμόνοιαν ἄλλη, ταύτην δὲ γράφω ὁμοῦ μὲ τὴν ὁμόνοιαν τοῦ Γλυκύ· ἦχος δ΄ *Εετερεετε*'. And on fol. 206v, 'λεγόμενον ἡ μεγάλη καταβασία, τοῦ Ἀβασιώτου, ἦχος δ΄ *Ὡς Ἄννα ανενανε ... τεριρεμ ... ὡς Ἄννα ἡ προφῆτις*'. Both instances in this codex concern the finale, the *perissai*, and fulfill a kind of concord.

76 Athos, Konstamonitou 86, fol. 68v: 'ὁμόνοια κυροῦ Γρηγορίου, ἦχος δ΄ *Ερεετε* — ἑτέρα ὁμόνοια, τοῦ Κοντοπετρῆ, *Ερετερε*'; fol. 69r, 'ἑτέρα ὁμόνοια, ἦχος δ΄ *Ερερουτερε*'; cfr Stathēs 1975–: Vol. 1, 660.

77 In the margin on fol. 345v is written *kai exō ison holoi*.

78 A particular instance of the perissē is given on fol. 45r of this codex: '*Δόξα — Καὶ νῦν, καὶ πάλιν ἠχίζει ὁ δομέστικος τὴν περισσήν· Νεανες Τὴν ζωηφόρον σου ἔγερσιν Κύριε δοξάζω ου μεωουεγγεεν*'. Hence, the verse is repeated with the more melismatic style and the insertion of ēchētic syllables in the cadence.

79 In Athens, Nat. Libr. 2604 (year 1463), and from fol. 194r there exists an entire unit of perissai hōs *heuromen apo tou lampadariou athebolaion*; they consist of large *dichora* compositions, with katabasiai and homonoiai, at the end of the hexapsalmos and are followed by dekapentasyllabic compositions, *Ριφεὶς Ἀδάμ*, and the like. On fol. 235r there is an interesting note regarding perissai, as well as in Athos, Docheiariou 315, fol. 174r; cfr Stathēs 1975–: Vol. 1, 354.

CHAPTER 3

The tradition of the kalophonic melos

THE FORMATION AND TRADITION OF THE RELATED CODICES BEGINNING FROM THE FOURTEENTH CENTURY

So far, the contents of the earliest known codex, the Athens, Nat. Libr. 2458 from the year 1336 (p. 49), was summarized above. This codex is the bearer of the new trends and tendencies of the compositional art, in other words, the codification of kalophony as it reached that year through the evolutionary road taken over the time-span of a century. Together with the development and the spreading of the kalophonic melos, from the year 1336 onward, an analogous formation of large divisions in the contents according to the forms and order [*taxis*] of the daily offices is noticed in the manuscript tradition of these melē. As a natural consequence, a new type of manuscript, the *Akolouthiai* or, commonly named, *Papadikē* was enriched and widened en masse in order to receive the continuously growing output of the kalophonic melos according to groups of similar compositions. From the year 1336 to the decade of the Fall of Constantinople, there exists a group of approximately sixty *Papadikai*, following the order of contents comparable to that of Athens, Nat. Libr. 2458. As to the kalophonic stichēra, their anagrams or anapodismoi, the katanyktika and the kratēmata, these codices dedicate a large number of folios, sometimes reaching half or even more of the codex. This swelling of the *Papadikai* during the first quarter of the fifteenth century breeds the creation of other codices whose contents are large unities of similar kalophonic melē. Thus, from this fundamental bearer of kalophony, the *Papadikē*, emanate the codices known as the *Kratēmatarion, Mathēmatarion* or *Kalophōnikon Stichērarion*, as well as the *Oikēmatarion*, and mainly the Akathistos.[1]

Meanwhile, under the names *Akolouthiai* (during the fourteenth and fifteenth centuries) or later as *Anthologia*, along with the psalmic mathēmata that organically belonged to it, the *Papadikē* never ceased to contain the mathēmata for the formal feasts of the year, as well as a collection of select kratēmata. Furthermore, from the end of the seventeenth century, they also contained a collection of kalophonic heirmoi. It should be noted here that the *Papadikai* or *Anthologiai* comprise forty or more per cent of the entire catalogue of extant Byzantine music manuscripts, so it is not difficult to envision their usefulness and usage. Also evident is the extent, value and exhaustive research involved in all aspects of the study of Byzantine chant, its development and morphology, and that is to be gleaned from them. Accordingly, it is necessary for us to review the manuscript tradition of the kalophonic melos according to the four types of codices mentioned above, beginning with the *Papadikē*.

The Papadikē

In order to draft a complete image of the contents of the *Papadikē*, the place and expanse held by the kalophonic melē including the kratēmata, the place of the dekapentasyllabic mathēmata and how they were eventually separated from the *Papadikē* creating separate music books of similar hymnic content, it is prudent and useful to present here a comprehensive description of the *Papadikē* written in the year 1458 by Manuel Doukas the lampadarios and Chrysaphēs — Athos, Iviron 1120.[2] The fundamental reason for selecting this *Papadikē* is that it is the largest and most complete codifying of the music tradition at the close of the Byzantine period. Other than this, it is also useful, I believe, for us to have a complete description of the psalmic mathēmata of the kalophonic verses for the vespers, the polyeleos and

[1] For the text of the Akathistus cfr Christ 1871: 140–147; Trypanis 1968: 17–39.
[2] Cfr Lampros 1888: Vol. 2, 252; 1966: Vol. 2, 252; Stathēs 1975–: Vol. 4, unpublished.

The tradition of the kalophonic melos

the Amōmos with its kratēmata, thus providing a well-rounded overview of the kalophony of Byzantine melopœïa.[3] After the description of this manuscript, the necessary references to chronologically earlier and later *Papadikai* will be addressed.

ΠΑΠΑΔΙΚΗ — Iviron 1120 — scribe: Manuel Chrysaphēs, year 1458, fols. 674 (+30).

This paper codex measures 18.2 x 12.2 cm. According to the last numbering of the folios of this huge but most important codex, the first folio is numbered 1 — inner folio, two errors occurred: from number 463 it continues with number 444 and from number 569 to 560. The repetition of certain numbers received a small 'χ' from me indicating the repetition, thus, 463χ, 464χ, 465χ and so on, and 560χ, 561χ, 562χ, etc.

Fols. 2r–29v. The normal *protheōria* 'ἀρχὴ σὺν θεῷ ἁγίῳ τῶν σημαδίων τῆς ψαλτικῆς τέχνης ... συντεθειμένης παρὰ τῶν κατὰ καιροὺς ἀναδειχθέντων ποιητῶν, παλαιῶν τε καὶ νέων' and the work of Manuel Chrysaphēs (fol. 12r) *On the theory of the art of chanting;* other methodoi interspersed (fols. 7r–10) by Xēros, Manuel Chrysaphēs, Iohannes Koukouzelēs.

Fol. 30r: 'Ἀκολουθίαι συντεθεῖσαι παρὰ κυροῦ Ἰωάννου μαΐστορος τοῦ Κουκουζέλη. Ἀρχὴ σὺν θεῷ τοῦ μεγάλου ἑσπερινοῦ, ποιηθέντος παρὰ διαφόρων ποιητῶν παλαιῶν. Ἄρχεται ὁ δομέστικος ἡσύχῳ φωνῇ εἰς ἦχον πλ. δ' Ἀνοίξαντός σου'. Fol. 30v: 'Ἕτερος μέγας ἑσπερινὸς ποιηθεὶς παρὰ λαμπαδαρίου Μανουὴλ τοῦ Χρυσάφη, πλ. δ' Ἀνοίξαντός σου – Ἀποστρέψαντός σου'.

The rest of the verse follows according to the compositions of: Iohannes Koukouzelēs, Georgios Panaretos, Iohannes lampadarios Kladas, Manuel

---

3 In reality, through the analytical description of this codex we are provided with almost half of the entire repertoire of kalophony, the other half of the *Mathēmatarion*, the other half provided with the *initia* of Chourmouzios' eight-tomed *Mathēmatarion* below. If then we have before us the *Pandektē*, huge *Papadikē* of Anastasius Baïas, Athos, Xeropotamou 307, of the years 1767 and 1770 (744 folios), in which is contained the larger part of Manuel Chrysaphes' *Papadikē* plus the compositions of the new teachers, as well as the collection of kolophonic heirmoi, we will be well situated for a global view of the kalophonic melos. For a description of Athos, Xeropotamou 307 cfr Stathēs 1975–: Vol. 1, 107–117.

Chrysaphēs, Xenos Korōnēs, Iohannes Kampanes, Georgios Kontopetres, Agathon, Manuel Korōnēs and protopsaltes, priest of Ampelokepiotes, Georgios Moschianos, domestikos Kassianos, Ioakeim monachos, Nikon monachos, 'παλαιόν, άπό χορού δλοι όμου, Πάντα εν σοφία'.

Fol. 43v: 'Είτα γίνεται συναπτή και μετά τήν έκφώνησιν άρχεται ό δομέστικος του β΄χορού, πλ. δ΄ Μακάριος άνήρ· έτέρα άρχή, Μανουήλ λαμπαδαρίου του Χρυσάφη, πλ. δ΄ Μακάριος άνήρ'.

All the verses of the three first psalms according to composition: Manuel lampadarios, Chalibourēs, *hagiosophitikon*, Xenos Korōnēs, Iohannes maïstōr Koukouzelēs, Iohannes Kladas, Dokeianos, Manuel Agallianos, *palaion*, Panaretos, [Iohannes] Xēros. — (fol. 50r) 'Ενταύθα γίνεται ή καλοφωνία. Άρχή της βας στάσεως'; *palaion*, Geōrgios Kontopetrēs, Tzaknopoulos, domestikos [Philippos] Gabalas. — (fol. 60r) 'Στάσις τρίτη· άρχεται ό δομέστικος του αριστερού χορού'; *frangikon*, Theodōros Argyropoulos, Chōmatianos, [Kōnstantinos] Magoulas, (fol. 67v) 'έτερον άπό τον Κουκουμάν Δόξα—Καί νυν, τά κομμάτια έκ δευτέρου δλα'.

Fols. 70r–203v: 'Στίχοι καλοφωνικοί του μεγάλου εσπερινού'. [Prologoi, kratēmata; analytically:] (fol. 70r) κυρού Ιωάννου μαΐστορος του Κουκουζέλη, πλ. δ΄ *Ίνα τί εφρύαξαν έθνη* —(fol. 71v) του αύτου, πλ. δ΄ *Ίνα τί εφρύαξαν* —(fols. 74r, 76b, 78r) Ξένου πρωτοψάλτου του Κορώνη, πλ. δ΄ *Ίνα τί εφρύαξαν* —(fols. 80r, 81v) Ιωάννου Κουκουζέλη, πλ. δ΄ *Παρέστησαν οι βασιλείς* —(fol. 82r) του λαμπροτάτου μαΐστορος κυρού Ιωάννου του Κουκουζέλη, λεγόμενον ή βιόλα· λέγεται και καμπάνα, πλ. δ΄ *Ananenna* [kratēma: in the lower margin is a note referring to the red *parallagai*]: ση[μείωσις] τά κόκκινα πάντα είσί του λαμπαδαρίου κυρού Ιωάννου [Κλαδά] —(fol. 85r) πρόλογος, πλ. δ΄ *Παρέστησαν* —του μακαρίτου και ώς άληθώς μαΐστορος κυρού Ιωάννου του Κουκουζέλη, λεγόμενον έθνικόν και μαργαρίτης, πλ. δ΄ *Ερρετεντεν* —(fol. 87v) του θαυμασιωτάτου μαΐστορος κυρού Ιωάννου του Κουκουζέλη, ό χορός, πλ. δ΄ *Ανεενα* —(fol. 90r) πρόλογος του Κορώνη, πλ. δ΄ *Και οι άρχοντες* —Ιωάννου μαΐστορος Κουκουζέλη, ό τροχός, έπλατύνθη καί παρά κυρού Ιωάννου λαμπαδαρίου, πλ. δ΄ *Ερρετεϊτέ* —(fol. 91v) πρόλογος, Μανουήλ λαμπαδαρίου του Χρυσάφη, πλ. δ΄ *Και οι άρχοντες* —(fol. 92r) Ιωάννου Κουκουζέλη, λεγόμενον του βασιλέως, πλ. δ΄ *Νεανε* —(fol. 94v) πρόλογος Ιωάννου μαΐστορος, πλ. δ΄ *Κατά του κυρίου* —(fol. 95r) Ιωάννου πρωτοψάλτου του Γλυκέος, ήδύτατον πάνυ, πλ. δ΄ *Τοτοτο* —(fol. 96v) πρόλογος, Κορώνη, πλ. δ΄ *Κατά του κυρίου* —(fol. 97r) πρωτοψάλτου Ξένου του Κορώνη, λεγόμενον ροδάνιν, πλ. δ΄ *Ανεανε* —(fol. 99r) πρόλογος του Κορώνη, πλ. δ΄ *Διαρρήξωμεν* —*Ερρετερε* —(fol. 100v) Μανουήλ λαμπαδαρίου Χρυσάφη, πρόλογος, πλ. δ΄ *Διαρρήξωμεν* —Ξένου Κορώνη, πλ. δ΄ *Ανεανε* —(fol. 102v) πρόλογος, πλ. δ΄, *Και άπορρίψωμεν* —(fol. 103r) Κορώνη, λεγόμενον τό πάνυ ώραΐον, πλ. δ΄ *Ανενανεϊνα* —(fol. 105r) πρόλογος, πλ. δ΄ *Διαρρήξωμεν* —Ιωάννου λαμπαδαρίου του Κλαδά, λεγόμενον ό ανακαράς, πλ. δ΄ *Ερρετερρε* —(fol. 107v) πρόλογος, πλ. δ΄ *Και*

The tradition of the kalophonic melos 99

ἀπορρίψωμεν —(fol. 108r) Ἰωάννου Κλαδᾶ πλ. δ΄ *Ερρετερρε* —(fol. 109r) λαμπαδαρίου Μανουὴλ Χρυσάφη, ἀηδών, πλ. δ΄ *Ανενε* —(fol. 111r) πρόλογος τοῦ δομεστίκου κὺρ Γεωργίου τοῦ Κοντοπετρῆ, πλ. δ΄ *Διαρρήξωμεν* —(fol. 111v) Ἰωάννου μαΐστορος τοῦ Κουκουζέλη, λεγόμενον ὁ ἀνυφαντής, πλ. β΄ *Ανανενα* —(fol. 113v) πρόλογος, Ἰωακεὶμ μοναχοῦ, πλ. δ΄ *Καὶ ἀπορρίψωμεν* —(fol. 114r) Ἰωάννου Κουκουζέλη, πλ. β΄ *Ερρεντεντεν* —(fol. 116v) Ἰωάννου μαΐστορος Κουκουζέλη, πλ. δ΄ *Ὁ κατοικῶν ἐν οὐρανοῖς* —(fol. 118r) Ἰωάννου Κουκουζέλη, πρόλογος, πλ. δ΄ *Ὁ κατοικῶν* —(fol. 118v) Ἰωάννου Κουκουζέλη, φθορικόν, ἦχος δ΄ *Τετερρετερε* —(fol. 120r) Ἰωάννου πρωτοψάλτου τοῦ Γλυκέος, ἰσοφωνία, ἦχος δ΄ *Τοτοτορροτο* —(fol. 120r) Ξένου τοῦ Κορώνη, ἦχος δ΄ *Τοτοτο* —(fol. 122r) πρόλογος, Μανουὴλ Χρυσάφη, ὀργανικὸς ἦχος δ΄ *Ὁ κατοικῶν* —τοῦ αὐτοῦ, γλυκύτατον, ὀργανικόν, λεγόμενον τερπνόν, ἦχος δ΄ *Τοτορροτο* —(fol. 124r) Μανουὴλ λαμπαδαρίου τοῦ Χρυσάφη, πρόλογος, ἦχος δ΄ *Εερρε* —(fol. 124v) πρόλογος τοῦ αὐτοῦ, ἦχος δ΄ *Καὶ ὁ Κύριος ἡμῶν* —ἡ λεγομένη κιννύρα, ἦχος δ΄ *Τέεετερρε* —(fol. 126r) Ἰωάννου μαΐστορος τοῦ Κουκουζέλη, πλ. δ΄ *Τότε λαλήσει* —(fol. 127r) πρόλογος, πλ. δ΄ *Τότε λαλήσει* —(fol. 127v) δομεστίκου Γεωργίου Κοντοπετρῆ, δ΄ *Τέετερρε* —(fol. 129r) Ἰωάννου Κουκουζέλη, φθορικόν, πλ. δ΄ *Ερρεντεν* —(fol. 131v) Γεωργίου δομεστίκου Κοντοπετρῆ, πρόλογος, πλ. δ΄ *Ἐγὼ κατεστάθην* —(fol. 132r) Μανουὴλ Χρυσάφη, δεδεμένον, πλ. β΄ *Ανενενε* —(fol. 133v) πρόλογος, τοῦ αὐτοῦ, πλ. δ΄ *Ἐπὶ Σιὼν ὄρος* —(fol. 134r) Μανουὴλ Χρυσάφη, πάνυ καλόν, πλ. β΄ *Ανενανε* —(fol. 136r) πρόλογος τοῦ αὐτοῦ, πλ. δ΄ *Διαγγελῶν τὸ πρόσταγμα* —Ἰωάννου τοῦ Γλυκέος, λεγόμενον ὁ σουρλᾶς, πλ. β΄ *Τοτοτο* —(fol. 137v) πρόλογος, Ξένου τοῦ Κορώνη, πλ. δ΄ *Κύριος εἶπε πρός με* —*Ερρετερρε* —(fol. 139r) στίχος ποιηθεὶς παρὰ Μανουὴλ λαμπαδαρίου τοῦ Χρυσάφη, δι' ὁρισμοῦ τοῦ ἁγίου τοῦ μακαρίτου βασιλέως καὶ αὐθέντου ἡμῶν κυροῦ Κωνσταντίνου, πλ. δ΄ *Ἐγὼ σήμερον γεγέννηκά σε* [noted in the bottom margin:] σφόδρα μοι δοκεῖ γλυκύτατον —(fol. 141r) Ἰωάννου Κουκουζέλη, πλ. δ΄ *Αἴτησαι παρ' ἐμοῦ* —(fol. 143r) Ἰωάννου Κουκουζέλη, πλ. δ΄ *Ὡς σκεύη κεραμέως* —(fol. 143v) τοῦ αὐτοῦ, πλ. β΄ *Νεχεανε* —(fol. 145v) πρόλογος Μανουὴλ Χρυσάφη, πλ. δ΄ *Καὶ νῦν βασιλεῖς* —(fol. 146r) Ἰωάννου μαΐστορος τοῦ Κουκουζέλη, δύσκολον, πλ. β΄ *Ερερερε* —(fol. 148r) πρόλογος ἡμέτερος [Manuel Chrysaphēs], πλ. δ΄ *Καὶ παιδεύθητε* —δεδεμένον ὅλον μετὰ τῆς φθορᾶς [νενανω], πλ. β΄ *Ανενανε* —(fol. 150r) ποίημα τοῦ θαυμασιωτάτου καὶ διδασκάλου τῶν διδασκάλων κυροῦ Ἰωάννου μαΐστορος τοῦ Κουκουζέλη, πάνυ καλόν, πλ. δ΄ *Δουλεύσατε τῷ Κυρίῳ* —(fol. 152v) ποίημα κὺρ Γαβριὴλ τοῦ ἀπὸ τῶν Ξανθοπούλων, γλυκύτατον, βαρὺς *Καὶ ἀγαλλιᾶσθε αὐτῷ* —(fol. 154v) πρωτοψάλτου Ξένου τοῦ Κορώνη, πλ. α΄ *Δουλεύσατε τῷ Κυρίῳ* —(fol. 155r) τοῦ αὐτοῦ, τὸ μικρὸν σημαντήρι, πλ. α΄ *Τοτοτο* —(fol. 157r) πρόλογος, τοῦ Κορώνη, πλ. α΄ *Καὶ ἀγαλλιᾶσθε* —(fol. 157v) Ἰωάννου μαΐστορος τοῦ Κουκουζέλη, θαυμαστόν, λεγόμενον πάνυ ὡραῖος, πλ. α΄ *Ανενενε* —(fol. 160r) πρόλογος τοῦ Κορώνη, πλ. β΄ *Καὶ ἀγαλλιᾶσθε* —(fol. 160v) Ξένου τοῦ Κορώνη, πάνυ καλόν, πλ. β΄ *Ανενανε* —(fol. 163r) πρόλογος Ἰωάννου λαμπαδαρίου [Κλαδᾶ], βαρὺς *Δουλεύσατε τῷ Κυρίῳ* —(fol. 163v) Κορώνη, βαρὺς *Ανενενανε* —(fol. 165v) πρόλογος, βαρὺς *Δράξασθε παιδείας* —(fol. 166r) Μανουὴλ λαμπαδαρίου Χρυσάφη, λεγόμενον πάνυ ὡραῖος, βαρὺς *Ανενανε* —(fol. 167v) Μανουὴλ Χρυσάφη, βαρὺς *Καὶ ἀπολεῖσθε* —τοῦ αὐτοῦ [in the bottom margin]: ἐποιήθη ἐν τῇ

Σερβία· ώς δοκεῖ μοι πάνυ καλόν, βαρὺς Τοτοτο —(fol. 169v) Ἰωάννου δομεστίκου τοῦ Τζακνοπούλου, πλ. δ´ *Δράξασθε παιδείας* —(fol. 171r) Δημητρίου τοῦ Δοκειανοῦ, πλ. δ´ *Ὅταν ἐκκαυθῇ* —(fol. 172v) πρόλογος, δομεστίκου τοῦ Κασσᾶ ἀπὸ τῆς Κύπρου, δ´ *Ερρερερε* —(fol. 173r) πρόλογος, Ἰωάννου Κουκουζέλη, πλ. δ´ *Δόξα Πατρί* —(fol.173v) Δημητρίου Δοκειανοῦ, πλ. δ´ *Ανενανεϊνα* —(fol. 175r) πρόλογος, Κουκουζέλη, πλ. δ´ *Δόξα Πατρί* —πάνυ καλόν, πλ. δ´ *Ερρετεντεν* —(fol. 177v) τοῦ αὐτοῦ, λεγόμενον τοῦ Παπαδοπούλου, πλ. δ´ *Ερρετεντεν* —(fol. 179v) τοῦ αὐτοῦ, λεπτότατον, πλ. δ´ *Ανεανε* —(fol. 181r) τοῦ αὐτοῦ, παρόμοιον τοῦ χοροῦ, κάλλιστον πλ. δ´ *Ανενανεϊνα* —(fol. 183v) πρόλογος, πλ. δ´ *Καί νῦν καί ἀεί* —Ξένου τοῦ Κορώνη, πλ. δ´ *Νεανενε* —(fol. 185r) πρόλογος τοῦ Μαΐστορος, τρίτος *Δόξα Πατρί* —(fol. 185v) τρίτος, πλ. δ´ *νανα Ανανενανε* —(fol. 187r) πρόλογος, Ξένου τοῦ Κορώνη, τρίτος *Δόξα* —*Καί νῦν* —(fol. 187v) Νικηφόρου δομεστίκου τοῦ Ἠθικοῦ, τρίτος *Ανενανε* —(fol. 188v) πρόλογος τοῦ Κοντοπετρῆ, δ´ *Δόξα* —*Καί νῦν* —(fol. 189r) πρόλογος, Μανουὴλ Χρυσάφη, πλ. β´ *Δόξα* —*Καί νῦν* —Γρηγορίου ἱερομονάχου τοῦ Ἀλυάτου, δύσκολον φθορικόν, πλ. β´ *Ανεενενε* —(fol. 192v) πρόλογος τοῦ αὐτοῦ, πλ. δ´ *Νενενεανε* —(fol. 192v) πρόλογος, τοῦ αὐτοῦ, πλ. δ´ *Δόξα* —*Καί νῦν* —(fol. 193r) Γαβριὴλ ἐκ τῶν Ξανθοπούλων, πλ. δ´ *Ετερρερε* —(fol. 195v) πρόλογος, Μανουὴλ λαμπαδαρίου τοῦ Χρυσάφη· μουσικὸς ὀργανικός· δ´ *Ετετε* —*Δόξα Πατρί* —(fol. 196r) Ἀργυροπούλου ἐκ τῆς Ῥόδου, λεγόμενον ῥόδιον, δ´ *Τοτοτο* —(fol. 197v) πρόλογος, μουσικός, ὀργανικός, ψαλλόμενος διὰ τριῶν μελῶν ἐντέχνως, Μανουὴλ λαμπαδαρίου τοῦ Χρυσάφη, δ´ *Ετεντεντεν* —(fol. 198v) πρόλογος Ἰωάννου Κουκουζέλη, δ´ *Δόξα* —*Καί νῦν* —*Τοτοτοτο* —(fol. 199v) πρόλογος τοῦ Γλυκέος, δ´ *Ερρερερε* —(fol. 200r) πρόλογος, Μανουὴλ Γαζῆ, δ´ *Ερερερε* —(fol. 200v) πρόλογος, δ´ *Δόξα Πατρί* —Δημητρίου Δοκειανοῦ, δ´ λέγετος μέσος *Νενανε* —(fol. 202r) πρόλογος, Ἰωάννου λαμπαδαρίου, δ´ *Δόξα* —*Καί νῦν* —*Τοτοτοτο*.

(fol. 203v) Εἶτα γίνεται μικρὰ συναπτή, καὶ μετὰ τὴν ἐκφώνησιν ἄρχεται ὁ πρωτοψάλτης ἢ ὁ δομέστικος τὸ *Κύριε ἐκέκραξα* εἰς ἦχον τῆς ἑορτῆς, κατ᾽ ἦχον —(fol. 207v) ἠχήματα κατ᾽ ἦχον ψαλλόμενα ἐν τῇ εἰσόδῳ τοῦ ἑσπερινοῦ· Ἰωάννου Κουκουζέλη, Ἰωάννου Γλυκέος, Μανουὴλ Χρυσάφη, Ξένου Κορώνη, Ἰωάννου Κλαδᾶ —(fol. 223r) ἀρχὴ τῶν μικρῶν καὶ μεγάλων δοχῶν τῆς ὅλης ἑβδομάδος —(fol. 226v) ἐνταῦθα γίνεται καλοφωνία, εἴ τι βούλει —(fol. 227r) ἐνταῦθα γίνεται καλοφωνία· ποίημα τοῦ μαΐστορος κυροῦ Ἰωάννου τοῦ Κουκουζέλη, μετ᾽ ἐπιφωνημάτων, πλ. δ´ *Ενεδύσατο Κύριος* —(fol. 228v) πρόλογος Ἰωακεὶμ μοναχοῦ, δ´ *Τῷ οἴκῳ σου πρέπει* —(fol. 229r) τῇ Κυριακῇ πρωΐ, πλ. β´ *Ἀνάστηθι Κύριε* —Ἰωάννου Κουκουζέλη, *Ἐξομολογήσομαί σοι* —(fol. 232r) προκείμενα τὰ μεγάλα, ἄτινα ψάλλονται τῇ ἑβδομάδι τῆς Διακαινησίμου· τῇ ἁγίᾳ καὶ μεγάλῃ Κυριακῇ τοῦ Πάσχα ..., βαρὺς *Τίς Θεὸς μέγας*.

The series of prokeimena, by pairs: small and great doche. The prokeimena *Μὴ ἀποστρέψῃς* (fol. 234v) and ἕτερα ψαλλόμενα εἰς τὰς ἑορτὰς τῆς Θεοτόκου, *Μεγαλύνει ἡ ψυχή μου*᾽ follow.

(Fol. 236) Τέλος τοῦ ἑσπερινοῦ. —Μετὰ ταῦτα ἄρχεται ὁ Ορθρος· καὶ μετὰ τὸν ἑξάψαλμον γίνεται μεγάλη συναπτή, καὶ μετὰ τὴν ἐκφώνησιν ἄρχεται ὁ δομέστικος τὸ Θεὸς Κύριος — (fol. 238v) Ἀλληλούια —(fol. 241r) Μετὰ τὴν συνήθη στιχολογίαν ψάλλεται ὁ πολυέλεος, ὁ λεγόμενος Λατρινός· ἔχει δὲ οὗτος ἀλληλουϊάρια παλαιά τε καὶ νέα. Ὁ δομέστικος ἀπ' ἔξω, ἦχος α΄ *Δοῦλοι Κύριον* —ἐσωτέρᾳ φωνῇ ἀπὸ χοροῦ, *Αἰνεῖτε*.

The entire Polyeleos; the verses according to composition — with allagmata — by composer: *latrinon*, Iohannes Koukouzelēs, Michael Mystakon, Agallianos, Xenos Korōnēs, Demetrios Dokeianos, Iohannes lampadarios [Kladas], Gregorios domestikos, Longinos hieromonachos, Phokas and laosynaptes of the Great Church, Kontopetres, Andreas, Nikephoros Ethikos. On fols. 250–253 there are dekapentasyllabic and verses for the last verses of the polyeleos for feasts. From fol. 254r begins the second stasis of the Latrinos, mode II, *Ἐξομολογεῖσθε* —(fol. 261r) ᾀσματικὸν κυροῦ Μιχαὴλ τοῦ Μυστάκωνος, πλ. δ΄ *Ἐξομολογεῖσθε*.

(Fol. 262r) Ἕτερος πολυέλεος, ὃς καλεῖται Κουκουμᾶς, ποιηθεὶς παρὰ τοῦ Κουκουμᾶ καὶ μαΐστορος, ψαλλόμενος εἰς δεσποτικὰς ἑορτὰς καὶ εἰς μεγάλους ἁγίους, ἦχος α΄ *Δοῦλοι Κύριον*.

The entire polyeleos, compositions as follows: Κουκουμᾶ, Μανουὴλ Χρυσάφη, Κωνσταντίνου Μαγουλᾶ, Μανουὴλ Πλαγίτου, Μανουὴλ τοῦ Κούρτεση, τοῦ Γλυκέος τοῦ δυσικοῦ ἡ βουλγάρα *[Καὶ τὸ μνημόσυνόν σου]*, Γρηγορίου δομεστίκου τοῦ Γλυκέος, Κορνηλίου μοναχοῦ, Ἰωάννου μαΐστορος τοῦ Κουκουζέλη, τοῦ Μυστάκωνος δίχορος· οὕτως ἐψάλλετο ἐν Κωνσταντινουπόλει, πλ. α΄ *Οἶκος Ἰσραὴλ — Οἶκος Ἀαρὼν* (with ēchēmata), τοῦ Κλωβᾶ, Νικηφόρου Ἠθικοῦ. The last verses with verses fitting for the feasts. —(fol. 277r) 'πολυέλεος, ἡ Δευτέρα στάσις, ὃς λέγεται τετράστιχος, ποιηθεὶς παρὰ τοῦ Κουκουμᾶ, ἦχος α΄ *Ἐξομολογεῖσθε*'. The polyeleos finishes as an oktaēchos; allagmata in each verse. The verse, II plagal *Καὶ δόντι τὴν γῆν αὐτῶν* is characterized as 'ἡ βουλγάρα' on fol. 278v. —(fol. 280r) Αἱματικὸν ἐκ τῶν ᾠδῶν, κυροῦ Χριστοφόρου τοῦ Μυστάκωνος, πλ. Δ΄ *Αὕτη ἡ πύλη τοῦ Κυρίου* (with kratēma). —(fol. 281r) Πολυέλεος ποιηθεὶς παρὰ Μανουὴλ λαμπαδαρίου τοῦ Χρυσάφη, εἰς τὴν ὁδὸν τοῦ Κουκουμᾶ. Ὁ δομέστικος ἔξω φωνῇ· ἦχος α΄ *Δοῦλοι, Κύριον*. —The entire Polyeleos. The last verses contain dekapentasyllablic references. —(fol. 291v) Στίχος καλοφωνικὸς τοῦ μακαρίτου μαΐστορος κυροῦ Ἰωάννου τοῦ Κουκουζέλη· α΄ *Εὐλογητὸς Κύριος ἐκ Σιών*. —(fol. 223r) Πολυέλεος κατ' ἦχον ὁ μέγας, ποιηθεὶς παρὰ τοῦ Κουκουμᾶ· ὁ δεξιὸς χορός, α΄ *Ἐξομολογεῖσθε*. The entire polyeleos, oktaēchos with allagmata and anaphōnēmata. At the end there are epiphōnēmata chanted 'μετὰ βαστακτῶν'.

(Fol. 305r) Καλοφωνία τοῦ πολυελέου. Στίχος καλοφωνικός, ποιηθεὶς παρὰ τοῦ Ξένου πρωτοψάλτου τοῦ Κορώνη, ἦχος α΄ *Στόμα ἔχουσι*. —(fol. 307r) πρόλογος, Ἰωάννου

Κουκουζέλου, πλ. α' *Στόμα έχουσι.* —(fol. 307v) τοῦ αὐτοῦ, τὸ μέγα σημαντήρι, πλ. α' *Τοτοτο.* —(fol. 309v) πρόλογος, τοῦ Κορώνη, πλ. α' *Ὀφθαλμοὺς ἔχουσι.* —(fol. 310v) πρόλογος, τοῦ Κορώνη, πλ. α' *Ὀφθαλμὸς ἔχουσι.* —(fol. 311r) Ἰωάννου Κουκουζέλη, τὸ ὀργανικόν, πλ. α' *Τοτοτο.* —(fol. 312v) πρόλογος, τοῦ Κορώνη, πλ. α' *Ὦτα ἔχουσι.* —(fol. 313r) τοῦ Κορώνη, λεγόμενον τὰ ῥοδάκινα, πλ. α' *Ἀνενανεϊνα.* —(fol. 314v) πρόλογος τοῦ μαΐστορος, α' *Ὦτα ἔχουσι.* —(fol. 315r) Δημητρίου τοῦ Δοκειανοῦ, τετράφωνος α' *Ἀνανανα.* —(fol. 316r) Ἰωάννου μαΐστορος τοῦ Κουκουζέλη, πάνυ ἔντεχνον καὶ λεπτότατον, α' *Οὐδὲ γάρ ἐστι πνεῦμα.* —(fol. 317v) πρόλογος, α' *Οὐδὲ γάρ.* —Νικηφόρου δομεστίκου τοῦ Ἠθικοῦ, α' *Ἀνεανε.* —(fol. 319r) Τὸ αὐτὸ καλλωπισμένον παρὰ κυροῦ Ἰωάννου τοῦ λαμπαδαρίου, α' *Ἀνεανε.* —(fol. 320r) πρόλογος, πλ. α' *Οἶκος Ἰσραήλ.* —Ἰωάννου Κουκουζέλη, *Ἀνενανεϊνα.* —(fol. 322v) πρόλογος, πλ. α' *Οἶκος Ἀαρών.* — Ἰωάννου πρωτοψάλτου τοῦ Γλυκέος, λεγόμενον τοῦ μεγάλου πριμικηρίου πλ. α' *Ἀνενανε* —(fol. 324r) τοῦ Ἠθικοῦ, πλ. α' *Ἀνενανε* —(fol. 325r) πρόλογος, Κορώνη, πλ. α' *Ὅμοιοι αὐτοῖς* —Ἰωάννου μαΐστορος τοῦ Κουκουζέλη, λεγόμενον πολεμικόν, πλ. α' *Τοτοτο* —(fol. 328r) τοῦ αὐτοῦ, λεγόμενον βουλγάρικον, πλ. α' *Τοτοτο* —(fol. 328r) τοῦ αὐτοῦ, ἡ ἀηδών, πλ. α' *Ἀνεενα* —(fol. 329v) πρόλογος, μαΐστορος Ἰωάννου, πλ. α' *Οἶκος Ἰσραήλ.* —(fol. 330r) τὸ μικρὸν σημαντάρι, πλ. β' *Τοτοτο.* —(fol. 332r) πρόλογος, πλ. α' *Οἶκος Λευί.* —(fol. 332v) Ξένου Κορώνη, ἐκαλλωπίσθη δὲ παρὰ τοῦ Κλωβᾶ, πλ. α' *Τοτοτο.* —(fol. 333v) τοῦ αὐτοῦ, ἡ ἀηδών, πλ. α' *Ἀνενανε.*

(Fol. 335r) Ἕτερα καλλιφωνία τοῦ πολυελέου, εἰς τοὺς πρώτους καὶ βαρέους (sic.). Πρόλογος, α' *Στόμα ἔχουσι.* —Ἰωάννου μαΐστορος Κουκουζέλη, α' *Τετετε* —(fol. 336v) τοῦ αὐτοῦ, ἕτερον, α' *Τετετε.* —(fol. 337r) τοῦ αὐτοῦ, α' *Τερρετερρε.* —(fol. 338r) πρόλογος, α' *Στόμα ἔχουσι.* —(fol. 338v) Ξένου τοῦ Κορώνη, μέσος α' *Τετετε* —(fol. 339v) πρόλογος, τοῦ Κορώνη, βαρὺς *Ὀφθαλμοὺς ἔχουσι* —Μανουὴλ δομεστίκου Ἀγαλλιανοῦ, βαρὺς *Ἀνεενανε.* —(fol. 341r) πρόλογος, Μανουὴλ λαμπαδαρίου, πρωτόβαρυς *Ὦτα ἔχουσι.* —Ξένου τοῦ Κορώνη, παρόμοιον, πρωτόβαρυς *Ἀνεϊνα.* —(fol. 342v) πρόλογος, α' *Οὐδὲ γάρ ἐστι.* —Ἰωάννου λαμπαδαρίου, πέρσικον, α' *Τετετε.* —(fol. 343v) τοῦ αὐτοῦ, βαρὺς *Οἶκος Ἀαρών.* —ἦχος α' *Τετετε.* —(fol. 348r) πρόλογος τοῦ χαριτωνύμου μαΐστορος, βαρὺς *Ερρετερε.* —(fol. 352v) ἕτερος πρόλογος εἰς τὸν Ἄμωμον τῶν ἁγίων· εἰς ἱεράρχας, βαρὺς *Ἄξιόν ἐστιν μακαρίζειν σε τὸ Ἱεράρχην.*

(Fol. 353r) Ἀντίφωνον ψαλλόμενον εἰς τὰς ἑορτὰς τῆς ὑπεραγίας Θεοτόκου, καὶ εἰς τὰς δεσποτικὰς ἑορτάς. Ὁ δομέστικος ἀπ' ἔξω, ἦχος α' *Λόγον ἀγαθόν.* —(fol. 360r) ἕτερον ἀντίφωνον ..., τρίτος *Ἐπὶ τῶν ποταμῶν Βαβυλῶνος* —(fol. 366r) ἕτερον ἀντίφωνον ψαλλόμενον εἰς Ἀποστόλους, εἰς μάρτυρας, εἰς προφήτας, εἰς ὁσίους καὶ εἰς ἱεράρχας. Ὁ δομέστικος ἀπ' ἔξω, ἦχος δ' *Τὸν Κύριον, ἀλληλούια.* —εἶτα ἔσω, ὅλοι ὁμοῦ *Μακάριος ἀνήρ.* —(fol. 377r) ἕτερον ἀντίφωνον ψαλλόμενον εἰς τὴν σύναξιν τῶν Ἀσωμάτων καὶ εἰς τὴν Χριστοῦ γέννησιν· τοῦ Ἠθικοῦ, πλ. β' *Αἰνεῖτε τὸν Κύριον* .... —(fol. 379v) ἕτερον ἀντίφωνον ψαλλόμενον εἰς τὴν Μεταμόρφωσιν τοῦ Κυρίου ..., ποιηθὲν παρὰ τοῦ Ἀνεώτου καὶ ἑτέρων. Εἰ βούλει ψάλλε καὶ εἰς τὰ Φῶτα, καὶ εἰς τὴν Ἀνάληψιν μετὰ τῶν ἐκεῖσε στίχων,

The tradition of the kalophonic melos

βαρὺς *Τὰ ἐλέη σου Κύριε* —The verse compositions of all the above antiphons are by the main composers of the fourteenth and fifteenth centuries.

(Fol. 388r) Εἶτα οἱ ἀναβαθμοὶ καὶ τὸ προκείμενον τῆς ἑορτῆς ἢ τῆς Κυριακῆς, καὶ εὐθὺς τὸ *Πᾶσα πνοή*, ἦχος δ'. —ὁ δομέστικος ἀπ' ἔξω, δ' *Τὸν Κύριον* —(fol. 388v) εἶτα γίνεται καλοφωνία, παλαιόν, ἦχος α' *Πᾶσα πνοή.* —(fol. 390r) Ἀναγραμματισμός, Ἰωάννου Κουκουζέλη, ἦχος α' *Πᾶσα πνοή.* —(fol. 392r) ἕτερον, τοῦ αὐτοῦ μαΐστορος Ἰωάννου, πλ. δ'. —(fol. 393r) *Ἕτερον, πρὸς τὸ Ἐγὼ σήμερον γεγέννηκά σε*, Μανουὴλ λαμπαδαρίου τοῦ Χρυσάφη, πλ. δ' *Πᾶσα πνοή.* —(fol. 395r) Εἶτα τὸ Εὐαγγέλιον καὶ μετ' αὐτὸ τὸν πεντηκοστόν· εἶτα ..., παλαιόν, Ἰωάννου τοῦ Κομνηνοῦ, πλ. β' *Ἀναστὰς ὁ Ἰησοῦς.* —(fol. 395v) Ἀναγραμματισμὸς εἰς τὸ αὐτό· ποίημα Νικολάου τοῦ Παλαμᾶ, ἐκαλλωπίσθη δὲ καὶ παρὰ κυροῦ Μάρκου Καρίνθου· ὕστερον δὲ καὶ παρ' ἐμοῦ [Manuel Chrysaphēs]· δ' *Ἔδωκεν ἡμῖν.* —(fol. 397r–v) [...] καὶ εὐθὺς τὸν εἱρμὸν τῆς ζ' ᾠδῆς *Ὁ παῖδας ἐκ καμίνου.* —(fol. 397v) Μεγαλυνάριον εἰς τὴν εἴσοδον τῆς Θεοτόκου, εἰς τὴν θ' ᾠδήν, δ' *Ἄγγελοι τὴν εἴσοδον.* —Τὸ αὐτὸ καὶ καλοφωνικόν, Ἰωάννου Κουκουζέλη, δ' *Ἄγγελοι τὴν εἴσοδον.*

The fols. 398r–410v contain the megalynaria of the great feasts with the corresponding kalophonic megalynaria by the composers Iohannes Koukouzelēs, Iohannes Kladas, Manuel Chrysaphēs, Iohannes Glykys. On fol. 409r *Ἑτέρα ἐπιβολή, τοῦ μαΐστορος, δ' Ἐν τῇ ἐγέρσει.*

(Fol. 411r) Εἰς τοὺς αἴνους τὸ *Πᾶσα πνοή*, κατ' ἦχον. —Ὅτε οὐκ ἔστι μαγάλη δοξολογία ψάλλεται τοῦτο· *Αἰνεῖτε τὸν Κύριον.* —(fol. 413v) Μετὰ τὸ ἑωθινὸν ἰδιόμελον καὶ τὸ Ὑπερευλογημένη, γίνεται ἡ μεγάλη δοξολογία. Εἶτα τὸ Ἅγιος ὁ Θεὸς ἐκ τρίτου, ὕστερον δὲ τοῦτο· πλ. β' *Ἅγιος ὁ Θεός* [asmatikon]. —(fol. 414r) Μανουὴλ Χρυσάφη, ἕτερον, δ' —ἕτερον ἀσματικόν, πλ. δ' *Α-ουαγγ-άγιος ὁ Θεός.*

(Fol. 414v) Ἄμωμος ψαλλόμενος εἰς τὴν θεόσωμον ταφὴν τοῦ Κυρίου ἡμῶν Ἰησοῦ Χριστοῦ καὶ εἰς τὴν κοίμησιν τῆς ὑπεραγίας Θεοτόκου καὶ εἰς τὸν Πρόδρομον. Ὁ δομέστικος ἀπ' ἔξω, πλ. α' *Εὐλογητὸς εἶ Κύριε ... Ἄμωμοι ἐν ὁδῷ.* —(fol. 425v) ἡ καλοφωνία τοῦ Ἀμώμου. Πρόλογος τοῦ Κορώνη· ἦχος β' *Μακαρίζομέν σε* —*Τοτοτο* —(fol. 427r) πρωτοψάλτου τοῦ Κορώνη, β' *Τοτοτο* —(fol. 428v) πρόλογος, β' *Μακαρίζομέν σε* —(fol. 429r) Ἰωάννου Κουκουζέλη, β' *Ερρετερρε* —(fol. 430r) πρόλογος, β' *Μακαρίζομέν σε* —(fol. 432r) πρόλογος, β' *Μακαρίζομέν σε* —Ξένου τοῦ Κορώνη, β' *Τοτοτοτο* —(fol. 433v) πρόλογος εἰς τὴν δ' στάσιν, πλ. α' *Ἄξιόν ἐστιν.*

(Fols. 434v–435r) Ἀπὸ τοῦ μέλους τῶν περισσῶν τὸ Ριφεὶς Ἀδάμ, μετεποιήθη καὶ ἐπλατύνθη καὶ ἐκαλλωπίσθη παρὰ κὺρ Ἰωάννου τοῦ λαμπαδαρίου εἰς ἐγκώμια τῆς Θεοτόκου· ψάλλεται δὲ εἰς τὸ τέλος τῆς Ἀκολουθίας, δίχορον, ἦχος α' *Ἄνωθεν οἱ προφῆται.* —(fol. 437r) Ἐκ τῶν περισσῶν, τοῦ μακαρίτου λαμπαδαρίου κυροῦ Ἰωάννου, ἦχος α' *Ἡμεῖς δὲ ταῦτα βλέποντες* (dekapentasyllabic theotokion).

(Fols. 440r-443v) Ἀκολουθία ψαλλομένη τῇ Κυριακῇ τῶν ἁγίων προπατόρων πρὸ τῆς Χριστοῦ γεννήσεως, ἤτοι τῆς καμίνου.

Compositions of Xenos Korōnēs, Manuel Chrysaphēs and Manuel Gaze (Cf. Velimirovič 1962).

(Fols. 444r-449v) Ἀσματικαὶ [ᾠδαί]· ᾠδὴ γ΄, ποίημα τοῦ Ἀνδρειωμένου, πλ. δ΄ *Ἑτοίμη ἡ καρδία μου* [and the rest, odes iv-ix]. —(fol. 450v) ἕτερον, ποιηθὲν μετὰ τὴν ἅλωσιν τῆς Κωνσταντινουπόλεως, Μανουὴλ λαμπαδαρίου τοῦ Χρυσάφη, πλ. δ΄ *Ὁ Θεὸς ἤλθωσαν ἔθνη*.

(Fol. 453r) Ἄμωμος ψαλλόμενος εἰς κοιμηθέντας κοσμικούς, ποιηθεὶς παρὰ διαφόρων ποιητῶν καὶ παρὰ τοῦ Φαρδιβούκη ἐκείνου καὶ τοῦ λαμπαδαρίου κὺρ Ἰωάννου. Ὁ δομέστικος ἀπ᾽ ἔξω, β΄ *Ἄμωμοι ἐν ὁδῷ*. —εἶτα ἔσω ὅλοι, *Μακάριοι οἱ ἄμωμοι*.

The three stases of the Amōmos: some kalophonic verses and the so-called '*archontika*' in the third stasis. Compositions of Phardiboukes, Iohannes Kladas, *palaion*, Iohannes Glykes, Ethikos, Manourgas, Keladenos, Korōnēs, *thessalonikaion*, Kampanes, Gregorios domestikos, 'synoptikon', Manuel domestikos of Thebes, Manuel Chrysaphēs.

(Fol. 459χr) Ἕτερος Ἄμωμος ψαλλόμενος εἰς κοιμηθέντας μοναχούς. Ὁ δομέστικος ἀπ᾽ ἔξω· πλ. α΄ *Εὐλογητὸς εἶ Κύριε... Μακάριοι οἱ ἄμωμοι*. —(fol. 474r) εἶτα τὰ εὐλογητάρια. Ὁπόταν ἐκδημήσῃ τις καὶ φέρουσιν αὐτὸν ἐν τῇ ἐκκλησίᾳ, ψάλλουσι τὸ Ἅγιος ὁ Θεός, μετὰ μέλους· Ἰωάννου πατριάρχου, νεναννω. —Τοῦτο ψάλλεται καὶ εἰς τὸν Ἐπιτάφιον τῷ Μεγάλῳ Σαββάτῳ.

The verses of the Amōmos on fols. 459χr-473v of the composers Iohannes lampadarios, *palaion*, Manuel Chrysaphēs, Nikephoros Ethikos, Xenos Korōnēs, Markos metropolitan of Corinth, priest Michael of the Orphanage, priest Michael Panaretos, Klobas, of Periphemoy, Konstantinos Gabras, Spanos.

(Fol. 474v) Ἡ καλοφωνία τοῦ Ἀμώμου κατὰ στάσιν. Στιχηρὸν νεκρώσιμον, μέλος κυροῦ Ἰωάννου λαμπαδαρίου τοῦ Κλαδᾶ, ἦχος α΄ *Ποία τοῦ βίου τρυφή*. —(fol. 475v) τοῦ αὐτοῦ, β΄ *Οἴμοι, οἷον ἀγῶνα*. —(fol. 476v) τοῦ αὐτοῦ, τρίτος *Πάντα ματαιότης*. —(fol. 478r) τοῦ αὐτοῦ, δ΄ *Ὄντως φοβερώτατον*. —(fol. 479r) Ἰωάννου Κουκουζέλη, δ΄ *Ὄντως φοβερώτατον*. —(fol. 480r) Ἰωάννου Κουκουζέλη, πλ. α΄ *Οἴμοι, τὸ τέλος ἄνθρωπε*. —(fol. 481r) Στίχοι κατανυκτικοὶ νεκρώσιμοι, ποιηθέντες παρὰ κυροῦ Μελισσηνοῦ τοῦ φιλοσόφου, καὶ μελισθέντες παρὰ τοῦ Κορώνη, πλ. α΄ *Πληθὺς ἀνθρώπων ἅπασα*. —(fol. 482r) Δεύτερος πούς, νεναννω *Πῶς παρελύθη τὸ διπλοῦν*. —(fol. 482v) τοῦ αὐτοῦ [Κορώνη], νεναννω *Εἰ θέλεις, ἄνθρωπε, μαθεῖν*. —(fol. 483v) Κουκουζέλη, πλ. δ΄ *Στῆθι*

The tradition of the kalophonic melos 105

καὶ βλέψον ἄνθρωπε. —(fol. 484v) Μανουὴλ Χρυσάφη, πλ. δ' Θρηνῶ καὶ ὀδύρομαι. —(fol. 486r) ἀναγραμματισμός,'Ιωάννου Κουκουζέλη, πλ. δ' Ὦ τοῦ θαύματος. —(fol. 487v) Οἶκος τοῦ κυρίου Ἀνδρέου. Οὗτος ψάλλεται μετὰ τὸ κοντάκιον, εἰς τὴν ζ' ᾠδήν, πλ. δ' Αὐτὸς μόνος ὑπάρχεις ἀθάνατος.

(Fol. 489r) Ἀρχὴ τῆς θείας καὶ ἱερᾶς Λειτουργίας ....

Contains the melē of the Trisagion and the chants instead of the Trisagion. The Δύναμις, Ἅγιος ὁ Θεὸς with kratēmata by Koukouzelēs and Korōnēs (fol. 490rv), as well as Δύναμις,Ὅσοι εἰς Χριστὸν asmatikon (fol. 492v) — Korōnēs (fol. 493r), Manuel Chrysaphēs (fol. 493v). There are also 'synoptika' melē, mostly syntoma, without kratēmata.

(fol. 496r) 'Μετὰ τὴν ἀνάγνωσιν τοῦ Ἀποστόλου εὐθὺς τὸ Ἀλληλούια, κατ' ἤχον'. A rich collection; compositions of Andreas Sigeros, Agallianos, Manuel Chrysaphēs, Theophylaktos Argyropoulos, Theodoulos monachos, Konstantinos Magoulas, Xenos Korōnēs, Iohannes Koukouzelēs, Christophoros Mystakon, Manuel Kourteses, Iohannes Kladas, Manuel Blateros.

(Fol. 504r) Ἀρχὴ τῶν χερουβικῶν ὕμνων, κατ' ἤχον.

Basic collection of the main compositions. From fol. 524r those of the Liturgy of St. Basil by Ethikos, Georgios Panaretos, Manuel Chrysaphēs, Xenos Korōnēs Ἐπὶ σοὶ χαίρει (fol. 526r). — (fol. 526r) 'Ἀρχὴ τῶν κατ' ἤχον κοινωνικῶν'. A rich collection of communion hymns Αἰνεῖτε — Ποτήριον σωτηρίου, Εἰς μνημόσυνον and some others, kat' echon. Then the following Πληρωθήτω τὸ στόμα μου by Andreas (fol. 526χv), Εἴη τὸ ὄνομα Κυρίου 'ὅτε δίδοται τὸ κατακλαστόν, παλαιὸν' (fol. 563χr). — (fol. 565χr) "Ὅτε γίνεται χειροτονία διακόνου' — (fol. 565χv) "Ὅτε μέλλῃ ὁ βασιλεὺς διέρχεσθαι εἰς προσκύνησιν τῶν ἁγίων εἰκόνων καὶ νὰ λάβῃ ἐκ τοῦ κατακλαστοῦ, Πολυχρόνιον — Εἰς δὲ τοὺς ἀρχιερεῖς τοῦτο, δ' Τὸν δεσπότην'.

(Fol. 566χr) Ἀρχὴ τῆς θείας Λειτουργίας τῶν Προηγιασμένων. Μετὰ τὴν συμπλήρωσιν τῶν ἀναγνωσμάτων ἄρχεται ὁ δομέστικος ἀπὸ χοροῦ, πλ. β' Κατευθυνθήτω. —Εἶτα εὐθὺς ἄρχεται ὁ μονοφωνάρης γεγονωτέρᾳ τῇ φωνῇ ταῦτα, β' Κύριε ἐκέκραξα. —εἶτα, πάλιν τὸ Κατευθυνθήτω· εἶτα τοῦτο, πλ. β' Μὴ ἐκκλίνῃς. —(fol. 567χv) ὁ δομέστικος ἀπ' ἔξω τὸ τέλος Ἔπαρσις τῶν χειρῶν μου —ἕτερον τέλος, δ' Θυσία ἑσπερινή. —(fol. 568χr) Χερουβικόν, τοῦ ἁγίου Ἰωάννου τοῦ Δαμασκηνοῦ, πλ. β' Νῦν αἱ δυνάμεις [and compositions of] Ἰωάννου Κουκουζέλη, Λογγίνου ἱερομονάχου, Δημητρίου Δοκειανοῦ, Μανουὴλ Χρυσάφη. —(fol. 572r) ἀρχὴ τῶν κατ' ἤχον κοινωνικῶν. Κοινωνικὸν ἀσματικὸν [ἀνώνυμον], ἦχος α' Γεύσασθε. [Rich collection of compositions for this communion.]

At the end of this collection, Τοῦ δείπνου σου — Σιγησάτω — Ἐξηγέρθη — Σῶμα Χριστοῦ, various compositions.

(Fol. 586r) Τιμιωτέρα ἡ λεγομένη ἁγιορείτικος· ψάλλεται δὲ εἰς παρακλήσεις καὶ παννυχίδας καὶ ἐν τῇ τραπέζῃ, ἀπὸ χοροῦ, πλ. β΄ δίφωνος Ἄξιόν ἐστιν ὡς ἀληθῶς. — (fol. 587r) ἑτέρα, κυροῦ Ἰωάννου μαΐστορος τοῦ Κουκουζέλη, ἀπὸ χοροῦ, νενανω Ἄξιόν ἐστιν. —(fol. 588r) ἀρχὴ σὺν Θεῷ ἁγίῳ τῶν κατ᾽ ἦχον μεγαλυναρίων εἰς τὴν ὑπεραγίαν Θεοτόκον. Κυροῦ Ξένου πρωτοψάλτου τοῦ Κορώνη· ἦχος α΄ Σὲ μεγαλύνομεν.

Contains a rich collection of megalynaria, kalophonic compositions with dekapentasyllabic or other verses of metrical improvisation up to fol. 616r. Compositions by: Xenos Korōnēs, Iohannes Kladas, Manuel Chrysaphēs, Iohannes Koukouzelēs, Georgios Kontopetres, Gerasimos Chalkeopoulos, Georgios Panaretos. — (fol. 616v) Τιμιωτέρα the *hagioreitike*, allagma at the 9th ode Καθεῖλε δυνάστας, νενανω, Ἐξαπέστειλε κενούς — (fol. 617r) Staurotheotokion, Manuel Chrysaphēs, δ΄ Ὅτε σὲ εἶδεν ἐν σταυρῷ — (618v) Kontakion at the Akathist, composed by kyr Iohannes the lampadarios, πλ. δ΄ Τῇ ὑπερμάχῳ — (fol. 620r) by Gazes, πλ. α΄ Σῶμα Χριστοῦ — (fol. 620v) πλ. α΄ Χριστὸς ἀνέστη.

(Fol. 621r) Εἱρμοὶ καλοφωνικοί, ψαλλόμενοι τῇ ἁγίᾳ καὶ μεγάλῃ Κυριακῇ τοῦ Πάσχα· κὺρ λαμπαδαρίου τοῦ Κλαδᾶ [and Manuel Chrysaphēs]. —(fol. 631v) Εἱρμοὶ καλοφωνικοὶ ψαλλόμενοι εἰς τὸν μεγαλομάρτυρα Δημήτριον καὶ εἰς ἑτέρους ἁγίους· κυροῦ Μανουὴλ τοῦ Πλαγίτου· ἦχος β΄ [odes i–ix] Τῷ κυρίῳ ἄσωμεν —Δεῦτε λαοί.

(Fol. 637r) Κοντάκιον μετὰ τῶν οἴκων, ψαλλόμενον τῷ Σαββάτῳ τῆς Ἀκαθίστου· κυροῦ Ἰωάννου μαΐστορος τοῦ Κουκουζέλη, πλ. δ΄ Τῇ ὑπερμάχῳ. —(fol. 639r) Ἀκάθιστος ποιηθεῖσα παρὰ κυροῦ Ἰωάννου λαμπαδαρίου τοῦ Κλαδᾶ· μιμούμενος κατὰ τὸ δυνατὸν τὴν παλαιάν, ὡς αὐτὸς γράφει, δ΄ Ἄγγελος πρωτοστάτης. —(fol. 645r) ἕτερος [οἶκος], ποιηθεὶς παρὰ λαμπαδαρίου Μανουὴλ τοῦ Χρυσάφη, δ΄ Ἄγγελος πρωτοστάτης. —[τοῦ αὐτοῦ καὶ] (fol. 649v) δ΄ Βλέπουσα ἡ ἁγία. —(fol. 652v) δ΄ Ἤκουσαν οἱ ποιμένες. — (fol. 657r) νενανω Ὦ πανύμνητε μῆτερ. —(fol. 661r) ποίημα κυροῦ Ἰωάννου μαΐστορος τοῦ Κουκουζέλη, δ΄ Γνῶσιν ἄγνωστον γνῶναι. —(fol. 665r) τοῦ αὐτοῦ, δ΄ Θεοδρόμον ἀστέρα. —(fol. 666r) Ἰωάννου λαμπαδαρίου, νεναvω Ξένον τόκον. —(fol. 668r) Ἀρχὴ τῶν ἕνδεκα ἑωθινῶν, ποιηθέντα παρὰ κυροῦ Λέοντος τοῦ σοφωτάτου βασιλέως.

The eleventh, a little worn, fol. 674. On fol. 674v, on the bottom half of the page is the scribe's colophon in red letters:

† Ἐτελειώθη τὸ παρὸν βιβλίον αἱ ἀκολουθίαι πᾶσαι τῆς Ψαλτικῆς διὰ χειρὸς Μανουὴλ δούκα λαμπαδαρίου τοῦ Χρυ[σάφ]η ἐν ἔτει ,ςλξς΄, ἰνδικτιῶνος ς΄ [μηνὸς Ἰου]λλίου ...

ἡμέρα ... καὶ οἱ βλέ[ποντες καὶ ἀναγινώσκ]οντες τοῦτο εὔχεσθέ μοι διὰ [τὴν] τοῦ Κυρίου ἀγάπην.

This enormous and exquisite, but especially very important Papadikē by Manuel Chrysaphēs, is in relatively good condition. The binding is old and probably original, bound from dark red leather on wooden plates; the almond and star ornamentations are preserved. The paper is off-white, thin, with a soft gloss. Experienced and refined hand in double verses, 15 of equal length. Black ink and faded rose.
— The complete description of the codex in the fourth, unpublished volume of my catalogue *Τὰ Χειρόγραφα Βυζαντινῆς Μουσικῆς — Ἅγιον Ὄρος* (Stathēs 1975–).

As is easily discerned, this *Papadikē* by Manuel Doukas Chrysaphēs is most significant, certainly having been written in AD 1458, that is, after the fall of Constantinople, and by such a learned man who was also one of the most important *maïstores* of Byzantine Music. Manuel Chrysaphēs wished to codify the Byzantine chant tradition and to preserve it, handing it down in a single volume to Hellenism's years of occupation. In this endeavour, he enriched the codex with compositions from many teachers and borrowed many kratēmata from the *Kratēmatarion*.

Reviewing the codex's contents, we are able to distinguish which compositions were separated and later created their own codex of similar material.

The contents of the folios 280r, 397r–410v, 434v–446, 444r–452v, 474v–486r, 588v–618 and 621r–636 belong mainly to the *Mathēmatarion*. They are, however, also anthologized in the *Papadikē* as they are necessary for practical reasons. In his *Papadikē*, Chrysaphēs did not collect many mathēmata, i.e., kalophonic stichēra and anagrams, as did other compilers of their *Papadikai*, in a special unit after the communion hymns; the reason for this is that Manuel Chrysaphēs wrote a separate codex — the *Kalophonic Stichērarion* — Athos, Iviron 975,[4] where he put all the mathēmata according to their order of use in the liturgical calendar.

The oikoi on folios 487v, 618v and 637r–667r belong predominantly to the *Oikēmatarion* or *Kontakarion*. The oikoi as mathēmata, but particularly

---

4 Cfr Lampros 1888; 1966: Vol. 2, 243. The codex carries the clear indications that it was written by Manuel Chrysaphes. The similarity of the scribal hand, but especially the internal evidence, allow us to assert this; cfr Stathēs 1975–: Vol. 3, 759 sq.

the Akathistos, are anthologized in the *Kratēmataria* (see below, p. 110 sq.) and thus create a special, mixed codex. The position of the oikoi in the *Kratēmataria* are always either at the beginning or at the end.

Today there are nearly sixty extant *Papadikai* between the years 1336 and 1458 — the dates of Athens, Nat. Libr. 2458 and the Athos, Iviron 1120, used extensively in this publication.[5] In these *Papadikai* the entire output of Byzantine melopœïa is codified as concerns the kalophonic melos of the Papadikē, that is, the psalmic mathēmata and one part of the genuine 'mathēmata proper' [*kath'ayto mathēmata*], more precisely, of the kalophonic stichēra with their anagrams and anapodismoi, katanyktika and kratēmata.

From these important codices, the most noteworthy are Athens, Nat. Libr. 2622 (c. 1341–1360); Athens, Nat. Lib. 2062[6] (third quarter of the fourteenth century), Nat. Lib. 2061 (after 1391), Nat. Lib. 2444, Nat. Lib. 904, Nat. Lib. 905, Nat. Lib. 906, Nat. Lib. 2454, Nat. Lib. 2600 (fourteenth century, at least), Nat. Lib. 2406 (year 1453),[7] Nat. Lib. 2837 (year 1457), Nat. Lib. 899, Nat. Lib. 2599, and Nat. Lib. 2401 (fifteenth century); and the Athos, Koutloumousiou 457 (fourteenth century, 2nd half) and Koutloumousiou 399 (mid-fourteenth century), Athos, Iviron 985 (year 1425), Iviron 984 (fifteenth century, first half), Iviron 973 (fifteenth century, beginning), Iviron 974 (fifteenth century, first half), Athos, Koutloumousiou 456 (year 1443), Athos, Philotheou 122 (end of fourteenth century–beginning of fifteenth century), Athos, Konstamonitou 86 (fifteenth century, first half),[8] Athos, M. Lavra I 185 (mid-fourteenth century), M. Lavra I 178 (year 1377), I 79, E 173 (year 1436), E 46 (year 1436), E 148 (fifteenth century, first half).

From these codices again, Athos, Koutloumousiou 457, through its epigraphs but also its general contents, provides useful information on

---

5 A table of approximately two-thirds of all *Papadikai* is available in Conomos 1972: 47–48.
6 Along with Athos, Koutloumousiou 457, the Athens, Nat. Libr. 2062 and 2061 are important for the study of the asmatic cathedral office.
7 Much useful information on this codex can be found in Velimirović 1966a.
8 A complete description is found in Stathēs 1975–: Vol. 1, 656–668.

the chief triad of kalophonic composers, namely, Iohannes Glykys, Xenos Korōnēs, and Iohannes Koukouzelēs (see below, p. 125 sq.). This codex contains neatly divided units of vesporal kalophonic verses (fol. 23r sq.), anapodismoi of the megalynaria (fol. 90v sq.), kratēmata (fol. 264r sq.) and the 'eklogē of some anapodismoi, and often also stichēra for feasts of the entire year, all compositions of the maïstōr Koukouzelēs and protopsaltes Korōnēs' (fol. 352r sq.). The other important codex, Koutloumousiou 456 of the year 1443, contains the following large divisions: fol. 120r, 'Beginning with holy God, of the anagrams'; containing only anagrams, about 80 belonging to Iohannes Koukouzelēs; — fol. 200r, 'Stichēra, with God, chanted at the formal feasts of the entire year' — fol. 264r, 'Kratēmata, with God, *kat' ēchon*, the most excellent from many' — fol. 389r, 'Katanyktika, with God, *kat' ēchon* and theotokia, as well as heirmoi and verses put to melody, staurotheotokia and stichēra nekrosima'.[9]

In the years after the Fall of Constantinople, the *Papadikē* eidos remained the same. Little by little, however, the melē of the asmatic vespers and orthros were excluded and only the kalophonic verses were preserved. The *Papadikē* was duplicated into hundreds of manuscripts during the post-Byzantine period, particularly during the second half of the seventeenth and the second half of the eighteenth centuries. During these periods many old compositions gave up their place to those from newer teachers. However, these *Papadikai* often contained only the newer compositions owing to the proliferation of these new composers. The principal codex writers are the eminent teachers in the second half of the seventeenth century: Chrysaphēs the new, Germanos Neōn Patrōn, Balasios hiereus, Kosmas the Ibēritēs and Macedonian, and Athanasios hieromonachos the Ibēritēs. In the first half of the eighteenth century, *Papadikai* are produced by Antonios oikonomos of the Great Church, Michael hiereus from Chios, Anatolios the hagioritēs, Pavlos hiereus, Iohannes protopsaltes, Païsios hieromonachos and others; during the second half of the same century

---

9 For a complete description, Athos, Koutloumousiou 456 and Koutloumousiou 457, cfr Stathēs 1975–: Vol. 3, 345–366.

Theodoulos monachos, Serapheim Lauriotēs, Anastasios Baïas,[10] Demetrios Lōtos, Damaskenos Agraphorendiniotēs and many others[11] will continue the tradition.

After the reformation of the New Method, Gregorios and Chourmouzios create their *exēgēseis* of these *Papadikai*: Gregorios' *Papadikē* was published as the four-tomed *Pandektē* in Constantinople during the years 1850–1851 (Ioannēs Lampadarios and Stephanos Domestikos 1850–1851). Compared to the *Papadikē* of the fourteenth and fifteenth century, this *Papadikē* is new, except for the *Mathēmatarion* and great anoixantaria, and contains all the mathēmata of the new composers of the eighteenth and first half of the nineteenth century. Chourmouzios' five-tomed autograph manuscript *Papadikē*, however — MΠT 703–706 and 722 — is the *exēgēsis* of the old Byzantine *Papadikē*, just as it was in the second half of the seventeenth century, plus the additions of the great composers of that century.[12]

The Kratēmatarion

The *Kratēmatarion* is the music book that usually contains the kratēmata of Byzantine melopœïa organized according to mode [*kat' ēchon*]. A kratēma is a composition whose basic characteristic are the meaningless syllables used as its text. These syllables are normally *Anane, Anena, Tototo, Tororon,*

---

10   It was mentioned above that Athos, Xeropotamou 307 is an autograph of Anastasios Baïas and we highly recommend it as a prototype for comparative study with other *Papadikai*.
11   It is difficult to discuss to all *Papadikai* codices here. The reader is referred, however, to the following main ones described in Stathēs 1975–: Athos, Docheiariou 337 (year 1764, autograph of Demetrios Lotos — Anthology of the old teachers), Docheiariou 338 (year 1767 — autograph of Demetrios Lotos — Anthology of the new teachers); Athos Xeropotamou 330 (years 1781–1782 — autograph of Demetrios Lōtos — *New Papadikē*) and Athos, Gregoriou 4 (year 1744, autograph of Machael hiereus).
12   The publishers of the first scores of printed Byzantine chant selected melē from the *exegesis Papadikai* of Gregorios and Chourmouzios for their *Tameion Anthologias* and *Anthologia publications*.

Tititi, Tiriri, Errere, Terrere, Tetete and *Terirem*.[13] Parallel to the use of these syllables, the kratēmata are also known by the names *nenanismata*, *terentismata* and *teretismos*. The designation *ēchēmata*, which was originally used for all the kratēmata, refers specifically to the kratēmata using the syllables *Anane, Anena*, and *Tenena*. This particular instance is interesting because we can accurately establish the genesis of the kratēmata through these very syllables.

From very early on in Byzantine melopœïa, the tendency of the composers [*melodoi*] and, hence, of the chanters was to compose and chant with a certain virtuosity and embellishment. This embellishment emanated from the role of the domestikos, as initiator of the *enēchēmata* or *epēchēmata* or *enēchēseis* of the modes with their polysyllabic introductory enēchētic *theseis*[14] or phrases, that is, *Ananes, Neanes, Nana* or *Nenanō*,

13 Early attempts at discerning the origin of the *terentismata* include Bamboudakes 1933: 353–363 and Eustratiades 1938. In Athos, Gregoriou 4, fol. 24v there is the following note: 'Τάρεν, ὄργανον μουσικόν· τερέτισμα καὶ ἀσματεριτίζει τοῖς μουσικοῖς κρουμάτιόν (sic) τι κατίθισται (sic) τὸ λεγόμενον τάρεν, ἀφοῦ τερετίζειν λέγεται τὸ ᾄδειν κατὰ ἀλλοίωσιν τοῦ ἄλφα εἰς ἔψιλον· καὶ τερετίσματα ᾠδαὶ ἀπατηλαὶ ἢ ᾄσματα ἔκλυτα ἀπὸ τῆς μεταφορᾶς τοῦ τέττιγος ἢ τῆς χελιδῶνος [possibly ἀηδόνος?]'; cfr Stathēs 1975–: Vol. 2, 590.

14 The ēchēmata, as epibolē of each mode and with the correct syllables, are found in manuscripts from the tenth century on and pronounce the eight modes. This very instance reaches far back to the genesis of the oktōēchia. Constantinus Porpherogennitus (Vogt 1967: 90–93) mentions use of the meaningless syllables. The fact that something similar exists in western music, the so-called *Noeane*, which scholarly consensus attributes to Byzantine origin is interesting. Raasted's comments are worth noting: 'The intonation system of Byzantine chant can be studied in musical Mss from the beginning of the 10th century onwards ... The western *Noeane* formulas can be traced back to the time of Charlemagne. These formulas, obviously of Byzantine extraction or inspiration ... For our present purpose the importance of the *Noaeane* formulas lies in the very existence of such phenomena in Western Europe about AD 800, and in the fact that the western theorists themselves felt these formulas as to be of Byzantine origin... The dissimilarities between the unstable Gregorian *Noeane* formulas and the much more stable Byzantine standard ἠχήματα are in a way more interesting than the fundamental similarity of the Byzantine and Gregorian systems' (Raasted 1966: 154–161). Cfr Huglo 1972: 81–90; Wellesz 1980: 303–309.

etc., and which had a double function. This is distinctly affirmed in the manuscripts through the witnesses 'echizei ho domestikos ...'.[15] Early on, the doxastika idiomela of the main feasts were chanted dichora[16] kata stichon [by two choirs according to verse], with ēchēmata. The same occurs in the asmatic type of hymns; the asmatic *Hagios ho Theos* and the asmatic cherubic hymns both receive ēchēmata.[17]

As we have observed, this praxis is introduced into the kalophonic verses of the vespers, orthros and Divine Liturgy wherever anagrammatisation of the text is called for. Thus, a condition was provided for the development and evolution of the form [eidos] of the kratēmata. The term kratēma[18] is conventional then and demonstrates that the *teretismoi* or *nenanismoi* compositions 'hold' [*kratoun*] and augment the melos, lengthening the

15 In a Typikon from the year 1573 in Dmitrievski and Orthodox Eastern Church 1965: Vol. 3, 342 we read: 'Εἶτα δοξάζει ὁ δομέστικος τοῦ α´ χοροῦ εἰς ἦχον πλ. β´, Καὶ νῦν ὁ ἕτερος· ἐντεῦθεν ἠχίζει ὁ πρῶτος καὶ ψάλλομεν στάσιν μίαν, ἠχίζει καὶ ὁ δεύτερος πάλιν τὸ αὐτό, δηλονότι δευτεροῦμεν ὅλον τὸ στιχηρὸν κατὰ στάσιν, τὸ δὲ τέλος τοῦ στιχηροῦ ἐκ γ´'. Sinai Gr. 1527 (sixteenth century) also offers an interesting indication: 'Λέγουσι δὲ οἱ ψάλται διὰ μέσου καὶ ἠχίσματα εἰς ἦχον πλ. δ´' (Velimirović 1962: 388, v. 132 on). The ēchismata-ēchēmata between verses developed into full kratēmata. This is clear from the witnesses below. Athens, Nat. Libr. 2406 (year 1453), fol. 151v: "Ἠχίσματα δὲ λέγομεν κρατημάτων πλαγίου τετάρτου· ἀνάλογα πρὸς τὸν διπλασμὸν τῆς φωνῆς τῶν παίδων· εἰς δὲ τὸ τέλος τοῦ ἠχίσματος λέγομεν ἀπὸ χοροῦ πάντες εἰς τὴν αὐτὴν φωνήν, οὕτως· πλ. δ´ *Εὐλογητὸς εἶ Κύριε*'; fol. 161r: "Ἕτερον ἤχισμα, τοῦ μαΐστορος, πλ. δ´". The meaningless syllables used are *Nene ane toto terere*. It is a complete kratēma, that is, ēchisma-ēchēma equals kratēma. This formula is valid earlier also; already by 1336, in Athens, Nat. Libr. 2458, at fols. 42v, 45v and 69v we find 'ἤχημα τοῦ μαΐστορος κυροῦ Ἰωάννου τοῦ Κουκουζέλη' in a mixed form: *Neenene* for the first part and *Terrere* for the second.

16 *Dichora* are the troparia and general compositions which are chanted verse by verse antiphonally by two choirs. The main *dichora* doxastika during the thirteenth century are the following, as preserved in Paris, BnF Coislin 41: Σήμερον γεννᾶται (fol. 65v), Προτυπῶν τὴν ἀνάστασιν (fol. 134r), Τῇ ἀθανάτῳ κοιμήσει (fol. 138r), Σήμερον ὁ Χριστὸς ἐν Ἰορδάνῃ (fol. 170r), Πρὸ ἓξ ἡμερῶν (fol. 187v), Σήμερον κρεμᾶται (fol. 208v), Ἀναστάσεως ἡμέρα (fol. 212r) and Βασιλεῦ οὐράνιε (fol. 230r).

17 Cfr Conomos 1972: 123–145.

18 The term, as has already been mentioned, is found early; cfr Athens, Nat. Libr. 2458 from the year 1336, fol. 203r: 'κράτημα κατ᾽ ἦχον'.

The tradition of the kalophonic melos

duration of the Offices. This reality is the more correct interpretation of the situation, that is, of the existence and the purpose of the nonsense syllables.[19]

The kratēmata are the colophon of Byzantine melopœïa from the aspect of artistic sound. They are rhythmic, intense and follow diverse types, but always contain a clearly discernible architectural structure. The meaningless syllables constrained the composers to concentrate all their attention to the melos in order to sustain the listener's attention and create a pleasant sound.

The kratēmata hold another important detail. They are the connecting link between ecclesiastical and secular [*exōterikē*] music. Many kratēmata entitled *organika* or *mousika* are in reality the melos of a secular song or musical arrangement for a particular instrument, usually the tambour. Others echo the melos of a particular geographic area, nationality or the name of a musical instrument; compare the titles *thettalikon, ethnikon, persikon, viola, ho anakaras,*[20] *to rodani, ho choros, he papadopoula,* etc.[21] During the seventeenth century, the secular kratēmata are anthologized in a separate unity; '*hetera kratēmata, ethnika, pany charmosyna ...*' [other kratēmata, national, very joyous][22] and the *Anthologies* are even host to

---

19 In Ioannēs Lampadarios and Stephanos Domestikos 1850–1851: Vol. 4, 885–891 there exist naïve interpretations, as in the chapter 'Regarding the *terere*, and why it is chanted in the Church.' At the request of the protopsaltes Chandakos Demetriou Ntamias, one Gerasimos Blachos Krēs attempted an interpretation in the year 1649. In that interpretation he holds that the *teretismata* are the words that cannot be spoken (II Corinthians 12:4) the apostle Paul heard from the angels. In another interpretation five reasons are enumerated through which the *teretismata* are expressed. Cfr Conomos 1972: 262–286.

20 From the Arabic *naqqāra*, and in English as *nakers*, these are small kettle drums of Saracen origin. They were known in Moorish Spain since the early eightth century, but enter western music literature from the time of the Crusades. There is evidence for their use in the courts of Edward I (1304) and Louis IX (1314–1316); cfr Blades and Bowles ; Farmer 1949; Montagu 1976.

21 Cfr the analytical description of the *Kratēmatarion*, Athos, Xeropotamou 287 (year 1724) and the name designations in Stathēs 1975–: Vol. 1, 51–55.

22 Cfr Athos, Panteleimon 901 (from the year 1734), fol. 151r; Panteleimon 1008 (autograph of Balasios hiereus, end of seventeenth century), fols. 352r–362r; Stathēs 1975–: Vol. 2, 177, 426 respectively. Composers of the *ethnikon* kratēmata are Arsenios

Persian songs and *nenanismata* of characteristic syllables: *tadirten, tadillitana, gelele, chilitil* ....[23] This very form of the kratēmata is the open window to the influence on and preservation of secular-eastern music in the Byzantine melos, and flourishes during the seventeenth and eighteenth centuries.

We also observe that the kratēmata are the necessary element for the kalophonic compositions. These compositions, however, contain their own unique kratēmata — i.e., the mathēmata. Few are the instances when kratēmata come into the *Kratēmatarion* from the *Mathēmatarion* as an example of a suitable kratēma. The *Kratēmatarion*, then, is independent and is its own form [*eidos*], notwithstanding the countless kratēmata contained in it and drawn from kalophonic compositions. Of course, we also come across the so-called *prologoi* in the *Kratēmataria*, that is, usually the last verse of a kalophonic verse and a full kratēma that follows.

In the second half of the eighteenth century the teachers composed kratēmata suitable to the kalophonic heirmoi and it is mainly these last kratēmata that were transcribed into the New Method and published in printed form in a special section at the end of the book known as the *Kalophonic Heirmologion* (Grēgorios Prōtopsaltēs and Theodōros Phōkaeus 1835: 189–262).

During the fourteenth and fifteenth centuries the kratēmata were an organic part of the *Papadikē* and, as we have seen, also of the *Oikēmatarion*, mainly because of the Akathistos, as is the Athos, Iviron 972 (fifteenth century, first half). The unmixed *Kratēmatarion* appears later, toward the

---

mikros, Theophanēs Karykēs, Chrysaphēs the new, Germanos Neōn Patrōn, Petros Bereketēs and others. Each of these kratēmata usually also bear a unique name like *mouschali, nagmes, naï, persikon, ismaēlitikon*.

23   Athos, Iviron 1189 (autograph of Leontios Koukouzelēs in the year 1562), fols. 120r–125r. Cfr Athos, Iviron 1080 (autograph of Kosmas Makedonos from the year 1668), fols. 130r–v and 1203 (autograph of Athanasios Kapetanos, c. 1700), fols. 239r–240v (Stathēs 1976: 185–187) and the photographs of the Persian song from Iviron 1189 on pp. 203–213. Other Persian songs with kratēmata are found in Athos Xeropotamou 330, fol. 379r (Stathēs 1975–: Vol. 1, 202) and Athos, Panteleimon 994, fols. 323v–324v (Stathēs 1975–: Vol. 2, 379–380).

end of the seventeenth century, as in the Athos codices Iviron 1089 (of the year 1695), Iviron 1203 (c. 1700, written by Athanasios Kapetanos) and Iviron 1073 (eighteenth century, beginning). In the post-Byzantine period, the existence of the mixed *Oikēmatarion–Kratēmatarion* and *Kratēmatarion–Oikēmatarion* were more common. The collection of old, great [*megala*] kratēmata contain a number that fluctuates around 128 kratēmata, as in the Athos, Xeropotamou 287 (the year 1724).[24] Beautiful *Kratēmataria–Oikēmataria* were written by Kosmas Macedōn.[25] Chourmouzios Chartophylax did *exēgēseis* into the New Method resulting in a two-volume *Kratēmatarion*.[26]

The Kalophōnon Sticherarion or Mathēmatarion

The *Kalophōnon Sticherarion* or *Mathēmatarion* appears around the first half of the fifteenth century as an independent music codex and develops out of the related parts of the *Papadikai*, as we observed above. The writing and production of a codex such as this became necessary so that the similar compositions created by the great musicians could be collected. The codex received its maximum size during the Byzantine period from Manuel Chrysaphēs.[27] The *Mathēmatarion* contains[28] mainly the kalophonic stichēra, the mathēmata for all the feasts of the *Mēnologion* from 1 September to 31 August and from the Sunday of the Publican and Pharisee to the Sunday of All Saints — the *Triōdion* and *Pentēkostarion*. Beyond this,

---

24   On fol. 239v of this codex is the note 'ἅπαντά εἰσι κρατήματα ρκη´ [128]'. An important and rich *Kratēmatarion* is the Athos, Hagiou Pavlou 146 (206/79) from the year 1758 (autograph of Theodosios hierodiakonos Chios).
25   The reader is referred mainly to Athos, Iviron 1080 (year 1668), 1141 and 1150.
26   ΜΠΤ 710–711. Some other kratēmata are included in Tome V of the same *Papadikē*, 722, fols. 363r–420v. For *kratēmata* and the *Kratēmatarion* cfr Anastasiou 2005.
27   After Iohannes Koukouzelēs, Manuel Chrysaphēs is the second *kallopistēs* of the kalophonic stichēra of the earlier composers and was an excellent melourgos himself, enriching the *Mathēmatarion* with a great number of new compositions.
28   For a general introduction to the contents of the *Mathēmatarion* cfr Stathēs 1975–: Vol. 1, λη´-λθ´.

the *Mathēmataria* also contain the theotokia mathēmata and anagrams that belong to them, usually ordered according to mode and followed by the katanyktika mathēmata and staurotheotokia in the same unity. In these last two parts, the theotokia mathēmata and the katanyktika, are found the majority of dekapentasyllabic mathēmata, which is a separate branch of Byzantine hymnography.[29] The heirmoi or troparia of the odes as texts for the mathēmata are usually contained in the unit of the theotokia. The kontakia or oikoi of the kontakia, if they are theotokia, are also placed with the theotokia; if they are not found with the theotokia then they are collected in the section of the particular feasts to which they belong. There also exist a few instances where there is a collection of select kratēmata at the end of the *Mathēmatarion*. On a few occasions the kalophonic verses of the vespers and orthros,[30] sometimes in the *Kratēmatarion*, but more often in the *Kontakaria*, can be found among the *Mathēmataria* and psalmic mathēmata.

In the established contents-repertoire of the *Mathēmataria*, the appearance of the movement of the theotokion mathēmata group to the beginning of the codex is often noticed, due mainly to the artistic value of these compositions, as well as the scribe's reverence for the Theotokos. Usually in these instances, and especially during the seventeenth and eighteenth centuries after the unity containing the theotokia, the phēmai and polychronismoi to archons and archbishops follow. Otherwise, this section of anthems and polychronismoi is anthologized in the *Papadikai* and *Anthologiai* after the orthros.

In the manuscript tradition of the post-Byzantine period, there also exists the *Anthology of the Mathēmatarion [Anthologion tou Mathēmatariou]*, which contains mainly the kalophonic stichēra and mathēmata for the commemorations of the celebrated saints and the great feasts of the Lord and

---

29   Stathēs 1977.
30   Cfr Athos, Iviron 972 (fifteenth century) containing some oikoi and the Akathistos twice, ēchēmata, theotokia mathēmata, katanyktika and the kalophonic verses of Psalm 2. The same holds for the *Mathēmatarion* of David Raidestēnos in Athos, Iviron 1006 and Athens, Nat. Libr. 2604 from the year 1463.

the Theotokos. Only the foremost and renowned texts and katanyktika melē are gathered from the other types into the *Anthology of the Mathēmatarion*. One of the first attempts to gather all the kalophonic compositions into one codex was by David Raidestēnos in the Athos, Iviron 1006,[31] written in the year 1431. In 1434, Markos hieromonachos of the Xanthopouloi hands down a similar codex of kalophonic compositions, the Athos, Vatopedi 1527.[32] A little later, shortly after the fall of Constantinople, Manuel Chrysaphēs writes the most extensive *Mathēmatarion* with 475 folios, the Athos, Iviron 975. Still, the codex lacks a title; the only indications in the epigraphs are 'select stichēra' [*stichēra eklekta*] or 'kalophonic stichēra and anagrams' [*kalophōnika stichēra kai anagrammatismoi*]. From them, however, is derived the title *Stichērarion Kalophōnikon* or *Kalophōnon*, as in the Athos, Vatopedi 1498 (fifteenth century).[33] This tradition continues for a century after the fall of Constantinople.[34] We can observe *Stichērarion Kalophōnikon* as a title or, from the epigraph of the first folio, 'Beginning with holy God of the stichēra and anagrams of the feasts for the entire year', and the like.

31 The main units of the codex are (fol. 3r) kalophonic verses from the great vespers, various composers, with many prologoi and kratēmata, (fol. 37r) other kalophonic verses from the Polyeleos (also with prologoi and kratēmata), (fol. 64r) the *Timiōtera hagioreitike* chanted at table, mode II plagal Ἄξιόν ἐστιν, (fol. 65v) *Timiōtera kat' ēchon* anagrams by Korone, mode I Σὲ μεγαλύνομεν· Τὴν ὄντως Θεοτόκον, (fol. 83v) katanyktika, staurotheotokia, theotokia kat' ēchon, (fol. 147r) select stichēra and anagrams for the entire year.
32 Cfr Chatzegiakoumes 1975: 337–338; Eustratiades and Archadios 1924: 238.
33 Eustratiades and Archadios 1924: 235; Wellesz 1980: 145.
34 From the years of the Fall to the middle of the seventeenth century there is a series of important manuscript *Mathēmataria*. The following are indicative: Athos Iviron 977 (mid-fifteenth–sixteenth century, 355 fols.), Hagiou Pavlou 101 (from the same period), Iviron 976 (seventeenth century, 423 fols.), Koutloumousiou 438 (seventeenth century), Panteleimon 938 (seventeenth century), Sinai Gr. 1234 (fifteenth century), Sinai Gr. 1259 (seventeenth century), Meteoron, Metamorphosis 317 (fifteenth century) and Metamorphosis 44 (sixteenth century), Athens, Nat. Libr. 937 and Nat. Libr. 938 (a two-volume *Mathēmatarion*, rich in content, from the middle of the seventeenth century).

Nevertheless, around the middle of the sixteenth century the term *Mathēmatarion* becomes characteristic of the codex. In the Athos, Iviron 1204, fol. 1r we read: '*Mathēmatarion Anthologion*, with holy God, of stichēra and anagrams for the entire year by various composers. Month of September 1, by kyr Manuel Chrysaphēs ....'[35] From here on, the term *Mathēmatarion* is stereotypically given to the rich manuscript tradition of this type, as well as during the entire seventeenth century, especially the second half, during which Kosmas hieromonachos the Ibēritēs and Macedonian[36] lives and produces an entire series of important codices. The tradition continues during the eighteenth century also,[37] the greatest production occurring during the second half of that century.

In the volumes of my work, *The Manuscripts of Byzantine Music — the Holy Mountain* that have already been published (Stathēs 1975–), the

[35] This codex was most likely copied by the hieromonk Leontios Koukouzelēs, also responsible for Athos, Iviron 1189 and Iviron 964 from the year 1562. Iviron 964 is also a *Mathēmatarion*, bearing the title (fol. 1r) 'Ἀρχὴ σὺν Θεῷ ἁγίῳ τῶν καλοφωνικῶν καὶ ἀναγραμματισμῶν τοῦ ὅλου ἐνιαυτοῦ, ψαλλόμενα ἐν ταῖς ἐπισήμοις ἑορταῖς'. From fol. 341r, *kratēmata eklekta*. This is an important *Mathēmatarion* because we find in it a witness for the content of the genre. Regarding Leontios Koukouzelēs and his three codices cfr Stathēs 1976: 185–186.

[36] The largest number of Kosmas' manuscripts are at Iviron (Stathēs 1977: 119). His most important *Mathēmataria* are the Athos, Iviron 911 (from the year 1670, of the old teachers, 446 fols.), Iviron 978 and Iviron 980, which are mixed codices beginning with the *Stichērarion* and then adding the *Mathēmatarion* (beginning on fol. 183r). Other noteworthy *Mathēmataria* from the seventeenth century include Iviron 1205 (mid-seventeenth century), Iviron 1156 (end of sixteenth–beginning of seventeenth century, autograph by Gerasimos hagioreitēs), Iviron 1112 (first half of the seventeenth century, autograph of Nathanael Nikaias), which is a *Stichērarion* for the months September–February with kalophonic stichēra throughout, Iviron 1051 (from the year 1673) and 1079 (autograph of Germanos Neōn Patrōn), M. Lavra Λ 166.

[37] Isolated instances in the *Mathēmatarion* hold significance, as with Athos, Iviron 967 (first half of eighteenth century), as with the witness of the attempt to collect all the kalophonic troparia into one volume, and the compendium of the festal kalophonic heirmoi *poiethenton para diaphorōn poiētōn haper psallontai meta paradoseōs* (fol. 312r); cfr the similar Athos, Iviron 988 (year 1734).

The tradition of the kalophonic melos

following *Mathēmataria* have been analytically catalogued. From them a clear picture of the *Mathēmatarion* repertoire can be realized.[38]

- Xēropotamou 276 (by Anatolios the hagiorite, first half of eighteenth century)
- Xēropotamou 383 (second half of the fifteenth century, extensive)
- Docheiariou 334 (year 1726)
- Docheiariou 339 (year 1768, by Dēmētrios Lōtos — substantial *Mathēmatarion* of compositions by the new teachers of the seventeenth century and eighteenth century)
- Docheiariou 379 (first half of the seventeenth century, 396 folios — quite rich)
- Dionysiou 569 (year 1685, by Kosmas Makedonas, 388 folios)
- Agiou Pavlou 101 (fifteenth–sixteenth century)
- Agiou Pavlou 128 (eighteenth century, by Theodosios of Chios)
- Koutloumousiou 427 (sixteenth century, 277 folios)
- Koutloumousiou 431 (eighteenth century, 283 folios)
- Koutloumousiou 438 (sixteenth century, 296 folios)
- Koutloumousiou 462 (fifteenth–sixteenth century, 369 folios)
- Philotheou 135 (sixteenth century, 520 folios)
- Iviron 960 (eighteenth century, 663 folios)
- Iviron 964 (year 1562, 680 folios)
- Iviron 967 (eighteenth century, 694 folios)
- Iviron 975 (fifteenth century, 759 folios)
- Iviron 988 (year 1734, 844 folios)
- Iviron 1000 (sixteenth century, 907 folios)

Chourmouzios Chartophylax's monumental exegetical work of Byzantine and post-Byzantine compositions, selected from various codices, resulted in

---

38 All the mathēmata produced over time are recorded in these *Mathēmataria*. The existence of distinct *Mathēmataria* containing the compositions of the seventeenth-century teachers points directly to a flourishing of the form [*eidos*] and of melopœïa in general during that century.

an eight-volume *Mathēmatarion*[39] of Byzantine composers. Furthermore, in another two volumes[40] of the *Papadikē* he included the theotokia mathēmata and the mathēmata of the feasts for the entire year with a clear concentration on the composers of the seventeenth century. In turn, in his own *Papadikē*, Grēgorios Protopsaltes collected into one volume — eventually (Ioannēs Lampadarios and Stephanos Domestikos 1850–1851: Vol. 3) — the most necessary mathēmata of the year. Other *exēgētai*[41] like Matthaios Batopedēnos, Nikolaos Docheiaritēs, Iohasaph Dionysiatēs, Theophanēs Pantokratorinos and Apostolos Kōnstas Chios passed down *Mathēmataria* during the first half of the nineteenth century.

Kontakarion or Oikēmatarion and the Akathistos

When we speak of kontakia and oikoi in Byzantine melopœïa, we have in mind the separation between the *prooimion* or *koukoulion* and the first oikos of all the other oikoi belonging to a single kontakion exactly as these two troparia were placed between the sixth and seventh odes of the canons in the Office of the Orthros. Nevertheless, the term kontakion was first introduced into hymnography during the ninth century.[42] The kontakion, then, i.e., the koukoulion and the first oikos, became widely known throughout the liturgical books. It followed that the kalophonic composers used the texts of these first two troparia for melic composition. The Akathistos is the exception to this rule in that the composers would use all its oikoi for composition.

The kalophonic handling of the kontakia is an evolution of the embellishment of the melos of the older *Kontakaria* known with the name *Psaltikon* (cfr p. 120 above). The oikos Αὐτὸς μόνος ὑπάρχεις ἀθάνατος

---

39 Referring specifically to the ΜΠΤ 727–734.
40 ΜΠΤ 706 and 722.
41 These other *exēgētai* also added their own mathemata compositions to these *Mathēmataria*.
42 In Wellesz 1980: 179 we read, 'even the name *kontakion* only occurs for the first time in the ninth century'.

of Andreas Sigeros or Iohannes Glykys[43] found its place early on in the *Papadikai*, as did the oikos Ἄγγελος πρωτοστάτης,[44] with or without the prooimion Τῇ ὑπερμάχῳ. By contrast, other oikoi to the Theotokos, like *Εἰ καὶ ἐν τάφῳ*, *Τὸν πρὸ ἡλίου*[45] and *Ἔκτεινόν σου παλάμα*, by Iohannes Kladas[46] were gradually introduced into the *Papadikai* and *Mathēmataria*.

The *Kalophōnikon Kontakarion* or *Oikēmatarion* containing oikoi for the feasts of the entire year was not widely distributed in the manuscript tradition. Conversely, the Akathistos had a wide influence and tradition, either according to the composition of the old teachers or the virtuosic and great arrangement by Iohannes lampadarios Kladas. In this instance, we find the indiscriminate *Oikēmatarion* or *Akathistos* for a title. Manuel Chrysaphēs' assertion is significant:

> Τῶν οἴκων δέ γε πρῶτος ποιητὴς ὁ Ἀνανεώτης ὑπῆρξε καὶ δεύτερος ὁ Γλυκὺς τὸν Ἀνανεώτην μιμούμενος· ἔπειτα τρίτος ὁ Ἠθικὸς ὀνομαζόμενος, ὃς διδασκάλοις ἑπόμενος τοῖς εἰρημένοις δυσί, καὶ μετὰ πάντας αὐτοὺς ὁ χαριτώνυμος Κουκουζέλης, ὅς, εἰ καὶ μέγας τῷ ὄντι διδάσκαλος ἦν, εἴπετο δ' ὅμως κατ' ἴχνος αὐτοῖς, καὶ οὐδέν τι τῶν ἐκείνοις δοξάντων καὶ δοκιμασθέντων καλῶς, δεῖν ᾤετο καινοτομεῖν, διὸ οὐδὲ ἐκαινοτόμει· ὁ δὲ λαμπαδάριος Ἰωάννης τούτων ὕστερος ὢν καὶ κατ' οὐδὲν ἐλαττούμενος τῶν προτέρων καὶ ἂν ταῖς λέξεσι γράφων ἰδίᾳ χειρὶ ἔφη· «ἀκάθιστος ποιηθεῖσα παρ' ἐμοῦ Ἰωάννου λαμπαδαρίου τοῦ Κλαδᾶ, μιμουμένη κατὰ τὸ δυνατὸν τὴν παλαιὰν ἀκάθιστον[47] καὶ οὐκ ᾐσχύνετο γράφων οὕτως, εἰ μὴ μᾶλλον καὶ ἐσεμνύνετο. (Manuel Chrysaphēs and Conomos 1985: 44,143–44,157)

> The first composer of oikoi was Aneotes and the second was Glykys, who imitated Aneotes; next, the third was named Ethikos, who followed the aforementioned two writers as teacher and, after all of these, Iohannes Koukouzelēs who, even though he was truly great, was a teacher and did not depart from the science of his predecessors. Therefore, he followed in their footsteps and decided not to change anything

---

43 And in the kalophonic Messina, San. Salvatore 161, fol. 81v, mentioned above and Athens, Nat. Libr. 2458, fols. 136v–138r.
44 Athens, Nat. Libr. 2458, fol. 191r.
45 Athens, Nat. Libr. 886, fol. 489r and Athos, Iviron 972, fol. 301v.
46 Cfr Athos, Iviron 972, fol. 217r.
47 *Akathistos* is the general title of the work in the manuscript tradition; the version mentioned by Manuel Chrysaphēs here as an autograph of Iohannes Kladas is not indicated.

they had considered and proved sound. Thus he made no innovations. Iohannes the lampadarios, who came after these men and who was in no way inferior to his predecessors, wrote with his own hand these words, saying: 'Akathistos composed by me, Iohannes Kladas, the lampadarios, imitating the old Akathistos as closely as possible'. He was not ashamed so to write, but rather took pride. (Manuel Chrysaphēs and Conomos 1985: 45)

The above witness is of interest for the list of composers of the kalophonic oikoi (in this case, the Akathistos) and because of the antiquity of this category of kalophony, as well as the tradition of the imitation of the melos in the older compositions by the newer composers. Through it the natural evolution of the kalophonic tradition of the *Kontakarion* is revealed, but also the general origin of the form [*eidos*] of the mathēmata as coming out of the *Psaltikon*, i.e., the *Kontakarion*. Chrysaphēs speaks about oikoi and, hence, the *Oikēmatarion* book, referring only to the Akathistos.

The above assertion by Chrysaphēs is confirmed by the witnesses in the Athos, Iviron 972, written during the first half of the fifteenth century and containing the old Akathistos, that of Iohannes Kladas, some mathēmata, ēchēmata and kratēmata, as well as kalophonic verses for the vespers. The following are specifically mentioned: (fol. 165) 'Akathistos chanted on Saturday of the fifth week of the holy Fast; by kyr Iohannes and protopsaltes Glykys; smaller than the great Akathistos, more technical and sweeter; mode IV plagal, $Τῇ\ ὑπερμάχῳ$ — (fol. 17v) The oikos, $Ἄγγελος\ πρωτοστάτης$ — (fol. 30r) Another Akathistos; by the domestikos kyr Michael Aneōtes, kallōpismos by Iohannes Koukouzelēs; mode IV plagal, $Τῇ\ ὑπερμάχῳ$ —(fol. 31v) the oikos, $Ἄγγελος\ πρωτοστάτης$ —(fol. 37v) Another Akathistos, by the protopsaltes Iohannes Glykys; mode IV plagal, $Τῇ\ ὑπερμάχῳ$ —(fol. 38v) nenano $Ἄγγελος\ πρωτοστάτης$ —(fol. 44v) by Ēthikos kyr Nikēphoros; mode II plagal nenano, $Βλέπουσα\ ἡ\ ἁγία$'. The entire Akathistos is completed according to the compositions of the new writers up to fol. 108v — mostly Koukouzelēs and Glykys and Tzaknopoulos (fol. 75v —$Πᾶσα\ φύσις$) and Xenos Korōnes (fol. 1r —$Ἄγγελος\ πρωτοστάτης$, and fol. 117v —$Τῇ\ ὑπερμάχῳ$). Kladas' entire Akathistos is on fols 119v–216v.

As concerns the composers of the oikoi, Grēgorios Bounēs Alyatēs bears witness to their chronological order and to the development of their melos at the beginning of his *Kontakarion*, the Sinai Gr. 1262 from the year 1437,[48] which is also the best example of the *Kalophonic Kontakarion* codex type.

It should be noted here that circumstances also exist of the *syntmēsis* of the kalophonic oikoi of the Akathistos in Crete by Benediktos Episkopopoulos (c. 1600), as well as many ancient kalophonic compositions by Cretan musicians of the period — the last quarter of the sixteenth and the first quarter of the seventeenth centuries.[49] The opposite tendency to the embellishment and elongation is perceived through an abridgment called *syntmēsis* consisting of a removal of repetition and kratēmata from the old compositions. The epigraph by Benedict Episkopopoulos in the Athos, Koutloumousiou 448 (fol. 2r) is very characteristic. Ὁι εἰκοσιτέσσαρεις οἶκοι τῆς ὑπεραγίας Θεοτόκου, ποιηθέντες παρά τινων παλαιῶν διδασκάλων ἐντέχνως καὶ μεθοδικῶς, πλὴν δὲ εἰς πλάτος, καὶ διὰ τοῦτο οἱ νῦν οὐ ψάλλουσι τούτους· λέγω δὲ διὰ ῥαθυμίαν, ἕτεροι δὲ πάλιν δι᾽ ἀπραξίαν: (τοσοῦτον παρὰ πάντων ἀργῶσιν). Ἔδοξε γοῦν κἀμοὶ ἵνα μὴ ἀνενέργητοι μείνωσι εἰς τὸ ἐξῆς, παρά τινων εὐλαβῶν εἰς δόξαν αὐτῆς τῆς ὑπεραγίας Θεοτόκου, ἀλλὰ μᾶλλον ψάλλεσθαι, Βενεδίκτῳ πρεσβυτέρῳ τῷ Ἐπισκοποπούλῳ συνθέναι καὶ γράψαι ὡς ἐν βραχεῖ ἐπακολουθῶν τὰς ἐκείνων μεθόδους, καὶ τοῦτο οὐ καταφρονῶν ἐκείνους, ἀλλὰ μᾶλλον ἐπαινῶν καὶ μακαρίζων τὰ πλεῖστα. Κὺρ Βενεδίκτου Ἐπισκοποπούλου, οἶκος ὁ α΄, ἦχος α΄ Ἄγγελος πρωτοστάτης.[50]

In the post-Byzantine period, the Akathist of Iohannes Kladas was more widely distributed than the old Akathistos compositions. Athos, Docheiariou 381 (end of the sixteenth century)[51] is an *Oikēmatarion* of the old teachers. On the other hand, Athos, Docheiariou 388 (beginning

48 Cfr p. 25, above.
49 Cfr Stathēs 1977: 111–113.
50 The other 23 oikoi follow in a two-part form, with one short kratēma and kratēmata by Demetrios Damias. In this particular instance we do not have abridgements of older, particular compositions, but new melē with an intense, contemporary Cretan idiom. Other than the oikoi, the codex contains a rich *Mathēmatarion* of theotokia, either of original compositions of the Cretan melopoioi Demetrios Damias, Antonios Episkopopoulos, Nikolaos hiereus Strianos, Benedictos Episkopopoulos, Iohannes Phokas and Iohannes hiereus Plousiadēnos, or rare, original works by older composers newly arranged by the above Cretan composers.
51 Cfr Stathēs 1975–: Vol. 1, 542–543.

of the seventeenth century)[52] contains Kladas' Akathistos with insertions [*parembolai*] between the first and second oikoi of six compositions by Manuel Chrysaphēs and Iohannes Koukouzelēs. Other illustrious codex *Oikēmataria* include Athos, Iviron 1080 (year 1668, written by Kosmas the Macedonian), Xēropotamou 287 (year 1724, written by Anatolios hieromonachos), Docheiarion 342 (year 1734, written by Iohannes Trapezountios), Hagiou Pavlou 146 (year 1758, written by Theodosios hierodiakonos of Chios), and many others.

Balasios hiereus, Petros Bereketēs,[53] and later, Anastasios Rapsaniōtēs,[54] Demetrios Lōtos[55] and Petros Peloponnēsios also composed oikoi of the Akathistos. Chourmouzios Chartophylax wrote two volumes[56] of *exēgēseis* containing the Akathistos of Kladas, as well as other oikoi according to the compositions of Manuel Chrysaphēs and Balasios hiereus.[57]

THE PRINCIPAL COMPOSERS OF THE KALOPHONIC MELOS OF THE MATHĒMATARION

In this section we have chosen not to dwell on the composers' lives and works, even of the more important among them, for the simple reason that such a venture would fill a many-paged volume owing to the collection of data. Furthermore, almost all composers of Byzantine melopœïa delved into the kalophonic melos, the great ones even more so. In another of my

52 Cfr Stathēs 1975–: Vol. 1, 559–560.
53 Cfr the description of the *Hapanta* of his mathēmata below, pp. 226 sq.
54 Cfr fols. 334r–354r of Athos, Xenophontos 137 (end of eighteenth century) where the oikoi of Anastasios Rapsaniōtēs are anthologized in Chatzegiakoumes 1975: 380 and Stathēs 1975–: Vol. 2, 82.
55 Athos, Xenophontos 330 (year 1782), fols. 351r, 353r is an autograph; cfr Stathēs 1975–: Vol. 1, 201.
56 ΜΠΤ 711 and 710.
57 On the Akathistos cfr Krētikou 2004.

dissertations (Stathēs 1977: 97–124), I dedicated an entire chapter to this theme, that is, to the precise discernment of the biographical details of the composers and writers of the dekapentasyllabic hymnographic texts. The composers described there are also the principal representatives of the kalophonic melos.

It is sufficient simply to list the names of the main composers of mathēmata here according to five large groups whose musical genius and activity exemplify one or more composers. This will also produce an outline of the development of the *Mathēmatarion* melos according to five definitive stages in the shaping and tradition of form.

The brilliant ensemble of composers: Nikēphoros Ēthikos, Iohannes Glykys, Iohannes Koukouzelēs, and Xenos Korōnēs (first half of the fourteenth century)

To the accounts by Manuel Chrysaphēs and Grēgorios Bounēs Alyatēs in the middle of the fifteenth century regarding the chronology of teachers following Iohannes Glykys, Iohannes Koukouzelēs and Xenos Korōnēs we add, from the codex Athos, Koutloumousiou 457 (second half of the fourteenth century): Ἀρχὴ σὺν Θεῷ ἁγίῳ τοῦ μεγάλου ἑσπερινοῦ, ἀπὸ χοροῦ· περιέχει δὲ ἀλλάγματα παλαιά τε καὶ νέα, διαφόρων ποιητῶν, τοῦ τε θαυμαστοῦ πρωτοψάλτου τοῦ Γλυκὺ καὶ τῶν διαδόχων αὐτοῦ καὶ φοιτητῶν κυροῦ Ξένου καὶ πρωτοψάλτου τοῦ Κορώνη καὶ τοῦ Παπαδοπούλου κυροῦ Ἰωάννου καὶ μαΐστορος τοῦ Κουκουζέλη,[58] σὺν αὐτοῖς καὶ ἑτέρων πολλῶν' [Beginning with holy God of the great vespers, from the choir [*apo chorou*]; containing allagmata old and new by various authors, the wondrous protopsaltes Glykys and his successors and students, kyr Xenos the protopsaltes

---

58 And on fols. 23r and 352r the names Koukouzelēs and Korōnēs are mentioned together, '*tou maïstoros kyrou Iohannou tou Koukouzelou kai a 'psaltou kyr Xenou tou Korōnē*'. At the beginning of this codex there existed an icon showing Iohannes Glykys seated, holding a baton, as 'the ison', and below him are sitting Iohannes Koukouzelēs and Xenos Korōnēs. This illustration was most likely stolen by Uspensky, by whom it was published and republished in Petrov and Kodov 1973: 42.

Korōnēs and Papadopoulos kyr Iohannes the maïstōr Koukouzelēs, with them many others]. According to the account of Manuel Chrysaphēs and other evidence stating that his compositions were embellished by Koukouzelēs, Nikēphoros Ēthikos is chronologically the oldest, at least before Koukouzelēs and Korōnēs, flourishing around the end of the thirteenth and beginning of the fourteenth centuries.[59]

Having codified the kalophonic tradition and setting the boundaries through their *Methodoi of theseis and kratēmata of the Psaltic Art*, these four teachers are the source of Byzantine melopœïa in all its forms for the centuries that follow up to our own time. In the *Papadikai* we find the *Method of the theseis* [*Methodos tōn theseōn*][60] by Iohannes Glykys, as well as the well-known other method by Iohannes Koukouzelēs, known as the *Mega Ison*. Iohannes Koukouzelēs also composed a *methodos kalophōnias*[61] through the kratēmata and Xenos Korōnēs composed two *methodoi* of the kratēmata.[62] It seems, though, that the personage of Iohannes Koukouzelēs was the most imposing of the four, as evidenced in the manuscript tradition.[63] A number of conditions contributed to this popularity: first, the stabilisation of the repertoire of the *Heirmologion* and its dissemination under the established form of the *Heirmologia* Sinai Gr. 1256 (of the year

59 Cfr Stathēs 1977: 99–103 regarding these four composers.
60 Athos, Konstamonitou 86 (first half of fifteenth century), fol. 13v; Stathēs 1975–: Vol. 1, 656. Manuel Chrysaphes mentions, 'οὐδεμία ἦν ἂν χρεία οὐδ' ἀνάγκη τοῦ τὸν μὲν Γλυκὺν Ἰωάννην πεποιηκέναι τὰς μεθόδους τῶν κατὰ τὴν Ψαλτικὴν θέσεων, τὸν δὲ Μαΐστορα Ἰωάννην μετ' αὐτὸν τὴν ἑτέραν μέθοδον καὶ τὰ σημάδια ψαλτά ...' [there would have been no need for Ioannes Glykys to have composed methods for the *theseis* in chanting and after him for the maistōr Ioannes to have composed another method and the chanted signs] (Manuel Chrysaphēs and Conomos 1985: 40,69–74; 41); also cfr Troelsgård 1997.
61 Athos, Dionysiou 570, fol. 108r: *hetera methodos tēs kalophōnias tou maïstoros, ēchos a Neeeena*.
62 Cfr Stathēs 1977: 103n1.
63 In Athos, Iviron 1205 (mid-eighteenth century), fol. 273r, we find: *Iōannou tou Koukouzelē kai Papadopoulou, didaskalou tōn didaskalōn kai maïstoros tōn maïstorōn*. Manuel Chrysaphes often gives Koukouzelēs the names *charitonymos* and *megas didaskalos*.

1309) and St. Petersburg–Leningrad, Nat. Libr. of Russia Gr. 121 (of the year 1302), in which the name Iohannes Koukouzelēs is found; secondly, the subsequent codification of the form of the anagrams,[64] together with the mathēmata in general, and the *methodoi* of the signs [*sēmadia*] and the *theseis*; and finally, above and beyond the other two points, the large production of kalophonic compositions and their collection in the new type of music codex known as the *Papadikē* would, over and over again, perpetuate the name of 'teacher of teachers' [*didaskalos tōn didaskalōn*], Iohannes Koukouzelēs, 'the true maïstōr' [*ontōs maïstōr*].[65]

We have already commemorated the names of the four primary composers of the kalophonic melos of the preceded era. Their contemporaries and successors were many, and the names more often encountered include Geōrgios Kontopetrēs — Koukouzelēs' student — Geōrgios Panaretos, Phardiboukēs [prōtopapas of the Church of the Holy Apostles], Dēmētrios Dokeianos, Kornēlios monachos, Koukoumas [Nikolaos the maïstōr], Christophoros Mystakōn, Manuel Plagitēs hiereus and Tzaknopoulos.[66] The *Papadikē* from the year 1336, Athens, Nat. Libr. 2458 contains compositions of even more musicians.

---

64 On fol. 275r of Athos, Iviron 1205 (middle of seventeenth century) the following note can be found: 'Γίνωσκε ὅτι τοῦ παρόντος ἀναγραμματισμοῦ τὸ καθ' ὅλον στιχηρὸν ἄρχεται πλ. δ'· διὰ τοῦτο γοῦν τελειοῖ καὶ ὁ ἀναγραμματισμὸς τὸν αὐτὸν ἦχον.' This regards the anagram in mode II plagal *Τῶν θλιβομένων τὸ συμπαθές*, corroborating with what Manuel Chrysaphes writes concerning the technique of Koukouzelēs' anagrams. Cfr p. 70.

65 To the witnesses regarding the life of Koukouzelēs, that he lived and flourished from the beginning of the fourteenth century up to 1336, let us add Athens, Nat. Libr. 884 *Sticherarion*, written by one Athanasios in the year 1341 '*ex antigraphou pany diorthōmenou ontos kakeinou tou palai Koukouzelē...*' (fol. 390v). We conclude, then, that Koukouzelēs must have died before the year 1341.

66 These composers wrote mele mostly for the *Papadikē*. Dokeianos, however, Kontopetrēs and Manuel Plagitēs also wrote for the *Mathēmatarion*.

Melourgoi contemporary to Iohannes Kladas the lampadarios (c. 1400)

Evidence in the manuscripts regarding the fact that Iohannes Kladas was lampadarios 'of the pious royal clergy' [*tou euagous basilikou klērou*] and contemporary of the patriarch Mattheos I (1396–1410) helps in his chronological placement around 1400 and afterwards.[67] His importance for the *Mathēmatarion* lies primarily in his masterful composition of the Akathistos. His occupation with this work afforded him the opportunity to produce many other mathēmata. In any event, it seems his main concern was the composition of works that complete the compositional lacunae of the previous teachers. For this reason he composed megalynaria theotokia, dogmatic theotokia[68] and asmatic heirmoi for the Paschal canon. We can easily observe that Kladas dedicated his genius to the hymnody of the Theotokos. Kladas' production of dekapentasyllabic katanyktika mathēmata and kratēmata[69] is also considerable and of great importance.

Primary composers of kalophonic compositions that were contemporary with Iohannes Kladas — first quarter of fifteenth century — are Iohannes Laskarēs the Sērpaganos,[70] Manuel Argyropoulos, Manuel

---

67 Kladas, as the melic arranger of the verses for Iohannes Laskares, and regarding whom we have a clear witness in the year 1418 (Stathēs 1977: 95–97, 103–104), is the musical genius of the first quarter of the fifteenth century.

68 In Athos, Dionysiou 570 (autograph of I. Plousiadenos), fol. 205v, we read: 'ἐκ τῶν ιϛ´ θεοτοκίων τῆς Ὀκτωήχου, ἃ ἐποίησε μέρος ὁ θαυμαστὸς λαμπαδάριος, μέρος δ᾽ ἄλλοι τινὲς ἐποίησαν· ἐπειδὴ οὐχ εὑρίσκονται πάντα τοῦ λαμπαδαρίου … ἃ οὐκ ἔφθασεν ὁ λαμπαδάρης ποιῆσαι'.

69 All the compositions of Iohannes Kladas were widely distributed. The communion of the Pre-sanctified *Γεύσασθε* is still chanted today. In addition, his contribution to the papadikon melos is significant, especially for anoixantaria, verses of the *Makarios anēr* and the Amōmos. Athos, Konstamonitou 86 attributes the entire structure of the great vespers after the abandonment of the asmatic cathedral office to Kladas; at fol. 50v, we read: "Ὄπισθεν προεγράφη ὁ μεγάλος ἑσπερινὸς εἰς πλάτος, καθὼς ἐψάλλετο ἐν τῇ Θεσσαλονίκῃ. Ὁ δὲ προκείμενος γέγονεν παρὰ τοῦ λαμπαδαρίου κυροῦ Ἰωάννου τοῦ Κλαδᾶ καὶ ἑτέρων ποιητῶν'. And at fol. 35v: "Ταῦτα τὰ τριαδικὰ [anoixantaria] τοῦ λαμπαδαρίου κὺρ Ἰωάννου' (Stathēs 1975–: Vol. 1, 658).

70 Regarding Iohannes Laskaris and Manuel Argyropoulos cfr Stathēs 1977: 95–97. Iohannes Laskaris created a *Methodos of the Parallagē* and relationship between the modes; cfr Athos, Dionysiou 570, fols. 40r–42r and Bentas 1971.

Blatēros, Nikolaos Palamas of Anchialus, Bartholomaios domestikos of Lavra (second half and toward the end of the fourteenth century) and Manuel Gazēs.[71]

Melourgoi contemporary to Manuel Chrysaphēs the lampadarios (c. 1453)

Manuel Chrysaphēs along with Grēgorios Bounēs Alyatēs are two talented composers from the years of the Fall of Constantinople onward who, by instinct, codified the music produced by the Byzantine composers in a sequence of beautifully prepared codices.[72] The importance of Manuel Chrysaphēs for the compositions of the *Mathēmatarion* comes from the fact that he had embellished many old compositions and added a large number of his own new ones. Theodosios hierodiakonos of Chios preserves the following account in his autograph *Mathēmatarion* from the years 1755–1765, Athos, Hagiou Pavlou 128 [=Lambrou 186/59], p. 61: Ἀρχὴ σὺν Θεῷ ἁγίῳ τῶν στιχηρῶν τοῦ ὅλου ἐνιαυτοῦ, ποιηθέντων παρὰ διαφόρων ποιητῶν, καλλωπισθέντων δὲ παρὰ κὺρ Ἰωάννου μαΐστορος τοῦ Κουκουζέλη· ὕστερον δὲ παρὰ κὺρ Μανουὴλ τοῦ Χρυσάφου᾽ [Beginning with holy God of the stichēra for the entire year, created by various composers, embellished [*kallōpisthentōn*] by kyr Iohannes maïstōr Koukouzelēs, later also by kyr Manuel Chrysaphēs]. Elsewhere, the scribe of the Athos, Iviron 1205 (beginning of the seventeenth century) praises Manuel Chrysaphēs[73] in iambic verse. He puts to melody the compositional remaining genus lacunae, mainly asmatic heirmoi,[74] festal stichēra according to the letters of the alphabet, as well as a plethora of mathēmata, easily confirmed through the analytical description of Chourmouzios' *Mathēmatarion* (see below pp. 173 sq.). Regarding his theoretical treatise *On the Theory of the Psaltic*

71 Cfr Adamis 1974: 738–739.
72 Cfr Patrinelis 1969: 71, 82; 1973; Vogel and Gardthausen 1909: 92.
73 Cfr fol. 346r: ʽΦερωνύμως κέκτησαι χρυσᾶ τὰ μέλη·/ἡδύτατον δὲ πλεῖστον ὡς ὑπὲρ μέλιʼ.
74 In the *Mathēmatarion*, Athos, Docheiariou 379 (mid-seventeenth century), containing many compositions by Manuel Chrysaphes (about one-third of the entire contents), also preserves asmatic heirmoi for Christmas (fols. 105r–113v) and the Annunciation (fols. 156r–168v); cfr Stathēs 1975–: Vol. I, 529, 531).

Art (Manuel Chrysaphēs and Conomos 1985), he left an indisputable guide for the research of the Psaltic Art during the two centuries of Byzantine kalophony, the fourteenth and fifteenth centuries.

Parallel to Manuel Chrysaphēs' activity, the great contribution of the teacher Grēgorios Bounēs monachos[75] is worth mentioning here, mostly because of his Method, *Νε οὕτως οὖν ἀνάβαινε οὕτως καὶ κατάβαινε*[76] and the *dyskolon* kratēmata in mode II plagal. Grēgorios Bounēs is the benchmark and demarcation for those who come after, as the colophon of Athos, Xeropotamou 308 from the year 1676 leaves us to understand.[77]

Amongst other important composers for kalophony, we must include the names Gerasimos hieromonachos Chalkeopoulos — a student of Manuel Chrysaphēs[78] — Markos the metropolitan of Corinth from Xanthopouloi Monastery, Gabriēl of the Xanthopouloi Monastery, Anthimos abbot of the Lavra, Geōrgios Sgouropoulos, Iohasaph monachos and Iohannes Plousiadēnos hiereus (second half of the fifteenth century).[79] Also worth mentioning are Iohannes and Thōmas Kordokotoi in Cyprus.[80]

---

75 In Athens, Nat. Libr. 2406 (year 1453), fol. 269v we read: "Ἕτερον τοῦ μοναχοῦ Γρηγορίου τοῦ Ἀλυάτου, πρῶτον σχέδιον, βαρὺς *Αἰνεῖτε τὸν Κύριον*' (Patrinelis 1969: 71; 1973).

76 Cfr Athos, Xeropotamou 307, fol. 131; Stathēs 1975–: Vol. 1, 107.

77 Xeropotamou 307 (year 1679), fol. 409r: '[...] καὶ ἀμαθὴς ἀπὸ καλλιγραφίαν· πλὴν εἶναι καλὸν ἀντίβολον τοῦ παλαιοῦ διδασκάλου κυροῦ Γρηγορίου τοῦ Ἀλυάτου ...' (Stathēs 1975–: Vol. 1, 118). An autograph *Sticherarion* by Gregorios is Athos, Dionysiou 564 from the year 1445 in Stathēs 1975–: Vol. 2, 668–669.

78 This is often repeated in the manuscripts, but is admitted by Manuel himself in the prologue to his treatise: 'Ἐπεὶ δὲ νῦν ὁ ἐν Ἱερομονάχοις Γεράσιμος τῶν ἡμετέρων μαθητῶν τυγχάνων, σπουδαῖός τέ ἐστι καὶ φιλομαθὴς καὶ τῶν οὐδέν τι παραδραμεῖν αὐτὸν βούλεται ...' [One of my pupils, the hieromonk Gerasimos, who is full of zeal and eager to learn and does not want nay sound teaching to escape him ...] (Manuel Chrysaphēs and Conomos 1985: 36,20–23).

79 Many of his compositions can be found in his autograph Athos, Dionysiou 570, also in Kosmas Makedōn' *Mathēmatarion*, Athos, Dionysiou 569 (year 1689).

80 Cfr Chatzegiakoumes 1975: 315.

The sixteenth- and seventeenth-century transmitters and renewers of the tradition

One century after the Fall of Constantinople, musical activity is mostly limited to the stereotypical repetition of the Byzantine melos and its dissemination through the copying of older codices. Hence, the unaltered *Sticheraria, Mathemataria*[81] and *Papadikai* hymnbooks are duplicated. An early attempt at differentiation is noticed in the *Heirmologion* with a shortening of its melos. Individual creativity, however, was never absent.[82] Nevertheless, the places where we will witness a musical development and activity with tendencies to variation in the melos and eventual creation of a new tradition is mainly on the islands of Crete and Cyprus, mostly due to the political situation in those localities and possibly also due to their special relationship with the God–trodden Mount Sinai.

We observed above the circumstances of the creation of a new tradition for the melos of the twenty-four oikoi of the Akathistos by Benediktos Episkopopoulos. That name introduces us to a group of Cretan composers who either wrote original compositions, abridged, or passed on the older ones as they chanted them. These composers include Benediktos and Antonios Episkopopoulos, Kosmas Baranēs, Dēmētrios Damias, Ignatios Phrielos, Nikolaos Strianos hiereus, and cover the chronological period from the last quarter of the sixteenth century to approximately the middle of the seventeenth.[83]

The new trends around the middle of the sixteenth century are represented in Cyprus by Hieronymos Tragōdistēs and, later, around the end of the same century, Kōnstantinos Phlangēs. In the Athos, Koutloumousiou 427, fol. 24r we read: Ἀναποδισμοὶ ὅλου τοῦ ἐνιαυτοῦ ἀπὸ ἀρχῆς Σεπτεμβρίου ἄχρι ὅλου τοῦ Αὐγούστου· ἐκαλλωπίσθησαν δὲ παρὰ τοῦ κυροῦ Κωνσταντίνου

---

81   It was mentioned above how the Athos, Iviron 964 *Mathēmatarion* from the middle of the sixteenth century is representative of the stable tradition of the old teachers.
82   The new names most often encountered is Angelos hiereus ex Athenōn, Alexios hiereus bouleutēs ek Krētēs, Eleutherios hiereus and others; cfr Athos Docheiariou 379 and Panteleimon 938.
83   Cfr Giannopoulos 2004; Stathēs 1977: 111–113.

Φλαγγῆ' ['*anapodismoi* for the entire year, beginning with September through to August']. *Kallōpismos* here does not mean the lengthening of an older composition, but a newly created composition afresh; it is worth mentioning that with the exception of the first mathēma, none contains a kratēma. The melos is of a unique, Cypriot tradition.

During the first half of the seventeenth century, important musicians will continue the Byzantine tradition proper: Gerasimos monachos the Hagioreitēs,[84] Kōnstantinos of Anchialus, Klēmēs Lesbios or Mytēlinaios,[85] Gennadios monachos of Anchialus and Geōrgios Raidestēnos the protopsaltes. In the second half of the seventh century we find ourselves before a renewal of Byzantine melopœïa.

The new four-member ensemble of brilliant composers, Panagiotēs Chrysaphēs the new and protopsaltes, Germanos Neōn Patrōn, Balasios hiereus and nomophylax and Petros Bereketēs the melōdos are the counterweight of the old masters of the first half of the fourteenth century. Essentially, these four teachers, together with their contemporaries Kosmas hieromonachos Ibēritēs the Macedonian, Damianos hieromonachos Batopedēnos, Athanasios the Patriarch from Andrianoupolis, Athanasios Ibēritēs, Daniel monachos, Pankratios monachos Ibēritēs and others,[86] would leave a monumental corpus of works. These works become the bridge by which we access the Byzantine compositions, simultaneously creating the basis upon which the new compositional evolution[87] is constructed. These composers, in any event, created so large a number of mathēmata[88] as to merit the creation of a new hymnbook, the *Mathēmatarion of the new teachers* [*tōn neōn didaskalōn*].

---

84   Cfr Stathēs 1977: 114.
85   Cfr Chatzegiakoumes 1975: 46–47; Stathēs 1977: 114.
86   The codices Athos, Docheiariou 339 (*Mathēmatarion* from the year 1768) and Docheiariou 338 (*Anthologion* from the year 1767), Xeropotamou 330 (*Nea Papadikē* from the year 1781 and autograph of Demetrios Lotos) contain almost all the compositions of the new teachers; cfr Stathēs 1975–: Vol. 1, 406–427, 189–206.
87   During this period we see the *Stichēraria meta tinos kainophanous kallopismou*, as well as the *kallopisthen Heirmologion* and *Kalophōnikon Heirmologion*.
88   Cfr Athos, Docheiariou 339 *Mathēmatarion*.

Last appearance of the form of the mathēmata in the eighteenth and nineteenth centuries

The figure of Petros Bereketēs[89] dominates the first quarter of the eighteenth century. His contemporaries are Antonios the priest and oikonomos[90] of the Great Church and Panagiotēs Chalatzoglou, protopsaltes c. 1728. From this time to the year 1769, the figure of Iohannes Trapezountios[91] — domestikos, lampadarios, protopsaltes — dominates for almost half a century. To him we add and recognize Daniel the protopsaltes, Petros lampadarios Peloponnēsios, Iakovos protopsaltes, Petros Byzantios, office holders of the Great Church.[92] In addition, worthwhile work was left by Theodosios hierodiakonos of Chios and his pupil Dēmētrios Lōtos, protopsaltes of Smyrna,[93] Anastasios Rapsaniōtēs, Theodoulos Aineitēs[94] and Melētios Sinaïtēs the new.

Representatives of the kalophonic melos of the *Mathēmatarion* during the nineteenth century are the exegetes Grēgorios protopsaltes and Chourmouzios Chartophylax,[95] Kōnstantinos protopsaltes[96] and Iohannes lampadarios.[97] Beyond their importance for other reasons,[98] the hagiorite teachers Matthaios Batopedēnos, Nikolaos Docheiaritēs and Iohasaph

---

89 Cfr Stathēs 1971: 223–241.
90 Cfr Chatzegiakoumes 1975: 266.
91 Cfr Patrinelis 1969: 76–78; 1973.
92 Cfr Patrinelis 1969; 1973: 78–89.
93 Theodosios hierodiakonos, writer of Athos, Hagiou Pavlou 146 in the year 1758, often mentions in his manuscripts that he was D. Lotos' teacher. For a general overview regarding Demetrios Lotos cfr Stathē 1973.
94 For the musical work of Anastasius Rapsaniōtēs, protopsaltes of Larisa and Theodoulos monachos Aineitēs refer to the indicies in Stathēs 1975–.
95 Cfr Anatolikiōtēs 2004; Giannopoulos 2002.
96 Cfr Terzopoulos 2004.
97 In Ioannēs Lampadarios and Stephanos Domestikos 1850–1851: Vol. 3, 474–539 there are six new mathēmata by Iohannes lampadarios, who was co-editor of the monumental work in 1851 with Stephanos domestikos, the later lampadarios.
98 Referring specifically to the exegetical work see Stathēs 1975–: Vol. 2, ιδ´–ιε´.

Dionysiatēs are recognized as significant composers of kalophonic melē of the *Papadikē* and mathēmata.[99]

From the middle of the nineteenth century, the production of mathēmata declines; the new times do not allow for the luxury of musical time consumption. Wherever time allows, however, mainly in the vigils of the monasteries on Mount Athos, the turn toward well-accepted compositions of mathēmata was firm — Bereketēs' Θεοτόκε Παρθένε, the pasapnoaria of Iohannes Trapezountios, Koukouzelēs' Ἄνωθεν οἱ προφῆται and the mathēmata of the Polyeleos. This praxis, still intact today, is the best declaraton of the diachronic character of the Byzantine melos, as well as the coexistence of the old and new compositions of the same *Psaltikē*, the same chant tradition, both Byzantine and post–Byzantine.

99   For the main mathēmata of Matthaios Batopedēnos, cfr the autograph Athos, Panteleimon 1207 (Typikarion Koimeseos Theotokou 6) from the year 1837 (Stathēs 1975–: Vol. 2, 644–646). With regards to the mathēmata of Iohasaph Dionysiatēs, cfr especially the autograph Athos, Dionysiou 707 (year 1858) from fol. 239r on, for stichēra and tetraēcha apolytikia and oktōēcha (Stathēs 1975–: Vol. 2, 793–795).

CHAPTER 4

The analysis of the mathēmata

THE TEXT OF THE MATHĒMATA

In the previous chapter the texts used for the mathēmata were briefly discussed. An in-depth analysis will be presented here in this chapter.

It should be noted that on the very basis of their text, the mathēmata are divided into two large categories: (a) the category of the psalmic mathēmata, which are mainly found in the *Papadikē*, and (b) the category of the mathēmata proper [*kath' heauto*], whose text is not psalmic.

First Category: psalmic verses

A distinction must be made at the outset within this category with regards to the following texts: (i) the verses of the Ninth Biblical Ode, usually the last two —Καθεῖλε δυνάστας ἀπὸ θρόνων and Ἀντελάβετο Ἰσραὴλ παιδὸς αὐτοῦ (Luke 1:52–53, 54–55, respectively); (ii) the Trisagion hymn —Ἅγιος ὁ Θεός, ἅγιος ἰσχυρός, ἅγιος ἀθάνατος, ἐλέησον ἡμᾶς; (iii) the cherubic hymn —Οἱ τὰ χερουβὶμ μυστικῶς εἰκονίζοντες and the hymns used instead of the cherubic hymn —Σιγησάτω πᾶσα σάρξ βροτεία, Νῦν αἱ δυνάμεις τῶν οὐρανῶν, and Τοῦ δείπνου σου τοῦ μυστικοῦ; as well as (iv) some psalmic communion hymns like Ποτήριον σωτηρίου, Εἰς πᾶσαν τὴν γῆν, Σωτηρίαν εἰργάσω and others for the feasts throughout the liturgical year, some of which are the product of early Christian hymnographic activity, with the exception of those lifted out of the New Testament, like Σῶμα Χριστοῦ, Ὁ τρώγων μου τὴν σάρκα and Ἐπεφάνη ἡ χάρις. Although they are not all texts derived from the Psalms of David, they are examined, however, with the psalmic mathēmata since they belong to this category organically.

1. Kalophonic verses of the vespers

The foremost kalophonic verses of the vespers were lifted from Psalm 2: Ἵνα τί ἐφρύαξαν ἔθνη [*Why do the heathen rage*], either as it stands or in some anagrammatical form, verse by verse, consecutively, or with references to other verses; nevertheless, in either form the verses of the second Psalm served as the text for kalophony.[1] After the kalophonic verses of Psalm 2, psalmic mathēmata for the vespers include the prokeimena called *dochai*. Each prokeimenon verse has a triple performance: (i.) it is first chanted, usually first as a half-verse in a simple style, then a second verse follows; next, (ii.) the entire first verse is chanted — this is called a small or simple *dochē*; finally, (iii.) the great and virtuosic *dochē* is added, that is, the same text of the entire verse, but with a kalophonic performance.[2] Here is a list of the virtuosic *dochai*:

a) Prokeimena for the week:

— Sunday evening: mode I plagal Ἰδοὺ δὴ εὐλογεῖτε τὸν Κύριον (Psalm 133)
— Monday evening: mode I plagal Κύριος εἰσακούσεταί μου (Psalm 4)
— Tuesday evening: mode I plagal Τὸ ἔλεος σου Κύριε καταδιώξοι με (Psalm 22)
— Wednesday evening: mode I plagal Ὁ Θεὸς ἐν τῷ ὀνόματί σου σῶσόν με (Psalm 53)
— Thursday evening: mode II plagal Ἡ βοήθειά μου παρὰ Κυρίου (Psalm 120)

---

1   Cfr Athos, Iviron 1120, fols. 70r sq. These verses and the kratēmata were transcribed into the New Method of analytical notation, mainly by Chourmouzios, included in his *Papadikē*, ΜΠΤ 703; the kratēmata are found in the *Kratēmatarion*. Before Chourmouzios there exist *exēgēseis* by Petros Byzantios; cfr Athos, Xeropotamou 318.
2   In Athos, Iviron 1120, fols. 223r sq.: *Archē tōn mikrōn kai megalōn dochōn tēs holēs hebdomados*.

— Friday evening: mode barys Ὁ Θεὸς ἀντιλήπτωρ μου εἶ (Psalm 58)
— Saturday evening: mode II plagal Ὁ Κύριος ἐβασίλευσεν (Psalm 92)

b) Prokeimena for the Week of New Creation (Pascha week):

— Sunday of Pascha, in the evening: mode barys: Τίς Θεὸς μέγας (Psalm 76)
— Monday in the Week of New Creation: mode barys Ὁ Θεὸς ἡμῶν ἐν τῷ οὐρανῷ (Psalm 113)
— Tuesday in the Week of New Creation: mode IV plagal Φωνῇ μου πρὸς Κύριον (Psalm 141)
— Wednesday in the Week of New Creation: mode barys Ἐνώτισαι ὁ Θεὸς τὴν προσευχήν μου (Psalm 54)
— Thursday in the Week of New Creation: Mode barys Ἀγαπήσω σε, Κύριε, ἡ ἰσχύς μου (Psalm 17)
— Friday in the Week of New Creation and in the Great Fast: mode IV plagal Ἔδωκας κληρονομίαν (Psalm 61)
— Saturday in the Week of New Creation and in the Great Fast: mode IV plagal Μὴ ἀποστρέψῃς[3] (Psalm 68)

The melos of these mathēmata are handed down anonymously.[4] Among them, however, the prokeimena of the week are kalophonically composed eponymously by various authors.[5]

Also belonging to the prokeimena group are the *epiphōnēmata*. These are the Ἐνεδύσατο Κύριος (Psalm 92) with epiphōnēma Δύναμιν ἐνεδύσατο καὶ περιεζώσατο by Iohannes Koukouzelēs or Δύναμιν ἐνεδύσατο ὁ Κύριος καὶ περιεζώσατο by Gregorios Alyatēs, and others.

---

3   Cfr Thodberg and Hamann 1966: 15–16.
4   The *exēgēsis* into the New Method by Chourmouzios is in MΠT 703, fols. 410v–490v.
5   Athos, Iviron 1120, fols. 223r–235v. Daniel hieromonachos composed these at the beginning of the eighteenth century, as did Theodoulos monachos; cfr Chatzegiakoumes 1975: 289; Stathēs 1975–.

2. Kalophonic verses of the orthros

Psalmic verses used as text for mathēmata in the orthros include the following:

a) The Prokeimena

The prokeimena, especially those for Sunday; again, that is the virtuosic *dochē Ἀνάστηθι, Κύριε, ὁ Θεός μου* and the kalophonic composition by Iohannes Koukouzelēs with epiphōnēmata *Ἐξομολογήσομαί σοι, Κύριε* with epiphōnēma the *Ὑψωθήτω ἡ χείρ σου, Κύριε, μὴ ἐπιλάθῃ τῶν πενήτων σου εἰς τέλος.*

b) The pasapnoaria of the heōthinon Gospel

After the *anabathmoi* [Hymns of Ascent] in the Office of the Orthros [Matins] and their prokeimenon there is a second prokeimenon, the *Pasa pnoē* —Πᾶσα πνοή [*Let every thing that hath breath praise the Lord*] (Ps. 150); the contemporary anagram — *Praise, every thing that has breath, the Lord* — has its roots in this ancient tradition, which is borne witness to by the antiphon of the domestikos *ἀπ' ἔξω· Τὸν Κύριον.*[6] After that kalophony is made the verses of Psalm 148 are harmoniously anagrammatized. Preceding them the final verse of Psalm 150, *Πᾶσα πνοὴ αἰνεσάτω τὸν Κύριον*, is used, and this was determinate in the creation of the title *pasapnoarion* (plural, *pasapnoaria*). Many kalophonic pasapnoaria have been handed down from the fifteenth century on.

c) The Megalynaria and the kalophonic verses of the Ninth Biblical Ode

From the six verses of the Ninth Biblical Ode (Luke 1:46–55, 68–79) the last two are of interest to us: *Καθεῖλε δυνάστας ἀπὸ θρόνων* and *Ἀντελάβετο Ἰσραὴλ παιδὸς αὐτοῦ.* Especially from the seventeenth century on, these verses

---

6   Athos, Iviron 1120, fol. 388r.

were the texts for kalophonic mathēmata (except for the above exceptions).[7] Before this century, and especially in the fourteenth and fifteenth centuries, the verse Μεγαλύνει ἡ ψυχή μου τὸν Κύριον with the troparion Ἄξιόν ἐστιν ὡς ἀληθῶς was also kalophony texts anagrammatized in various ways and enriched with encomiastic hymnographic phrases.[8] It was in this way that the ground was prepared for the 'free' verse, not conforming to normal metres, encomiastic at first; afterwards, dekapentasyllabic verse was gradually introduced. These *theotokia*, however, are the megalynaria that belong to the collection of theotokia mathēmata along with the other megalynaria verses unique to the Ninth Ode of the canons for the feasts.

d) The kalophonic verses of the Polyeleoi

From the verses of the Polyeleoi, the last verses of Psalm 134 Δοῦλοι Κύριον [*Ye servants of the Lord*] (Ps. 134:15–21) were especially used for kalophony, specifically:

— Τὰ εἴδωλα τῶν ἐθνῶν, ἀργύριον καὶ χρυσίον
— Στόμα ἔχουσι καὶ οὐ λαλήσουσι
— Ὀφθαλμοὺς ἔχουσι καὶ οὐκ ὄψονται
— Ὦτα ἔχουσι καὶ οὐκ ἐνωτισθήσονται
— Οὐδὲ γάρ ἐστι πνεῦμα ἐν αὐτοῖς
— Ὅμοιοι αὐτοῖς γένοιντο οἱ ποιοῦντες αὐτά
— Οἶκος Ἰσραήλ, εὐλογήσατε τὸν Κύριον
— Οἶκος Ἀαρών, εὐλογήσατε τὸν Κύριον
— Οἶκος Λευί, εὐλογήσατε τὸν Κύριον
— Οἱ φοβούμενοι τὸν Κύριον, εὐλογήσατε τὸν Κύριον
— Εὐλογητὸς Κύριος ἐκ Σιὼν
— Δόξα Πατρί· Καὶ νῦν καὶ ἀεί.

7 For example, Athos, Iviron 1120, fol. 616v.
8 In Athos, Iviron 1120, fol. 588r–616v there are many instances; at fol. 616v: Τιμιωτέρα ἡ ἁγιορείτικη· ἄλλαγμα εἰς τὴν θ´ ᾠδήν, Καθεῖλε δυνάστας· ἦχος πλ. β´ νενανω Ἐξαπέστειλε κενούς.

Of significance here is the fact that short dekapentasyllabic compositions were added to these verses when the need arose to emphasize a particular feast, i.e., of the Theotokos, the Forerunner, the Apostles, the Archangels, the Transfiguration, some Hierarch or Great Martyr, the Elevation of the Precious Cross, as well as the Nativity of Christ, the Theophany, the Ascension and Pentecost. In the section of Polyeleoi[9] in Manuel Chrysaphēs' *Papadikē*, we find these types of dekapentasyllabic compositions.

From the other Polyeleoi Psalms, specifically, Ἐξομολογεῖσθε τῷ Κυρίῳ (Psalm 135), Ἐπὶ τῶν ποταμῶν Βαβυλῶνος (Psalm 136), Λόγον ἀγαθόν (Psalm 44) and the other *eklogai*, very few verses are put to kalophonic melodies, even during the post-Byzantine period.[10]

e) The asmatic trisagia of the Great Doxology[11]

3. *Kalophonic verses and kalophony of the Divine Liturgy*

While keeping the previously mentioned distinction between psalmic and non-psalmic texts in mind, kalophony in the Divine Liturgy concerns the following types:

— the Δύναμις, Ἅγιος ὁ Θεός and those compositions used 'instead of' during the Great Feasts of the Lord, specifically, the Δύναμις, Ὅσοι εἰς Χριστόν and Δύναμις, Τὸν Σταυρόν Σου προσκυνοῦμεν;

---

9   Notice in Athos, Iviron 1120, fol. 241r–293r.
10   Cfr Chaldaiakēs 2003.
11   These compositions can also be found in Athos, Iviron 1120, fols 413v–414v. The custom continued into the post-Byzantine period and noteworthy kalophonic compositions are found after the great doxologies of the seventeenth and eighteenth century. And due to the lengthiness of these compositions we have the wondrous syntomon asmatic trisagia for the Doxology by Petros Bereketēs (Stathēs 1971: 234), which can be found published in Euthymiades 1978: Vol. 2, 517–525.

The analysis of the mathēmata

— the allelouiaria[12] chanted after the Epistle reading. We have many such important *kat' ēchon* compositions by both the old and new teachers;[13]
— the cherubim hymns, and especially the asmatic and *dichora*,[14] as well as those used instead of the cherubic hymn, *Νῦν αἱ δυνάμεις, Τοῦ δείπνου σου τοῦ μυστικοῦ, Σιγησάτω πᾶσα σάρξ βροτεία*;[15]
— the koinonika (communion hymns) for Sundays (*Αἰνεῖτε*, Psalm 148:1), for weekdays and the annual feasts, as well as the *Γεύσασθε* (Psalm 33: 9a) of the Liturgy of the Presanctified Gifts; and
— the kalophonic verses at the end of the Divine Liturgy — mainly the *Πληρωθήτω τὸ στόμα μου αἰνέσεώς σου Κύριε* and *Εἴη τὸ ὄνομα Κυρίου εὐλογημένον*,[16] as well as the *Εὐλογήσω τὸν Κύριον ἐν παντὶ καιρῷ*.

One interesting instance of kalophony also exists, which is alternated in the manuscripts by scribes between the Orthros and the Divine Liturgy. It is the Amōmos (Psalm 118) of the funeral service in its various forms. In saying 'its various forms' is meant the existence of a different order of the Amōmos for the burial of the Divine Body of our Lord (Service of Good Friday) and the Dormition of the Theotokos (15 August) and for the Forerunner and Baptist, John — 'εἰς τὴν θεόσωμον ταφὴν τοῦ Κυρίου

---

12 Cfr Dmitrievski and Orthodox Eastern Church 1965: Vol. III, 3, 424; Thodberg and Hamann 1966: 11.
13 Athens, Nat. Libr. 2458, fol. 161v: *To cheroubikon asmatikon, apo chorou, ēchos b*; cfr Athens, Nat. Libr. 2406, fols. 239r sq. The flow of an asmatic cheroubikon is interesting from the perspective that it provides performance data, sometimes *apo chorou* or *eita ho monophōnarēs, anaphōnei ho domestikos*, and *kai legei kratēma hoion thelei ho domestikos* (Athos, Philotheou 122, fols. 203–206). D. Conomos comments, 'What may have been quite an early setting (the ascriptions ἀσματικὸν and παλαιὸν testify to this) has emerged in the 14th and 15th century Byzantine musical manuscripts as a Kalophonic potpourri with internal alternatives, interpolated kratemata and soloistic coloratura' (Conomos 1972: 123 sq.).
14 Cfr Athos, Philotheou 137 (beginning of the seventeenth century), in which are three *dichora* cheroubika and one other by Kosmas monachos Baranēs, with the addition of explanatory verses.
15 Cfr Karagounēs 2003.
16 Athos, Iviron 1120, fols. 526χv and 565χr.

ἡμῶν Ἰησοῦ Χριστοῦ καὶ εἰς τὴν κοίμησιν τῆς ὑπεραγίας Θεοτόκου καὶ εἰς τὸν Πρόδρομον'[17] — a different order of the Amōmos for the funeral of a lay person — 'εἰς κοιμηθέντας'[18] — and, finally, another order for monastics — 'εἰς τοὺς κοιμηθέντας μαναχούς'.[19] Kalophony in the first instance occurs in the prologoi *Μακαρίζομέν σε* — depending on the circumstance — and in the kratēmata.[20] In the second circumstance, kalophony occurs in some verses from the first two *staseis* and especially in the so-called *archontika*[21] of the third stasis, i.e. the verses beginning with Ἄρχοντες κατεδίωξάν με δωρεάν (Ps. 118:161). Such kalophonic verses were composed by many of the old teachers. Also of interest is the asmatic *nekrōsimon* [for the dead] Trisagion chanted as the body is carried out, especially owing to the use of the supplicatory melos of the nenanō phthora.

The best known and most widely disseminated is the kalophony of the Amōmos, which occurs in the troparia of the eight modes attributed to Iohannes Damascenus[22] after the stichologia of the third stasis, Ποία τοῦ βίου τρυφή; Οἴμοι, οἶον ἀγῶνα ἔχει ἡ ψυχή; Πάντα ματαιότης τὰ ἀνθρώπινα; Ὄντως φοβερώτατον, and Θρηνῶ καὶ ὀδύρομαι, as well as the oikos Αὐτὸς μόνος ὑπάρχεις ἀθάνατος,[23] chanted after the koukoulion the same kontakion attributed to Anastasius the monk, Μετὰ τῶν ἁγίων ἀνάπαυσον.[24]

The contritional character of these troparia is the inspiration for this large group of nekrōsima, at the start, dekapentasyllabic troparia and by

17 Athos, Iviron 1120, fol. 414v.
18 Athos, Iviron 985 (year 1425, autograph of Manouel Blatēros), fol. 104r.
19 Athos, Iviron 985, fol. 116v. On fol. 124r there is the following note: *kai euthys ginetai prologos, ēchos b, kalophōnikon Tēn aeimakariston*.
20 Cfr the previous note. In this codex, Athos, Iviron 985, fol. 130r, the following: Τοῦτο ψάλλεται δίχορον, μέλος θεσσαλονικαῖον, ἦχος τρίτος Αἱ γενεαὶ πᾶσαι; on fol. 130v, again, the same, mode IV Τὴν ὄντως Θεοτόκον, with kratēma, in other words, a kalophonic usage; cfr Iviron 1120, fols. 425v–433v.
21 The nekrōsimon Trisagion is noteworthy from the perspective that it is the oldest melos which was first to receive *exēgēsis* into the analytical notation by Balasios hiereus, around the year 1670; cfr Athos, Iviron 1250, fols. 211v–212v.
22 Cfr Zerbou 1862: 413–414.
23 Cfr Athos, Iviron 1120, fols. 474v–478v.
24 Cfr Trypanis 1968: 51–63.

extension the so-called and more generally referred to *katanyktika* dekapentasyllabic troparia, which will be discussed below.

Second Category: the mathēmata, proper

It has already been mentioned that the text of this second category of the mathēmata proper is not psalmic, not even New Testamental; the text of these mathēmata proper are purely hymnographic. Depending on the service, troparia are selected from texts of the various forms of Byzantine hymnography.

1. Kontakia or Oikoi

In the beginning the entire Akathistos Hymn was used, specifically, the prooimion or koukoulion (Τῇ ὑπερμάχῳ στρατηγῷ) and the twenty-four oikoi. Beyond the masterful composition of the entire Akathistos by Iohannes Kladas the lampadarios there exist many oikoi, often the same ones, used as mathēmata, composed by various old writers, but also by the new composers of the seventeenth through eighteenth centuries (see above pp. 120 sq.).

In addition to the Akathistos as mathēma, kontakia of the great feasts were also put to melody, albeit on a limited scale because of the primary position held by the stichēra idiomela.

2. Heirmoi or Troparia of the Canon Odes

In comparison to the kontakia, the heirmoi and troparia of the odes of the canons were also favourite texts. The heirmoi of the ninth ode of the canons of the feasts of the Theotokos were chosen, as well as the great feasts of the Master, the Nativity and Theophany, either with their characteristic verses or without. The second position of prominence is held by the heirmoi of the Resurrectional canon Ἀναστάσεως ἡμέρα[25] and some of its troparia, followed by some other heirmoi[26] and canon troparia, mainly theotokia, whose texts were all used for kalophonic composition.[27]

The distinction should now be made between kalophonic heirmoi as mathēmata and kalophonic heirmoi as a new, unmixed type of the seventeenth and eighteenth centuries. The new type of kalophonic heirmos contains only one element of kalophony, the kratēma. They utilized no anagrams, neither the widened nor lengthened embellished melos. The embellishment found in this type does not exceed the general parameters of the heirmologic melos, but is simply varied and 'beautified' [*kallōpizetai*], remaining within the bounds of the syntomon melodic development; it is always applied to a single word or to one complete phrasal period expressed by the text.

3. Stichēra idiomela

The most customary case for mathēmata is the one using as its text a single stichēron idiomelon. The Byzantine and post-Byzantine writers for kalophonic composition used almost half the number of stichēra idiomela

---

25 Athos, Iviron 964 from the year 1562 contains all the collected kalophonic heirmoi for Pascha; cfr fol. 230r: Τῇ ἁγίᾳ καὶ μεγάλῃ Κυριακῇ τοῦ Πάσχα, εἱρμοὶ καλοφωνικοὶ ψαλλόμενοι ὕστερον εἰς τὴν καταβασίαν, ποίημα κὺρ Μανουὴλ μαΐστορος τοῦ Χρυσάφου. Other compositions follow.

26 In the *Mathēmatarion*, Athos, Docheiariou 379 (first half of seventeenth century) we find: fol. 105r, Ἑιρμοὶ καλοφωνικοί, ἔντεχνοι, ψαλλόμενοι εἰς τὴν ἑορτὴν τῶν Χριστουγέννων, ποιηθέντες παρὰ κὺρ Μανουὴλ τοῦ Χρυσάφη, ψάλλονται ἀργὰ καὶ ἴσα; fol. 156r, Μηνὶ Μαρτίῳ κε΄ [...], εἱρμοὶ ἀσματικοὶ ποιηθέντες παρὰ κὺρ Μανουὴλ τοῦ Χρυσάφη· ψάλλονται καὶ τῆς Ἀκαθίστου; fol. 313r, Εἱρμοὶ ψαλλόμενοι τῇ ἁγίᾳ καὶ μεγάλῃ Κυριακῇ τοῦ Πάσχα, ποίημα τοῦ Κλαδᾶ' [and many others]. Cfr Stathēs 1975–: Vol. 1, 529, 531, 537. In the Athos, Koutloumousiou 457 (2nd half of fourteenth century), fol. 345v: ʽεἱρμοὶ ψαλλόμενοι εἰς τὴν μνήμην τοῦ ἁγίου Δημητρίου, ποίημα τοῦ πρωτοψάλτου Θεσσαλονίκης κὺρ Μανουὴλ τοῦ Πλαγίου· ἦχος β΄ Δεῦτε λαοί; cfr Athos, Iviron 973, fols. 68r and Iviron 1120, fol. 631v sq.

27 In Chourmouzios' eight-tomed *Mathēmatarion* catalogued below it is easy to distinguish the heirmoi and canon troparia.

The analysis of the mathēmata

from the *Sticherarion*. This large number of kalophonic idiomela resulted in the creation of a specialized hymnbook, the *Kalophonic* or *Kalophōnon Sticherarion*, i.e., the *Mathēmatarion*, as we have seen. The kalophonic idiomela follow the order of the feasts of the menologion from 1 September to 31 August, as well as the *Triōdion* and *Pentēkostarion*.

From more than one, and often many, of the stichēra idiomela of the vespers, litē, aposticha and ainoi of the feasts of the Master, the Mother of God and of the celebrated Saints, the best and most eloquent are chosen, the lyric or dramatic, as well as those that are easily distinguished into rhythmic feet. These preferences resulted in the composition of many of these stichēra and, at times, select rhythmic feet and anagrams were composed from them by many teachers. This selection usually occurs at the great feasts of the Lord and the feast of the sacred Forerunner. At the feasts of the Mother of God, the Akathist Hymn and the many theotokia heirmoi, i.e., the megalynaria, normally exhaust the themes. The dogmatika theotokia of the *Oktōēchos* (*Anastasimatarion*)[28] from the *Sticherarion* were primarily favoured for the feasts of the Mother of God.

4. Prosomoia: stichēra, kathismata

The stichēra prosomoia and, more rarely, the kathismata, with the exception of their theotokia, were used to a limited scale as texts for mathēmata. This is observed on the feasts of saints of later inclusion, whose services originally lacked stichēra idiomela. Usually, the preferred stichēra prosomoia and kathismata are excellent poetic texts of high quality. Prosomoia stichēra and kathismata are more common from the seventeenth century on, primarily because by this time the older teachers had already composed most of the stichēra idiomela as mathēmata.[29]

---

28 Athos, Iviron 964 (year 1562), fol. 311r: Ἀρχὴ σὺν Θεῷ ἁγίῳ τῶν δογματικῶν θεοτοκίων κατ' ἦχον'; cfr Athos, Philotheou 136 (1st half of seventeenth century), fol. 196r: Ἀρχὴ σὺν Θεῷ ἁγίῳ τῶν δογματικῶν στιχηρῶν τῆς Ὀκτωήχου· ποιηθέντα παρὰ μακαριωτάτου κυροῦ Ἰωάννου λαμπαδαρίου' [Kladas].

29 The more well-known, as far as being anthologized more often, are those by Chrysaphes the new, Ἐν φωναῖς ἀλαλάξωμεν (for the elevation of the Cross, 14 Sept.)

5. Exaposteilaria

The circumstances by which the texts of some exaposteilaria were used for the composition of mathēmata are quite rare. Mostly, some mathēmata were composed from exaposteilaria anastasima and of the Theotokos.[30]

6. Apolytikia

The apolytikia of the feasts of the Lord, formal Saint and hierarch commemorations, were widely used as texts for the composition of mathēmata, especially during the seventeenth to eighteenth centuries. Furthermore, from the end of the seventeenth century to the middle of the nineteenth century, the custom was to compose the apolytikia as *dichora* and as *tetraēcha* or *oktaēcha*, beginning from the mode proper to the apolytikion. This came about mainly due to the influence of the masterpiece *oktaēchon*, Θεοτόκε Παρθένε by Petros Bereketēs, chanted as third troparion in the service of the artoklasia belonging to the vigil. The dichora apolytikia as mathēmata[31] mainly occupy this position of the theotokion in the vigil, with very few exceptions.

7. Doxastika of the Polyeleos

The doxastika of the Polyeleos were the focus of melic embellishment from early on. The simplest type utilizes the insertion of a single kratēma after the Δόξα Πατρί and Καί νῦν, something that also occurs in the anoixantaria and *Makarios anēr*. The most artistic is the inclusion of a single triadikon troparion after the Δόξα Πατρί and a theotokion after the Καί νῦν. More

---

and Πανήγυρις φαιδρά (for the feast of St. Spyridon, 12 Dec.). Relatively well-known are also the kathismata, as mathēmata, of Petros Bereketēs, Βίον ἄϋλον (St. Catherine, 25 Nov.), Τήν ὡραιότητα τῆς παρθενίας σου (Theotokos), and Petros Peloponnēsios' Λίαν εὔφρανας (St. Euphemia, 11 July).

30 The most disseminated is Germanos Neōn Patrōn's Χρυσοπλοκώτατε πύργε.
31 These compositions are mainly for the feasts of Christmas, Theophany, Sunday of Palms, Ascension and Transfiguration.

common is the addition of new, 'free' verses and, subsequently, of dekapentasyllabic verses, especially theotokia encomia to the Theotokos. On occasion, the older composers lifted these theotokia verses from the last verses of the Polyeleos by the older composers, i.e., Οἶκος Ἀαρών ... Τοὺς ὀρθοδόξους ἄνακτας ....[32]

8. New compositions with 'free' verse of metrical improvisation

There exist a small number of mathēmata, especially theotokia makaristaria, which incorporate verse not conforming to established metres. These verses follow immediately after the introduction of a mathēma utilising a phrase from the Ἄξιόν ἐστι — Σὲ μεγαλύνομεν, Τὴν κλίμακα τὴν οὐράνιον,[33] etc. Their symbolisms were borrowed from various types of hymnography.

Certainly, this reference to and independence from, the established forms of hymnography, as well as the accompanying freedom and poetic inspiration, was instrumental in the introduction of the dekapentasyllabic verse.

9. Phēmai and polychronismoi

The acclamation of the civil and ecclesiastical authorities, patriarchs, archbishops, bishops, metropolitans, abbots, is an ancient practice in the Church. Compositional texts used for the ecclesiastical authorities include the following:

— Τὸν δεσπότην καὶ ἀρχιερέα ἡμῶν,
— Ἄνωθεν οἱ προφῆταί σε προκατήγγειλαν,
— Σήμερον στολίζεται ἡ Ἐκκλησία,

---

[32] Athos, Iviron 1120, fols. 251v–253v and 275r–276v.
[33] In some Polyeleos verses, as above, can be found encomiastic or paracletic verses of metrical improvisation. Specifically, cfr Athos, Iviron 1006 (of the year 1431), fol. 65v sq. On fol. 69r: 'ποίημα τοῦ λαμπαδαρίου [Iohannes Kladas], πρὸς τὸ Οὗτος γὰρ ἐκήρυξεν, ἦχος β' Σὲ μεγαλύνομεν... Τὴν ἀπαρχὴν τῆς ἡμῶν σωτηρίας' or fol. 82v, 'ἕτερον παρόμοιον, τοῦ Κορώνη, ἦχος πλ. δ' Τὴν ἄχραντον καὶ ἄσπιλον'.

— Σήμερον φαιδρῶς προϋπαντήσωμεν,
— Ὡς ζωηφόρος, ὡς παραδείσου ὡραιότερος,[34]

also, influenced mainly by the civic polychronismoi, the

— Πολυχρόνιον ποιῆσαι Κύριος ὁ Θεός.[35]

From the many ancient polychronismoi,[36] the main form to be used and transmitted is the following:

34 In Chryasphēs the New's autograph from the year 1671, Athos, Xenophontos 128, on fol. 223v, we find: ἕτερον μάθημα, ἡμέτερον, ὀργανικόν, ὅπερ καὶ αὐτὸ γέγονε δι' αἰτήσεως [...] τοῦ πατριάρχου κυρίου κὺρ Νεκταρίου Ἱεροσολύμων. Ψάλλεται δὲ ἔνδον τοῦ ἁγίου καὶ ζωοποιοῦ Τάφου, ὅταν ἐνδύνουσιν (sic) τὸν πατριάρχην· ἦχος δ' [Ὡς ζωηφόρος] ὡς παραδείσου ὡραιότερος; cfr Stathēs 1975–: Vol. 2, 64. Except for the civil phemai, most are used during the bishop's preparation Kairos service before vesting for the Divine Liturgy.

35 In manuscripts from the seventeenth century on there are many polychronismoi to the patriarchs and metropolitans of various thrones. In the previously mentioned Chrysaphes the new autograph, Xenophontos 128 there are, for example, two such polychronismoi: fol. 119v, πρὸς ἔπαινον τοῦ πατριάρχου· ἦχος δ' Πολυχρόνιον ποιῆσαι ... κ. Μεθόδιον; fol. 121r, ἕτερον, ἡμέτερον εἰς τὸν θρόνον Μητροφάνους τοῦ Κυζίκου· ἦχος δ' Πολυχρόνιον. Many of these are composed by Germanos Neōn Patrōn, Balasios hiereus and nomophylax, Athanasios the Patriarch and Petros Beretekēs.

36 From the many related witnesses, the following is presented: Athos, Iviron 973 (beginning of the fifteenth century), fol. 358v: 'μετὰ δὲ τὸ λέγειν τὰ τροπάρια εἰσέρχεται καὶ ἀναβιβάζεται ὁ αὐτοκράτωρ ἄναξ ἐν τῇ προσκυνήσει αὐτοῦ· ὁ δὲ πρωτοψάλτης καὶ οἱ μετ' αὐτοῦ δομέστικοι μετὰ τῆς εὐφήμης (sic) ψάλλουσιν οὕτω τὸ τοιοῦτον στιχηρὸν' [two verses in the bottom margin in red ink, mode I Ὁ Χριστὸς ἐγεννήθη ὁ στέψας σε βασιλέα] λέγεται δὲ τρὶς ἢ καὶ πολλάκις καὶ εὐθὺς τὸ πολυχρόνιον πρὸς τὸν βασιλέα'; fol. 359r: 'τελειωθείσης δὲ τῆς προσκυνήσεως ψάλλομεν τοῦτο ἐν τῇ ἑσπέρᾳ τῆς ἑορτῆς πρὸς τὸν βασιλέα· τοῦ πρωτοψάλτου Κορώνη, παρεκβολή· ἦχος α' Πολυχρόνιον ποιῆσαι ὁ Θεός ... τὴν ἁγίαν βασιλείαν σας'. See also Athens, Nat. Libr. 2458, fol. 144r, 'Πολλὰ τὰ ἔτη τῶν βασιλέων'.
A similar rubric is given in Athos, Philotheou 122, fol. 189r, where a similar phēmē for the patriarch is to be found: Ἰωσὴφ τοῦ παναγιωτάτου καὶ οἰκουμενικοῦ Πατριάρχου πολλὰ τὰ ἔτη and ὁ δομέστικος ἔξω φωνῇ εἰς διπλασμόν, Κύριε σῶσον τοὺς βασιλεῖς, ὁ ἕτερος δομέστικος πάλιν τὸ αὐτό· ἦχος πλ. δ' Καὶ ἐπάκουσον ἡμῶν'.

— Πολυχρόνιον ποιῆσαι Κύριος ὁ Θεὸς τὸν ἐκλαμπρότατον ...[37]

The nature of the phēmai and polychronismoi is such that from early on space was left for inspiration in the form of free encomiastic expression. The absence of specific troparia for these circumstances resulted in resorting to exoteric poetry via the borrowing of metre and expression. Thus, the dekapentasyllabic verse entered the polychronismoi, sometimes as simple encomium and at other times as autonomous compositions, usually of a triadic character:

— Λόγε Πατρὸς καὶ συμφυὲς πνεῦμα, ταυτότης μία.[38]

These compositions are of great interest mostly because they unite both political and ecclesiastical leaders in their acclamation; and, in this circumstance we find ourselves enter a time in which political verse was marginally introduced into worship.

10. The dekapentasyllabic compositions

Lastly, the new dekapentasyllabic verse, the so-called *politikon* compositions, were also used as texts for the mathēmata. This circumstance, especially when the writer of the verses is also its melic composer, is distinctly interesting. Excluding a few exceptions, the dekapentasyllabic compositions are normally anagrammatized during melic composition. They are often divided into metered feet.

---

37 In Verpeaux and Codinus 1976: VI, 46 the following text is given: Πολυχρόνιον ποιῆσαι ὁ Θεὸς τὴν ἁγίαν καὶ κρατείαν βασιλείαν σας εἰς πολλὰ ἔτη; and, Πολυχρόνιον ποιῆσαι ὁ Θεὸς τὴν θεοπρόβλεπτον, θεόστεπτον καὶ θεοφρούρητον κρατείαν καὶ ἁγίαν βασιλείαν σας εἰς πολλὰ ἔτη.
38 Cfr Stathēs 1977: 255–259, 73–74, 82.

THE FORMS BASED ON CONTENT

With the exception of the psalmic mathēmata of the first large category, based on their content, these mathēmata are ordered according to the following forms of Byzantine hymnographic poetry, under the name by which they are often referred to in the manuscripts.

Triadika (triadic – trinitarian)

The troparia called *triadika* are those whose text refers to the Holy Trinity, Father, Son and Holy Spirit. Primarily, the hymns for Pentecost and the Holy Spirit have a triadic character. In the papadic genus of Byzantine melopœïa, the pre-eminent triadic hymns are the great anoixantaria, due to the addition of triadic references in each mode, i.e.,

— Ἀνοίξαντός σου τὴν χεῖρα τὰ σύμπαντα πλησθήσονται χρηστότητος· δόξα σοι ὁ Θεός. (Io. Koukouzelēs)
— Ἀντανελεῖς τὸ πνεῦμα αὐτῶν καὶ ἐκλείψουσι· Δόξα σοι Πάτερ, δόξα σοι Υἱέ, δόξα σοι τὸ Πνεῦμα τὸ ἅγιον (Io. Koukouzelēs)
— Ὁ ἐπιβλέπων ἐπὶ τὴν γῆν καὶ ποιῶν αὐτὴν τρέμειν
— Ἄναρχε Πάτερ, Υἱὲ συνάναρχε καὶ Πνεῦμα τὸ θεῖον καὶ σύνθρονον· σὲ προσκυνοῦμεν καὶ δοξάζομεν· ἐν μιᾷ θεότητι βοῶμεν, δόξα σοι ὁ Θεός[39] (Arkadios)

For this reason, the anoixantaria in many manuscripts are referred to with the characterisation, '*archē tōn triadikōn*' [beginning of the triadic].[40]

---

39 These verses were taken from an Athens codex belonging to the Institute of Byzantine Musicology 1. All the verses of the great anoixantaria have received *exēgēsis* in (Chourmouzios Chartophylax 1824: 1–36).
40 Cfr Athos, Konstamonitou 86 (1st half of fifteenth century), fol. 35v: 'Ταῦτα τὰ τριαδικὰ τοῦ λαμπαδαρίου κὺρ Ἰωάννου' (Stathēs 1975–: Vol. 1, 658); Docheiariou 341 (year 1822), fols. 1r, 6r (Stathēs 1975–: Vol. 1, 430); Panteleimon 1008 (autograph

Beyond this, all the doxastika stichēra and troparia of the odes of the canons are triadic because of the doxology *Δόξα Πατρί καί Υίῷ καί ἁγίῳ Πνεύματι*. There also exist entire canons that are triadic in nature, those chanted in the mesonyktikon [pannychis, midnight office], as well as other troparia labelled *triadika*. From the above-mentioned forms, triadic mathēmata include the following:

— the trisagios and cheroubic hymns and
— from the mathēmata proper, kontakia or triadic oikoi, heirmoi or triadic troparia of the odes, stichēra idiomela and prosomoia, the doxastika of the polyeleoi, dekapentasyllabic compositions, either autonomous or with some polychronismos.

Anastasima (resurrectional)

Anastasima mathēmata are those whose text refers to the Resurrection of the Lord. The stichēra idiomela of the *Anastasimatarion* are always resurrectional. They are also the heirmoi and troparia from the *Heirmologion* of the resurrectional canons of the *Oktōēchos* for this main day of the Lord's Resurrection, Sunday.

There also exists a small group of troparia known as the *stauroanastasima* (of the Cross and the Resurrection). Their similar characteristic is that the text of the same troparion refers to both the Lord's Cross and Resurrection together.

Dogmatika (dogmatic)

Dogmatika mathēmata are mainly the dogmatic stichēra of the *Oktōēchos* attributed by Iohannes Damascenus, and which refer to the Mother of God.

---

of Balasios), fol. 17r: 'Ἀρχὴ σὺν Θεῷ ἁγίῳ τοῦ μεγάλου ἑσπερινοῦ, ἤτοι τὰ καλούμενα τριαδικά, ἐποιήθησαν δὲ παρὰ διαφόρων ποιητῶν, πάνυ ἔντεχνα καὶ κατανυκτικά' (Stathēs 1975–: Vol. 2, 418). Also cfr Velimirović 1966b: 317–337; Williams 1972: 211–229.

In them, the Orthodox dogma is revealed and the wondrous symbolisms and types of the Old Testament regarding the holy Theotokos are woven into the texts. The basic doctrine these dogmatika hymns speak to is that of the incarnation of our Lord.

The dogmatika are anthologized in the old *Sticheraria*; the sixteen dogmatika of the modes were mainly preferred as mathēmata, i.e., the doxastika of the vespers and aposticha in the *Oktōēchos*.

Doxastika

Doxastika are mainly stichēra idiomela preceded by the verse Δόξα Πατρί καὶ Υἱῷ καὶ ἁγίῳ Πνεύματι, but their content is not of a Trinitarian character. There are three doxastika in the vespers and two in the orthros of the daily Office. The doxastika for the commemorations of saints and feasts of the Mother of God are of a festal character, and commonly make use of the salutations [χαίροις ...], praise, and invocation [σπεῦσον, ἐλθέ]. Kalophony first appeared in the doxastika of the more important feasts, especially through the introduction of ēchēmata and their division into parts for two choirs [*dichora*]. The tradition of the oktaēcha [literally, eight-mode] doxastika has its beginnings in this application; this in turn had its influence of some oktaēcha compositions in certain mathēmata, as we shall see below.

Theotokia

Generally, all the troparia in which the Theotokos is hymned, magnified, blessed, praised and glorified are called theotokia. The primary theotokia, par excellence, are all the heirmoi and troparia of the ninth odes of the canons. By extension, the final troparion of each ode is dedicated to the honour of the Theotokos.

From the stichēra idiomela and prosomoia, theotokia are those following the verse *Καὶ νῦν καὶ ἀεί* .... Beyond this, all the hymnography for the feasts of the Theotokos is considered theotokion hymnography. It follows that theotokia mathēmata are:

The analysis of the mathēmata 153

— the megalynaria and verses Καθεῖλε δυνάστας — Ἀντελάβετο Ἰσραὴλ of the Ninth Biblical Ode, and the
— kontakia or oikoi, primarily the Akathistos Hymn, stichēra idiomela and prosomoia, kathismata, the theotokia exaposteilaria, apolytikia, the theotokia Καὶ νῦν ... of the Polyeleos, encomia in free verse and the dekapentasyllabic compositions.

The theotokia can be placed into the following categories based on their content.

11. Megalynaria[41]

Megalynaria are the theotokia heirmoi and troparia of the ninth ode of the canons, when preceded by the verse Μεγάλυνον ψυχήν μου τὴν τιμιωτέραν ... or other suitable verses.[42] Megalynaria also include the many mathēmata, Ἄξιόν ἐστιν ὡς ἀληθῶς, usually with anagrams, mainly because the primary heirmos Τὴν τιμιωτέραν τῶν χερουβίμ ... ends with the word μεγαλύνομεν.

12. Encomia

As mathēmata, encomia theotokia are mainly new compositions in free or dekapentasyllabic verse. Few are classified precisely as encomia or encomiastic verses; the well-known Ἄνωθεν οἱ προφῆται by Iohannes Koukouzelēs and two other similar mathēmata by Iohannes Kladas, all based on Kladas' dekapentasyllabic Σὲ προκατήγγειλε χορὸς τῶν προφητῶν ἁπάντων, and other

---

41 The word *megalynarion* comes from the first word of the Ninth Biblical Ode, known in Latin as the *magnificat*. Mary's words begin, in Greek, μεγαλύνει ἡ ψυχή μου, utilising the verb μεγαλύνω; thus, the term *megaly-narion* is attained; cfr Mazera-Mamalē 2007.

42 'Suitable verses', according to the occasion, include the following: Ἄγγελοι τὴν εἴσοδον τῆς Παρθένου ..., or Ἄγγελοι τὴν κοίμησιν τῆς παναγνου ..., or Ἀκατάληπτόν ἐστιν ..., Θεοτόκε ἡ ἐλπίς ..., or Εὐαγγελίζου γῆ χαρὰν μεγάλην or Ὁ ἄγγελος ἐβόα ...; cfr Athos, Iviron 985 (year 1425, autograph of Manuel Blatēros), fols. 43v–62r; Iviron 974 (first half of fifteenth century), fols. 68v–82v; Athens, Nat. Libr. 2458, fol. 554r–v.

compositions like the Ἄσωμεν πάντες ἄσωμεν τὴν μόνην Θεοτόκον[43] are primarily understood as belonging to this category.

13. Staurotheotokia

This group of theotokia troparia in which the subject matter concerns the Mother of God's lament before the Cross and the Crucified One are characterized as staurotheotokia. Usually as prosomoia, they are found throughout the *Paraklētikē* in the Wednesday and Friday Office.

Leo VI Sapiens (ninth–tenth centuries) Imperator's staurotheotokia stichēra idiomela compositions[44] are famous and contained in almost all the complete old *Stichēraria*. Some of these works became the text for compositions of the kalophonic melos — i.e., mathēmata. The ideas, images, laments of the Theotokos, symbolisms and references to the human state before the Fall in Eden are most wondrously presented in Leo's stichēra idiomela, as is his tendency toward metrically free verse that would become the basis for the creation of a group of staurotheotokia mathēmata in dekapentasyllabic verse.

14. Makaristaria

Makaristaria troparia in the Amōmos to the Theotokos and the burial of the divine Body of the Lord comprise prologoi similar to the Μακαρίζομέν σε, Θεοτόκε ἁγνή ...[45] and are followed with a kratēma.

---

43 Kosmas Ibēritēs and Makedōn gives the following title, 'ἕτερον ἐκ τῶν ἡμετέρων, ἐγκωμιαστικὸν καὶ ὀκτάηχον εἰς Κυρίαν καὶ Δέσποιναν ἡμῶν Θεοτόκον' (Athos, Dionysiou 569, fol. 382v (year 1685)). Also in another of his autograph codices, the Iviron 970, fol. 266: 'ἐγγόμιον (sic) ὀκτάηχον'.

44 Leo VI Sapiens Imperator is especially known for having composed hymns for the Saturday of Lazarus (the day before the Sunday of Palms) and the feast of the Universal Exaltation of the Sacred Cross (14 September).

45 Cfr Athos, Iviron 1120, fols. 425–432r: 'ἡ καλοφωνία τοῦ Ἀμώμου· πρόλογος τοῦ [Ξένου] Κορώνη· ἦχος β' *Μακαρίζομέν σε, Τοτοτο* ...'.

15. Katanyktika

Katanyktika[46] troparia are those whose texts refer to death, the futility of earthly things, the judgement before the impartial judge and repentance, which man must pursue. These elements have the specific purpose of bringing man's soul to contrition, moving it toward repentance. There exist entire katanyktika canons, katanyktika kathismata and katanyktika stichēra, though very few have been used as texts for kalophonic composition. Instead, an entire group of new dekapentasyllabic verses were created by numerous great composers and maïstores of Byzantine melopœïa, many of which are examples of superb poetry and arrangements, according to both their words and melos.[47]

16. Nekrōsima

The stichēra, usually idiomela, that refer to death used at the end of the funeral service (Amōmos) are known as *nekrōsima*.[48] Many of these stichēra were put to melody as mathēmata and were widely disseminated.

17. Pentēkostaria

Pentēkostaria[49] are the stichēra idiomela chanted in the orthros after the first verse of the 50th Psalm. Many pentēkostaria for the commemorations of saints are idiomela from the Litē, because it is the idiomela of the litē that contains a vibrant hymnic, laudatory character. The resurrectional pentēkostarion troparion each Sunday is Ἀναστὰς ὁ Ἰησοῦς ἀπὸ τοῦ τάφου, and for the Sundays of the great Fast, Τὰ πλήθη τῶν πεπραγμένων μοι

---

46   From the Greek word κατάνυξις, meaning *contrition*; cfr Liddell *et al.* 1996: sv. κατάνυξις, 2.
47   Many of the dekapentasyllabic katanyktika have a dual character; that is, they are theotokia-katanyktika, despotika-katanyktika, etc.; cfr Stathēs 1977: 71–73, 79, 217–235 where some of the best-known are published.
48   From the Greek verb νεκρ-όω, to *mortify*.
49   The name is derived from the Greek word for the number 'fifty', *pentēkostos*.

δεινῶν.⁵⁰ The two troparia said immediately before Τὰ πλήθη, namely, Τῆς μετανοίας ἄνοιξόν μοι ... and Τῆς σωτηρίας εὔθυνόν μοι ... are also considered pentēkostaria. These texts are frequent themes for mathēmata. There are also a few pentēkostaria in the manuscripts written in free verse, or in pure dekapentasyllabic verse. This arose out of the desire to offer encomiastic glorification for the commemorated saint through the use of appropriate phrases found in the troparia of the Office.⁵¹

THE MORPHOLOGICAL TYPES OF COMPOSITION OF THE MATHĒMATA PROPER

Being now thoroughly acquainted with the genesis of Byzantine melopœïa and its categories, to which the forms of the mathēmata belong based on their contents, let us focus on the form of the mathēmata from a purely musical point of view. The purpose of our research is the morphological analysis of the mathēmata, an analysis as it concerns the structure of their compositions, as well as the distinct parts from which they are constructed. As a branch of musicology, morphology is a necessary presupposition for the understanding of a musical composition and, therefore, for the correct evaluation of melic compositions. It is, in other words, a measure by which music is artistically critiqued.

As described above, two large groups were delineated based on the poetic text of the mathēmata: first, the group of mathēmata whose text consists either of psalmic verse or of ancient Christian hymnology and

50 The term *pentēkostarion* is found often in the manuscripts. Some examples: Athos, Philotheou 125 (fifteenth century), fol. 9r: 'Τροπάρια, ἅτινα λέγονται πεντηκοστάρια· ψαλλόμενα τῇ ἁγίᾳ Τεσσαρακοστῇ, ἀντὶ τὸ Ἀναστὰς ὁ Ἰησοῦς· μίαν Κυριακὴν τὸ ἓν καὶ ἄλλην τὸ ἄλλον· ἦχος πλ. β' Τὰ πλήθη; fol. 9v: ἕτερον· ἦχος πλ. δ' Τῆς μετανοίας ἄνοιξόν μοι'.
51 Cfr Stathēs 1977: 79–80, 235–251.

The analysis of the mathēmata

second, the group of mathēmata proper, whose text is lifted from the different forms of Byzantine hymnography (oikoi, but mainly stichēra, heirmoi, etc.). The morphological analysis will be limited now only to the second group of mathēmata proper found in the *Mathēmatarion*. This is dictated for two reasons. First, these mathēmata represent the more perfected form of kalophony and, as a result, the points mentioned will generally also hold true for the other group of mathēmata. Second, in most cases the psalmic mathēmata belong to the *Papadikē* and make up the larger portion of all that resulted from melic composition. It is surely impossible to speak in morphological detail regarding every aspect of our subject; on the other hand, these different forms have already been the subjects of study by others in the field.

Again, from the *Mathēmatarion* we can distinguish between the *Oikēmatarion* — the Akathistos by Kladas — otherwise a unique codex-book, and then all the rest of the oikoi composed by other melodists also found in the *Mathēmataria*, since they normally represent a more complex form in relation to the first. The analysis of these specific mathēmata and the designation of morphological types of their compositions relates to the general form of the oikoi.

For our morphological analysis of the mathēmata, it is of crucial importance that we, as analysts, must always have before us the following three defining elements, without which kalophony does not exist:

1) the kalophonic melos, ornate and skilled;
2) the anagrams and repetitions of the text; and
3) the ēchēmata and kratēmata in the beginning or middle.

At least two of the elements are found in the mathēmata and often — at least in the anapodismoi and anagrams — all three. Fundamentally and in the simplest of circumstances, the first element is always present, the kalophonic, skilled, virtuosic melos in whose unfolding is almost always found the repetitions of both words and meanings, as well as the insertions [*parembolai*] of ēchēmata for the extending of the melody. Accordingly, even on its own the skilled melos constitutes a mathēma. The anagrams also constitute a mathēma with the skilful melos they entail. When the kratēmata are inserted into the skilled melos, either with or without anagrams, they constitute the fullest form of mathēma. However, from a morphological perspective, in and of itself a kratēma does not constitute a mathēma. When introduced into the skilled melos through two, three, or four movements — known as *staseis* — the kratēma becomes the determining factor in the identification of the mathēma type. Hence, the kratēma alone is not autonomously self-contained and does not serve as an organic necessity in the akolouthiai,[52] as it is usually *inserted* or introduced into a kalophonic composition, or, more clearly, is tacked on to the end of a single part of a kalophonic composition. It logically follows then, as a mathēma unit we understand a section of text with the kratēma that follows and never the other way around.

Consequently, a number of different structure types can be identified in the mathēmata form, whose careful study produces the following six types:

1) the simple type
2) the single-part type
3) the two-part type
4) the three-part type
5) the four-part type
6) the multi-part type

The definition of these basic underlying types or forms of mathēmata refer to the single, twofold, or threefold, etc., insertion of a kratēma into a composition and the resulting distinction of one, two, or three parts of the same piece. Since, however, as it is with all developed entities, the most fully developed form of melopœïa, i.e., mathēma, has a beginning, middle and end, the above part distinction relating to the main, middle part of a single or multi-part kalophonic composition.

A short introduction normally precedes this main, middle part, of which various types exist depending on the artisan's embellishment. In

---

52   Sometimes the indication 'εἰ βούλει λέγε κράτημα' or 'κράτημα οἷον βούλει' is found in the manuscripts, showing that the kratēma was not always necessary.

most circumstances, though, the introduction receives the melos of the paraklētikē *thesis* — expressed thus,

and which, depending on the mode in use produces a different melos, even though the basic melic shape is similar.[53] In some circumstances, this melos of the paraklētikē *thesis* is followed by a short introductory phrase on the first syllable of the poetic text. Instead of the melos of the paraklētikē *thesis*, we occasionally encounter an introductory melodic phrase that is not very long and which introduces us to the characteristic idea of the mode, often quite reminiscent of the modal enēchetic *theseis*.[54]

The following is an interesting case. After an introduction of one of the above two types, a quick ēchēma follows, that is, a melos on the first vowel of the first syllable of the text. However, this first vowel is usually pronounced using the foreign, inserted consonants χ, ν[55] and κ. Even when it develops into a kratēma, τενενα, τεριρεμ, etc., this ēchēma is understood as part of the introduction; moreover, one such introductory kratēma is clearly marked in the manuscripts as a prelude via the word *prologos*.

[53] The paraklētikē is one of the great hypostatic signs of cheironomy or aphonous signs of Byzantine notation and is used for a lengthening of the melos, as well as an imposition of an introductory melos. The *Protheōriai of the Papadikai* address its effect; cfr Chrysanthos ek Madyton 1832: § 417, 186; Gabriel hieromonachos *et al.* 1985: 290, 308, 311, 372; Karas 1933: Table IV; Stathēs 1978: 66.

[54] Cfr the introductory periods in the mathēmata *Οἱ μαθηταί σου*, *Λόγε* of Markos Korinthou and *Ἄγγελοι διηκόνουν* by Manuel Chrysaphēs in ΜΠΤ 732, 240v, and 243v, respectively, both in mode II plagal. In both cases the thesis of the paraklētikē adds an entire music period to the composition. Also compare fols. 240v and 243v in the plates below.

[55] The element used for the ν sound in these instances is not a letter of the Greek alphabet and has two forms, ꙋ and Ꙋ. ꙋ is used with the vowels α, ι, ο, ω and ου and Ꙋ with the vowels ε and αι. Their use, as with the γγ and ου is observed in manuscripts from the end of the thirteenth century, in the *enēchēmata Ananeanes* and *Neanes*. Cfr Conomos 1972: 261–268.

There are also limited instances of kalophonic stichēra where the argon stichēraric melos of the troparion is *apo chorou* [from the choir] instead of some other introduction, exactly as an introductory period and where 'kalophony is performed' [*eita ginetai kalophōnia*].[56] In any case, the occasions where one or the other type of introduction is not found in a mathēma are few.

All the mathēmata finish with a conclusion that is always the final phrase of the text and never a kratēma. The finale is counted as one of the parts of a mathēma for this reason, but is at the same time an organic and inseparable segment of the entire composition. The concluding phrase in the anagrams is either used as its starting phrase or has already been used within the composition; if something like this occurs, the melos is either completely new or at least partially varied. The final section of the kratēma in the two-part, three-part, all the way up to the multi-parted types is usually introduced before the text's final phrase. The ending that follows is either a kalophonic melos or *apo chorou*, which assumes the argon stichēraric melos. Occasionally two melē are found in this ending phrase; this is noted as *heteron telos* [another ending]. Alternatively, after the ending of the kalophonic melos, the *apo chorou* ending lifted from the *Stichērarion* is added. In these cases it is not clear if both musical periods were chanted or if one of the two were chosen for performance.

The following distinction must also be considered. *Epibolai* and *parekbolai*[57] are other elements sometimes found in the mathēmata. If they do not consist of a homogeneous continuation, that is if it is not a text — kalophonic melos on a text or kratēma on a kratēma, but a text on a kratēma or

---

56 In the kalophonic stichēron Προτυπῶν τὴν ἀνάστασιν by Theodoros Manougras in the present volume (p. 239 sq.) this very instance arises; instead of another introduction we have the *apo chorou* argon stichēraric melos followed by kalophony. In this circumstance the kalophony has its own introduction via the paraklētikē melos, followed by a melic lengthening. The reader is reminded of Chrysaphes' comment about how the composers 'took pride after not departing from the model provided by the effort of the older composers' (Manuel Chrysaphēs and Conomos 1985: 45).
57 On fol. 236r in the plates below there is an epibolē of Korōnēs, a kratēma.

The analysis of the mathēmata

a kratēma on a text — it is considered as another part of the composition and contributes to the formation of one or another mathēma type form.

To summarize, the following are easily identified. Three things can almost always be distinguished in the mathēmata: [i.] a beginning, [ii.] a middle and [iii.] an end; this would correspond to a type of [i.] introduction, [ii.] main, middle part and [iii.] ending or finale. The [i.] introduction and [iii.] ending are organic, indispensable sections of the whole composition and are not 'parts'. It is the introduction of a kratēma once, twice, three times or more that imposes the distinction into separate 'parts'. By 'part' is meant a piece of text kalophonically put to melody with the kratēma that follows.

Thus, the following is the basic diagram for the structure of the mathēmata:

> introduction + main melos [text — kratēma] + ending

If two kratēmata are inserted into the main part, the part is then divided into two: (1) 'text — kratēma' and, again, (2) 'text — kratēma'. The type created is then a two-part type. If three kratēmata are inserted we have the three-part type, if four, a four-part type, and so on.

Regarding the [i.] introduction, as illustrated above, it follows that in most cases an introduction exists; however, in rare cases we do not find an introduction. In these cases, a short ēchēma is developed, either after the introduction or on the first syllable of the text. Furthermore, the ēchēma occasionally develops into a kratēma-prologos or a kratēma is immediately introduced. This multiplicity of types of introductions makes it necessary to assign more specific morphological types. The reason for this is the following: contained within the beginning of the mathēmata, always, (a) there is or is not a short introduction (introduction A), and (b) an ēchēma or kratēma is developed from a pre-existing or not, short introduction (introduction B).

Accordingly, the following table of morphological types of mathēmata can finally be presented:

1. Simple type:
     a. only the kalophonic melos　　　　　　　(Simple A)
     b. with an ēchēma inserted　　　　　　　　(Simple B)
     c. with an ēchēma or kratēma in the beginning　(Simple C)

2. Single-part:
     a. introduction A + a single part + ending　(Single A)
     b. introduction B + a single part + ending　(Single B)

3. Two-part:
     a. introduction A + two parts + ending　(Two-part A)
     b. introduction B + two parts + ending　(Two-part B)

4. Three-part:
     a. introduction A + three parts + ending　(Three-part A)
     b. introduction B + three parts + ending　(Three-part B)

5. Four-part:
     a. introduction A + four parts + ending　(Four-part A)
     b. introduction B + four parts + ending　(Four-part B)

6. Multi-part:
     a. five or more parts (the oikoi)　(Multi-part A)
     b. the dichora　　　　　　　　　　(Multi-part B)
     c. the polyēcha　　　　　　　　　　(Multi-part C)
     d. the oktaēcha　　　　　　　　　　(Multi-part D)[58]

With the exception of the simple type, the diagram below illustrates the various types of mathēmata.

---

[58] I used abbreviations of these morphological types of the mathēmata transcribed by Chourmouzios in Part Two of the present work (πολ. α-δ, ἁπλ. α-γ, μον. α-β, διμ. α-β, τριμ. α-β, τετρ. α-β). Thus, it is possible for anyone to consult the table there for any of the mathēmata in his *Mathēmatarion*.

The analysis of the mathēmata

Table 3. Mathēmata Types.

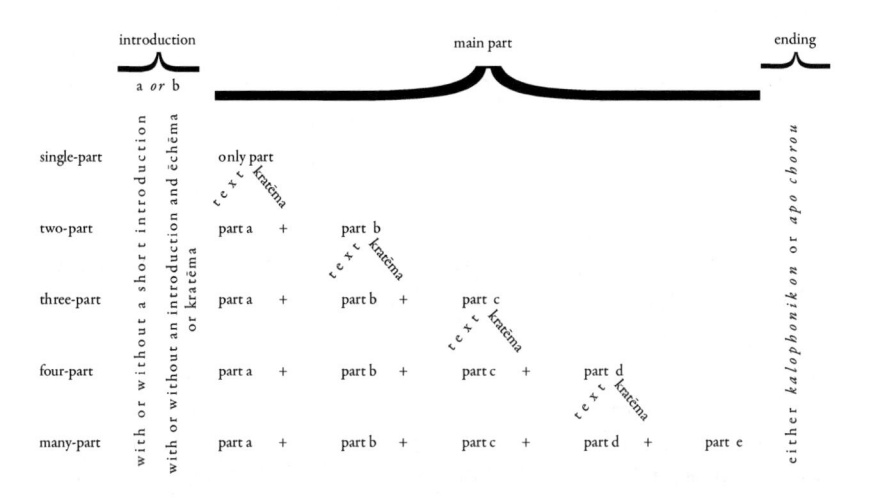

	introduction	main part				ending
	a *or* b					
single-part		only part *text / kratēma*				
two-part	with or without a short introduction	part a +	part b *text / kratēma*			either *kalophonikon* or *apo chorou*
three-part	with or without an introduction and ēchēma or kratēma	part a +	part b +	part c *text / kratēma*		
four-part		part a +	part b +	part c +	part d *text / kratēma*	
many-part		part a +	part b +	part c +	part d +	part e

These morphological types relate to the external shape of the kalophonic compositions and its architectural structure, so to speak. As learned above, it is upon this structure that kalophony is founded and constructed. I would now like to dwell on some of the esoteric consequences of kalophony, which include the melic lengthening, the development of the ēchēmata, the modulation between modes, the repetitions using the word *palin*, the enechetic supplications using *lege*, the *theseis* with which the kratēmata are initiated, and, finally, the vocal range, *ambitus* or number of voices utilized in each mode via kalophony.

The main attribute of kalophony is the melismatic style and the melic extending that results from it. Melic augmentation is achieved by the composer's persistence to accentuate a single syllable of a word or all the syllables of that word. In this way the vowels, fit where the phonetic signs are repeated. To avoid the anaesthetic and monotonous sound of the pronounced vowels, foreign consonants are introduced — χ, κ and ν; from the end of the thirteenth century, the ν sound is expressed in two ways. With the ꞁ for the vowels α, ι, ο, ω, ου and with the originally for ε and αι. Thus, the vowels are aesthetically completed, but the entire melic period is also separated into *theseis* of smaller melic periods.[59]

Especially in the introductions of the mathēmata, the development of the ēchēmata distinguish their melic elaboration in the following manner. The introduced foreign consonants, usually ν and χ, are pronounced at each vowel and not at the beginning of the melic phrase alone. It is noteworthy that the ēchēma is always analogously developed with skilled and like-sounding syllables, as in the following examples: Ἐν ... νενενεε ... εχεχε ... Ἐν Σιναίῳ τῷ ὄρει,[60] or Ἄ ... ναχαα ... ναχαα Ἅπας ἐγκωμίων,[61] or Χρυ ... υ νυχυυνυχυυ ... Χρυσοπλοκώτατε πύργε.[62]

The most necessary aspects regarding the modulations of modes using the phthorai have already been mentioned above.[63] Melic modulations can be observed in all the mathēmata, the most important being modulations from genus to genus. Through the skilled modulation of the melos from mode to mode, mainly of another genus, i.e., from a diatonic mode to a chromatic or vice versa, the composer's theoretical cultivation and knowledge of the relationships between modes and their individual characteristic musical ideas are necessary. Through this change, a transition from ethos to ethos[64] is accomplished, but also the modulation to another vocal sphere, since each mode has a specific vocal range and scope dependent on the particular plagalisation, whether it is an authentic mode or a plagal mode

---

59 A characteristic example can be observed in the Theodore Manougra's kalophōnikon stichēron published in the plates below at Τότε παραλαμβάνεις and the words παραλαμβάνεις, Πέτρον, Ἰάκωβον, Ἰωάννην (fols. 234v–235v). The small kratēmata with their melic lengthening at παραλαμβάνεις prolong the melodist's emphasis of the word and does not divide the composition into short parts.

60 ΜΠΤ 706, fol. 109r–v.

61 ΜΠΤ 706, fol. 264r–v.

62 ΜΠΤ 706, fol. 281v.

63 Cfr footnote 17 on p. 59 in the present work and Chrysanthos ek Madyton 1832: 176–177.

64 Cfr Chrysanthos ek Madyton 1832: 176–177 regarding the ethos of melopœïa: diastaltic or elevating, systaltic or depressing and hesychastic or soothing (Aristides Quintilianus 1963: I 19,20; Cleonides Mus. 1916: 13,25). The change of ethos has a direct relationship with the change in intervals, rhythm and tempo of chant.

reaching a doubling.[65] In this way, the melos is embellished, the desired emphasis of textual meanings is created and resulting in continuous pleasure to the listener, in addition to an attentive participation in the meaning of what is being chanted.

Mode I is normally expended in its expression, that is, in its *tetraphōnia* (a musical third), its *naon*, its *meson* – *barys* and its *plagal*. Mode II alternates with its plagal, embellished with temporary diatonic borrowings. Mode III alternates with the modes IV plagal and I. Mode IV alternates with its plagal and the *nenanō* melos. The plagal modes remain within their normal ranges.[66] This technique of modulations affected through the use of phthorai is wonderfully expressed by Manuel Chrysaphēs in his chapter *On Phthorai* (Manuel Chrysaphēs and Conomos 1985: 48–67).

The word *palin* is often encountered in the mathēmata and indicates the repetition of a musical period; the term can be compared to the contemporary *da capo*. The repetition, however, does not necessarily refer to the same music; for this reason we observe changes in the melos[67] or even an entirely different melos.[68] The melos that adorns this word is clearly an enechetic melos and assists in the introduction and insertion of the mode to which the mathēma belongs. The same role is played by the word *lege*, introducing a new meaning and almost always a new melic scheme.[69] Indeed, it seems to be addressed either to the domestikon or monophōnarēs,[70] requiring the use of kalophony. In the *Mathēmatarion*, however, it does not seem to have this meaning. The word's melic content is most definitely

---

65 Cfr Gabriel hieromonachos *et al.* 1985: X, 585–590.
66 Cfr Chrysanthos ek Madyton 1832: § 388, 173–174.
67 In the anagram by Iohannes Koukouzelēs Οὐρανοὶ ἔφριξαν (fols. 247v–248r below) the repetition contains a slight change in the melos. It is characteristic that other copies, such as Athos, Xenophontos 120, fol. 70χr, do not have the πάλιν and the repetition of the musical period.
68 Cfr the kalophonic repetitions in Ἄγγελοι ἐν οὐρανοῖς by Symeon Psēritzēs: πάλιν-ναχα Ἄγγελοι, or πάλιν-συνελθόντες, or πάλιν-ἀθλητικοῖς αἵμασι (Athos, Xeroponamou 120, fols. 77v, 79v, 80v).
69 In the above work a kratēma is introduced with the word *lege* (fol. 78v).
70 Cfr Conomos 1972: 306–310.

enechetic, because of this it is easily possible that it consist of a single echematic *thesis*.[71]

The composer at any point within the composition makes the introduction or insertion of kratēmata freely when they contain two, three or many parts. In the dichora, polyēcha and oktaēcha compositions, the kratēmata fulfil an entire foot or verse and full isometry is usually observed. In the single-part mathēmata types, the kratēma is introduced before the last two phrases of the text. In the two-part types, the first part is normally longer than the second. The great composers anticipate the introduction of the kratēma either through the use of the word *lege*[72] or with the isolation and related melic lengthening of the last syllable of the word where the kratēma is to begin. In this last case, they begin the kratēma with similar sounding syllables, like τετετε, if the last syllable of the word is τε,[73] or τιτιτι if it is τι, or τοτοτο,[74] or τατατα. Other times, and with great frequency, it can be preceded by a *nenanisma* νενενα or τενενα and the *teretismos* follows in the forms τιτιτι, τορροροv, τερερρε, τεριρεμ, etc.

Finally, concerning the modulation of modes, it is interesting to note here the vocal range, the *ambitus* of the mathēmata in each mode. Regarding this, hieromonachos Gabriel's teaching is clear in his *One the eight modes*, and from which we can summarily draw the following: Each mode 'has its own distinguishing idea, which appears in each mode as colour; for each mode's idea distinguishes it from the other modes' (Gabriel hieromonachos *et al.* 1985: 76,428–429). The first mode has the form of tetraphony, *mesotēta* and the so-called *naon*, that is, another two tones beyond tetraphony. The four authentic modes have as their common characteristic the

---

71 In the mathēma by Markos Korinthou Οἱ μαθηταί σου (fol. 241r below), characteristically, the word *palin* is interchanged with the enēchēma *Echenena* ... in the nenanō melos; the continuation consists of a full repetition of the text and melos: οἱ μαθηταί σου, Λόγε.
72 As in footnote 68 on p. 165.
73 As Iohannes Koukouzelēs does in his Οὐρανοὶ ἔφριξαν at the word τότε (ΜΠΤ 732, fol. 250r).
74 The kratēma by Korōnēs in the kalophonic piece by Manougras adapts to the syllable –το in ἐπεσκέπετο (ΜΠΤ 732, fol. 236r).

The analysis of the mathēmata

fact that they advance another three tones and have tetraphony. 'Again, another common element in them is the making of mesoi. They are called mesoi because they are found between the authentic and plagal modes. [...] From these [the authentic] the plagioi are found, which are each different from the authentic; for the ideas of the authentic are different from the ideas of the plagals and [that] the authentic advance up to three notes higher. With the plagal modes they are lower; for they advance up to three, four, five, six seven and eight intervals; at this point they stop and advance no more' (Gabriel hieromonachos *et al.* 1985: 78,453–455; 82,507–513).

Consequently, the mathēmata belonging to the authentic modes move in relatively high intervals, especially in mode IV, and those belonging to the plagal modes 'lay' [*plagiazoun*] on the lower intervals. The kalophonic compositions in the plagal modes extend within the middle range when their melos is unmixed and without phthorai. In all cases, however, the desired modulations are accomplished with the use of phthorai and, by extension, the stretching of the vocal range upwards and downwards, within which the melos progresses according to the artist's desire and technical abilities.

*

The morphological themes belonging to the mathēmata have been exhausted with all that has been said above. The morphological types, as defined and as much as they were developed, are clear and any further discussion for each is unnecessary in this context. Individually, the following points are summarized:

- The katanyktika were mainly composed using the simple type of mathēma,[75] and sometimes the second and third feet of some stichēra, as well as some old [*palaia*] compositions.

---

75   Cfr the *Mathēmatarion* of Chourmouzios, MΠT 733.

- The mathēmata with lengthy poetic texts usually[76] belong to the single-part type, and this, because two parembolai or three kratēmata would make for an extremely long arrangement.
- The majority of the oikoi of the Akathistos belong to the multi-part type, exactly because of the breadth and variety of meaning, at which point the old teachers and Iohannes Kladas, but also newer composers,[77] introduced many *staseis* of kratēmata for finer emphasis and distinction in meaning. When they are not polyēcha or oktaēcha, the dichora also contain many parts, whose number depends on the total number of verses contained in the troparion and which were normally chanted antiphonally.[78]
- The polyēcha are almost always dichora and usually tetraēcha, as are the new compositions of certain apolytikia.[79]
- Oktaēcha mathēmata, not always dichora, are largely compositions from the seventeenth and beginning of the nineteenth century. The principal compositions[80] are those by Balasios hiereus, Ἄγγελος πρωτοστάτης and Ὕψιστε πάντων ὕψιστε, and Petros Bereketēs' dichoron Θεοτόκε Παρθένε and Ψάλλοντές σου τὸν τόκον. In the nineteenth century we also discern the festal apolytikia already mentioned above[81] by Nikolaos Docheiaritēs, Matthaios Batopedēnos, Iohasaph Dionysiatēs,

---

76 Kalophonic composition with the imposition [*epibolē*] of a single kratēma, but in the middle, they were classified as 2-part compositions mainly because the text receiving the kalophonic melos is very long.
77 Cfr above, p. 120.
78 The primary *dichora* are the three doxastika from the Ninth Hour of Christmas, Theophany and Holy Saturday, as well as the artistic [*entechnon*] Τῇ ὑπερμάχῳ of the Akathistos. In these instances, instead of kratēmata we have ēchēmata and not even that in the Τῇ ὑπερμάχῳ.
79 Cfr footnote 99 above, p. 134.
80 Noteworthy oktaēcha mathēmata in the *Papadikē* are the following: the *hymnodikon* (Athos, Iviron 951, fol. 40v) pasapnoarion by Klement hieromonachos of Lesbos, the theotokion by Kōnstantinos of Ankialus Τὴν ὄντως Θεοτόκον, and Damianos Batopedinos' Ἄξιόν ἐστιν (Ioannēs Lampadarios and Stephanos Domestikos 1850–1851: Vol. II, 509–523).
81 Cfr footnote 99 above, p. 134.

as well as the *Ρόδον τὸ ἀμάραντον* by Chourmouzios Chartophylax.[82] In the multi-part compositions there also exists an introduction [*eisagōgē*], usually the melos of the paraklētikē *thesis* in mode I and *telos thesis*, which in the oktaēcha belong to the first, initial mode used by the particular composition.

By the grace of God, this much[83] was discovered through the examination of the eidos and structures of the mathēmata of Byzantine ecclesiastical melopœïa.

---

82   Cfr Grēgorios Prōtopsaltēs 1834: 394–403.
83   It is natural that every detail of the topic of the musical setting of each and every mathēma has not been exhausted. This could be a matter of special investigation and study in and of itself, given the opportunity. In the present work an attempt was made to define a framework in which a taxonomy of the mathēmata could be attained to classify the manifestations of an elevated art form, the Psaltic Art [*Psaltikē*]. For the complete comprehension of this art form and its creations, according to Gabriel hieromonachos, *habitus* [*hexis*] is necessary. 'Of course, without the experience of Psaltikē one cannot well understand this (Gabriel hieromonachos *et al.* 1985: X, 586–587).

PART TWO

Incipits and texts

CHAPTER 5

Incipits of the Anagrams and mathēmata in the Mathēmatarion transcribed by Chourmouzios

INTRODUCTORY NOTE

'Chourmouzios Chatophylax and Grēgorios lampadarios–protopsaltes are the two music teachers and benefactors of the nation' (Chrysanthos ek Madyton 1832: ϛ´)[1] who, immediately after the reformation of the notational system for Byzantine Music and the resulting New Method of analytical notation in 1814, undertook the huge task of transcribing the manuscript tradition into the analytical notation, this major offshoot of Byzantine and Post-Byzantine melopœïa. Unfortunately, Grēgorios died young, in 1821, leaving behind 18 manuscripts of exegetical labour.[2] Chourmouzios was blessed to live longer, until 1840; for the duration of approximately twenty-five years, devotedly working night and day, he passed down thirty-four multi-folio manuscript codices in which are preserved the truly momentous repertory of Byzantine and Post-Byzantine melopœïa transcribed into the New Method. Today, these codices are preserved in the Manuscripts Department of the National Library of Greece, in Athens.

Directly relating to the present discussion of the anagrams and mathēmata of the Psaltic Art of the Byzantine period chiefly, but also the post-Byzantine, detailed knowledge is invaluable; herein lies the value of the analytical transcription *exēgēseis* passed down to us in the New Method by these *exēgētai* and *didaskaloi*, Chourmouzios and Grēgorios. The list of

---

1 Regarding these personalities, cfr Chatzegiakoumes 1975: 282–286, 389–391; Papadopoulos 1890: 329–332; Stathēs 1975–: Vol. 2, ια´-ιε´.
2 Cfr Stathēs 2007.

heading and *incipits* below is provided as an important resource for those engaged in the study of *Mathēmatarion* and Byzantine kalophony.

Turning to the exegetical work of Chourmouzios Chartophylax, we come to the realisation that almost half of the bulk of his exegetical work is dedicated to the *Mathēmatarion*. Twelve and a half of Chourmouzios' autograph manuscripts contain kalophonic compositions — anagrams, anapodismoi, and mathēmata — works of the old and new composers. From these codices, eight are of great importance, making up the eight-tome *Mathēmatarion* of the old composers (fourteenth through fifteenth centuries), i.e., the codices of the collection of the Metochion of the All-holy Sepulchre in Constantinople [*Metochion tou Panagiou Taphou* (MΠT)] Mss. 727–734. Chourmouzios generated his *Mathēmatarion* by collecting the compositions from the many manuscript *Mathēmataria*, taking great care to include every composition, which he accomplished to a great degree. Unfortunately, however, Chourmouzios did not fully succeed in doing so; specifically he did not have the time to perform the *exēgēseis* of all the mathēmata of the newer teachers, those of the seventeenth and eighteenth centuries. In the *Mathēmatarion* of the *Papadikē* preserved in MΠT 706 and 722, he included the theotokia mathēmata, as well as the festal mathēmata. These were followed by the more eloquent kratēmata and placed in a special unit at the end of MΠT 722; these last kratēmata were carefully selected from the works of the older and newer (seventeenth-century) composers. We come across compositions by Chrysaphēs the new, Balasios hiereus and Germanos Neōn Patrōn, but only a small fraction of the actual mathēmata produced by these newer composers. Chourmouzios made an exception for the work of Petros Bereketēs, all of whose works he transcribed and included in the second half of MΠT 712 — the *Hapanta*. Finally, in MΠT 713–714 he included the *Oikēmatarion* containing the entire Akathistos by Iohannes Kladas and some oikoi by Manuel Chrysaphēs, Iohannes Koukouzelēs and Balasios hiereus.

In these twelve and a half codices is contained, then, the repertory of the form of the *Mathēmatarion* of Byzantine and post-Byzantine melopœïa, the category of the authentic mathēmata transcribed into the New Method. Below is the analytical description of these codices, except for the *Oikēmatarion*, revealing the richness of the kalophonic output of the Byzantine and post-Byzantine composers. The consecutive numbering of the compositions in the eight-volume *Mathēmatarion* is my own, while Chourmouzios does number the compositions in codices 706 and 722. Also of my own addition is the parenthetic description of the morphological type to which each mathēma belongs; this is, of course, in accordance to the types discussed in Chapter IV.

So that we have a complete picture of the mathēmata transcribed into the New Method, we add that the two-volume *Oikēmatarion* contains the following oikoi.

> Athens, Nat. Libr. ΜΠΤ 713, fols. 1r–484r, Ἄγγελος πρωτοστάτης up to Σῶσαι θέλων τὸν κόσμον of Iohannes Kladas' Akathistos; cod. ΜΠΤ 714, fols. 1r–85r, Τεῖχος εἶ τῶν παρθένων up to Ὦ πανύμνητε μῆτερ by Iohannes Kladas. Following, on folios 85v–261r are included the oikoi (fol. 85r) by Manuel Chrysaphēs, Ἄγγελος πρωτοστάτης; (fol. 112v) by the same Chrysaphēs, Βλέπουσα ἡ ἁγία; (fol. 128v) Ἤκουσαν οἱ ποιμένες; (fol. 146v) Ὦ πανύμνητε μῆτερ; (fol. 161v) by Iohannes Koukouzelēs, Γνῶσιν ἄγνωστον γνῶναι; (fol. 179v) also by Koukouzelēs, Θεοδρόμον ἀστέρα; (187v) by Balasios hiereus, Ἄγγελος πρωτοστάτης; (fol. 206v) also by Balasios, Πᾶσα φύσις ἀγγέλων.

Except for these mathēmata proper, Chourmouzios also created transcriptions of the majority of the other kalophonic compositions from the *Papadikē*, i.e., the psalmic mathēmata, kalophonic verses, prokeimena, trisagia, cheroubika and koinonika, which he included in his three-volume *Papadikē* (ΜΠΤ 703–705) and the *Hapanta* of Petros Bereketēs (ΜΠΤ 712). In his *Papadikē*, Chourmouzios combined the most artistic compositions of the old and new composers. The general scheme followed by these codices of the *Papadikē* creates the following units:

> Codex Athens, Nat. Libr. ΜΠΤ 703 (year 1818): (fols. 227v–347r) kalophonic verses from the second Psalm, put to melody by various composers (15 verses) —(fols. 410v–490r) prokeimena for the entire week, called *dochai; pany dyskola* [according to the epiphōnēmata of Koukouzelēs' Ἐνεδύσατο ὁ Κύριος (fol. 442r); and, Ἐξομολογήσομαί σοι Κύριε, (fol. 457v); and, the kallōpismos by Manuel Chrysaphēs Ὁ Κύριος ἐβασίλευσε, τεριρεμ (fol. 449r); and, Iohannes Koukouzelēs, annagram from the Θεοτόκε Παρθένε, chanted in the artoklasia; Mode I, tetraphōnos Κεχαριτωμένη χαῖρε (fol. 490r)].

> Codex Athens, Nat. Libr. ΜΠΤ 704: (fols. 13v–153v) Polyeleoi, (fols. 153r–197r) pasapnoaria kat' ēchon, by various poets, (fols. 199v–215r) *Timiōterai* kat' ēchon,

(fols. 255v–264r) asmatika trisagia, (fols. 264v–289r) various polychronismoi, (fols. 289r–345v) the Divine Liturgy of Chrysostom — trisagia, cheroubika.

Codex Athens, Nat. Libr. ΜΠΤ 705 (year 1829): (fols. 1r–77v) cheroubika, (fols. 78r–224v) Sunday, weekday and festive communion hymns, (fol. 224v) *thessalonikaion Εὐλογήσω τὸν Κύριον*, (fol. 225r) by Nikephoros Ēthikos, mode I *Κε Εἴη τὸ ὄνομα Κυρίου*, and the same hymn by (fol. 226r) Manuel Chrysaphēs — mode II plagal nenanō, (fol. 227r–v) *palaion* mode IV plagal and Gabriel of Anchialus, mode II plagal nenanō.

Regarding the exegetic work of Grēgorios lampadarios, later protopsaltes, as it relates to the *Mathēmatarion* type, let it be said here that it includes all the mathēmata by Petros Bereketēs. These are contained in Gregory's autograph manuscript Athens, Nat. Libr. ΜΠΤ 754 (years 1817–1818), along with some mathēmata by old and new composers included in the volume of his *Mathēmatarion* of the *Papadikē*, published as volume 3 of the four-volume *Pandektē* published in the year 1851 (Ioannēs Lampadarios and Stephanos Domestikos 1850–1851).

ΜΠΤ 727: MATHĒMATARION (VOLUME I)

370 + i–iv folios

The first three-fifths of fol. 1r were left unused to receive the epititlos and title, which were never added. The indication for the first kalophonic stichēron of the Indiction (1 September) is also missing.

1. 1r [... ἦχος α΄] *Ἐπέστη ἡ εἴσοδος* (2-part B)

2. 9v Ἕτερον στιχηρὸν εἰς τὴν αὐτὴν ἑορτήν, κὺρ Ἰωάννου μαΐστορος τοῦ Καλλίστου, ἐκαλλωπίσθη δὲ παρὰ κὺρ Ἰωάννου μαΐστορος τοῦ Κουκουζέλου· ἦχος πλ. α΄ *Σὺ βασιλεῦ ὁ ὢν καὶ διαμένων* (single B)

3. 14v Δεύτερος πούς· ἦχος πλ. β΄ *Τοὺς πιστοτάτους βασιλεῖς* (2-part A)

4. 21r Ἕτερον στιχηρὸν εἰς τὸν ἅγιον Συμεών, μελισθὲν παρὰ κὺρ Βαρθολομαίου· ἦχος β΄ *Τὸ μνημόσυνόν σου* (single B)

Incipits of the Anagrams and mathēmata in the Mathēmatarion 177

5. 26v Δεύτερος πούς· ἦχος πλ. β΄ *Εἰ καὶ μετέστης ἐξ ἡμῶν* (2-part A)

6. 32r Ἕτερον στιχηρὸν εἰς τὸν αὐτὸν ἅγιον, κὺρ Ἰωάννου πρωτοψάλτου τοῦ Γλυκέος· ἦχος β΄ *Ἡ τῶν λειψάνων σου θήκη* (2-part A)

7. 36r Ἰωάννου λαμπαδαρίου τοῦ Κλαδᾶ· ἦχος β΄ *Ἀξίως ἀγάλλεται* (single A)

8. 37v Δεύτερος πούς· ἦχος δ΄ *Ἔχων οὖν πρὸς Κύριον* (single B)

9. 41v Ἕτερον στιχηρὸν εἰς τὸν αὐτὸν ἅγιον· κὺρ Μανουὴλ τοῦ Χρυσάφου καὶ μαΐστορος· πλ. Β΄ *νενανω Θεία χάρις* (single B)

10. 49r εἰς τὰς β΄ Σεπτεμβρίου, μνήμη τοῦ ἁγίου καὶ ἐνδόξου μεγαλομάρτυρος Μάμαντος· στιχηρὸν Ἰωάννου μαΐστορος τοῦ Κουκουζέλη· ἦχος β΄ *Νέον φυτόν* (single B)

11. 54r Δεύτερος πούς· ἦχος πλ. β΄ *Διὰ μαρτυρίου εὐλόγησέ σε* (2-part B)

12. 58r Ἕτερον στιχηρὸν εἰς τὸν αὐτὸν ἅγιον· κὺρ Μανουὴλ μαΐστορος τοῦ Χρυσάφου· ἦχος δ΄ *Δεῦτε συμφώνως* (single B)

13. 65v εἰς τὰς γ΄ Σεπτεμβρίου. Μνήμη τοῦ ἁγίου ἐνδόξου ἱερομάρτυρος Ἀνθίμου ἐπισκόπου Νικομηδείας· στιχηρὸν κὺρ Ἰωάννου μαΐστορος τοῦ Κουκουζέλου· ἦχος πλ. β΄ *Ἱερεὺς ἐννομώτατος* (3-part B)

14. 72r εἰς τὰς η΄ Σεπτεμβρίου. Ἰωάννου μαΐστορος Κουκουζέλη· ἦχος δ΄ *Ἡ παγκόσμιος χαρά* (3-part B)

15. 81v Ἕτερον [...] Μανουὴλ Χρυσάφου· ἦχος δ΄ *Στεῖρα ἄγονος* (single B)

16. 88v Δεύτερος πούς· ἦχος α΄ *Οὐκέτι γυναῖκες* (single A)

17. 94v Ἕτερον [...] τοῦ Ἀβασιώτου, ἐκαλλωπίσθη δὲ παρὰ κὺρ Ἰωάννου μαΐστορος τοῦ Κουκουζέλη· πλ. β΄ *Σήμερον ὁ τοῖς νοεροῖς* (3-part B)

18. 102v Ἀναγραμματισμὸς ἀπὸ τὸ αὐτὸ σιχηρὸν [...], τοῦ Ἰωάννου Κουκουζέλη· ἦχος πλ. β΄ *Ἐξ ἀκάρπου γὰρ ρίζης* (sinlge-part A)

19. 106v Τὸ αὐτὸ στιχηρὸν [...] καὶ παρὰ Ἰωάννου Κλαδᾶ· ἦχος πλ. β΄ *Σήμερον ὁ τοῖς νοεροῖς* (single B)

20. 111v Δεύτερος πούς· ἦχος β΄ *Ἐξ ἀκάρπου γὰρ ρίζης* (single B)

21. 115v Ἕτερον [...] κὺρ Γερμανοῦ, ἐκαλλωπίσθη δὲ παρὰ Ἰωάννου τοῦ Κουκουζέλου· ἦχος πλ. β΄ *Αὕτη ἡ ἡμέρα Κυρίου* (single A)

22. 119v Τὸ αὐτὸ στιχηρόν, εἰς τὴν αὐτὴν ἑορτήν, καλλωπισθὲν παρὰ τοῦ Κορώνη. ἦχος πλ. β΄ *Αὕτη ἡ ἡμέρα Κυρίου* (2-part A)

23. 124v Δεύτερος πούς· ἦχος πλ. β΄ *Καὶ ἡ κατ' ἀνατολὰς πύλη* (2-part A)

24. 130v Ἀναγραμματισμὸς ἀπὸ τὸ αὐτὸ στιχηρὸν [...], τοῦ ἐν ἱερομονάχοις κὺρ Γρηγορίου ἐκ τῆς Σηλυβρίας· ἦχος πλ. β΄ νενανω *Μόνη καὶ μόνον εἰσάγουσα* (single A)

25. 137r Ἕτερον στιχηρὸν [...], Ξένου τοῦ Κορώνη· πλ. β΄ *Σήμερον στειρωτικαὶ* (single B)

26. 142r Δεύτερος πούς· ἦχος β΄ *Ἐμφανίζουσα τῷ κόσμῳ* (single B)

27. 144v Ἕτερον [...], Ἰωάννου τοῦ Κλαδᾶ· πλ. δ΄ *Δεῦτε ἅπαντες πιστοί* (single A)

28. 154v Ἕτερον [...], Μανουὴλ τοῦ Χρυσάφου· πλ. δ΄ *Ἐν εὐσήμῳ ἡμέρᾳ* (single B)

29. 163r Πεντηκοστάριον εἰς τὴν αὐτὴν ἑορτήν· κὺρ Νικηφόρου τοῦ Ἠθικοῦ· ἦχος α΄ *Νοερῶς οἱ προφῆται* (single A)

30. 168r Σεπτεμβρίου ιγ΄, τὰ ἐγκαίνια τῆς Χριστοῦ ἀναστάσεως. Τελεῖται δὲ ἡ τοιαύτη ἀκολουθία καὶ εἰς ἑτέρους ναούς, κατὰ τὸν καιρὸν ὃν ἐθρονίσθη ὁ εἰρημένος ναός, καὶ ἐν τῷ σεβασμίῳ ναῷ τοῦ Προδρόμου τῆς Πέτρας· στιχηρὸν τοῦ Ἠθικου· ἦχος α΄ πα *Ἄρατε πύλας* (multi-part *dichoron*) Ἤχημα ἐκτενὲς (fol. 169v) «οἱ ἐκτὸς» *Ἄρατε πύλας* — (fol. 171r) «οἱ ἐντός, πρῶτον ἠχίζει ὁ δομέστικος καὶ οἱ ἐκτὸς λέγουσι τὸ αὐτό· ἦχος α΄ *Ανανα* (ēchēma) —*Τίς ἐστίν* —(fol. 172v) «καὶ πάλιν οἱ ἐκτός· ὁ δομέστικος ἠχίζει· ἦχος α΄ πα» *Ανανε* ... (ēchēma) —(fol. 173v) «ἄλλο» *Αχαανε* (ēchēma) — (fol. 174r) «ὅλοι» *Κύριος τῶν δυνάμεων* —(fol. 175r) «ἡνωμένοι ὅλοι», ἦχος α΄ *Ἄρατε πύλας* «ἐκ τρίτου» —(fol. 175r) «εἰσέρχονται γοῦν ἐν τῷ ναῷ καὶ λέγουσι τὸ ἀπολυτίκιον, καὶ τελεῖται ἡ θεία Λειτουργία».

31. 175r Τοῦ αὐτοῦ [Νικηφόρου Ἠθικοῦ]· ἦχος δ΄ Δι *Ὡς τοῦ ἄνω στερώματος* (with ēchēma *αγια ... αναχα*, thrice)

32. 179v Ἀντὶ χερουβικοῦ τοῦ Σιγησάτω, καὶ κοινωνικοῦ, τὸ αὐτὸ ἦχος πλ. δ΄ *Κύριε ἠγάπησας εὐπρέπειαν*

33. 181v Ἕτερον [κοινωνικὸν] τοῦ αὐτοῦ· ἦχος πλ. α΄ *Εἰς μνημόσυνον*

34. 183r Τῇ αὐτῇ ἡμέρᾳ στιχηρὸν τοῦ ἐγκαινιασμοῦ· κὺρ Νικηφόρου τοῦ Ἠθικοῦ· ἦχος β΄ βου *Τὸν ἐγκαινισμὸν τελοῦντες* (simple A)

35. 187r Σεπτεμβρίου ιδ΄. Ἡ ὕψωσις τοῦ τιμίου καὶ ζωοποιοῦ Σταυροῦ· στιχηρὸν κὺρ Ἰωάννου τοῦ Γλυκέος· ἦχος β΄ βου *Σύ μου σκέπη κραταιὰ* (single B)

36. 192r Ἀναγραμματισμὸς ἀπὸ τὸ αὐτὸ στιχηρόν, τοῦ μαΐστορος κὺρ Ἰωάννου τοῦ Κουκουζέλη· ἦχος πλ. β΄ *Ἵνα πίστει καὶ πόθῳ* (single A)

37. 196r Ἕτερον στιχηρὸν [...], τοῦ Θαλασσινοῦ· ἦχος πλ. β΄ *Σήμερον ξύλον ἐφανερώθη* (4-part B)

Incipits of the Anagrams and mathēmata in the Mathēmatarion 179

38.	204v	Ἀναγραμματισμὸς ἀπὸ τὸ αὐτὸ στιχηρόν· Ἰωάννου μαΐστορος τοῦ Κουκουζέλη· ἦχος πλ. β΄ *Διὰ πιστῶν βασιλέων* (single B)
39.	209r	Ἕτερον στιχηρὸν [...], Μανουὴλ μαΐστορος τοῦ Χρυσάφου· ἦχος πλ. δ΄ *Ὅνπερ πάλαι Μωσῆς* (single B)
40.	217v	Πεντηκοστάριον εἰς τὴν αὐτὴν ἑορτήν, παλαιόν· ἦχος α΄ *Παρακοὴ καὶ συμβολὴ* (simple A)
41.	220v	Ἕτερον σιχηρὸν [...], Ἰωάννου πρωτοψάλτου τοῦ Γλυκέος· ἦχος δ΄ *Χριστοῦ σταυρὸς τετραμερὴς* (single B)
42.	224v	Ἕτερον [...], Ξένου τοῦ Κορώνη· ἦχος πλ. δ΄ *Ξύλον ἐξόριστον Ἐδὲμ* (single A)
43.	231r	Ὠιδὴ θ΄, εἰς τὴν αὐτὴν ἑορτήν, κὺρ Γερασίμου ἱερομονάχου τοῦ Χαλκεοπούλου· ἦχος πλ. δ΄ *Μυστικὸς εἶ Θεοτόκε* (single A)
44.	236v	Σεπτεμβρίου ιε΄, τοῦ ἁγίου καὶ ἐνδόξου μεγαλομάρτυρος Νικήτα· στιχηρὸν τοῦ Γλυκέος· πλ. δ΄ *Τῆς νίκης ἐπώνυμος* (multi-part A)
45.	245v	Σεπτεμβρίου ις΄, μνήμη [...] ἁγίας Εὐφημίας· στιχηρὸν τοῦ Γλυκέος· ἦχος πλ. β΄ *Ἐκ δεξιῶν τοῦ σωτῆρος* (3-part B)
46.	255r	Ἀναγραμματισμὸς ἀπὸ τὸ αὐτὸ στιχηρὸν εἰς τὴν αὐτὴν ἁγίαν, μελισθεὶς παρὰ κὺρ Ἰωάννου λαμπαδαρίου τοῦ εὐαγοῦς βασιλικοῦ κλήρου, τοῦ ἐπιλεγομένου Κλαδᾶ· ἦχος πλ. β΄ νενανω *Αὐτῆς ταῖς ἱκεσίαις* (single B)
47.	260v	Ἕτερον στιχηρὸν [...], παρὰ κὺρ Δημητρίου Μαρκοπούλου, ἐκαλλωπίσθη δὲ παρὰ κυρίου Μανουὴλ μαΐστορος Χρυσάφου· πλ. δ΄ *Πᾶσα γλῶσσα κινείσθω* (3-part B)
48.	271v	Ἕτερον [...], Νικηφόρου Ἠθικοῦ· πλ. δ΄ *Πᾶσα γλῶσσα κινείσθω* (3-part B)
49.	281v	Σεπτεμβρίου κε΄, μνήμη τῆς ὁσίας [...] Εὐφροσύνης· στιχηρὸν μελισθὲν παρὰ κὺρ Ξένου τοῦ Κορώνη· ἦχος β΄ βου *Τὸ καθαρὸν τῆς ἁγνείας σου* (2-part B)
50.	291r	Ἀναγραμματισμὸς ἀπὸ τὸ αὐτὸ στιχηρὸν [...], Κωνσταντίνου δομεστίκου τοῦ Μαγουλᾶ· πλ. β΄ νενανω *Ἀλλ' αἴτησαι εἰρήνην* (single B)
51.	296v	Ἀναγραμματισμὸς ἀπὸ τὸ Καθαρὸν τῆς ἁγνείας σου· ἦχος πλ. β΄ νενανω *Ἔλαθες τοῦ Βελίαρ* (single B)
52.	300r	Σεπτεμβρίου κς΄, ἡ μετάστασις τοῦ ἁγίου [...] Ἰωάννου τοῦ Θεολόγου· στιχηρὸν [...] τοῦ Γλυκέος· ἦχος α΄ *Ἐξ ὧν ἡ Ἐκκλησία* (single B)
53.	306r	Δεύτερος πούς· ἦχος α΄ *Ἐξ ὧν ἡ Ἐκκλησία* (single B)
54.	310r	Ἕτερον στιχηρὸν [...], Ξένου Κορώνη· ἦχος β΄ *Τὸν υἱὸν τῆς βροντῆς* (single B)

55. 315r Δεύτερος πούς· ἦχος β΄ *Τὸν ἠγαπημένον Ἰωάννην* (single B)

56. 320r Ἕτερον στιχηρὸν [...] μελισθὲν παρὰ κὺρ Νικηφόρου τοῦ Ἠθικοῦ· ἦχος β΄ *Τὴν τῶν ἀποστόλων ἀκρότητα* (single B)

57. 325r Ἕτερον στιχηρὸν [...], παρὰ τοῦ μαΐστορος κὺρ Ἰωάννου τοῦ Κουκουζέλη· ἦχος β΄΄ *Θεολόγε παρθένε* (2-part B)

58. 330r Ἕτερον στιχηρόν, παλαιόν· ἦχος δ΄ *Ἀναπεσὼν ἐν τῷ στήθει* (3-part B)

59. 337v Ἀναγραμματισμὸς ἀπὸ τὸ αὐτὸ στιχηρὸν [...] παρὰ μαΐστορος κὺρ Ἰωάννου τοῦ Κουκουζέλη· ἦχος πλ. Β΄΄ *Ἐν ἀρχῇ ἦν ὁ λόγος* (2-part A)

60. 343v Ἕτερον στιχηρὸν [...] Μανουὴλ τοῦ Χρυσάφου· ἦχος δ΄ *Ἀναπεσὼν ἐν τῷ στήθει* (single B)

61. 350r Ἕτερον στιχηρὸν [...], Γερμανοῦ μοναχοῦ· πλ. β΄ *Ἀπόστολε Χριστοῦ* (single B)

62. 354r Δεύτερος πούς· ἦχος πλ. β΄ *Τὸ ἐν ἀρχῇ τρανώσας* (single B)

63. 359v Ἀναγραμματισμὸς ἀπὸ τὸ αὐτὸ στιχηρὸν [...], Κωνσταντίνου τοῦ Μαγουλᾶ· πλ. β΄ *νενανω Παρρησίαν ἔχων* (single B)

64. 365r Ἕτερον στιχηρὸν [...] ἐμελίσθη παρὰ τοῦ Καμπάνη· ἦχος πλ. δ΄ *Εὐαγγελιστὰ Ἰωάννη* (single B)

ΜΠΤ 728: MATHĒMATARION (VOLUME II)

349 + i–iii folios

Μαθηματάριον τόμος δεύτερος, ἐξηγηθέντος παρὰ Χουρμουζίου διδασκάλου καὶ Χαρτοφύλακος τῆς τοῦ Χριστοῦ Μεγάλης Ἐκκλησίας. Μὴν Ὀκτώβριος, εἰς τὴν α΄, τοῦ ἁγίου ἐνδόξου ἀποστόλου Ἀνανίου, καὶ τοῦ ὁσίου πατρὸς ἡμῶν Ῥωμανοῦ τοῦ μελῳδοῦ.

65. 1r Στιχηρόν, Νικηφόρου τοῦ Ἠθικοῦ· ἦχος πλ. δ΄ *Μαθητὰ τοῦ σωτῆρος* (single A)

66. 5v Ὀκτωβρίου β΄, τοῦ ἁγίου [...] Κυπριανοῦ· στιχηρόν, Μανουὴλ τοῦ Χρυσάφου· ἦχος β΄ *Τὸν φωστῆρα τὸν θεολαμπῆ* (single A)

67. 12r Δεύτερος πούς· ἦχος πλ. β΄ *Μετ᾽ ἀγγέλων γὰρ ἀγάλλεται* (single B)

68.	17r	Ὀκτωβρίου γ΄, τοῦ ἁγίου [...] Διονυσίου τοῦ ἀρεοπαγίτου. Στιχηρὸν ὃ ψάλλεται καὶ εἰς πάντας ἱερομάρτυρας, ἐμελίσθη δὲ παρὰ κὺρ Μανουὴλ τοῦ Χρυσάφου· ἦχος πλ. δ΄ *Ἐν ἱερεῦσι καὶ μάρτυσι* (single B)
69.	23r	Ὀκτωβρίου ς΄, τοῦ ἁγίου [...] ἀποστόλου Θωμᾶ, μελισθὲν παρὰ κὺρ Φιλίππου τοῦ Γαβαλᾶ· ἦχος α΄ *Χριστῷ ἠκολούθησας* (single B)
70.	29v	Ὁ δεύτερος πούς· ἦχος πλ. β΄ *Ὅθεν γενόμενος* (single B)
71.	31r	Ἕτερον στιχηρὸν [...], Ξένου τοῦ Κορώνη· πλ. β΄ *Ὡς ὑπηρέτης τοῦ Λόγου* (single A)
72.	35r	Ὁ δεύτερος πούς· ἦχος πλ. β΄ *Ὅθεν τῇ σαγήνῃ* (single B)
73.	38v	Ὀκτωβρίου ζ΄, τῶν ἁγίων [...] Σεργίου καὶ Βάκχου· στιχηρὸν μελισθὲν παρὰ κυρίου Ἀνδρέου τοῦ Σιγηροῦ, ἐκαλλωπίσθη δὲ καὶ ἐπλατύνθη παρὰ κυρίου Μανουὴλ τοῦ Χρυσάφου· ἦχος γ΄ *Ἤ τί καλόν, ἤ τί τερπνόν* (single B)
74.	43r	Ὁ δεύτερος πούς· ἦχος δ΄ *Οὕς γὰρ ἡ δύσις ἀδελφοὺς* (single B)
75.	47v	Ἕτερον στιχηρὸν [...] παρὰ τοῦ Κοντοπετρῆ· ἦχος δ΄ *Σέργιος καὶ Βάκχος* (single B)
76.	53r	Ὀκτωβρίου η΄, τῆς ὁσίας μητρὸς ἡμῶν Πελαγίας· στιχηρόν, ὃ ψάλλεται καὶ εἰς τὴν ὁσίαν Μαρίαν τὴν Αἰγυπτίαν, μελισθὲν παρα κὺρ Ἰωάννου τοῦ Γλυκέος καὶ πρωτοψάλτου· ἦχος δ΄ *Ὅπου ἐπλεόνασεν ἡ ἁμαρτία* (single B)
77.	56v	Ποὺς [β΄]· ἦχος γ΄ *Ἐν προσευχαῖς καὶ δάκρυσι* (single B)
78.	58v	Ποὺς [γ΄]· ἦχος β΄ *Καὶ τὸ τέλος εὐπρόσδεκτον* (simple C)
79.	60v	Ὀκτωβρίου ιβ΄, τῶν ἁγίων μεγάλων μαρτύρων Πρόβου, Ταράχου καὶ Ἀνδρονίκου· στιχηρὸν ὃ ψάλλεται καὶ εἰς ἑτέρους μάρτυρας ἡνωμένους, καὶ εἰς τοὺς ἁγίους τεσσαράκοντα μάρτυρας· ἐμελίσθη παρὰ κὺρ Μανουὴλ τοῦ Χρυσάφου· ἦχος δ΄ *Στρατευθέντες τῷ Χριστῷ* (single B)
80.	67v	Ὁ δεύτερος πούς· ἦχος β΄ *Πρόβε, τὸ κλέος* (single B)
81.	71v	Ὀκτωβρίου ιδ΄ [...], Ξένου τοῦ Κορώνη· ἦχος πλ. δ΄ *Τὰ θύματα τὰ λογικὰ* (single B)
82.	77r	Ὁ δεύτερος πούς· ἦχος γ΄ *Διὸ ταῖς εὐχαῖς αὐτῶν* (single B)
83.	80r	Ὀκτωβρίου ιη΄, τοῦ ἁγίου [...] εὐαγγελιστοῦ Λουκᾶ· στιχηρὸν μελισθὲν παρὰ τοῦ Θαλασσινοῦ· ἦχος πλ. β΄ *Πάνσοφε ἁλιεῦ* (single B)
84.	85r	Ὀκτωβρίου ιθ΄, τοῦ ἁγίου [...] Ἀνδρέου τοῦ ἐν Κρήτῃ· στιχηρόν, τοῦ Ἠθικοῦ· ἦχος πλ. β΄ *Σήμερον ἁγιάζει* (single B)

85. 90r   Ὁ δεύτερος πούς· ἦχος β´ *Ποιμένες σὺν ὁσίοις* (single B)

86. 94r   Ἕτερον στιχηρὸν εἰς τὸν αὐτὸν ἅγιον· ψάλλεται δὲ καὶ εἰς τὸ ἅγιον Στέφανον τὸν νέον καὶ Θεόδωρον τὸν Στουδίτην, ἐμελίσθη δὲ παρὰ κυρίου Μανουὴλ τοῦ Χρυσάφου· ἦχος α´ *Εὐφραίνεται σήμερον* (single B)

87. 100r Ὁ δεύτερος πούς· ἦχος γ´ *Ὁ τῶν ὁσίων καὶ τῶν δικαίων* (single B)

88. 104v Ὀκτωβρίου κβ´, τοῦ ἁγίου [...] Ἀβερκίου· στιχηρὸν, ἦχος γ´ *Ἀρχιερεῦ ὅσιε* (single B)

89. 108v Ὀκτωβρίου κγ´, εἰς τὴν ἑορτὴν τοῦ ἁγίου [...] ἀποστόλου Ἰακώβου τοῦ ἀδελφοθέου· στιχηρὸν Ξένου τοῦ Κορώνη· ἦχος πλ. β´ *Αἵματι τοῦ μαρτυρίου* (single B)

90. 113r Πούς δεύτερος· ἦχος πλ. β´ *Ὅθεν ὑπὸ Ἰουδαίων* (single B)

91. 116r Ὀκτωβρίου κδ´ [...] τοῦ ἁγίου Ἀθανασίου πατριάρχου Κωνσταντινουπόλεως· στιχηρὸν Ξένου τοῦ Κορώνη· ἦχος πλ. β´ *Ἀθανάσιε πάτερ* (single B)

92. 120r Δεύτερος πούς· ἦχος πλ. β´ *Τῶν φιλτάτων σου τέκνων* (single B)

93. 125r Ὀκτωβρίου κζ´, εἰς τὴν ἑορτὴν τοῦ ἁγίου καὶ ἐνδόξου μεγαλομάρτυρος καὶ ἐν θαύμασι περιβοήτου Δημητρίου τοῦ μυροβλήτου· στιχηρὸν τοῦ Καμπάνη, ἐκαλλωπίσθη δὲ παρὰ τοῦ Γλυκέος· ἦχος α´ *Εὐφραίνου ἐν Κυρίῳ* (3-part B)

94. 130v Δεύτερος πούς, ἐκαλλωπίσθη δὲ παρὰ τοῦ Κορώνη· ἦχος γ´ *Δημήτριον τὸν πανένδοξον* (single B)

95. 136v Ἕτερον στιχηρὸν [...], Ἰωάννου τοῦ Κουκουζέλη· ἦχος γ´ *Δημήτριον τὸν πανένδοξον* (single A)

96. 139v Ἀναγραμματισμὸς ἀπὸ τὸ αὐτὸ στιχηρόν· Ἰωάννου μαΐστορος τοῦ Κουκουζέλη· ἦχος α´ *Ἀπόλαυε τῶν θαυμάτων* (single A)

97. 143v Εἰς τὴν αὐτὴν ἑορτήν, Φωκᾶ πρωτοψάλτου· ἦχος α´ *Τῇ τῶν ἀσμάτων τερπνότητι* (single B)

98. 146v Δεύτερος πούς· ἦχος α´ *Πρόκειται γὰρ ἡμῖν* (single B)

99. 148v Τρίτος πούς· ἦχος β´ *Καὶ γὰρ τὰς τῶν ἀνόμων* (single B)

100. 150r Ἀναγραμματισμὸς ἐκ τοῦ αὐτοῦ στιχηροῦ· Ἰωάννου μαΐστορος τοῦ Κουκουζέλη· ἦχος α´ *Καὶ τὰ νικητήρια* (single A)

101. 153v Ἕτερον στιχηρὸν, Μανουὴλ Χρυσάφου· ἦχος α´ *Τῇ τῶν ἀσμάτων τερπνότητι* (single B)

102. 159r Ὁ δεύτερος πούς· ἦχος δ´ *Καὶ γὰρ τὰς τῶν τυράννων* (single B)

Incipits of the Anagrams and mathēmata in the Mathēmatarion 183

103. 164r Ἕτερον στιχηρὸν εἰς τὸν αὐτὸν ἅγιον· μέλος Φωκᾶ μητροπολίτου Φιλαδελφείας, ἐκαλλωπίσθη δὲ παρὰ Ἰωάννου μαΐστορος τοῦ Κουκουζέλου· ἦχος πλ. δ ΄ *Ἔχει μὲν ἡ θεοτάτη σου ψυχὴ* (single B)

104. 169v Ὁ δεύτερος πούς· ἦχος γ ΄ *Ἔχει δὲ καὶ τὸ πανέντιμον* (single B)

105. 172v Τρίτος πούς· ἦχος δ ΄ *Ἔνθα προστρέχοντες* (2-part B)

106. 175v Ἕτερον στιχηρόν, Ἰωάννου μαΐστορος τοῦ Κουκουζέλη· ἦχος πλ. β ΄ *Φρούρησον πανένδοξε* (single A)

107. 178r Ἕτερον στιχηρόν, Ἰωάννου τοῦ Γλυκέος· πλ. δ ΄ *Ὁ τῆς ἀληθείας ἀήττητος* (single B)

108. 183r Ὁ δεύτερος πούς· ἦχος γ ΄ *Ὦ τερπνῆς προσενέξεως* (single B)

109. 186v Στίχοι εἰς τὸν αὐτὸν ἅγιον, ποιηθέντες παρὰ τοῦ μοναχοῦ Μόσχου, μελισθέντες δὲ παρὰ τοῦ μαΐστορος Ἰωάννου τοῦ Κουκουζέλου· ἦχος πλ. δ ΄ *Κατὰ τὴν ἀσματίζουσαν* (single A)

110. 190v Ἕτεροι στίχοι εἰς τὸν αὐτὸν ἅγιον· γράμματα καὶ μέλος Μανουὴλ τοῦ Χρυσάφου· ἦχος δ ΄ *Τὸν στρατιώτην τὸν λαμπρὸν* (single A)

111. 194v Τῇ αὐτῇ ἡμέρᾳ εἰς τὴν ἀνάμνησιν τοῦ σεισμοῦ· στιχηρὸν τοῦ Γλυκέος· ἦχος πλ. β ΄ *Φοβερός εἶ Κύριε* (simple A)

***

112. 198v Μὴν Νοέμβριος. Εἰς τὴν πρώτην, τῶν ἁγίων [...] Κοσμᾶ καὶ Δαμιανοῦ· στιχηρόν, Ἰωάννου τοῦ Γλυκέος· ἦχος β ΄ *Μαγάλων ἀξιωθέντες δωρεῶν* (single B)

113. 201r Δεύτερος πούς· ἦχος δ ΄ *Ὤφθητε ἀγγέλων συνόμιλοι* (single B)

114. 203v Ἕτερον στιχηρόν [...] παλαιόν, ἐκαλλωπίσθη παρὰ τοῦ μαΐστορος Ἰωάννου τοῦ Κουκουζέλου· ἦχος πλ. β ΄ *Ἀτελεύτητος ὑπάρχει* (2-part B)

115. 207v Ἀναγραμματισμὸς ἀπὸ τὸ αὐτὸ στιχηρὸν [...], Ἰωάννου μαΐστορος τοῦ Κουκουζέλου· ἦχος β ΄ *Τῶν ἀνιάτων ἀλγηδόνων* (single A)

116. 210v Ἕτερον στιχηρὸν [...], Μανουὴλ τοῦ Χρυσάφου· ἦχος πλ. δ ΄ *Τίς μὴ θαυμάσῃ* (single B)

117. 216v Πούς δεύτερος· ἦχος γ ΄ *Ὦ δυὰς ἁγία* (single B)

118. 221r Νοεμβρίου β ΄ [...], στιχηρὸν Νικηφόρου τοῦ Ἠθικοῦ· ἦχος β ΄ *Δεῦτε ἀγαλλιασώμεθα* (single B)

119. 224v Δεύτερος πούς· ἦχος πλ. β ΄ *Χαίροις, Ἀκίνδυνε* (single B)

120. 228v Νοεμβρίου η΄ [...], Νικηφόρου τοῦ Ἠθικοῦ· ἦχος α΄ *Ὁ ταξιάρχης τῶν ἄνω δυνάμεων* (single B)

121. 232r Ὁ δεύτερος πούς· ἦχος πλ. α΄ *Ὁ καθ' ἑκάστην μεθ' ἡμῶν* (single A)

122. 235v Ἕτερον στιχηρὸν [...]· ἦχος πλ. α΄ *Ὅπου ἐπισκιάσει* (single B)

123. 241v Ἀναγραμματισμὸς ἀπὸ τὸ αὐτὸ στιχηρὸν [...], Κωνσταντίνου τοῦ Μαγουλᾶ· ἦχος πλ. α΄ *Τῇ μεσιτείᾳ σου λυτρούμενος* (single A)

124. 246v Ἕτερον στιχηρὸν [...], θεσσαλονικαῖον· ἦχος πλ. β΄ *Συγχάρητε ἡμῖν* (single B)

125. 249v Ἕτερον μέλος, τὸ αὐτὸ στιχηρόν, πολίτικον· ἦχος πλ. β΄ *Συγχάρητε ἡμῖν* (single B)

126. 235r Ἕτερον στιχηρὸν [...], Ἰωάννου τοῦ Κουκουζέλου· ἦχος β΄ *Ὁ πρωτοστάτης γὰρ ἡμῶν* (single A)

127. 255r Ὁ δεύτερος πούς. [ἦχος β΄] *Τὴν σήμερον ἡμέραν* (single B)

128. 258v Ἀναγραμματισμὸς ἀπὸ τὸ αὐτὸ στιχηρὸν [...], τοῦ μαΐστορος· ἦχος πλ. β΄ *Σκέπασον ἡμᾶς* (single B)

129. 262r Ἕτερος ἀναγραμματισμὸς εἰς τὰ αὐτὰ γράμματα, ὅστις, ὥς φασιν, ἐστὶ τοῦ Κουκουζέλου, ἄδηλον ὅμως· ἦχος πλ. α΄ *Σκέπασον ἡμᾶς* (single A)

130. 267r Ἕτερον στιχηρὸν [...] παλαιόν· πλ. δ΄ *Ὡς ταξιάρχης καὶ πρόμαχος* (single B)

131. 273v Ἕτερον στιχηρὸν [...], Κωνσταντίνου τοῦ Μαγουλᾶ· ἦχος πλ. δ΄ *Ὡς ταξιάρχης καὶ πρόμαχος* (single A)

132. 277v Πεντηκοστάριον εἰς τὴν αὐτὴν ἑορτὴν τῶν Ἀσωμάτων· Ἰωάννου τοῦ Γλυκέος· ἦχος α΄ *Ἄρχον δυνάμεων Θεοῦ* (single B)

133. 280v Ἕτερον στιχηρὸν [...], ἦχος α΄ *Ἄρχον δυνάμεων Θεοῦ* (single A)

134. 282v Δεύτερος πούς· πλ. β΄ *Σύντριψον ἔθνη καὶ λαούς* (single B)

135. 284v Τρίτος πούς· ἦχος β΄ *Καὶ προπορεύου πρόμαχος* (singe-part B)

136. 286v Ἕτερον [...], Ἰωάννου μαΐστορος τοῦ Κουκουζέλου· ἦχος β΄ *Καὶ προπορεύου πρόμαχος* (single A)

137. 288r [Πούς]· ἦχος α΄ *Τοὺς δὲ τοῦ στέφους ἀρχηγούς* (single A)

138. 290r Ἀναγραμματισμὸς ἀπὸ τὸ αὐτὸ στιχηρὸν [...], Ἰωάννου μαΐστορος τοῦ Κουκουζέλου· ἦχος πλ. β΄ *Τοὺς ὀρθοδόξους ἄνακτας* (single A)

139. 292v Νοεμβρίου ιβ΄ [...]· στιχηρὸν Ἰωάννου μαΐστορος τοῦ Κουκουζέλου· ἦχος β΄ *Δεῦτε φιλάθλοι* (single B)

Incipits of the Anagrams and mathēmata in the Mathēmatarion 185

140. 295v   Δεύτερος πούς· ήχος πλ. β' *Διό καί καρτερικῶς* (2-part A)

141. 298r   Νοεμβρίου ιβ' [...], τοῦ Γλυκέος· ἦχος β' *Ἡ πηγή τοῦ ἐλέους* (single B)

142. 301r   Δεύτερος πούς· ἦχος β' ἐκ τοῦ Νη *Φιλευσπλάγχνῳ γὰρ στοργῇ* (single B)

143. 303r   Νοεμβρίου ιγ', ἡ κοίμησις τοῦ ἐν ἁγίοις πατρὸς ἡμῶν [...] Ἰωάννου τοῦ Χρυσοστόμου· στιχηρὸν Νικηφόρου τοῦ Ἠθικοῦ· ἦχος α' *Φωστὴρ Ἰωάννη* (single B)

144. 306r   Ὁ δεύτερος πούς· ἦχος δ' *Σύ, τοῦ παναχράντου* (single B)

145. 308v   Ἕτερον στιχηρὸν [...] παλαιόν, ἐκαλλωπίσθη δὲ παρὰ τοῦ μαΐστορος· ἦχος β' *Σὲ τὸν μέγαν ἀρχιερέα* (single B)

146. 310v   Δεύτερος πούς· ἦχος πλ. δ' *Τῆς μετανοίας τὸ κήρυκα* (2-part B)

147. 315v   Ἀναγραμματισμὸς ἀπὸ τοῦ αὐτοῦ στιχηροῦ [...], τοῦ Κουκουζέλη· ἦχος πλ. β' *Ἀνευφημοῦντες πόθῳ* (single A)

148. 319r   Ἕτερον στιχηρὸν [...], Μανουὴλ Χρυσάφου· ἦχος δ' *Πέγονας, Χρυσόστομε* (single B)

149. 324r   Ἕτερον στιχηρὸν [...], Ἰωάννου μαΐστορος τοῦ Καλλίστου· ἦχος πλ. β' *Ὅσιε τρισμάκαρ* (3-part B)

150. 329v   Ἕτερον στιχηρὸν [...] παλαιόν, ἐκαλλωπίσθη παρὰ τοῦ Κουκουζέλη· ἦχος πλ. β' *Σάλπιγξ χρυσόφωνος* (single B)

151. 332r   Ὁ δεύτερος πούς· [ἦχος πλ. β'] *Χρυσουργῶν γὰρ* (single B)

152. 334r   Ἀναγραμματισμὸς ἀπὸ τὸ αὐτὸ στιχηρὸν [...], Ἰωάννου τοῦ Κουκουζέλη· πλ. β' *Προφητικῶς γὰρ ἐξῆλθε* (single A)

153. 336v   Ἕτερον στιχηρὸν [...], Νικηφόρου δομεστίκου τοῦ Ἠθικοῦ· ἦχος πλ. δ' *Χρυσέοις ἔπεσι* (single B)

154. 339v   Ὁ δεύτερος πούς· [ἦχος πλ. δ'] *Διὸ στέφανον* (single B)

155. 341v   Ἀναγραμματισμὸς ἀπὸ τὸ Ἔπρεπε τῇ βασιλίδι τῶν πόλεων, εἰς τὸν αὐτὸν ἅγιον, Μανουὴλ τοῦ Χρυσάφου· ἦχος πλ. δ' *Χρυσολόγε καὶ Χρυσόστομε* (single A)

156. 345r   Μὴν Νοεμβρίῳ ιζ', μνήμη τοῦ ἐν ἁγίοις πατρὸς ἡμῶν Γρηγορίου Νεοκαισαρείας τοῦ θαυματουργοῦ· ἀναγραμματισμὸς ἀπὸ τὸ, Τὸν περιβόητον ἐν θαύμασι, Νικολάου ἱερέως καὶ χαρτοφύλακος Αἴνου· ἦχος δ' *Λίμνη γὰρ ἐχερσοῦτο* (single B)

ΜΠΤ 729: MATHĒMATARION (VOLUME III)

371 + i–v folios

	1r	Τόμος τρίτος τοῦ Μαθηματαρίου, ἐξηγηθεὶς ἐκ τοῦ παλαιοῦ παρὰ Χουρμουζίου διδασκάλου τῆς Νέας Μεθόδου τῆς Μουσικῆς καὶ Χαρτοφύλακος τῆς τοῦ Χριστοῦ Μεγάλης Ἐκκλησίας. Μὴν Νοέμβριος εἰς τὴν κα΄, ἡ ἐν τῷ ναῷ εἴσοδος τῆς ὑπεραγίας Δεσποίνης ἡμῶν Θεοτόκου καὶ ἀειπαρθένου Μαρίας.
157.		Στιχηρόν, Μανουὴλ τοῦ Χρυσάφου· ἦχος α΄ *Ἀγαλλιάσθω σήμερον* (single B)
158.	5v	Ὁ δεύτερος πούς· [ἦχος α΄] *Ἀγαλλιάσθω ὁ Δαβίδ* (single B)
159.	10r	Ἕτερον στιχηρὸν [...] Μανουὴλ τοῦ Χρυσάφου· ἦχος β΄ *Σήμερον τῷ ναῷ προσάγεται* (single B)
160.	14v	Ἕτερον στιχηρὸν [...], Μανουὴλ τοῦ Χρυσάφου· ἦχος δ΄ *Σήμερον ὁ θεοχώρητος ναός* (single B)
161.	19r	Ὁ δεύτερος πούς· ἦχος πλ. δ΄ *Μεθ᾽ ὧν καὶ ἡμεῖς* (single B)
162.	22r	Ἀναγραμματισμὸς ἀπὸ τὸ Σήμερον τὰ στίφη [...], Μανουὴλ τοῦ Χρυσάφου· ἦχος πλ. β΄ *Ἅπαντες οὖν χαρμονικῶς* (single B)
163.	27v	Ἕτερον στιχηρὸν [...] τοῦ Καμπάνη· πλ. δ΄ *Μετὰ τὸ τεχθῆναί σε* (2-part B)
164.	31v	Παρεκβολή, Ξένου τοῦ Κορώνη· ἦχος α΄ *Παρεγένου ἐν ναῷ Κυρίου Τοτοτο* (single A)
165.	33r	Δεύτερος πούς· ἦχος λεγετος βου *Τότε καὶ Γαβριὴλ* (single B)
166.	35r	Τρίτος πούς· πλ. δ΄ *Τὰ οὐράνια πάντα* (the kratēma is a parembolē by Kladas) (single B)
167.	38v	Ἀναγραμματισμὸς ἀπὸ τὸ αὐτὸ στιχηρὸν [...], Ἰωάννου Κουκουζέλου· ἦχος πλ. α΄ *Ἄσπιλε, ἀμόλυντε* (single A)
168.	42r	Ἀναγραμματισμὸς ἀπὸ τὸ αὐτὸ στιχηρὸν [...], Μανουὴλ τοῦ Χρυσάφου· ἦχος πλ. δ΄ *Μήτηρ Θεοῦ* (single A)
169.	46v	Ἕτερον στιχηρὸν [...], Μανουὴλ τοῦ Χρυσάφου· πλ. δ΄ *Ὁ Δαβὶδ προανεφώνει σοι* (single B)
170.	51r	Δεύτερος πούς· ἦχος δ΄ *Σήμερον ἐν τῷ ναῷ* (single B)
171.	55r	Μεγαλυνάριον εἰς τὴν αὐτὴν ἑορτὴν τῶν εἰσοδίων Ἰωάννου πρωτοψάλτου τοῦ Γλυκέος· ἦχος δ΄ *Ἄγγελοι τὴν εἴσοδον* (simple A)

172. 56v Ἕτερον μεγαλυνάριον [...], Ἰωάννου τοῦ Κουκουζέλου· ἦχος δ΄ Ἄγγελοι τὴν εἴσοδον (single B)

173. 58v Πεντηκοστάριον εἰς τὴν αὐτὴν ἑορτὴν τῶν εἰσοδίων, παλαιόν· ἦχος α΄ Εὔφραίνου Ἰωακείμ (2-part B)

174. 63r Ἕτερον πεντηκοστάριον [...], Ἰωάννου τοῦ Γλυκέος· ἦχος α΄ Τὴν πύλην, κόρη, τῆς Ἐδέμ (simple A)

175. 65v Δεύτερος πούς· ἦχος δ΄ Ἀλλ᾿ ὦ Παρθένε ἄχραντε (single A)

176. 69r Νοεμβρίου κη΄, τοῦ ἁγίου καὶ ἐνδόξου ὁσιομάρτυρος Στεφάνου τοῦ νέου· στιχηρόν, ὃ ψάλλεται καὶ εἰς πάντας τοὺς ὁμολογητάς· Μανουὴλ τοῦ Χρυσάφου· ἦχος πλ. δ΄ Τὸ κατ᾿ εἰκόνα τηρήσας (single B)

177. 73v Δεύτερος πούς· ἦχος πλ. δ΄ Διὸ παρρησίαν κεκτημένος (single B)

178. 77v Νοεμβρίου λ΄, τοῦ ἁγίου [...] Ἀνδρέου τοῦ πρωτοκλήτου· Μανουὴλ τοῦ Χρυσάφου· ἦχος α΄ Ὁ πρωτόκλητος μαθητής (single B)

179. 81r Ἕτερον στιχηρὸν [...], Μανουὴλ τοῦ Χρυσάφου· ἦχος τρίτος Τὸν συναίμονα Πέτρου (single B)

180. 85r Ὁ δεύτερος πούς· ἦχος τρίτος Τοῦ γὰρ Ἰησοῦ τὰ διδάγματα (single B)

181. 87v Ἕτερον στιχηρὸν [...], Νικηφόρου τοῦ Ἠθικοῦ· ἦχος πλ. δ΄ Τὸν κήρυκα τῆς πίστεως (single B)

182. 90v Τὸ αὐτὸ στιχηρὸν ποιηθὲν καὶ παρὰ τοῦ μοναχοῦ Κορνηλίου· ἦχος πλ. δ΄ Τὸν κήρυκα τῆς πίστεως (single B)

183. 93v Ὁ δεύτερος πούς· ἦχος δ΄ Οὗτος γὰρ τοὺς ἀνθρώπους (1-part B) «οὗτός ἐστιν ὁ Κορνήλιος ὁ ποιήσας τὸ Στόμα ἔχουσι» (note in codex)

***

184. 96v Μὴν Δεκέμβριος· εἰς τὰς δ΄, τοῦ ὁσίου πατρὸς ἡμῶν καὶ ὁμολογητοῦ Ἰωάννου μοναχοῦ καὶ πρεσβυτέρου τοῦ Δαμασκηνοῦ, καὶ τῆς ὁσίας μεγαλομάρτυρος Βαρβάρας. Στιχηρὸν τοῦ ὁσίου, ἐμελίσθη παρὰ δομεστίκου Νικηφόρου τοῦ Ἠθικοῦ· ἦχος α΄ Τὴν χεῖρα τὴν σήν, Ἰωάννη (single A)

185. 100r Δεύτερος πούς· ἦχος τρίτος Σὺ δὲ καὶ σαυτὸν (single A)

186. 103r Ἕτερον στιχηρὸν [...], Ἰωάννου τοῦ Καλλίστου, ἐκαλλωπίσθη δὲ παρὰ τοῦ μαΐστορος [Ἰω. Κουκουζέλη]· πλ. α΄ Τὴν χεῖρά σου τὴν ἐκμηθεῖσαν (single B)

187. 107r Ἕτερον στιχηρὸν εἰς τὸν αὐτὸν ἅγιον· γράμματα καὶ μέλος Μανουὴλ τοῦ Χρυσάφου· πλ. δ΄ Λαμπρῶς πανηγυρίσωμεν (single A)

188. 111r   Δεύτερος πούς· ήχος δ' *Ούτος γάρ ανεδείχθη* (single A)

189. 116v   Εις την αγίαν Βαρβάραν· τοῦ Κλωβᾶ, ἐκαλλωπίσθη δὲ παρὰ τοῦ μαΐστορος· ἦχος β' *Τὴν πανήγυριν σήμερον* (single B)

190. 120v   Δεκεμβρίου ε', τοῦ ὁσίου [...] Σάββα τοῦ ἡγιασμένου· στιχηρὸν Κορνηλίου μοναχοῦ· ἦχος πλ. β' *Ὅσιε πάτερ* (single B)

191. 123r   Πούς [δεύτερος]· ἦχος πλ. β' *Διὸ ἐν τοῖς οὐρανοῖς* (single A)

192. 125v   Ἀναγραμματισμὸς ἀπὸ τὸ αὐτὸ στιχηρὸν [...] Ἰωάννου τοῦ Κουκουζέλου· πλ. β' *Τῶν δαιμόνων ὤλεσας* (single B)

193. 128v   Δεκεμβρίου ς', τοῦ ἁγίου [...] Νικολάου· στιχηρὸν Μανουὴλ τοῦ Χρυσάφου· ἦχος α' *Ἄνθρωπε τοῦ Θεοῦ* (single B)

194. 133r   Ἕτερον στιχηρὸν [...] Μανουὴλ λαμπαδαρίου τοῦ Χρυσάφου· ἦχος β' *Κανόνα πίστεως* (single B)

195. 135v   Ἕτερον στιχηρὸν εἰς τὸν αὐτὸν ἅγιον, τοῦ Καμπάνη πρωτοψάλτου Θεσσαλονίκης· πλ. α' *Σαλπίσωμεν ἐν σάλπιγγι* (single B)
[Παρεμβολὴ] τοῦ Κορώνη· *Ἐν σάλπιγγι ᾀσμάτων Τέριρεμ*

196. 139r   Δεύτερος πούς· ἦχος πλ. α' *Βασιλεῖς καὶ ἄρχοντες* (2-part A)

197. 140v   Ἕτερον τοῦ Κορώνη· ἦχος δ' *Οὓς κρατουμένους τρεῖς* (single A)

198. 145v   Ἀναγραμματισμὸς ἀπὸ τὸ αὐτὸ στιχηρὸν [...], Ἰωάννου τοῦ Κουκουζέλη· ἦχος πλ. α' *Πανάγιε Νικόλαε* (single B)

199. 149v   Ἕτερον στιχηρὸν [...], Ἰωάννου τοῦ Γλυκέος· ἦχος πλ. β' *Ἱεραρχῶν τὴν καλλονὴν* (single B)

200. 152v   Δεύτερος πούς· ἦχος πλ. β' *Χαίροις τῶν Μυρέων* (single A) (with ἐπιβολὴ Χρυσάφου [Μανουὴλ]; note on fol. 155r)

201. 157r   Ἀναγραμματισμὸς ἀπὸ τὸ αὐτὸ στιχηρὸν· Μανουὴλ τοῦ Χρυσάφου· ἦχος πλ. β' *Συνελθόντες οὖν φιλέορτοι* (single A)

202. 161v   Εἰς τὸν αὐτὸν ἅγιον· ἀναγραμματισμὸς ἀπὸ τό, Κληρονόμε Θεοῦ, πρὸς τὸ Ἀνευφημοῦντες πόθῳ· ἦχος πλ. β' *Ἡ ζωή σου ἔνδοξος* (single A)

203. 165v   Ἕτερον στιχηρὸν [...], Μανουὴ τοῦ Ἀργυροῦ· ἦχος πλ. β' *Ἄνθρωπε τοῦ Θεοῦ* (single A)

204. 170r   Ἕτερον στιχηρὸν τοῦ Καμπάνη [...]· ἦχος πλ. δ' *Τῶν ἀνδραγαθημάτων σου* (single B)

Incipits of the Anagrams and mathēmata in the Mathēmatarion 189

205. 172v Δεύτερος πούς· ἐκαλλωπίσθη παρὰ τοῦ Κουκουζέλου· [ἦχος πλ. β'] *Τίς γὰρ ἀκούων* (single B)

206. 176r Ἀναγραμματισμὸς ἀπὸ τὸ αὐτὸ στιχηρόν, Ἰωάννου τοῦ μαΐστορος· ἦχος πλ. β' *Τῶν θλιβομένων τὸ συμπαθές* (single A)

207. 179r Δεκεμβρίου ια', τοῦ ὁσίου [...] Δανιὴλ τοῦ Στυλίτου· στιχηρὸν Ἰωάννου πρωτοψάλτου τοῦ Γλυκέος, ὃ ψάλλεται καὶ εἰς ἑτέρους ἁγίους· ἦχος πλ. α' *Τὸ ἐμπιστευθέν σοι τάλαντον* (simple C)

208. 181v Ὁ δεύτερος πούς· ἦχος πλ. α' *Στῦλος καὶ ἑδραίωμα* (simple C)

209. 83v Δεκεμβρίου ιβ', τοῦ ἐν ἁγίοις πατρὸς ἡμῶν Σπυρίδωνος [...]· στιχηρὸν Μανουὴλ τοῦ Χρυσάφου· ἦχος α'. *Ὅσιε πάτερ* (single B)

210. 187v Ὁ δεύτερος πούς· ἦχος τρίτος *Νεκροὺς δὲ πάλιν ἤγειρας* (single B)

211. 191r Ἕτερον στιχηρὸν [...], Ἰωάννου τοῦ Γλυκέος· ἦχος β' *Ἱεραρχῶν τὸ θεῖον κειμήλιον* (single B)

212. 194v Δεύτερος πούς· πλ. β' νενανω *Ὅθεν τῆς ἐκκλησίας* (simple C)

213. 198r Εἰς τὸν αὐτὸν ἅγιον, ἀναγραμματισμὸς ἀπὸ τὸ Ὅσιε πάτερ, Μανουὴλ τοῦ Χρυσάφου· ἦχος δ' *Ἀλλ' ὦ πατέρων ἀξιάγαστε* (single A)

214. 202v Δεκεμβρίου ιγ' [...], στιχηρὸν παλαιόν· ἦχος πλ. α' *Τῶν τυραννούντων τὰ θράση* (single B)

215. 205v Ποὺς δεύτερος· ἦχος τρίτος *Εὐστράτιε καὶ Αὐξέντιε* (single B)

216. 207v Δεκεμβρίου ιε', τοῦ ἁγίου [...] Ἐλευθερίου· στιχηρὸν Ξένου τοῦ Κορώνη· ἦχος β' *Τὸν ἐν μάρτυσι μάρτυρα* (single B)

217. 210v Δεύτερος πούς· ἦχος τρίτος *Ὅτι καθεῖλεν ἀνδρικῶς* (2-part A)

218. 214r Δεκεμβρίου ιζ', τοῦ ἁγίου προφήτου Δανιὴλ καὶ τῶν ἁγίων τριῶν παίδων· στιχηρὸν Ἰωάννου τοῦ Γλυκέος· ἦχος β' νη *Πνευματικῶς ἡμᾶς, πιστοί* (simple A)

219. 215v Ὁ μονοφωνάρης ἀπ' ἔξω· πούς [β'], ἦχος β' *Οὗτος γὰρ ὁ προφήτης* (single B)

220. 218v Τρίτος πούς· ἦχος τρίτος *Οὐ γὰρ ἐχώνευσεν αὐτούς* (single B)

221. 220v Τέταρτος πούς· ἦχος πλ. β' *Ὁ διαγαγὼν ἡμᾶς* (simple C)

222. 222r Ἕτερον στιχηρὸν [...], Μανουὴλ τοῦ Χρυσάφου· ἦχος πλ. β' *Δανιὴλ ἀνὴρ ἐπιθυμιῶν* (simple C)

223. 226r Δεκεμβρίου κβ', τῆς ἁγίας [...] Ἀναστασίας· στιχηρὸν Κωνσταντίνου τοῦ Μαγουλᾶ· ἦχος β' *Τῆς ἀναστάσεως εἴληφας* (simple C)

224. 229r Έτερον στιχηρὸν [...], Ἰωάννου πρωτοψάλτου τοῦ Γλυκέος· ἦχος πλ. α´ Προεόρτιος ἡμέρα (simple C)

225. 231v Ποὺς δεύτερος· ἦχος τρίτος Ἰδοὺ ἡ Παρθένος (simple C)

226. 235r Στιχηρὸν προεόρτιον [...] Ἰωάννου Κουκουζέλου· ἦχος πλ. Β´ Σπήλαιον εὐτρεπίζου (3-part A)

227. 238v Στιχηρὰ τῶν Χριστοῦ γεννῶν μελισθέντα παρὰ διαφόρων ποιητῶν. Στιχηρόν, μέλος παλαιόν. Ἀπὸ χοροῦ· ἦχος πλ. δ´ Βηθλεὲμ ἑτοιμάζου —(fol. 239v) εἶτα γίνεται καλλιφωνία· ἦχος τρίτος (fol. 240r) Ἡ ἀλήθεια ἦλθεν (simple B) (240v) [Ἐπιβολὴ] τοῦ Κορώνη· ἦχος δ´ Ἦλθεν ἡ ἀλήθεια (single A) (242v) Ἕτερον τοῦ Κουκουζέλου· ἦχος δ´ Ἦλθεν ἡ ἀλήθεια (single A)

228. 244v Δεύτερος ποὺς· ἦχος δ´ Καὶ Θεὸς ἀνθρώποις (simple C) (245v) [Παρεκβολὴ] τοῦ Κορώνη· Μορφωθείς, τεριρεμ (simple C)

229. 247r Ἕτερον τοῦ Κουκουζέλου· πλ. δ´ Μορφωθείς, (simple C)

230. 248v Ἀναγραμματισμὸς ἀπὸ τὸ αὐτὸ στιχηρόν· Ἰωάννου τοῦ Κουκουζέλου· ἦχος β´ νη Ἀδὰμ ἀνανεοῦται (single A)

231. 250v Ἕτερος ἀναγραμματισμὸς ἀπὸ τὸ αὐτὸ στιχηρόν, Ἰωάννου τοῦ Κουκουζέλου· ἦχος πλ. δ´ Ἀδὰμ ἀνανεοῦται (2-part A)

232. 254v Ἕτερον ἐξ αὐτῶν· Φιλανθρωπηνοῦ τοῦ Εὐνούχου· ἦχος τρίτος Νῦν προφητικὴ πρόρρησις (simple C)

233. 254v Τοῦ Κουκουζέλη· [παρεκβολὴ] Νῦν προφητικὴ πρόρρησις (2-part A)

234. 258v Δεύτερος ποὺς· ἦχος τρίτος Ἐξ οὗ γάρ μοι ἐξελεύσεται (single B)

235. 261r Ἀναγραμματισμὸς τοῦ μαΐστορος, ἀπὸ τὸ αὐτὸ στιχηρόν· ἦχος πλ. α´ Ἐκ Παρθένου κόρης (single A)

236. 264r Ἕτερον στιχηρὸν ἐξ αὐτῶν, παλαιόν, ἐκαλλωπίσθη δὲ παρὰ Ἰωάννου μαΐστορος τοῦ Κουκουζέλη· ἦχος πλ. δ´ ἀπὸ χοροῦ Τάδε λέγει Ἰωσήφ —(fol. 264v) εἶτα ἄρχεται ὁ μονοφωνάρης· νενανω Μαρία, τί τὸ δρᾶμα (2-part A)

237. 268v Ἀναγραμματισμὸς ἀπὸ τὸ αὐτὸ στιχηρόν, τοῦ μαΐστορος· ἦχος πλ. δ´ Οὐκέτι φέρω λοιπόν (simple A)

238. 273r Ἕτερον στιχηρὸν ἐξ αὐτῶν, παλαιόν, ἐκαλλωπίσθη δὲ παρὰ τοῦ Κουκουζέλου· ἦχος πλ. β´ Οὗτος ὁ Θεὸς ἡμῶν —(fol. 275r) «κείμενον» Υἱὸς μονογενὴς —(fol. 276v) «ἀπὸ χοροῦ».

239. 276r Ἕτερον στιχηρὸν ἐξ αὐτῶν, τοῦ Καμπάνη· τινὲς δέ φασι τοῦ Καλλίστου· ἦχος πλ. δ´ Πρὸ τῆς γεννήσεως —(2-part A) — (with parekbolē by Koukouzelēs) Αἱ νοεραὶ στρατιαί, τεριρεμ (fol. 277v)

240.	279v	Τὸ αὐτὸ στιχηρόν, ἐκαλλωπίσθη δὲ παρὰ τοῦ Κορώνη καὶ παρὰ τοῦ Χρυσάφου· ἦχος πλ. δ´ *Πρὸ τῆς γεννήσεως* (single A)
241.	282r	[Παρεκβολή] τοῦ Κουκουζέλου· πλ. δ´ *Τέριρεμ, Τρόμῳ ὁρῶσαι*
242.	283r	Ἕτερον [πλ. δ´] *Τρόμῳ ὁρῶσαι* (single A)
243.	285r	Παλαιὸν [παρεκβολή]· *Καὶ τῇ φάτνῃ τῶν ἀλόγων* (single A)
244.	286v	Ἕτερον στιχηρὸν ἐξ αὐτῶν· Θεοδώρου τοῦ Μανουγρᾶ· ἦχος τρίτος *Ἰωσὴφ εἰπὲ ἡμῖν* (single A)
245.	289v	Παρεκβολὴ τοῦ μαΐστορος· ἦχος πλ. α´ *Πέπεισμαι ὅτι Θεός* (single A)
246.	291v	Ἀναγραμματισμὸς ἀπὸ τὸ αὐτὸ στιχηρόν· Κωνσταντίνου δομεστίκου τοῦ Μαγουλᾶ· ἦχος βαρὺς Ζω *Ὁ σαρκωθεὶς δι' ἡμᾶς* (2-part A)
247.	297r	Ἕτερον στιχηρὸν ἐξ αὐτῶν· Κωνσταντίνου δομεστίκου τοῦ Μαγουλᾶ· ἦχος α´ κε *Δεῦτε πιστοί* (single A)
248.	301v	Ἕτερον στιχηρὸν ἐξ αὐτῶν, Θεοδώρου τοῦ Μανουγρᾶ· ἦχος δ´ *Ἄκουε οὐρανὲ* (3-part A)
249.	304r	[Παρεκβολή] τοῦ Κουκουζέλου· βου *Ἐπιλαβέτω τρόμος* (single A)
250.	306v	Ἕτερον [παρεκβολή]· βου *Ἐπιλαβέτω τρόμος* (single A)
251.	309r	Ἀπὸ χοροῦ· βου *Ὅτι Θεός τε καὶ κτίστης* (simple B)
252.	312r	Ἀναγραμματισμὸς ἀπὸ τὸ αὐτὸ στιχηρόν· τοῦ μαΐστορος Κουκουζέλη· ἦχος πλ. δ´ *Ὦ βάθος πλούτου* (single A)
253.	316r	Ἕτερον στιχηρὸν ἐξ αὐτῶν· Μανουὴλ τοῦ Χρυσάφου· ἦχος πλ. α´ *Δεῦτε χριστοφόροι λαοί* (single B)
254.	320r	Ἀναγραμματισμὸς ἀπὸ τὸ αὐτὸ στιχηρόν· Μανουὴλ τοῦ Χρυσάφου· ἦχος πλ. δ´ *Τί τὸ ἐν σοί* (single A)
255.	324v	Ἕτερον στιχηρὸν ἐξ αὐτῶν, Λέοντος τοῦ Ἀλμυριώτου· ἦχος βαρὺς Ζω *Ἐξεπλήττετο ὁ Ἡρώδης* (3-part B)
256.	334v	Ἀναγραμματισμὸς ἀπὸ τὸ αὐτὸ στιχηρόν· Ἰωάννου τοῦ Κουκουζέλου· ἦχος τρίτος *Μητέρες ἠτεκνοῦντο* (single B)
257.	341r	Ἕτερον στιχηρὸν ἐξ αὐτῶν· Μανουὴλ τοῦ Χρυσάφου· ἦχος β´ *Ὁ Ἰωσήφ, Παρθένε* (4-part B)
258.	346v	Ἕτερον στιχηρὸν ἐξ αὐτῶν· τοῦ Κουκουμᾶ· ἦχος πλ. β´ ἀπὸ χοροῦ *Σήμερον γεννᾶται* —(fol. 348v)· εἶτα ἄρχεται ὁ μονοφωνάρης· πλ. β´ *Θεὸς ἐν φάτνῃ ἀνακέκλιται* (4-part A)

259. 354v   Ἕτερον ψαλλόμενον ἐν Κωνσταντινουπόλει· ἀσματικόν· ἦχος πλ. β΄ *Δόξα Πατρί* —καὶ ὁ ἕτερος χορός· πλ. β΄ *Καὶ νῦν καὶ ἀεί* (fol. 355r) εἶτα ἀναγιγνώσκεται ἐν τῷ μέσῳ παρὰ τοῦ κανονάρχου καὶ εὐθὺς ἠχίζει ὁ δομέστικος, εἰς ἦχον πλ. τοῦ β΄ *Νεεεχεανες Σήμερον γεννᾶται* (multi-part B). (With ēchēmata between the feet.)

260. 360r   Ἕτερον θετταλικόν· ἦχος πλ. β΄ *Νεχεανες, Σήμερον γεννᾶται* (with ēchēmata and long kratēmata; very melismatic) — (multi-part B)

261. 366v   Εἰς τὴν πρόσκυψιν τοῦ βασιλέως· ἦχος δ΄ *Ὁ Χριστὸς ἐγεννήθη*

262. 367r   Εἶτα τὸ πολυχρόνιον· Ξένου τοῦ Κορώνη καὶ πρωτοψάλτου· ἦχος α΄ *Πολυχρόνιον ποιῆσαι* (single B)

263. 369v   Τὸ αὐτὸ συνοπτικώτερον· συντμηθὲν παρὰ τοῦ Χρυσάφου· ἦχος α΄ *Πολυχρόνιον ποιῆσαι* (single B)

ΜΠΤ 730: MATHĒMATARION (VOLUME IV)

241 + i–ii folios

1r   Τέταρτος τόμος τοῦ Μαθηματαρίου, ἐξηγηθεὶς ἐκ τοῦ παλαιοῦ καὶ γραφεὶς παρὰ Χουρμουζίου διδασκάλου τῆς Νέας Μεθόδου τῆς Μουσικῆς, καὶ Χαρτοφύλακος τῆς τοῦ Χριστοῦ Μεγάλης Ἐκκλησίας.

264.   Δεκεμβρίου κε΄, ἡ κατὰ σάρκα γέννησις τοῦ Κυρίου ἡμῶν Ἰησοῦ Χριστοῦ· στιχηρὸν Μανουὴλ τοῦ Χρυσάφου· ἦχος δ΄ *Εὐφραίνεσθε δίκαιοι* (single A)

265. 6r   Ἕτερον στιχηρὸν [...], Μανουὴλ τοῦ Χρυσάφου· ἦχος πλ. Β΄ *Χορεύουσιν ἄγγελοι* (single B)

266. 10v Εἰς τὸν ὄρθρον, τὸ πεντηκοστάριον· ἦχος β΄ *Τὰ σύμπαντα σήμερον* (simple A)

267. 11r Εἶτα ψάλλεται τὸ παρόν, πρὸς τό, Ἀναστὰς ὁ Ἰησοῦς· ἦχος πλ. β΄ *Γεννηθεὶς ὁ Ἰησοῦς ἐν τῷ σπηλαίῳ* (simple B)

268. 13v Ἕτερον πεντηκοστάριον εἰς τὴν αὐτὴν ἑορτήν, Ἰωάννου τοῦ Γλυκέος· ἐκαλλωπίσθη παρὰ τοῦ Κορώνη· ἦχος α΄ *Μετὰ ποιμένων μάγοι* (single A)

269. 16v Ὁ δεύτερος πούς· ἦχος α΄ *Τῷ ἐκ Παρθένου ἀνατείλαντι* (2-part B)

270. 20r   Τὸ αὐτὸ πεντηκοστάριον συντομηθὲν καὶ καλλωπισθὲν παρὰ Μανουὴλ τοῦ
           Χρυσάφου· ἦχος α´ Μετὰ ποιμένων μάγοι (2-part A)

271. 25v   Ἀναγραμματισμὸς ἀπὸ τὸ αὐτὸ στιχηρὸν [...], Ἰωάννου μαΐστορος τοῦ
           Κουκουζέλου· ἦχος βαρὺς Δόξα ἐν ὑψίστοις (2-part A)

272. 28v   Εἱρμοὶ ἀσματικοὶ μετὰ ἠχημάτων, εἰς τὴν αὐτὴν ἑορτήν, ψαλλόμενοι εἰς τὴν
           καταβασίαν· μελισθέντες παρὰ Μανουὴλ τοῦ Χρυσάφου· ἦχος α´ Τῷ Κυρίῳ
           ᾄσωμεν — Χροστὸς γεννᾶται δοξάσατε (2-part A, as are the following)

273. 32v   Ὠιδὴ γ´, ἦχος α´ Ἅγιος εἶ Κύριε — Τῷ πρὸ τῶν αἰώνων

274. 36r   Ὠιδὴ δ´, ἦχος α´ Δόξα τῇ δυνάμει σου — Ῥάβδος ἐκ τῆς ῥίζης

275. 41r   Ὠιδὴ ε´, ἦχος α´ Κύριε ὁ Θεὸς — Θεὸς ὢν εἰρήνης

276. 44v   Ὠιδὴ ϛ´, ἦχος α´ Ὡς τὸν προφήτην — Σπλάγχνων Ἰωνᾶν

277. 48v   Ὠιδὴ ζ´, ἦχος α´ Αἰνοῦμεν — Θαύματος ὑπερφυοῦς

278. 53v   Ὠιδὴ η´, ἦχος α´ Τῶν πατέρων — Οἱ παῖδες εὐσεβείᾳ

279. 57r   Ὠιδὴ θ´, ἦχος α´ Μεγάλυνον ψυχή μου — Μυστήριον ξένον

280. 62v   Μεγαλυνάριον εἰς τὴν αὐτὴν ἑορτήν· Ἰωάννου τοῦ Γλυκέος· ἦχος α´ Μεγάλυνον,
           ψυχή μου (2-part B)

281. 64v   Ἕτερον μεγαλυνάριον [...], Ξένου τοῦ Κορώνη· ἦχος α´ Μεγάλυνον ψυχή μου
           (2-part B)

282. 67r   Ἕτερον μεγαλυνάριον [...], Μανουὴλ τοῦ Χρυσάφου· ἦχος α´ Μεγάλυνον ψυχή
           μου

283. 71v   Ἕτερον μαγαλυνάριον [...], Ἰωάννου Κουκουζέλου· ἦχος α´ Μεγάλυνον ψυχή
           μου — Μυστήριον ξένον (single B)

284. 74r   Ἕτερον μαγαλυνάριον [...], Κωνσταντίνου τοῦ Μαγουλᾶ· ἦχος α´ Μεγάλυνον
           ψυχή μου — Ῥᾷον σιωπὴν (single B)

285. 78v   Εἰς τοὺς αἴνους ψάλλεται εἰς τὸ Καὶ νῦν· ἀσματικὸν μετὰ ἠχημάτων, τοῦ
           Κουκουζέλου· ἦχος β´ Καὶ νῦν — Σήμερον ὁ Χριστὸς

286. 84v   Ἕτερον συννοπτικώτερον, ψάλλεται δὲ δίχορον· ἦχος β´ Νεχεανες ... Σήμερον ὁ
           Χριστὸς ἐν Βηθλεὲμ (multi-part B)

287. 87r   Δεκεμβρίου κζ´ [...], στιχηρὸν τοῦ ἁγίου Στεφάνου· ἐμελίσθη παρὰ Δαβὶδ
           μοναχοῦ τοῦ Ραιδεστηνοῦ· ἦχος δ´ Στέφανος ἡ καλὴ ἀπαρχὴ (single B)

288. 93r   Ἕτερον στιχηρὸν εἰς τὸν αὐτὸν ἅγιον Μανουὴλ τοῦ Χρυσάφου· ἦχος πλ. α´
           Πρωτομάρτυς ἀπόστολε (single B)

289. 99r Ἕτερον στιχηρὸν [...], Μανουὴλ τοῦ Θηβαίου· ἦχος πλ. β´ *Πρῶτος ἐν μάρτυσι* (single B)

290. 102v Δεύτερος πούς· ἦχος πλ. Β´ *Τοὺς τὴν σεπτήν σου* (simple C)

291. 104r Ἕτερον στιχηρὸν [...], Ἰωάννου Κουκουζέλου· πλ. δ´ *Χαίροις ἐν Κυρίῳ* (simple C)

292. 107r Δεύτερος πούς· ἐπλατύνθη καὶ παρὰ τοῦ Χρυσάφου· πλ. δ´ *Καὶ τὴν πλάνην τῶν ἀνόμων* (simple C)

293. 110r Ἕτερον στιχηρὸν τῇ αὐτῇ ἡμέρᾳ, εἰς τὸν ἅγιον Θεόδωρον τὸν γραπτόν, Ἰωάννου τοῦ Κουκουζέλου· ἦχος πλ. β´ *Ἐν ὥρᾳ φρικτῇ* (single B)

294. 114v Δεύτερος πούς· ἦχος πλ. α´ *Εὕρω σε, πάτερ Θεόδωρε* (single A)

295. 116v Ἕτερον στιχηρὸν καὶ εἰς τοὺς δύο αὐταδέλφους Θεόδωρον καὶ Θεοφάνην· Ἰωάννου τοῦ Γλυκέος· ἦχος πλ. β´ *Τὴν ξυνωρίδα τὴν σεπτήν* (single B)

296. 120r Δεύτερος πούς· ἦχος πλ. β´ *Χαίρετε τῶν δογμάτων φρουροί* (simple)

297. 122v Μηνὶ Δεκεμβρίου κθ´, τῶν ἁγίων νηπίων [...], στιχηρὸν τοῦ Καρβουναριώτου· ἦχος πλ. δ´ *Ἡρώδης ὁ παράνομος* (single A)

298. 125v Πούς δεύτερος· ἦχος β´ *Ἡ δὲ Ἐλισάβετ* (2-part B)

299. 128v Δεκεμβρίου λα´, τοῦ ἁγίου [...] Ζωτικοῦ τοῦ Ὀρφανοτρόφου· στιχηρὸν Μανουὴλ τοῦ Χρυσάφου· ἦχος δ´ *Ζωτικὲ ἀθλοφόρε* (single B)

***

300. 132v Μὴν Ἰανουάριος, εἰς τὴν α´, μνήμη τοῦ ἐν ἁγίοις [...] Βασιλείου τοῦ μεγάλου· στιχηρὸν τοῦ Ἀναπαρδᾶ· ἦχος α´ *Ὦ θεία καὶ ἱερά* (single B)

301. 134v Δεύτερος πούς· ἦχος πλ. β´ *Σὺ γὰρ τοῦ θείου πόθου* (simple A)

302. 137r Τὸ αὐτὸ στιχηρὸν ποιηθὲν καὶ παρὰ Μανουὴλ τοῦ Χρυσάφου· ἦχος α´ *Ὦ θεία καὶ ἱερά* (single B)

303. 141r Ἀναγραμματισμὸς ἀπὸ τὸ αὐτὸ στιχηρόν· Ἰωάννου τοῦ Κουκουζέλου· ἦχος βαρύς Ζω *Μνημόνευε καὶ ἡμῶν* (single A)

304. 143v Ἕτερον στιχηρὸν [...], Γρηγορίου δομεστίκου· ἦχος α´ *Πάντων τῶν ἁγίων* (simple A)

305. 145r Ἐπιβολή, τοῦ Χρυσάφου· λεγετος *Πάντων τῶν ἁγίων* (single A)

306. 146v Πούς δεύτερος· ἦχος πλ. Α´ *Ὡς Παῦλος ἐκβοῶν* (simple A)

Incipits of the Anagrams and mathēmata in the Mathēmatarion 195

307. 148v Ἕτερον στιχηρὸν [...], Ἰωάννου τοῦ Κουκουζέλου· ἦχος α΄ *Τίς ἀσθενεῖ* (single A)

308. 151r Ἀναγραμματισμὸς [...] ἀπὸ τὸ Ὁ τῇ χάριν τῶν θαυμάτων, Μανουὴλ τοῦ Χρυσάφου· ἦχος πλ. β΄ *Ἀρχιερέων ἐδείχθης* (single A)

309. 155v Ἕτερον στιχηρὸν [...], ψάλλεται δὲ καὶ εἰς ἑτέρους ἱεράρχας· Μανουὴλ τοῦ Χρυσάφου· πλ. β΄ *Ἐξεχύθη ἡ χάρις* (single B)

310. 159r Ἕτερον στιχηρὸν [...], Ἰωάννου τοῦ Κουκουζέλου· ἦχος πλ. δ΄ *Σοφίας ἐραστής* (single A)

311. 161v Δεύτερος πούς· ἦχος πλ. δ΄ *Καὶ θεία μελέτη νόμου* (single A)

312. 164r Τρίτος πούς· ἦχος πλ. δ΄ *Διὸ σάρκα καὶ κόσμον* (single A)

313. 166r Τὸ αὐτὸ στιχηρὸν ἐνωθὲν μετὰ τῶν ποδῶν αὐτοῦ καὶ συντομηθὲν παρὰ Γερασίμου· πλ. δ΄ *Σοφίας ἐραστής* (single A)

314. 170v Στιχηρὰ τροπάρια τῶν Ὡρῶν τῶν Φώτων, μελισθέντα μὲν παρὰ διαφόρων ποιητῶν, καλλωπισθέντα δὲ παρὰ Ἰωάννου τοῦ Κουκουζέλου καὶ μαΐστορος, παλαιόν· πλ. δ΄ *Σήμερον τῶν ὑδάτων* (simple C)

315. 172v Ἐπιβολὴ τοῦ Κορώνη· *Τοοτο — Σήμερον τῶν ὑδάτων* (simple C)

316. 173v Ἑτέρα ἐπιβολή, τοῦ Κουκουζέλου· πλ. δ΄ *Σήμερον τῶν ὑδάτων, Τοοτο* (single A)

317. 175v Δεύτερος πούς· ἦχος πλ. δ΄ *Καὶ τῶν ἰδίων ναμάτων* (single B)

318. 178r [Πατεκβολή]· *Δεσπότην ὁρῶν ῥιπτόμενον, Τοοτο* (single A)

319. 180r Ἕτερον στιχηρὸν ἐξ αὐτῶν, Ἰωάννου τοῦ Κουκουζέλου· ἦχος πλ. δ΄ *Ὡς ἄνθρωπος ἐν ποταμῷ* (simple C)

320. 183v Ἀναγραμματισμὸς ἀπὸ τὸ αὐτὸ στιχηρόν, Ἰωάννου τοῦ Κουκουζέλου· ἦχος πλ. δ΄ *Διὰ τὰς ἁμαρτίας ἡμῶν* (single A)

321. 186r Ἕτερον στιχηρὸν ἐξ αὐτῶν· τοῦ Καμπάνη· ἦχος πλ. δ΄ *Πρὸς τὴν φωνὴν τοῦ βοῶντος* (simple A)

322. 188v [Ἐπιβολὴ] τοῦ Κουκουζέλου· πλ. δ΄ *Βάπτισμα αἰτῶν* (simple C)

323. 190v [Ἐπιβολὴ] τοῦ Κουκουζέλου· *Τέριρεμ, Ἁγίασον ἐμέ* (simple C)

324. 191v Ἀναγραμματισμὸς ἀπὸ τὸ αὐτὸ στιχηρόν· Ἰωάννου τοῦ Κουκουζέλου καὶ μαΐστορος· *Ὁ αἴρων τὴν ἁμαρτίαν* (single A)

325. 194v Ἕτερον στιχηρὸν ἐξ αὐτῶν· τοῦ τίνος ἐστίν, ἄδηλον· ἦχος πλ. δ΄ *Ἡ τοῦ προδρόμου καὶ βαπτιστοῦ* (2-part B)

326. 200v Ἕτερον στιχηρὸν ἐξ αὐτῶν, παλαιόν· τινὲς δέ φασι Γερμανοῦ μοναχοῦ· ἦχος πλ. β΄ *Σήμερον ἡ ψαλμική* (2-part A)

327. 204v Ἕτερον στιχηρὸν ἐξ αὐτῶν· τοῦ Μανουγρᾶ· ἦχος πλ. α΄ *Τί ἀναχαιτίζῃ σου* (single A)

328. 208v Δεύτερος πούς· ἦχος πλ. α΄ *Ὅτι οὐκ εἴωθα* (single B)

329. 210r Ἀναγραμματισμὸς ἀπὸ τὸ αὐτὸ στιχηρόν, τοῦ Κουκουζέλου, ὥς φασιν· ἦχος πλ. α΄ *Ὁ Ἰωάννης συμμαρτυρεῖ μοι* (simple A)

330. 214r Ἕτερον στιχηρόν, Λέοντος τοῦ Ἁλμυριώτου· ἦχος βαρὺς Ζω *Θάμβος ἦν κατιδεῖν* (single A)

331. 219r Παλαιὸν [ἐπιβολή]· βαρὺς *Καὶ χοροὶ ἀγγέλων* (single B)

332. 221r Ἕτερον στιχηρὸν ἐξ αὐτῶν, Ἰωάννου μαΐστορος τοῦ Καλλίστου· ἦχος πλ. α΄ *Τὴν χεῖρά σου* (with two epibolai kratēmata by Koukouzelēs, fols. 222r and 229v) (multi-part B)

333. 232r Ἕτερον ἀσματικόν, ψαλλόμενον δίχορον· ὁ δομέστικος ἠχίζει τὸ Δόξα· ἦχος πλ. α΄ *Δόξα πατρὶ — Τὴν χεῖρά σου* (multi-part B)

334. 237r Ἕτερον συνοπτικώτερον, δίχορον, ὁ δομέστικος ἠχίζει· πλ. α΄ *Ανεανες — Τὴν χεῖρά σου* (multi-part B)

335. 240r Ἰανουαρίου ϛ΄, τὰ ἅγια Θεοφάνεια [...], στιχηρὸν Ξένου τοῦ Κορώνη· ἦχος β΄ *Εἴδοσάν σε ὕδατα* (single B)

336. 244r Ἕτερον στιχηρὸν εἰς τὴν αὐτὴν ἑορτήν, παλαιόν· ἦχος δ΄ *Ἔτρεμεν ἡ χεὶρ τοῦ βαπτιστοῦ* (single B)

337. 246v Δεύτερος πούς· ἦχος δ΄ *Ἐστράφη Ἰορδάνης ποταμός* (3-part B)

338. 250r Ἀναγραμμαστισμὸς [...] ἀπὸ τὸ αὐτὸ στιχηρόν, τοῦ Κουκουζέλου· ἦχος πλ. δ΄ *Ἀλλὰ πᾶσαν ἐπλήρωσας* (single A)

339. 253v Ἕτερον στιχηρὸν [...], Μανουὴλ τοῦ Χρυσάφου· ἦχος πλ. δ΄ *Σήμερον ἡ κτίσις φωτίζεται* (single B)

340. 259r Ἕτερον στιχηρὸν παλαιόν, τινὲς δέ φασι τοῦ Γλυκέος· ἦχος πλ. δ΄, ἀπὸ χοροῦ *Σήμερον ἡ κτίσις φωτίζεται* — (fol. 259v) ὁ μονοφωνάρης ἀπ᾽ ἔξω· πλ. δ΄ *Ὅπου γὰρ βασιλέως παρουσία* (3-part B)

341. 264v Ἀναγραμματισμὸς ἀπὸ τὸ αὐτὸ στιχηρὸν τοῦ Κουκουζέλου· ἦχος πλ. δ΄ Γα *Ἴδωμεν πάντες ἴδωμεν* (single A)

342. 268v Εἰς τὸν ὄρθρον μετὰ τὸν πεντηκοστόν, τὸ παρὸν πεντηκοστάριον· ἦχος β΄ *Τὰ σύμπαντα σήμερον* (single A)

343. — Εἶτα ψάλλεται τὸ Βαπτισθεὶς ὁ Ἰησοῦς, πρὸς τὸ Ἀναστὰς ὁ Ἰησοῦς, τοῦ Γλυκέος· ἦχος πλ. β΄ *Βαπτισθεὶς ὁ Ἰησοῦς* (simple B)

344. 271r Στιχηρὸν πρὸ τῆς ὀγδόης ᾠδῆς· Ἰωάννου λαμπαδαρίου τοῦ Κλαδᾶ· ἦχος β΄ *Τριάδος ἡ φανέρωσις* (2-part B)

345. 274r Μεγαλυνάριον εἰς τὴν αὐτὴν ἑορτήν· Ξένου τοῦ Κορώνη· ἦχος β΄ *Μεγάλυνον ψυχή μου* (single B)

346. 277r Ἕτερον μεγαλυνάριον [...], Ξένου τοῦ Κορώνη· ἦχος β΄ *Μεγάλυνον ψυχή μου* (single B)

347. 279v Ἕτερον μεγαλυνάριον [...], Ξένου τοῦ Κορώνη· ἦχος β΄ *Μεγάλυνον ψυχή μου* (single B)

348. 282r Ἕτερον μεγαλυνάριον [...] Ἰωάννου μαΐστορος τοῦ Κουκουζέλου· ἦχος β΄ *Μεγάλυνον ψυχή μου — Γλῶσσα πᾶσα ἀπορεῖ* (single B)

349. 286r Στιχηρὸν ἀσματικὸν εἰς τοὺς αἴνους, Ἰωάννου τοῦ Γλυκέος, δίχορον· ἦχος β΄ βου *Δόξα Πατρὶ* — (fol. 286v) ὁ ἕτερος χορὸς *Καὶ νῦν καὶ ἀεὶ* —(fol. 287r) *Σήμερον ὁ Χριστὸς* —(fol. 288r) ἠχήματα *Νεεεχε νε* (multi-part B)

350. 293r Ἕτερον ἀσματικὸν δίχορον, Ξένου τοῦ Κορώνη· ἦχος β΄ νη, ἀπὸ χοροῦ *Σήμερον ὁ Χριστὸς* — Ὁ μονοφωνάρης *Σήμερον ὁ Χριστὸς* — (multi-part B) — (The asmatikon is chanted exchanging verses of the text of the sticheron between the choir and the monophōnarēs using the kalophonic melos)

351. 298v Εἶτα γίνεται μεγάλη δοξολογία καὶ ἀπόλυσις. Ἰανουαρίου ζ΄ [...], στιχηρὸν τοῦ Μανουγρᾶ· ἦχος πλ. β΄ *νενανω Ἔνσαρκε λύχνε* (single B) — (the kratēma by Chrysaphēs, fol. 300v)

352. 301v Ἰανουαρίου ιε΄ [...], στιχηρὸν Ἰωάννου τοῦ Γλυκέος· ἦχος β΄ *Ἀρνησάμενος κόσμον* (single B) —(the kratēma by Chrysaphēs, fol. 304r)

353. 305v Ἰανουαρίου ιζ΄ [...], στιχηρὸν Νικηφόρου τοῦ Ἠθικοῦ· ἦχος β΄ κε *Τὸν ἐπὶ γῆς ἄγγελον* (single B)

354. 308r Δεύτερος πούς· ἦχος πλ. β΄ *Πεφυτευμένος γὰρ* (single A)

355. 309v Ἕτερον στιχηρὸν [...], Ἰωάννου μαΐστορος Παπαδοπούλου τοῦ Κουκουζέλου· ψάλλεται δὲ καὶ εἰς ἑτέρους ὁσίους· ἦχος πλ. α΄ *Ὅσιε πάτερ* (single B)

356. 312v Δεύτερος πούς· ἦχος α΄ *Ἵνα ὅταν ἔλθῃ* (single B)

357. 314r Ἕτερον στιχηρὸν [...], τοῦ Καρβουναριώτου· ἦχος πλ. δ΄ Γα *Τῶν μοναστῶν τὰ πλήθη* (the kratēma, fol. 318v, epibolē by Koukouzelēs — 4-part B)

358. 319v Ἕτερον ἐκ τῆς Κρήτης· ἐκαλλωπίσθη δὲ παρὰ τοῦ Χρυσάφου· ἦχος πλ. δ΄ *Τῶν μοναστῶν τὰ πλήθη* (single B)

359. 321v Ἀναγραμματισμὸς [...] ἀπὸ τὸ αὐτὸ στιχηρόν· Μανουὴλ τοῦ Χρυσάφου· πλ. δ΄ *Ἀγγέλων συνόμιλε* (single A)

360. 325v Ἕτερος ἀναγραμματισμὸς [...] ἀπὸ τὸ αὐτὸ στιχηρόν· Μανουὴλ τοῦ Χρυσάφου· πλ. δ΄ *Μακάριος εἶ* (single A)

361. 329v Ἰανουαρίου ιη΄, τοῦ ἐν ἁγίοις πατρὸς ἡμῶν Ἀθανασίου [...], στιχηρὸν τοῦ Ἠθικοῦ· ἦχος τρίτος *Πάλιν ἡμῖν ὁ Χρυσορρόας* — (the kratēma by Chrysaphēs, fol. 332r) — (single A)

362. 334r Ἕτερον στιχηρὸν εἰς τὸν αὐτὸν ἅγιον, ψάλλεται δὲ καὶ εἰς ἑτέρους ἱεράρχας· ἐμελίσθη παρὰ Μανουὴλ τοῦ ὡς ἀληθῶς Χρυσάφου· ἦχος πλ. β΄ *Χριστοῦ τὸν ἱεράρχην* (single B)

363. 339r Ἀναγραμματισμὸς [...] ἀπὸ τὸ αυτὸ στιχηρόν· Κωνσταντίνου τοῦ Μαγουλᾶ· πλ. β΄ νενανω *Ὂν καὶ πρεσβεύει* (single A)

364. 342v Ἰανουαρίου κ΄, τοῦ ὁσίου καὶ θεοφόρου πατρὸς ἡμῶν Εὐθυμίου τοῦ μεγάλου· στιχηρὸν Ἰωάννου μαΐστορος τοῦ Κουκουζέλου· ἦχος β΄ *Εὐθυμεῖτε, ἔλεγε* (single B)

365. 344v Ποὺς δεύτερος· ἦχος β΄ νη *Ἐνεφύης δὲ γαστρί* (single B)

366. 346v Ἕτερον στιχηρὸν [...], Ξένου τοῦ Κορώνη· ἦχος β΄ βου *Τῶν ἐν τῷ βίῳ πραγμάτων* (single B)

367. 348v Ποὺς δεύτερος· ἦχος τρίτος *Τρυφὴν ἐμίσησας* (single B)

368. 352r Ἕτερον στιχηρὸν εἰς τὸν αὐτὸν ἅγιον, ψάλλεται δὲ καὶ εἰς ἑτέρους ὁσίους· Ἰωάννου μαΐστορος τοῦ Κουκουζέλου· ἦχος πλ. α΄ *Ὅσιε πάτερ* (single B)

369. 355r Ποὺς δεύτερος· ἦχος α΄ κε *Ἐλθὼν γὰρ ὁ Χριστός* (single-art B)

370. 357r Μηνὶ Ἰανουαρίου κα΄, τοῦ ἁγίου καὶ ἐνδόξου μεγαλομάρτυρος Εὐγενίου τοῦ Τραπεζουντίου· στιχηρὸν Ἰωάννου πρωτοψάλτου τοῦ Γλυκέος· ἦχος β΄ βου *Δεῦτε φιλάθλοι* (2-part A)

371. 359r Δεύτερος ποὺς· ἦχος τρίτος *Εὐγένιος τῆς Τραπεζοῦντος* (single B)

372. 362v Ἕτερον στιχηρὸν εἰς τὸν αὐτὸν ἅγιον· Μιχαὴλ τοῦ Ἀλμυριώτου· ἦχος πλ. β΄ *Εἰ καὶ τῷ θρόνῳ τῆς δόξης* (single B)

373. 367v Ἀναγραμματισμὸς ἀπὸ τό, Τὴν ἐπὶ γῆς εὔκλειαν, εἰς τὸν αὐτὸν ἅγιον· Μανουὴλ τοῦ Χρυσάφου· πλ. δ΄ *Ἀλλ' ὦ μαρτύρων καλλονὴ* (single A)

Incipits of the Anagrams and mathēmata in the Mathēmatarion 199

374. 373r Ἰανουαρίου κγ΄, τοῦ ἁγίου ἱερομάρτυρος Κλήμεντος, ἐπισκόπου Ἀγκύρας· στιχηρὸν Ξένου τοῦ Κορώνη, πλ. δ΄ *Τὴν τῶν χρόνων τετραχῶς περίοδον* (single B)

375. 376r Ποὺς δεύτερος· ἦχος πλ. δ΄ *Ἀλλ' οὔτε πῦρ, οὔτε ξίφος* (single B)

376. 378v Μηνὶ Ἰανουαρίου κε΄, τοῦ ἐν ἁγίοις πατρὸς ἡμῶν Γρηγορίου πατριάρχου Κωνσταντινουπόλεως τοῦ Θεολόγου· στιχηρὸν Ἀνδρέου Σιγηροῦ, ἦχος α΄ πα *Τὴν λύραν τοῦ πνεύματος* — (fol. 380v, text by Chrysaphēs [epibolē], fol. 381r)

377. 382r Δεύτερος πούς· ἦχος πλ. β΄ *Σὺ εἶ ὁ ποιμὴν ὁ καλός* — (single B) — (with epibolē by Chrysaphēs, fol. 383v, *Καὶ σὺν Παύλῳ χορεύεις*)

378. 384v Ἕτερον στιχηρὸν εἰς τὸν αὐτὸν ἅγιον, Ἰωάννου μαΐστορος τοῦ Κουκουζέλη· ἦχος δ΄ *Λόγῳ Θεοῦ ἀνοίξας* (single B)

379. 387v Δεύτερος πούς· ἦχος τρίτος Διὸ ταῖς σαῖς *ἐλλαμφθέντες* (single B)

380. 390r Ἕτερον στιχηρὸν εἰς τὸν αὐτὸν ἅγιον, Ξένου τοῦ Κορώνη· ἦχος πλ. δ΄ *Ἡ γρήγορος γλῶσσα* (single B)

381. 393r Ποὺς δεύτερος· ἦχος δεύτερος *Καὶ θεοφθόγγοις δόγμασι* (single B)

382. 395r Ἰανουαρίου κζ΄, ἡ ἐπάνοδος τοῦ λειψάνου τοῦ ἐν ἁγίοις πατρὸς ἡμῶν Ἰωάννου τοῦ Χρυσοστόμου· στιχηρὸν τοῦ Καλλίστου, ἐκαλλωπίσθη δὲ παρὰ Ἰωάννου τοῦ Κουκουζέλου· ἦχος δ΄ *Οὐκ ἔδει σε, Χρυσόστομε* (single A)

383. 397v Ὁ δεύτερος πούς· πλ. δ΄ *Ὅθεν ἠγμένη ἡ ἀνακτορικὴ* — (with [epibolē] by Chrysaphēs, fol. 400v)

384. 401v Τρίτος πούς· ἦχος πλ. δ΄ *Τὸ ὕψος τῆς ταπεινοφροσύνης* — (single B) — (with epibolē of the kratēma by Koukouzelēs (fol. 402v) and prologos (fol. 403r); ends *apo chorou*)

385. 403v Ἰανουαρίου λ΄, τῶν τριῶν Ἱεραρχῶν [...], στιχηρὸν τοῦ Γλυκέος· ἦχος α΄ πα *Πᾶσα πνοὴ λογικὴ* — (single B) — (the kratēma by Chrysaphēs, fol. 406r)

386. 406v Ἕτερον στιχηρὸν [...], Ξένου τοῦ Κορώνη· ἦχος β΄ *Φωστῆρες ἐξέλαμψαν* (single B)

387. 409r Δεύτερος πούς· ἦχος πλ. β΄ νη *Ἡ γὰρ τοῦ πνεύματος* — (simple C) — (fol. 411v, text [kratēma] — fol. 412r *apo chorou*)

388. 412v Ἕτερον στιχηρὸν [...] Μανουὴλ τοῦ Χρυσάφου· ἦχος βαρὺς Ζω *Δεῦτε ἅπαντες πιστοί* (single B)

389. 417v Ἕτερον στιχηρὸν εἰς τὴν αὐτὴν ἑορτήν, πρὸς τό, Τὰ θύματα τὰ λογικά· μέλος Ξένου τοῦ Κορώνη· πλ. δ΄ *Τοὺς κήρυκας τοὺς ἱερούς* (single B)

ΜΠΤ 731: MATHĒMATARION (VOLUME V)

393 + i–iv folios

ΙΓ   Τόμος πέμπτος τοῦ Μαθηματαρίου, ἐξηγηθεὶς κατὰ τὴν Νέαν τῆς Μουσικῆς Μέθοδον, παρὰ Χουρμουζίου διδασκάλου τῆς κοινῆς τοῦ Γένους Σχολῆς τῆς ῥηθείσης Μεθόδου, καὶ Χαρτοφύλακος τῆς τοῦ Χριστοῦ Μεγάλης Ἐκκλησίας. Μὴν Φεβρουάριος, εἰς τὴν α΄, τοῦ ἁγίου μεγαλομάρτυρος Τρύφωνος·

390.   Στιχηρὸν Ἰωάννου τοῦ Γλυκέος· πλ. δ΄ *Τρύφων ὁ στερρός* (single B)

391. 4r   Δεύτερος πούς· *Οὗτος νοητῶς τοὺς πιστοὺς* (single B)

392. 6r   Τρίτος πούς· ἦχος τρίτος *Τούτῳ καὶ ἡμεῖς* (single B)

393. 9r   Φεβρουαρίου β΄, ἡ Ὑπαπαντὴ τοῦ Κυρίου· στιχηρὸν τοῦ Ἠθικοῦ· ἦχος β΄ βου *Συμεὼν ἐν ταῖς ἀγκάλαις* (single B)

394. 12r   Δεύτερος πούς· ἦχος α΄ *Οὗτός ἐστιν ὁ ἐν τοῖς προφήταις* (single B)

395. 14v   Ἕτερον στιχηρὸν [...], Ξένου τοῦ Κορώνη· ἦχος β΄ *Τὸν ἱερὸν ἡ ἱερὰ* — (single B) — (the kratēma τοῦ λαμπαδαρίου, fol. 15v)

396. 16r   Δεύτερος πούς· ἦχος πλ. β΄ νενανω *Καὶ ἐβόησε, νῦν ἀπολύοις* (single B)

397. 18r   Ἕτερον στιχηρὸν [...], Γερμανοῦ μοναχοῦ· ἦχος πλ. β΄, ἀπὸ χοροῦ *Ἀνοιγέσθω ἡ πύλη* — (fol. 18v) Εἶτα γίνεται καλλιφωνία, ὁ δομέστικος *Ὁ γὰρ ἄναρχος λόγος* — (fol. 19r) τοῦ Κουκουζέλη (kratēma) — (2-part A)

398. 23v   Ἀναγραμματισμὸς ἀπὸ τὸ αὐτὸ στιχηρόν· Ἰωάννου μαΐστορος τοῦ Κουκουζέλη· ἦχος β΄ *Ὁ ἐλθὼν εἰς τὸν κόσμον* (single B)

399. 26v   Ἕτερον στιχηρὸν [...], τοῦ τίνος ἐστὶν ἄδηλον· ἦχος βαρὺς *Κατακόσμησον τὸν νυμφῶνα* (3-part B)

400. 32r   Ἀναγραμματισμὸς ἀπὸ τὸ αὐτὸ στιχηρόν· Ἰωάννου τοῦ Κουκουζέλου· ἦχος πλ. δ΄ *Αὕτη γὰρ θρόνος* (single A)

401. 36r   Ἕτερον στιχηρὸν [...], Μανουὴλ Χρυσάφου· βαρὺς *Φῶς εἰς ἀποκάλυψιν* (single B)

402. 40v   Ἕτερον [...] Μανουὴλ τοῦ Χρυσάφου· πλ. δ΄ *Ὁ τοῖς χερουβὶμ* (single B)

403. 46r   Πεντηκοστάριον εἰς τὴν αὐτὴν ἑορτήν, παλαιόν· ἦχος πλ. β΄, ἀπὸ χοροῦ *Χριστὸν ὡς βρέφος σήμερον* (simple A)

Incipits of the Anagrams and mathēmata in the Mathēmatarion 201

404. 48v   Μεγαλυνάριον εἰς τὴν αὐτὴν ἑορτήν, μελισθὲν παρὰ Ἰωάννου λαμπαδαρίου τοῦ εὐαγοῦς βασιλικοῦ κλήρου, ἐπονομαζομένου Κλαδᾶ· ἦχος α΄ δ΄φωνος Ἀκατάληπτόν ἐστι (2-part B)

405. 53r   Ἕτερον μεγαλυνάριον [...], Ἰωάννου πρωτοψάλτου τοῦ Γλυκέος· ἦχος β΄ Ἀκατάληπτόν ἐστι (simple A)

406. 54r   Ἕτερον μεγαλυνάριον [...], Ἰωάννου τοῦ Κουκουζέλου· ἦχος τρίτος Ἀκατάληπτόν ἐστι (single B)

407. 57r   Φεβρουαρίου ια΄, τοῦ ἁγίου καὶ ἐνδόξου μεγαλομάρτυρος Βλασίου [...], στιχηρὸν Ξένου τοῦ Κορώνη· ἦχος δ΄ Ὡς καλὸς παιδοτρίβης (single B)

408. 60v   Δεύτερος πούς· [πλ. β΄] Μεθ᾽ ὧν τὸν δρόμον (single B)

409. 62v   Φεβρουαρίου κγ΄, τοῦ ἁγίου ἱερομάρτυρος Πολυκάρπου· στιχηρὸν τοῦ Ἠθικοῦ· ἦχος δ΄ Ἀμφότερα σὺ (simple C)

410. 64v   Φεβρουαρίου κδ΄ [...], στιχηρὸν Μανουὴλ τοῦ Χρυσάφου· ἦχος πλ. β΄ Τὴν πάνσεπτον κάραν (single B)

***

411. 68r   Μὴν Μάρτιος· εἰς τὰς θ΄, τῶν ἁγίων μ΄ μαρτύρων· στιχηρὸν Ξένου τοῦ Κορώνη· ἦχος β΄ βου Τὴν λίμνην ὡς παράδεισον (single B)

412. 71v   Δεύτερος πούς· Οὐκ ἐδειλίασαν οἱ γενναῖοι (single B)

413. 74r   Ἕτερον στιχηρὸν Νικολάου τοῦ Λιμνηνοῦ· ἦχος β΄ Τὴν λίμνην ὡς παράδεισον (single B)

414. 76r-v Δεύτερος πούς· [πλ. β΄] Οὐκ ἔπτηξαν τὸν λογισμὸν (single B)

415. 79r   Ἕτερον στιχηρὸν εἰς τὴν αὐτὴν ἑορτήν, παλαιόν· ἐκαλλωπίσθη δὲ παρὰ τοῦ Κουκουζέλου, ὕστερον δὲ συνετμήθη καὶ ἡνώθη μετὰ τῶν ποδῶν αὐτοῦ, παρὰ Μανουὴλ τοῦ Χρυσάφου· ἦχος β΄ βου Τὴν τετραδεκάριθμον χορείαν (single B)

416. 83r-v Δεύτερος πούς· [ἦχος β΄] Ἐλάφρυνον τὸ βάρος (single B) (with epibolē by the maïstōr, fol. 85r, Ἐβάφησαν ἡμῶν)

417. 88r   Ἕτερον στιχηρὸν [...], Ἰωάννου μαΐστορος τοῦ Κουκουζέλου· ἦχος β΄ βου Προφητικῶς μὲν ἐβόα (2-part B) (with parekbolē by Chrysaphēs, fol. 90v, Διὰ πυρός)

418. 93r   Ἕτερον στιχηρὸν [...], Γερμανοῦ μοναχοῦ, ἐκαλλωπίσθη δὲ παρὰ τοῦ Χρυσάφου· πλ. β΄ Φέροντες τὰ παρόντα (single B)

419. 97v Ἀναγραμματισμὸς ἀπὸ τὸ αὐτὸ στιχηρὸν [...], Μανουὴλ τοῦ Χρυσάφου· ἦχος πλ. β' *Μὴ οὖν ἐκκλίνωμεν* (single A)

420. 102r Μαρτίου κε', ὁ εὐαγγελισμὸς τῆς Θεοτόκου· στιχηρὸν Μιχαὴλ τοῦ Πατζάδος· ἦχος α' *Ἀπεστάλη ἄγγελος* (single B) (with parekbolē by Koukouzelēs, ἦχος β' *Εἰς πόλιν τῆς Γαλιλαίας, τεριρεμ*, fol. 104v)

421. 106r Δεύτερος πούς· ἦχος πλ. β' *Εὐαγγελίσασθαι αὐτῇ* (single B)

422. 107v Τρίτος πούς· ἦχος α' *Ἀπεστάλη δοῦλος ἀσώματος* (4-part A)

423. 112r Τέταρτος πούς· ἦχος α' *Χαῖρε θρόνε πυρίμορφε* (single A)

424. 114v Πέμπτος πούς· [ἦχος β'] *Χαῖρε ὄρος ἀλατόμητον* (single B)

425. 118v Ἕτερον στιχηρὸν [...], Ἰωάννου τοῦ Κουκουζέλου· ἦχος β' *Εὐαγγελίζεται ὁ Γαβριὴλ* (single B)

426. 121v Δεύτερος πούς· [ἦχος β'] *Χαῖρε ἀνύμφευτε μήτηρ* (single A)

427. 124r Τρίτος πούς· ἦχος πλ. δ' *Ὄφις ἐξηπάτησεν* (single A)

428. 126r Ἕτερον πρὸς τό, Ὁ διδάσκαλος λέγει, μεταβληθὲν παρὰ κὺρ Γερασίμου τοῦ Χαλκεοπούλου· ἦχος πλ. β' *Εὐαγγελίζεται ὁ Γαβριὴλ* (single A)

429. 131r Ἕτερον στιχηρὸν [...], Μανουὴλ τοῦ Χρυσάφου· ἦχος β' βου *Τὸ ἀπ' αἰῶνος μυστήριον* (single B)

430. 136r Δεύτερος πούς· ἦχος β' *Εὐφραινέσθω ἡ φύσις* (single B)

431. 139r Ἕτερον στιχηρὸν [...], Μανουὴλ τοῦ Χρυσάφου· ἦχος δ' *Γλῶσσα ἣν οὐκ ἔγνω* (single B)

432. 143v Ἀναγραμματισμὸς τοῦ Κουκουζέλη, μεταβληθεὶς εἰς ἕτερα γράμματα, παρὰ Μανουὴλ τοῦ Χρυσάφου· ἦχος πλ. β' νενανω *Χαῖρε κεχαριτωμένη* (single A)

433. 146v Ἕτερον στιχηρὸν [...], Γερασίμου τοῦ Χαλκεοπούλου· πλ. δ' *Εὐφραινέσθωσαν οἱ οὐρανοί* (simple C)

434. 152r Ἀναγραμματισμὸς ἀπὸ τὸ αὐτὸ στιχηρὸν [...], Μανουὴλ τοῦ Χρυσάφου· πλ. δ' *Χαῖρε κεχαριτωμένη* (single A)

435. 156v Ἕτερον εἰς τὴν αὐτὴν ἑορτήν· ἀναποδισμὸς ἐκ τοῦ Θεοτόκε Παρθένε, Ἰωάσαφ· ἦχος α' *κε Κεχαριτωμένη χαῖρε* (single A)

436. 160r Πεντηκοστάριον εἰς τὴν αὐτὴν ἑορτήν· Μανουὴλ τοῦ Χρυσάφου· πλ. β' *Σὲ προκατήγγειλε χορός* (single A)

437. 162v Εἱρμοὶ ἀσματικοὶ μετὰ ἠχημάτων εἰς τὴν αὐτὴν ἑορτήν, ἀλλὰ δὴ καὶ εἰς τὴν εἴσοδον αὐτῆς καὶ εἰς τὴν κοίμησιν, ψαλλόμενοι ὕστερον εἰς τὴν καταβασίαν,

μελισθέντες παρὰ Μανουὴλ τοῦ Χρυσάφου· ἦχος δ΄, ᾠδὴ α΄ *Τῷ Κυρίῳ ᾄσωμεν* — *Ἀνοίξω τὸ στόμα μου* (with ēchēmata and at times kratēmata)

438. 166r   Ὠιδὴ γ΄, ἦχος δ΄ *Ἅγιος εἶ Κύριε* — *Τοὺς σοὺς ὑμνολόγους*

439. 169r   Ὠιδὴ δ΄, ἦχος δ΄ *Δόξᾳ τῇ δυνάμει σου* — *Ὁ καθήμενος*

440. 173r   Ἕτερος εἱρμὸς εἰς τὴν εἴσοδον καὶ εἰς τὴν κοίμησιν· ἦχος δ΄ *Τὴν ἀνεξιχνίαστον*

441. 175v   Ὠιδὴ ε΄, ἦχος δ΄ *Κύριε ὁ Θεὸς* — *Ἐξέστη τὰ σύμπαντα*

442. 179v   Ὠδὴ ς΄, ἦχος δ΄ *Ὡς τὸν προφήτην* — *Ἐβόησε προτυπῶν*

443. 183r   Ὠιδὴ η΄, ἦχος δ΄ *Αἰνοῦμεν* — *Ἄκουε κόρη*

444. 187r   Ἕτερος εἱρμὸς εἰς τὴν κοίμησιν· ᾠδὴ η΄, ἦχος δ΄ *Παῖδας εὐαγεῖς*

445. 189v   Ὠιδὴ θ΄, ἦχος δ΄ *Εὐαγγελίζου* — *Ὡς ἐμψύχῳ*

446. 194v   Ἕτερος εἱρμὸς εἰς τὴν κοίμησιν· ἦχος δ΄ *Ὑπεραγία Θεοτόκε* — *Ἅπας γηγενὴς*

447. 199r   Μεγαλυνάριον εἰς τὴν ἑορτὴν τοῦ Εὐαγγελισμοῦ, Ἰωάννου μαΐστορος τοῦ Κουκουζέλου· ἦχος δ΄ *Εὐαγγελίζου γῆ* (single B)

448. 203r   Ἕτερον μεγαλυνάριον, Ἰωάννου λαμπαδαρίου τοῦ Κλαδᾶ· ἦχος δ΄ *Εὐαγγελίζου* — *Ὡς ἐμψύχῳ* (2-part B)

***

449. 209r   Μὴν Ἀπρίλιος, εἰς τὴν α΄, Μαρίας τῆς Αἰγυπτίας· Ἰωάννου τοῦ Κλαδᾶ· πλ. δ΄ *Μέγας ὁ Κύριος ἡμῶν* (single B)

450. 213v   Δεύτερος πούς· ἦχος τρίτος *Νηστείαις καὶ δεήσεσι* (single A)

451. 215v   Ἀπρίλιος κγ΄, Γεωργίου μεγαλομάρτυρος τοῦ τροπαιοφόρου· στιχηρὸν Μανουὴλ τοῦ Χρυσάφου· ἦχος α΄ *Ὁ λαμπρὸς ἀριστεὺς* (single B)

452. 220r   Ἕτερον στιχηρὸν [...], Ξένου τοῦ Κορώνη· ἦχος α΄ *Τοῦ μεγάλου βασιλέως* (single A)

453. 223r   Δεύτερος πούς· ἦχος πλ. β΄ *Τὸ γὰρ σῶμά σου* (single B)

454. 225v   Ἀναγραμματισμὸς ἀπὸ τὸ αὐτὸ στιχηρόν· Κωνσταντίνου δομεστίκου τοῦ Μαγουλᾶ· ἦχος πλ. α΄ *Χριστὸν γὰρ ὃν ἐπόθησας* (single A)

455. 228v   Ἕτερος εἰς τὸν αὐτὸν ἅγιον, Ἰωάννου τοῦ Γλυκέος· ἦχος δ΄ *Ἀσμάτων χορεύοντες* (single B)

456. 230v   Τοῦ Κουκουζέλου· πλ. δ΄ *Διὸ πάντες κράξωμεν* (single A)

457. 232r Ἕτερον στιχηρὸν […], τοῦ Καρβουναριώτου, ἐκαλλωπίσθη δὲ παρὰ τοῦ Χρυσάφου· ἦχος δ΄ *Τὸν νοερὸν ἀδάμαντα* (single B)

458. 234r Δεύτερος πούς· ἦχος πλ. β΄ *Γεώργιον τὸν ἀοίδιμον* (2-part B)(with parembolē by Chrysaphēs, fol. 236v *Γεώργιον ὑμνήσωμεν*, with kratēma)

459. 239v Ἀναγραμματισμὸς ἐκ τοῦ αὐτοῦ στιχηροῦ […], τοῦ Χρυσάφου· ἦχος δ΄ *Γεώργιον τὸν ἀοίδιμον* (single A)

460. 243r Τὸ αὐτὸ στιχηρὸν μελισθὲν παρὰ Γρηγορίου Μπούνη τοῦ Ἀλυάτου· ἦχος δ΄ *Τὸν νοερὸν ἀδάμαντα* (single B)

461. 247v Ἕτερον στιχηρὸν […], Μιχαὴλ τοῦ Πατζάδος· ἐκαλλωπίσθη δὲ παρὰ τοῦ Κουκουζέλου· ἦχος πλ. α΄ *Ἀνέτειλε τὸ ἔαρ* (single B)

462. 250r Δεύτερος πούς· ἦχος πλ. α΄ *Ἡ τοῦ ἀθλοφόρου μνήμη* (single B)

463. 252v Τρίτος πούς· ἦοχς πλ. α΄ *Οὗτος γὰρ ὡς καλὸς* (single A)

464. 255r Ἀναγραμματισμὸς ἀπὸ τοῦ αὐτοῦ στιχηροῦ […], Ἰωάννου τοῦ Κουκουζέλου· ἦχος α΄ *Οὐκ ἠλέησε τὸ σκεῦος* (single A)

465. 257v Τοῦ αὐτοῦ· ἦχος πλ. β΄ *Αὐτῷ βοήσωμεν* — (as *prologos* with a kratēma — fol. 258v *heteros prologos*)

466. 259v Πεντηκοστάριον εἰς τὸν αὐτὸν ἅγιον· Ἰωάννου τοῦ Κουκουζέλου· ἦχος β΄ βου *Ὡς ῥόδον ἐπεξήνθησεν* (single A)

467. 262r Ἀπριλίου κε΄, τοῦ ἁγίου ἀποστόλου καὶ εὐαγγελιστοῦ Μάρκου· στιχηρὸν τοῦ Κοντοπετρῆ· ἦχος πλ. β΄ *Σοῦ ἐξεχύθη χάρις* (single B)

468. 265r Δεύτερος πούς· ἦχος πλ. β΄ *Διδάσκων τὰ λογικὰ* (single B)

***

469. 268r Μὴν Μάιος· εἰς τὰς θ΄, τοῦ ἁγίου μεγαλομάρτυρος Χριστοφόρου· Μανουὴλ τοῦ Χρυσάφου· πλ. β΄ *Ἐπέστη σήμερον* (single B)

470. 272r Δεύτερος πούς· [ἦχος β΄] *Ὅθεν καὶ ἀπέλαβες* (single B)

471. 274v Μαΐου ιβ΄, Ἐπιφανίου ἐπισκόπου Κύπρου· Κωνσταντίνου δομεστίκου τοῦ Μαγουλᾶ· ἦχος α΄ *Τοῦ θεοφόρου πατρὸς* (single B)

472. 278r Δεύτερος πούς· ἦχος δ΄ *Ὡς Παύλου μιμητὴς* (single B)

473. 281r Ἀναποδισμὸς ἀπὸ τὸ Φοβερὸς μέν, τοῦ αὐτοῦ [Χρυσάφου]· ἦχος πλ. β΄ *Παρρησίαν ἔχων* (single A)

Incipits of the Anagrams and mathēmata in the Mathēmatarion 205

474. 284r   Μαΐου ιε΄, Ἀχιλλίου ἐπισκόπου Λαρίσης τοῦ ὁμολογητοῦ· Ἰωάννου Κουκουζέλου· ἦχος β΄ βου *Ὡς ἀστὴρ πολύφωτος* (single B)

475. 286v   Δεύτερος πούς· ἦχος πλ. β΄ *Τῶν γὰρ σεπτῶν εἰκόνων* (single B)

476. 289r   Μαΐου κα΄, Κωνσταντίνου καὶ Ἑλένης· στιχηρὸν παλαιόν, ἐκαλλωπίσθη δὲ παρὰ τοῦ Κουκουζέλου· ἦχος β΄ βου *Τοῦ εὐσεβοῦς Κωνσταντίνου* (single B)

477. 291v   Ἕτερον στιχηρὸν [...], Νικηφόρου τοῦ Ἠθικοῦ· ἦχος β΄ βου *Οὐκ ἐξ ἀνθρώπων τὴν κλῆσιν* (single B)

478. 294r   Δεύτερος πούς· ἦχος πλ. β΄ *Τὸ γὰρ σημεῖον τοῦ σταυροῦ* (single B)

479. 296r   Ἕτερον στιχηρὸν [...] Ἰωάννου τοῦ Γλυκέος· πλ. δ΄ *Σέλας φαεινὸν* (single B)

480. 298v   Δεύτερος πούς· ἦχος τρίτος *Ἤκουσας ἐκεῖθεν* (simple C)

481. 300r   Τρίτος πούς· ἦχος δ΄ *Ὀρθοδόξων βασιλέων* (single B)

482. 302r–v   Ἀναγραμματισμὸς ἀπὸ τὸ αὐτὸ στιχηρόν· Μανουὴλ τοῦ Χρυσάφου· ἦχος πλ. δ΄ *Κωνσταντῖνε ἰσαπόστολε* (single B)

483. 306v   Ἕτερον στιχηρὸν παλαιόν, ἐκαλλωπίσθη δὲ παρὰ Ἰωάννου τοῦ Κουκουζέλου· ἦχος πλ. δ΄ *Ὁ τῶν ἀνάκτων ἄναξ* (single B)

484. 308v   Δεύτερος πούς· ἦχος πλ. δ΄ *Αὐτὸς οὐρανόθεν* (single B)

485. 310r   Τρίτος πούς· ἦχος β΄ *Ἐν τούτῳ, ἔφησας, νίκα* (single B)

486. 313r   Μαΐου κθ΄, Θεοδοσίας ὁσιομάρτυρος· στιχηρὸν Μανουὴλ τοῦ Χρυσάφου· ἦχος τρίτος *Τὴν νοητὴν χελιδόνα* (single B)

487. 316r   Δεύτερος πούς· ἦχος β΄ *Ἵνα ταῖς πρεσβείαις αὐτῆς* (single B)

488. 319r   Στίχοι εἰς τὴν αὐτὴν ἁγίαν, στιχουργηθέντες παρὰ Μάρκου ἰατροῦ, τοῦ μεγάλου στρατοπεδάρχου, μελισθέντες δὲ παρὰ Μανουὴλ τοῦ Χρυσάφου· ἦχος δ΄ *Τὴν νυμφευθεῖσαν τῷ Χριστῷ* (single A)

***

489. 322v   Ἰουνίου η΄, Θεοδώρου τοῦ στρατηλάτου· στιχηρὸν τοῦ Καλλίστου, καλλωπισμὸς τοῦ Κουκουζέλου· ἦχος πλ. δ΄ *Τῶν τοῦ Θεοῦ δωρεῶν* (single B)

490. 324v   Τὸ αὐτὸ στιχηρὸν καὶ πολίτικον· πλ. δ΄ *Τῶν τοῦ Θεοῦ δωρεῶν* (single B)

491. 326v   Δεύτερος πούς· πλ. δ΄ *Πάντες εὐφημήσωμεν* (single B)

492. 329r   Τρίτος πούς· ἦχος τρίτος *Τῆς οἰκουμένης τὸν ὑπέρμαχον* (single B)

493. 330v   Ἑτέρα ἐπιβολή, τοῦ Κουκουζέλου· ἦχος δ΄ *Μακαρίσωμεν πάντες* (single A)

494. 332v Ἀναγραμματισμὸς ἀπὸ τὸ αὐτὸ στιχηρόν, Γεωργίου τοῦ Σγουροπούλου· ἦχος πλ. δ´ *Τῆς οἰκουμένης τὸν ὑπέρμαχον* (single A)

495. 335v Στιχηρὸν εἰς τὸν ἅγιον Βαρθολομαῖον· Ἰωάννου τοῦ Γλυκέος· ἦχος πλ. δ´ *Ἀπόστολε τοῦ σωτῆρος* (single B)

496. 338r Ἰουνίου ιη´, Λεοντίου μεγαλομάρτυρος· στιχηρὸν Ἰωάννου τοῦ Κουκουζέλου· ἦχος α´ *Ἀθλοφόρε Λεόντιε* (single B)

497. 340r Δεύτερος πούς· ἦχος πλ. α´ *Ἀλλ᾿ ἀνδείως ἀθλήσας* (single B)

498. 343r Τὸ αὐτὸ στιχηρὸν ποιηθὲν καὶ παρὰ Ἰωάννου λαμπαδαρίου τοῦ Κλαδᾶ, καλλωπισθὲν δὲ παρὰ Μανουὴλ τοῦ Χρυσάφου· ἔτι γὰρ νέος ὢν ἐποίησεν αὐτό, διὰ τοιοῦτο ἐδεήθη καλλωπισμοῦ· ἦχος α´ δ´φωνος κε *Ἀθλοφόρε Λεόντιε* (single A)

499. 345v Ποὺς [δεύτερος]· ἦχος πλ. β´ *Τὰ τῶν εἰδώλων σεβάσματα* (single B)

500. 347v Ἰουνίου κδ´, τὸ γενέσιον τοῦ Προδρόμου· στιχηρὸν τοῦ Χρυσάφου· ἦχος β´ βου *Τὸν ἐκ προφήτου προφήτην* (single B)

501. 351r Ἀναγραμματισμὸς ἀπὸ τὸ αὐτὸ στιχηρόν· Κωνσταντίνου τοῦ Μαγουλᾶ· ἦχος α´ δ´φωνος κε *Δωρηθῆναι εἰρήνην* (single A)

502. 354r Ἕτερον στιχηρὸν εἰς τὴν αὐτὴν ἑορτήν· Γαβριὴλ ἱερομονάχου ἐκ τῶν Ξανθοπούλων· ἦχος β´ βου *Ἦλθεν ἡ φωνὴ τῆς χάριτος* (single B)

503. 357r Ἕτερον στιχηρὸν [...], Μανουὴλ τοῦ Χρυσάφου· ἦχος δ´ *Λύει τοῦ Ζαχαρίου* (single B)

504. 360v [Ποὺς δεύτερος]· ἦχος β´ *Ὢ καὶ εὐηγγελίσθη* (single A)

505. 362v Ἕτερον στιχηρὸν [...], τοῦ Καρβουναριώτου, ἐκαλλωπίσθη δὲ παρὰ τοῦ Χρυσάφου· ἦχος πλ. α´ *Τὸν ἐν προφήταις ὅρον* (single B)

506. 366r Δεύτερος πούς· ἦχος α´, τοῦ Χρυσάφου· *Σήμερον ἡ Ἐλισάβετ* (single B)

507. 370r Ἕτερον στιχηρὸν εἰς τὴν αὐτὴν ἑορτήν· ψάλλεται καὶ εἰς τὴν σύλληψιν αὐτοῦ· τοῦ Χρυσάφου· ἦχος πλ. β´ *Ἡ Ἐλισάβετ συνέλαβε* (single A)

508. 373v Ἕτερον στιχηρὸν εἰς τὴν αὐτὴν ἑορτήν, Νικολάου τοῦ Καμπάνη· ἐκαλλωπίσθη δὲ παρὰ τοῦ Κουκουζέλη, καὶ Μανουὴλ τοῦ Χρυσάφου· ἦχος πλ. δ´ *Πρέπει τῷ Ἰωάννῃ* (single A)

509. 375r Ἕτερον [παρεκβολή], Ἰωάννου τοῦ Κουκουζέλου· ἦχος πλ. δ´ *Τῶν ᾀσμάτων πρέπει τερπνότης* (single A)

510. 376v Ἕτερον [παρεκβολή], πολίτικον· ἦχος πλ. δ´ *Ἡ τερπνότης*, τιτιτι

Incipits of the Anagrams and mathēmata in the Mathēmatarion 207

511. 377r Δεύτερος πούς· ἦχος β´ *Οὗτος γὰρ ἐκήρυξε* (3-part A)

512. 380v Ἀναγραμματισμὸς ἀπὸ τὸ αὐτὸ στιχηρόν·Ἰωάννου τοῦ Κουκουζέλου· ἦχος δ´ *Ὁ τὸν ἀμνὸν προμηνύων* (single A)

513. 383r Ἕτερος ἀναγραμματισμὸς ἀπὸ τὸ αὐτὸ στιχηρόν· Μανουὴλ τοῦ Χρυσάφου· ἦχος πλ. δ´ *Τοῦ βασιλέως ὁ στρατιώτης* (2-part A)

514. 387r Ἕτερον στιχηρὸν εἰς τὴν αὐτὴν ἑορτήν·Ἰωάννου Κλαδᾶ τοῦ περιφήμου· ἦχος πλ. δ´ *Γα Βλέπε τὴν Ἐλισάβετ* (single B)

515. 390r Ἰουνίου κζ´, Σαμψὼν τοῦ ξενοδόχου· στιχηρὸν Μανουὴλ τοῦ Χρυσάφου· ἦχος πλ. δ´ *Τὸν ἄρτον σου τοῖς πένησι* (single B)

ΜΠΤ 732: ΜΑΤΗĒΜΑΤΑRION (VOLUME VI)

390 + i–ii folios

1r Τόμος ἕκτος τοῦ Μαθηματαρίου, ἐξηγηθεὶς κατὰ τὴν Νέαν τῆς Μουσικῆς Μέθοδον παρὰ Χουρμουζίου διδασκάλου τῆς κοινῆς τοῦ Γένους Σχολῆς τῆς ῥηθείσης Μεθόδου καὶ Χαρτοφύλακος τῆς τῦ Χριστοῦ Μεγάλης Ἐκκλησίας.

516. Ἰουνίου κθ´, τῶν ἁγίων καὶ ἐνδόξων ἀποστόλων Πέτρου καὶ Παύλου· στιχηρὸν πρὸς τό, Ἀναστάσεως ἡμέρα, μεταβληθὲν παρὰ Μανουὴλ τοῦ Χρυσάφου· ἦχος α´ *Τοὺς φωστῆρας τοὺς μεγάλους* (single B)

517. 5r Ἕτερον στιχηρὸν […], τοῦ Κομνηνοῦ, ἐκαλλωπίσθη δὲ παρὰ τοῦ Χρυσάφου· ἦχος β´ *Πέτρε κορυφαῖε* (single A)

518. 7v Ἕτερον στιχηρὸν […],Ἰωάννου τοῦ Κουκουζέλου· ἦχος β´ *βου Παῦλε, στόμα Κυρίου* (single A)

519. 10r Δεύτερος πούς· ἦχος β´ *Ὅθεν ἄρρητα εἶδες* (single B)

520. 11v Ἀναγραμματισμὸς ἀπὸ τὸ αὐτὸ στιχηρόν·Ἰωάννου τοῦ Κουκουζέλου· ἦχος πλ. β´ *Δεῦτε σὺν ἐμοί* (single A)

521. 14r Ἕτερον στιχηρὸν […], Μανουὴλ τοῦ Χρυσάφου· τρίτος *Οἱ τῆς ἄνω Ἱερουσαλήμ* (single B)

522. 17v Ἕτερον στιχηρὸν […], Νικολάου τοῦ Καμπάνη, ἐκαλλωπίσθη δὲ παρὰ τοῦ Κουκουζέλου· ἦχος δ´ *Τῷ τριττῷ τῆς ἐρωτήσεως* (single B)

523. 20v   Δεύτερος πούς· ἦχος δ' *Κύριε, πάντα γινώσκεις* (simple A)

524. 23r   Ἀναγραμματισμὸς ἀπὸ τὸ αὐτὸ στιχηρόν· Ἰωάννου τοῦ Κουκουζέλου καὶ μαΐστορος· ἦχος δ' *Ὅθεν πρὸς αὐτὸν ὁ σωτήρ* (single B)

525. 27r   Ἕτερον στιχηρὸν [...], Βαρθολομαίου μοναχοῦ, ἐκαλλωπίσθη δὲ παρὰ τοῦ Χρυσάφου· ἦχος πλ. α' *Ἡ σοφία τοῦ Θεοῦ* (single B)

526. 30v   Ἀναποδισμὸς ἀπὸ τὸ αὐτὸ στιχηρόν· Ἰωάννου τοῦ μαΐστορος· ἦχος πλ. α' *Στηρίξατε ποίμνην* (single A)

527. 34v   Ἕτερον στιχηρὸν [...], δομεστίκου Νικηφόρου τοῦ Ἠθικοῦ· ἦχος πλ. β' *Ἑορτὴ χαρμόσυνος* (single A)

528. 39r   Τὸ αὐτὸ στιχηρὸν μελισθὲν καὶ παρὰ Μανουὴλ τοῦ Χρυσάφου· οὐ γινώσκων γὰρ ἦν τὸ προγραφὲν (sic)· ἦχος πλ. β' *Ἑορτὴ χαρμόσυνος* (single A)

529. 42r   Δεύτερος πούς· ἦχος πλ. β' *Χαῖρε, Πέτρε ἀπόστολε* (single B)

530. 45r   Ἕτερον στιχηρὸν [...], Ξένου τοῦ Κορώνη· ἦχος πλ. β' *Τοὺς τῆς εὐσεβείας* (single B)

531. 49v   Ἰουνίου λ', τῶν ἁγίων ἀποστόλων τῶν δώδεκα· στιχηρὸν Μανουὴλ τοῦ Χρυσάφου· ἦχος πλ. δ' *Τοὺς μαθητὰς τοῦ σωτῆρος* (single B)

***

532. 54v   Μὴν Ἰούλιος· εἰς τὰς β', ἡ κατάθεσις τῆς τιμίας ἐσθῆτος τῆς Θεοτόκου· στιχηρὸν Ἰωάννου τοῦ Γλυκέος· ἦχος β' *Φρένα καθάραντες* (single B)

533. 58r   Δεύτερος πούς· ἦχος β' *Ὡς γὰρ παλάτιον τερπνὸν* (single B)

534. 60r   Ἰουλίου ε', τοῦ ὁσίου πατρὸς ἡμῶν Ἀθανασίου τοῦ ἐν τῷ Ἄθῳ· στιχηρὸν τοῦ Κουκουζέλου· ἦχος β' *Περικυκλοῦντες τὴν λάρνακα* (single A)

535. 62v   Δεύτερος πούς· ἦχος πλ. β' *Οὐ δάκρυα χέομεν* (single A)

536. 64v   Ἀναγραμματισμὸς [...], τοῦ μαΐστορος· ἦχος πλ. β' *Ἡ καὶ πρεσβεύει* (single A)

537. 67v   Ἕτερον στιχηρὸν [...], Γερασίμου ἱερομονάχου· πλ. β' *Ὡς ἔνθεος ἡ ζωή σου* (2-part A)

538. 71r   Ἕτερον στιχηρὸν [...], Ξένου τοῦ Κορώνη· πλ. δ' *Τὴν τοῦ Κυρίου πτωχείαν* (single B)

539. 74r   Πούς δεύτερος· ἦχος δ' *Διὸ πλήρης τῶν σῶν θαυμάτων* (single B)

540. 76v   [Πούς ἄλλος]· ἦχος πλ. β' *Καὶ πρέσβευε τῷ Κυρίῳ* (single A)

Incipits of the Anagrams and mathēmata in the Mathēmatarion 209

541. 78v Τὸ αὐτὸ στιχηρὸν συντομηθὲν καὶ κατὰ τὸ δοκοῦν καλλωπισθὲν παρὰ Γερασίμου· ἦχος πλ. δ΄ *Τὴν τοῦ Κυρίου πτωχείαν* (simple C)

542. 82r Ἰουλίου η΄, τοῦ ἁγίου μεγαλομάρτυρος Προκοπίου· στιχηρὸν Μανουὴλ τοῦ Χρυσάφου· ἦχος α΄ *Ἀθλοφόρε τοῦ Χριστοῦ* (single A)

543. 85v Ἕτερον στιχηρὸν [...], Νεοφύτου τοῦ Ἠθικοῦ· πλ. β΄ *Ἐξέλαμψε σήμερον* (single B)

544. 88v Ποὺς δεύτερος· ἦχος πλ. β΄ *Ὅθεν καὶ προστρέχοντες* (single B)

545. 90v Ἰουλίου ια΄, τῆς ὁσίας μητρὸς ἡμῶν Εὐφημίας τῆς νέας, τῆς κειμένης ἐν τῇ μονῇ τοῦ Ζωτικοῦ τοῦ Ὀρφανοτρόφου· στιχηρὸν Μανουὴλ τοῦ Χρυσάφου· τρίτος *Τὴν νοητὴν χελιδόνα* (single B)

546. 93v Δεύτερος ποὺς· ἦχος β΄ *Ἵνα ταῖς προσβείαις αὐτῆς* (single B)

547. 97r Ἰουλίου ιε΄ [...], στιχηρὸν τοῦ Χρυσάφου· πλ. β΄ *Δεῦτε καὶ θεάσασθε* (single A)

548. 100r Ἕτερον στιχηρὸν [...], Ἰωάννου τοῦ Γλυκέος· πλ. δ΄ *Ὁ τριετὴς τὴν τριάδα* (single B)

549. 103r Ἀναγραμματισμὸς ἀπὸ τὸ αὐτὸ στιχηρόν· Ἰωάννου τοῦ Κουκουζέλου· πλ. δ΄ *Παῦσον, ὦ μῆτερ μου* (single B)

550. 105v Ἰουλίου ιζ΄, τῆς ἁγίας Μαρίνης· στιχηρὸν τοῦ Κλαβᾶ, ἐκαλλωπίσθη δὲ παρὰ τοῦ Κουκουζέλου· ἦχος β΄ *Ἐν πόλει τοῦ Θεοῦ ἡμῶν* (single B)

551. 108r Δεύτερος ποὺς· ἦχος πλ. β΄ *Τὴν λαμπάδα ἄσβεστον* (single B) — (note at the end (fol. 111r): εἶτα γίνεται καλλιφωνία)

552. 111r Ἕτερον στιχηρὸν [...], Μανουὴλ τοῦ Χρυσάφου· ἦχος β΄ *βου Ἐν φωνῇ ἀγαλλιάσεως* (single B)

   115r Τὸ αὐτὸ ἀπὸ τοῦ, λέγε, εἰς ἦχον τέταρτον *Λέγε, ὑπὲρ σοῦ τὰς σάρκας μου*

553. 116v Ἰουλίους κ΄, τοῦ ἁγίου ἐνδόξου προφήτου Ἠλιοὺ τοῦ Θεσβίτου· στιχηρὸν τοῦ Ἠθικοῦ· ἦχος α΄ *Ἠλίας ὁ ζηλωτής* (3-part B)

554. 121r Ἕτερον [...], τοῦ Γλυκέος, ἐκαλλωπίσθη παρὰ τοῦ Χρυσάφου· ἦχος δ΄ *Ἐν πυρίνῳ ἅρματι* (single B)

555. 124v Ἰουλίου κβ΄, τῆς ἁγίας καὶ ἰσαποστόλου Μαρίας τῆς Μαγδαληνῆς· στιχηρὸν Γρηγορίου Μπούνη τοῦ Ἀλυάτου· ἦχος πλ. β΄ *Πρώτη κατιδοῦσα* (single B)

556. 128r Ποὺς [δεύτερος]· ἦχος β΄ *Τὴν ἀθυμίαν ἀποθέμενοι* (single B)

557. 129r Ἕτερον στιχηρὸν εἰς τὴν αὐτὴν ἁγίαν, ψάλλεται δὲ καὶ τῇ Κυριακῇ τῶν Μυροφόρων· Μανουὴλ τοῦ Χρυσάφου· ἦχος πλ. δ' *Τῷ ἑκουσίως πτωχεύσαντι* (single B)

558. 134r Ἰουλίου κε', ἡ κοίμησις τῆς ἁγίας Ἄννης· στιχηρὸν Δημητρίου ἱερέως τοῦ Συνοδινοῦ· ἦχος πλ. δ' *Οἱ ἐξ ἀκάρπων λαγόνων* (single B)

559. 136v Δεύτερος πούς· ἦχος δ' *Οὗτοι μεταστάντες* (single B)

560. 139r Τρίτος πούς· ἦχος δ' *Οὓς καὶ ἡμεῖς συνελθόντες* (single B)

561. 141r Ἕτερον στιχηρὸν [...], Ξένου τοῦ Κορώνη· πλ. δ' *Δεῦτε πᾶσα κτίσις* (4-part B)

562. 146v Ἰουλίου κζ', τοῦ ἁγίου μεγαλομάρτυρος καὶ ἰαματικοῦ Παντελεήμονος· στιχηρὸν Ἰωάννου τοῦ Κομνηνοῦ, ἐκαλλωπίσθη παρὰ τοῦ Χρυσάφου· ἦχος β' *Μητρὸς εὐσεβοῦς* (single B)

563. 150r Ἕτερον [...], Ἰωάννου τοῦ Γλυκέος· πλ. β' *Ἡ παμφαὴς τοῦ μάρτυρος* (the kratēma is characterized as an parekbolē, fol. 253v) (2-part B)

564. 154r Ἕτερον στιχηρὸν [...], τοῦ Καμπάνη, ἐκαλλωπίσθη δὲ παρὰ τοῦ Κουκουζέλου πλ. β' *Ἐξέλαμψε σήμερον* (2-part A)

565. 157r Ἕτερος πούς· ἦχος πλ. β' *Ἐπέστη γὰρ νῦν ἡμῖν* (single B)

566. 159v Ἕτερον στιχηρὸν [...], Μανουὴλ τοῦ Χρυσάφου· πλ. δ' *Μητρικὴν ἀγάπην* (single B)

567. 164r Ἰουλίου κη', τῆς ὁσίας μητρὸς ἡμῶν Εἰρήνης, τῆς κειμένης ἐν τῇ μονῇ τοῦ Ἀλείψη· στιχηρὸν τοῦ Κουκουζέλου· τρίτος *Τὴν ἁγνὴν περιστερὰν* (single B)

568. 167r Δεύτερος πούς· ἦχος α' δ' φωνος *Ὅπως ταῖς πρεσβείαις αὐτῆς* (single B)

569. 169v Ἀναγραμματισμὸς ἀπὸ τὸ αὐτὸ στιχηρὸν [...], Μανουὴλ τοῦ ὡς ἀληθῶς Χρυσάφου· τρίτος *Εἰρήνην τὴν ἀοίδιμον* (single A)

570. 173r Ἰουλίου λα', Εὐδοκίμου τοῦ δικαίου καὶ θαυματουργοῦ· στιχηρὸν Ἰωάννου τοῦ Γλυκέος· ἦχος α' *Πῶς μὴ θαυμάσωμεν* (single B)

571. 175r Ἑτέρα ἐπιβολή, τοῦ μαΐστορος· ἦχος δ' *Πῶς μὴ θαυμάσωμεν* (single A)

572. 176v Δεύτερος πούς· ἦχος α' *Τὸ πρᾶον καὶ ταπεινὸν* (the kratēma as epibolē of Chrysaphēs, fol. 178r *Ἐν πάσαις ταῖς ἀρεταῖς*) (single B)

573. 179r Τρίτος πούς· τοῦ Κουκουζέλου· [ἦχος πλ. β'] *Ὅθεν ἀπόκειταί σοι* (single B)

574. 181r Ἀναγραμματισμὸς ἀπὸ τὸ αὐτὸ στιχηρὸν· τοῦ Χρυσάφου, ἦχος δ' *Ὅθεν ἀπόκειταί σοι* (single B)

Incipits of the Anagrams and mathēmata in the Mathēmatarion   211

575. 185r Ἕτερον στιχηρὸν εἰς τὸν αὐτὸν ἅγιον· τοῦ Χρυσάφου· ἦχος α΄ Ἡ θήκη τῶν λειψάνων σου (single B) Ἑτέρα ἐπιβολή, τοῦ αὐτοῦ· ἦχος πλ. α΄ Ἀγάλλεται μετὰ ἀγγέλων (single A)

***

576. 190r Μὴν Αὔγουστος· εἰς τὴν α΄, τῶν ἁγίων ἑπτὰ παίδων τῶν Μακαββαίων καὶ τῆς μητρὸς αὐτῶν Σολομονῆς καὶ τοῦ διδασκάλου αὐτῶν Ἐλεαζάρου· στιχηρὸν τοῦ Ἠθικοῦ· ἦχος α΄ Ἡ πολύαθλος μήτηρ (2-part B)

577. 194r Ἕτερον στιχηρὸν [...], Ξένου τοῦ Κορώνη· ἦχος δ΄ Τὸν κατὰ τῶν Μακαββαίων (the kratēma by Chrysaphēs, fol. 196r–v) (single B)

578. 197r Δεύτερος πούς· ἦχος τρίτος Τύραννος βασιλεὺς (single B)

579. 199r Ἕτερον στιχηρὸν [...], Κωνσταντίνου τοῦ Μαγουλᾶ· ἦχος πλ. δ΄ Ψυχαὶ δικαίων (single B)

580. 203r Δεύτερος πούς· ἦχος δ΄ Εὐσεβῶς γὰρ συντραφέντες (single B)

581. 206r Τρίτος πούς· ἦχος β΄ νη Ψυχὴν ἀνδρείαν (single B)

582. 211v [Αὐγούστου] γ΄, τῆς ἁγίας Θεοδώρας τῆς ἐν Θεσσαλονίκῃ· στιχηρὸν τοῦ Κουκουζέλου· ἦχος πλ. β΄ Τὴν τῶν πειρασμῶν προσβολὴν (single B)

583. 213v Δεύτερος πούς· [ἦχος πλ. β΄] Ἀλλ᾽ ἐκορέσθης ὕδατος (simple A)

584. 216r Πνετηκοσταρίον εἰς τὴν αὐτὴν ἁγίαν· Ἰωάννου τοῦ Κουκουζέλου, οἱ δὲ λόγοι τοῦ Στάχυος· ἦχος β΄ Ἡ μυροχεύμων θάλασσα (single A)

585. 219r Αὐγούστου ς΄, ἡ ἁγία Μεταμόρφωσις τοῦ Κυρίου, στιχηρὸν Νεοφύτου μοναχοῦ τοῦ Ἠθικοῦ· ἦχος δ΄ Εἰς ὄρος ὑψηλὸν (the kratēma as ἐπιβολὴ τοῦ Χρυσάφου, fol. 222r) (single B)

586. 222v Δεύτερος πούς· πλ. δ΄ Συλλαλοῦντες δὲ τῷ Χριστῷ (single B)

587. 225r Ἕτερον [πούς]· πλ. δ΄ Ὦ καὶ φωνὴ ἐκ τοῦ πατρὸς (single B)

588. 226v Ἕτερον στιχηρὸν [...], Γερασίμου ἱερομονάχου τοῦ Χαλκεοπούλου· ἦχος δ΄ Ὅρος τὸ ποτὲ ζοφῶδες (single B)

589. 231r Ἀναγραμματισμὸς εἰς τὴν αὐτὴν ἑορτήν, ἀπὸ τοῦ, Τῆς θεότητός σου, σωτήρ· τοῦ Μαγουλᾶ· ἦχος πλ. α΄ Μεθ᾽ ὧν καὶ ἡμεῖς (single A)

590. 234r Ἀναγραμματισμὸς εἰς τὴν αὐτὴν ἑορτήν, Θεοδώρου τοῦ Μανουγρᾶ, ἐκαλλωπίσθη δὲ παρὰ Ξένου τοῦ Κορώνη· ἦχος πλ. β΄ δίφωνος, ὁ δομέστικος ἀπὸ χοροῦ Προτυπῶν τὴν ἀνάστασιν τὴν σὴν — (fol. 234v) εἶτα γίνεται καλλιφωνία· ὁ

δομέστικος άπ' έξω *Τότε παραλαμβάνεις* — (the kratēma epibolē by Korōnēs, fol. 236r–v) (2-part B)

591. 237r [Πούς β'], τοῦ Μαΐστορος· ἦχος β' *Τὸ Θαβώριον ὄρος* (single A)

592. 238v Ἀπὸ χοροῦ, παλαιόν· ἦχος δ' *Οἱ μαθηταί σου, Λόγε* (single A)

593. 240v Ἕτερος πούς· Μάρκου μητροπολίτου Κορίνθου· ἦχος πλ. β' *Οἱ μαθηταί σου, Λόγε* (single B)

594. 243v Ἀναγραμματισμὸς ἀπὸ τὸ αὐτὸ στιχηρόν· Μανουὴλ τοῦ Χρυσάφου· ἦχος πλ. β' *Ἄγγελοι διηκόνουν* (single A)

595. 247v Ἕτερος ἀναγραμματισμὸς ἀπὸ τὸ αὐτὸ στιχηρόν, Ἰωάννου τοῦ Κουκουζέλου· ἦχος α' δ' φωνος *Οὐρανοὶ ἔφριξαν* (2-part A)

596. 251v Ἕτερον στιχηρὸν [...], Μανουὴλ τοῦ Χρυσάφου· ἦχος πλ. δ' *Παρέλαβεν ὁ Χριστός* (2-part B)

597. 256r Δεύτερος πούς· ἦχος πλ. β' *Ἔβλεπον γὰρ τὰ ἱμάτιά σου* (single B)

598. 259v Ἕτερον στιχηρὸν εἰς τὴν αὐτὴν ἑορτήν, τά τε γράμματα καὶ τὸ μέλος Μανουὴλ τοῦ Χρυσάφου· ἦχος βαρὺς Ζω *Μετεμορφώθης ἐπὶ τὸ Θαβώριον* (single B)

599. 264r Ἕτερον στιχηρὸν [...], Μανουὴλ τοῦ Χρυσάφου· ἦχος πλ. δ' *Παρέλαβεν ὁ Χριστός* (2-part B)

600. 269r Ἀναγραμματισμὸς ἀπὸ τὸ αὐτὸ στιχηρὸν εἰς τὴν αὐτὴν ἑορτήν, Μανουὴλ τοῦ Χρυσάφου· ἦχος πλ. δ' *Οὗτός ἐστιν ὁ υἱός μου* (single A)

601. 273v Ἀναγραμματισμὸς ἀπὸ τό, Ἐν τῷ ὄρει τῷ Θαβὼρ, Γρηγορίου ἱερομονάχου τοῦ ἐκ Σηλυβρίας· ἦχος β' *Καὶ ὁδήγησον ἐν τῇ τρίβῳ* (single A)

602. 276r Πεντηκοστάριον εἰς τὴν αὐτὴν ἑορτήν, παλαιόν· ἦχος πλ. β' νενανω *Τὴν λάμψιν τοῦ προσώπου σου* — (on fol. 278v an indication: εἰ βούλει, *καλλιφωνίαν Τετεριρεμ* — ἀπὸ χοροῦ)

603. 278v Αὐγούστου ιε', ἡ σεβασμία κοίμησις τῆς Θεοτόκου· στιχηρὸν παλαιόν, καλλωπισμὸς τοῦ Κουκουζέλη· ἦχος β' *Ἡ τῶν οὐρανῶν ὑψηλοτέρα* (2-part A)

604. 283v Ἀναγραμματισμὸς ἀπὸ τὸ αὐτὸ στιχηρόν, τοῦ Κουκουζέλου· ἦχος β' *Καὶ σὺν αὐτῇ πληροῦται* (single A)

605. 286r Ἕτερος, ἀναποδισμὸς ἀπὸ τό, Δεῦτε τὴν παγκόσμιον κοίμησιν, Κωνσταντίνου Μαγουλᾶ· ἦχος β' *Σὲ γὰρ χριστιανῶν τὸ γένος* (single A)

606. 290v Ἕτερον στιχηρὸν [...], Μανουὴλ τοῦ Χρυσάφου· ἦχος δ' *Τὴν πάνσεπτόν σου κοίμησιν* (single B)

Incipits of the Anagrams and mathēmata in the Mathēmatarion 213

607. 294v Ἕτερον στιχηρὸν [...], Μιχαὴλ τοῦ Πατζάδος· ἦχος πλ. β΄ *Τῇ ἀθανάτῳ σου κοιμήσει* (4-part B) — (two kratēmata, fols. 269r and 298r by Koukouzelēs)

608. 300v Ἀναγραμματισμὸς ἀπὸ τὸ αὐτὸ στιχηρὸν εἰς τὴν αὐτὴν ἑορτήν· Ἰωάννου τοῦ μαΐστορος· ἦχος πλ. β΄ νενανω *Χαῖρε κεχαριτωμένη* (single A)

609. 303v Ἕτερον στιχηρὸν [...], Συμεὼν τοῦ Ψηρίτζη, ἐκκαλωπίσθη δὲ παρὰ τοῦ μαΐστορος· πλ. β΄ *Ὅτε ἡ μετάστασις* (2-part A) (the kratēma as *parekbolē tou maïstoros*, fol. 305v)

610. 307r Τὸ αὐτὸ στιχηρὸν καλλωπισθὲν καὶ παρὰ Ξένου τοῦ Κορώνη, πολίτικον· ἦχος πλ. β΄ *Ὅτε ἡ μετάστασις* (2-part A)

611. 309v Δεύτερος πούς· ἦχος πλ. β΄ *Καὶ οἱ μὲν ἀτενίζοντες* (2-part B)

612. 314v Ἀπὸ τὸ αὐτὸ στιχηρὸν ἀναγραμματισμός, Ἰωάννου τοῦ μαΐστορος· ἦχος πλ. β΄ *Ἀλλ' ὦ Παρθένε ἄχραντε* (single A)

613. 318r Ἕτερος ἀναγραμματισμὸς ἀπὸ τὸ αὐτὸ στιχηρὸν [...], Μανουὴλ τοῦ Χρυσάφου· πλ. β΄ *Ὦ Παρθένε, ὁρῶ σε* (single A)

614. 322v Ἕτερον στιχηρὸν [...] παλαιόν· πλ. β΄ *Συντρέχει χορός* (simple A)

615. 324v Πεντηκοστάριον εἰς τὴν αὐτὴν ἑορτήν, Νικηφόρου μοναχοῦ τοῦ Ἠθικοῦ· ἦχος πλ. β΄ *Τῇ βασιλίδι παρέστησαν* (3-part B)

616. 328r Μεγαλυνάριον εἰς τὴν αὐτὴν ἑορτήν, ἄφθορον, Μανουὴλ τοῦ Χρυσάφου· ἦχος α΄ ναος κε *Αἱ γενεαὶ πᾶσαι — Νενίκηνται* (single B)

617. 331v Ἕτερον μεγαλυνάριον εἰς τὴν αὐτὴν ἑορτήν, Ἰωάννου λαμπαδαρίου τοῦ Κλαδᾶ· δ΄ *Ἅγια, Ἄγγελοι τὴν κοίμησιν — Ἅπας γηγενής* (2-part B)

618. 336r Ἕτερον μεγαλυνάριον εἰς τὴν αὐτὴν ἑορτήν, Κωνσταντίνου τοῦ Μαγουλᾶ· ἦχος δ΄ *Ἅπας γηγενής* (single B)

619. 339v Αὐγούστου κβ΄, τοῦ ἁγίου μεγαλομάρτυρος Ἀγαθονίκου· στιχηρὸν Ξένου τοῦ Κορώνη· ἦχος α΄ *Φερωνύμως ἐκλήθης* (single B)

620. 342v Δεύτερος πούς· ἦχος α΄ *Τῷ γὰρ θείῳ ἔρωτι* (single B)

621. 345v Ἕτερον στιχηρὸν [...], Μανουὴλ Χρυσάφου· πλ. δ΄ *Φερωνύμως τὴν κλῆσιν* (single B)

622. 349v Αὐγούστου κθ΄, ἡ ἀποτομὴ τῆς τιμίας κεφαλῆς τοῦ Προδρόμου· στιχηρὸν Κωνσταντίνου τοῦ Μαγουλᾶ· ἦχος α΄ *Τί σὲ καλέσωμεν* (single B)

623. 353r Ἕτερον στιχηρὸν [...], Μιχαὴλ τοῦ Πατζάδος, ἐκαλλωπίσθη παρὰ τοῦ Κουκουζέλου· πλ. β΄ *Γενεθλίων τελουμένων* (single B)

624. 356r Δεύτερος πούς· πλ. β ' καὶ πλ. α ' *Τοῦ γὰρ Προδρόμου ἡ κεφαλή* (simple A)

625. 359r Ἀναγραμματισμὸς ἀπὸ τὸ αὐτὸ στιχηρόν· Ξένου τοῦ Κορώνη· ἦχος πλ. β ' *Ἀλλ' ἡμεῖς τὸν βαπτιστήν* (single A)

626. 362v Ἕτερον στιχηρὸν [...], τοῦ Καρβουναριώτου· ἐκαλλωπίσθη παρὰ τοῦ Μαγουλᾶ, ὕστερον δὲ καὶ παρὰ Ἰωάννου μαΐστορος τοῦ Κουκουζέλου· ἦχος πλ. β ' *Πάλιν Ἡρωδιὰς μαίνεται* (fol. 366v ἀπὸ χοροῦ *Ὁ βαπτιστὴς ἀπετέμνετο* — fol. 367r καλλιφωνία (kratēma not written) — fol. 367v τοῦ Κουκουζέλου *Τέτετε* — fol. 368v ἀπὸ χοροῦ *Τὴν εἰρήνην παράσχου ταῖς ψυχαῖς ἡμῶν*) (3-part B)

627. 368v Ἀναγραμματισμὸς ἀπὸ τὸ αὐτὸ στιχηρὸν [...], Ἰωάννου τοῦ Κουκουζέλου· πλ. β ' *Ὦ ὄρχισμα δόλιον* (single A)

628. 371r Ἀπὸ τὸ αὐτὸ στιχηρὸν ἀναγραμματισμὸς Μανουὴλ τοῦ Χρυσάφου· πλ. β ' *Πρεσβείαις, Κύριε, τοῦ προδρόμου* (single A)

629. 374r Ἕτερον στιχηρὸν [...], Μανουὴλ τοῦ Χρυσάφου· πλ. δ ' *Πρόδρομε τοῦ σωτῆρος* — (fol. 375r, ἐντεῦθεν ἄρχεται ἡ ἔμπροσθεν ἐν ἄλλοις διαφορετικὴ γραμμή) (single A)

630. 378v Πεντηκοστάριον εἰς τὴν αὐτὴν ἑορτήν· οἱ μὲν λόγοι τοῦ μοναχοῦ Μόσχου, τὸ δὲ μέλος Ἰωάννου τοῦ Κουκουζέλου· ἦχος πλ. α ' *Λαμπρά σου τὰ γενέσια* (2-part A)

631. 381r Ἕτερον πεντηκοστάριον [...]· πλ. β ' *Τὴν κεφαλὴν τοῦ βαπτιστοῦ*

632. 384r Δεύτερος πούς· ἦχος δ ' *Ἀλλ' ὦ προφῆτα, πρόδρομε* (single A)

633. 386r Αὐγούστου λα ', ἡ κατάθεσις τῆς τιμίας ζώνης τῆς Θεοτόκου· στιχηρὸν τοῦ Ἠθικοῦ ἦχος β ' βου *Ὡς στέφανον ὑπέρλαμπρον* (single B)

634. 388v Δεύτερος πούς· [ἦχος β '] *Χαῖρε διάδημα τίμιον* (single B)

ΜΠΤ 733: MATHĒMATARION (VOLUME VII — TRIŌDION)

327 folios

1r Τόμος ἕβδομος τοῦ Μαθηματαρίου. Ἀρχὴ σὺν Θεῷ ἁγίῳ τῶν στιχηρῶν τῆς ἁγίας καὶ μεγάλης Τεσσαρακοστῆς, ἀρχομένων ἀπὸ τῆς Κυριακῆς τοῦ Τελώνου καὶ τοῦ Φαρισαίου καὶ καταληγόντων ἄχρι τῆς Κυριακῆς τῶν ἁγίων Πάντων.

Incipits of the Anagrams and mathēmata in the Mathēmatarion 215

635.   Στιχηρὸν τῆς Κυριακῆς τοῦ Τελώνου καὶ τοῦ Φαρισαίου· Μανουὴλ μαΐστορος τοῦ Χρυσάφου· ἦχος α΄ *Μὴ προσευξώμεθα φαρισαϊκῶς* (single B)

636. 4r   Ἕτερον στιχηρόν, τῇ αὐτῇ ἡμέρᾳ, Ξένου τοῦ Κορώνη· ἦχος πλ. δ΄ *Παντοκράτορ Κύριε* (simple A)

637. 7r   Τῇ Κυριακῇ τοῦ Ἀσώτου· στιχηρὸν Δημητρίου τοῦ Δοκειανοῦ· ἦχος β΄ *Ὦ πόσων ἀγαθῶν* (simple A)

638. 9v   Τὸ αὐτὸ στιχηρὸν μελισθὲν καὶ παρὰ Νικηφόρου τοῦ Ἠθικοῦ· ἦχος β΄ *Ὦ πόσων ἀγαθῶν* (2-part A)

639. 13r Ἕτερον στιχηρόν [...], Ἰωάννου τοῦ Γλυκέος· πλ. β΄ *Πάτερ ἀγαθέ* (simple A)

640. 16r Τῷ σαββάτῳ τῶν ψυχῶν· στιχηρὸν Ἰωάννου τοῦ Κλαδᾶ· ἦχος α΄ *Ποία τοῦ βίου τρυφή* (simple)

641. 19v Νεκρώσιμον· ἦχος α΄ δ΄ *φωνος Ἄφωνον βλέποντες, νεκρόν* (simple A)

642. 22v Ἕτερον νεκρώσιμον, ὡς ἀπὸ προσώπου νεκροῦ πρὸς ζῶντας· ἦχος β΄ *Ὦ ἀπάτη τοῦ βίου* (simple A)

643. 25v Ἰωάννου λαμπαδαρίου [Κλαδᾶ]· ἦχος β΄ *Οἴμοι, οἷον ἀγῶνα* (simple A)

644. 28r Ἕτερον νεκρώσιμον, Ἰωάννου Κλαδᾶ· τρίτος *Πάντα ματαιότης* (simple A)

645. 31r Ἕτερον, Ἰωάννου τοῦ Κλαδᾶ· ἦχος δ΄ *Ὄντως φοβερώτατον* (simple A)

646. 34v Τὸ αὐτὸ στιχηρὸν μελισθὲν καὶ παρὰ Ἰωάννου μαΐστορος τοῦ Κουκουζέλου· ἦχος δ΄ *Ὄντως φοβερώτατον* (simple A)

647. 37r Ἕτερον στιχηρόν, Ξένου τοῦ Κορώνη· πλ. α΄ *Δεῦτε ἀδελφοί* (simple A)

648. 39v Ἕτερον, Ξένου τοῦ Κορώνη· πλ. β΄ *Ὁρῶντές με ἄφωνον* (simple A)

649. 44v Ἕτερον, τὰ μὲν γράμματα Μελισσηνοῦ τοῦ φιλοσόφου, τὸ δὲ μέλος Ξένου τοῦ Κορώνη· πλ. β΄ *Πληθὺς ἀνθρώπων ἅπασα* (simple A)

650. 48r Ἀναγραμματισμὸς ἀπὸ τό, Θρηνῶ καὶ ὀδύρομαι, Ἰωάννου τοῦ Κουκουζέλου· ἦχος πλ. δ΄ *Ὦ τοῦ θαύματος* (simple A)

651. 51v Τῇ Κυριακῇ τῆς Ἀπόκρεω, στιχηρὸν τοῦ Καρβουναριώτου· ἐκαλλωπίσθη δὲ παρὰ Μανουὴλ τοῦ Χρυσάφου· ἦχος πλ. β΄ νεναvω *Ὦ ποία ὥρα τότε* (simple C)

652. 55v Ἕτερον στιχηρόν, παλαιὸν [...], ἐκαλλωπίσθη δὲ παρὰ Μανουὴλ τοῦ Χρυσάφου· πλ. δ΄ *Ὅταν τίθωνται θρόνοι* (simple C)

653. 58r Ἕτερον στιχηρόν [...], τοῦ Καρβουναριώτου· ἐκαλλωπίσθη δὲ παρὰ μαΐστορος τοῦ Κουκουζέλου· πλ. δ΄ *Οἴμοι, μέλαινα ψυχή* (simple A)

654. 61v   Ἀναγραμματισμὸς ἀπὸ τὸ αὐτὸ στιχηρόν· Ἰωάννου μαΐστορος τοῦ Κουκουζέλου· πλ. δ΄ *Λοιπόν, ὦ ψυχὴ* (simple A)

655. 64r   Τῇ Κυριακῇ τῆς Τυροφάγου, εἰς τὴν ἐξορίαν τοῦ Ἀδάμ· στιχηρὸν Ξένου τοῦ Κορώνη· πλ. β΄ *Ἐκάθισεν Ἀδάμ* (simple A)

656. 67v   Ἀναγραμματισμὸς ἀπὸ τὸ αὐτὸ στιχηρόν· Ἰωάννου τοῦ Κουκουζέλου· πλ. β΄ *Ἀλλ' ὦ παράδεισε* (simple A)

657. 70r   Ἕτερον στιχηρὸν τῇ αὐτῇ ἡμέρᾳ· Μανουὴλ μαΐστορος τοῦ Χρυσάφου· πλ. β΄ *Ἐξεβλήθη Ἀδάμ* (simple C)

658. 73v   Ἕτερον [...], Ἰωάννου Κουκουζέλου· πλ. β΄ *Ἥλιος ἀκτῖνας ἔδυνεν* (simple A)

659. 76r   Ἕτερον στιχηρὸν [...], Ἰωάννου λαμπαδαρίου τοῦ Κλαδᾶ· πλ. β΄ *νενανω Παράδεισε ἁγιώτατε* (single B)

660. 78r–v Ἐκ τῶν περισσῶν· Ἰωάννου τοῦ Γλυκέος· ἦχος πλ. β΄ *Ἐκάθησεν ἀπέναντι* (single A)

661. 81v   Ἕτερον ἐξ αὐτῶν· Ξένου τοῦ Κορώνη· ἦχος τρίτος *Εὑρίσκω τὴν εἰσέλευσιν* (single A)

662. 84v   Ἕτερον, Ξένου τοῦ Κορώνη· πλ. α΄ *Ἀλλὰ πενθῶν* (single A)

663. 87v   Ἕτερον, Ἰωάννου [...] Κουκουζέλου· πλ. δ΄ *Ἀλλὰ πενθῶν* (single A)

664. 90v   Ἕτερον [...], Νικηφόρου τοῦ Ἠθικοῦ· ἦχος β΄· *Ἀδὰμ ὁ πρῶτος ἄνθρωπος* (simple A)

665. 92v   Ἕτερον, Ξένου τοῦ Κορώνη· πλ. β΄ *Ἀδὰμ ὁ φύλαξ τῆς Ἐδὲμ* (simple A)

666. 94v   Πεντηκοστάριον, ψαλλόμενον τῇ ἁγίᾳ Τεσσαρακοστῇ, παλαιόν· ἦχος πλ. β΄ καὶ δ΄ *Τὰ πλήθη τῶν πεπραγμένων μοι* (simple B)

667. 96r   Τὸ αὐτὸ ποιηθὲν καὶ παρὰ Ἰωάννου τοῦ Λάσκαρη· ἦχος πλ. β΄ *Τὰ πλήθη τῶν πεπραγμένων μοι* (simple B)

668. 99r   Ἕτερον πεντηκοστάριον παλαιόν· καλλωπισμὸς τοῦ Κουκουζέλου· πλ. δ΄ *Τῆς μετανοίας ἄνοιξόν μοι* (single B)

669. 102r Ἀναγραμματισμὸς ἀπὸ τὸ αὐτὸ στιχηρόν, Ἰωάννου τοῦ Κουκουζέλου· πλ. δ΄ *Ὡς οἰκτίρμων κάθαρον* (single A)

670. 105r Τῇ Δευτέρᾳ τῆς Α΄ ἑβδομάδος τῶν Νηστειῶν· στιχηρὸν Θεοδούλου μοναχοῦ· ἦχος β΄ *Πᾶσαν ἁμαρτίαν* (single A)

Incipits of the Anagrams and mathēmata in the Mathēmatarion 217

671. 107v   Σαββάτῳ πρώτῳ τῶν Νηστειῶν, τοῦ ἁγίου μεγαλομάρτυρος Θεοδώρου τοῦ Τύρωνος· στιχηρὸν Ἰωάννου τοῦ Γλυκέος· ἦχος β΄ βου *Τὴν θεοδώρητον χάριν* (single B)

672. 110r   Δεύτερος πούς· ἦχος δ΄ *Μάταιον δρασμὸν ἐπέχεις* (single B)

673. 112r–v Ἕτερον στιχηρὸν […], Μανουὴλ μαΐστορος τοῦ Χρυσάφου· ἦχος δ΄ *Χορεύουσι στίφη μαρτύρων* (single B)

674. 115v   Ἕτερον στιχηρὸν […], Ἰωάννου πρωτοψάλτου τοῦ Γλυκέος· ἦχος πλ. β΄ *Ἁγιωσύνης δωρεά* (single B)

675. 118r   Ἀναγραμματισμὸς εἰς τὸν αὐτὸν ἅγιον, πρὸς τὸ Ἴδωμεν πάντες· μέλος Ἰωάννου τοῦ Κουκουζέλου· πλ. δ΄ *Γα Ἴδωμεν πάντες τῶν ἰαμάτων* (single A)

676. 120v   Τῇ Κυριακῇ τῆς Ὀρθοδοξίας, στιχηρὸν τοῦ Πατζάδος ἐκαλλωπίσθη πρῶτον παρὰ τοῦ Κουκουζέλου, εἶτα συνετμήθη καὶ ἡνώθη καὶ δεύτερον ἐκαλλωπίσθη παρὰ Χρυσάφου τοῦ μαΐστορος· ἦχος β΄ βου *Ἡ χάρις ἐπέλαμψε* —(the kratēma as epibolē by Chrysaphēs, fol. 124r) (single B)

677. 125r   Τῇ Κυριακῇ τῆς Σταυροπροσκυνήσεως· στιχηρὸν τοῦ Ἠθικοῦ, ἐκαλλωπίσθη δὲ παρὰ Ἰωάννου τοῦ Κουκουζέλου· ἦχος δ΄ *Ὁ συμμαχήσας, Κύριε* (single B)

678. 127r   Χρυσάφου, προσθήκη· *Κατάβαλε τῷ ὅπλῳ τοῦ σταυροῦ* (3-part A)

679. 130r   Ἀναγραμματισμὸς Ἰωάννου μαΐστορος Κουκουζέλου· πλ. δ΄ *Ἵνα σώσῃ κόσμον* (single A)

680. 133r   Ἕτερον στιχηρὸν εἰς τὴν αὐτὴν ἑορτήν· τὰ μὲν γράμματα Λέοντος τοῦ σοφοῦ βασιλέως, τὸ δὲ μέλος Μανουὴλ τοῦ Χρυσάφου· ἦχος πλ. δ΄ *Σήμερον, ὁ ἀπρόσιτος τῇ οὐσίᾳ* (single A)

681. 137v   Στίχοι εἰς τὴν αὐτὴν ἑορτήν, ποιηθέντες παρὰ διακόνου νομοφύλακος τοῦ Διασίτου, μελισθέντες δὲ εἰς ὀκτὼ ἤχους παρὰ Ἰωάννου τοῦ Γλυκέος· ἄρχου, ἦχος α΄ πα *Φαιδρῶς πανηγυρίζοντες σταυροῦ τῇ προσκυνήσει* 139r, Καλοφωνία· ἦχος α΄ *Οἱ βασιλεῖς ἀγάλλονται σταυροῦ τῇ προσκυνήσει* — (the kratēma as epibolē by Chrysaphēs, fol. 140r) (single A)

682. 140v   Ἦχος β΄ *Ἡ τοῦ σταυροῦ προσκύνησις εἰς δόξαν τοῖς κρατοῦσι* (simple)

683. 141v   Ἦχος τρίτος *Ἰδοὺ σταυροῦ προσκύνησις, αὐτάνακτες, σκιρτᾶτε*

684. 142v   Ἦχος δ΄ *Χριστοῦ σταυρὸς τετραμερὴς ἀρτίως προσκυνεῖται*

685. 144r   Ἦχος πλ. α΄ *Ἀειθαλῆ παράδεισον Χριστοῦ ἡ ἐκκλησία*

686. 145v   Ἦχος πλ. β΄ *Οἱ στεφηφόροι τὸν σταυρὸν προκείμενον ὁρῶντες*

687. 146v   Ἦχος βαρὺς *Ὑμῖν δὲ τοίνυν γένοιτο καυχᾶσθαι στεφηφόροι*

688. 149r   Ἦχος πλ. δ΄ Θνῄσκεις ἐν ξύλῳ σταυρικῷ ζωῶν τὸν τεθνηκότα

689. 150v   Σταυροθεοτοκία κατ' ἦχον, ψαλλόμενα εἰς τὴν αὐτὴν ἑορτήν, ἀλλὰ δὲ καὶ τῇ μεγάλῃ Παρασκευῇ καὶ τῷ μεγάλῳ Σαββάτῳ. Τὸ παρὸν τοῦ μαΐστορος Ἰωάννου τοῦ Κουκουζέλου· ἦχος α΄ ναος κε *Ἰδοὺ γὰρ κτίσις ἅπασα* (simple A)

690. 153r   Ἰωάννου [...] Κουκουζέλου· ἦχος α΄ κε *Εἰ καὶ σταυρὸν ὑπομένεις* (simple B)

691. 154v   Ἕτερον, Ξένου τοῦ Κορώνη· ἦχος α΄ *Σφαγήν σου τὴν ἄδικον* (simple A)

692. 157r   Ἕτερον· ἦχος β΄ *Τοῦτον ἰδοῦσα πρὸς σφαγὴν* (single A)

693. 159r   [...] Ἰωάννου [...] Κουκουζέλου· τρίτος *Τέκνον μου, πλάστα δυνατέ* (simple A)

694. 160v   Ἕτερον, Μανουὴλ τοῦ Χρυσάφου, τά τε γράμματα καὶ τὸ μέλος· ἦχος δ΄ *Ὅτε σὲ εἶδεν ἐν σταυρῷ* (simple A)

695. 163r   [...] Ξένου τοῦ Κορώνη· πλ. α΄ *Ὡραῖος κάλλει πεφυκὼς* (single A)

696. 164v   Ἕτερον, Ἰωάννου μαΐστορος Παπαδοπούλου τοῦ Κουκουζέλη· πλ. α΄ *Σταυρῷ σε προσηλούμενον* (simple A)

697. 167r   Ἕτερον, τοῦ αὐτοῦ Κουκουζέλου [...]· πλ. α΄ *Ὁρῶσα ξύλῳ σε σταυροῦ* (simple A)

698. 169v   (698α) Ἕτερον τοῦ αὐτοῦ Ἰωάννου τοῦ Κουκουζέλου· ψάλλεται δὲ εἰς τρεῖς ἤχους· πλ. α΄, πλ. β΄, καὶ λεγετον, ἤτοι πα, πα (πλ. β΄) καὶ βου. Χρεία λοιπὸν ἐξηγηθῆναι ἐν ἑκάστῃ ἰδέᾳ τῶν εἰρημένων ἤχων κατὰ μέρος. Τὸ παρὸν ἦχος πλ. α΄ πα *Πάθος σου βλέπων σταυρικὸν* (simple A) (698β–171v) Τὸ αὐτὸ στιχηρὸν εἰς τὴν ἰδέαν τοῦ λεγετος βου (698γ–174r) Τὸ αὐτὸ στιχηρὸν εἰς τὴν ἰδέαν τοῦ πλ. β΄ πα

699. 176r   Ἕτερον, Ξένου τοῦ Κορώνη· πλ. β΄ *Ἄνανδρος μήτηρ ἐν σταυρῷ* (simple C)

700. 179r   Ἕτερον, Ξένου τοῦ Κορώνη· πλ. β΄ *Ἄνανδρος μήτηρ ἐν σταυρῷ* (simple A)

701. 180v   Ἕτερον, τοῦ αὐτοῦ Ξένου τοῦ Κορώνη· πλ. β΄ νενανω *Τῆς ἀκηράτου σου πλευρᾶς* (simple A)

702. 183r   Ἕτερον, Ἰωάννου μαΐστορος τοῦ Κουκουζέλη· πλ. β΄ νενανω *Φεῦ, τί τὸ ξένον καὶ φρικτὸν* (simple A)

703. 184v   Τοῦ αὐτοῦ Ἰωάννου τοῦ Κουκουζέλη· βαρὺς *Μήτηρ Παρθένος σταυρικὸν* (simple A)

704. 186v   Ἕτερον, Ξένου τοῦ Κορώνη καὶ πρωτοψάλτου· βαρὺς *Ἰδοὺ ρομφαίᾳ τῇ ψυχῇ* (simple A)

Incipits of the Anagrams and mathēmata in the Mathēmatarion 219

705. 188v   Ἕτερον, Μανουὴλ τοῦ Χρυσάφου, τά τε γράμματα καὶ μέλος· ἦχος βαρὺς *Βλέπουσα πάλαι τὸν υἱὸν* (simple A)

706. 191v   Ἕτερον, Ξένου τοῦ Κορώνη· πλ. δ´ *Ὡς προσκυνῶ τὰ πάθη σου* (simple A)

707. 193r   Ἕτερον, Ἰωάννου Κουκουζέλου· πλ. δ´ *Ὅτε τὸ πάθος τὸ φρικτὸν* (simple A)

708. 195r   Ἕτερον, τοῦ αὐτοῦ Κουκουζέλου· πλ. δ´ *Ἡ δὲ τεκοῦσα, δέσποτα* (simple A)

709. 196v   Ἕτερον τοῦ αὐτοῦ Κουκουζέλου· πλ. δ´ *Ὡς ἐκ νεφῶν, ἐξ ὀφθαλμῶν* (simple A)

710. 198v   Ἕτερον τοῦ αὐτοῦ Ἰωάννου τοῦ Κουκουζέλου· ἦχος πλ. δ´ *Αἱμοχαρής, ἀπάνθρωπος* (simple A)

711. 200r   Τοῦ αὐτοῦ Κουκουζέλου· πλ. δ´ *Παρισταμένη τῷ σταυρῷ* (simple A)

712. 202r   [...] τοῦ αὐτοῦ Κουκουζέλου· πλ. δ´ *Πάθος ὁρῶσα σταυρικὸν* (simple A)

713. 203v   [...] τοῦ αὐτοῦ Κουκουζέλου· πλ. δ´ *Ἐγὼ δὲ πῶς τὸ πάθος σου* (simpla A)

714. 205v   Τῷ σαββάτῳ τοῦ ἁγίου καὶ δικαίου Λαζάρου· στιχηρὸν Ξένου τοῦ Κορώνη· ἦχος δ´ *Τεταρταῖον ἤγειρας* (2-part B)

715. 209v   Ἕτερον στιχηρὸν εἰς τὴν αὐτὴν ἑορτήν· Μανουὴλ τοῦ Χρυσάφου· ἦχος δ´ *Μάρθα, Μαρία ἐβόα*

716. 211r   Ἕτερον στιχηρὸν [...], τοῦ αὐτοῦ Μανουὴλ τοῦ Χρυσάφου· ἦχος πλ. δ´ *Τα Τὴν ψυχωφελῆ πληρώσαντες* (2-part A)

717. 215r   Τῇ Κυριακῇ τῶν Βαΐων, στιχηρὸν τοῦ Μαγουλᾶ, ἐκαλλωπίσθη δὲ παρὰ Μανουὴλ τοῦ Χρυσάφου· ἦχος δ´ *Ὁ πλεῖστος ὄχλος* (single B)

718. 217v   Τοῦ αὐτοῦ Μανουὴλ τοῦ Χρυσάφου [...] ἦχος δ´ *Ἐξέλθετε ἔθνη* (single A)

719. 221r   Ἕτερον στιηρὸν εἰς τὴν αὐτὴν ἑορτήν, Ἰωάννου πρωτοψάλτου τοῦ Γλυκέο· ἦχος πλ. β´ *Σήμερον ἡ χάρις* (single B) (the kratēma as epibolē by Chrysaphēs, fol. 222v)

720. 223v   Ἀναγραμματισμὸς ἀπὸ τὸ αὐτὸ στιχηρόν, Ἰωάννου μαΐστορος τοῦ Κουκουζέλου· πλ. β´ *Εὐλογημένος ὁ ἐρχόμενος* (single A)

721. 225r–v Ἕτερον στιχηρὸν εἰς τὴν αὐτὴν ἑορτήν, Θεοδώρου τοῦ Μουνουγρᾶ· ἐκαλλωπίσθη δὲ παρὰ τοῦ Κορώνη· ἦχος πλ. β´ νενανω, ἀπὸ χοροῦ *Πρὸ ἓξ ἡμερῶν* — εἶτα ἄρχεται ἡ καλλιφωνία· *Κύριε, ποῦ θέλεις* (4-part A)

722. 229r   Ἕτερον, Ἰωάννου μαΐστορος τοῦ Κουκουζέλου· πλ. δ´ *Ὁ δὲ ἀπέστειλεν αὐτοὺς* (2-part A) — (on fol. 232r–v, ἕτερον [παρεκβολή]· *Βαστάζοντα*)

723. 232v   Ἀναγραμματισμὸς ἀπὸ τὸ αὐτὸ στιχηρὸν [...], Ἰωάννου λαμπαδαρίου τοῦ Κλαδᾶ· ἦχος πλ. β´ *Ὁ διδάσκαλος λέγει* (single A)

724. 235v   Τὸ αὐτὸ στιχηρόν, μελισθὲν παρὰ Κωνσταντίνου τοῦ Μανουγρᾶ, καλλωπισθὲν δὲ παρὰ Μανουὴλ τοῦ Χρυσάφου· πλ. β ' νενανω *Πρὸ ἐξ ἡμερῶν* (single B) — (the kratēma contains a short prologos, as epibolē by Chrysaphēs, fol. 237v–239r)

725. 239r   Τῇ ἁγίᾳ καὶ μεγάλῃ Δευτέρᾳ· στιχηρὸν Ἰωάννου πρωτοψάλτου τοῦ Γλυκέος· πλ. δ ' *Δευτέραν Εὔαν* (single A)

726. 241v   Τῇ ἁγίᾳ καὶ μεγάλῃ Τρίτῃ· στιχηρὸν τοῦ Πατζάδος· ἦχος α ' *Ἐν ταῖς λαμπρότησι τῶν ἁγίων σου* (simple A)

727. 243r   Ἕτερον στιχηρὸν τῇ αὐτῇ ἡμέρᾳ· Ἰωάννου πρωτοψάλτου τοῦ Γλυκέος· ἦχος δ ' *Τοῦ κρύψαντος τὸ τάλαντον* (simple A)

728. 244v   Τῇ ἁγίᾳ καὶ μεγάλῃ Πέμπτῃ· στιχηρὸν τοῦ Ἁλμυριώτου· ἦχος α ' *Ὅτε ἡ ἁμαρτωλὸς* (simple C)

729. 246r   Ἕτερον, τῇ αὐτῇ ἡμέρᾳ· Μελετίου μοναχοῦ· ἦχος πλ. δ ' *Κύριε, ἡ ἐν πολλαῖς ἁμαρτίαις* (simple C)

730. 251r   Τῇ ἁγίᾳ καὶ μεγάλῃ Πέμπτῃ, στιχηρὸν τοῦ Πατζάδος· ἦχος β ' βου *Συντρέχει, λοιπὸν* (simple C)

731. 253v   Ἕτερον στιχηρὸν τῇ αὐτῇ ἡμέρᾳ, τοῦ Καμπάνη· ἦχος β ' βου *Ἰούδας ὁ δοῦλος* (simple C)

732. 256r   Ἕτερον στιχηρὸν [...], Ἀνδρέου Σιγηροῦ· πλ. δ ' *Μηδείς, ὦ πιστοί* (3-part A)

733. 259r   Ἕτερον [...], Ἰωάννου [...] Κλαδᾶ· πλ. δ ' *Ὁ τρόπος σου δολιότητος*

734. 261r   Ἕτερον στιχηρὸν· ἑσπέρας ἐκ τῶν ἀντιφώνων· Γοτθίας τοῦ Μανουγρᾶ· τρίτος *Σήμερον γρηγορεῖ ὁ Ἰούδας* (simple C)

735. 263r   Ἕτερον στιχηρὸν ἐξ αὐτῶν, τοῦ Μανουγρᾶ· ἦχος βαρὺς Ζω ἀπὸ χοροῦ *Κύριε, ἐπὶ τὸ πάθος* — Εἶτα γίνεται ἡ καλλιφωνία, ἀπ' ἔξω *Κἂν μίαν ὥραν* (simple C)

736. 265r   Ἕτερον ἐξ αὐτῶν, τοῦ Καρφᾶ· τρίτος *Ἔστησαν τὰ τριάκοντα ἀργύρια* (3-part B)

737. 268r   Ἕτερον στιχηρὸν ἐξ αὐτῶν, τοῦ Ἁλμυριώτου· πλ. β ' *Ὁ ἀναβαλλόμενος τὸ φῶς* (single A)

738. 271r   Ἕτερον ἐξ αὐτῶν, τοῦ Καμπάνη· ἐκαλλωπίσθη παρὰ τοῦ Γλυκέος· ἦχος πλ. δ ' *Μικρὰν φωνὴν ἀφῆκεν* (single A)

739. 273r   Τῇ ἁγίᾳ καὶ μεγάλῃ Παρασκευῇ· στιχηρὸν Λέοντος τοῦ Ἁλμυριώτου· ἐκαλλωπίσθη δὲ παρὰ Μανουὴλ τοῦ Χρυσάφου· τρίτος *Δύο καὶ πονηρὰ* (2-part B)

740. 278r   Ἕτερον στιχηρὸν [...] τοῦ Καμπάνη· ἐκαλλωπίσθη δὲ παρὰ τοῦ Χρυσάφου· τρίτος *Ἕκαστον μέλος* (single B)

Incipits of the Anagrams and mathēmata in the Mathēmatarion 221

741. 281r   Ἕτερον στιχηρὸν [...], Ἰωάννου τοῦ Κουκουζέλη, θαυμαστόν· ἦχος β΄ βου Ἐπί ξύλου βλέπουσα (single B)

742. 284r   Ἕτερον στιχηρὸν [...], τοῦ Καμπάνη, ἐκαλλωπίσθη δὲ παρὰ τοῦ Χρυσάφου· πλ. δ΄ Κύριε, ἀναβαίνοντός σου (simple C)

743. 287r   Ἕτερον τῇ αὐτῇ ἡμέρᾳ [τῶν αὐτῶν]· πλ. δ΄ Ἤδη βάπτεται κάλαμος (single B)

744. 290r   Τροπάρια τῶν ἁγίων Παθῶν· Ὥρα πρώτη, τοῦ Καρβουναριώτου, ἐκαλλωπίσθη δὲ παρὰ Ἰωάννου τοῦ Κουκουζέλου· πλ. δ΄ Σήμερον τοῦ ναοῦ τὸ καταπέτασμα (single B)

745. 293r   Ἕτερον ἐξ αὐτῶν· Μανουὴλ τοῦ Χρυσάφου· ἦχος πλ. δ΄ Τοῖς συλλαβοῦσί σε (simple A)

746. 295v   Ἕτερον ἐξ αὐτῶν, τοῦ Καμπάνη· ἐκαλλωπίσθη παρὰ Μανουὴλ τοῦ Χρυσάφου· πλ. δ΄ Διὰ τὸν φόβον τὸν Ἰουδαίων (simple C)

747. 298r   Ἀναγραμματισμὸς ἀπὸ τοῦ, Τάδε λέγει Κύριος τοῖς Ἰουδαίοις· Ἰωάννου μαΐστορος τοῦ Κουκουζέλου· πλ. δ΄ Οὐκέτι στέγω, λοιπόν (simple A)

748. 300v   Ἕτερον ἐξ αὐτῶν, παλαιόν· πλ. δ΄ ἀπὸ χοροῦ Οἱ νομοθέται τοῦ Ἰσραὴλ (simple A)

749. 302r   Ἕτερον στιχηρὸν ἐξ αὐτῶν, Λέοντος τοῦ Ἁλμυριώτου· ἐκαλλωπίσθη παρὰ Ἰωάννου τοῦ Γλυκέος καὶ Ξένου τοῦ Κορώνη· ἦχος β΄ Ὅτε τῷ σταυρῷ προσήλωσαν (3-part B)

750. 306r   Ἕτερον, [ἀναγραμματισμὸς] Ἰωάννου τοῦ Κουκουζέλου· ἦχος πλ. β΄ Τίς ὑμᾶς ἐρρύσατο (single A)

751. 308v   Ἕτερον, β΄ πούς· Ἰωάννου τοῦ Γλυκέος· πλ. α΄ Ἐβόα πρὸς αὐτούς (4-part A)

752. 312r   Ἀναγραμματισμὸς ἀπὸ τὸ αὐτὸ στιχηρόν· Δημητρίου Δοκειανοῦ· ἦχος πλ. δ΄ Λοιπόν, καλῶ τὰ ἔθνη (simple A)

753. 314v   Τῷ ἁγίῳ καὶ μεγάλῳ Σαββάτῳ· στιχηρὸν Νικολάου τοῦ Καλλίστου, ἐκαλλωπίσθη δὲ παρὰ Ἰωάννου Κουκουζέλου καὶ Ξένου τοῦ Κορώνη· ἦχος πλ. α΄ Σὲ τὸν ἀναβαλλόμενον (single A)

754. 320r   Ἀναγραμματισμὸς ἀπὸ τὸ αὐτὸ στιχηρόν, Ἰωάννου τοῦ Κουκουζέλου· ἦχος πλ. α΄ Μεγαλύνω τὰ πάθη (simple A)

755. 323v   Ἕτερος ἀναγραμματισμὸς ἀπὸ τοῦ, Δεῦτε ἴδωμεν, Μανουὴλ μαΐστορος τοῦ Χρυσάφου· πλ. β΄ Ἀναπεσὼν κεκοίμησαι (simple A)

ΜΠΤ 734: MATHĒMATARION (VOLUME VIII — PENTĒCOSTARION)

224 folios

	1r	Τόμος ὄγδοος τοῦ Μαθηματαρίου.
756.		Τῇ ἁγίᾳ καὶ μεγάλῃ Κυριακῇ τοῦ Πάσχα. Εἱρμοὶ καλοφωνικοί, ψαλλόμενοι εἰς τὴν καταβασίαν, μελισθέντες παρὰ Ἰωάννου λαμπαδαρίου τοῦ Κλαδᾶ καὶ Μανουὴλ τοῦ Χρυσάφου. Ὁ παρὼν τοῦ λαμπαδαρίου· ἦχος α΄ *Ἀναστάσεως ἡμέρα* (2-part Β)
757.	5r	Ὠιδὴ γ΄, Μανουὴλ Χρυσάφου· α΄ δ΄ φωνος *Δεῦτε πόμα πίωμεν* (single A)
758.	9r	Ὠιδὴ δ΄, Μανουὴλ Χρυσάφου· ἦχος α΄ *Ἐπὶ τῆς θείας φυλακῆς* (single B)
759.	14r	Ὠιδὴ ε΄, Μανουὴλ Χρυσάφου· α΄ δ΄ φωνος *Ὀρθρίσωμεν ὄρθρου βαθέος* (simple C)
760.	18r	Ὠιδὴ ς΄, Ἰωάννου Κλαδᾶ· α΄ δ΄ φωνος *Κατῆλθες ἐν τοῖς κατωτάτοις* (single B)
761.	22v	Μετὰ τὸ Συναξάριον, τὸ Ἀναστὰς ὁ Ἰησοῦς, ῥηθέντος τοῦ Ἀνάστασιν Χριστοῦ, πρῶτον· Ἰωάννου Γλυκέος, ἀπὸ χοροῦ· ἦχος πλ. β΄ καὶ δ΄, ἀλλ' ἡ ἰδέα τοῦ πλ. β΄ ἐν ἀρχῇ ἐστι μόνον· *Ἀναστὰς ὁ Ἰησοῦς* (simple A) 761β fol. 23r: Τὸ αὐτὸ ἀπ' ἀρχῆς, μὲ τὴν ἰδέαν τοῦ δ΄· ἦχος δ΄ *Ἀναστὰς ὁ Ἰησοῦς* (simple A)
762.	24v	Ἀπὸ τὸ αὐτὸ στιχηρόν, ἀναποδισμός· Παλαμᾶ τοῦ ἐξ Ἀγχιάλου, ἐκαλλωπίσθη δὲ παρὰ Μάρκου μητροπολίτου Κορίνθου· ἦχος πλ. δ΄ *Ἔδωκεν ἡμῖν* (single A)
763.	28r	Ὠιδὴ ζ΄, Μανουὴλ Χρυσάφου· ἦχος α΄ *Ὁ παῖδας ἐκ καμίνου* (single B)
764.	31r	Ὠιδὴ η΄, Ἰωάννου τοῦ Κλαδᾶ· ἦχος α΄ *Αὕτη ἡ κλητή* (2-part A)
765.	34r	Ὠιδὴ θ΄, Ἰωάννου τοῦ Γλυκέος· ἦχος α΄ *Φωτίζου, φωτίζου* (single B) 765β fol.36v: Ἑτέρα ἐπιβολή, τοῦ Κουκουζέλου· ἦχος δ΄ *Ἐν τῇ ἐγέρσει, τιτιτι*
766.	37v	Ἕτερον ἐκ τῆς αὐτῆς ᾠδῆς, Βαρθολομαίου μοναχοῦ καὶ δομεστίκου τῆς Λαύρας· ἦχος α΄ *Ὤ θείας, ὦ φίλης* (single a)
767.	40r	Ἕτερον, Ξένου τοῦ Κορώνη, πρὸς τὸ Χαίροις ἡ καλλονή· ἦχος α΄ *Ὤ θείας, ὦ φίλης* (single a)
768.	42r	Ἕτερον ἐκ τῆς αὐτῆς ᾠδῆς, Ξένου τοῦ Κορώνη· ἦχος α΄ *Ὤ πάσχα τὸ μέγα* (single A)

769.	44v	Εἰς τοὺς αἴνους, στιχηρὰ μελισθέντα παρὰ Μανουὴλ μαΐστορος τοῦ Χρυσάφου· ἦχος πλ. α΄ *Πάσχα ἱερὸν* (single A)
770.	47r	Ἕτερον, τοῦ αὐτοῦ Χρυσάφου· πλ. α΄ *Δεῦτε ἀπὸ θέας* (single A)
771.	50r	Ἕτερον, τοῦ αὐτοῦ Χρυσάφου· πλ. α΄ *Αἱ μυροφόροι γυναῖκες* (single A)
772.	52r	Ἕτερον, Μόσχου τοῦ Κομνηνοῦ, ἐκαλλωπίσθη δὲ παρὰ τοῦ Χρυσάφου· ἦχος πλ. α΄, ἀπὸ χοροῦ *Ἀναστάσεως ἡμέρα* (simple A)
773.	54r	Ἀναγραμματισμὸς ἀπὸ τὸ αὐτὸ στιχηρόν· Θεοδούλου μοναχοῦ· ἦχος πλ. α΄ *Χριστὸς ἀνέστη* (single A)
774.	57r	Στίχοι εἰς τὴν αὐτὴν ἑορτήν, μελισθέντες παρὰ Ἰωάννου τοῦ Κουκουζέλου· ἦχος δ΄ *Λέλυται φύσις τῶν βροτῶν* (single A)
775.	59r	Ἕτερον, Ξένου τοῦ Κορώνη· ἦχος δ΄ *Ἄναξ ἀνάκτων ἥλιος* (single A)
776.	61r	Στιχηρὰ ἀναστάσιμα τοῦ ἁγίου Ἰωάννου τοῦ Δαμασκηνοῦ, ψαλλόμενα κατ' ἦχον τῇ ἁγίᾳ καὶ μεγάλῃ Κυριακῇ τοῦ Πάσχα, ἐν πάσῃ τῇ Πεντηκοστῇ καὶ ἐν ταῖς ἀναστασίμοις ἡμέραις· μελισθέντα παρὰ Ἰωάσαφ τοῦ νέου Κουκουζέλου· ἦχος α΄ *Ἀγαλλιάσθω ἡ κτίσις* (single B)
777.	64v	Ἕτερον στιχηρὸν ἐξ αὐτῶν, τοῦ αὐτοῦ Ἰωάσαφ· ἦχος β΄ βου *Χαίρετε λαοί* (single B)
778.	67v	[...] τοῦ αὐτοῦ Ἰωάσαφ· τρίτος *Χαρᾶς τὰ πάντα* (single A)
779.	71r	[...] τοῦ αὐτοῦ Ἰωάσαφ, λέγεται δὲ καὶ τῇ Κυριακῇ τῶν Μυροφόρων· ἦχος δ΄ νη *Μετὰ δακρύων γυναῖκες* (single A)
780.	74v	[...] τοῦ αὐτοῦ Ἰωάσαφ· πλ. α΄ *Μέγα θαῦμα* (single A)
781.	77v	[...] τοῦ αὐτοῦ Ἰωάσαφ· πλ. β΄ *Τὴν ἀνάστασίν σου* (single A)
782.	80v	[...] τοῦ αὐτοῦ Ἰωάσαφ· βαρὺς *Φοβερὸς ὤφθης, Κύριε* (single A)
783.	83v	[...] τοῦ αὐτοῦ Ἰωάσαφ· πλ. δ΄ *Ὦ δέσποτα τῶν ἁπάντων* (single A)
784.	87r	Τῇ Παρασκευῇ τῆς Διακαινησίμου, ἑορτάζομεν τὴν ὑπεραγίαν Θεοτόκον τὴν Ζωοδόχον Πηγήν· στιχηρὸν Ξένου τοῦ Κορώνη· ἦχος α΄ *Τὴν ζωοδόχον πηγὴν τὴν ἀέναον* (single B)
785.	89v	Δεύτερος πούς· ἦχος πλ. β΄ *Τοῦ οὐρανοῦ τε καὶ γῆς* (single B)
786.	91v	Ἕτερον στιχηρὸν [...], Ἰωάννου Κουκουζέλου· ἦχος α΄ *Ὁ ποταμὸς τῶν δωρεῶν* (single A)
787.	94r	Ἕτερον [...], Ἰωακεὶμ μοναχοῦ· ἦχος α΄ *Χαῖρε τῆς χάριτος πηγὴ* (single A)

788. 97v Ἕτερον στιχηρὸν θεοτοκίον εἰς τὴν αὐτὴν ἑορτήν· Ξένου τοῦ Κορώνη· ἦχος β´ *Ζῶσα ὑπάρχουσα πηγή* (single A)

789. 100r Ἕτερον [...], Μανουὴλ Χρυσάφου· τρίτος *Σὲ τὴν ἀθάνατον πηγὴν* (single B)

790. 103r Τῇ Κυριακῇ τοῦ Θωμᾶ· στιχηρὸν τοῦ Μανουγρᾶ, ἐκαλλωπίσθη δὲ παρὰ Γεωργίου δομεστίκου τοῦ Κοντοπετρῆ· ἦχος πλ. α´ *Φιλάνθρωπε, μέγα* (single B)

791. 105r Δεύτερος πούς· ἦχος πλ. β´ *Πῶς ἐσαρκώθης* (single B)

792. 107v Τῇ Κυριακῇ τῶν Μυροφόρων· στιχηρὸ Μανουὴλ τοῦ Χρυσάφου· ἦχος α´ *Ἦλθον ἐπὶ τὸ μνημεῖον* (single B)

793. 111r Ἕτερον στιχηρὸν [...], τοῦ Μανουγρᾶ· ἦχος β´ *Ἔρραναν μύρα* (single B)

794. 113r Ἕτερον [...], Ξένου τοῦ Κορώνη· τρίτος *Εἰς τὰ μνῆμά σε ἐπεζήτησεν* (simple C)

795. 115v Δεύτερος πούς· τρίτος πα *Ζεῦγος δὲ ζωηφόρων ἀγγέλων* (simple C)

796. 118r Τρίτος πούς· ἦχος πλ. β´ *Αὐτὴ δὲ στραφεῖσα* (single B)

797. 120r Ἕτερον στιχηρὸν [...], Θεοδούλου μοναχοῦ· τρίτος *Κρυπτόμενον τὸν Πέτρον* (single B)

798. 123v Τῇ Κυριακῇ τοῦ Παραλύτου· στιχηρὸν τοῦ Καμπάνη· ἦχος α´ *Ἄταφος νεκρὸς* (single A)

799. 126v Τῇ Τετάρτῃ τῆς Μεσοπεντηκοστῆς, στιχηρὸν τοῦ Χρυσάφου· ἦχος δ´ *Φωτισθέντες, ἀδελφοί* (single B)

800. 129r–v Ἕτερον στιχηρὸν [...], τοῦ Χρυσάφου· πλ. δ´ *Μεσούσης τῆς ἑορτῆς* (single B)

801. 133v Τῇ Κυριακῇ τῆς Σαμαρείτιδος· στιχηρὸν Καλλίστου τοῦ Πατζάδος· ἦχος β´ *Ἐπὶ τὸ φρέαρ ὡς ἦλθεν* (simple C)

802. 135r Ἕτερον στιχηρὸν [...], Ξένου τοῦ Κορώνη· πλ. β´ *Παρὰ τὸ φρέαρ* (single B)

803. 137v Δεύτερος πούς· πλ. β´ *Ὕδωρ αἰτῶν* (single B)

804. 140r Ἕτερον [...] Μανουὴλ Χρυσάφου· πλ. δ´ *Ὡς ὤφθης ἐν σαρκὶ* (single B)

805. 143r Τῇ Κυριακῇ τοῦ Τυφλοῦ· στιχηρὸν Ξένου τοῦ Κορώνη· ἦχος πλ. δ´ *Δικαιοσύνης ἥλιε* (simple C)

806. 146r Δεύτερος πούς· [ἦχος β´] *Καὶ ἡμῶν τὰ ὄμματα* (single B)

807. 148v Ἕτερον στιχηρὸν [...], Ἰωάννου Κλαδᾶ· πλ. δ´ *Τίς λαλήσει* (single B)

808. 150v Δεύτερος πούς· ἦχος τρίτος *Οὐ μόνον γὰρ τοῦ σώματος* (single B)

Incipits of the Anagrams and mathēmata in the Mathēmatarion 225

809.	152r	Τῇ Πέμπτῃ τῆς ἁγίας τοῦ Χριστοῦ καὶ Θεοῦ ἡμῶν Ἀναλήψεως· στιχηρὸν Φιλίππου τοῦ Γαβαλᾶ· ἦχος α΄ *Ἀνελθὼν εἰς οὐρανοὺς* (single B)
810.	155r	Ἕτερον [...], Ἰωάννου τοῦ Γλυκέος· β΄ βου *Ἀναλαμβανομένου σου*
810β	156r:	Παρεκβολὴ τοῦ Κουκουζέλου· ἦχος πλ. α΄ *Ἑτέρα τῇ ἑτέρᾳ*
811.	157r	Δεύτερος πούς· ἦχος δ΄ *Τίς οὗτος, καί φησι* (2-part B)
812.	160r	Ἀναποδισμός, ἀπὸ τὸ αὐτὸ στιχηρόν, δομεστίκου τοῦ Εὐγενικοῦ· ἦχος δ΄ *Ἀπέστειλας ἡμῖν, Χριστὲ* (single B)
813.	163r	Ἕτερον [...], Μανουὴλ Χρυσάφου· ἦχος δ΄ *Ὅτε ἀνελήφθης* (single B)
814.	167r	Ἀναγραμματισμὸς ἀπὸ τό, Κύριε οἱ ἀπόστολοι, Γρηγορίου τοῦ ἐκ Σηλυβρίας· ἦχος πλ. β΄ *Ἀλλ᾽ ἀπόστειλον ὡς ὑπέσχου ὑμῖν* (single A)
815.	170r	Ἕτερον στιχηρὸν [...], τοῦ Παλαμᾶ· ἐκαλλωπίσθη παρὰ Μάρκου μητροπολίτου, ὕστερον δὲ καὶ παρὰ Χρυσάφου· ἦχος πλ. β΄ *Δέσποτα, μὴ ἐάσῃς ἡμᾶς* (single A)
816.	172v	Ἕτερον [...], Γρηγορίου Μπούνη· πλ. β΄ *Ἀνέβη ὁ Θεὸς* (single B)
817.	175v	Ἕτερον [...], Μανουὴλ Χρυσάφου· πλ. δ΄ *Ἀνελήφθης ἐν δόξῃ* (single B)
818.	180r	Ἕτερον στιχηρὸν εἰς τὴν αὐτὴν ἑορτήν, Θεοδούλου μοναχοῦ· τοῦτο ψάλλεται καὶ ἐν ὅλῃ τῇ Πεντηκοστῇ· ἦχος πλ. δ΄ *Πιστεύω σου τὴν ἔνσαρκον* (single A)
819.	183v	Τῇ Κυριακῇ τῶν ἁγίων τριακοσίων δέκα καὶ ὀκτὼ θεοφόρων Πατέρων τῶν ἐν Νικαίᾳ, Νικολάου τοῦ Καλλίστου [anagram]· ἦχος πλ. δ΄ *Ὢ θεία παρεμβολὴ* (4-part A)
820.	188r	Τῇ Κυριακῇ τῆς Πεντηκοστῆς· στιχηρὸν Ξένου τοῦ Κορώνη· ἦχος β΄ βου *Ἐν ταῖς αὐλαῖς σου* (2-part B)
821.	191r	Ἕτερον [...], Ἰωάννου τοῦ Γλυκέος· ἦχος δ΄ *Τὸ πνεῦμα τὸ ἅγιον* (2-part B)
822.	194r	Ἕτερον [...], Ξένου τοῦ Κορώνη· πλ. β΄ *Βασιλεῦ οὐράνιε* (3-part B)
823.	198r	Ἕτερον στιχηρὸν [...]· πλ. δ΄ *Γλῶσσαί ποτε συνεχέθησαν* (single B)
824.	200r	Δεύτερος πούς· ἦχος τρίτος *Ἐκεῖ κατεδίκασε* (single B)
825.	202r	Ἀναγραμματισμὸς ἀπὸ τὸ αὐτὸ στιχηρόν· Ἰωάννου τοῦ Κουκουζέλου· ἦχος πλ. δ΄ *Τότε κατηργεῖτο* (single B)
826.	205r	Ἕτερον [...], Μανουὴλ Χρυσάφου· πλ. δ΄ *Δεῦτε λαοί* (single B)
827.	208v	Δεύτερος πούς· ἦχος τρίτος *Ἅγιος ὁ Θεὸς* (simple C)

828. 211v Τῇ Κυριακῇ τῶν ἁγίων Πάντων· στιχηρὸν Μανουὴλ τοῦ Χρυσάφου· ἦχος α΄ *Δεῦτε πάντες οἱ πιστοί* (single B)

829. 215r Ἕτερον στιχηρὸν εἰς τὴν αὐτὴν ἑορτήν, Φιλίππου τοῦ Γαβαλᾶ· ἦχος δ΄ *Τὴν τετραπέρατον ἑορτὴν* (single B)

830. 218r Ἕτερον [...], Συμεὼν τοῦ Ψηρίτζη· ἦχος δ΄ *Ἄγγελοι ἐν οὐρανοῖς* (3-part A)

831. 221r Ἕτερον στιχηρὸν εἰς τὴν αὐτὴν ἑορτήν· Μάρκου μητροπολίτου Κορίνθου· ἦχος πλ. δ΄ *Ἀσματικὴν χορείαν κροτήσωμεν* (2-part A)

832. 224v Τέλος καὶ τῷ Θεῷ χάρις.

ΜΠΤ 706: PAPADIKĒ (THEOTOKIŌN)

484 + i–iv folios

ir Ἀρχὴ σὺν Θεῷ ἁγίῳ τῶν κατ᾽ ἦχον θεοτοκίων μαθημάτων τῆς Παπαδικῆς, μελισθέντων παρὰ διαφόρων παλαιῶν μουσικῶν διδασκάλων, τὸ νῦν δὲ ἐξηγηθέντων κατὰ τὴν Νέαν τῆς μουσικῆς Μέθοδον παρὰ Χουρμουζίου διδασκάλου καὶ Χαρτοφύλακος τῆς τοῦ Χριστοῦ Μεγάλης Ἐκκλησίας.

1. ir Τὸ παρὸν ἐμελίσθη παρὰ Ξένου τοῦ Κορώνη καὶ πρωτοψάλτου· ἦχος α΄ πα *Ποίαν σοι ἐπάξιον ᾠδὴν* (single A)

2. 6v Κὺρ Χρυσάφου τοῦ νέου· ἦχος α΄ πα *Ποίαν σοι ἐπάξιον* (single B)

3. 13v Κὺρ Ἰωάννου τοῦ Κλαδᾶ· ἦχος α΄ πα *Τῇ ἀειπαρθένῳ καὶ μητρὶ* (single A)

4. 18r Κὺρ Ἰωάννου τοῦ Κλαδᾶ· ἦχος α΄ πα *Τῶν οὐρανίων ταγμάτων* (single A)

5. 24v Ἀναγραμματισμὸς Φωκᾶ λαμπαδαρίου· ἦχος α΄ πα *Ἣν πάλαι προκατήγγειλαν οἱ θαυμαστοὶ προφῆται* (2-part B)

6. 31r Κὺρ Ξένου τοῦ Κορώνη· ἦχος α΄ τετράφωνος κε *Σὲ μεγαλύνομεν, τὴν ὄντως Θεοτόκον* (single A)

7. 35v Κλήμεντος ἱερομονάχου· ἦχος α΄ τετράφωνος κε *Σὲ μεγαλύνομεν* (single A)

8. 40r Χρυσάφου τοῦ νέου· ἦχος α΄ τετράφωνος κε *Σῶσον τὸν λαόν σου* (single B)

9. 49v Μπαλασίου ἱερέως· ἦχος α΄ τετράφωνος κε *Κόλπων οὐκ ἐκστὰς* (single A)

Incipits of the Anagrams and mathēmata in the Mathēmatarion 227

10. 56r Μπαλασίου ἱερεώς· ἦχος α΄ δ΄ φωνος κε *Ἄπας ἐγκωμίων* (single B)

11. 64r Μπαλασίου ἱερέως· ἦχος α΄ πα *Ἐκύκλωσεν ἡμᾶς* (single A)

12. 68r Γερμανοῦ Νέων Πατρῶν· ἦχος α΄ πα *Ῥίζης ἐκ Δαβὶδ* (single B)

13. 74v Ἀναγραμματισμὸς τοῦ Νέων Πατρῶν [Γερμανοῦ]· ἦχος α΄ πα *Ἦν πάλαι προκατήγγειλαν* (2-part B)

14. 83r Μανουὴλ τοῦ Χρυσάφου· ἦχος β΄ βου *Τὴν πᾶσαν ἐλπίδα μου* (single A)

15. 88v Κὺρ Μαουὴλ τοῦ Χρυσάφου, κατανυκτικόν· ἦχος β΄ *Πάντων προστατεύεις, ἀγαθή* (single A)

16. 93r Νικηφόρου τοῦ Ἠθικοῦ· ἦχος β΄ *Ἐν λύπαις σε παράκλησιν* (single A)

17. 98r Ξένου τοῦ Κορώνῃ, εἰς τὴν παράκλησιν· ἦχος β΄ *Διάσωσον ἀπὸ κινδύνων* (simple B)

18. 102r Μπαλασίου ἱερέως· ἦχος β΄ *Πάντα ὑπὲρ ἔννοιαν* (single A)

19. 109r Καλλωπισμὸς Κωνσταντίνου τοῦ Μαγουλᾶ· ἦχος τρίτος *Ἐν Σιναίῳ τῷ ὄρει* (single B)

20. 115r Μανουὴλ τοῦ Χρυσάφου· ἦχος τρίτος *Μέγιστον θαῦμα* (single A)

21. 122v Μανουὴλ τοῦ Χρυσάφου· τρίτος *Τὴν ὡραιότητα τῆς παρθενίας σου* (single A)

22. 130v Κωνσταντίνου τοῦ Μαγουλᾶ· ἦχος τρίτος *Παιδοτόκον Παρθένον* (single A)

23. 137r Μπαλασίου ἱερέως· ἦχος τρίτος *Ἐν Σιναίῳ τῷ ὄρει* (single A)

24. 142v Μπαλασίου ἱερέως· ἦχος τρίτος *Θρόνος πάγχρυσος* (single A)

25. 149v Ἰωάννου τοῦ Κουκουζέλου· ἦχος δ΄ *Τὴν ὄντως Θεοτόκον* (single A)

26. 155v Μανουὴλ τοῦ Χρυσάφου· ἦχος δ΄ *Σὲ τὸ καθαρώτατον* (2-part A)

27. 163v Κωνσταντίνου τοῦ ἐξ Ἀγχιάλου· ἦχος δ΄ *Ἐσείσθησαν λαοί* (single B)

28. 170r Μανουὴλ τοῦ Χρυσάφου· γράμματα καὶ μέλος· ἦχος δ΄ *Βασίλισσα πανύμνητε παρθενομῆτορ κόρη* (single A)

29. 176r Ἰωάννου τοῦ Κλαδᾶ· ἦχος δ΄ *Ἐσείσθησαν λαοί* (single B)

30. 182r Κωνσταντίνου τοῦ Μαγουλᾶ· ἦχος δ΄ *Ἄπας γηγενής* (single B)

31. 187v Γεωργίου τοῦ Ραιδεστηνοῦ· ἦχος δ΄ *Σὲ μεγαλύνομεν, τὴν ὄντως Θεοτόκον* (single B)

32. 193r Μανουὴλ (?) τοῦ νέου Χρυσάφου· ἦχος δ΄ *Ἴδι τοῦ πτωχοῦ λαοῦ σου* (single B)

33. 200v Χρυσάφου τοῦ νέου· ἦχος δ΄ *Ρόδον τὸ ἀμάραντον* (single B)
34. 209v Χρυσάφου τοῦ νέου· ἦχος δ΄ *Ὡς ζωηφόρος* (single A)
35. 216r Γερμανοῦ Νέων Πατρῶν· ἦχος δ΄ *Πυρίμορφον ὄχημα* (single B)
36. 225v Μπαλασίου ἱερεώς· ἦχος δ΄ *Χρυσοπολοκώτατε πύργε* (single B)
37. 233v Μπαλασίου ἱερεύς· ἦχος δ΄ *Δάμαλις τὸν μόσχον* (single A)
38. 238r Μπαλασίου ἱερέυς· ἦχος δ΄ *Τὸ τοῦ ὑψίστου ἡγιασμένον* (single A)
39. 245v Ἰωάννου τοῦ Κλαδᾶ· ἦχος πλ. α΄ *πα Ἡσαῖα χόρευε* (single A)
40. 250v Μανουὴλ τοῦ Χρυσάφου· ἦχος πλ. α΄ *πα Μακαρίζομέν σε* (single B)
41. 255v Ξένου τοῦ Κορώνη· ἦχος πλ. α΄ *Χαίροις ἡ καλλονὴ Ἰακώβ* (single A)
    41α 260r: Ἑτέρα ἐπιβολὴ· ἦχος πλ. α΄ *Χαίροις παντευλόγητε* (single A)
    41β 261r: Ποὺς δεύτερος· ἦχος πλ. α΄ *Γαστὴρ θεοχώρητε* (single A)
42. 264r Ἰωάννου τοῦ Κλαδᾶ· ἦχος πλ. α΄ *Ἅπας ἐγκωμίων* (simple A)
43. 268v Ξένου τοῦ Κορώνη· ἦχος πλ. α΄ *Τὴν ζωοδόχον πηγὴν* (single B)
    43α 272v: Ποὺς δεύτερος· ἦχος πλ. β΄ *Τοῦ οὐρανοῦ καὶ τῆς γῆς ἡ πλατυτέρα* (single B)
44. 276r Χρυσάφου τοῦ νέου· ἦχος πλ. α΄ *Θεοτόκε Παρθένε* (single A)
45. 281v Γερμανοῦ Νέων Πατρῶν· ἦχος πλ. α΄ *Χρυσοπλοκώτατε πύργε* (single B)
46. 286v Γερμανοῦ Νέων Πατρῶν· ἦχος πλ. α΄ *Ἣν πάλαι προκατήγγειλαν* (2-part B)
47. 294r Μπαλασίου ἱερέως· ἦχος πλ. α΄ *Ἐν θρόνῳ καθήμενος* (single A)
48. 298r Μπαλασίου ἱερέως· ἦχος πλ. α΄ *Τὴν ζωοδόχον πηγὴν* (single B)
49. 304v Μπαλασίου ἱερέως· ἦχος πλ. α΄ *Μέγα θαῦμα* (single B)
    310r: Ἀρχὴ τοῦ πλαγίου δευτέρου ἤχου.
50. 310r Ξένου τοῦ Κορώνη· ἦχος πλ. β΄ *Τοὺς Θεοτόκον σε ἐκ ψυχῆς* (single A)
51. 315r Ξένου τοῦ Κορώνη· ἦχος πλ. β΄ *Μεταβολὴ τῶν θλιβομένων* (simple A)
52. 319r Θεοδώρου τοῦ Γαβαλᾶ [β΄ ποὺς]· ἦχος πλ. β΄ *Δέσποινα τοῦ κόσμου* (simple C)
53. 324r Τοῦ ἐν ἁγίου πατρὸς ἡμῶν Ἰωάννου τοῦ Δαμασκηνοῦ· ἦχος πλ. β΄ *Προστασία τῶν χριστιανῶν* (simple A)
54. 326v Μανουὴλ λαμπαδαρίου τοῦ Χρυσάφου· πλ. β΄ *Τὸ θαῦμα τοῦ τόκου σου* (single A)

55.	333v	Μανουὴλ λαμπαδαρίου τοῦ Χρυσάφου· πλ. β´ *Τῆς εὐσπλαγχνίας τὴν πύλην* (single A)
56.	338r	Ἰωάννου τοῦ Κουκουζέλη· πλ. β´ *νενανω Ἄνωθεν οἱ προφῆται* (single A)
57.	342v	Ἰωάννου λαμπαδαρίου τοῦ Κλαδᾶ· πλ. β´νενανω *Ἄνωθεν οἱ προφῆται* (single A)
58.	349v	Μανουὴλ τοῦ Χρυσάφου· πλ. β´ *Σὲ πάντες μεγαλύνομεν* (simple C)
59.	354r	Μπαλασίου ἱερέως· πλ. β´ νενανω *Σὲ προκατήγγειλε χορὸς τῶν προφητῶν ἐνθέως* (simple A)
60.	360v	Μπαλασίου ἱερέως· ἦχος πλ. β´ *Ὁ μέγας προέγραψε* (single A)
61.	365r	Ἰωάννου μαΐστορος τοῦ Κουκουζέλη· ἦχος βαρὺς *Ἄνωθεν οἱ προφῆται* (2-part A)
62.	370r	Ἰωάννου τοῦ Κλαδᾶ· ἦχος βαρὺς *Ἄνωθεν οἱ προφῆται* (2-part A)
63.	378v	Μανουὴλ τοῦ Χρυσάφου· ἦχος βαρὺς *Τὴν ὄντως Θεοτόκον* (single A)
64.	385r	Γερμανοῦ Νέων Πατρῶν· ἦχος βαρὺς *Χαῖρε κεχαριτωμένη* (single B)
65.	393r	Μπαλασίου ἱερέως· βαρὺς *Ὑπὸ τὴν σήν, Δέσποινα, σκέπην* (single A)
66.	398v	Μπαλασίου ἱερέως· βαρὺς *Ψάλλων Δαβὶδ σὸς προπάτωρ* (single A) 404v Ἀρχὴ τοῦ πλαγίου τετάρτου ἤχου.
67.	404v	Τὸ παρὸν κὺρ [Μανουὴλ] Χρυσάφου, τά τε γράμματα καὶ τὸ μέλος· ἦχος πλ. δ´ *Ψαλμοῖς καὶ ὕμνοις σὲ ὑμνῶ* (single B)
68.	413v	Τοῦ αὐτοῦ κὺρ Χρυσάφου· πλ. δ´ *Δέσποινα πρόσδεξαι* (single B)
69.	421r	Τοῦ αὐτοῦ κὺρ Χρυσάφου· πλ. δ´ *Ταῖς πρεσβείαις τῆς Θεοτόκου* (single A)
70.	425v	Ἰωάννου τοῦ Κλαδᾶ· πλ. δ´ *Ὁ ναός σου, Θεοτόκε* (single A)
71.	429v	Ἰωάσαφ μοναχοῦ· πλ. δ´ *Τὴν Θεοτόκον Μαρίαν* (single A)
72.	434v	Μανουὴλ τοῦ Ἀργυροπούλου· πλ. δ´ *Βασίλισσα παντάνασσα* (simple A)
73.	439r	Μανουὴλ τοῦ νέου Χρυσάφου· πλ. δ´ *Ἐν ὕμνοις εὐχαρίστοις* (single A)
74.	446r	Τοῦ αὐτοῦ Μανουὴλ τοῦ νέου Χρυσάφου· πλ. δ´ *Ἔντεινε καὶ κατευοδοῦ* (single A)
75.	452r	Τοῦ αὐτοῦ νέου Χρυσάφου· πλ. δ´ *Ῥυσθείημεν τῶν δεινῶν* (single A)
76.	458r	Μπαλασίου ἱερέως· πλ. δ´ *Πρός τίνα καταφύγω* (single B)
77.	466r	Μπαλασίου ἱερέως· πλ. δ´ *Ἐξέστη ἐπὶ τούτῳ ὁ οὐρανός* (single A)

78.	473v	Μπαλασίου ιερέως· ήχος πλ. δ´ *Πῶς σου τὴν χάριν ὑμνῆσαι με* (single A)
79.	479v	Μπαλασίου ιερέως· ήχος πλ. δ´ *Ψαλμοῖς σε ἀνυμνοῦμεν* (single A)
	484r	Τέλος τοῦ πρώτου τόμου τῶν μαθημάτων τῆς Παπαδικῆς [...].

ΜΠΤ 706: PAPADIKĒ (VOLUME V)

430 folios

	1r	Ὁ τῆς Παπαδικῆς τόμος ὁ τελευταῖος, ὅστις περιέχει τὰ τοῦ ἐνιαυτοῦ μαθήματα καί τινα ὀργανικὰ κρατήματα ἐν τῷ τέλει, ἐξηγηθέντα καὶ γραφέντα παρὰ Χουρμουζίου διδασκάλου καὶ Χαρτοφύλοκος τῆς τοῦ Χριστοῦ Μεγάλης Ἐκκλησίας.
80.	1r	Σεπτεμβρίου η´, Μπαλασίου ιερέως· πλ. δ´ *Ἐν εὐσήμῳ ἡμέρᾳ* (single A) (fol. 6r: ζήτει τὸ λοιπὸν κράτημα εἰς τό, *Ψαλμοῖς σε ἀνυμνοῦμεν*)
81.	6r	Σεπτεμβρίου ιδ´, κὺρ Χρυσάφου [νέου]· ήχος δ´ *Ὡς ἐμεγαλύνθη* (single A)
82.	12r	Χρυσάφου [νέου], εἰς τὴν αὐτὴν ἑορτήν· ήχος δ´ *Ἐν φωναῖς ἀλαλάξωμεν* (single A)
83.	17v	Σεπτεμβρίου κς´, Χρυσάφου τοῦ νέου· ήχος α´ *Ποταμοὶ θεολογίας* (single B)
84.	23r	Ὀκτωβρίου κς´, εἰς τὴν ἑορτὴν τοῦ ἁγίου μεγαλομάρτυρος Δημητρίου, Μανουὴλ τοῦ Χρυσάφου· ήχος δ´ *Τὸν στρατιώτην τὸν λαμπρόν* (single B)
85.	28v	Νοεμβρίου η´ [...], Κωνσταντίνου Μανουγρᾶ· πλ. α´ *Τῇ μεσιτείᾳ σου* (single A)
86.	35r	Χρυσάφου τοῦ νέου · α´ δ´ φωνος κε *Πυρίμορφοι ἀρχάγγελοι* (single B)
87.	44v	Εἰς τὴν αὐτὴν ἑορτήν, Μπαλασίου ιερέως· ήχος δ´ *Ἄρχον δυνάμεων Θεοῦ* (single B)
88.	51v	Νοεμβρίου κα´ [...], κὺρ Μανουὴλ [Χρυσάφου]· ήχος α´ δ´ φωνος κε *Ἀγαλλιάσθω ὁ Δαβίδ* (single B)
89.	56v	Δεκεμβρίου ε´, εἰς τὴν ἑορτὴν τοῦ ἁγίου πατρὸς ἡμῶν Σάββα τοῦ ἡγιασμένου· Μπαλασίου ιερέως· πλ. δ´ *Τῶν μοναστῶν τὰ πλήθη* (2-part B)
90.	64r	Δεκεμβρίου ς´ [...], Χρυσάφου τοῦ νέου· ήχος α´ *Νέος Ἀβραάμ* (single B)

Incipits of the Anagrams and mathēmata in the Mathēmatarion 231

91.	70r	Εἰς τὴν αὐτὴν ἑορτήν, Γερμανοῦ Νέων Πατρῶν· πλ. α' *Σαλπίσωμεν* (single B)
92.	78v	Εἰς τὴν αὐτὴν ἑορτήν, Μπαλασίου ἱερέως· ἦχος α' *Ἄνθρωπε τοῦ Θεοῦ* (single A)
93.	83v	Δεκεμβρίου ιβ' [...], Χρυσάφου τοῦ νέου· ἦχος α' *Πανήγυρις φαιδρά* (single B)
94.	89v	Δεκεμβρίου κβ' [...], Ἰωάννου τοῦ Κουκουζέλου· βαρὺς [πρωτόβαρυς] *Δόξα ἐν ὑψίστοις Θεῷ* (2-part A)
95.	94r	Εἰς τὴν αὐτὴν ἑορτήν, Μανουὴλ Χρυσάφου· ἦχος δ' *Εὐφραίνεσθε δίκαιοι* (single A)
96.	102r	Εἰς τὴν αὐτὴν ἑορτήν, Χρυσάφου τοῦ νέου· ἦχος α' *Οἱ παῖδες εὐσεβείᾳ* (2-part B)
97.	108v	Εἰς τὴν αὐτὴν ἑορτήν, Μπαλασίου ἱερέως· ἦχος α' *Χριστὸς γεννᾶται* (single A)
98.	115v	Ἰανουαρίου α', εἰς τὴν ἑορτὴν τοῦ ἐν ἁγίοις πατρὸς ἡμῶν Βασιλείου τοῦ μεγάλου· Μανουὴλ τοῦ Χρυσάφου· ἦχος α' *Ὦ θεία καὶ ἱερά* (single A)
99.	121r	Ἰανουαρίου ς' [...], Ἰωάννου Κουκουζέλου· βαρὺς *Δόξα ἐν ὑψίστοις Θεῷ* (2-part A)
100.	126v	Εἰς τὴν αὐτὴν ἑορτήν, Χρυσάφου τοῦ νέου· ἦχος δ' *Ἡ τριάς, ὁ Θεὸς ἡμῶν* (single B)
101.	132v	Εἰς τὴν αὐτὴν ἑορτήν, Μπαλασίου· πλ. δ' *Σήμερον ἡ κτίσις φωτίζεται* (single A)
102.	142r	Φεβρουαρίου β' [...], Μανουὴλ Χρυσάφου· βαρὺς *Φῶς εἰς ἀποκάλυψιν* (single B)
103.	151r	Μαρτίου κε' [...], Μανουὴλ Χρυσάφου· ἦχος δ' *Γλῶσσαν ἣν οὐκ ἔγνω* (single B)
104.	157v	Ἀπριλίου κγ' [...], Χρυσάφου νέου· α' δ' *φωνος Δεῦτε φιλοθεάμονες* (single B)
105.	166r	Εἰς τὴν αὐτὴν ἑορτήν, Μανουὴλ Χρυσάφου· ἦχος α' *Χριστὸν γὰρ ὃν ἐπόθησας* (single A)
106.	174r	Ἰουνίου κδ' [...], Μανουὴλ Χρυσάφου· ἦχος δ' *Λύει τοῦ Ζαχαρίου* (single B)
107.	180r	Ἰουνίου κθ' [...], Μανουὴλ Χρυσάφου· ἦχος δ' *Μακάριόν σε* (single A)
108.	186r	Ἰουλίου κς' [...], Χρυσάφου τοῦ νέου· ἦχος δ' *Ἅπας νῦν βροτός* (single B)
109.	123r	Αὐγούστου ς' [...], Μπαλασίου ἱερέως· πλ. δ' *Παρέλαβεν ὁ Χριστός* (2-part A)

110. 200v Αὐγούστου ιε´ [...], Χρυσάφου τοῦ νέου· ἦχος α´ *Ἡ δημιουργικὴ* (single B)

111. 207v Γερμανοῦ Νέων Πατρῶν [...]· ἦχος α´ *Νενίκηνται τῆς φύσεως* (single A)

112. 213v Τῇ Κυριακῇ τῆς Τυροφάγου, εἰς τὴν ἐξορίαν τοῦ Ἀδάμ· Ἰωάννου λαμπαδαρίου τοῦ Κλαδᾶ· πλ. β´ νενανω *Παράδεισε ἁγιώτατε* (single B)

33b. 220v Τῇ Κυριακῇ τῆς Ὀρθοδοξίας· Χρυσάφου τοῦ νέου· ἦχος δ´ *Λάμπρυνον τῇ θείᾳ σου δόξῃ* (single A)

113. 227v Εἰς τὸν Ἀκάθιστον ὕμνον, μέλος παλαιόν, δίχορον καὶ ἔντεχνον· ἦχος πλ. δ´ *Τῇ ὑπερμάχῳ* (πλ. α´) κατακλείεται δι᾽ ἀργοῦ ὁμοίου μέλους τοῦ Ἀλληλούϊα [τρίς])

114. 231r Ἕτερον σύντομον· ἦχος πλ. δ´ *Τῇ ὑπερμάχῳ*

115. 232v Ἕτερον συντομώτερον· ἦχος πλ. δ´ *Τῇ ὑπερμάχῳ*

116. 233r Ἰωάννου τοῦ Κλαδᾶ, ἔντεχνον· ἦχος πλ. δ´ *Τῇ ὑπερμάχῳ* (2-part A)

117. 241r Γεωργίου τοῦ Ραιδεστηνοῦ· ἦχος πλ. α´ *Τῇ ὑπερμάχῳ* (single A)

118. 246r Μπαλασίου ἱερέως· ἦχος α´ *Τῇ ὑπερμάχῳ* (2-part B)

119. 259r Τῇ Κυριακῇ τῶν Βαΐων· Μπαλασίου ἱερέως· ἦχος πλ. δ´ *Χαῖρε καὶ εὐφραίνου* (single A)

120. 246v Εἰς τὴν αὐτὴν ἑορτήν, Μπαλασίου· ἦχος δ´ *Ἐκ στόματος νηπίων* (2-part B)

121. 270r Ἀναγραμματισμὸς τοῦ Κουκουζέλους, ἀπὸ τό, Σὲ τὸν ἀναβαλλόμενον· ἦχος πλ. α´ *Μεγαλύνω τὰ πάθη σου* (simple A)

122. 276v Εἰς τὴν λαμπροφόρον ἀνάστασιν τοῦ Κυρίου· Μανουὴλ τοῦ Χρυσάφου· ἦχος πλ. α´ *Δόξα Πατρί, Καὶ νῦν· Ἀναστάσεως ἡμέρα* (single A)

123. 282r Ἕτερον [...], Χρυσάφου τοῦ νέου· ἦχος α´ *Χριστὸς ἀνέστη* (single B)

124. 289v Εἰς τὴν αὐτὴ ἑορτήν, Χρυσάφου τοῦ νέου· ἦχος α´ δ´ φωνος κε *Ἆρον κύκλῳ τοὺς ὀφθαλμούς σου* (single B)

125. 296r Εἰς τὴν αὐτὴν ἑορτήν, Γερμανοῦ ἀρχιερέως Νέων Πατρῶν· ἦχος α´ *Ἀναστάσεως ἡμέρα* (single B)

126. 303v Εἰς τὴν αὐτὴν ἑορτήν, Μπαλασίου ἱερέως· ἦχος α´ *Ὁ ἄγγελος ἐβόα* (single B)

127. 310r Εἰς τὴν Ἀνάληψιν τοῦ Κυρίου, Μπαλασίου ἱερέως· ἦχος πλ. β´ *Ἀνέβη ὁ Θεός* (single A)

128. 316v Τῇ Κυριακῇ τῆς Πεντηκοστῆς, Χρυσάφου τοῦ νέου· ἦχος δ´ *Χαίροις ἄνασσα* (single B)

129. 322r Εἰς τὴν αὐτὴν ἑορτήν, Μπαλασίου ἱερέως· ἦχος α´ *Πάντα χορηγεῖ* (single B)

Incipits of the Anagrams and mathēmata in the Mathēmatarion 233

130. 329r Εἰς τὴν αὐτὴν ἑορτήν, Χρυσάφου τοῦ νέου· ἦχος α΄ *Τὸν πατέρα προσκυνήσωμεν* (single B)

131. 337v Ἄμωμος ἔντεχνος, καλλωπισθεὶς παρὰ Χρυσάφου τοῦ νέου· ἦχος β΄ *Δι Ἄμωμοι ἐν ὁδῷ*. (fol. 340r) Στάσις δευτέρα, πλ. α΄ *Αἱ χεῖρές σου*· (fol. 342v) Στάσις τρίτη· πλ. δ΄ *Γα Καὶ ἐλέησόν με, ἀλληλούια* [At the *archontika* there is the *lege* for the epibolē of the kratēma.]

132. 346r Κατανυκτικόν, Ἰωάννου τοῦ Κλαδᾶ· ἦχος α΄ δ΄ φωνος κε *Οὐδείς μοι τότε βοηθός* (simple A)

133. 348r Ἕτερον κατανυκτικόν, Μανουὴλ λαμπαραδίου τοῦ Χρυσάφου· ἦχος βαρὺς Ζω *Τὴν τετραυματισμένην μου* (single A)

134. 353v Ἕτερον [...], Ἰωάννου Κλαδᾶ· ἦχος β΄ *Οἴμοι, οἷον ἀγῶνα* (simple C)

135. 358r Ἕτερον [...], Ἰωάννου Κλαδᾶ· πλ. α΄ *Ἄνθρωπε, θρήνησον πικρῶς* (simple A)

***

363r Ἀρχὴ τῶν κατ᾽ ἦχον κρατημάτων.

136. 363r Τὸ παρὸν ἐκαλλωπίσθη παρὰ τοῦ Πρασίνου· ἦχος α΄ δ΄ φωνος *Αχανανενανε*

137. 367r Καλλωπισμὸς τοῦ Καρύκη· ἦχος β΄ *Νεχεανες Αχανενε*

138. 369r Μανουὴλ τοῦ Χρυσάφου· ἦχος τρίτος *Ανεενενανε, τεριρεμ*

139. 371v Μανουὴλ τοῦ Χρυσάφου· ἦχος δ΄ *Αναα Τεριρεμ*

140. 373v Μανουὴλ τοῦ Χρυσάφου· πλ. α΄ *Ανενε Εριρεμ*

141. 376v Γρηγορίου ἱερομονάχου Μπούνη τοῦ Ἀλυάτου· ἦχος πλ. β΄ *Νεε Τεετουτερερον*

142. 379v Μανουὴλ λαμπαδαρίου Χρυσάφου· βαρὺς *Αχανανε Τεριρεν*

143. 381v Μανουὴλ λαμπαδαρίου Χρυσάφου· πλ. δ΄ *Νεαγιε Τερρερε*

144. 384r Ἕτερα κρατήματα χαρμόσυνα. Τὸ παρὸν Ἀρσενίου τοῦ μικροῦ· ἦχος α΄ δ΄ φωνος κε *Ανενε Εριρερεμ*

145. 386v Θεοφάνους πατριάρχου τοῦ Καρύκη· πλ. α΄ *Ανεενεε*

146. 389r Θεοφάνους πατριάρχου τοῦ Καρύκη· πλ. α΄ *Ανεενε*

147. 393r Ἀρσενίου τοῦ μικροῦ, ὀργανικόν, ἐκ τοῦ δὶς διαπασῶν· ἦχος δ΄ *Ανεενε Ααααγια*

148. 398r Ἀρσενίου τοῦ μικροῦ· λέγεται δὲ σύριγξ· πλ. α΄ *Ανεεχε*

149. 401v Γεωργίου τοῦ Ραιδεστηνοῦ· πλ. δ΄ *Ανεενεε*

150.	406v	Χρυσάφου τοῦ νέου· πλ. α' *Ανεενεχε*
151.	411r	Γερμανοῦ ἀρχιερέως Νέων Πατρῶν· πλ. α' *Ααανανε*
152.	417r	Ἀρσενίου ἱερομονάχου τοῦ μικροῦ καὶ μουσικωτάτου· πρωτόβαρυς *Ανανενα*
153.	421v	Χουμουζίου ἱερέως· βαρὺς *Νεεανενενανα*
154.	425r	Παναγιώτου πρωτοψάλτου· βαρὺς *Τεριρερερερεμ*
155.	427v	Χουμουζίου ἱερέως· πλ. δ' *Ανεενενενα*
	430r	Ὅδε τῆς Παπαδικῆς τόμος ὁ τελευταῖος ἐξηγήθη καὶ ἐγράφη παρ' ἐμοῦ Χουρμουζίου Χαρτοφύλακος τῆς τοῦ Χριστοῦ μεγάλης Ἐκκλησίας ἐν ἔτει σωτηρίῳ χιλιοστῷ ὀκτακοσιοστῷ δεκάτῳ ἐννάτῳ, κατὰ μῆνα Ἰούνιον.

ΜΠΤ 712: HAPANTA OF PETROS BEREKETĒS

225 + i–iii folios
N.B. Only the mathēmata of Petros Bereketēs from the *hapanta* are recorded here.

1.	62v	Ὅταν ἐνδύεται ὁ ἀρχιερεύς· ἦχος δ' *Σὲ μεγαλύνομεν· Ἄσπιλε παναμώμητε*
2.	64r	Ἐγκώμιον εἰς τὸν αὐτοκράτορα Ρωσίας· α' δ' φωνος *Δεῦτε, χριστοφόροι λαοί*
3.	121r	Ἀρχὴ τῶν κατ' ἦχον θεοτοκίων· τὸ παρόν, ἦχος α' δ' φωνος κε *Ὦ τῶν ὑπὲρ νοῦν* (single B)
4.	123r	Ἦχος β' *βου Θεοτόκε, μὴ παρίδης* (single B)
5.	124v	Ἦχος β' *Ἐπίβλεψον ἐν εὐμενίᾳ* (single B)
6.	125v	Ἦχος τρίτος *Πάναγνε, ἡ μόνη* (single B)
7.	127v	Ἦχος τρίτος *Τὴν ὡραιότητα τῆς παρθενίας σου* (2-part A)
8.	129r	Ἦχος τρίτος *Τὴν πᾶσαν ἐλπίδα μου* (single B)
9.	130v	Ἦχος δ' *Ὡς ζωηφόρος, ὡς παραδείσου* (single A)
10.	133v	Ἦχος δ' *Ἐκ παντοίων κινδύνων* (single A)
11.	134v	Ὀκτάηχον δίχορον· ἄρχου, ἦχος α' πα *Θεοτόκε Παρθένε* (multi-part B)

Incipits of the Anagrams and mathēmata in the Mathēmatarion 235

12. 136v Ἦχος πλ. α´ Ὦ Δέσποινα πανάχραντε (single A)
13. 139v Ἦχος πλ. β´ Θεοτόκε, σὺ εἶ ἡ ἄμπελος (single A)
14. 141r Ἦχος βαρὺς Ζω Σὲ μεγαλύνομεν· Τὴν πύλην τὴν οὐράνιον (single A)
15. 143v Ἦχος πλ. δ´ Ψαλμοῖς καὶ ὕμνοις σὲ ὑμνῶ (single A)
16. 146r Ἦχος πλ. δ´ Οἱ ἐλπίδα καὶ στήριγμα (single A)

***

147v–148r Μαθήματα τῶν ἑορτῶν τοῦ ἐνιαυτοῦ, τοῦ Τριῳδίου καὶ τοῦ Πεντηκοσταρίου·

17. Σεπτεμβρίου α´, ἦχος πλ. α´ Σὺ βασιλεύων ἀεί (single A)
18. 149v Τῶν ἐγκαινίων· ἦχος α´ Ἐγκαινίζου ἡ νέα Ἱερουσαλὴμ (single A)
19. 151v Τοῦ τιμίου Προδρόμου· ἦχος πλ. β´ νενανω Ἡ Ἐλισάβετ συνέλαβε (single A)
20. 152v Τοῦ ἁγίου Ἰωάννου τοῦ Θεολόγου· πλ. δ´ Εὐαγγελιστὰ Ἰωάννη (single A)
21. 154r Τοῦ ἁγίου Λουκᾶ τοῦ Εὐαγγελιστοῦ· πλ. δ´ Δαβιτικῶς συνελθόντες (single A)
22. 155v Τῶν ἁγίων Ἀναργύρων· ἦχος β´ Ἡ πηγὴ τῶν ἰαμάτων (single A)
23. 156v Εἰς ἱεράρχας· ἦχος πλ. β´ νενανω Ὅσιε τρισμάκαρ (single A)
24. 157v Ματθαίου τοῦ Εὐαγγελιστοῦ· πλ. δ´ Κροτήσωμεν ἐν ᾄσμασι (single A)
25. 159r–v Τῆς ἁγίας Αἰκατερίνης· ἦχος β´ Βίον ἄυλον ἐξησκημένη (single A)
26. 160v Ἀνδρέου τοῦ πρωτοκλήτου· ἦχος δ´ Τὴν τῶν ἰχθύων ἄγραν (single A)
27. 162r Τῇ Κυριακῇ τῶν προπατόρων· τρίτος Τῶν προπατόρων τὸ σύστημα (single A)
28. 163v Δανιὴλ τοῦ προφήτου· ἦχος πλ. β´ νενανω Δανιὴλ ἀνὴρ ἐπιθυμιῶν (single A)
29. 165r Τοῦ ἁγίου Σπυρίδωνος· ἦχος α´ Πανήγυρις φαιδρὰ (single B)
30. 167r Ἰανουαρίου α´, τοῦ ἁγίου Βασιλείου· ἦχος α´ κε Ὦ θεία καὶ ἱερὰ (single A)
31. 168v Εἰς τὸν μέγαν Ἀθανάσιον· πλ. β´ νενανω Χριστοῦ τὸν ἱεράρχην (single B)
32. 170v Τοῦ ἁγίου Κωνσταντίνου· πλ. δ´ Προάναρχε, ἀθάνατε (single A)
33. 173r Τοῦ προφήτου Ἠλιού· πλ. δ´ Ἱλάσθητί μοι, σωτήρ (single A)
34. 174v Εἰς τὴν ἁγίαν Κυριακὴν καὶ εἰς ἄλλας ὁσιομάρτυρας· ἦχος β´ Ἐν πόλει τοῦ Θεοῦ ἡμῶν (single A)
35. 176r Εἰς τὴν κοίμησιν τῆς Θεοτόκου· ἦχος δ´ Ἐν τῇ μεταστάσει σου (single A)

***

36. 177v Τριώδιον. Τῇ Κυριακῇ τοῦ Τελώνου καὶ τοῦ Φαρισαίου· ἦχος α' *Μὴ προσευξώμεθα φαρισαϊκῶς* (single A)

37. 179r Τῇ Κυριακῇ τοῦ Ἀσώτου· ἦχος β' *Ὦ πόσων ἀγαθῶν* (single A)

38. 180v Τῇ Κυριακῇ τῶν Ἀπόκρεω· πλ. δ' *Οἴμοι μέλαινα ψυχὴ* (single A)

39. 182v Τῇ Κυριακῇ τῆς Ὀρθοδοξίας· ἦχος δ' *Ἱερογραφίαις εἰκόνων* (single B)

40. 184r Κυριακῇ τῆς Σταυροπροσκυνήσεως· ἦχος α' *Ἐν ξύλῳ τέθνηκας* (single B)

41. 186v Τοῦ ἁγίου Ἰωάννου τῆς κλίμακος· πλ. α' *Ὅσιε πάτερ* (single A)

42. 188r Εἰς τὸν Ἀκάθιστον ὕμνον, ὀκτάηχον καὶ ἔντεχνον· ἄρχου α' πα *Ψάλλοντές σου τὸν τόκον* (2-part B)

43. 194r Ἕτερος οἶκος· ἦχος πλ. δ' *Ὦ πανύμνητε μῆτερ* (2-part B)

44. 197r Τῆς ὁσίας Μαρίας τῆς Αἰγυπτίας· ἦχος δ' *Ἐθαυματούργησε Χριστὲ* (single B)

45. 198v Τῇ Μ. Πέμπτῃ· πλ. δ' *Ζωῆς τοῦ ἄρτου τράπεζα* (single A)

***

46. 200v Ἀρχὴ τοῦ Πεντηκοσταρίου· εἰς τὴν ἀνάστασιν τοῦ Κυρίου· ἦχος πα *Ἀναστάσεως ἡμέρα λαμπρυνθῶμεν λαοί* (single B)

47. 203v Τῇ Κυριακῇ τοῦ Θωμᾶ· ἦχος α' πα *Τῶν θυρῶν κεκλεισμένων* (single B)

48. 205v Τῇ Κυριακῇ τῶν Μυροφόρων· πλ. α' *Σὲ τὸν ἀναβαλλόμενον* (single A)

49. 207v Τῇ Κυριακῇ τοῦ Παραλύτου· πλ. δ' *Κύριε, τὸν παράλυτον* (single A)

50. 209v Τῇ Τετάρτῃ τῆς Μεσοπεντηκοστῆς· ἦχος δ' *Φωτισθέντες, ἀδελφοὶ* (single A)

51. 211r Τῇ Κυριακῇ τῆς Σαμαρείτιδος· πλ. δ' *Ὡς ὤφθης ἐν σαρκὶ* (single A)

52. 212v Τῇ Κυριακῇ τοῦ Τυφλοῦ· πλ. δ' *Δικαιοσύνης ἥλιε* (single A)

53. 214v Τῶν ἁγίων Πατέρων· ἦχος πλ. β' *Τὰς μυστικὰς σήμερον* (single A)

54. 216r Τῇ Κυριακῇ τῶν ἁγίων Πάντων· ἦχος α' δ' φωνος *Δεῦτε πάντες οἱ πιστοὶ* (single A)

***

1. 218r Κράτημα ἐθνικόν, καλούμενον ναγμὲς· ἦχος α' πα *Αανενα Τεριρεμ*

2. 220r Ἕτερον, ἦχος τρίτος *Αανενενα Τεριρεμ*

3. 220v Ἕτερον, καλούμενον μουσκάλι· ἦχος δ΄ βου *Αανενεχε* ... *Τέριρεμ*[3]
4. 222v Ἕτερον, καὶ τοῦτο μουσκάλι· ἦχος πλ. δ΄ *Εεενεε* ... *Τέριρεμ*
   225r Τέλος καὶ τῷ Θεῷ χάρις.

[3] This kratēma was recorded and can be found on Stathēs *et al.* 1975.

CHAPTER 6

Reproduction of the kalophonic stichēron Προτυπων την αναστασιν from the feast of the transfiguration

PRELIMINARY REMARKS

Chosen from the kalophonic sea of the Byzantine Psaltic Art is the cluster of compositions — feet, anapodismoi, anagrams — for the kalophonic stichēron idiomelon for the Transfiguration *Προτυπὼν τὴν ἀνάστασιν* [*Prefiguring the resurrection*]. The reason for this choice came down to a combination of things, all having to do with the variety of morphological types of these compositions, and with the length of the chronological periods covered by them — (end of thirteenth and mid-fifteenth century). They also represent the technical and melourgic genius of the main composers of the Psaltic Art, from Theodoros Manougras to Manuel Chrysaphēs.

These mathēmata are published as reproductions lifted from Chourmouzios Chartophylax's Athens, Nat. Libr. ΜΠΤ 732 (sixth tome of the *Mathēmatarion*), fols. 234r–251v, as he made the exēgēsis into the New Method of analytical notation. This was predetermined for purely aesthetic reasons, due to the beauty of its melos. All these compositions are also found in the synoptic notation, as written in the various *Mathēmataria* mentioned above. Anyone seeking a particular reference can refer to Athens, Nat. Libr. 886, fols. 379v–387r, or Xeropotamou 383, fols. 204v–209r. Clearly, those accustomed to analysing the compositions and gathering their conclusions using codices in the old notation are also capable of doing the same in the new analytical notation.

Below is only an example of the correlation between the old synoptic and new analytical Byzantine notations. This correlation divides the melos into theses, with the clear distinction the exēgēsis and analytical transcription of the melos offers in the New Method. The topic of exēgēsis or its correctness is not addressed here. The topic has, however, been addressed by this author in other, specialized studies, as well as in (Stathēs 1978).

The metrophony of the old synoptic notation is noted using Latin characters, showing the degree within the scale. The melos of the theses, which is the *exēgēsis* and analytical transcription of the New Method, was written by the author on the staff, notwithstanding the reservations regarding the correct expression of the intervals. The correct chromatic changes of the intervals are indicated on the first staff with the use of single-lined hypheses and three-lined dieses.

Athens, Nat. Libr. 886 (end of fifteenth century), fol. 379v.
Athens, Nat. Libr. ΜΠΤ 732 (manuscript-*exēgēsis* by Chourmouzios, around the year 1825), fol. 234r.

Transcriptions of the kalophonic stichēron
προτυπων την αναστασιν

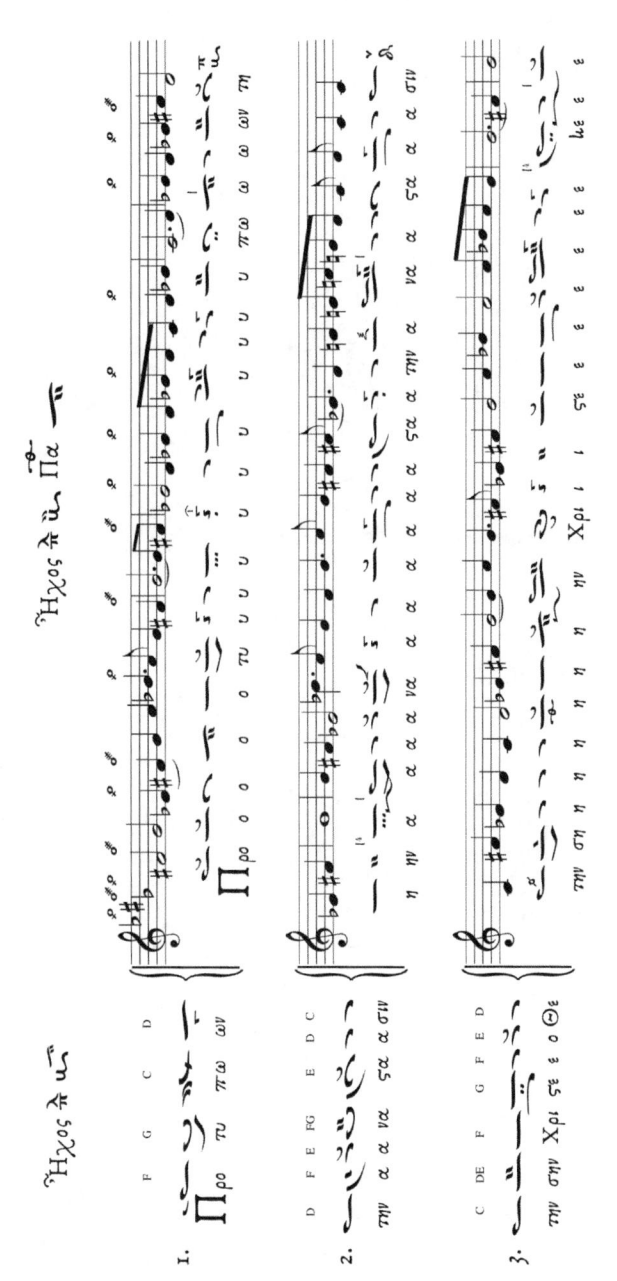

Transcriptions of the kalophonic sticherōn προτυπων την αναστασιν 243

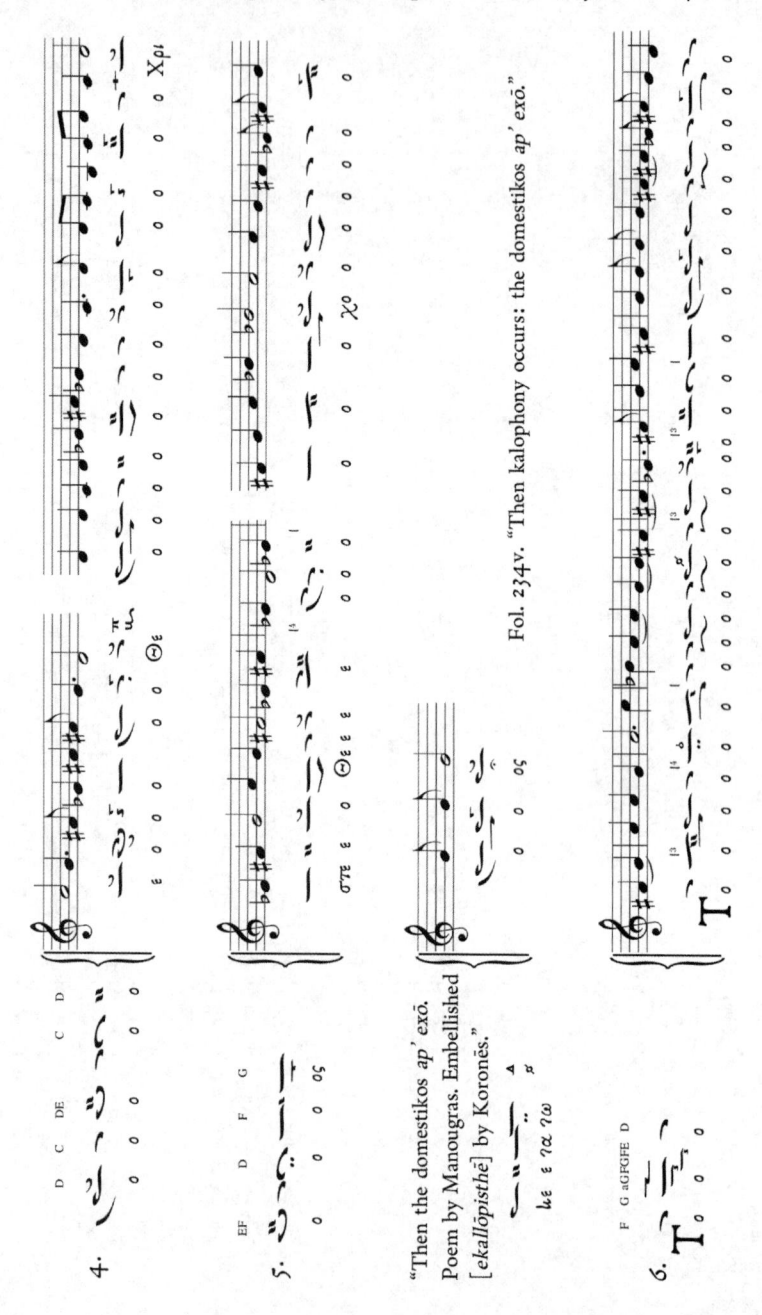

244　　　*Transcriptions of the kalophonic stichēron προτυπων την αναστασιν*

"Then the domestikos *ap' exō*.
Poem by Manougras. Embellished
[*ekallōpisthē*] by Koronēs."

Fol. 234v. "Then kalophony occurs: the domestikos *ap' exō*."

Transcriptions of the kalophonic sticheron προτυπων την αναστασιν 245

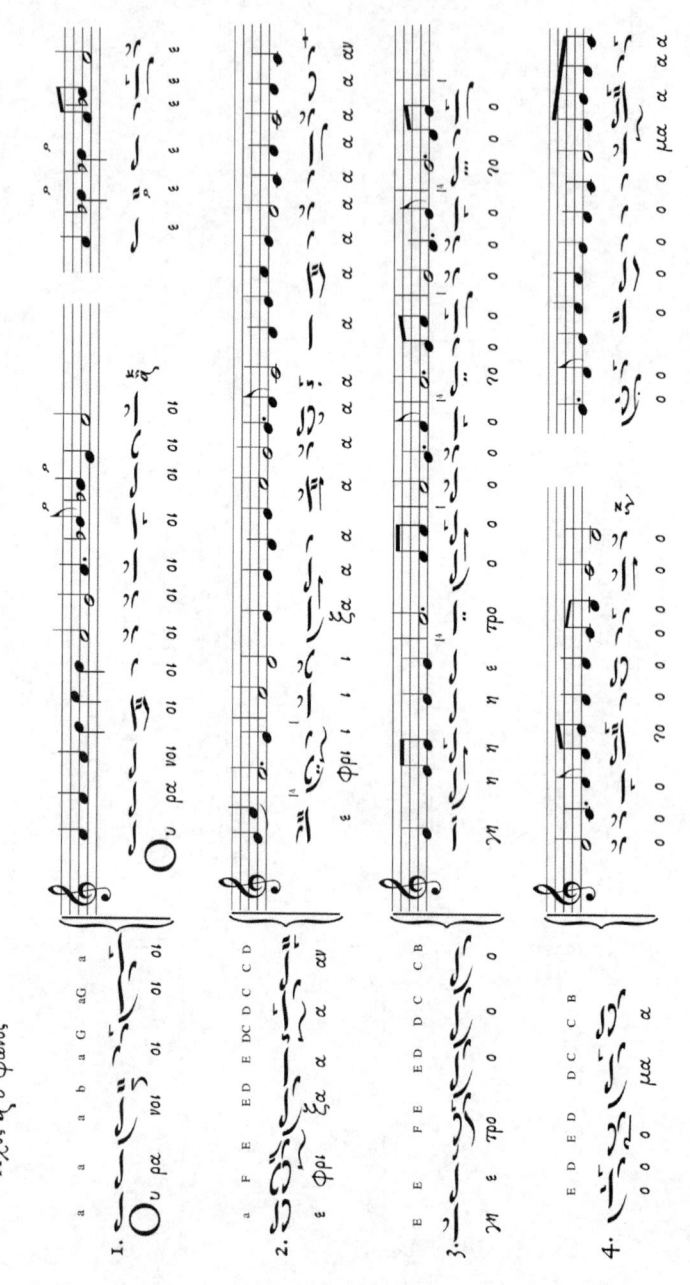

246 Transcriptions of the kalophonic sticherōn προτυπων την αναστασιν

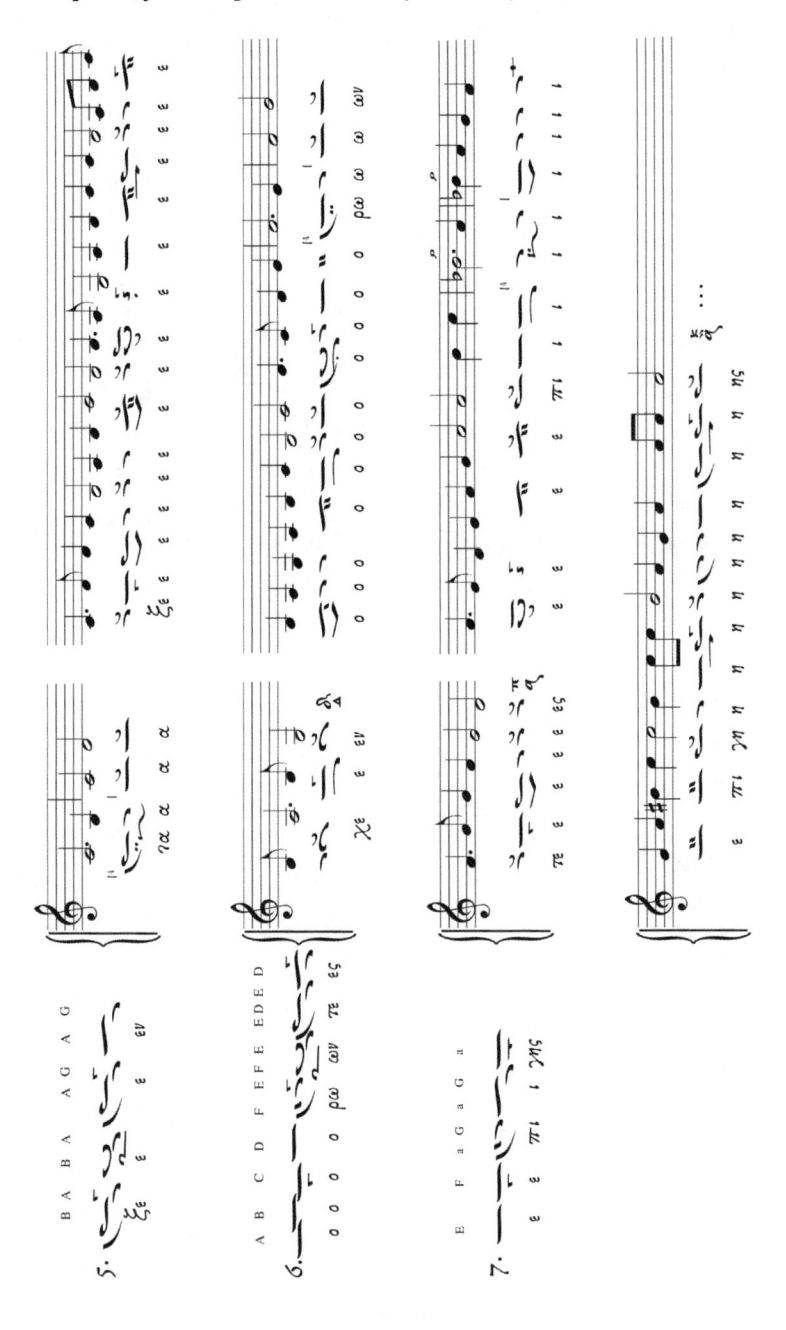

Transcriptions of the kalophonic stichēron προτυπων την αναστασιν

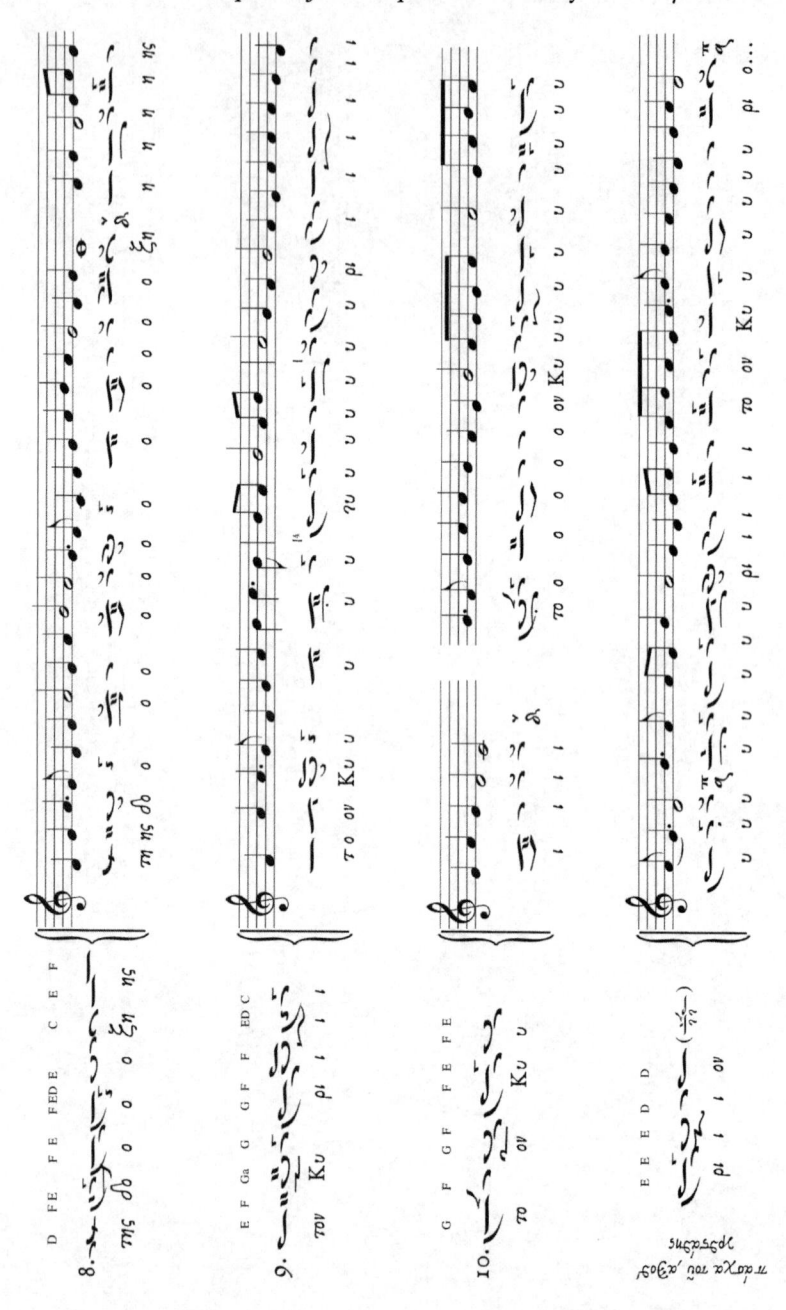

Transcriptions of the kalophonic sticherōn προτυπων την αναστασιν

Wishing to emphasize the composition of the elements of kalophony, as such, they are made clear via the poetic text, especially the anagrams and repeats. Therefore, we place here the complete text of the sticheron and thereafter the text of each mathēma as found in the kalophonic utilisation by each composer. What is strived for as the final goal is the aesthetic, pleasing sound of these examples of the kalophony of Byzantine melic composition, nonetheless, still remains unexpressed. As is always the case with music texts, they speak only in the tongue of each interpreter.

Text of the Doxastikon of the vespers for the feast of the Transfiguration

Προτυπῶν τὴν ἀνάστασιν τὴν σήν,
Χριστὲ ὁ Θεός,
Τότε παραλαμβάνεις τοὺς τρεῖς σου μαθητάς,
Πέτρον καὶ Ἰάκωβον καὶ Ἰωάννην,
ἐν τῷ Θαβὼρ ἀνελθών.
Σοῦ δέ, Σωτήρ, μεταμορφωμένου
τὸ Θαβώριον ὄρος φωτὶ ἐσκέπετο.
Οἱ μαθηταί σου, Λόγε,
ἔρριψαν ἑαυτοὺς ἐν τῷ ἐδάφει τῆς γῆς,
μὴ φέροντες ὁρᾶν τὴν ἀθέατον μορφήν.
Ἄγγελοι διηκόνουν φόβῳ καὶ τρόμῳ.
Οὐρανοὶ ἔφριξαν,
γῆ ἐτρόμαξεν,
ὁρῶντες ἐπὶ γῆς
τῆς δόξης τὸν Κύριον.[1]

---

1 The following translation can be found in Orthodox Eastern Church. *et al.* 1969: 471: Prefiguring, O Christ our God, Thy Resurrection, Thou hast taken with Thee in Thy ascent upon Mount Tabor Thy three disciples, Peter, James, and John. When Thou wast transfigured, O Saviour, Mount Tabor was covered with light. Thy disciples, O Word, cast themselves down upon the ground, unable to gaze upon the Form that none may see. The angels ministered in fear and tranbling, the heavens shook and the earth quaked, as they beheld upon earth the Lord of Glory.

THE TEXT OF THE KALOPHONIC STICHĒRON FROM THE CHOURMOUZIOS MATHĒMATARION (ΜΠΤ 732)

Fol. 234r Another [*heteron*] stichēron for the same feast, by Theodōros Manougras. Beautified [*ekallōpisthē*] by Xenos Korōnēs. The domestikos, from the choir [*apo chorou*]: mode II plagal πα [*diphōnos*]

Προτυπῶν τὴν ἀνάστασιν τὴν σήν,
Χριστὲ ὁ Θεός,

Then kalophony occurs; the domestikos *ap' exō*.

Τὸ χοχοχο ... τότε παραλμβάνεις
τότε παραλαμβά χαχα νεις τιιτιιιχιτιριριν
παραλαμβάνεις τοὺς τρεῖ κιχιτιτιριρι ...
τοὺς τρεῖς σου μαθητά, τοὺς τρεῖς σου μαθητὰς
τότε παραλαμβά χαχαχα παραλαμβάνεις
παραλαμβάνεις Πέτρο χοχοχο Πέτρον Πέτρον
καὶ Ἰάκωβο χοχοχον καὶ Ἰωά χαχαχα καὶ Ἰωάννην
Πέτρον καὶ Ἰάκωβον καὶ Ἰωάννην
ἐν τῷ Θαβὼρ ἀνελθών.
Σοῦ νουχουχου, σοῦ δὲ Σωτὴρ μεταμορφουμένου
τὸ Θαβώριον ὄρος φωτὶ ἐσκέπετο.

By Korōnēs

Τοτοτο τορον το
Τὸ Θαβώριον ὄρος φωτί, φωτὶ ἐσκέ χεχε ἐσκέπετο.

Fol. 237r. By the maïstōr [*Iohannes Koukouzeles*]; mode II.

Τὸ Θαβώριον ὄρος, ὄρος τὸ Θαβώριον
φωτὶ ἐσκέπε φωτὶ ἐσκέπετο
ὄρος τὸ Θαβώτιον σοῦ μεταμορφωμένου,
Χριστὲ Σωτήρ, Χριστὲ Σωτήρ,
ἐσκέπετο τὸ Θα τὸ Θαβώ τὸ Θαβώριον ὄρος
φωτὶ ἐσκέ, ἐσκέπε, φωτὶ ἐσκέπετο
σοῦ μεταμορφουμέ, μεταμορφουμένου

ἐσκέπετο καπνῷ τὸ ὄρος, τὸ ὄρος τὸ Θαβώριον·
τοτοτο τεριτεμ [long kratēma]
φωτὶ ἐσκέπε ἐσκέπετο τὸ ὄρος τὸ Θαβώριον.

Fol. 238v. *Apo chorou, palaion; [mode] IV [hagia]*

Οἱ μαθηταί σου Λό χο Λόγε
Ε ε ν α ϊ ν ε ἔρριψα τα τα τα
ἔρρι ἔρριψαν ἑαυτοὺς
ἐν τῷ ἐδά χα χα φει τῆς γῆ χη η τῆς γῆς
μὴ μὴ φέροντες ὁρᾶ χα να χα ὁρᾶν
τὴν τὴν ἀθε νεε τὴν ἀθεατο χοον μο-
τὴν ἀθέατον μορφήν.
Ἄγγε ἄγγελοι διηκόνουν
φόβῳ καὶ τρόμῳ χω χω χω καὶ τρόμῳ.
Οὐρανοὶ χοι οι οὐρανοὶ ἔφρι ἔφριξαν·
γῆ ἐτρόμα α α α γῆ ἐτρόμαξε εχεε ἐτρόμαξεν.
Οὐρανοὶ ἔφρι ἔφριξαν να χα χα ἔφριξαν
γῆ ἐτρόμαξε· τε τε τε [short kratēma]
Γῆ ἐτρό χοοο μαξε ενεχε ἐτρόμαξεν
ὁρῶντες ἐπὶ γῆς.

Fol. 240v. *Another [heteros] foot, by Markos metropolitan of Corinth; mode II plagal πα.*

Οἱ οι οι οι χοι οι Τιτιριριν [kratēma]
Οἱ μαθηταί σου Λο ο ο Λόγε εχεενενανε
Οἱ μαθηταί σου Λο Λόγε.
ἔ εεε ἔρρι ιι ἔριψαν ἑαυτοὺ χου χου ο νου ου ἑαυτοὺς
ἔρρι ἔρριψαν ἔρριψαν ἑαυτοὺ χου χου χο ν ἑαυτοὺς
ἐν τῷ ἐδάφει τῆς γῆς — λέγε—
μὴ φέροντες ὁρᾶ χα χα να χα ὁρᾶν
τὴν ἀθέατον μορφὴ κι κι κι μορφήν.
Ἄγγελοι διηκόνουν φο φόβῳ καὶ τρόμῳ χω χω χω καὶ τρόμῳ.
Οὐρανοὶ χοι χοι χοι οὐρανοὶ ἔφριξαν·
γῆ ἐτρόμα γῆ ἐτρόμαξε
ἐτρόμαξεν ἡ γῆ ἐτρόμαξε
ἐτρόμαξεν ἡ γῆ ἐτρόμα ἐτρόμαξεν
ὁρῶντες ἐπὶ γῆς δόξης τὸν Κυ χυ ν ν ν, τὸν Κύριον

Fol. 243v. *Anagram from the same sticheron; by Manuel Chrysaphēs; mode II plagal* πα.

Ἄ χα α χα ἄγγε ἄγγελοι διηχι διηκόνουν
φόβῳ καὶ τρό ο χο ο χο καὶ τρό καὶ τρό χο καὶ τρόμῳ
Οὐρανοὶ χο ι χο ι χο ι ἔφρι ἔφριξαν·
γῆ γῆ ἔτρο γῆ ἐτρόμα γῆ ἐτρόμαξεν
ὁρῶντες ἐπὶ γῆς τῆς δόξης τὸν Κύριον.
Τὴν σήν, Χριστέ, προτυπῶν ἀνα χα ἀνάστα ἀνάστασιν
παραλαμβάνεις τότε τοὺς τρεῖς σου μαθη μαθητὰς
Πέτρον καὶ Ἰα χα χα χα κω καὶ Ἰάκωβον
καὶ χα ι χα ι καὶ Ἰωάννην
ἐν τῷ Θαβὼρ ἀνελθών.
Σοῦ δέ, Σωτήρ, μεταμορφουμένου
τὸ Θαβώριον ὄ χο χο ο νο χο ὄρος
φωτὶ ἔσκε χε νε φωτὶ ἐσκέπετο.
Οἱ μαθηταί σου, Λο Λόγε
ἔρριψα χα α αν ἑαυτοὺς
ἐν τῷ ἐδάφει τῆς γῆς,
μὴ φέροντες ὁρᾷ μὴ φέροντες ὁρᾶν
τὴν ἐθέατον μορφήν.
Ἄγγελοι διηκόνουν
φό χο χο χο βῳ καὶ τρό χο ο ο,
φόβῳ καὶ τρόμῳ χω χω χω καὶ τρόμῳ.
Οὐρανοὶ ἔφριξαν
γῆ ἐτρό ἐτρόμα, γῆ ἐτρόμαξεν
ὁρῶντες ἐπὶ γῆς
τῆς δόξης τὸν Κύ χυ χυ χυ ριον·
γῆ ἐτρό γῆ ἐτρόμαξεν
ὁρῶντες ἐπὶ ἐπὶ γῆς Τι τι τι τεριρεμ
ὁρῶντες ἐπὶ γῆς
τῆς δόξης τὸν Κύ τὸν Κύ τὸν Κύριον

Another ending.

τῆς δό χοχοχο ξης τὸν Κύ τὸν Κύ τὸν Κύριον.

Fol. 247v. Another [heteron] anagram from the same sticheron; by Iohannes Koukouzeles; mode I tetraphōnos κε.

Οὐρανοὶ ἔφριξαν,
γῆ ἐτρόμαξεν
ὁρῶντες ἐπὶ ἐπὶ γῆς
τῆς δόξης τὸν Κύρι τὸν Κύρι τὸν Κύριον. —πάλιν—
Οὐρανοὶ ἔφριξαν
γῆ ἐτρόμαξεν
ὁρῶντες ἐπὶ ἐπὶ γῆς
τῆς δόξης τὸν Κύρι τὸν Κύρι τὸν Κύριον.
Τὸ Θαβώριον ὄρο τὸ ὄρος
φωτι ιιχιι ὲ φωτὶ ἐσκέπε φωτὶ ἐσκέπετο χοχοχο ἐσκέπετο
ὄχοοο νο ὄρος τὸ Θαβώρι τὸ Θαβώριον.
Σοῦ μεταμορφουμένου, Χριστὲ Σωτὴ Χριστὲ Σωτήρ,
ἄγγε ἄγγελοι διηκόνουν
φόβῳ φόβῳ καὶ τρό καὶ τρόμῳ.
Οἱ μαθηταί σου, Λόγε,
ἔρριψαν ἑαυτοὺς
ἐν τῷ ἐδάφει τῆς γῆς,
σοῦ μεταμορφωμένου
ἐν τῷ Θαβὼρ ἀνελθὼν
τὴν σήν, Χριστέ, προτυπῶν ἀνα χα ἀνάστα ἀνάστασιν
παραλαμβάνεις Πέτρον Ἰακω Ἰάκωβον καὶ Ἰωάννην τότε τότε τεεε τε ετε [short kratēma]
Σοῦ μεταμορφουμένου Χριστὲ χεε Σωτή, Σωτήρ μου
Οὐρανοὶ ἔφρι ἔφριξαν
γῆ ἐτρομα ἐτρόμαξεν
Τεετεριρερετε [long kratēma]
ὁρῶντες ἐπὶ γῆς τῆς δόξης τὸν Κύριον.

Images of MПТ 732

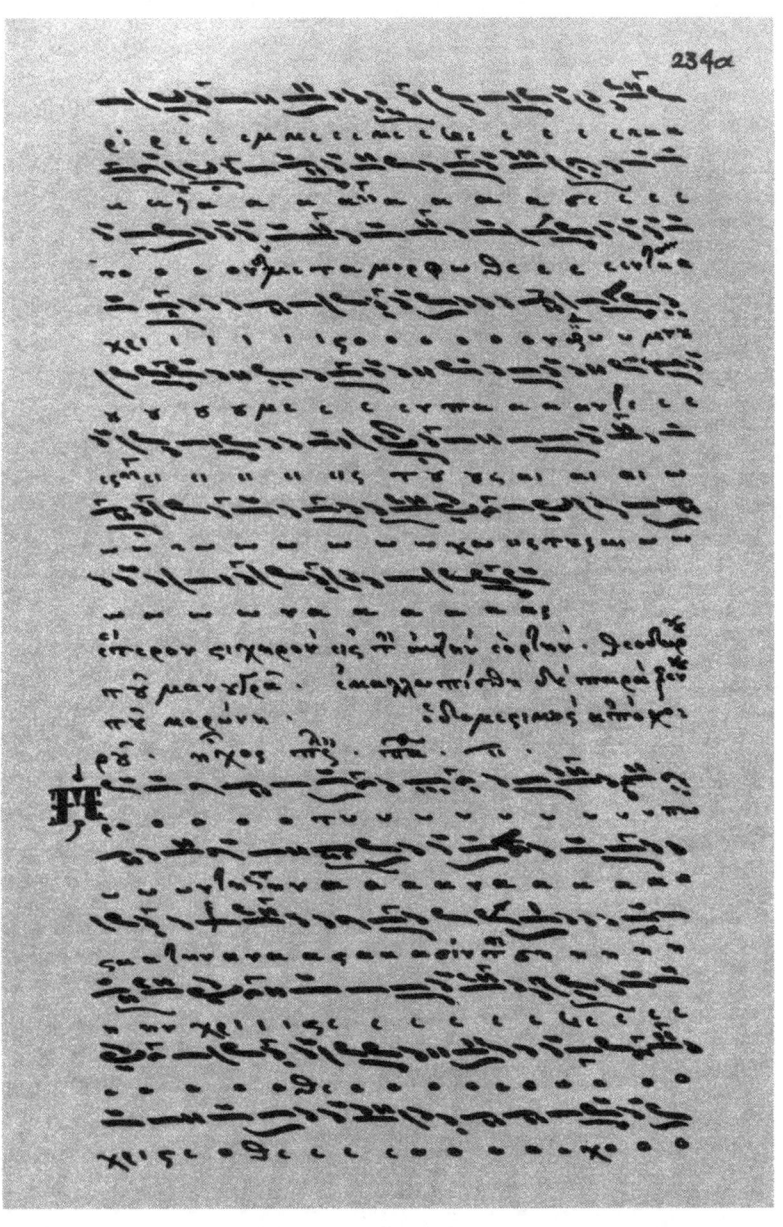

Plate I. ΜΠΤ 732, fol. 234r

Plate II. ΜΠΤ 732, fol. 234v

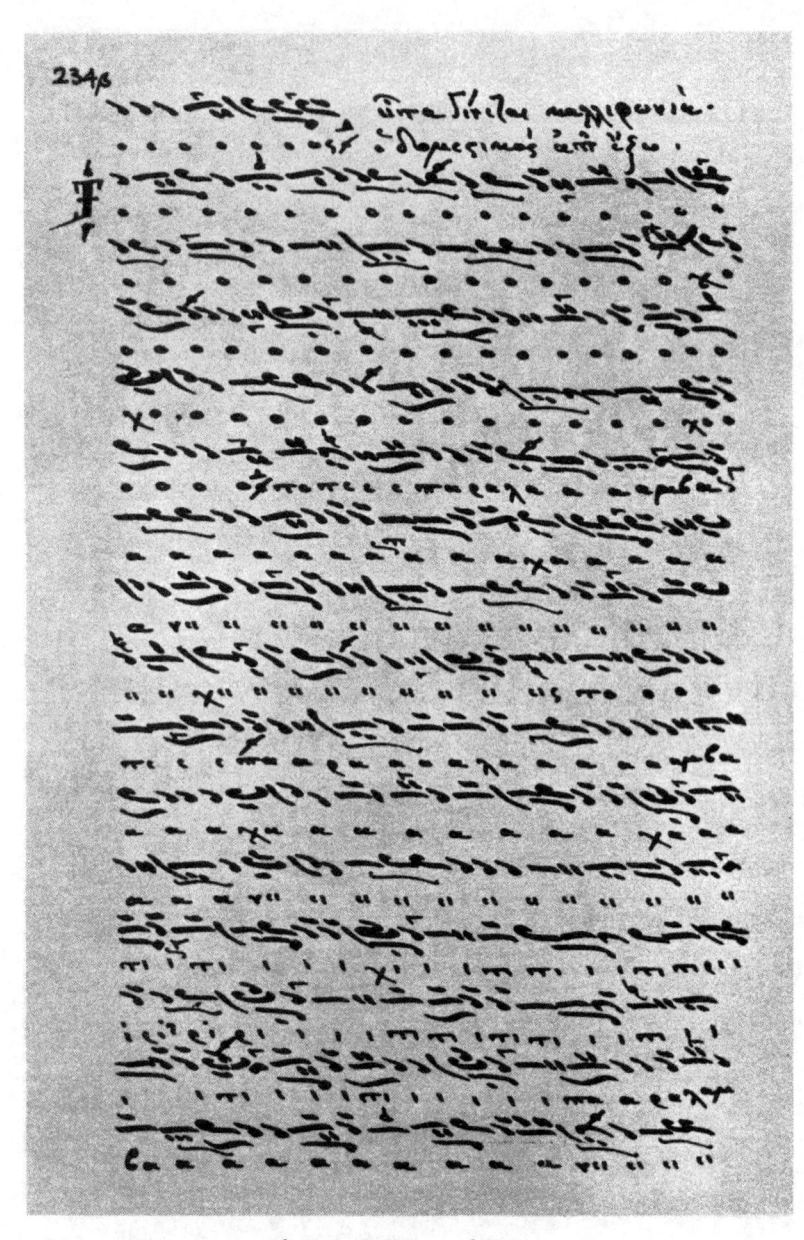

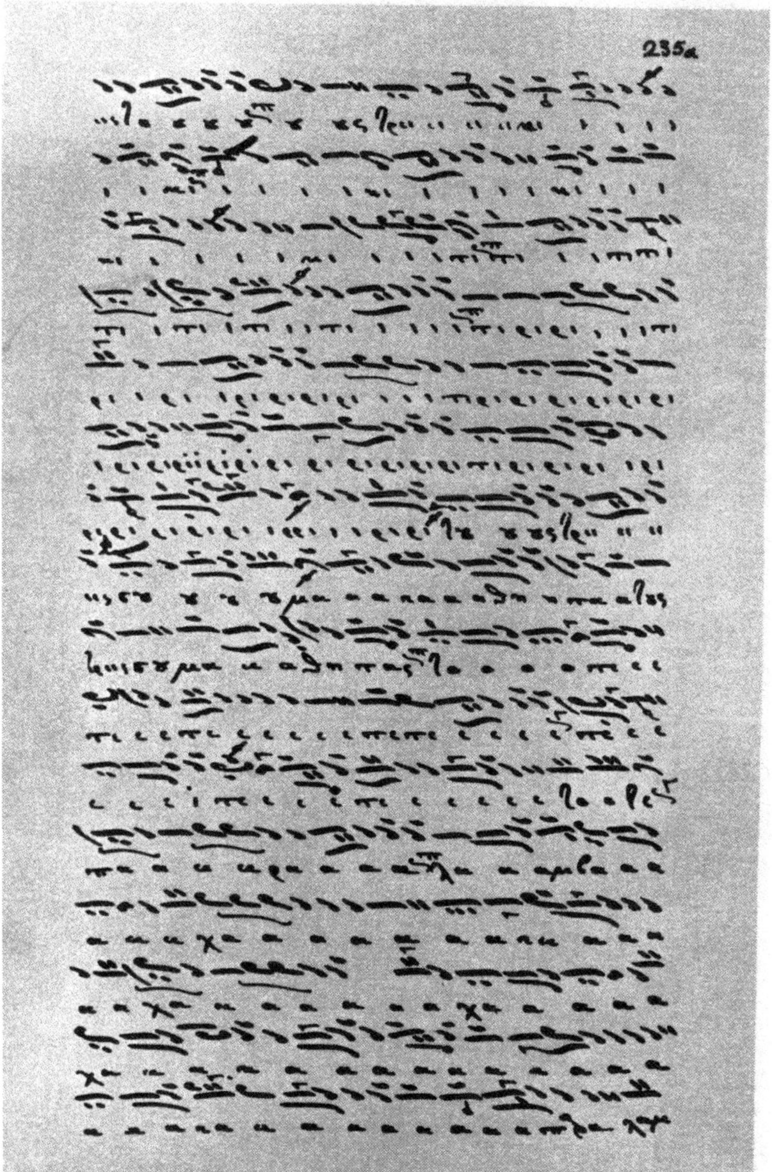

Plate III. ΜΠΤ 732, fol. 235r

Plate IV. ΜΠΤ 732, fol. 235v

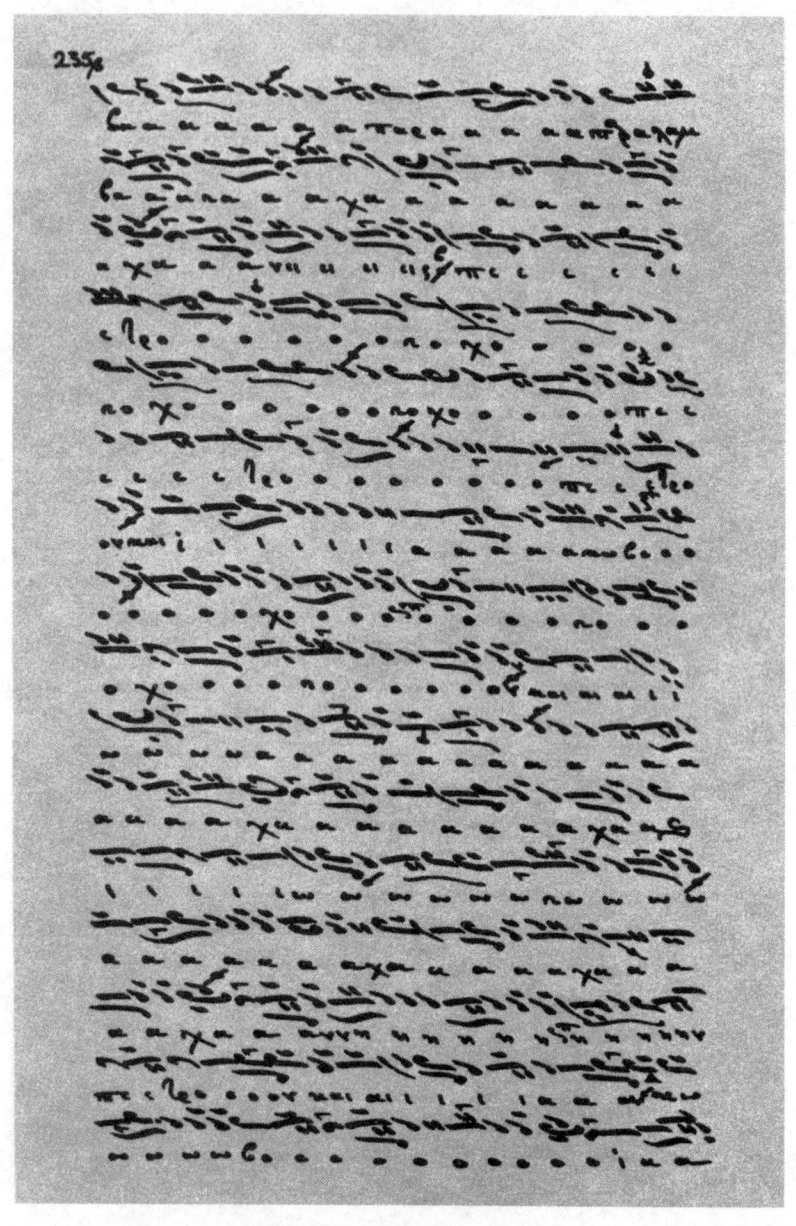

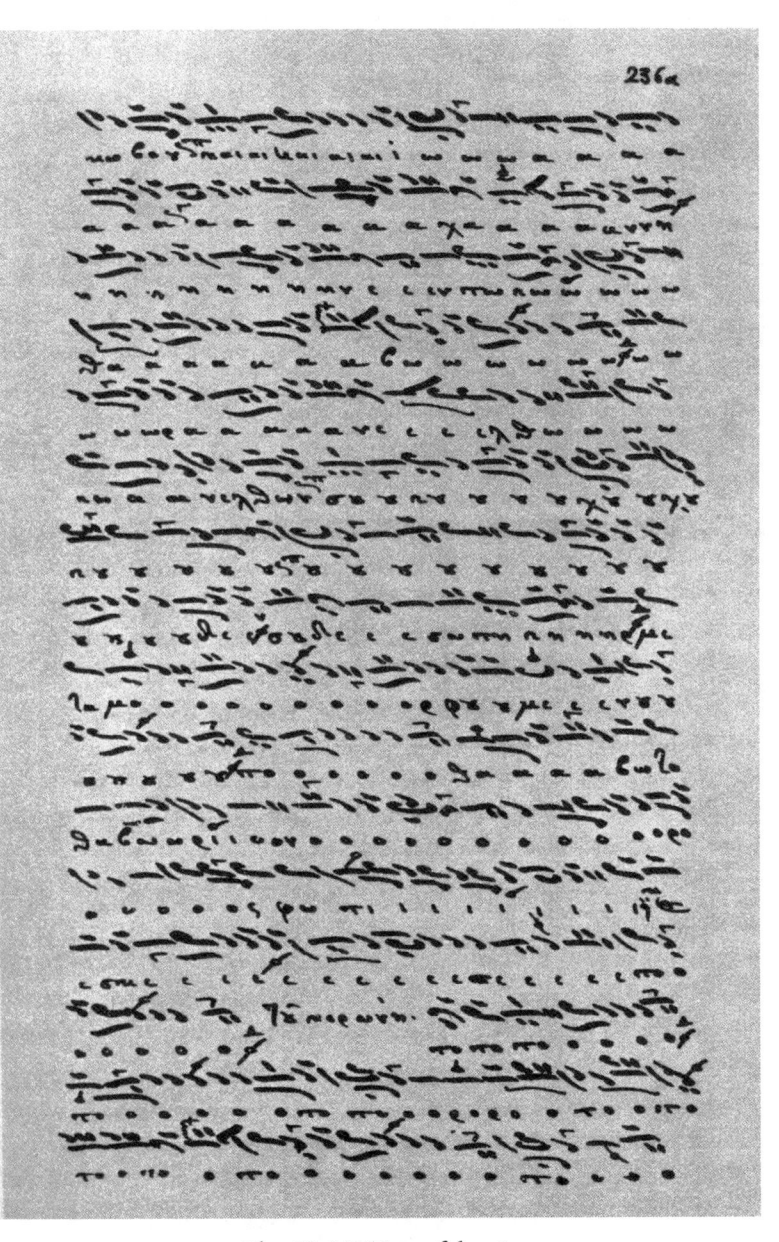

Plate V. МПТ 732, fol. 236r

Plate VI. ΜΠΤ 732, fol. 236v

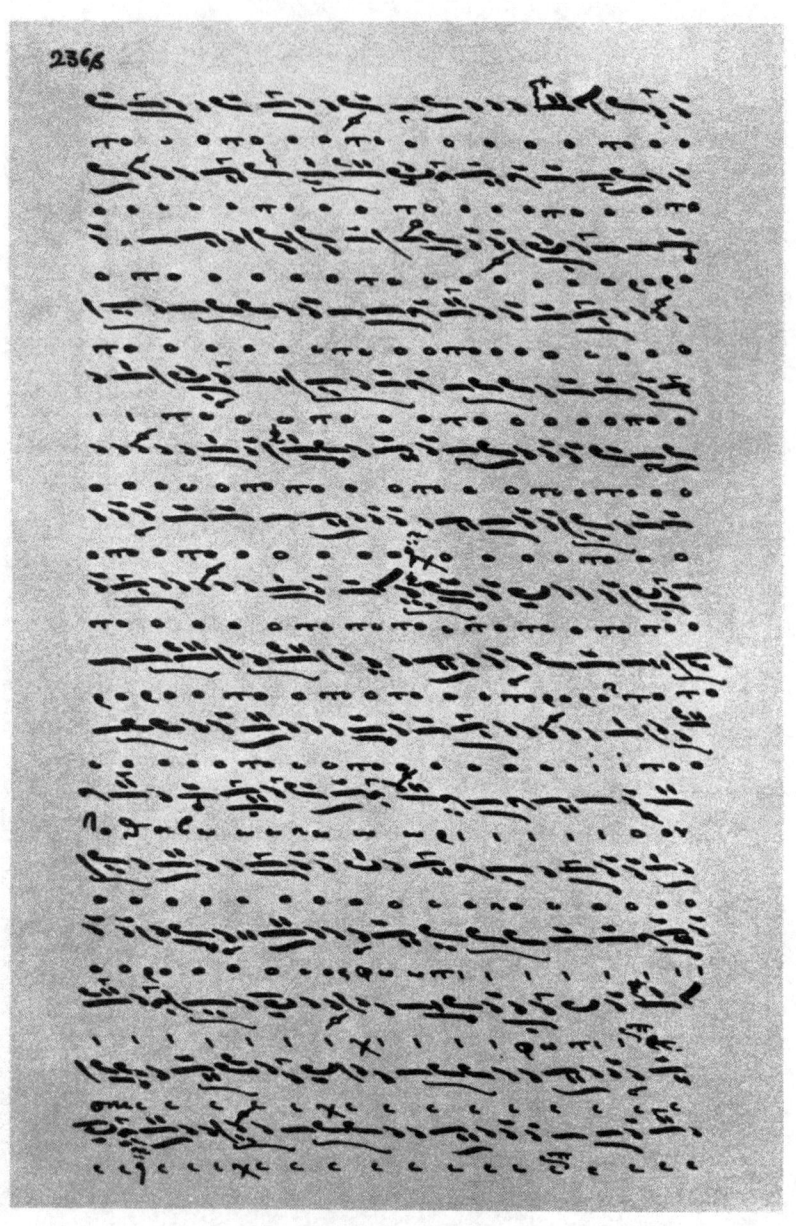

Plate VII. ΜΠΤ 732, fol. 237r

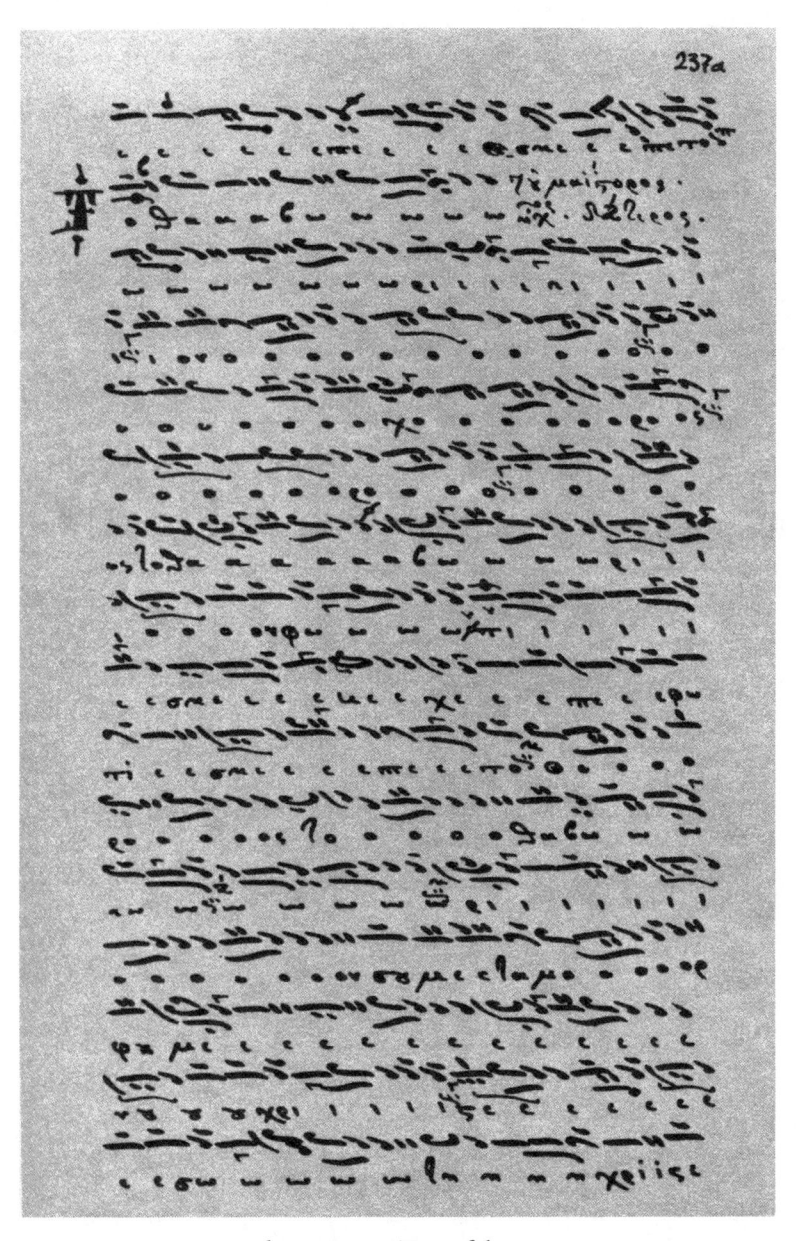

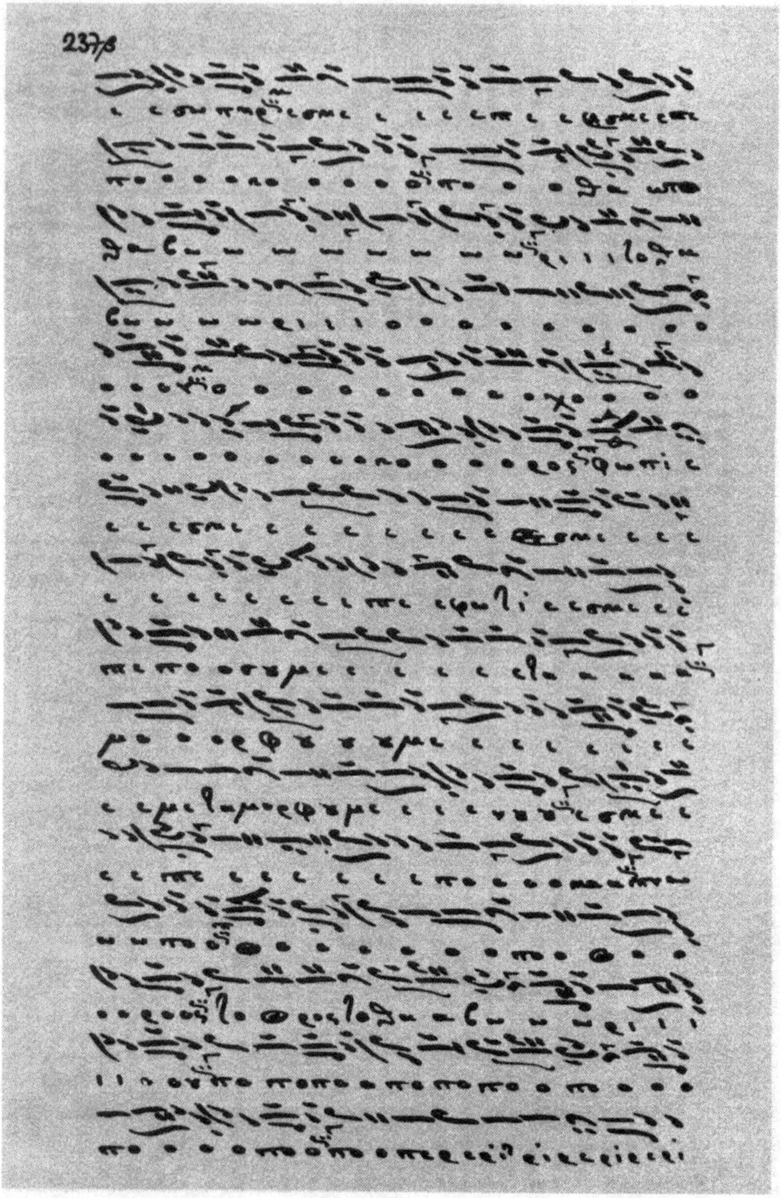

Plate VIII. МПТ 732, fol. 237v

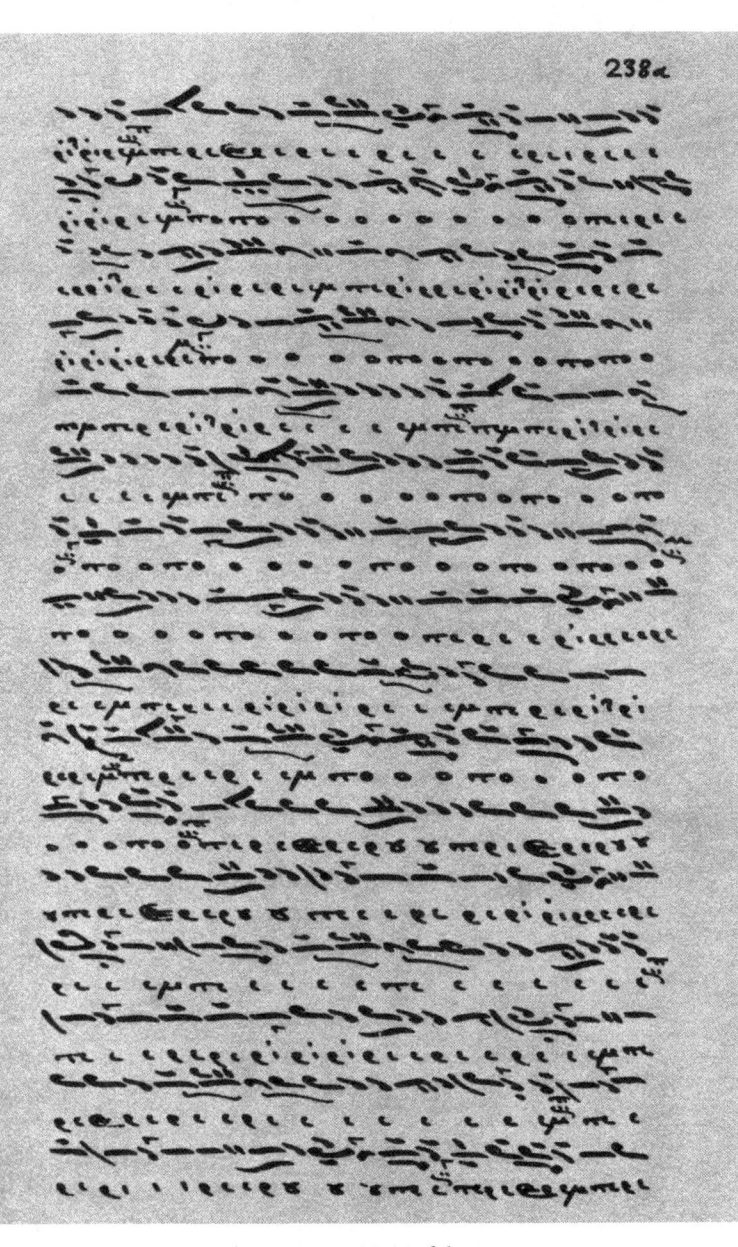

Plate IX. МПТ 732, fol. 238r

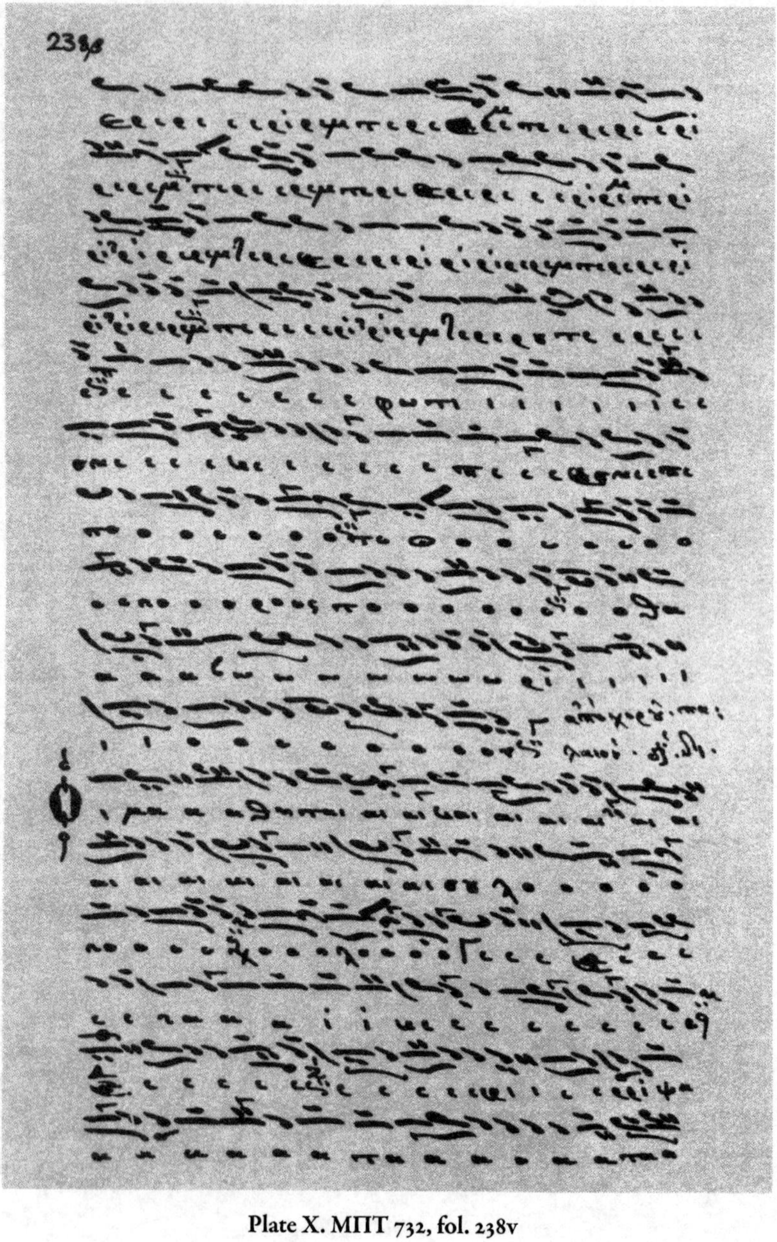

Plate X. ΜΠΤ 732, fol. 238v

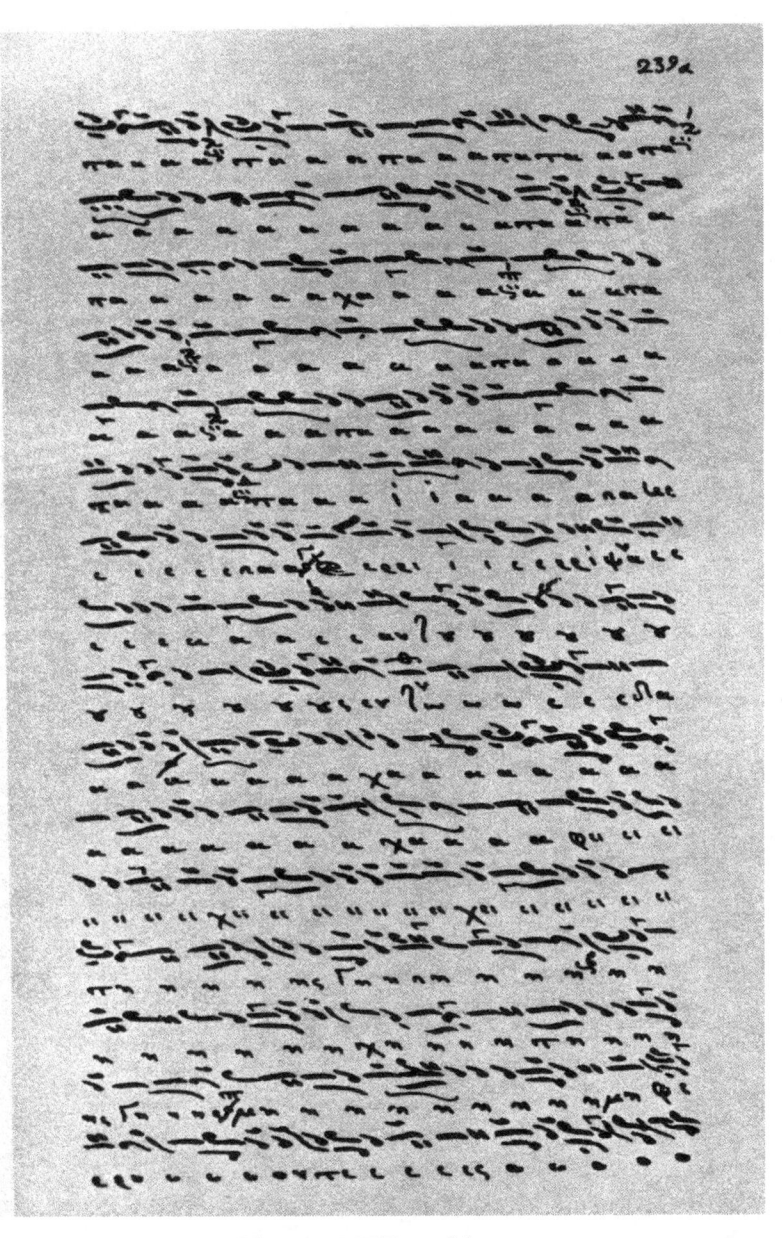

Plate XI. MΠT 732, fol. 239r

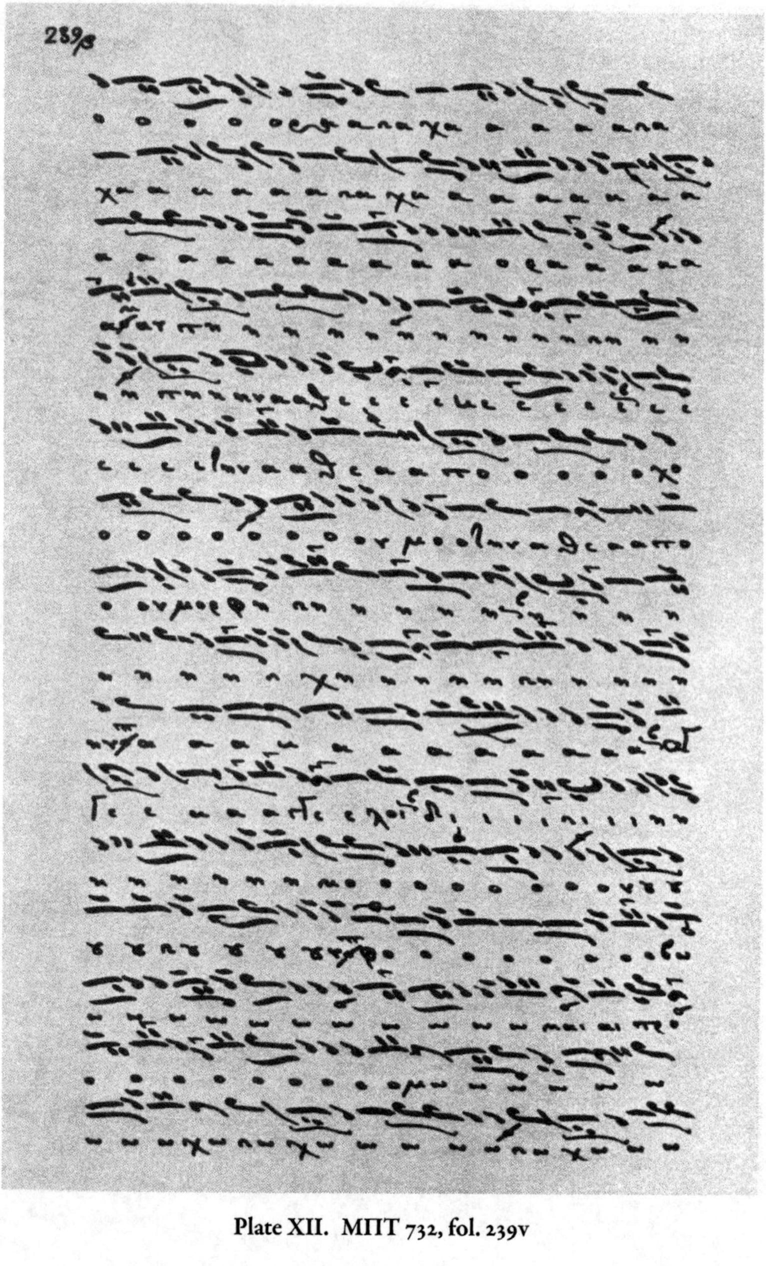

Plate XII. МПТ 732, fol. 239v

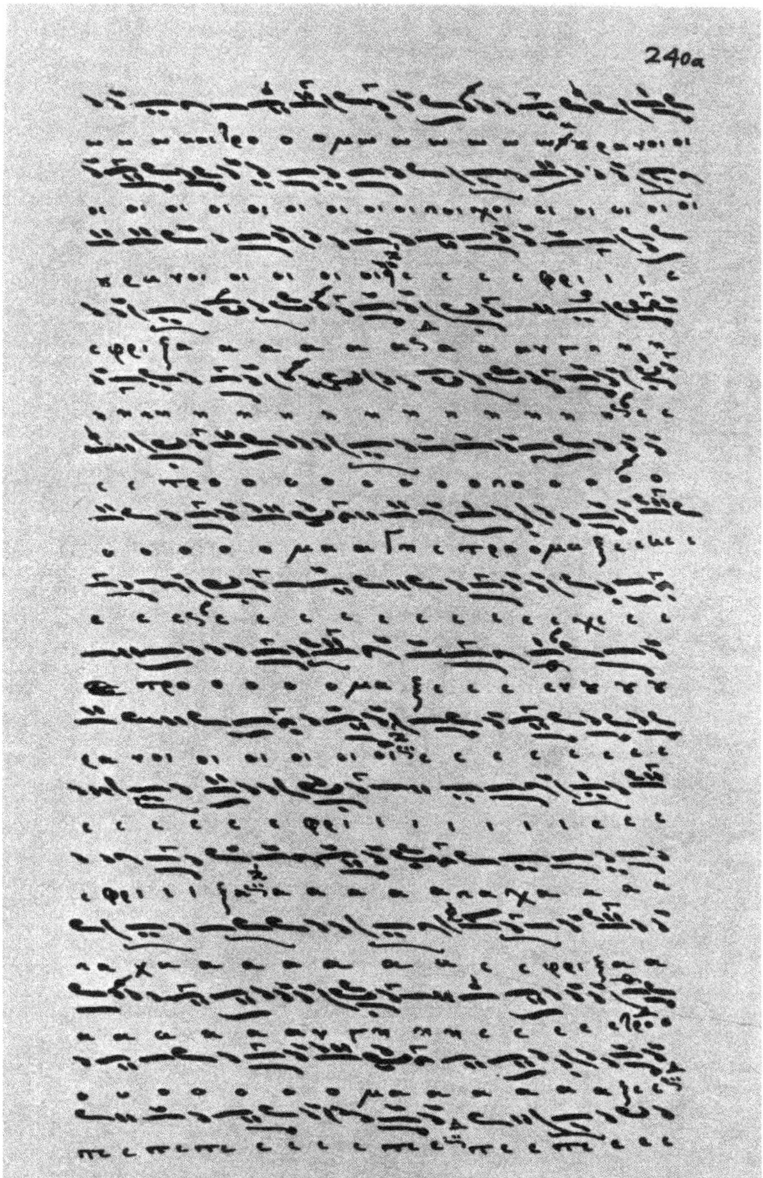

Plate XIII. MΠT 732, fol. 240r

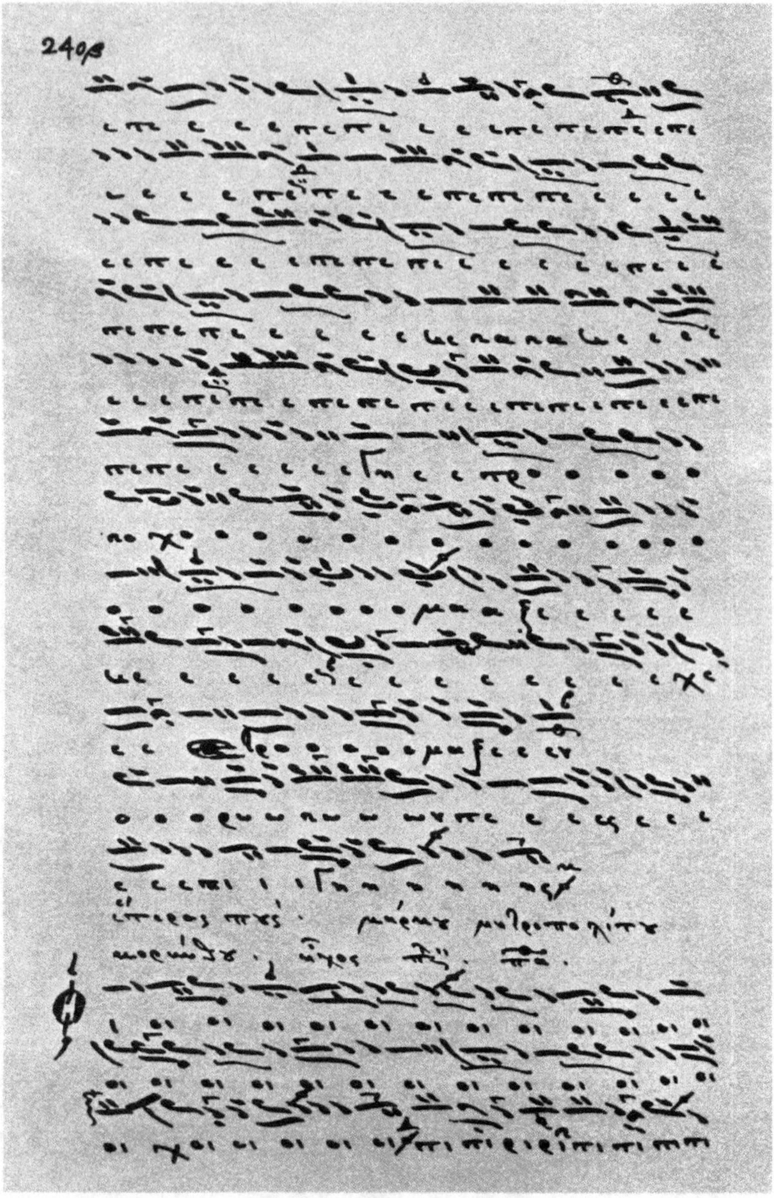

Plate XIV. ΜΠΤ 732, fol. 240v

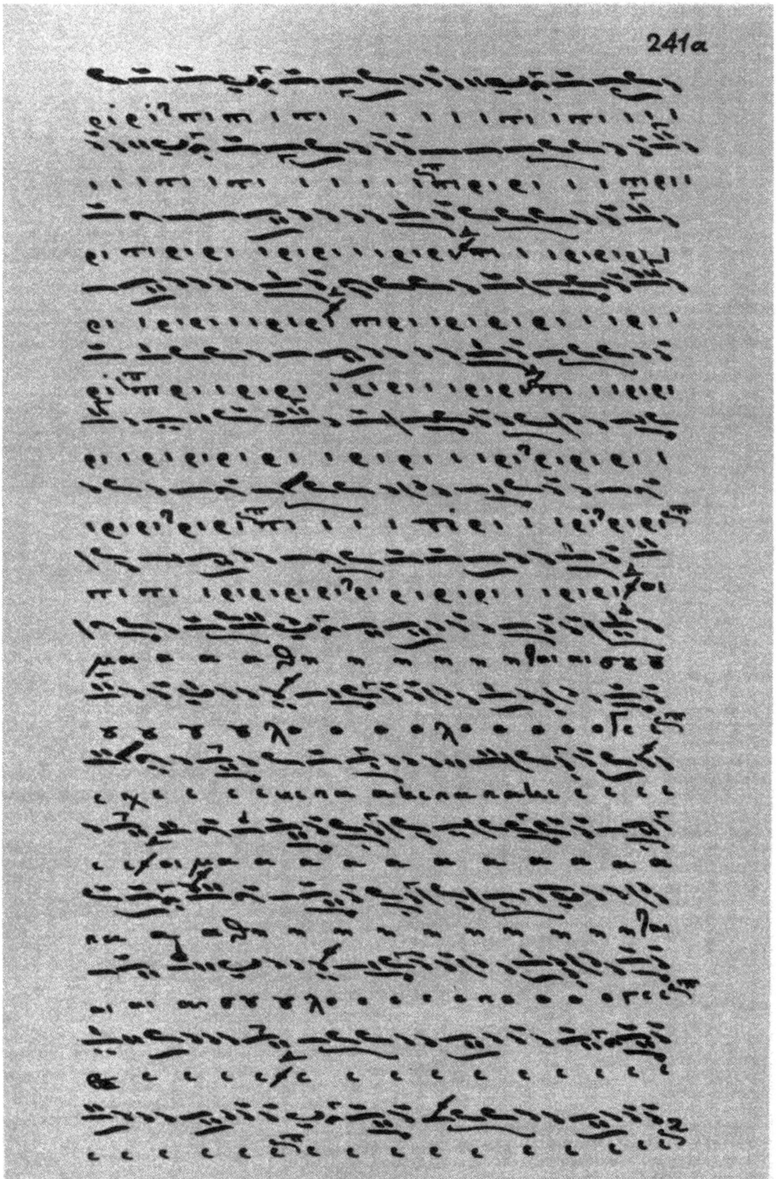

Plate XV. MΠT 732, fol. 241r

Plate XVI. МПТ 732, fol. 241v

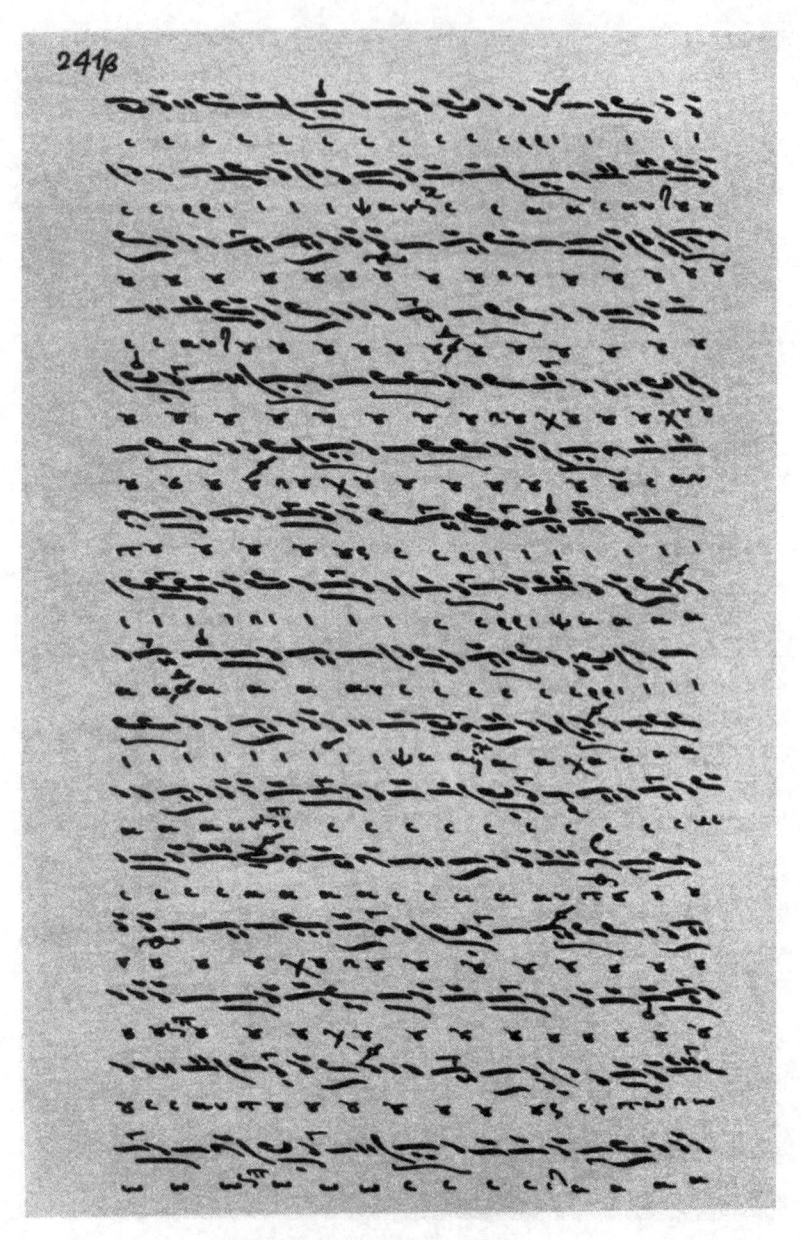

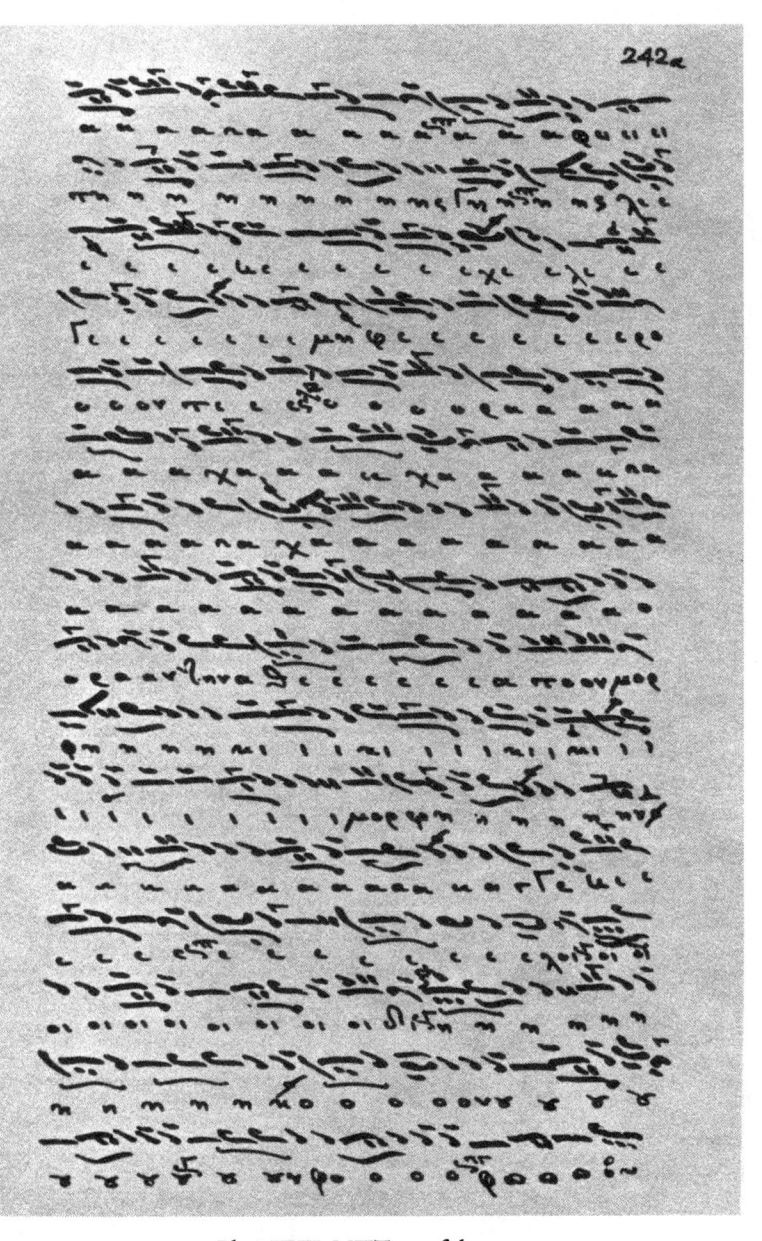

Plate XVII. МПТ 732, fol. 242r

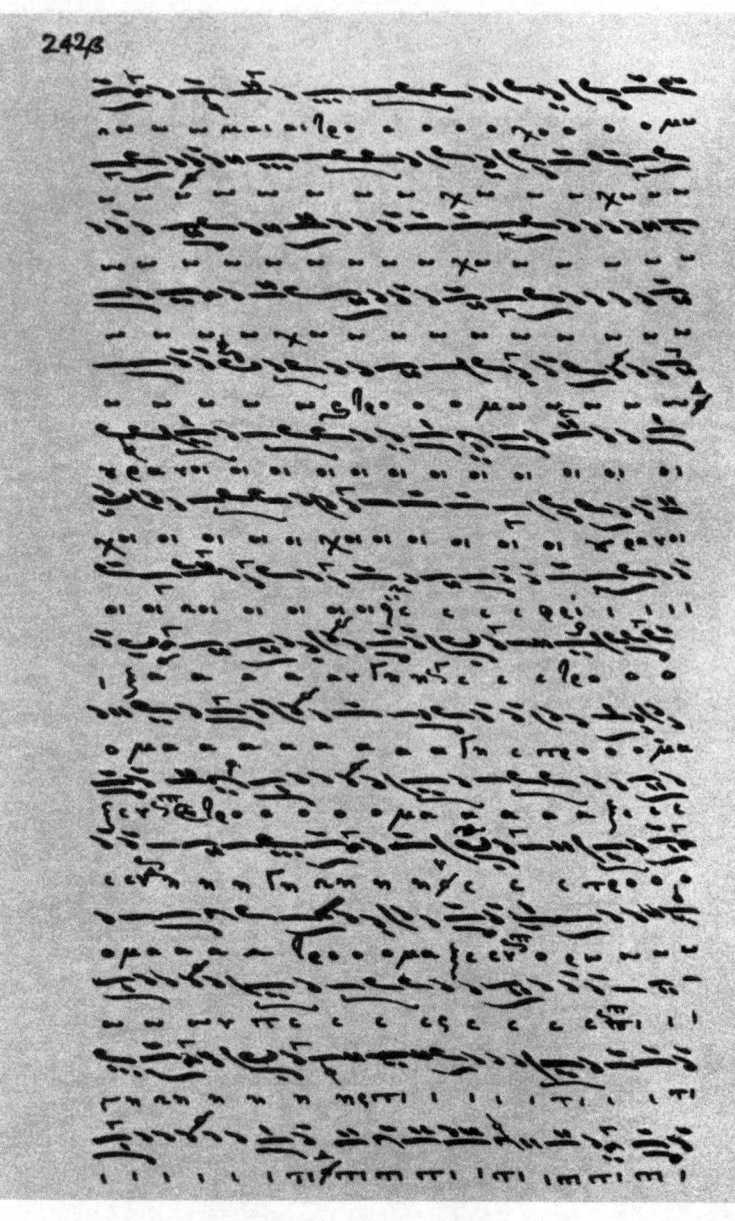

Plate XVIII. MΠT 732, fol. 242v

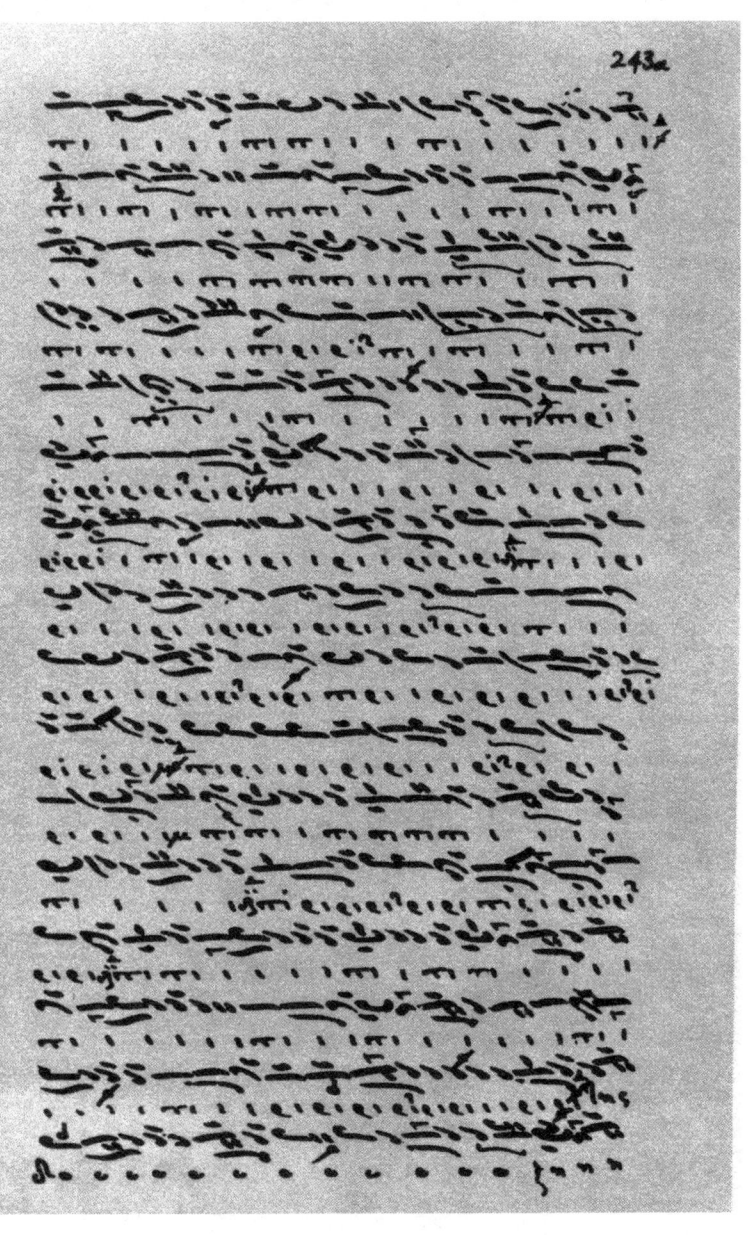

Plate XIX. MIT 732, fol. 243r

Plate XX. ΜΠΤ 732, fol. 243v

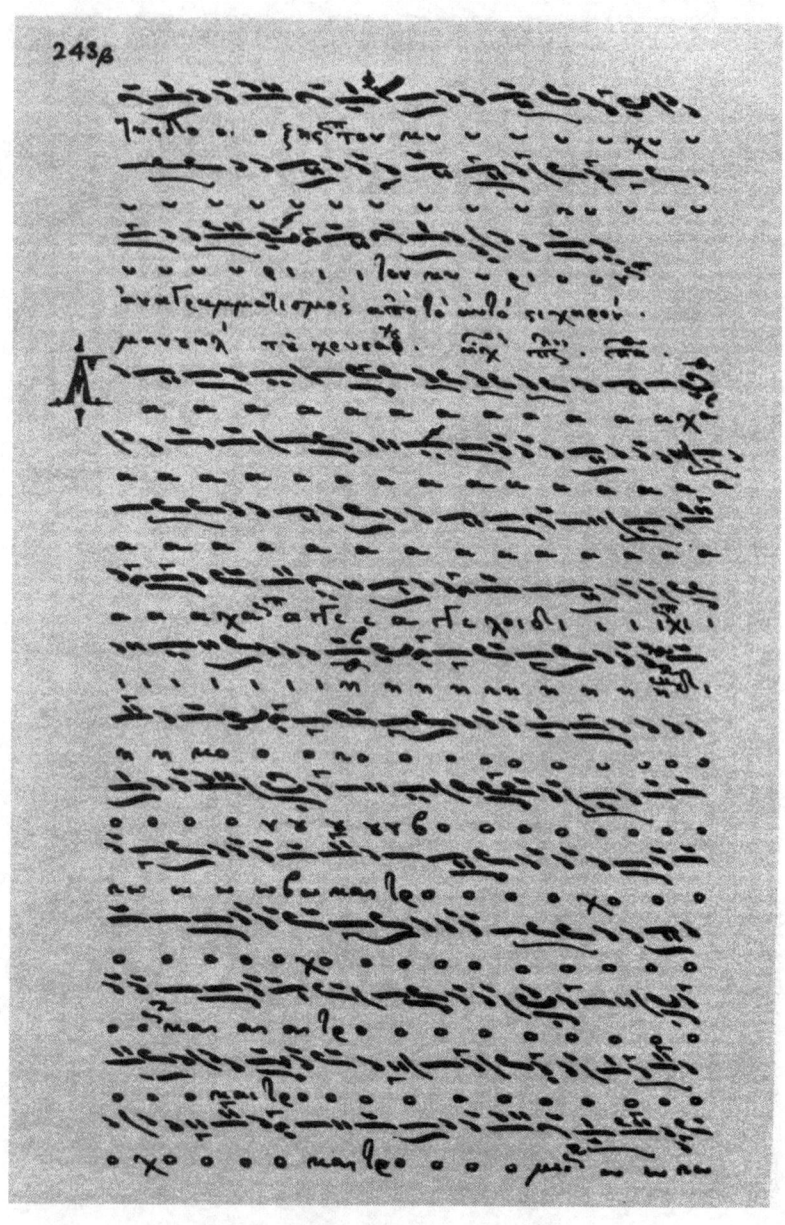

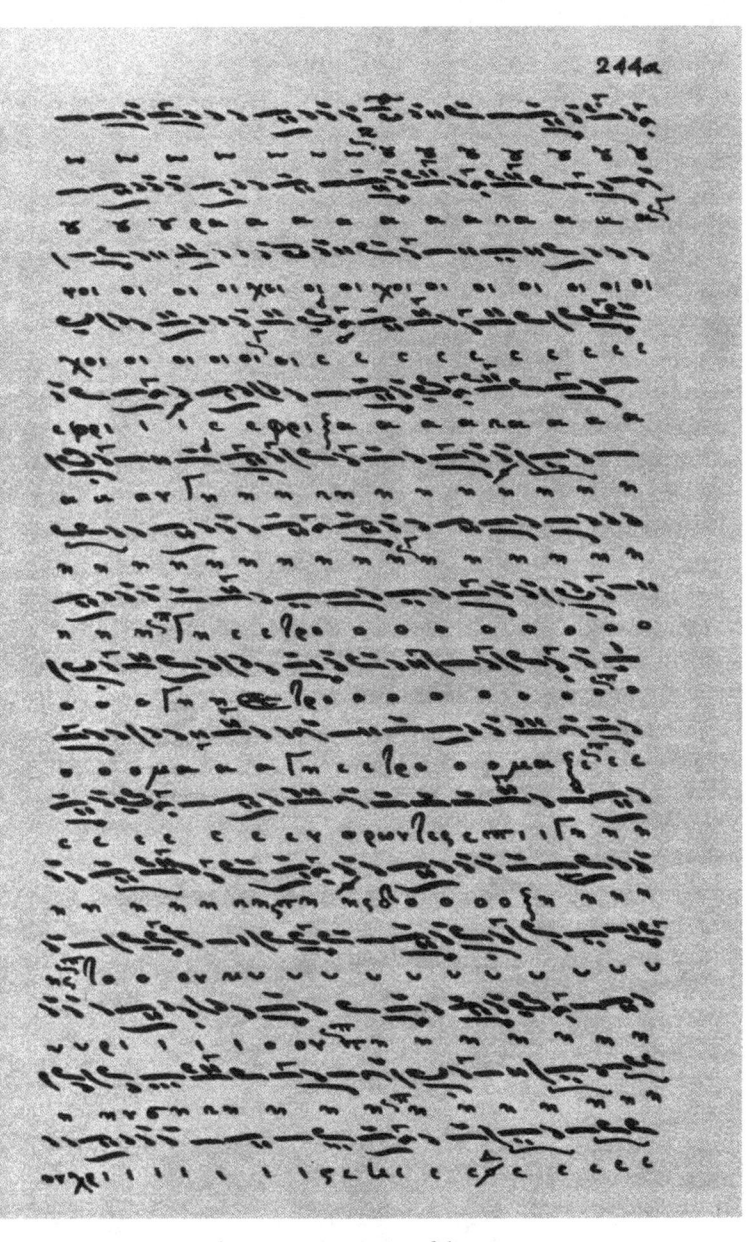

Plate XXI. МПТ 732, fol. 244r

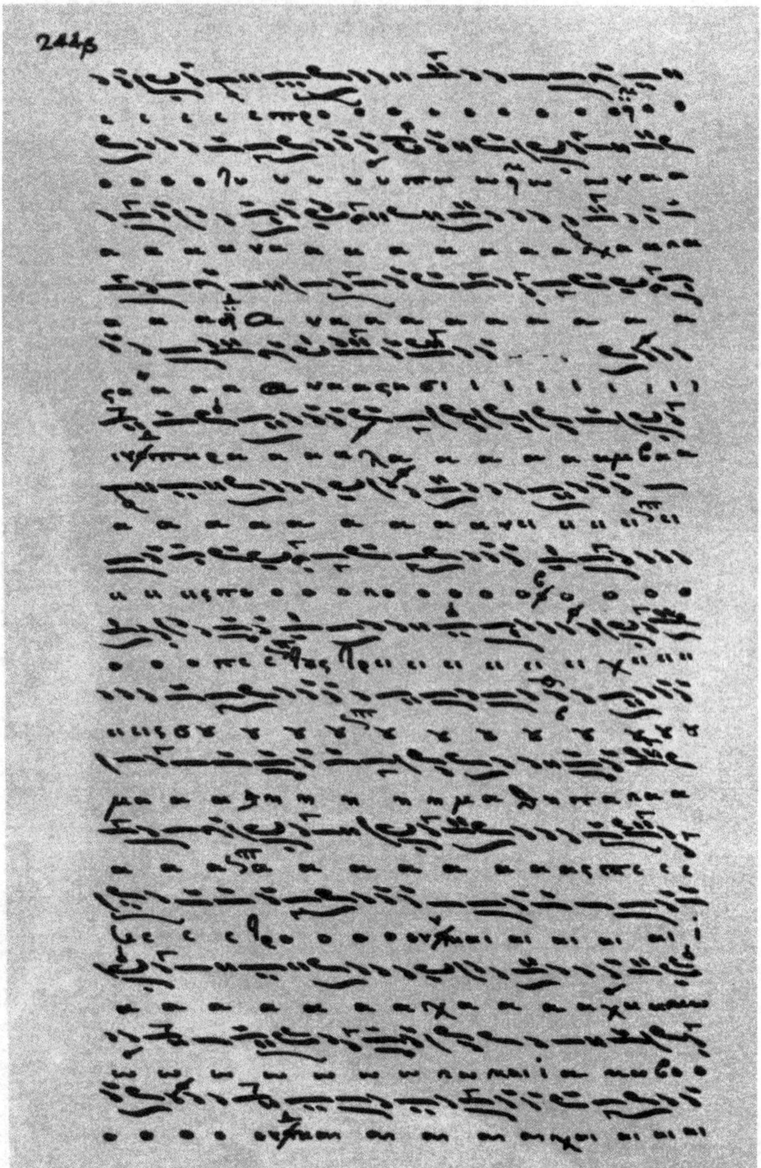

Plate XXII. МПТ 732, fol. 244v

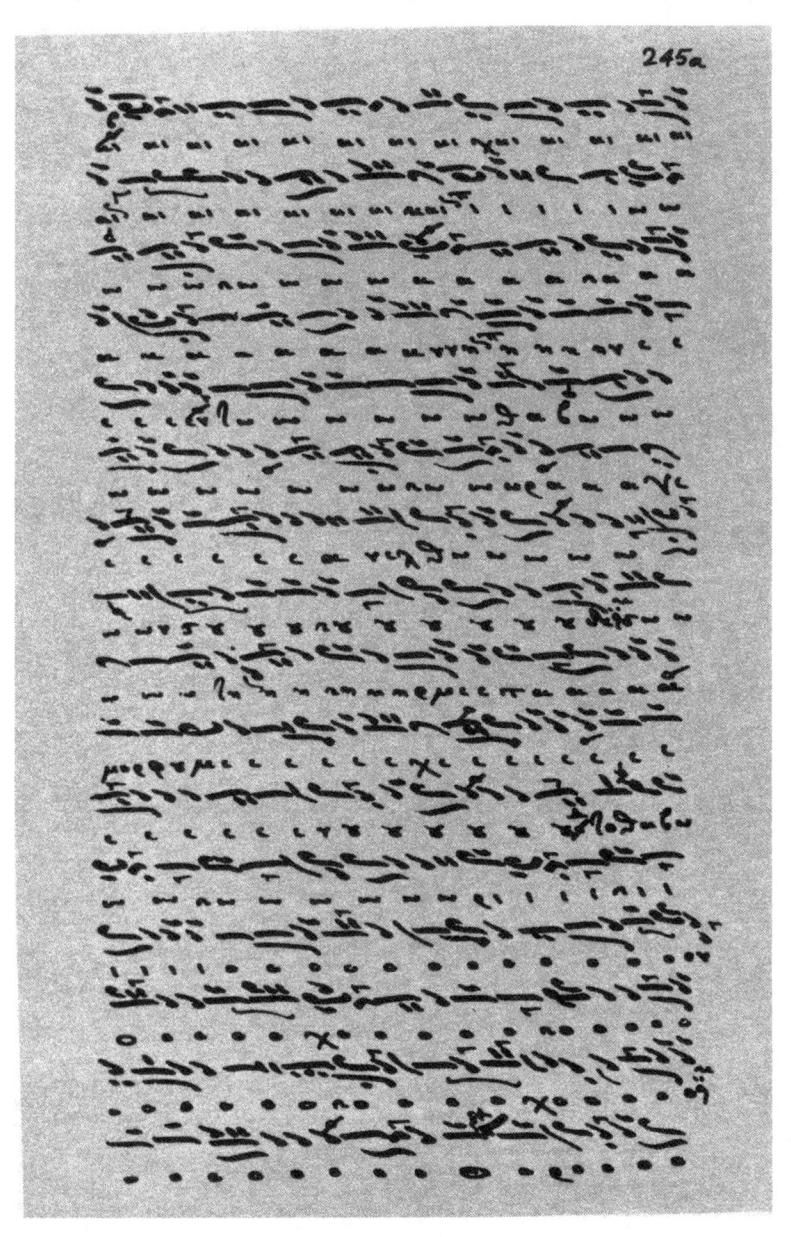

Plate XXIII. MΠT 732, fol. 245r

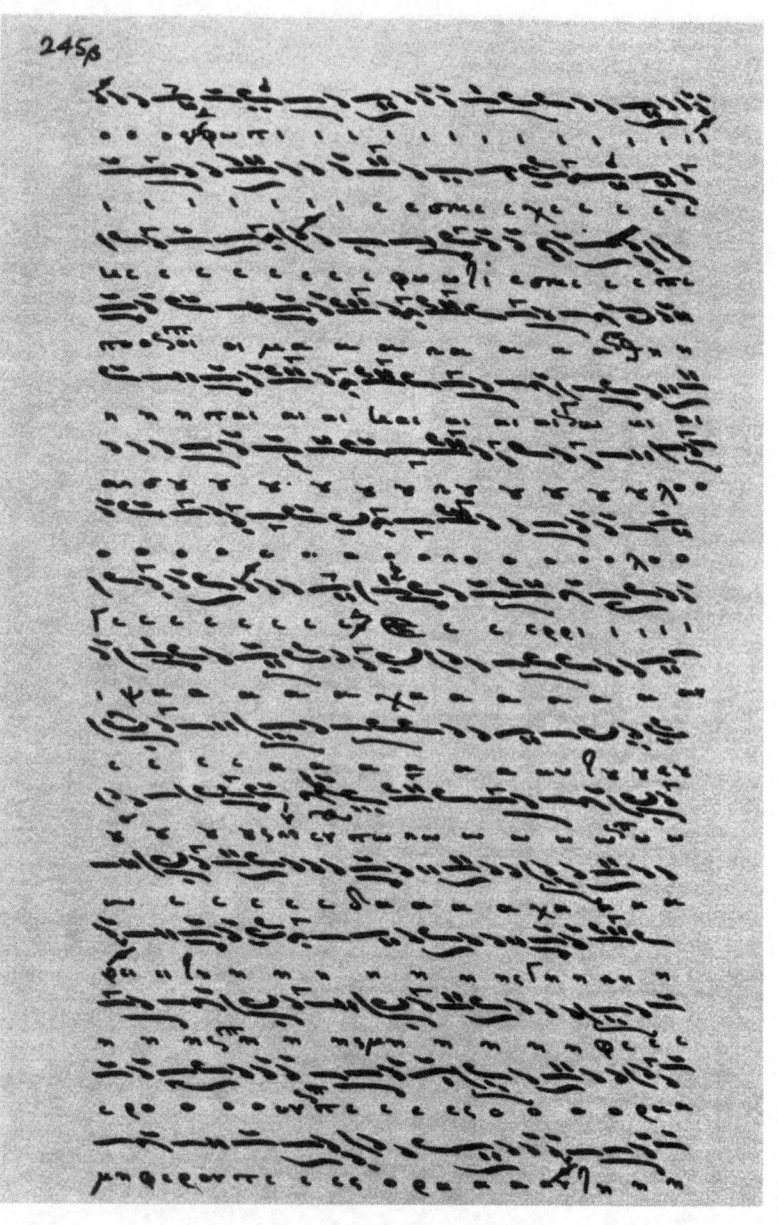

Plate XXIV. МПТ 732, fol. 245v

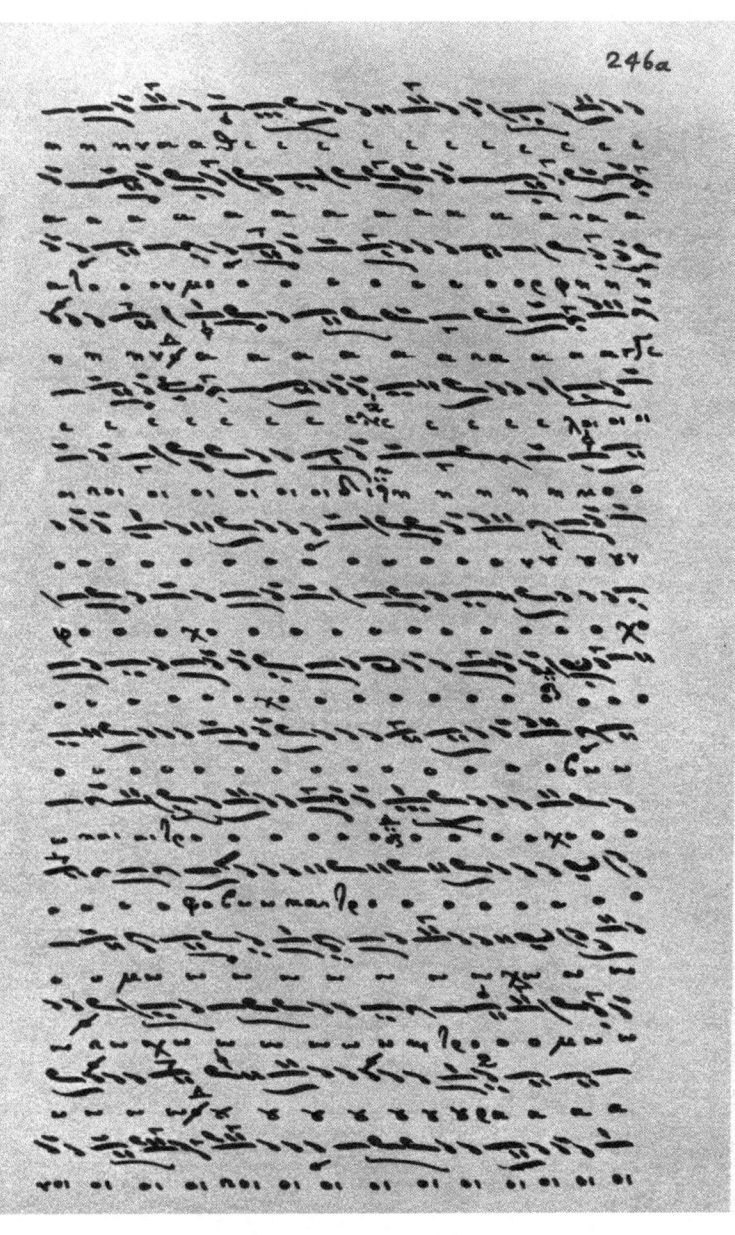

Plate XXV. MΠT 732, fol. 246r

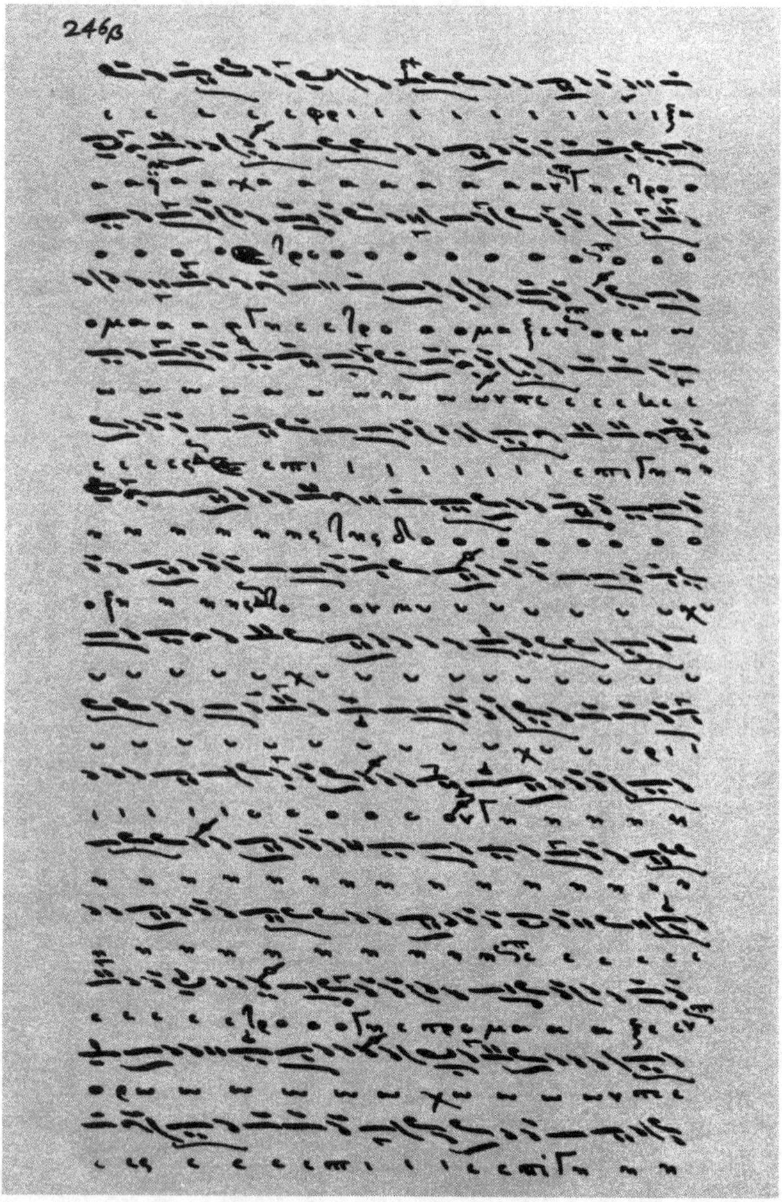

Plate XXVI. МПТ 732, fol. 246v

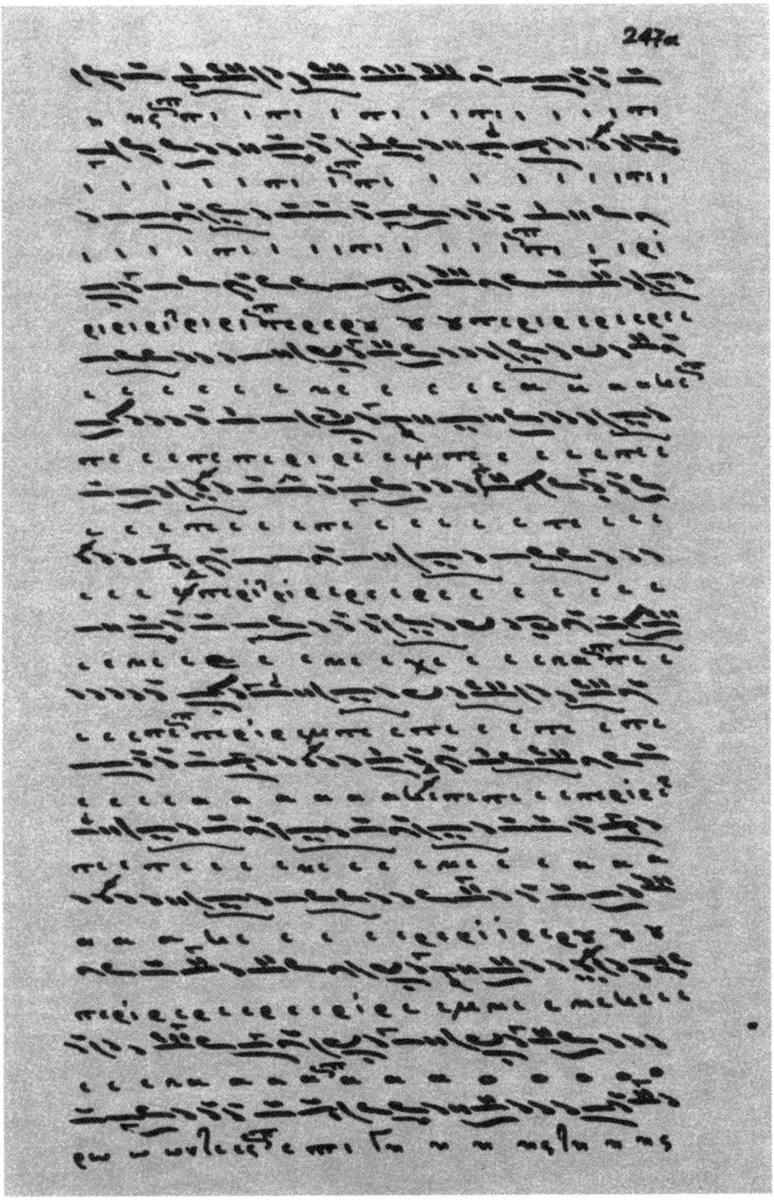

Plate XXVII. МПТ 732, fol. 247r

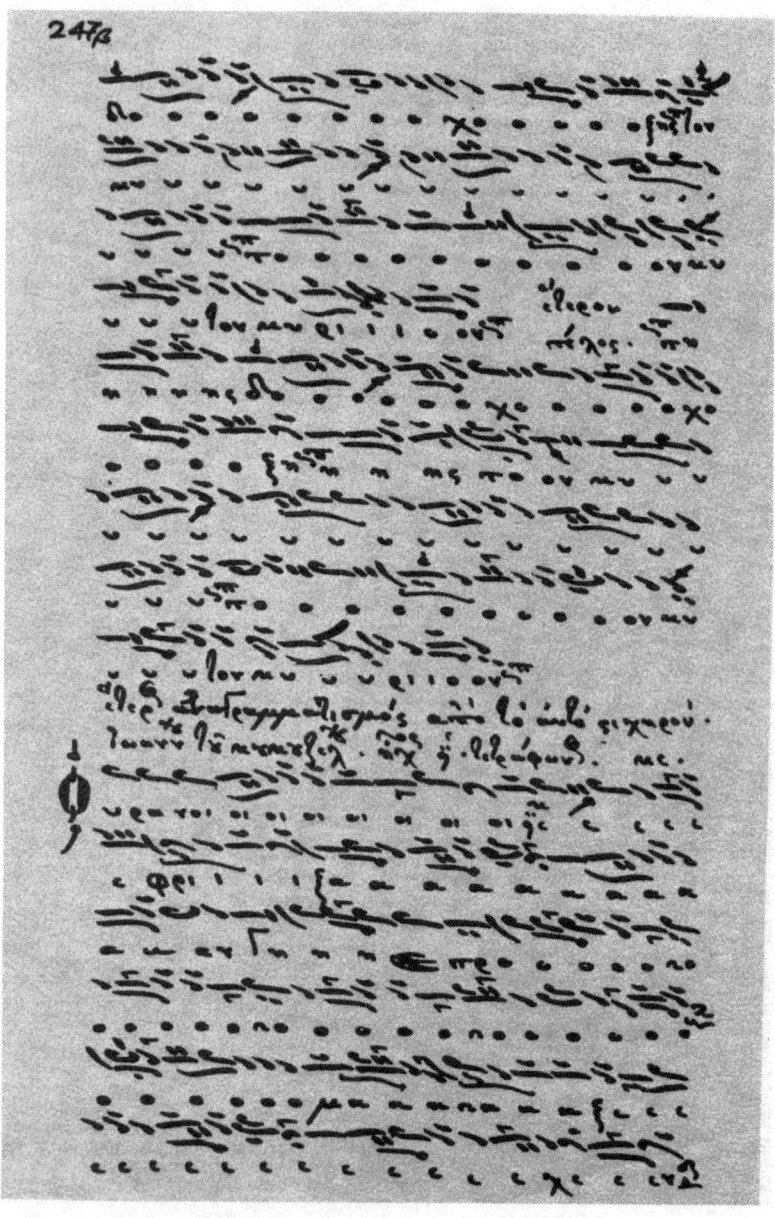

Plate XXVIII. ΜΠΤ 732, fol. 247v

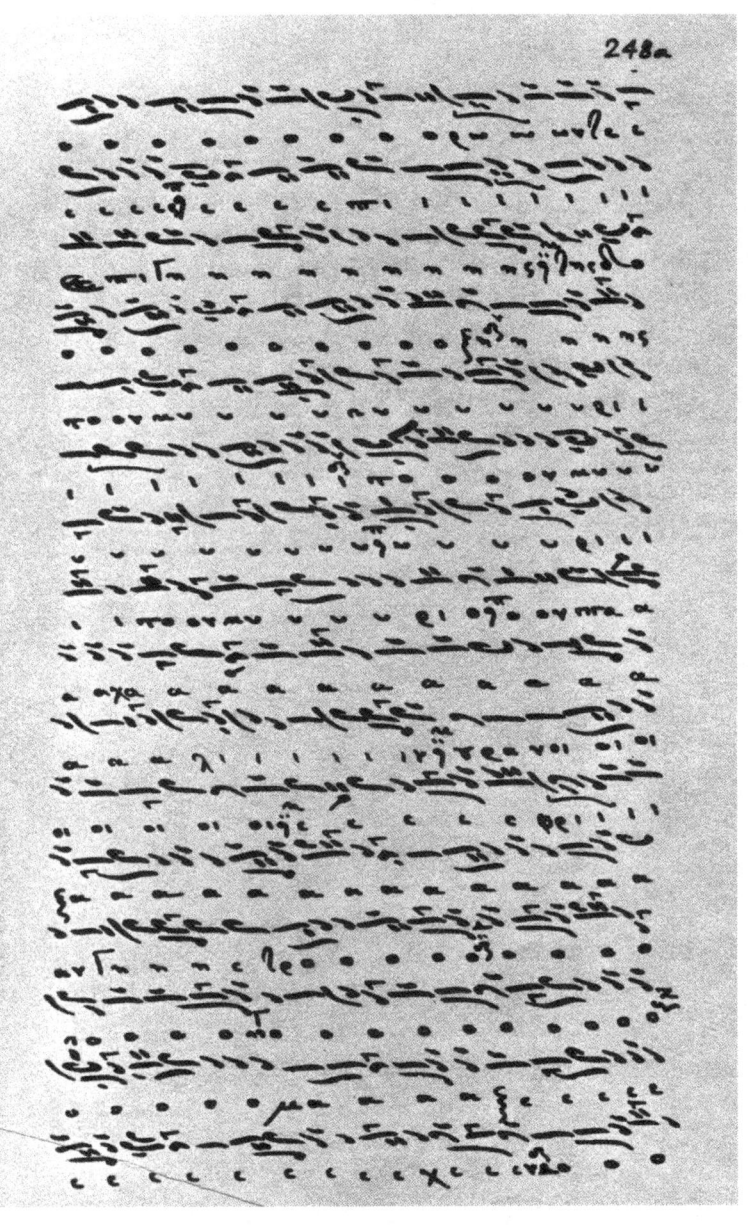

Plate XXIX. МПТ 732, fol. 248r

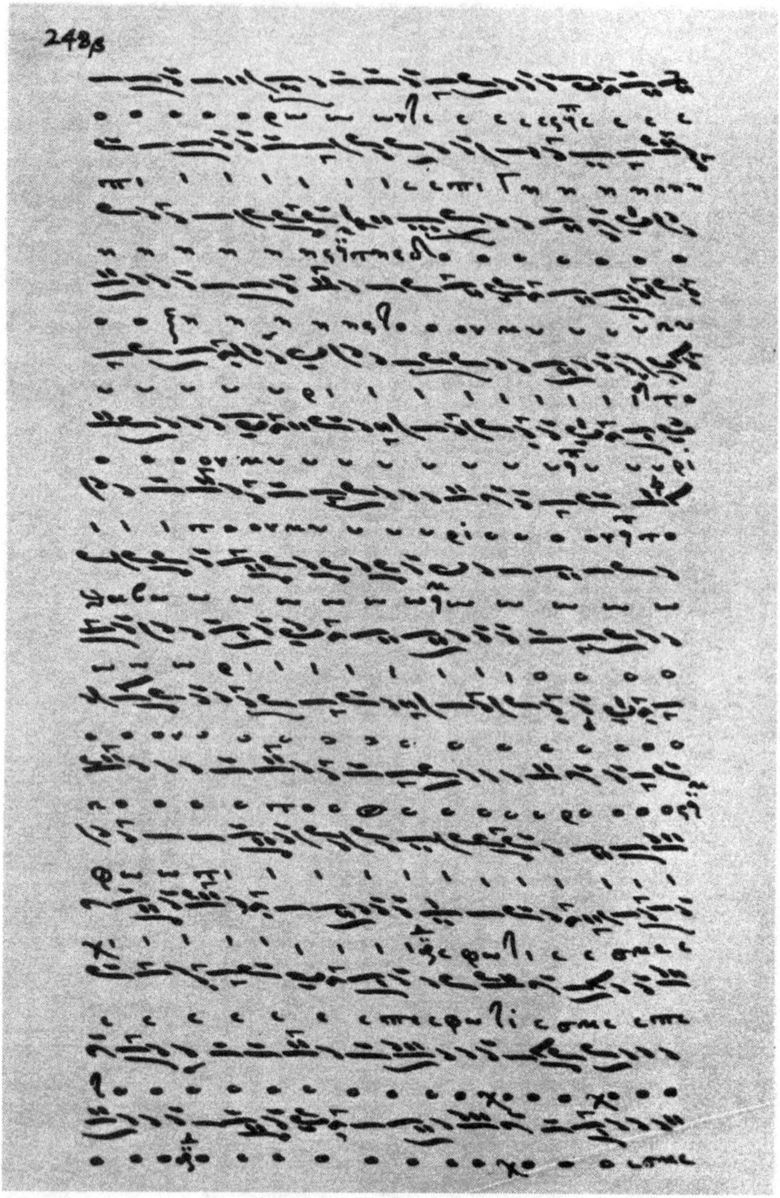

Plate XXX. MΠT 732, fol. 248v

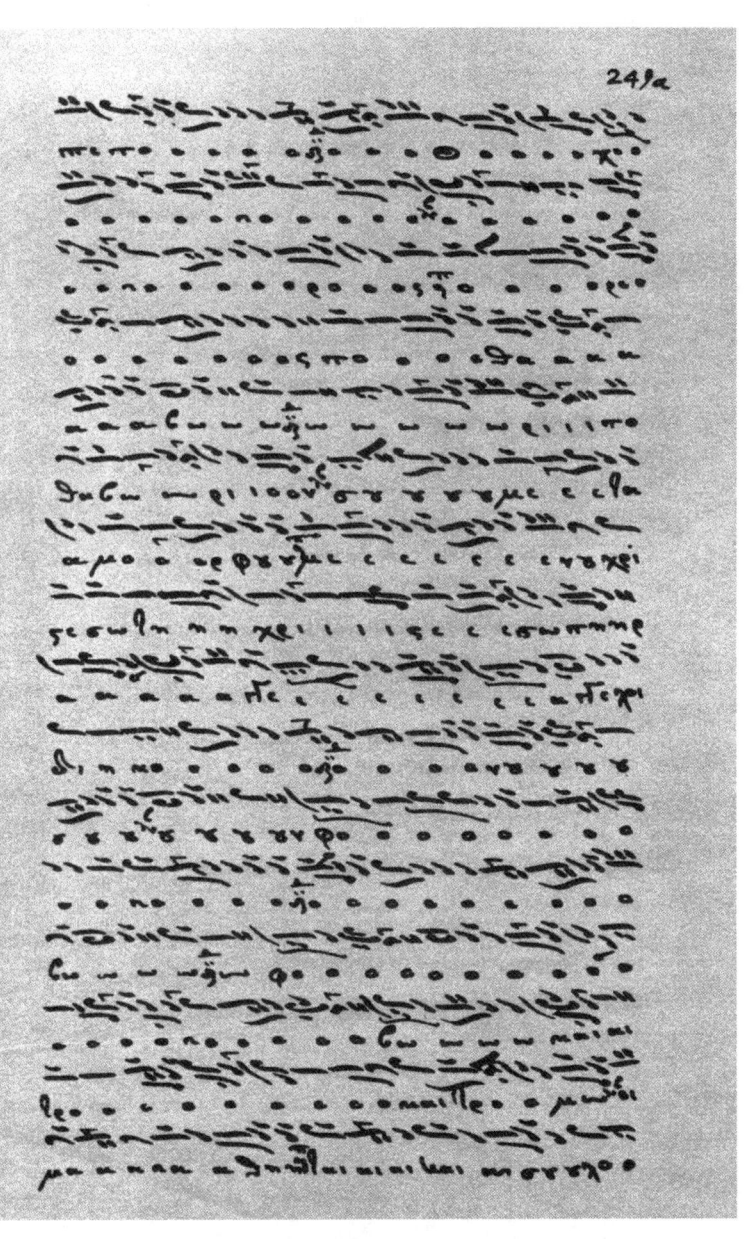

Plate XXXI. ΜΠΤ 732, fol. 249r

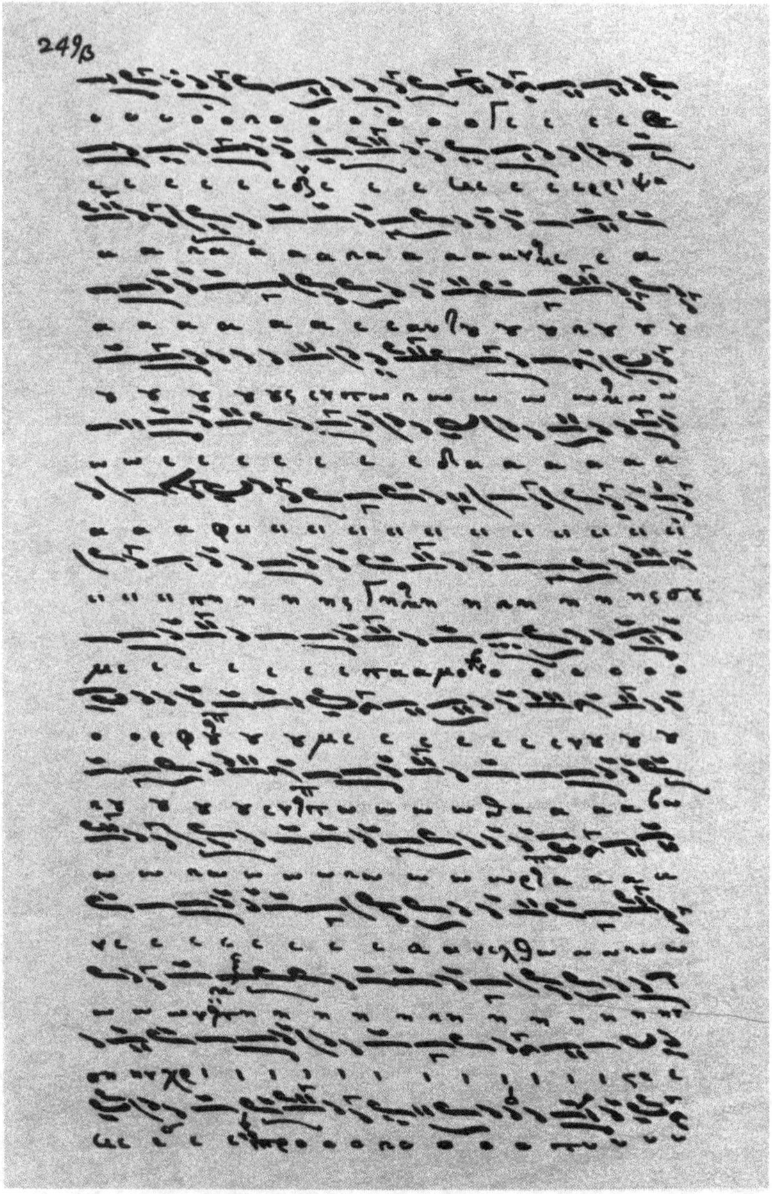

Plate XXXII. MΠT 732, fol. 249v

Images of МПТ *732*

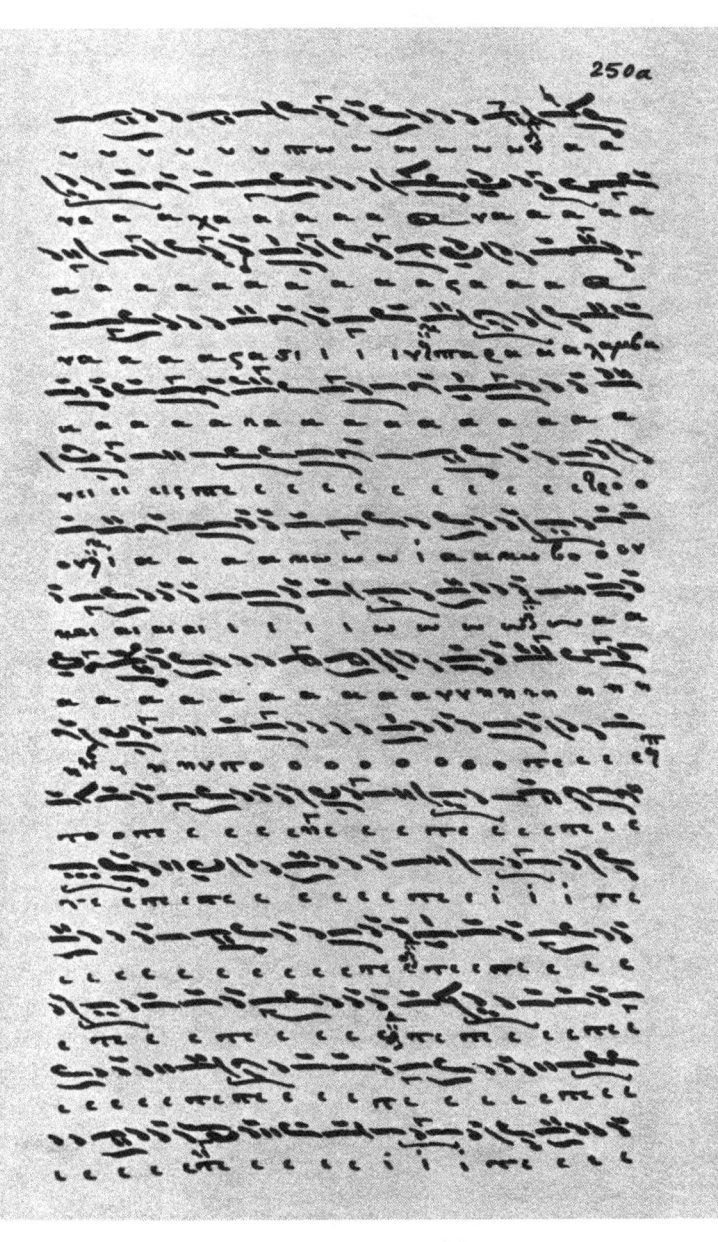

Plate XXXIII. МПТ 732, fol. 250r

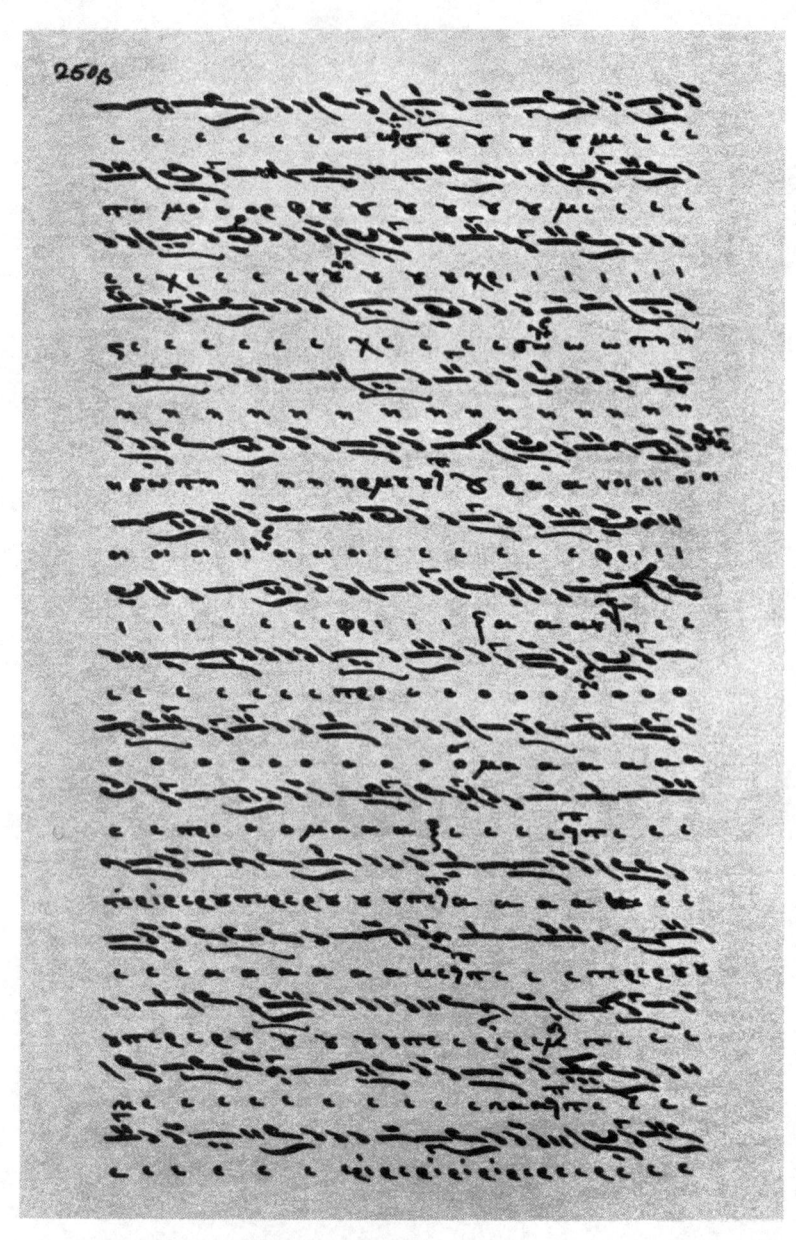

Plate XXXIV. МПТ 732, fol. 250v

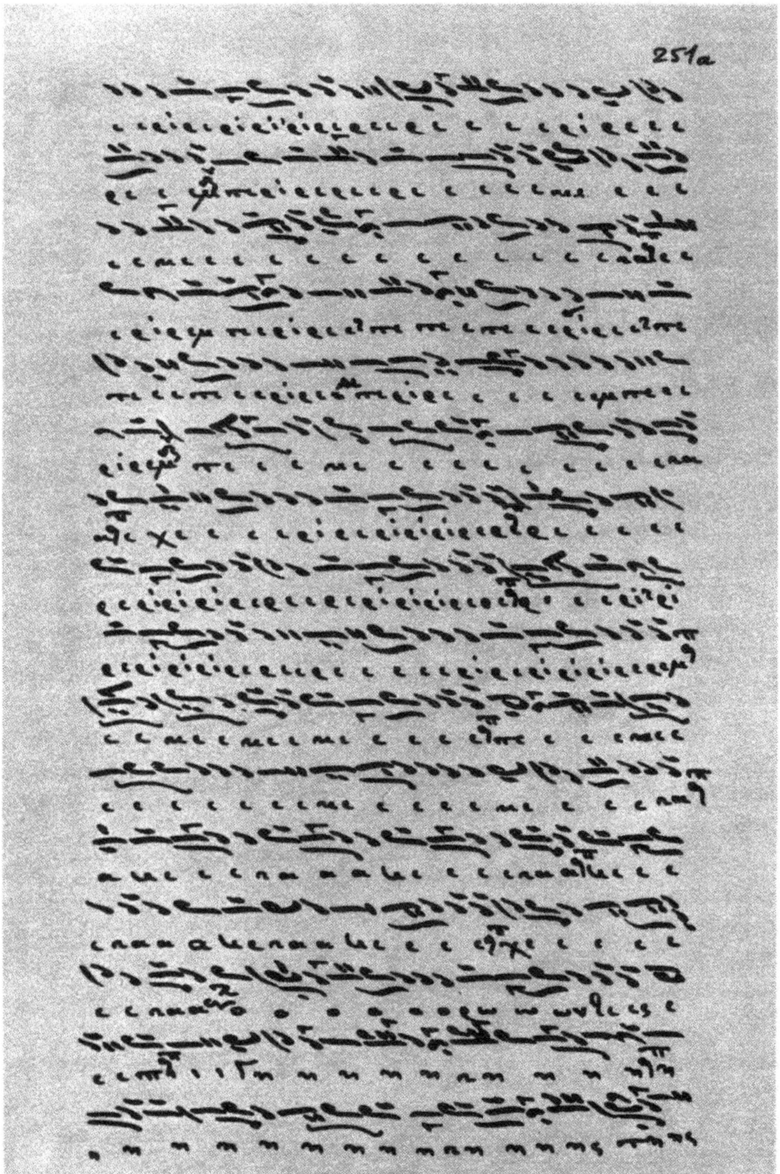

Images of МПТ 732

Plate XXXV. МПТ 732, fol. 251r

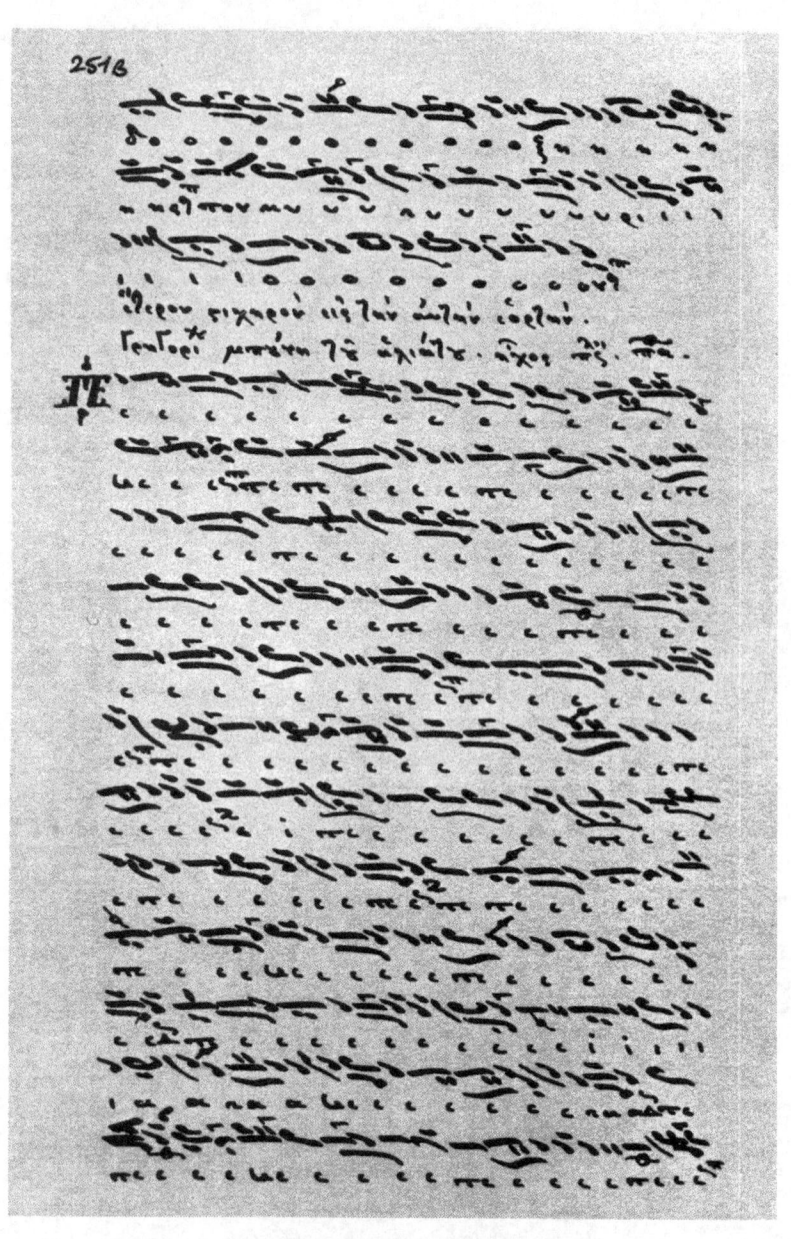

Plate XXXVI. MΠT 732, fol. 251v

Epilogue

The examination of the anagrams and mathēmata of Byzantine and post-Byzantine melic composition made necessary the general review regarding kalophony as a phenomenon and independent art form. As was natural, this research spread to all themes connected to kalophony; firstly, the related terminology and periods or stations of notational development and melopœïa parallel to the first creators and perpetuators of the forms, and then the text and morphological types of these compositions. Having journeyed the greater portion of the ocean of Byzantine and post-Byzantine melic compositional output, we have reached the final harbour, a termination of the present difficult research that is also the beginning of only a first attempt at coming to terms with the themes related to kalophony.

The mathēmata of Byzantine melic composition, namely, the kalophonic stichēra idiomela with their anagrams, feet and anapodismoi, mainly, but also all the rest of the kalophonic forms, are the artistic creation through which art, and here *Psaltikē*, is appreciated in all its grandeur and becomes an object of awe. Regarding this, in these arrangements the Chant reaches a point of artistic autonomy and becomes confident in its tradition of succession, passed down to the many-member choir of its initiates and tutors — domestikoi, lampadarioi, protopsaltai. They are the ones who raised the magnificent monument of monophonic vocal music that accompanied and continues to accompany the offered prayers and petitions, doxologies and praises of the people named after Christ, the Greek Orthodox, during the daily offices.

It is useful to enumerate and underline here the main points addressed and studied in this detailed examination of kalophony in summary form, listing the significant offering to scholarly knowledge which my weakness has attained.

1. Kalophony appeared after the re-taking of Constantinople and the dismantling of the Frankish conquest, finding fertile soil in the general climate of renaissance and splendour of Byzantine civilization during the empire of Andronicus II (1282–1328).
2. The lengthening of the melos that led directly to the anagrams and text repetitions, not to mention the insertion of the kratēmata, is the main characteristic of the new Psaltic technique of the Byzantines', in addition to the simultaneous tendency toward the art form's autonomy and coming into its own class.
3. The eponymous compositions indicate the competitiveness among composers and the creation of a class of artists, the *maïstores* and domestikoi, the kalophōnarēs or monophōnarēs, who were professional music teachers and were celebrated and admired by their fellow, contemporary and later artists.
4. The insertion of kalophony contributed to the shaping of the cathedral, asmatic typos or office of services, as well as the tradition of unique music codices, mainly the *Papadikē* and *Mathēmatarion*.
5. Kalophony spread from the psalmic verses to the *Konkatarion* and from there to the *Stichērarion*, where it developed into its strongest breadth. Hence, we have two categories of kalophony: the psalmic mathēmata and the mathēmata proper, whose texts are stichēra idiomela, heirmoi, kontakia or dekapentasyllabic compositions.
6. Regarding the melos and development of the Psaltic Art, the mathēmata, as free, creative composition and momentary intellectual revelations are the colophon of Byzantine and post-Byzantine melopœïa and greatly contributed to the art form's attainment to unmatchable achievements.
7. The theoretical treatises by Manuel Chrysaphēs and Gabriel hieromonachos, but also the methods of kalophony by various authors, concern themselves with the forms of melic compositional kalophony, and through it interpret and promote the art form. The kalophonic compositions are pre-eminent, skilled creations of artistic value.
8. The poets of the anagrams and mathēmata were the primary composers of their time. The structures and forms of these compositions were

Epilogue

defined by their first creators, Iohannes Koukouzelēs, Nikephoros Ethikos, Iohannes Glykys and Xenos Korōnēs.

9. Morphologically, the mathēmata belong to the following basic types: simple, single-part, two-part, three-part, four-part and multi-part, with a varied introduction, and a finale. The variety and adaptability in the morphological structure, together with the embellished, skilled melos characterize a highly artistic monophonic chant created by the latter Byzantine spirit, in many ways pioneering the finalized forms that would come to be used in polyphonic music.

Today, the anagrams and mathēmata have been withdrawn from liturgical use and are only chanted in the monastic vigils; this kalophony, disseminated and elevated through the anagrams and mathēmata, is the criterion for the understanding and preservation of a tradition and art such as is the Psaltic Art.

Bibliography

MANUSCRIPTS USED

ATHOS

Chilandariou

146 (XVIIIth century, beginning)

Dionysiou

564 (AD 1445)
567 (AD 1685)
570 (XVth century, end)
707 (AD 1858)

Docheiariou

334 (AD 1726)
337 (AD 1764)
338 (AD 1767)
339 (AD 1768)
341 (AD 1822)
342 (AD 1734)
361 (c. AD 1800)
379 (XVIIth century, first half)
381 (XVIth century, end)
388 (XVIIth century)
389 (AD 1807)
123 [*Typikarion*] (mid-IX century)

Gregoriou

03 (XVIIth century, end)
04 (AD 1744)

Hagiou Pavlou

101 [198/71] (XVth–XVIth century)
128 [186/59] (AD 1755–1765)
146 [206/79] (AD 1758)

Iviron

961 (XVIIth century, end)
964 (AD 1562)
967 (mid-XVIIIth century)
970 (AD 1686)
972 (XVth century, first half)
973 (XVth century, beginning)
974 (XVth century, first half)
975 (mid-XVth century)
977 (XVth century end–XVIth century)
978 (c. AD 1680)
980 (c. AD 1680)
984 (XVth century, first half)
985 (AD 1425)

988 (AD 1734)
991 (AD 1670)
1006 (AD 1431)
1048 (AD 1686)
1051 (AD 1673)
1061 (XVIIIth century, first half)
1073 (XVIIIth century, beginning)
1074 (AD 1682)
1079 (XVIIth century, second half)
1080 (AD 1668)
1089 (AD 1695)
1108 (mid-XVIIth century)
1112 (XVIIth century, first half)
1120 (AD 1458)
1141 (XVIIth century, second half)
1150 (XVIIth century, second half)
1154 (XVIIth century, first half)
1155 (XVIIth century, first half)
1156 (XVIth century, end–XVIIth century)
1189 (AD 1562)
1192 (XVIIth century, beginning)
1203 (c. AD 1700)
1204 (mid-XVIth century)
1205 (XVIIth century, beginning)
1250 (c. AD 1670)

Koutloumousiou

399 (mid-XIVth century)
427 (mid-XVIth century)
446 (AD 1757)
448 (c. AD 1600)
455 (XVth–XVIth century)
456 (AD 1443)

457 (XIVth century, second half)
588 (XVIIIth century, second half)

Konstamonitou

86 (XVth century, first half)

M. Lavra

Γ 67 (Xth century)
Ε 46 (AD 1436)
Ε 148 (XVth century, first half)
Ι 79 (XVth century)
Ι 173 (AD 1436)
Ι 178 (AD 1377)
Ι 185 (mid-XIVth century)
Κ 158
Λ 166 (XVIIth century)

Panteleimon

901 (AD 1734)
917 (mid-XIXth century)
927 (XVIIIth century, second half)
938 (XVIth century, beginning)
959 (XVIIth century, end)
994 (mid-XVIIIth century)
1008 (XVIIth century, end)
1207 (AD 1837 [*Typikarion Koimeseos Theotokou o6*])

Philotheou

122 (XIVth–XVth century)
125 (XVth century)

Bibliography

136 (XVIIth century, first half)
137 (XVIIth century, beginning)

Vatopedi

1498 (mid-XVth century)
1527 (AD 1434)

Xenophontos

120 (AD 1825)
128 (AD 1671)
137 (XVIIIth century, end)
159 (AD 1610)
183 (mid-XIXth century)

ATHENS

Hidryma Byzantines Mousikologias (IBM)

01 (c. AD 1820)

Historikes kai Ethnologikes Hetaireias (IEE)

305 (AD 1750)

National Library of Greece (EBE)

884 (AD 1341)
886 (XVth century, end)
899 (mid-XVth century)
904 (XIVth century, end)
905 (XIVth century, end)
906 (XIVth century, end)
917 (XVIth century, first half)
937 (mid-XVIth century; Vol. 1)
938 (mid-XVIth century; Vol. 2)
2061 (post AD 1391)
2062 (c. first half of XIVth century)
2401 (XVth century)
2406 (AD 1453)
2444 (XIVth century, end)
2454 (XIVth century, end)
2456 (XVth century)
2458 (AD 1336)
2599 (XVth century)
2600 (XIVth century, end)
2601 (c. AD 1430)
2604 (AD 1463)
2622 (c. AD 1340–1360)
2837 (AD 1457)

CONSTANTINOPLE

Metochion Panagiou Taphou (MΠT)[1]

703 (AD 1818)
704 (AD 1819)
705 (AD 1829)
706 (AD 1819)
710 (AD 1817)
711 (AD 1817)
712 (AD 1837)
713 (XIXth century)

[1] All MΠT Mss. are Chourmouzios Chartophylax autographs except for 754, which is a Gregoios Lampadarios-Protopsaltes autograph.

714 (XIXth century)
722 (AD 1819)
727 (XIXth century)
728 (XIXth century)
729 (XIXth century)
730 (XIXth century)
731 (XIXth century)
732 (XIXth century)
733 (XIXth century)
734 (XIXth century)
754 (AD 1817–1818)

METEORA

Holy Transfiguration Monastery

44 (XVIth century)
317 (XVth century)

MESSINA

Bibl. Regionale Universitaria San Salvatore

161 (XIIIth century, end)

PARIS

Bibliotèque nationale de France (BnF)

Coislin 41 (AD 1244)
Suppl. Gr. 1047 (AD 1807)

PATMOS

Monastery of Saint John the Theologian

930 (AD 1665)

ROME

Grottaferrata Badia Graeca

Crypt. Γ.γ.IV (XIIIth–XIVth century)

SINAI

Saint Catherine's Monastery

1234 (XVth century)
1256 (AD 1309)
1259 (XVIth century)
1262 (AD 1437)
1527 (XVth century)
1764 (XVIIIth century)

ST. PETERSBURG
–LENINGRAD

National Library of Russia

121 (AD 1302)

VIENNA

Österreichische Nationalbibliothek

Theol. Gr. 181 (AD 1221)

WORKS CITED

Adamis, Michael (1974), 'An example of polyphony in Byzantine Music of the late Middle Ages,' *International Musicological Society: Report of the Eleventh Congress, Copenhagen 1972*, II, 737–747.

Alexandru, Maria (2011–2012), 'Byzantine Kalophonia, illustrated by St. John Koukouzeles' piece Φρουρησον πανενδοξε in honour of St. Demetrios from Thessalonike. Issues of notation and analysis,' *Studii și cercet. ist. art., Teatru, Musică, Cinematografie*, serie nouă, T. 5–6 (49–50), 57–105.

Anastasiou, Gregorios (2005), *Τὰ κρατήματα στὴν Ψαλτικὴ Τέχνη*, ed. Grēgorios Th. Stathēs (Meletai, 12; Athens: Institute of Byzantine Musicology).

Anatolikiōtēs, Dionysios N. M. (2004), *Ὁ Χουρμούζιος Χαρτοφύλαξ καὶ ἡ συμβολή του εἰς τὴν μουσικὴν μεταρρύθμισιν τοῦ 1814* (Athens: Kalamos).

Antoniades, Euangelos (1950), 'Περὶ τοῦ ἀσματικοῦ ἢ βυζαντινοῦ κοσμικοῦ τύπου τῶν ἀκολουθιῶν τῆς ἡμερονυκτίου προσευχῆς,' *Θεολογία*, 21, 43–56, 160–200, 339–353, 526–540.

Apostolopoulos, Thomas (2002), *Ὁ Ἀπόστολος Κώνστας ὁ Χίου καὶ ἡ συμβολή του στὴ θεωρία τῆς Μουσικῆς Τέχνης*, ed. Institute of Byzantine Musicology of the Holy Synod of the Church of Greece (Meletai, 4; Athens).

Aristides Quintilianus (1963), 'De musica,' in R. P. Winnington-Ingram (ed.), *Aristidis Quintiliani de musica libri tres*. (Leipzig: Teubner).

Aristoklis, Theodoros (1866), *Κωνσταντίου Α΄ τοῦ ἀπὸ Σιναίου· βιογραφία καὶ συγγραφαὶ αἱ ἐλάσσονες* (Constantinople).

Aristoxenus Tarentinus (1954), 'Elementa harmonica,' in R. da Rios (ed.), *Aristoxeni elementa harmonica* (Rome: Polygraphica), 5–92.

Asioli, Bonifazio and Coli, Antonio (1832), *Il maestro di composizione, ossia, Seguito del Trattato d'armonia: opera postuma*, 2 vols. (Milano: Ricordi).

Astruc, Charles, Concasty, Marie-Louise, and (France), Bibliothèque nationale (1989), *Catalogue des manuscrits grecs. Troisième partie, Le supplément grec* (Paris: La Bibliothèque).

Balageōrgos, Dēmētrios (2003), *Ὁ Θεόδουλος Μοναχὸς καὶ τὸ ἔργο τῶν συντμήσεων* (Athens).

Bamboudakes, Emmanuel (1933), 'Τὰ ἐν τῇ Βυζαντινῇ Μουσικῇ κρατήματα,' *Ἐπετηρὶς Ἑταιρείας Βυζαντινῶν Σπουδῶν*, 10, 353–362.

—— (1938), *Συμβολὴ εἰς τὴν σπουδὴν τῆς παρασημαντικῆς τῶν Βυζαντινῶν μουσικῶν, τόμος Α΄, Μέρος Γενικὸς* (Σάμος).

Barker, Andrew (1984), *Greek musical writings*, 2 vols. (Cambridge: Cambridge University Press).
Baumstark, Anton (1910), *Festbrievier und Kirchenjahr der syrischen Jakobiten* (Paderborn).
Baumstark, Anton and Botte, Bernard (1953), *Liturgie comparée: principes et méthodes pour l'étude historique des liturgies chrétiennes* (3. éd. / edn.; Chevetogne: Éditions de Chevetogne).
Baumstark, Anton, Botte, Bernard, and Cross, F. L. (1958), *Comparative liturgy* (London: Mowbray).
Beneshevich, V. N. (1937), *Les manuscrits grecs du Mont Sinaî et le monde savant de l'Europe depuis le XVIIe siècle jusq'é 1927* (Athen: Verlag der 'Byzantinisch-neugriechischen jahrbücher').
Bentas, Christos (1971), 'The Treatise on Music by John Laskaris', in Miloš Velimirović (ed.), *Studies in Eastern Chant* (II; London: Oxford University Press), 21–27.
Blades, James and Bowles, Edmund A. 'Nakers,' *Grove Music Online*.
Bugge, A. (1960), *Contacarium palaeoslavicum mosquense* (Union académique internationale Monumenta musicae Byzantinae, 6; Copenhague: E. Munksgaard).
Chaldaiakēs, Achileas (2003), *Ὁ Πολυέλεος στὴ βυζαντινὴ καὶ μεταβυζαντινὴ μελοποιία*, ed. Grēgorios Th. Stathēs (Meletai, 5; Athens: Institute of Byzantine Musicology).
Chatzegiakoumes, Manoles (1975), *Μουσικὰ χειρόγραφα τουρκοκρατίας (1453–1832)* (Athens).
Chourmouzios Chartophylax (1824), 'Ταμεῖον Ἀνθολογίας', (Constantinople).
—— (1901), 'Δοξαστάριον Ἀποστίχων', in Chourmouzios Chartophylax (ed.), (Thessalinikē: N. Christomanou).
Chourmouzios Chartophylax and Theodōros Phōkaeus (1859), *Δοξαστάριον περιέχον τὰ Δοξαστικὰ τῶν Ἀποστίχων* (Constantinople: Typois M. de Kastrou).
Christ, Wilhelm von (1871), *Anthologia graeca carminum christianorum*, ed. Matthaios K. b Paranikas (Lipsiae: B. G. Teubner).
Chrysanthos ek Madyton (1832), *Θεωρητικὸν μέγα τῆς μουσικῆς* (En Tergestē: Bais).
Cleonides Mus. (1916), 'Intriductio harmonica', in H. Menge (ed.), *Euclidis opera omnia* (8; Leipzig: Teubner), 186–222.
Cody, Aelred (1982), 'The Early History of the Octoechos in Syria', in Nina G. Garsoïan, Thomas F. Mathews, and Robert W. Thomson (eds.), *East of Byzantium: Syria and Armenia in the Formative Period* (Washington, D. C.: Dumbarton Oaks Symposium), 89–113.
Conomos, Dimitri E. (1972), 'Byzantine trisagia and cheroubika in the fourteenth and fifteenth centuries: a study of late Byzantine chant,' D Phil (University of Oxford).

Bibliography

—— (2001), 'Kalophonic chant.' Oxford University Press <http://www.oxfordmusiconline.com/subscriber/article/grove/music/14642>

Demetriou, Chrysostomos M. (1927), *Οἱ ἐξωκατάκοιλοι ἄρχοντες τῆς ἐν Κωνσταντινουπόλει Μεγάλης τοῦ Χριστοῦ Ἐκκλησίας* (Athens).

Dentakes, Basileios (1969), *Βυζαντινὴ ἐκκλησιαστικὴ Γραμματολογία· ἀπὸ τῶν ἀρχῶν τῆς 14ης ἑκατονταετηρίδος μέχρι τῆς ἁλώσεως (1328–1453)*.

Dmitrievski, Alekse and Orthodox Eastern Church (1965), *Opisanie liturgitseskich rukopisej*, 3 vols. (Hildesheim: G. Olms).

Eustratiades, Sophronios (1938), 'Ὁ Ἰωάννης Κουκουζέλης ὁ Μαΐστωρ καὶ ὁ χρόνος τῆς ἀκμῆς αὐτοῦ,' *Ἐπετηρὶς Ἑταιρείας Βυζαντινῶν Σπουδῶν*, 14, 3–86.

Eustratiades, Sophronios and Archadios, deacon (1924), *Κατάλογος τῶν ἐν τῇ ἱερᾷ μονῇ Βατοπεδίου ἀποκειμένων κωδίκων* (Paris).

Euthymiades, Abraam (1978), *Ὑμνολόγιον Φωναῖς Αἰσίαις, εἰς τόμους τρεῖς* (Thessalonike).

Farmer, Henry George (1949), 'Crusading Martial Music,' *Music & Letters*, 30 (Jul. 1949), 243–249.

Fleischer, Oskar (1904), *Die spätgriechische Tonschrift* (Berlin: G. Reimer).

Floros, Constantin (2009), *The origins of Russian music: introduction to the kondakarian notation* (Frankfurt am Main: Peter Lang) xix, 311 pp.

Floros, Constantin and Moran, Neil K. (2005), *Introduction to early medieval notation* (Enlarged 2nd edn., Detroit monographs in musicology/Studies in music, no 45; Warren, Mich.: Harmonie Park Press) xxiv 171 pp.

Frøyshov, Stig Simeon (2007), 'The Early Development of the Liturgical Eight-mode System in Jerusalem,' *St Vladimir's Theological Quarterly*, 51 (2–3), 139–178.

Gabriel hieromonachos and Schartau, Bjarne (1990), Über das Erfordernis von Schriftzeichen før die Musik der Griechen (Monumenta musicae Byzantinae Corpus scriptorum de re musica, 3; Vienna: Verlag der Österreichischen Akademie der Wissenschaften).

Gabriel hieromonachos, Hannick, Christian, and Wolfram, Gerda (1985), *Gabriel Hieromonachos: Abhandlung über den Kirchengesang* (Monumenta musicae Byzantinae Corpus scriptorum de re musica, Bd 1; Vienna: Österreichische Akademie der Wissenschaften).

Gastoué, Amédée (1907), *Introduction à la Paléographie musical byzantine [Catalogue des manuscrits de musique byzantine]* (Paris).

Giannopoulos, Emmanouel St. (2002), *Εἰσαγωγὴ εἰς τὸ Θεωρητικὸν καὶ πρακτικὸν τῆς ἐκκλησιαστικῆς μουσικῆς* (Thessalonike: University Studio Press).

—— (2004), *Ἡ ἄνθηση τῆς Ψαλτικῆς Τέχνης στὴν Κρήτη (1566–1669)*, ed. Grēgorios Th. Stathēs (Meletai, 11; Athens: Institute of Byzantine Musicology).

Goar, Jacques (1960), *Euchologion: sive rituale Graecorum* (2a edn.; Graz: Akademische Druck- u. Verlagsanstalt).

Grēgorios Prōtopsaltēs (1834), 'Ταμεῖον Ἀνθολογίας περιέχον ἅπασαν τὴν ἐκκλησιαστικὴν ἐνιαύσιον ἀκολουθίαν', (Constantinople: Kastrou).

Grēgorios Prōtopsaltēs and Theodōros Phōkaeus (1835), 'Εἱρμολόγιον Καλοφωνικὸν', (Constantinople: Ek tēs typographias Kastrou eis Galatan).

Gregorius Nazianzenus (1857–1866), 'Contra Julianum imperatorem 2 (orat. 5)', in J.-P. Migne (ed.), *Patrologiae cursis completus (series Graeca)* (35; Paris), 721–752.

Hierōnymos Tragōdistēs and Schartau, Bjarne (1990), *Über das Erfordernis von Schriftzeichen für die Musik der Griechen* (Monumenta musicae Byzantinae Corpus scriptorum de re musica, 3; Vienna: Verlag der Österreichischen Akademie der Wissenschaften).

Høeg, Carsten and Florence. Biblioteca mediceo-laurenziana. (1956), *Contacarium Ashburnhamense* (Copenhague: E. Minksgaard).

Huglo, Michel (1972), 'L'Introduction en Occident des formules Byzantines d'intonation', *Studies in Eastern Chant*, III, 81–90.

Iakōbos Prōtopsaltēs and Chourmouzios Chartophylax (1836), 'Δοξαστάριον', (Galata, Constantinople).

Ioannēs Lampadarios and Stephanos Domestikos (1850–1851), 'Πανδέκτη τῆς ἱερᾶς ἐκκλησιαστικῆς ὑμνῳδίας τοῦ ὅλου ἐνιαυτοῦ', (Constantinople: Ek tou Patriarckikou Typographeiou).

Ioannidou, Arsinoi (2009), 'The kalophonic settings of the 2nd psalm in the Byzantine tradition: a report on an on-going dissertation', *Byzantine Musical Culture. First International Conference — Greece 2007* (Paeanea: American Society of Byzantine Music and Hymnology (ASBMH)), 210–223.

Jeffery, Peter (2001), 'The Earliest Octōēchoi: the role of Jerusalem and Palestine in the Beginning of Modal Ordering', in idem (ed.), *The Study of Medieval Chant, Paths and Bridges, East and West. In Honoy of Kenneth Levy* (Woodbridge), 147–209.

Jung, Annette (1998), 'The Long Melisms in the Non-kalophonic Sticherarion,' (University of Copenhagen).

Karagounēs, Kōnstantinos (2003), *Ἡ παράδοση καὶ ἐξήγηση τοῦ μέλους τῶν Χερουβικῶν τῆς βυζαντινῆς καὶ μεταβυζαντινῆς μελοποιίας*, ed. Grēgorios Th. Stathēs (Meletai, 7; Athens: Institute of Byzantine Musicology).

Karas, Simon (1933), *Ἡ Βυζαντινὴ Μουσικὴ Σημειογραφία* (Athens).

King, C. W. (1888), *Julian the Emperor* (Bohn's Library; London: George Bell & Co).

Knös, Börje (1962), *L'histoire de la littérature néo-grecque; la période jusqu'en 1821* (Acta Universitatis Upsaliensis Studia Graeca Upsaliensia, 1; Stockholm: Almquist & Wiksell).

Komines, Athanasios (1968), *Πίνακες χρονολογημένων Πατμιακῶν κωδίκων* (Athens).

Konidares, Gerasimos (1970), *Ἐκκλησιαστικὴ Ἱστορία τῆς Ἑλλάδος* (Athens).

Krētikou, Flōra (2004), *Ὁ Ἀκάθιστος Ὕμνος στὴ βυζαντινὴ καὶ μεταβυζαντινὴ μελοποιία*, ed. Grēgorios Th. Stathēs (Meletai, 10; Athens: Institute of Byzantine Musicology).

—— (2008), 'Tradition and Innovation in the Postbyzantine Kalophonic Chant: A Study Based on Petros Bereketes' stanzas *Ψάλλοντες σου τον τόκον* and *Ω πανύμνητε μῆτερ*', in Gerda Wolfram (ed.), *Tradition and Innovation in Late- and Postbyzantine Liturgical Chant. Acta of the Congress held at Hernen Castle, the Netherlands, in April 2005* (Leuven, Paris, Dudley, MA: A. A. Bredius Foundation Peeters), 225–282.

Kyriazides, Agathangelos (1896), 'Ἐν Ἄνθος τῆς καθ' ἡμᾶς ἐκκλησιαστικῆς μουσικῆς', (Constantinople).

Lainas, Th. A. (1960), 'Ἡ Μητρόπολις Νέων Πατρῶν Ὑπάτης,' *Στερεοελλαδικὴ Ἑστία*, 1.

—— (1973), 'Γερμανὸς μητροπολίτης Νέων Πατρῶν – Ὑπάτης, μελῳδὸς τῆς φθίας,' *Στερεὰ Ἑλλάς*, 5 (48), 40–42.

Lampros, Spyridōn Paulou (1888), *Κατάλογος τῶν ἐν ταῖς βιβλιοθήκαις τοῦς ἁγίου ὄρους Ἑλληνικῶν κωδίκων* (Athens).

—— (1926), 'Κατάλογος κωδίκων τῆς Ἱστορικῆς καὶ Ἐθνολογικῆς Ἑταιρείας,' *Νέος Ἑλληνομνήμων*, 20.

—— (1966), *Catalogue of the Greek manuscripts on Mount Athos* (Amsterdam: A. M. Hakkert).

Levy, Kenneth (1963), 'A Hymn for Thursday in Holy Week,' *Journal of the American Musicological Society*, 16, 127–175.

—— (1976), 'Le "tournant décisif" dans l'histoire de la Musique Byzantine, 1071–1261', *Rapports et Co-rapports — Art et Archéologie. Congrès International d'Études Byzantines XVe* (Athens), 281–288.

Liddell, Henry George, Scott, Robert, and Jones, Henry Stuart (1996), *A Greek-English lexicon* (9th edn.; Oxford: Clarendon Press).

Lingas, Alexander (2004), 'Preliminary Reflections on Studying the Liturgical Place of Byzantine and Slavonic Melismatic Chant', in Gerda Wolfram (ed.), *Palaeobyzantine Notations III. Acts of the Congress held at Hermen Castle, The Netherlands, in March 2001* (Leuven, Paris, Dudley, MA: AA. Bredius Foundation Peeters), 147–156.

Mai, Angelo (1839), *Spicilegium romanum*, 10 vols. (Rome: Typis Collegii Urbani).

Manuel Chrysaphēs and Conomos, Dimitri E. (1985), *The treatise of Manuel Chrysaphes, the Lampadarios, On the theory of the art of chanting and on certain erroneous views that some hold about it (Mount Athos, Iviron Monastery MS 1120, July 1458)* (Monumenta musicae Byzantinae Corpus scriptorum de re musica, 2; Vienna: Verlag der Østerreichischen Akademie der Wissenschaften).

Manussaca, M. (1959), 'Recherches sur la vie de Jean Plousiadenos (Joseph de Méthone) 1419–1500,' *Revue des Études Byzantines*, 17, 28–51.

Mazera-Mamalē, Sebē (2007), *Τὰ Μεγαλυνάρια Θεοτοκία τῆς Ψαλτικῆς Τέχνης*, ed. Grēgorios Th. Stathēs (Meletai, 15; Athens: Institute of Byzantine Musicology).
Meibomius, Marcus (1652), *Antiquæ auctores septem Græce et Latine, M. Meibomius restituit ac notis explicavit* (Amstelodami: Apud L. Elzevirium).
Metsakes, Kariophiles (1971), *Βυζαντινή Ὑμνογραφία* (Thessalonike).
Montagu, Jeremy (1976), *The World of Medieval and Renaissance Musical Instruments* (Newton Abbot: David and Charles).
Morgan, Maureen M. (1972), 'The musical setting of Psalm 134 — the Polyeleos,' *Studies in Eastern Chant*, III, 112–123.
Murray, James Augustus Henry, Sir (1933), *The Oxford English dictionary: being a corrected re-issue with an introduction, supplement, and bibliography of a new English dictionary on historical principles*, 13 vols. (Oxford: Clarendon Press).
Orthodox Eastern Church and Apostolikē Diakonia (1960), *Τριῴδιον κατανυκτικόν* (Athens: Apostolikē Diakonia).
—— (1967–1973), *Μηναῖον*, 12 vols. (Athens: Apostolikē Diakonia of the Church of Greece).
—— (1976), *Παρακλητική, ἤτοι Ὀκτώηχος ἡ μεγάλη* (Athens: Apostolikē Diakonia of the Church of Greece).
Orthodox Eastern Church, Bartholomaios Koutloumousianos, and Andreola, Francesco (1837), *Πεντηκοστάριον χαρμόσυνον* (En Venetia: Ek tēs Ellēnikēs typographias Phranseskou Andreōla).
Orthodox Eastern Church., Mary, and Kallistos (1969), *The festal Menaion* (Service books of the Orthodox Church; London: Faber) 564 p.
Panagiotopoulos, D. G. (1947), *Θεωρία καὶ πρᾶξις τῆς βυζαντινῆς ἐκκλησιαστικῆς μουσικῆς* (Athens).
Papadopoulos, Georgios (1890), *Συμβολαὶ εἰς τὴν ἱστορίαν τῆς παρ' ἡμῖν ἐκκλησιαστικῆς Μουσικῆς* (Athens).
Papadopoulos-Kerameus, Athanasios (1891–1915), *Ἱεροσολυμιτικὴ βιβλιοθήκη*, 5 vols. (Αὐτοκρατορικὸς ὀρθόδοξος Παλαιστίνος σύλλογος; en Petroupolei).
Paschos, P. B. (1978), *Ὁ Ματθαῖος Βλάσταρης καὶ τὸ ὑμνογραφικὸν ἔργον του* (Thessalonike).
Patrinelis, Christos G. (1969), 'Πρωτοψάλται, Λαμπαδάριοι καὶ Δομέστικοι τῆς Μεγάλης Ἐκκλησίας (1453–1821),' *Μνημοσύνη*, 2, 63–95.
—— (1973), 'Protopsaltæ, Lampadarii, and Domestikoi of the Great Church during the post-Byzantine Period (1453–1821),' *Studies In Eastern Chant*, III (London), 141–170.
Petresco, J. D. (1932), *Les Idiomèles et le Canon de l'office de Noël* (Études de paléographie musicale byzantine — Bucharest; Paris: P. Geunther).
Petrov, Stoian V. and Kodov, Khristo (1973), *Starobulgarski muzikalni pametnitsi [Old Bulgarian Musical Documents]* (Sofia: Nauka i Izkustvo).

Philostorgius Cappadox (1981), 'Historia ecclesiastica (framenta ap. Photium)', in F. Winkelmann (ed.), *Philostorgius. Kirchengeschichte* (Die griechischen christlichen Schriftsteller; Berlin: Akademie Verlag), 4–150.

Phountoules, Ioannes (1976), 'Μαρτυρίαι τοῦ Θεσσαλονίκης Συμεὼν περὶ τῶν ναῶν τῆς Θεσσαλονίκης,' *Ἐπιστηπονικὴ Ἐπετηρὸς Θεολογικῆς Σχολῆς Ἀριστοτέλειον Πανεπιστήμιον Θεσσαλονίκης*, 21, 125–186.

Pitra, J. B. (1876), *Analecta sacra spicilegio Solesmensi parata*, 8 vols. (Parisiis: A. Jouby et Roger).

Psachos, K. A. (1917), *Ἡ παρασημαντικὴ τῆς βυζαντινῆς μουσικῆς* (Athens).

R. Palikarova, Verdeil (1953), *La musique byzantine chez les Bulgares et les Russes (du IXe au XIVe siécle)* (Série Subsidia; Copenhague: E. Munksgaard).

Raasted, Jørgen (1966), *Intonation formulas and modal signatures in Byzantine musical manuscripts* (Union académique internationale Monumenta musicae Byzantinae Subsidia, 7; Copenhagen: E. Munksgaard).

—— (1968), *Hirmologium Sabbaiticum. Codex Monasterii S. Sabbae 83; phototypice depictus*, 3 vols. (Union académique internationale Monumenta musicae, Byzantinae, 8:1, 8:2, 1; Hauniae: Munksgaard).

Rallēs, G. A. and Potlēs, M. (1852–1859), *Σύνταγμα τῶν θείων καὶ ἱερῶν κανόνων*, 6 vols. (Athens: Ek tēs tupografias G. Xartophulakos).

—— (1934), 'Περὶ τοῦ ἀξιώματος τοῦ λαμπαδαρίου,' *Πρακτικὰ Ἀκαδημίας Ἀθηνῶν*, 9, 259–261.

—— (1936), 'Περὶ τοῦ ἀξιώματος τοῦ πρωτοψάλτου,' *Πρακτικὰ Ἀκαδημίας Ἀθηνῶν*, 11, 66–69.

Riemann, Hugo (1909), *Die byzantinische Notenschrift im 10. bis 15. Jahrhundert* (Leipzig: Breitkopf und Järtel).

Rousanus, Pachomius (1903), 'Ἑρμηνεία εἰς τὴν Μουσικήν,' *Φόρμιγξ*, 2 (8).

Schartau, Bjarne (2008), 'Observations on the Transmission of the Kalophonic Œuvre of Ioannes (and Georgios) PLousiadenos', in Gerda Wolfram (ed.), *Tradition and Innovation in Late- and Postbyzantine Liturgical Chant. Acta of the Congress held at Hernen Castle, the Netherlands, in April 2005* (Leuven, Paris, Dudley, MA: A. A. Bredius Foundation Peeters), 129–158.

Socrates Scholasticus (1865), 'Historia Ecclesiastica', in J.-P. Migne (ed.), *Patrologiae Cursus Completus, Series Graeca Prior* (67; Paris), 30–842.

—— (1886), 'Socrates and Sozomenus Ecclesiastical Histories', in Philip Schaff (ed.), *Nicene and Post-Nicene Fathers Series II* (II; New York: Christian Literature Publishing Co.).

—— (2004–2007), 'Historia ecclesiastica', in P. Maraval and P. Périchon (eds.), *Socrate de Constantinople, Histoire ecclésiastique (Livres I–VII)* (Sources Chrétiennes 477,

493, 505, 506; Paris: Éditions du Cerf), 477: 44–262; 493: 18–258; 505:22–354; 506:20–158.

Spyrakou, Euangelia (2008), *Οι Χοροί Ψαλτών κατά την βυζαντινή παράδοση*, ed. Gr. Th. Stathes (Meletai, 14; Athens: Institute of Byzantine Musicology).

Stancev, Kr. and Tonceva, Elena (1978), 'Bulgarskite Pesnopenia bâb Byzantiiskite Akolytii,' *Mousikoznanie*, 2, 39–70.

Stathē, Penelopē (1973), "Ὁ φίλος τοῦ Κοραῆ Δημήτριος Λῶτος καὶ τὰ μουσικὰ χειρόγραφά του,' *Ἐρανιστής*, 10, 137–186.

Stathēs, Grēgorios Th. (1971), "Ἡ σύγχυση τῶν τριῶν Πέτρων (δηλ. Μπερεκέτη, Πελοποννησίου, Βυζαντίου),' *Βυζαντινά*, 3, 213–251.

—— (1972a), 'I Manoscritti e la tradizione musicale Bizantino-Sinaitica,' *Θεολογία*, 43 (1–2), 271–308.

—— (1972b), "Ἡ Βυζαντινὴ Μουσικὴ στὴ Λατρεία καὶ στὴν ἐπιστήμη· εἰσαγωγικὴ τετραλογία,' *Βυζαντινά*, 4, 389–438.

—— (1973), 'Problems connected with the transcription of the Old Byzantine Notation into the Pentagram', in Søren Sørensen and Peter Ryom (eds.), *International Musicological Society: Report of the Eleventh Congress, Copenhagen 1972* (2; Copenhagen: Wilhelm Hensen), 778–782.

—— (1975), "Ἡ παλαιὰ βυζαντινὴ σημειογραφία καὶ τὸ πρόβλημα μεταγραφῆς της εἰς τὸ πεντάγραμμον,' *Βυζαντινά*, 7, 193–220; pinakes 1–32.

—— (1975–), *Τὰ χειρόγραφα Βυζαντινῆς μουσικῆς· Ἅγιον Ὄρος*, 7 vols. (Athens: Ἱερὰ Σύνοδος τῆς Ἐκκλησίας τῆς Ἑλλάδος).

—— (1976), 'Τὸ ἀρχαιότερο, χρονολογημένο τὸ ἔτος 1562, δημοτικὸ τραφούδι μελισμένο μὲ τὴ βυζαντινὴ σημειογραφία,' *Πρακτικὰ Ἀκαδημίας Ἀθηνῶν*, 51, 184–219.

—— (1977), *Ἡ Δεκαπεντασύλλαβος Ὑμνογραφία ἐν τῇ Βυζαντινῇ Μελοποιίᾳ*, eds Μητροπολίτης Κοζάνης Διονύσιος and Γρ. Θ. Στάθης (Μελέται 1; Athens: Ἵδρυμα Βυζαντινῆς Μουσικολογίας).

—— (1978), *Ἡ ἐξήγησις τῆς παλαιᾶς Βυζαντινῆς σημειογραφίας*, eds Μητροπολίτης Κοζάνης Διονύσιος and Γρ. Θ. Στάθης (Μελέται 2; Athens: Ἵδρυμα Βυζαντινῆς Μουσικολογίας).

—— (1979a), *Οἱ ἀναγραμματισμοὶ καὶ τὰ μαθήματα τῆς βυζαντινῆς μελοποιίας*, eds Grēgorios Th. Stathēs and Dionysios metropolitan of Kozanē (Meletai, 3; Athens: Institute of Byzantine Musicology).

—— (1979b), 'An analysis of the sticheron Τὸν ἥλιον κρύψαντα by Germanos bishop of New Patras,' *Studies in Eastern Chant*, IV, 177–227.

—— (1983), 'The "abridgments" of Byzantine and post-Byzantine compositions,' *Cahiers de l'Institut du Moyen-Âge Grec et Latin*, 44, 16–38.

—— (1989), "Ἡ ἀσματικὴ διαφοροποίηση, ὅπως καταγράφεται στὸν κώδικα ΕΒΕ 2458 τοῦ ἔτους 1336', ΚΒ´ *Δημήτρια – Ἐπιστημονικὸ συμπόσιο. Χριστιανικὴ Θεσσαλονίκη*

– Παλαιολόγειος ἐποχή. Πατριαρχικὸν Ἵδρυμα Πατερικῶν Μελετῶν. Ἱερὰ Μονὴ Βλατάδων· 29–31 Ὀκτωβρίου 1987 (Thessalonike), 165–211.

—— (1992), 'Μπαλάσης ἱερεὺς καὶ νομοφύλαξ (β΄ ἥμισυ ΙΖ΄ αἰ.)· ἡ ζωὴ καὶ τὸ ἔργο του', Ἐθνικὸ καὶ Καποδιστριακὸ Πανεπιστήμιο Ἀθηνῶν. Ἐπίσημοι λόγοι ἀπὸ 26.2.1986 ἕως 31.8.1988 (29; Athens), 717–747.

—— (1997), 'Ἡ Μέθοδος τῶν θέσεων τοῦ Ἰωάννου Κουκουζέλη καὶ ἡ ἐφαρμογή της', in C. Troelsgård (ed.), *Byzantine Chant: tradition and reform. Acts of a Meeting held at the Danish Institute at Athens, 1993* (Monographs of the Danish Institute at Athens; Athens: The Danish Institute at Athens), 189–199 and 203–204.

—— (1998), 'Γερμανὸς ἀρχιερεὺς Νέων Πατρῶν (β΄ ἥμισυ ιζ΄ αἰῶνος)· ἡ ζωὴ καὶ τὸ ἔργο του', *Ἐθνικὸ καὶ Καποδιστριακὸ Πανεπιστήμιο Ἀθηνῶν. Ἐπίσημοι λόγοι ἀπὸ 31.8.1988 ἕως 31.8.1991* (30; Athens).

—— (2001), 'Οἱ "συντμήσεις" βυζαντινῶν καὶ μεταβυζαντινῶν συνθέσεων', *Τιμὴ πρὸς τὸν διδάσκαλον* (Athens: Anatoles to periechema), 588–612.

—— (2007), 'Τὰ Πρωτόγραφα τῆς ἐξηγήσεως', *Greek Research in Australia. Proceedings of the Biennial International Conference of Greek Studies. Flinders University, June 2005* (Adelaide), 378–387.

Stathēs, Grēgorios Th. and Maïstores tēs psaltikēs tecknēs (1988), 'Ἰωάννης Παπαδόπουλος ὁ Κουκουζέλης καὶ Μαΐστωρ (1270 περίπου – α΄ ἥμ. ιδ΄ αἰῶνος)', (Byzantine and Post-Byzantine Composers 6; Athens: Institute of Byzantine Musicology).

Stathēs, Grēgorios Th., Stanitsas, Thr., and Maïstores tēs psaltikēs tecknēs (1975), 'Πέτρος Μπερεκέτης ὁ μελωδός (α΄ τέταρτο τοῦ ΙΗ΄ αἰ.)· ἡ ζωὴ καὶ τὸ ἔργο τοῦ', (IBM 101 [I–II]; Athens).

—— (1977), 'Γρηγόριος Πρωτοψάλτης ὁ Βυζάντιος (1778–1821)· ἡ ζωὴ καὶ τὸ ἔργο του', (IBM 102 [I–II]; Athens).

Stephanides, Basileios (1900–1902), 'Σχεδίασμα περὶ μουσικῆς, ἰδιαίτερον ἐκκλησιαστικῆς', *Ἐργασίαι Ἐκκλησιαστικοῦ Μουσικοῦ Συλλόγου εἰς Παράρτημα Ἐκκλησιαστικῆς Ἀληθείας (Κωνσταντινούπολις)*, 5, 207–279.

Strunk, W. Oliver (1962), 'A Cypriote in Venice', *Natalicia musicologica: Knud Jeppesen, septuagenario* (Hafniae: Wilhelm Hansen), 271–373.

—— (1966a), *Specimina notationum antiquiorum: folia selecta ex variis codicibus saec. x, xi, & xii phototypice depicta* (Monumenta musicae Byzantinae, 7; Hauniae: E. Munksgaards forlag).

—— (1966b), 'H. J. W. Tillyard and the Recovery of a Lost Fragment', *Studies in Eastern Chant*, I, 95–103.

—— (1977a), 'Melody Construction in Byzantine Chant', *Essays on music in the Byzantine world* (New York: W. W. Norton), 191–201.

—— (1977b), 'The Byzantine Office at Hagia Sophia', *Essays on music in the Byzantine world* (New York: W. W. Norton), 112–150.
—— (1977c), 'St. Gregory Nazianzus and the Proper Hymns for Easter', *Essays on Music in the Byzantine World* (New York: W. W. Norton), 55–67.
—— (1977d), 'S. Salvatore di Messina and the Musical Tradition of Magna Graecia', *Essays on music in the Byzantine world* (New York: W. W. Norton), 45–54.
Symeon of Thessalonike and Simmons, H. L. N. (trans.) (1984), *Treatise on Prayer: an explanation of the services conducted in the Orthodox Church*, ed. N. M. Vaporis (The Archbishop Iakovos Library of Ecclesiastical and Historical Sources; Brookline: Hellenic College Press).
Symeon Thessalonicensis (1865), 'De sacra precatione', in J.-P. Migne (ed.), *Patrologiae Cursus Completus, Series Graeca Prior* (155; Paris), 535–670.
Tardo, Lorenzo (1931), 'I codici melurgici della Vaticana e il contributo alla musica bizantina del monachismo greco della Magna Grecia', *Archivo Storico per la Calabria e Lucania* (Rome).
—— (1935), 'Un manoscritto Καλοφωνικὸν del sec-XIII nella collezione melurgica bizantina della Biblioteca Universitaria di Messina', *Εἰς μνήμην Σπυρίδωνος Λάμπρου* (Athens), 170–176.
—— (1938), *L'antica melurgia bizantina nell'interpretazione della Scuola monastica di Grottaferrata* (Collezione meridionale Ser III: Il mezzogiorno artistico; Grottaferrata: S. Nilo, Badia greca di Grottaferrata di Maria Santissima).
Terzopoulos, Kōnstantinos (2004), *Ὁ πρωτοψάλτης τῆς Μεγάλης τοῦ Χριστοῦ Ἐκκλησίας Κωνσταντῖνος Βυζάντιος († 30 Ἰουνίου 1862)· ἡ συμβολή του στὴν Ψαλτικὴ Τέχνη*, ed. Gr. Th. Stathis (Meletai, 9; Athens: Institute of Byzantine Musicology).
Theodōros Phōkaeus (1842), *Κρηπὶς τοῦ θεωρητικοῦ καὶ πρακτικοῦ τῆς ἐκκλησιαστικῆς μουσικῆς* (Constantinople).
Theodōros Phōkaeus and Gregorios Prōtopsaltēs (1835), *Εἱρμολόγιον καλοφωνικόν* (En Konstantinoupolei: Ek tēs typographias Kastrou eis Galatan).
Thibaut, Jean Baptiste (1907), *Origine byzantine de la notation neumatique de l'église latine* (Bibl musicologique, 3; Par.).
Thodberg, Christian and Hamann, Holger (1966), *Der byzantinische Alleluiarionzyklus: Studien im kurzen Psaltikonstil* (Union académique internationale Monumenta musicae Byzantinae Subsidia, 8; Kopenhagen: E. Munksgaard).
Tiby, Ottavio (1938), *La musica bizantina: teoria e storia* (Letteratura musicale, 13; Milano: Fratelli Bocca).
Tillyard, H. J. W. (1935), *Handbook of the Middle Byzantine musical notation* (Union académique internationale Monumenta musicae byzantinae Subsidia, I, fasc l; Copenhague: Levin & Munksgaard).

Tomadakes, Nikolaos (1965a), Εἰσαγωγὴ εἰς τὴν Βυζαντινὴν Φιλολογίαν· βυζαντινὴ ὑμνογραφία καὶ ποίησις (Athens).
—— (1965b), Κλεὶς τῆς Βυζαντινῆς Φολολογίας (Athens).
Touliatos-Banker, D. (1976), 'The "chanted" vespers Service,' Κληρονομία, 8 (α), 107–126.
—— (1984), *The Byzantine Amomos Chant of the Fourteenth and Fifteenth Centuries*, ed. Panagiotis C. Christou (Analekta Blatadon; Thessaloniki: Patriarchal Institute for Patristic Studies).
Trembelas, Pan. (1949), Ἐκλογὴ ἑλληνικῆς ὀρθοδόξου ὑμνογραφίας (Athens).
Troelgård, Christian (2004), 'Thirteenth-century Byzantine Melismatic Chant and the Development of the Kalophonic Style', in Gerda Wolfram (ed.), *Palaeobyzantine Notations III. Acts of the Congress held at Hermen Castle, The Netherlands, in March 2001* (Eastern Christian Studies; Leuven, Paris, Dudley, MA: AA. Bredius Foundation Peeters), 67–90.
—— (2008), 'Long Intonations and Kalophonia: Traces of Stylistic Development in Late Byzantine Echemata', in Gerda Wolfram (ed.), *Tradition and Innovation in Late- and Postbyzantine Liturgical Chant. Acta of the Congress held at Hernen Castle, the Netherlands, in April 2005* (Eastern Christian Studies; Leuven, Paris, Dudley, MA: A. A. Bredius Foundation Peeters), 65–78.
Troelsgård, Christian (1997), 'The Development of a Didactic Poem. Some remarks on the Ἴσον, ὀλίγον, ὀξεῖα by Ioannes Glykys', in Christian Troelgård (ed.), *Byzantine Chant: tradition and reform. Acts of a Meeting held at the Danish Institute at Athens, 1993* (Monographs of the Danish Institute at Athens; Athens: The Danish Institute at Athens), 69–86.
Trypanis, C. A. (1968), *Fourteen early Byzantine cantica* (Wiener byzantinistische Studien, Bd 5; Vienna: Böhlaus) 171 p.
Velimirović, Miloš M. (1962), 'Liturgical Drama in Byzantium and Russia', *Dumbarton Oaks Papers*, 16, 351–385.
—— (1966a), 'Byzantine Composers in MS Athens 2406', *Essays presented to Egon Wellesz* (Oxford: Clarendon Press), 7–18.
—— (1966b), 'The Ptoemiac Psalm of Byzantine Vespers', in Laurence D. Berman and Elliot Forbes (eds.), *Words and Music: the scholar's view* (Cambridge, Mass.: Dept. of Music, Harvard University), 317–337.
Verpeaux, Jean and Codinus, George (1976), *Pseudo-Kodinos: traité des offices* (Monde byzantin, 1; Paris: Éditions du Centre national de la Recherche scientifique).
Vogel, Marie and Gardthausen, Viktor Emil (1909), *Die griechischen Schreiber des Mittelalters und der Renaissance* (Leipzig: O. Harrassowitz).
Vogt, Albert (1967), *Constantin VII Porphyrogénète Le livre des cérémonies* (Collection byzantine; Paris: Belles Lettres).

Wellesz, Egon (1916), 'Die Kirchenmusik im byzantinischen Reiche,' *Oriens Christianus*, 6 (Series II), 91–125.

—— (1947), *Eastern elements in western chant: studies in the early history of ecclesiastical music* (Monumenta musicae Byzantinae Subsidia, 2; Boston: Byzantine Institute).

—— (1980), *A history of Byzantine music and hymnography* (2nd edn.; Oxford: Clarendon Press).

Werner, Eric (1948), 'The origin of the eight modes of music (Octoechos): a study in musical symbolism,' *Hebrew Union College annual*, 21, 211–255.

Williams, Edward V. (1968), 'John Koukouzeles' reform of Byzantine chanting for great Vespers in the fourteenth century,' (Yale University).

—— (1971), 'The Treatment of the Text in the Kalophonic chanting of Psalm 2', *Studies in Eastern Chant* (Oxford), 173–193.

—— (1972), 'A Byzantine "Ars Nova": the 14th century Reforms of John Koukouzeles in the chanting of Great Vespers', *Aspects of the Balkans: continuity and change. Contributions to the International Balkan Conference held at UCLA, October 23–28, 1969* (The Hague: Mouton), 211–229.

Wulstan, David (1971), 'The origin of the modes', in Miloš M. Velimirović and Egon Wellesz (eds.), *Studies in Eastern Chant* (II; Oxford: Oxford University Press), 5–20.

Zakythenos, D. (1972), *Τὸ Βυζάντιον ἀπὸ τοῦ 1071 μέχρι τοῦ 1453* (Athens).

Zerbou, hieromonachou, Spyridonos, ed. (1862), *Εὐχολόγιον τὸ Μέγα* (Benetia: Ek tes hellenikes typographias tou Phoinikos).

Index of manuscripts

ATHOS

Chilandar
970	39 n. 104

Dionysiou
564	130 n. 77
569	119
569	130 n. 79, 154 n. 43
570	15 n. 40, 74 n. 45, 85 n. 61, 126 n. 61, 128 n. 68, 128 n. 70, 130 n. 79
707	134 n. 99

Docheiariou
334	119
337	110 n. 11
338	110 n. 11, 132 n. 86
339	119, 132 n. 86, 132 n. 88
341	150 n. 40
342	124
361	44 n. 116
379	18 n. 54, 119, 129 n. 74, 131 n. 82, 144 n. 26
381	123
388	123

Gregoriou
3	92 n. 74
4	110 n. 11, 111 n. 13

Hagiou Pavlou
101	117 n. 34, 119
128	72 n. 40, 119, 129
146	115 n. 24, 124, 133 n. 93

Iviron
96	61 n. 23
911	118 n. 36
951	168 n. 80
960	119
961	85 n. 62
964	61 n. 23, 118 n. 35, 119, 131 n. 81, 144 n. 25, 145 n. 28
967	118 n. 36, 119
970	39 n. 103, 154 n. 43
972	116 n. 30, 121 n. 45, n. 46
973	19 n. 54, 108, 144 n. 26, 148 n. 36
974	108, 153 n. 42
975	117, 119
976	117 n. 34
977	117 n. 34
978	118 n. 36
980	118 n. 36
984	108
985	108, 142 n. 18–19, 153 n. 42
988	118 n. 36, 119
991	61 n. 23, 74, 89 n. 69, 90

314   Index of manuscripts

1000	119		n. 60, 128 n. 69, 150
1006	147 n. 33		n. 40
1048	25 n. 65		
1051	118 n. 36	Koutloumousiou	
1073	115	399	108
1074	26 n. 68	427	119, 131
1079	118 n. 36	431	119
1080	114 n. 23, 115 n. 25, 124	438	117 n. 34, 119
		448	123
1089	115	455	92
1108	30 n. 77	456	73 n. 43, 93, 108, 109, 109 n. 9
1112	118 n. 36		
1120	11 n. 29, 12 n. 31, n. 32, n. 33, 22 n. 57, n. 58, 86 n. 64, 89 n. 68, 91 n. 72, 96, 97–107, 136 n. 1, 137 n. 5, 138 n. 6, 139 n. 7–8, 140 n. 9, n. 11, 141 n. 16, 142 n. 17, 142 n. 20, n. 23, 144 n. 26, 147 n. 32, 154 n. 45	457	11 n. 29, 12 b. 35, 19 n. 54, 93, 108, 109 n. 9, 125, 144 n. 26
		462	119
		588	12 n. 30, 18 n. 54
		M. Lavra	
		116	74 n. 44
		Γ 67	42, 64 n. 27
1141	115 n. 25	Γ 76	42
1150	115 n. 25	Λ 166	118 n. 36
1154	26 n. 69	Ε 148	108
1155	26 n. 69	Ε 173	108
1156	118 n. 36	Ε 46	108
1189	114 n. 23	Ι 178	108
1189	118 n. 35	Ι 185	108
1192	26 n. 70	Ι 79	108
1203	115	Κ 158	26 n. 70
1204	85 n. 63, 118		
1205	126 n. 63, 127 n. 64, 129	Panteleimon	
		1008	19 n. 54, 113 n. 22, 150 n. 40
1250	34, 39, 142 n. 21		
		1207	134 n. 99
Konstamonitou		901	113 n. 22
86	10, 11 n. 28, 13 n. 34, n 35, 91 n. 71, 93 n. 76, 108, 126	917	27 n. 71
		927	19 n. 54
		938	131 n. 82

Index of manuscripts

994	114 n. 23	**ATHENS**	
438	117 n. 34		
		Hidryma Byzantines Mousikologian (IBM)	
Philotheou			
122	108, 148 n. 36	01	150 n. 39
125	156 n. 50		
135	119	Historikes kai Ethnologikes Hetaireias (IEE)	
136	145 n. 28		
137	141 n. 14	305	15 n. 43
Vatopedi		National Library of Greece	
1498	61 n. 23, 117	866	92
1527	117	884	127 n. 65
		886	xv, 121 n. 45, 239, 240, 243–247
Xenophontos			
120	43 n. 113, 165 n. 67	899	55 n. 9, 84 n. 61, 108
128	38 n. 99, 148 n. 34–35	904	108
137	124 n. 54	905	108
159	26 n. 69	906	108
183	43 n. 113	917	40 n. 107
330	124 n. 55	937	117 n. 34
		938	117 n. 34
Xeropotamou		2047	11 n. 27
120	165 n. 68	2061	108
276	119	2062	108
279	27 n. 72	2401	55 n. 9, 108
282	76 n. 47	2406	55 n. 9, 87, 92, 92 n. 75, 93, 93 n. 79, 108, 112 n. 15, 130 n. 75, 141 n. 13
287	113 n. 21, 115, 124		
289	44 n. 116		
295	44 n. 116		
307	110 n. 10, 130 n. 76, n. 77	2444	55 n. 9, 108
		2454	108
318	136 n. 1	2456	55 n. 9
323	62 n. 24	2458	xiv, 22 n. 57, n. 58, 28, 51, 54 n. 8, 56, 60 n. 20, 70, 72, 73, 88 n. 66, 95, 108, 112 n. 15, 112 n. 18, 121 n. 43,
330	15 n. 43, 110 n. 11, 114 n. 23, 132 n. 86		
383	119, 239		
383	61 n. 21, 91 n. 71		

	n. 44, 127, 148 n. 36, 153 n. 42		73–74, 174, 207–214, 239, 243–247, 250–253, 257–292
2599	55 n. 9, 108, 141 n. 13		
2600	108	733	61 n. 22, 74 n. 44, 81 n. 57, 120 n. 39, 167 n. 75, 174, 214–221, 240
2601	93		
2604	116 n. 30		
2622	108		
2837	108	734	120 n. 39, 174, 222–226
2837	55 n. 9, 108		
		754	176

CONSTANTINOPLE

FIRENZE

Metochion Panagiou Taphou (MΠT)

703	57 n. 15, 110, 136 n. 1, 137 n. 4, 175	Biblioteca Medicea Laurenziana Ashburnhamense	
704	110, 175	64	29, 67
705	110, 175		
706	110, 120 n. 40, 164 n. 60–62, 174, 175, 226–234	METEORA	

Holy Transfiguration Monastery

710	115 n. 26, 124 n. 56	44	117 n. 34
711	115 n. 26, 124 n. 56	217	117 n. 34
712	175, 234–237		
713	174, 175	MESSINA	
714	174, 175		
722	110, 120 n. 40, 174, 175	Bibl. Regionale Universitaria (San Salvatore)	
727	72 n. 40, 120 n. 39, 174, 176–180	129	29
		161	56 n. 12, 68, 121 n. 43
728	92, 120 n. 39, 174, 180–185	MOSCOW	
729	79 n. 54, 81 n. 57, 90 n. 70, 92, 120 n. 39, 174, 185–192	Moscow Cathedral — Uspensky Sobor	
		09	29
730	192–199		
731	79 n. 55, 89 n. 69, 120 n. 39, 174, 200–207	PARIS	
732	Xv, 76 n. 47, 78 n. 51, 80 n. 56, 81 n. 57, 120 n. 39, 159 n. 54, 166 n.	Bibliotèque nationale de France (BnF)	
		Coislin 229	42

Index of manuscripts

Coislin 41   112 n. 16
Suppl. Gr. 1047   25 n. 61
Suppl. Gr. 1135   39 n. 104

PATMOS

Monastery of Saint John the Theologian
221   29

ROME

Grottaferrata Badia Graeca
Cod. Crypt. Γ.γ.4   56 n. 12, 68

SINAI

Saint Catherine's Monastery
Gr. 754   34
Gr. 1218   34
Gr. 1234   117 n. 34
Gr. 1256   67, 126
Gr. 1259   117 n. 34
Gr. 1262   68 n. 34, 122
Gr. 1527   112 n. 15

ST. PETERSBURG-LENINGRAD

National Library of Russia
121   67, 127

Index of topics and names

Aanes 14 n. 37
Abasiōtēs 66
abridgements *see* syntmēsis
acrostics 4 n. 6
agathon 90, 98
aghiopolitiki notation 43
aghioreitiki notation 43
agogē 24, 25 n. 60, 164 n. 64
ainoi 22–24
ainos 4
Akakios Chalkeopoulos 38 n. 98, 40
Akathistos 96, 108, 114, 120–124, 128, 143, 145, 153, 168
Akathistos, of Benediktos Episkopopoulos 131; of Iohannes Glykys 52–53; of Iohannes Kladas 143, 157, 174, 175; of kyr Iohannes the lampadarios 106
Akolouthiai 46, 51, 95–96
Alexios, hiereus bouleutēs ek Krētēs 131 n. 82
allagē 58
allagma xiii, 70, 86, 88, 101, 106, 125
Allelouiarion 23, 56, 68, 83 n. 59, 141
ambitus 163, 166
Ambrosian melos 5
Amomos 31, 52–55, 87–88, 97, 104, 128 n. 69, 141–142, 154–155
anagnōstēs 11
anagram – anagrammatismos 22, 31, 53, 59, 61, 66, 70–75, 82–83, 112, 157, 293–295
Anakaras, ho 91, 113
analogion 9

analytical notation *see* New Method
Ananes 14 n. 37, 45 n. 121, 111
Anapardas 67 n. 33
anaphōnēma xiii, 55, 86, 87–88, 101
anapodismos 53, 60, 70, 75–76, 81–82
anastasima, troparia 22–24, 146
Anastasimatarion 7 n. 14, 25, 145, 151;
    old – *palaion* 23; of Petros
    Peloponnēsios 23–24, 30;
    Syntomon 30
Anastasios Baïas 110
Anastasios Rapsaniōtēs 124, 133
Anatolios, the hagioritēs 109, 119, 124
anatrichisma 42
Ancient Greek music 17, 32 n. 80
Andreas 101
Andreas Sigeros 105, 121
Andrianoupolitēs 67 n. 33
Andronicus II xiii, 63, 65, 294
Aneanes 14 n. 37, 159 n. 55
Aneōtēs *see* Michael Aneōtēs
Angelos hiereus ex Athēnōn 131
Annunciation, feast of 77, 79 n. 55, 129 n. 74
Anoixantaria 22–23, 31, 51, 59 n. 19, 88, 110, 128 n. 69, 146, 150
Anthimos, abbot of Lavra 130
Anthologiai 17 n. 49, 28 n. 74, 43 n. 113, 62 n. 24, 96, 110 n. 12, 113, 116, 118, 132 n. 86
antikenōma 45 n. 119
antiphonal 22 n. 58, 112 n. 16, 168
antiphōnia 14, 17

antiphons 21, 22, 24, 27, 31, 51, 52, 55, 75 n. 46, 88, 138
antiphony 14, 17, 18
Antoniades, Euangelos 54 n. 8
Antonios Episkopopoulos 123 n. 50, 131
Antonios, oikonomos of the Great Church 109, 133
Anyphantēs, kratēma 99
ap' esō exō 42
aphōna sēmadia 16, 33, 44
apo chorou 12, 29, 81, 89 n. 67, 125, 141 n. 13, 160, 243, 250
apoderma 42
apolytarisma 92 n. 74
apolytikia 22, 24, 85, 134 n. 99, 146, 153, 168
aposticha 24, 30, 77, 145, 152
Apostolos Kōnstas Chios 15, 25 n. 60, 120
apostrophos 42
apothema 42
Archangels, feast of 79 n. 53, 140
archon of the kontakion 10
archontika 52, 55, 104, 142, 233
arga — argon 19 n. 54, 24–25
arga kai isa 144 n. 26
argon melos, dromos 24–27, 50 n. 3
argos meta melous 19 n. 54
Aristoxenus Tarentinus 18 n. 53, 32 n. 80
Arkadios, deacon 150
ars perfecta 9
Arsenios mikros 113 n. 22
asma 4, 54
asmatic form of composition 50
asmatic office 11 n. 27, 49, 75 n. 46, 109, 294
asmatika 22, 23, 31, 53–54, 63, 93, 112; cherubic 56, 141; doxastika 52; heirmoi 128–129; nekrōsimon 142; trisagia 52, 140–143, 176

Asmatikon, codex 28–29, 50
asmatologia 62
Athanasios, hieromonachos Ibēritēs 109, 132
Athanasios, Kapetanos 114 n. 23, 115
Athanasios, Patriarch from Andrianoupolis 39, 40, 132, 148 n. 35
Athanasios, scribe 127 n. 65
automelon 5

Balasios hiereus 25, 26, 28, 30, 38 n. 98, 39, 40, 109, 113 n. 22, 124, 132, 142 n. 21, 148 n. 35, 151 n. 40, 168, 174, 175
Bamboudakes, E. 111 n. 13
bareia 42, 45 n. 119
Bartholomaios, domestikos of the Lavra 129
barytis 18 n. 53
Basileios Stephanides 15 n. 45, 21 n. 56
Basilikos 67 n. 33
basis 17–18
bastaktai *see* Ison-isokratēma
bathy 42
Baumstark, A. 7 n. 14
bēma 9
Benediktos Episkopopoulos 123, 131
Benefactors of the nation 173
Boulgara 101
Boulgarikon 6 n. 11, 102

Cathedral, Rite, asmatic office 54, 75 n. 46, 108 n. 6, 128 n. 69
Chalibourēs 98
chamēlon 42
characteristic idea of the mode 84, 159, 166–167
characteristic melos 59 n. 17, 84
Charlemagne 111 n. 14
Chartres notation 41–43
Charytonymos 126

Index of topics and names

Chatzegiakoumes, Manoles 46 n. 123, 124 n. 54
cheironomia, cheironomy 16, 33, 39 n. 101, 43 n. 113, 44, 45, 58, 64, 159 n. 53
Cherubikon, cherubic hymn 21, 56, 90, 112, 135, 141
Chōmatianos 98
choreuma 42
choros, ho 9, 10, 18, 89, 91, 113
Chourmouzios Chartophylax xiv, 30, 35, 43 n. 113, 44 n. 116, 45 n. 117 and 123, 57 n. 15, 66, 76 n. 47, 90 n. 70, 92, 97 n. 3, 110, 115, 119, 124, 129, 133, 136 n. 1, 162 n. 58, 169, 173–175, 239, 243–248, 250–253
Christophoros Mystakōn 105, 127
chromatic genus 14 n. 37, 36, 164, 240
Chrysanthos Madytus 3, 14, 16, 22, 23–24, 27, 44 n. 113, 45 n. 117
Chrysostom, Liturgy of 176
Chrysostomus, Iohannes 7 n. 13, 79 n. 53
Coislin notation 34 n. 81, 41–43
common [*koinon*] melos 57
Constantine, the Great 79 n. 53
Constantinople xiii, xiv, 6, 31 n. 78, 34, 36, 46 n. 123, 51, 65, 66, 86, 95, 107, 109, 110, 117, 129, 131, 174, 294
Constantinus Porpherogennitus 111 n. 14
Crete 40, 123, 131
Crusades 113 n. 20
Cyprus 44 n. 114, 130, 131
Cyril Marmarēnos 15

da capo 165
Damaskenos Agraphorendiniotēs 110
Damianos hieromonachos, Batopedinos 132, 168 n. 80
Daniel monachos 132, 137 n. 5
Daniel prophet, feast of 79 n. 54
Daniel protopsaltes 44, 133

David Raidestēnos 116 n. 30, 117
death 155
deēsis 4
dekapentasyllabic, anagram 73; composition 51–53, 70, 73, 93 n. 79, 101, 125, 140, 149, 151, 153, 294; katanyktika 128, 155–156; mathēma 9, 96, 116; stichēron 79 n. 53; theotokion 103; troparia 142–143; verse 61, 72, 101, 106, 139, 147, 149, 153, 154
Demetrios, feast of 78
Demetrios Damias 123 n. 50, 131
Demetrios Dokeianos 101, 127
Demetrios Lōtōs 110, 119, 124, 132 n. 86, 133
despotika-katanyktika 155
diapason 18 n. 53
diatonic genus 14 n. 37
dichoron 168
Didaskalos tēs mousikēs 9, 45 n. 117, 54, 126 n. 63, 127
differentiation, of the melos 131
differentiation, of the music 44
diphōnos 14, 17, 250
diplasmos 17
diplophōnia 14, 17
disappearance of signs 33, 35, 40
disuse of signs 33, 35
dochai 22, 23, 31, 51, 55, 100, 136, 175; entechnoi 53
dogmatika 145, 151–152
domestikos, role of 10–11, 111–112
Dorian 17 n. 50
doubling *see* diplasmos
Doxastarion 23; of the Aposticha (Chourmouzios) 30; of Iakovos Protopsaltes 30, 46 n. 124; of Petros Lampadarios Peloponnēsios 30

doxastika 22, 23, 46 n. 124, 61 n.
    21, 63, 112, 151–152, 168 n.
    78; idiomela 112; of the
    Polyeleos 146–147
doxologiai 22, 51, 140, 151
dromos 25, 27
Durnad, Paul 42
dyo apostrophoi 45 n. 118
dyskolon 130
Dytikon, melos 6, 90, 98

Early Byzantine Notation 34
Ecclesiastical melos 6–7, 54 n. 8
Ecclesiastical offices see ophphikia
ēchadin 42
ēchēmata 4, 60–61, 68, 80, 87, 91, 93, 101,
    111, 112, 116 n. 30, 122, 152, 157, 159,
    161–164, 166, 168 n. 78, 178, 192,
    203; development of 163–164
ēchismata 60 n. 21, 112 n. 15
ēchoi see modes
Edward I 113 n. 20
eidē of melopœïa 5–7
eisodika — Entrance hymns 22–24, 52,
    91
Eleutherios hiereus 131 n. 82
enallagas 33, 58, 59 n. 17, 74
enarxis – initus 10
encomia 59 n. 19, 147, 153–154
encomiastic 139, 149, 156
enēchēmata 80, 111, 159 n. 55, 166 n. 71
energeia, function 33, 35, 45
epēchēmata 111
Ephraim Syrus 6 n. 10
epibolē xiii, 70, 86, 88–91, 111 n. 14, 160
    n. 57, 168 n. 76, 197, 199, 201, 210,
    212, 217, 219, 220, 233
epiphōnēmata 51, 55, 70, 86–87, 101, 137,
    138, 175
Epistle 11 n. 29, 52, 56, 141
epos 4

ethnikon melos 6, 91, 113
ethos of melopœïa 59, 164
Euclides 18 n. 53
Eudokimos, Saint 78
Eugenios domestikos 225
Eunouchos protopsaltes Philanthro-
    pinon 67 n. 33
exaposteilaria 22, 23, 24, 27, 146, 153
exarxis, initus 10
exēgēsis — metagraphē xiv, xv, 34–35,
    39–46, 76 n. 47, 110, 137 n. 4, 142
    n. 21, 150 n. 39, 173, 175, 239–240,
    243–248
exēgētai — exegetes 39, 120, 173
exēgēton 39 n. 103
exo ison holoi 93 n. 77
exōterikon melos 6–7

finale 29, 89 n. 67, 92, 93, 160, 161, 295
Fleischer, O. 35
Floros, Constantin xx n. 1
Frangikon melos 6, 90, 98
free verse 139, 147, 153, 154, 156
Frøyshov, S. 7 n. 14

Gabriel hieromonachos 13, 15, 17 n. 49,
    59 n. 17, 84, 130, 166–167, 169 n.
    83, 294
Gabriel of Anchialus 176
Gastoué, A. 35
Gennadius of Anchialus 132
George, Saint, feast of 79
Georgios, from Athens 30, 38
Georgios, Raidestēnos 39
Georgios Biolakēs 46 n. 124
Georgios Kontopetres 98, 106, 127
Georgios Moschianos 98
Georgios oikonomos from Athens
    30 n. 77, 38
Georgios Pachymeres 66 n. 32
Georgios Panaretos 97, 105, 106, 127

Index of topics and names 323

Georgios Sgouropoulos 130
Georgios, Raidestēnos II 46 n. 124, 132
Gerasimos Blachos Krēs 113 n. 19
Gerasimos Chalkeopoulos 106, 130
Gerasimos hagioreitēs 118 n. 36, 132
Germanos, monachos 66
Germanos Neōn Patrōn 26, 28, 30, 38, 109, 114 n. 22, 118 n. 36, 132, 146 n. 30, 148 n. 35, 174
Glykys 9
gorgon 42
Great Vespers 11, 21, 51, 117 n. 31, 125, 128 n. 69
Gregorian melos 5, 111 n. 14
Gregorios Bounēs Alyatēs 125, 129, 130, 137
Gregorios domestikos Glykys 67, 101, 104
Gregorios protopsaltes, lampadarios 25, 26 n. 71, 31, 35, 46 n. 123, 110, 114, 120, 133, 173, 176
Gregory Palamas, Saint 66
Gregory the Theologian, Nazianzus 7 n. 13
gronthismata 42

Hagia 251
Hagia Sophia xiv
harmōdion theseis 17 n. 48
harmonius 6 n. 10
harmony 4, 18
heirmoi 22, 24, 27, 31, 56, 61, 70, 91, 92, 109, 116, 128, 129, 143–144, 145, 151, 152, 153, 157, 294; kalphonic 28 n. 73, 31 n. 78, 50, 54, 62 n. 24, 85, 96, 97 n. 3, 114, 118 n. 37
heirmologikon melos, genus 22, 24–25, 26, 27, 29, 30–31, 38, 41, 42, 44 n. 116, 50, 62, 144
Heirmologion 25, 26, 27, 30–31, 38, 41–44, 46, 67, 126, 131, 132 n.

87, 151; of Cosmas the Macedonian and Germanos Neōn Patrōn 30–31; *Kalophōnikon* 24, 27, 62, 91, 114, 132 n. 87; Palaion, Old 31; of Petros Byzantios 24, 31; of Petros Peloponnēsios 25, 26, 30; *Syntomon* 26, 27 n. 71, 31; of Theophanēs Karykēs 26
hēmiphthora 42
hēmitonion 17 n. 50
heōthina 22, 23, 44 n. 116, 51, 55, 63, 75 n. 46, 89, 138
heptaphōnia 17
heptaphōnos 14, 17
heretics 7 n. 12
Herimologion, of Balasios hiereus and Nomophylax 25, 26, 30
Hesychastic controversy 65 n. 30, 70, 164 n. 64
Hieronymos Tragōdistēs 44 n. 114, 131
holoi homou 12, 81, 243
homalon 45 n. 119
Hymnodikon 168 n. 80
hymnōdoi 8
hymnographia, hymnography 5–9, 19, 50, 56, 116, 120, 143, 147, 152, 157
hymnographos, hymnographer 6, 8
hymnology 20, 64, 156
hymnos, hymn 4, 7 n. 13
hymns, heretical 6
hypakoai 22, 24, 29
hyperbatōs 14
hyphos 62
hypopsalma 75 n. 46
hypostases of cheironomy, great 14, 16, 33, 35, 39, 40, 43, 44, 45

Iakovos protopsaltes 44, 46 n. 124, 133; *Doxastarion* 23, 30
iambic dekapentasyllabic 72, 129
iconoclastic controversy 6, 7–8

idiomela 22, 23
idiomela stichera 24, 56, 68, 70, 75, 76,
    77, 143, 144–145, 151, 152, 153, 154,
    155, 293, 294
Ignatios Phrielos 131
in Thessalonike 51, 65
initus *see* enarxis
Institute of Byzantine Musicology of the
    Holy Synod of the Church of
    Greece xv–xvi, 150 n. 39
instrumental music 4
Introduction to the Mathēma 60 n. 21,
    91–92, 147, 158–169, 295
Iōakeim monachos 98
Iohannes Damascenus 4 n. 5, 7, 40 n.
    107, 142, 151
Iohannes Glykys 53, 66, 103, 109, 121, 122,
    125–127, 295
Iohannes hiereus Plousiadēnos 15, 74 n.
    45, 85 n. 61, 123 n. 50, 128, 130
Iohannes Kallistos the maïstōr 10, 176,
    185, 187, 190, 196, 199, 205
Iohannes Kampanēs 98
Iohannes Kladas 9, 12 n. 34, 97, 98, 101,
    103–106, 121–124, 128–129, 143,
    145 n. 29, 147 n. 33, 153, 157, 168,
    174, 175, 186
Iohannes Kordokotos 130
Iohannes Koukouzelēs Papadopoulos
    xiii, 9, 10, 18 n. 51, 26, 28, n. 74, 37
    n. 97, 43, 46, 50, 51, 52, 57, 60, 62,
    63, 64, 66, 67, 68 n. 34, 69, 71, 72,
    73, 74, 76 n. 47, 82, 85 n. 63, 86,
    87, 90, 97, 98, 101, 103, 105, 106,
    109, 114 n. 23, 115 n. 27, 121–124,
    125–129, 134, 137, 138, 150, 153, 165
    n. 66, 166 n. 73, 174, 175, 190, 196,
    197, 199, 202, 213, 246–248, 250,
    253, 295
Iohannes lampadarios 27 n. 71, 97, 101,
    104, 133

Iohannes Laskarēs the Sērpaganos 128
Iohannes Panaretos 98
Iohannes Trapezountios 124, 133,
    134
Iohasaph Dionysiatēs 45 n. 122, 120,
    133–134, 168
Iohasaph monachos 130
Iohasaph Neos Koukouzelēs 26, 39
Iohseph Tsarlinos 44 n. 114
Ismaēlitikon 6, 114 n. 22
ison-isokratēma, holders of the –
    isokratai 11–12, 14, 18–19,
    43, 124
ison saximata 42
Italy, Southern 65

John, Forerunner and Baptist, feast of
    71, 141

kalliphōnia 56–61, 81 n. 57
kallōpismos — kallopismoi xiii, 26, 30,
    38, 39, 44, 58, 62, 67 n. 33,
    68 n. 34, 76 n. 47, 81 n. 57, 88,
    122, 132, 175
kalogerikos 54
kalōphōnarēs 9, 12, 18, 53, 294
kalophōnia 38, 53, 54, 56–62
kalophōnikon 19, 56, 57, 61, 68,
    142 n. 19; *Heirmologion* 31,
    46, 62, 132 n. 87; *Kontaka-
    rion, Oikēmatarion* 120–124;
    Sticherarion 61, 68, 96, 117,
    164 n. 59
kalopismoi 66–67
kampana, kratēma 98
kampanēs 104
kanōn 5
kanonarchos 9, 11–12
Karas, Simon 26 n. 65, 38 n. 98
Karboounariōtēs 67, 194, 197, 204, 206,
    214, 215, 221

Index of topics and names

Karphas 220
Kassas domestikos 100
Kassianos domestikos 98
katabasiai 22, 24, 25 n. 63, 26, 27, 70, 86,
   93; megalē 92
katabatromikon 42
katanyktika 21, 31, 52, 53, 54, 61, 69, 83,
   85, 108, 109, 116, 117, 128, 143, 155,
   167
kath' heauto mathēma 66, 135
kathismata 22, 23, 24, 25, 27, 145, 153, 155
keimenon 81, 89
kekallopismenon 30, 58, 62, 68 n. 34
kekragaria 22, 23, 31, 40 n. 107, 44 n.
   116, 51
Keladēnos 104
Kinnyra, kratēma 99
klasma 42
Klēmēs Lesbios, Mytēlinaios 132
klimax, musical scale 17, 25 n. 60, 45,
   240
Klōbas 66, 101, 102, 104, 188
Kodov, K. 125 n. 58
koinonika — communion hymn 12, 22,
   23, 29, 31, 52, 56, 105, 107, 135, 141,
   175, 176
Komines, Athanasios 39 n. 100
Komnēnos 67 n. 33
kondeuma 42
Konidares, Gerasimos 65 n. 30
Kōnstantinos Anchialus 132, 168 n. 80
Konstantinos Gabras 104
Kōnstantinos Magoulas 67, 98, 105
Kōnstantinos Phlangēs 131
Kōnstantinos protopsaltes 133
Kontakarion, Oikēmatarion 29, 31, 46,
   96, 107, 114, 115, 120–124, 157,
   174, 175
kontakion 5, 10, 52, 69, 73, 106, 120, 142
Kornēlios monachos 101, 127, 187, 188
Kosmas Baranēs 131

Kosmas Ibēritēs the Macedonian 25 n.
   65, 39, 74, 89 n. 69, 90, 109, 114 n.
   23, 115, 118, 119, 124, 130 n. 79, 132,
   141 n. 14, 154 n. 43
koukoulion — prooimion 120, 142, 143
Koukoumas 87, 88, 101, 127, 191
kouphisma 45 n. 118
kratēmata 4, 110–115
kratēmata ek tōn exō 6 n. 11
Kratēmatarion 29, 31, 46, 96, 107,
   110–116, 136 n. 1
kratēmoÿporröon 45 n. 118
Kyriazides, Agathangelos 44 n. 113

Lainas, Theoktistos 26 n. 66
lampadarios 9–12
Lampros, Spyridon 96 n. 2, 107 n. 4
Latin occupation xiii, 6, 65, 69
Latrinon 101
lege 163, 165, 166, 233
lemoi, melōdēma 42
Leo VI Sapiens Imperitor 154
Leōn Almyriōtēs 67, 90, 191, 196, 198,
   220, 221
Leontios Koukouzelēs 85 n. 63, 114 n. 23,
   118 n. 35
Levy, Kenneth 63, 64 n. 28
Litē 70, 76, 145, 155
Longinos hieromonachos 101, 105
Louis IX 113 n. 20
lychnika 51
Lydian mode 17 n. 50
lyric poetry 3 n. 1

Maccabees, feast of 77
maïstor 9–10, 11 n. 24
Makarios anēr 10, 23, 31, 51, 86 n. 64, 88,
   91, 128 n. 69, 146
makarismoi 22, 24, 52
Makaristaria 147, 154
makrologia 68 n. 34

Manourgas *see* Theodōros Manourgas
Manuel Agallianos 90, 98, 101, 102, 105
Manuel Argyropoulos 10, 128, 229
Manuel Blatēros 105, 129, 142 n. 18,
    153 n. 42
Manuel Chrysaphēs Doukas, lampadarios
    and maïstor 10, 15, 16, 17 n. 48,
    20, 21, 59, 76 n. 47, 81 n. 58, 82, 83,
    91, 97, 99, 103, 104, 105, 106, 107,
    115, 117, 118, 121, 122, 124, 125, 126,
    127 n. 64, 129–130, 140, 159 n. 54,
    165, 174, 175, 176, 239, 252, 294
Manuel domestikos of Thebes 104, 194
Manuel Gazēs 106, 129
Manuel Korōnēs 98
Manuel Kourtesēs 105
Manuel Philēs 66 n. 32
Manuel Plagitēs 127
Margaritēs 98
Markos, metropolitan of Corinth 76 n.
    47, 104, 117, 130, 159, 166 n. 71,
    251
Markos hieromonachos of the
    Xanthopouloi 117
martyriai 33, 45, 80
mathēmata, psalmic 31, 55, 96, 108, 116,
    135–136, 138, 140, 150, 157, 175,
    294
mathēmata forms, two-part type 123,
    158, 160–163, 166, 295; three-part
    type xiii, 158–163, 295; four-part
    type 158, 161–163; multi-part
    type 158, 160, 162, 169, 295;
    simple type 158, 162, 167
Mathēmatarion 16, 22 n. 59, 29, 31, 32,
    46–47, 49–93, 96, 115–120,
    124–134, 173–225
Matthaios Batopedēnos 43 n. 113, 45 n.
    122, 47 n. 124, 120, 133, 134 n. 99,
    168
Matthaios Blastarēs 66 n. 32

Maximus Planoudēs 66 n. 32
Mega Ison 43 n. 113, 64, 126
megalynaria 21, 22, 23, 24, 31, 51, 55, 70,
    103, 106, 109, 128, 138–139, 145,
    153
megas rētōr 9 n. 18
Melētios Sinaïtēs 133
melic, elaboration 164; embellishment 146; expression 4, 16, 32,
    35, 60, 64–65, 81, 87, 149, 165,
    240; lengthening 160 n. 56, 163,
    164 n. 59, 166; modulations 164;
    period 164; shape/scheme 159,
    165
melographos 8
melismatikon 57
Melissēnos philosophos 104, 215
melodēmata 33, 42, 64
melōdia 4, 68
melōdos 8–9
melopœïa — melic composition 3, 20,
    24, 32, 74, 75, 82, 85, 86, 97,
    108, 110, 111, 113, 120, 124, 126,
    132, 149, 150, 155, 156, 157, 169,
    173, 174, 249, 293, 294
melopoios 8
melos — melē 3–8, 14
melos, genera of 22–32, 49
melourgia 3, 8
melourgos 8, 115 n. 27
mesoi, of the mode 14, 17, 167
Metochion of the All-holy Tomb
    (Jerusalem) 46 n. 123
Metrophōnia 14, 15 n. 38, 240
Michael Aneōtēs 121, 122
Michael hiereus Chios 109
Michael Mystakōn 101
Michael Panaretos, priest 104
Michael Patzados 66, 90
Middle Byzantine Notation xix, 36–39,
    42, 43, 46

Index of topics and names

mimesis — imitation 21, 68, 122
modes 7 n. 14, 9, 17, 18 n. 51, 33, 61 n.
    21, 84, 111, 128 n. 70, 142, 164,
    166
monastic 54, 142, 295
Monastic Republic of Mount Athos xix
monophōnarēs 18, 51, 53, 141 n. 13, 165,
    197, 294, 295
monophonic xiv, 18, 293, 295
Monumenta Musicæ Byzantinæ
    (MMB) 29
Moorish Spain 113 n. 20
Mount Sinai, Monastery of Saint
    Catherine 34, 131
Mount Tabor 80, 249 n. 1
Mouschali 114 n. 22
Mozambican melos 5
musicology 19, 38, 156
Musicology, Institute of xvi

Nagmes 114 n. 22
Naï 114 n. 22
nakers 113 n. 20
Naos 213, 218
Naqqāra 113 n. 20
National and Kapodistrian University of
    Athens xvi, xix
Neagie 14
Neanes 14, 45 n. 121, 111, 159 n. 55
Necheanes 14 n. 37
nekrōsima 109, 142, 155
Nektarios patriarch of Jerusalem
    148 n. 34
nenanismata 111, 114, 166
Nenanō 14 n. 37, 76, 111, 122, 142, 165,
    166 n. 71, 176
Neofytos Ēthikos 209, 211
Neos Glykys, Bereketēs 9
New Method, New Analytical Byzantine
    Notation xiv, 22, 31 n. 78, 34, 35,
    43 n. 113, 45, 46 n. 123, 110, 114,

115, 136 n. 1, 137 n. 4, 173, 174, 175,
    239–240
Nicēphoros Grēgoras 66 n. 32
Nicolaus Cabasilas 66
Nikēphoros Ēthikos 67, 101, 104, 125–
    126, 176, 295
Nikēphoros hieromonachos
    Docheiaritēs 45 n. 122
Nikolaos Docheiaritēs 120, 133, 168
Nikolaos hiereus Strianos 123 n. 50,
    131
Nikolaos Kallistos 67, 221, 225
Nikolaos Kampanēs 67, 180, 182, 186,
    188, 190, 195, 206, 207, 210, 220,
    221, 224
Nikolaos Koukoumas maïstōr 87, 88, 101,
    127, 191
Nikolaos Limnēnos 201
Nikolaos Palamas of Anchialus 129
Nikōn monachos 98
Noeane 7, 111 n. 14
nomophylax, office 9 n. 18
nonsense syllables 113
notational development 33, 35, 38, 293

octaves 17, 18 n. 53
Odēs, Biblical, canons 4, 24, 55, 116, 120,
    135, 138–139, 143–144, 151,
    152–153
Oikēmatarion see Kontakarion,
    Oikēmatarion
oikoi 21, 22, 23, 61, 107–108, 116,
    120–124, 131, 143, 151, 153, 157, 162,
    168, 174, 175
oikonomos, office 9 n. 18
oktaēcha 146, 152, 162, 166, 168,
    169
Oktōēchia 7, 18, 111 n. 14
Oktōēchos 7, 145, 151, 152
oligon 42, 43 n. 113
ophphikia 9–10; seventh pentad 10

organikon 6, 19 n. 54
Ottoman music 36
ouranisma 42
oxeia 42, 45 n. 118
oxytēs — oxytēta 3, 18 n. 53

Pachomios Rousanos 15
Païsios hieromonachos 109
Palaeologan Renaissance xix, 49, 63, 65
palaion 54, 76, 88 n. 66, 98, 104, 251
Palikarova Verdeil, R. 63
palin 163, 165, 166 n. 71
Panagiōtēs Chalatzoglou 28 n. 73, 133
Panagiōtēs Chrysaphēs, new 26, 30, 38,
    109, 114 n. 22, 132, 145 n. 29, 148
    n. 35, 174
Pankratios monachos Ibēritēs 132
papadic melos, genus 22, 23, 24, 27, 28,
    29, 31, 32, 39, 44, 46, 47, 49, 50,
    51, 57, 58, 150
Papadikai 11, 16, 17, 43 n. 113, 61 n. 21, 66,
    82, 86 n. 64, 91 n. 72, 95–110, 115,
    116, 121, 126, 131
Papadikai, Protheōria of the 17, 18 n. 51,
    61 n. 21, 97, 159 n. 53
Papadopoula 113
parakalesma 42
paraklētikē 154
Paraklētikē, thesis 42, 159–160, 169
parallagē 14, 15 n. 42, 18 n. 51, 45, 59 n.
    17, 128 n. 70
paramesos 14, 17
paraplagios 14
parasēmantikē 32 n. 80
parēchon 42
parekbolē xiii, 70, 86, 89–91, 190, 201,
    202, 210, 213
pasapnoaria 13 n. 35, 22, 23, 55, 134, 138,
    168 n. 80, 175
Paschos, P. B. 70 n. 36
Patriarchal School 65

pelaston 42, 45 n. 118
pentachord system 17–18
pentaphōnos 14, 17
pentaphony 13, 14, 17
pentēkostaria 73, 155–156
Pentēkostarion xv, 115, 145
Pereketi 28 n. 73
perissē 93 n. 78
Persikon 6, 113, 114 n. 22
petasma 42
Petresco, J. 35
Petros Bereketēs Melōdos 9, 28, 114 n. 22,
    124, 132, 133, 140 n. 11, 146, 148 n.
    35, 168, 174, 175, 176
Petros Byzantios 24–27, 30–31, 133,
    136 n. 1
Petros Ephesios 45 n. 122
Petros Hagiotaphitēs 45 n. 122
Petros Peloponnēsios Lambadarios
    23–26, 30, 43 n. 113, 44, 124,
    146 n. 29
Petrov, S. V. 125 n. 58
Phardiboukēs, prōtopapas of the Church
    of the Holy Apostles 54 n. 8,
    104, 127
phēmai 52, 85, 116, 147–151
Philippos Gabalas 98
Philostorgius Cappadox 7 n. 12
Phōkas laosynaptes of the Great
    Church 101, 123 n. 50
Phōkas Philadelpheias 66
phōnētika sēmadia 16, 33
Phrygian 17 n. 50
Phrygian mode 17 n. 50
phthongoi 3 n. 2, 14 n. 37, 18 n. 53;
    symphōnoi, symphonic tones 18
phthorai 33, 45, 58, 59, 83, 85, 142,
    164–167
phthorikon 86, 99, 100
phthorikon kai dyskolon 86
piasma 42

Index of topics and names

Pitra, J.-B. 5 n. 7
plagioi 17, 167
Plato, philosopher 3
Platysmos — expansion 59, 69, 79, 80
Plyēcha 162, 166, 168
poiēma 4
poiētēs 8
polemikon 102
politikon 54, 88 n. 66, 149
polychronismoi 85, 116, 147–151, 176
polyeleoi xiv, 21, 22, 23, 31, 51, 53, 55,
    59 n. 19, 60, 61, 75 n. 46, 87, 88,
    91, 96, 101, 117 n. 31, 134, 139–140,
    146–147, 151, 153, 173
polysyllabic phthongoi 14, 45, 111
pous — podes 75
prelude 60 n. 21, 75 n. 46, 91–92, 159
primikērios 9 n. 18, 10
prokeimena 12, 22 n. 57, 29, 51, 52, 55, 68,
    75 n. 46, 86, 100, 136–138, 175
prologos xiii, 5, 27 n. 72, 53, 70, 86,
    91–92, 142 n. 19, 159, 161
prooimion 120, 121, 143
proseuchē 4
prosomoia 5, 8, 22, 23, 24, 27, 85, 145, 151,
    152, 153, 154
prosomoiac 8, 27
prosthēkē 91 n. 71
prōtokanonarchos 11
prōtopapas 9 n. 18
prōtopsaltēs 9–12
Ps.-Codinus 10, 11
Psachos, K., Library of 46 n. 123
psalma 4
psalmōdia, psalmody 4, 7 n. 12, 16 n. 48,
    22, 24–27
psalmos 4
Psaltikē Technē, Psaltic Art xiii, xiv, xv,
    xvi, 19, 20, 21, 32, 54, 74 n. 45, 83,
    126, 130, 134, 169 n. 83, 173, 293,
    294–295

Psaltikon 22, 28–29, 46, 50, 63–64,
    67–68, 120, 122
psēphiston 42, 45 n. 119
psilon 42

Raasted, J. 7 n. 14, 34 n. 81, 63, 80–81,
    87 n. 65, 111
rapisma 42
Reform, Notaional, of Hierōnymos
    Tragōdistēs of Cyprus 44 n.
    114
Reform, Notaional, of the Three
    Teachers 34, 45, 110, 173
reuma 42
rhythms 3, 6 n. 10, 16 n. 48, 37, 113, 145,
    164 n. 64
Riemann, H. 35
Rodakina, ta, kratēma 102
Rodani, to 113
Rodion, to legomenon 100
round notation 34, 36, 38, 64
royal ceremonies 11
royal clergy 128

saximata 42
seisma 42
sēmadophōna — sēmadia 43, 44, 45,
    127
Sēmantēri, mega 102; mikron 99, 102
Serapheim Lauriotēs 110
Slavonic chant xx n. 1
Socrates Scholasticus 6 n. 10, 7 n. 12
    and 13
Sophotatē parallagē, methodos 18 n. 51
Soubatzoglou, N. K. 47 n. 124
Sourlas 99
Sozomenus 6 n. 10
Spanos 104
Spyridōn Batopedinos 47 n. 124
stauroanastasima 151
stauros 42, 45 n. 119

staurotheotokia 109, 116, 117 n. 31, 154
stichēra 5, 8, 21–24, 27, 31
stichēra, kalophonic 22 n. 59, 61, 68,
    80–84, 89, 95, 107, 108, 115, 116,
    117, 118 n. 36, 160, 293
stichēraric melos, genus 16, 22–24, 41,
    44, 46, 160; new 22, 23, 24, 41,
    44, 46; new argon 30; new syntomon 30; old 22, 23, 24, 30, 44,
    46, 47 n. 124
Stichērarion 17 n. 49, 21, 24, 44, 61,
    82, 127 n. 65, 145, 294; *Kalophonic* 46, 70, 75, 77, 80, 84, 96,
    107, 115–120, 145; *Old, Palaia* 30,
    34, 38, 44, 46 n. 124, 81 n. 58
stichēron idiomelon 5, 144–145
stichologia 29, 142
strangismata 42
Strunk, Oliver 35–50, 63
Symeon of Thessalonikē, Saint 11 n. 27,
    75 n. 46
Symeon Psēritzēs 67, 165 n. 68
Symphōnia, Symphony 18 n. 53, 19
synagma 42
synagma [meta staurou] 42
synaptē, great 10
syndesmos 45 n. 119
synthesis 4–5, 28 n. 74
syntmēsis 40, 41, 123 n. 50
syntomon 24, 25, 27, 30, 50 n. 3, 52, 54 n.
    8, 144; asmatic trisagia 140 n. 11;
    dromos 25, 27

table, at 117 n. 31
Tardo, L. 17 n. 49, 35, 68, 69
Taren 111 n. 13
telos 89
telos, heteron 160
telos, thesis 169
tempo *see* agogē
teretismoi 111, 112, 113 n. 19, 166

tetrachord system 17 n. 50, 18
tetraēcha 134 n. 99, 146, 168
tetraphōnia, tetraphony 13–14, 17, 165,
    175, 153, 166–167
tetraphōnos 14, 17
tetraphony 13, 165, 166, 167
Thalassinos 178, 181
thema 42
Theodōros Argyropoulos 98, 100
Theodōros Manourgas 67, 69 n. 35,
    76 n. 47, 97, 104, 160 n. 56, 239,
    243–248, 250
Theodōros Metochitēs 65
Theodōros Phōkaeus 3 n. 1, 30, 31 n. 78,
    46, 114
Theodosios hierodiakonos Chios 115 n.
    24, 119, 124, 129, 133
Theodoulos Aineitēs 133
Theodoulos monachos 105, 110, 133 n. 94,
    137 n. 5
Theophanēs hieromonachos
    Docheiaritēs 45 n. 122
Theophanēs Karykēs 26, 27, 39, 114 n. 22
Theophanēs Pantokratorinos 120
Theophylaktos Argyropoulos 105
theotokia 31, 52, 59 n. 19, 61, 69, 91 n. 72,
    109, 116, 117 n. 31, 120, 123 n. 50,
    128, 139, 144, 145, 147, 152–155,
    174; katanyktika 155 n. 47
theotokos 4, 51, 52, 69, 116, 117, 121, 128,
    140, 141, 143, 146, 147, 152, 154
Theseis, Method of 126
thesis — thesis 14–28, 39 n. 101, 40–46,
    58, 64, 111, 127, 159, 163, 164, 166,
    169
Thessalonikaion 54 n. 8, 88 n. 66, 104,
    176
Thettalikon 88 n. 66, 113
Thibaut, J. 35
Thodberg, Ch. 28 n. 75, 57 n. 13, 64
Thomas Kordokotos 130

Index of topics and names

Three Teachers, the 35, 45–46
Tiby, O. 35
Tillyard, H. J. W. 35–40
tinagma 42
transcription *see* exēgēsis — metagraphē
Transfiguration of the Lord, feast of
  xv, 68, 75, 140, 146 n. 31, 239,
  243–248, 249
transitional, exēgēmatic Byzantine
  Notation 34
triadika, triadic, trinitarian 55, 149,
  150–151, 152
triphōnia 85
triphōnos 14, 17
trisagion 34, 39 n. 103, 52, 56, 105, 135,
  142; nekrōsimon 39, 142 n. 21;
  nekrōsimon, Athēnaiïkon 39
Trochos 14 n. 37, 17, 18 n. 51
tromikon 42
Troparion 5, 14, 24, 59, 160, 168
tropic 18
tropos, modus, way 17, 64
Typika 22, 24

Typikon, asmatic (Cathedral Rite)
  75 n. 46
Typikon, diataxeis 11, 112 n. 15

Uspensky, Fyodor 29, 125 n. 58

Velimirovič, M. 108 n. 7, 112 n. 15
Verpeaux, J. 11 n. 24 and 26, 149 n. 37
verses, psalmic 5 n. 7, 50, 54, 57, 70, 135,
  156, 294
Viola 113
vocal music 4, 18, 293
vocal range 163, 164, 166, 167
vocal shape 164
Vogt, A. 111 n. 14

Wellesz, Egon 16 n. 47, 35–37
Williams, E. 59 n. 18

Xenos Korōnēs xiii, 51, 66, 67 n. 33, 76,
  81, 98, 101, 104, 105, 106, 109, 122,
  125–127, 243–248, 250, 295
xēros 97, 98

Studies in Eastern Orthodoxy

Edited by René Gothóni and Graham Speake

This series is concerned with Eastern Orthodox Christianity in its various manifestations. Originating as the church of the East Roman or Byzantine empire, Eastern Orthodoxy comprises the group of churches that owe allegiance to the Ecumenical Patriarchate in Constantinople. The Orthodox Church has exercised unparalleled influence over the history, thought, and culture of the region and remains one of the most dynamic and creative forces in Christendom today. The series will publish studies in English, both monographs and edited collections, in all areas of social, cultural, and political activity in which the Orthodox Church can be seen to have played a major role.

Vol. 1   Gregorios Stathis
         Introduction to Kalophony, the Byzantine *Ars Nova*:
         The *Anagrammatismoi* and *Mathēmata* of Byzantine Chant
         2014. ISBN 978-3-0343-0912-7

Vol. 2   James F. Wellington
         Christe Eleison!: The Invocation of Christ in Eastern Monastic Psalmody c.350–450.
         2014. ISBN 978-3-0343-1789-4